Sports Nutrition

A PRACTICE

MANUAL

FOR PROFESSIONALS

4th edition

Marie Dunford, PhD, RD, editor
Sports, Cardiovascular, and Wellness Nutritionists Dietetic Practice Group

**American
Dietetic
Association**

Diana Faulhaber, Publisher
Jason M. Muzinic, Acquisitions Editor
Elizabeth Nishiura, Production Editor

10 9 8 7 6 5 4 3 2 1

Library of Congress Cataloging-in-Publication Data

Sports nutrition: a practice manual for professionals / Sports, Cardiovascular, and Wellness Nutritionists
    Dietetic Practice Group. — 4th ed. / Marie Dunford, editor.
        p. ; cm.
    Includes bibliographical references and index.
    ISBN 0-88091-411-4
    1. Athletes—Nutrition.   2. Exercise—Physiological aspects.
    I. Dunford, Marie.   II. American Dietetic Association. Sports, Cardiovascular, and Wellness
    Nutritionists Dietetic Practice Group.
        [DNLM: 1. Nutrition. 2. Exercise—physiology. 3. Sports.
    QU 145 S7653 2005]
    TX361.A8S673 2005
    613.2'024'796—dc22

                                                                            2005010290

CONTENTS

ACKNOWLEDGMENTS

It has been a long journey from the inception to the completion of this project, but I won't recount the distance other than to thank the many people who helped along the way. Jason Muzinic, the acquisitions editor at the American Dietetic Association, provided a steady hand and wise counsel, as did Elizabeth Nishiura, the production editor. Chris Rosenbloom, the editor of the 3rd edition, was extraordinarily helpful, and I appreciate her knowledge, skill, professionalism, enthusiasm, and friendship. I was privileged to work with 25 different authors. They are the heart and soul of this book. More than 30 reviewers took time of out their busy schedules to offer constructive criticism. It is behind-the-scenes work that is not apparent but so vitally important. Special thanks goes to the Gatorade Sports Science Institute: without its financial support, this book would not have been possible. On a personal note, I would like to acknowledge my husband, Greg, for his love and support, and others on the pages of my book of counted joys—Matt, Michelle, Austin, Megan, and Monica.

Marie Dunford, PhD, RD
Nutrition educator
Kingsburg, CA

CONTRIBUTORS

Katherine A. Beals, PhD, RD, FACSM
Nutrition Specialist
Fleishman-Hillard, Inc.
Sacramento, CA

Louise M. Burke, PhD, APD, FACSM
Head, Department of Sports Nutrition
Australian Institute of Sport
Canberra, Australia

Ellen J. Coleman, MA, MPH, RD
Sports Dietitian
The Sport Clinic
Riverside, CA

Ann F. Cowlin, MA, CSM, CCE
Movement Specialist and Assistant Clinical Professor
Yale University
New Haven, CT

Cathryn R. Dooly, PhD, FACSM
Associate Professor
University of Illinois-Chicago
Chicago, IL

Marie Dunford, PhD, RD
Nutrition Educator
Kingsburg, CA

Martin J. Gibala, PhD
Associate Professor
McMaster University
Hamilton, Ontario, Canada

Diane L. Habash, PhD, RD
Bionutrition Research Manager
General Clinical Research Center
Ohio State University
Columbus, OH

Sally Hara, MS, RD, CDE
Nutrition Therapist/Owner
ProActive Nutrition, LLC
Kirkland, WA

Charlotte Hayes, MMSc, MS, RD, CDE
Director of Nutrition Services
Project Open Hand/Atlanta
Atlanta, GA

Leah Holbrook, RD
Coordinator, Heart Links Project
Stony Brook University Hospital and Medical Center
Stony Brook, NY

Krista R. Howarth, MSc
Doctoral candidate
McMaster University
Hamilton, Ontario, Canada

Satya S. Jonnalagadda, PhD, RD
Manager—Clinical Practice and Standards of Care
Novartis Medical Nutrition
St. Louis Park, MN

D. Enette Larson-Meyer, PhD, RD, FACSM
Assistant Professor and Director of Nutrition
    and Exercise Laboratory
University of Wyoming
Laramie, WY

Michele A. Macedonio, MS, RD
Nutrition Consultant, Sports Dietitian
Nutrition Strategies
Loveland, OH

Melinda M. Manore, PhD, RD
Professor
Oregon State University
Corvallis, OR

Christopher M. Modlesky, PhD
Assistant Professor
University of Delaware
Newark, DE

Bob Murray, PhD, FACSM
Director
Gatorade Sports Science Institute
Barrington, IL

Janet Walberg Rankin, PhD
Professor
Virginia Tech
Blacksburg, VA

Christine A. Rosenbloom, PhD, RD
Professor
Georgia State University
Atlanta, GA

Josephine Connolly Schoonen, MS, RD
Assistant Clinical Professor of Family Medicine
Stony Brook University Hospital and Medical Center
Stony Brook, NY

Bob Seebohar, MS, RD, CSCS
Performance Director/Sports Dietitian
Colorado Center for Altitude Training
    and Performance
Evergreen, CO

Rob Skinner, MS, RD, CSCS
Director, Homer Rice Center for Sports Performance
Georgia Tech Athletic Association
Atlanta, GA

Michael Smith, RD
Renal Dietitian
Gambro Healthcare
Fresno, CA

Leah Moore Thomas, MS, RD
Sports Dietitian
Georgia Tech Athletic Association
Atlanta, Georgia

Stella Lucia Volpe, PhD, RD, FACSM
Associate Professor and Miriam Stirl Term Endowed
    Chair in Nutrition
University of Pennsylvania
Philadelphia, PA

REVIEWERS

Hope Barkoukis, PhD, RD
Case Western Reserve University
Cleveland, OH

Gale B. Carey, PhD, FACSM
University of New Hampshire
Durham, NH

Amanda Gwinnup Carlson, MS
Athlete's Performance
Tempe, AZ

Kristine Clark, PhD, RD, FACSM
Pennsylvania State University
University Park, PA

Michael G. Coles, PhD
California State University, Fresno
Fresno, CA

Carole A. Conn, PhD, RD, FACSM
University of New Mexico
Albuquerque, NM

Suzanne Girard Eberle, MS, RD
Private practice
Portland, OR

Ellen M. Evans, PhD
University of Illinois
Urbana, IL

Reyna Franco, MS
Nutrition and Exercise Specialist
New York, NY

Marjorie Geiser, RD, NSCA-CPT
MEG Fitness
Running Springs, CA

Linda Houtkooper, PhD, RD
University of Arizona
Tucson, AZ

Asker Jeukendrup, PhD, Rnut, FACSM
University of Birmingham
Birmingham, UK

Christine Karpinski, MA, RD
Owner—Nutrition Edge, Inc.
West Chester, PA

Diane Keddy, MS, RD, FAED
Nutrition Therapist
Newport Beach, CA

Mark Kern, PhD, RD
San Diego State University
San Diego, CA

Charlotte Caperton-Kilburn, MS, RD
Private practice—NFL Performance
Charleston, SC

Susan Kundrat, MS, RD
Nutrition on the Move
Urbana, IL

Don Mankie, RD
Lewis-Gale Clinic
Salem, VA

Christina Scribner Reiter, MS, RD
Metropolitan State College of Denver
Denver, CO

Michelle Rockwell, MS, RD
University of Florida Athletic Association
Gainesville, FL

Brian Schilling, PhD, CSCS
University of Memphis
Memphis, TN

Leslie P. Schilling, MA, RD
Dietitian Associates, Inc.
Cordova, TN

Connie Schneider, PhD, RD
University of California Cooperative Extension, Fresno
Fresno, CA

Susan M. Shirreffs, PhD
Loughborough University
Loughborough, UK

Suzanne Nelson-Steen, DSc, RD
University of Washington
Seattle, WA

Patti Steinmuller, MS, RD
Montana State University-Bozeman
Bozeman, MT

C. Alan Titchenal, PhD, CNS
University of Hawaii at Manoa
Honolulu, HI

Mark Waldron, PhD
Nestlé Research Center
St. Louis, MO

Hilary Warner, MPH, RD
Nutrition Works! LLC
Bow, NH

Brian Zehetner, MS, RD, CSCS
Sports Nutrition Consultant
Las Vegas, NV

Paula Ziegler, PhD, RD, CFCS
Gerber Products Company
Parsippany, NJ

FOREWORD

Sports continue to be increasingly popular in the 21st century, not only for spectators but for participants as well. Individuals of all ages and abilities compete in a wide variety of athletic activities, not only for enjoyment but also for the thrill of victory. Relative to the latter, success in any given sport is dependent primarily on genetic endowment with physiologic, psychological, and biomechanical traits deemed vital to the performance requirements of that sport, and also on optimal development of those sport-specific traits through appropriate physical, mental, and skill training. Other than genetics and training, what the athlete eats is probably the most important determinant of success in sports.

In the past, nutrition advice for athletes was based primarily on hearsay, but since the late 1960s sports scientists have increased their focus on the role nutrition plays in sports performance. Literally thousands of studies, using methodologies ranging from basic laboratory tests of muscular strength to complex designs mimicking actual sports competition, have been conducted to evaluate the effects of various nutrients and nutritional strategies on exercise and sports performance. Over the years, such research has provided us with the scientific evidence to support prudent dietary recommendations for athletes competing in various sport endeavors.

Training for most sports involves exercise of some kind, and exercise programs for health-related benefits have become increasingly popular in industrialized nations. Research indicates that properly designed exercise programs may be very effective in the prevention of a host of chronic diseases, including cardiovascular disease, hypertension, obesity, diabetes, osteoporosis, and several forms of cancer. Although the vast majority of this text focuses on nutritional practices that may impact sports performance, various sections detail the role that nutrition, in concert with properly planned exercise programs, may play in prevention of chronic diseases or health problems in physically active individuals.

For the fourth edition of *Sports Nutrition: A Practice Guide for Professionals,* editor Marie Dunford has assembled an outstanding group of contributors, many internationally renowned in specific areas of sports nutrition. They have reviewed the current scientific literature, analyzed and synthesized the results, and interpreted those findings into prudent recommendations designed to enhance the health and performance of physically active individuals. Specific chapters highlight the importance of carbohydrates, proteins, fats, vitamins, minerals, fluids, and dietary supplements to sports performance, and other chapters provide related detailed dietary strategies for athletes based on age, gender, achievement level, varying rates of energy expenditure, and other considerations. Of particular significance, many chapters provide specific dietary guidelines for use when working with such athletes as well as excellent Internet sites for additional information.

This text provides the scientific basis to support prudent dietary recommendations for most athletes, and is de rigueur reading for any dietitian, strength coach, athletic trainer, or other professional who may influence the dietary decisions of athletes at all levels of competition.

Melvin H. Williams, PhD, FACSM
Eminent Scholar Emeritus
Department of Exercise Science, Sport, Physical Education, and Recreation
Old Dominion University
Norfolk, VA

Section 1

Sports Nutrition Basics

Sports nutrition requires an understanding of both exercise physiology and nutrition. Proper nutrition supports training and can improve performance, whereas improper nutrition can be detrimental to performance. Similarly, proper nutrition is important for the athlete's health and improper nutrition can be detrimental to both short-term and long-term health.

The foundations of sports nutrition are covered in the first section of this book. Each chapter is an overview of the current research. The book begins with a review of energy storage and transfer. The roles of carbohydrates, proteins, fats, vitamins, minerals, fluids, and electrolytes are detailed in individual chapters. The final chapter of this section reviews the scientific literature of some of the most popular dietary supplements and ergogenic aids and summarizes the safety and effectiveness of each to date.

Chapter 1

PHYSIOLOGY OF ANAEROBIC AND AEROBIC EXERCISE

Josephine Connolly Schoonen, MS, RD, and Leah Holbrook, RD

Introduction

This chapter focuses on the processes of energy storage and transfer. The energy to fuel physical movement and activity has its origin in the chemical bonds of food. This energy is stored and transferred within the body in many different ways. Eventually it is used to fuel all of the cells' activities, such as contracting muscle fibers or completing biochemical reactions. Physical performance, based on such factors as speed of muscle fiber contraction and number of muscle fibers contracted, depends largely on the energy available to the muscle fibers. Therefore, how energy is stored and transferred is an essential determinant of physical performance. The intensity and duration of the activity as well as nutritional status, level of physical conditioning, genetic endowment, and type of physical activity, affects these processes. Proper nutrition is essential for athletes to meet the energy demands of training and competition and optimize performance. Several excellent reviews discuss the use of energy systems during varying intensities of exercise (1–4).

Energy Storage

Energy is stored in the chemical bonds of macronutrients—dietary carbohydrates, fats, and proteins. Because amino acids from protein are primarily used for structure, function, and regulatory purposes, the chemical energy in protein is infrequently used as a fuel source for physical activity. The primary suppliers of chemical-bond energy for the body reside in fats and carbohydrates.

Dietary fats are digested to fatty acids, absorbed in the small intestine, transported in the bloodstream as lipoproteins and chylomicrons, and stored as triglycerides in adipose tissue and intramuscularly in skeletal muscle. Lipolysis results in triglyceride breakdown to yield fatty acids and glycerol. Fatty acids derived from lipolysis may be used for a variety of synthetic processes or used immediately for energy. Excess fatty acids are converted back to triglycerides for storage in adipose tissue and in lesser amounts within skeletal muscle tissue. Intramuscular triglycerides are an important fuel source, particularly during prolonged aerobic activity. Humans possess a virtually unlimited capacity to store fat and display a large variability in fat storage levels. Fat stores normally represent at least 100 times the amount of carbohydrate energy reserves. As noted in Table 1.1, energy stores in humans have been estimated to be approximately 400 kcal in liver glycogen, 1,500 kcal in muscle glycogen, 30,000 kcal in muscle protein, and 80,000 kcal or more in adipose tissue. Actual values will vary based on individual differences, diet, and the extent of body-fat stores and training (5).

Dietary carbohydrates are digested primarily in the small intestine, where enzymes break disaccharides, such as maltose and sucrose, into monosaccharides, such as glucose, fructose, and galactose. Monosaccharides are absorbed into the lining of the small intestines and travel via the portal vein to the liver, where lactose and galactose are converted to glucose. The liver stores glucose as glycogen and also releases glucose as needed into the bloodstream to maintain normal blood glucose levels. Once in the bloodstream, glucose is taken up by body tissues such as the brain and skeletal muscles.

Glucose may be used for synthetic processes, as an immediate energy source, or rearranged into long chains of glycogen and stored in liver and muscle tissue. The amount of glycogen typically stored is limited to approximately 100 g in the adult liver and 375 g in muscle tissue. Aerobic conditioning and dietary manipulations can increase muscle glycogen storage levels four- to five-fold (5). Dietary carbohydrates eaten in excess of the amount needed for energy or necessary to fill glycogen stores are converted into fatty acids and stored as triglycerides in adipose tissue.

By weight, fats provide more than twice the amount of energy, measured in kilocalories, than either carbohydrates or proteins. Therefore, fat is an efficient way to store energy while minimizing the weight of the energy storage that has to be carried—an evolutionary advantage. The energy in stored fat or glycogen remains in the chemical bonds of these substances. Muscle represents a substantial energy reserve. Small amounts of amino acids are normally used during aerobic exercise, but a prolonged semistarvation state forces the body to use muscle for energy and can negatively impact performance.

TABLE 1.1 Estimated Energy Stores in Humans

Energy Source	Storage Site	Approximate Energy, kcal
ATP/CP	Various tissues	5
Carbohydrate	Blood glucose	20
	Liver glycogen	400
	Muscle glycogen	1500
Fat	Serum free fatty acids	7
	Serum triglycerides	75
	Muscle triglycerides	2500
	Adipose tissue	80000+
Protein	Muscle protein	30000

Abbreviation: ATP/CP, Adenosine triphosphate/creatine phosphate.
Source: Data are from reference 5.

Energy is also stored as creatine phosphate (CP), which is also called phosphocreatine. Food sources of creatine include meat, poultry, fish, and other animal products. Most of the body's creatine is stored in skeletal muscle combined with phosphate. Creatine phosphate serves as an immediate energy source for high-power, very short–duration activities that last only a few seconds. Stored in small amounts in muscle, creatine phosphate can be quickly replenished during recovery periods from high-power activity. Supplementation with creatine can significantly increase intramuscular levels of creatine and creatine phosphate (6). Supplemental creatine as an ergogenic aid is discussed in Chapter 7.

The Energy Currency of the Cell

Adenosine triphosphate (ATP) is the energy currency of the cell. ATP is the only fuel used for biological work, such as muscle contraction, tissue repair and synthesis, and transportation of nutrients. Chemical-bond energy that is stored in various forms is used to synthesize ATP. Energy stored as ATP is transferred to the structure or compound within the cell that requires biological work. During this process a phosphate bond of ATP is broken and energy, adenosine diphosphate (ADP), and inorganic phosphate are released. The high-energy ATP is re-formed using chemical-bond energy from creatine phosphate, fatty acids, glucose, or muscle glycogen. Although the body stores only small amounts of ATP—approximately 80 to 100 g—enough energy to sustain maximum physical effort for a few seconds (7), ATP is continuously formed, used, and re-formed.

When the rate of metabolism increases, the demand for energy and ATP increases and the body immediately begins to break down energy stores. Different stored forms of energy are often used at the same time. The relative amounts of stored energy, as well as the method used to transfer the energy to ADP, depends on the intensity and duration of the activity, availability of fuels, type of activity, nutritional status and training level of the individual, and conditions in the cell. (5)

Energy Transfer

There are three systems used to transfer stored energy to form ATP: (*a*) the phosphagen system, (*b*) the glycolysis system (lactate system), and (*c*) the aerobic system.

The Phosphagen System

The phosphagen system (ATP-CP) is the first system used to transfer energy to form ATP when there is an increase in energy demand. This system does not require that oxygen be present. It is a direct, quick process. The chemical bond energy in the creatine phosphate molecule is transferred directly to an ADP molecule through an enzyme-catalyzed reaction. The amount of creatine phosphate stored in the body is approximately 4 to 6 times more than the amount of ATP stored (7). The combined energy stores of ATP and creatine phosphate are able to fuel muscle contraction for only a short time, depending on the intensity of exercise. For a 70-kg person, it is enough to fuel a 1-minute brisk walk or perform a maximum-effort sprint for 5 to 6 seconds (7). The ATP-CP system fuels high–power output, short-burst, all-out efforts in many sporting events, such as weightlifting, sprints and throws in track and field, and a serve in tennis. When the demand for energy persists and the ATP and creatine phosphate stores are depleted, the accumulation of the byproducts of ATP breakdown triggers the glycolysis system. This system provides energy at a slower rate and, therefore, the sustainable level of intensity and power output is substantially decreased.

The Anaerobic Glycolysis System

The glycolysis or lactate system allows for continued production of ATP for 60 to 180 seconds, whenever adequate oxygen for aerobic metabolism is not available in the active muscles (7). However, the glycolysis system can only use glucose for fuel. A net gain of two ATPs is produced when one molecule of glucose is converted to two molecules of pyruvate via anaerobic glycolysis. During strenuous, fast-paced exercise the production of hydrogen ions during glycolysis often exceeds the capacity on the electron transport chain to oxidize them. In these situations, excess hydrogen ions are combined with pyruvate to produce lactate. See Figure 1.1 for an abbreviated schematic of glycolysis.

Lactate formed during exercise is released into the bloodstream, and rapidly metabolized by cells with high oxidative capacity such as the heart and skeletal muscles. Lactate production increases as the intensity of exercise increases. As long as lactate entry into the blood from active muscles is matched by lactate clearance by the liver, lactate production is not problematic. However, if lactate is produced faster than it can be cleared, lactate accumulates in the blood. Lactate accumulation is associated with increased acidity within muscle cells and inhibition of fatty acid breakdown and use of fatty acids for fuel via aerobic metabolism. These factors contribute to fatigue and decreased exercise performance.

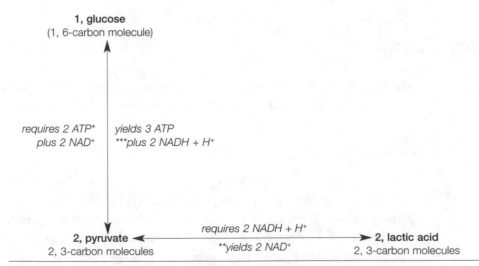

1, glucose
(1, 6-carbon molecule)

requires 2 ATP*   *yields 3 ATP*
plus 2 NAD+   ****plus 2 NADH + H+*

                    requires 2 NADH + H+
2, pyruvate ← → **2, lactic acid**
2, 3-carbon molecules   ***yields 2 NAD+*   2, 3-carbon molecules

* If the original glucose source is locally stored glycogen, then only 1 ATP is required.

** This regenerates the NAD+ necessary for glycolysis.

*** The NADH + H+ can be used later in the aerobic pathways when oxygen is available to produce more ATPs.

FIGURE 1.1.   The anaerobic glycolytic energy system.

Lactate threshold is a term used to describe an exercise level at which an imbalance occurs between lactate production and lactate clearance. Exercising beyond the lactate threshold results in continuously increasing blood lactate levels and a greater reliance on carbohydrate for fuel via anaerobic glycolysis. (7)

The lactate threshold for endurance-trained athletes does not occur until approximately 70% to 80% of their maximum aerobic exercise capacity. In contrast, among untrained individuals, the lactate threshold occurs at approximately 50% to 60% of their maximum aerobic exercise capacity. Adaptations to endurance training increase an athlete's lactate threshold by increasing the efficiency of the aerobic energy system and increase an athlete's capacity to sustain high levels of intensity and power output.

At rest, virtually all of the body's energy needs are met aerobically. With the initiation of physical activity, energy needs rapidly increase, and the oxygen supply to the active muscles is not immediately adequate to support this increased demand for energy exclusively through aerobic pathways. Therefore, until the rate of oxygen delivery increases, more energy is derived from glycolysis than from aerobic metabolism in active muscles. As activity continues, however, the proportion of energy derived from aerobic metabolism increases. Short-burst sprint activities lasting approximately 1 to 2 minutes, such as 100- or 200-meter swimming events, are fueled primarily by anaerobic ATP production. In addition, this system is important to fuel intermittent, high-intensity bursts of activity important in sports such as football, basketball, and soccer. A sprint to the finish line at the end of a 10-kilometer race is an example of ATP needs being met through anaerobic pathways.

The aerobic system is much more efficient than the anaerobic system with regard to ATP production. However, the rate of aerobic ATP production is slower than ATP produced anaerobically. See Table 1.2 for a comparison of the rate of ATP resynthesis by various aerobic and anaerobic processes. Because the rate of ATP production determines power output, anaerobic energy metabolism generates the highest level of power output. ATP-CP and glycolysis (lactate) are recruited to meet the demands for short-duration, high-power activities because ATP resynthesis is most rapid using anaerobic energy metabolism (8).

The Aerobic System

The aerobic system uses carbohydrates (glucose and glycogen), fats (fatty acids), or proteins (amino acids) as energy sources. This system requires that adequate oxygen be available within the cells' mitochondria. This system has two parts—the Krebs cycle and the electron transport chain. In the Krebs cycle, ATP is formed directly via substrate-level phosphorylation. Additional ATP is produced indirectly via electron transport. Electrons

TABLE 1.2 Maximal Rates of Adenosine Triphosphate (ATP) Resynthesis

	$\mu mol \cdot min^{-1} \, gram \, muscle^{-1}$
Creatine phosphate hydrolysis	440
Lactate formation	180
Carbohydrate oxidation	40
Fat oxidation	20

Source: Data are from reference 8.

are generated and carried to the electron transport chain by carriers, either by the reduction of nicotinamide adenine dinucleotide (NAD$^+$ to NADH + H$^+$) or flavin adenine dinucleotide (FAD to FADH$_2$). The electron transport chain consists of a series of coordinated oxidation-reduction reactions. During these reactions an H$^+$ gradient is formed and diffusion of these molecules causes energy to be released and captured in the formation of ATP molecules. Ultimately, oxygen accepts the electrons and is reduced to form water.

When oxygen is present the end product of glycolysis becomes pyruvate, which can be converted to acetyl coenzyme A and enter the Krebs cycle. Complete aerobic metabolism of a glucose molecule yields 38 ATP molecules. Figure 1.2 illustrates aerobic metabolism. Fatty acids are also used as substrates in the aerobic system. Stored fats represent an almost unlimited supply of energy—at least 80,000 to 120,000 kcal. This is in contrast to the approximate 1,000 to 2,000 kcal of stored carbohydrate energy, about 1% to 2% of the energy stored as fat (7,9). Although the majority of fatty acids are stored in adipose tissue, fat is also stored directly in muscle tissue as intramuscular triglycerides, an important fuel source especially during prolonged exercise. Additionally, fatty acids combine with protein for transport in the bloodstream.

Initiation of exercise leads to the release of hormones such as epinephrine, norepinephrine, and glucagon. These hormones activate enzymes that promote lipolysis and facilitate delivery of fatty acids to active muscles. During lipolysis, stored triglycerides are broken down to three fatty acids and a glycerol molecule. Fatty acids from adipose tissue

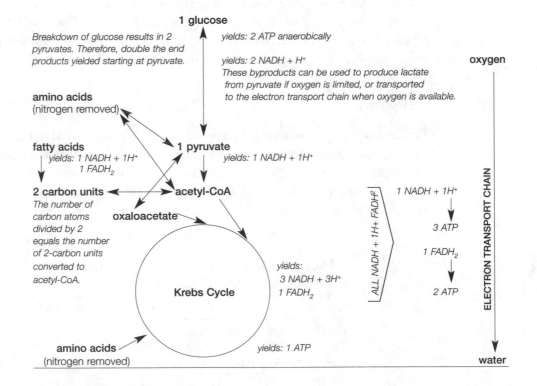

FIGURE 1.2.   The aerobic energy system.

diffuse into the bloodstream where they attach to transporter albumin molecules and are carried to active tissue. As the duration of physical activity increases, greater reliance on fatty acids in aerobic energy metabolism spares the use of muscle glycogen and blood glucose as fuel for physical activity. Because glycogen stores are relatively small compared to fat stores, use of fat to supply energy allows muscle cells to reserve glycogen for periods of exercise when oxygen delivery is inadequate and the cell must rely more heavily on anaerobic energy metabolism. Recall that, other than the small supplies of ATP-CP, only glucose can be used in anaerobic metabolism.

Fatty acids consist of long chains of carbon molecules, typically 16 to 18 carbon atoms, although chains can be as long as 24 carbon atoms. These long chains are first broken down to 2-carbon acetyl units through the process of beta oxidation. The number of ATPs produced from a fatty acid can be calculated using this formula:

$$\left\{\left[\left(\frac{\textit{Total Number of Carbon Units}}{2} - 1\right) \times 17\right] + 12\right\} - 1$$

For example, an 18-carbon fatty acid would yield 147 ATPs:

$$\left\{\left[\left(\frac{18}{2} - 1\right) \times 17\right] + 12\right\} - 1 = 147$$

The glycerol molecule resulting from the breakdown of a triglyceride also yields energy. It is a 3-carbon unit that is funneled into the glycolytic pathway approximately midway down. One glycerol molecule can produce 20 ATPs. A triglyceride with three 18-carbon fatty acids and a glycerol molecule would yield 461 ATPs. (See Figure 1.2.) Fats are obviously a rich energy source to fuel physical activity, but it is important to note that they can only be metabolized aerobically. If adequate oxygen is not available, greater reliance on anaerobic energy production and carbohydrate as the predominant fuel for physical activity will result.

Protein is composed of amino acids. Branched-chain amino acids (leucine, isoleucine, and valine) have long carbon chains that can yield energy via aerobic metabolism. Two other amino acids utilized in aerobic energy production are glutamine and aspartate. During endurance exercise, about 2% to 6% of energy needs can be supplied by this pathway.

Before amino acids can be used in aerobic energy metabolism, their nitrogen-containing groups must be removed. Excess nitrogen is eventually removed from the body by the kidneys as waste products in the urine. Because the formation of urine requires water, excess breakdown of protein increases the risk for dehydration. Different amino acids are funneled into the energy pathways at different points. The most ATP that can be produced from an amino acid is 15 ATPs. (See Figure 1.2.) However, use of amino acids for energy production involves the metabolic cost of excreting the nitrogen and the physiological cost of decreased muscle protein.

Protein is usually spared from entering energy production pathways and is conserved for tissue maintenance, repair, and growth. However, amino acids can be used to produce glucose or energy when glycogen stores are exhausted, which can occur secondary to low carbohydrate intake, low total energy intake, or during prolonged exercise. Additionally, failure of athletes to fully replenish glycogen stores after glycogen-depleting exercise training causes gradual depletion of glycogen stores over time. In these cases, protein stored in muscles can be broken down to synthesize glucose and provide energy for physical activity.

Even under conditions of normal glycogen storage, approximately 3% to 8% of energy needs are supplied by the use of branched-chain amino acids in aerobic metabolism. However, extensive use of protein for fuel results in decreased muscle protein and lean body mass. Although very lean bodies are typical of elite distance runners, a critical level of leg muscle mass is needed to develop the propulsive force required to sustain relatively high levels of power output for long periods. Even though a small percentage of the total fuel needed during prolonged exercise is normally met by oxidation of amino acids, a greater reliance on protein for fuel can be counterproductive to optimal physical performance.

Muscle Fiber Type and Energy Metabolism

There are two basic types of muscle fibers, slow-twitch and fast-twitch. The ratio of slow-twitch to fast-twitch muscle fibers depends largely on genetic predisposition. On average, 45% to 55% of human muscle fibers are slow-twitch fibers. However, training can affect the distribution of muscle fiber types. Athletes trained in sports requiring a high aerobic energy production, such as long-distance running, have up to 90% to 95% slow-twitch muscle fibers in the muscles engaged in the activity (7).

Type I, or slow-twitch, muscle fibers have a relatively slow speed of contraction and primarily use aerobic metabolic pathways. They have an abundance of mitochondria with high levels of enzymes necessary for aerobic energy production (ie, the enzymes necessary in the Krebs cycle and the electron transport chain). Type I muscle fibers also have a higher density of capillaries to transport oxygen and energy substrates and remove byproducts of energy metabolism such as carbon dioxide and lactate. A predominance of type I muscle fibers among endurance athletes is associated with high blood lactate thresholds. Pyruvate is more readily funneled into the Krebs cycle and less pyruvate is converted into lactate under conditions of high lactate thresholds. Therefore, type I fibers facilitate long-duration activities and take longer to fatigue.

Type II, or fast-twitch, muscle fibers have a relatively fast speed of contraction and have a high capacity for fast anaerobic energy production. Type II muscle fibers are subdivided into categories, two of which are well-defined. Type IIa muscle fibers have a high speed of contraction and fairly well-developed aerobic and anaerobic energy production systems. The type IIb muscle fiber types are the fastest, most glycolytic fiber types. Most activities require a combination of fast- and slow-twitch muscle fibers, sustaining relatively slow muscle contractions with occasional short bursts of fast muscle contraction. Activities that require the selective recruitment of type II muscle fibers, such as sprinting and high-intensity stop-and-go movements, depend more heavily on stored carbohydrate energy substrates. Therefore, these activities are associated with a more rapid depletion of glycogen stores.

Carbohydrate, Fat, and Protein Energy Metabolism

The storage and use of energy-containing nutrients—carbohydrates (glucose), proteins (amino acids), and fats (fatty acids)—is integrated. Excess intake of any of these nutrients can be burned aerobically or stored as fats. Although glucose can be used to synthesize amino acids and some amino acids can be used to synthesize glucose, fats cannot be converted to either carbohydrates or amino acids. Even where conversions are possible, these processes involve energy. For example, there is a 5% loss of energy when storing glucose as glycogen in muscles instead of using it immediately to produce ATP. This storage cost increases to 28% when converting glucose to fatty acids for storage (10).

A key point in energy metabolism is that the three energy systems are not simply used sequentially, with the ATP-CP system first, anaerobic glycolysis second, and aerobic metabolism last. All systems and energy substrates are often used simultaneously, with relative contributions varying according to such factors as intensity and duration of the activity, fuel availability, exercise training, nutritional status, and the cellular environment. While all three energy systems may work simultaneously, one system may predominate at any given time. For example, when high power output is demanded for a short duration, such as a maximal weight lift, reliance on the phosphagen system predominates. In contrast, during endurance cycling the aerobic energy system predominates until such time as a brief burst of power is required to pass an opponent or maintain high intensity going uphill. In these situations the anaerobic energy system is recruited more heavily.

In addition to exercise intensity, oxygen availability strongly influences the substrates and energy systems used to produce energy and power. Oxygen availability is an essential component of aerobic energy metabolism. When sufficient oxygen is available, 8.2 ATPs are produced aerobically per carbon atom of a fatty acid whereas only 6.2 ATPs are produced aerobically per carbon atom of one glucose molecule. Therefore, as long as oxygen supply is adequate and aerobic ATP production matches the demands of the activity for power output, greater reliance on fat as fuel is preferable.

However, when oxygen availability is low, the limited oxygen supply must be used efficiently. Under this condition, priority is given to the amount of ATP that can be produced for each oxygen molecule. Compared with 6.3 ATPs produced per oxygen molecule when metabolizing glucose aerobically, only 5.7 ATPs are produced per oxygen molecule when metabolizing fatty acids. Therefore, when oxygen is limited, glucose is the preferred fuel for aerobic metabolism, further highlighting the importance of adequate glycogen stores, especially for competitive, endurance athletes.

Although both glucose and fatty acids are potential substrates for aerobic energy production, fatty acid use depends on the simultaneous flow of at least some carbohydrates through the energy pathways. For example, carbohydrate is necessary to regenerate intermediate compounds in the Krebs cycle. Without adequate carbohydrate breakdown, fat mobilization from adipose tissue exceeds the capacity for fat oxidation. Therefore, instead of leading to ATP production, excess fatty acids are incompletely metabolized and result in the production of ketones, byproducts of incomplete fatty acid metabolism. Although highly oxidative tissues, such as the brain, heart, and skeletal muscles, can use ketones as fuel for aerobic metabolism, ketones are also excreted via respiration and in urine and sweat. Because they have been incompletely metabolized, excreted ketones represent an energy loss (11). In summary, inadequate carbohydrate intake is problematic, especially for those athletes whose performance depends on sustaining high-intensity exercise for prolonged periods.

Gender Differences in Energy Metabolism

There may be gender differences in energy metabolism. The majority of energy utilization research has been conducted with men and the results extrapolated to women. Walker and colleagues (12) briefly reviewed the literature on gender differences in substrate utilization, energy metabolism, and athletic performance. Their work demonstrates that although a glycogen-loading regimen (increasing carbohydrate intake with tapered exercise) increases carbohydrate oxidation and time to exhaustion when cycling at 80% maximum oxygen consumption (VO_{2max}), the resulting increase in glycogen stores is less among women than is demonstrated in men.

Work by Tarnopolsky et al (13) provides evidence that differences in carbohydrate loading are likely a result of lower total energy intake among women and, therefore, lower carbohydrate intake on a gram per kilogram of body weight basis by women than by men. According to Tarnopolsky's research, women might need to consume 8 g carbohydrate/kg daily when carbohydrate loading. Although enzymatic activity does not seem to differ between genders, hormonal effects and potential effects of the menstrual cycle need further investigation.

Summary

Energy is stored in the body in the form of creatine phosphate, carbohydrates (blood glucose, liver and muscle glycogen), fats (serum free fatty acids and triglycerides, muscle triglycerides, and adipose tissue), and protein (muscle). Dietary carbohydrates, fats, and proteins supply energy, with fats and carbohydrates being the primary sources used to fuel activity.

Three systems are used to transfer stored energy to form ATP: the phosphagen system (ATP-PC), the glycolysis system, and the aerobic system. The ATP-PC system provides rapid energy under anaerobic conditions, such as fueling a maximum-effort sprint for 5 seconds. The glycolysis system uses glucose under anaerobic conditions and fuels high-intensity activity for approximately 1 to 3 minutes. The aerobic system uses carbohydrates (glucose and glycogen), fats, and some proteins (amino acids) to fuel sustained activity. Energy metabolism is integrated. All three systems may work simultaneously, but one system may predominate based on several factors including the intensity and duration of the activity.

References

1. Gastin P. Energy system interaction and relative contribution during maximal exercise. *Sports Med.* 2001;31:725–741.
2. Conley KE, Kemper WF, Crowther GJ. Limits to sustainable muscle performance: between glycolysis and oxidative phosphorylation. *J Exp Biol.* 2001;204:3189–3194.
3. Noakes T. Physiological models to understand exercise fatigue and the adaptations that predict or enhance athletic performance. *Scand J Med Sci Sport*s. 2000;10:123–145.
4. Sahlin K, Tonkonogi M, Soderlund K. Energy supply and muscle fatigue in humans. *Acta Physiol Scand.* 1998;162:261–266.
5. Williams MH. *Nutrition for Health, Fitness, and Sport.* 7th ed. Boston, Mass: McGraw-Hill; 2005.
6. Mesa JL, Ruiz JR, Gonzalez-Gross MM, Gutierrez Sainz A, Castillo Garzon MJ. Oral creatine supplementation and skeletal muscle metabolism in physical exercise. *Sports Med.* 2002;32: 903–944.

7. McArdle W, Katch F, Katch V. *Exercise Physiology.* 5th ed. Baltimore, Md: Williams and Wilkins; 2004.

8. Maughan RJ, Burke LM. *Sports Nutrition: Handbook of Sports Medicine and Science.* Boston, Mass: Blackwell Science; 2002.

9. Linscheer WG, Vergroesen AJ. Lipids. In: Shils ME, Olson JA, Shike M, eds. *Modern Nutrition in Health and Disease.* 8th ed. Philadelphia, Pa: Lea & Febiger; 1994:47–88.

10. Macdonald I. Carbohydrates. In: Shils M, Olson JA, Shike M, eds. *Modern Nutrition in Health and Disease.* 8th ed. Philadelphia, Pa: Lea & Febiger, 1994:36–46.

11. Houston M. *Biochemistry Primer for Exercise Science.* 2nd ed. Champaign, Ill: Human Kinetics; 2001.

12. Walker JL, Heigenhauser JF, Hultman E, Spriet LL. Dietary carbohydrate, muscle glycogen content, and endurance performance in well-trained women. *J Appl Physiol.* 2000;88:2151–2158.

13. Tarnopolsky MA, Zawada C, Richmond LB, Carter S, Shearer J, Graham T, Phillips SM. Gender differences in carbohydrate loading are related to energy intake. *J Appl Physiol.* 2001;91:225–230.

Chapter 2

CARBOHYDRATE AND EXERCISE

ELLEN J. COLEMAN, MA, MPH, RD

Introduction

Carbohydrate is a primary fuel during physical activity; thus, adequate carbohydrate stores (muscle and liver glycogen and blood glucose) are critical for optimum athletic performance. Because carbohydrate stores are limited, consuming adequate carbohydrate on a daily basis is necessary to replenish muscle and liver glycogen between daily training sessions or competitive events. Consuming carbohydrate prior to exercise can help performance by "topping off" muscle and liver glycogen stores. Consuming carbohydrate during exercise can improve performance by maintaining blood glucose levels and carbohydrate oxidation. Finally, carbohydrate intake after glycogen-depleting exercise facilitates rapid refilling of carbohydrate stores, especially among athletes engaged in daily hard training or tournament activity.

Carbohydrate Availability During Exercise

Muscle glycogen represents the major source of carbohydrate in the body (300 to 400 g or 1,200 to 1,600 kcal), followed by liver glycogen (75 to 100 g or 300 to 400 kcal), and, lastly, blood glucose (25 g or 100 kcal). These amounts vary substantially among individuals, depending on factors such as dietary intake and state of training. Untrained individuals have muscle glycogen stores that are roughly 80 to 90 mmol/kg of wet muscle weight. Endurance athletes have muscle glycogen stores of 130 to 135 mmol/kg of wet muscle weight. Carbohydrate loading increases muscle glycogen stores to 210 to 230 mmol/kg of wet muscle weight (1).

Exercise energetics dictate that carbohydrate is the predominant fuel for exercise intensities at 65% of maximum oxygen consumption (VO_{2max}) or more—the level at which most athletes train and compete. Although both carbohydrate and fat contribute to energy production during exercise, fat oxidation alone cannot supply adenosine triphosphate (ATP) rapidly enough to support such high-intensity exercise. Although it is possible to exercise at light to moderate levels (< 60% of VO_{2max}) with low levels of muscle glycogen and blood glucose, it is impossible to meet the ATP requirements necessary for high-intensity, high–power output exercise when these fuels are depleted. Utilization of muscle glycogen is most rapid during the early stages of exercise and is exponentially related to exercise intensity (1).

There is a strong relationship between the pre-exercise muscle glycogen content and the length of time that exercise can be performed at 70% of VO_{2max}. The greater the pre-exercise glycogen content, the greater the endurance potential. Bergstrom et al (2) measured muscle glycogen content and compared the exercise time to exhaustion at 75% of VO_{2max} after 3 days of three diets varying in carbohydrate content. A low-carbohydrate diet (< 5% of energy from carbohydrate) produced a muscle glycogen content of 38 mmol/kg and supported only 1 hour of exercise. A mixed diet (50% energy from carbohydrate) produced a muscle glycogen content of 106 mmol/kg and enabled the subjects to exercise 115 minutes. However, a high-carbohydrate diet (≥ 82% of energy from carbohydrate) provided 204 mmol/kg of muscle glycogen and enabled the subjects to exercise for 170 minutes.

Liver glycogen stores maintain blood glucose levels both at rest and during exercise. At rest, the brain and central nervous system (CNS) utilize most of the blood glucose, and the muscle accounts for less than 20% of blood glucose utilization. During exercise, however, muscle glucose uptake can increase 30-fold, depending on exercise intensity and duration. Initially, the majority of hepatic glucose output comes from glycogenolysis; however, as the exercise duration increases and liver glycogen decreases, the contribution of glucose from gluconeogenesis increases (1).

At the beginning of exercise, hepatic glucose output matches the increased muscle glucose uptake so that blood glucose levels remain near resting levels. Although muscle glycogen is the primary source of carbohydrate during exercise intensities more than 65% of VO_{2max}, blood glucose becomes an increasingly important source of carbohydrate as muscle glycogen stores decrease. When hepatic glucose output can no longer keep up with muscle glucose uptake during prolonged exercise, the blood glucose decreases. Although a few athletes experience CNS symptoms typical of hypoglycemia, most athletes note local muscular fatigue and have to reduce their exercise intensity (1).

Liver glycogen stores can be depleted by a 15-hour fast and can decrease from a typical level of 490 mmol on a mixed diet to 60 mmol on a low-carbohydrate diet. A high-carbohydrate diet can increase liver glycogen content to approximately 900 mmol (1).

Daily Carbohydrate Recommendations

The relationship between muscle glycogen depletion and exhaustion is strongest at moderate training intensities (65% to 85% of VO_{2max}). Studies of runners have shown that high-carbohydrate diets replenished muscle glycogen levels (3,4) and maintained performance (4), whereas low-carbohydrate diets for 3 successive days resulted in low muscle glycogen levels (5). Athletes who train exhaustively on successive days should consume adequate carbohydrate and energy to delay onset of fatigue caused by the cumulative depletion of muscle glycogen. This includes athletes in sports that require repeated, near-maximal bursts of effort (such as football, basketball, and soccer) as well as endurance sports.

Jacobs and Sherman (1) conducted a literature review on the effectiveness of carbohydrate supplementation and chronic high-carbohydrate diets for improving endurance performance. They conclude that overwhelming evidence indicates carbohydrate supplementation before and during exercise improves endurance performance. The use of short-term dietary and training strategies to increase muscle glycogen stores (eg, carbohydrate loading) also improve performance. Although chronic high-carbohydrate diets maintain higher muscle glycogen concentrations than moderate-carbohydrate diets, the effect on performance is not clear. The authors note that research clearly demonstrates that a high-carbohydrate diet is necessary for optimal training adaptations and greater improvements in endurance performance in previously untrained individuals. Until research shows otherwise, Jacobs and Sherman conclude that a high-carbohydrate diet is still the best recommendation for endurance athletes (1).

Carbohydrate recommendations for athletes range from 6 to 10 g/kg/day (6,7). Burke and colleagues suggest an intake of 5 to 7 g/kg/day for general training needs and 7 to 10 g/kg/day for the increased needs of endurance athletes (8). Athletes participating in ultra-endurance events (those lasting longer than 4 hours) have the highest carbohydrate requirements, typically more than 11 g/kg/day or more than 600 g/day (9–11). Such high requirements are difficult to meet with conventional carbohydrate foods. Recommended daily carbohydrate intake is listed in Box 2.1.

Athletes should consume sufficient energy as well as carbohydrate. Consumption of a reduced-energy diet will impair endurance performance due to muscle and liver glycogen depletion (6,7). Adequate carbohydrate intake is also important for athletes in high-power activities (eg, wrestling, gymnastics, and dance) who have lost weight due to negative energy balances (7). Desire for weight loss and consumption of low-energy diets are prevalent among athletes in high-power activities. Negative energy balance can harm high-power performance due to impaired acid-base balance, reduced glycolytic enzyme levels, selective atrophy of type II muscle fibers, and abnormal sarcoplasmic reticulum function. Adequate dietary carbohydrate may ameliorate some of the damaging effects of energy restriction on the muscle (7).

For many athletes, energy and carbohydrate needs are greater during training than during competition. Some athletes involuntarily fail to increase energy intake to meet the energy demands of increased training. Costill et al (12) studied the effects of 10 days of increased training volume at a high intensity on muscle glycogen and swimming performance. Six swimmers self-selected a diet containing 4,700 kcal/day and 8.2 g carbohydrate/kg/day, whereas four swimmers self-selected a diet containing only 3,700 kcal/day and 5.3 g carbohydrate/kg/day. These four swimmers could not tolerate the heavier training demands and swam at significantly slower speeds, presumably due to a 20% decrease in muscle glycogen.

BOX 2.1   Recommended Daily Carbohydrate Intake

The typical US diet supplies 4 to 5 g carbohydrate/kg daily. Recommended daily intake for most trained athletes is

- 5 to 10 g carbohydrate/kg
- 5 to 7 g carbohydrate/kg for general training needs
- 7 to 10 g carbohydrate/kg for endurance athletes
- Ultraendurance athletes have exceptional needs and often need more than 11 g carbohydrate/kg

Low blood glucose and low muscle and/or liver glycogen concentrations can contribute to fatigue during other types of exercise. Building up and maintaining glycogen stores during training require an adequate intake of carbohydrate and energy. When adequate carbohydrate and energy are not consumed on a daily basis between training sessions, the pre-exercise muscle glycogen content gradually decreases and training or competitive performance may be impaired. Daily restoration of the body's carbohydrate reserves should be a priority for athletes involved in intense training.

Glycemic Index and Glycemic Load

A high-carbohydrate food may be classified by the type of carbohydrate (simple vs complex), by the form of carbohydrate (liquid vs solid), or by the glycemic index (GI) of the carbohydrate (low, moderate, or high). The simple vs complex and liquid vs solid classifications do not indicate the effect of carbohydrate-rich foods and fluids on blood glucose and insulin levels. The GI classification, however, does indicate the actual effects of carbohydrate-rich foods and fluids on blood glucose and has an effect on insulin levels (13). It is important to note that factors other than GI also affect insulin levels.

The GI is a ranking of foods based on their measured blood glucose response compared with a reference food, either glucose or white bread. The GI is calculated by measuring the incremental area under the blood glucose curve following ingestion of a test food providing 50 g carbohydrate, compared with the area under the blood glucose curve after a 50 g carbohydrate intake from the reference food. All tests are conducted after an overnight fast (13).

Generally, foods are divided into those that have a high GI (glucose, bread, potatoes, breakfast cereal, sports drinks), a moderate GI (sucrose, soft drinks, oats, tropical fruits such as bananas and mangos), or a low GI (fructose, milk, yogurt, lentils, pasta, nuts, cold climate fruits such as apples and oranges). The GIs of a large number of foods were published in the *American Journal of Clinical Nutrition* in 2002 (14).

The GI reflects the rate of digestion and absorption of a carbohydrate-rich food. Thus, the GI is influenced by the food form (including particle size, presence of intact grains, texture, and viscosity), the degree of food processing and cooking, the presence of fructose or lactose (both have a low GI), the ratio of amylopectin and amylose in starch (amylose has a slower rate of digestion), starch-protein or starch-fat interactions, and the presence of antinutrients (compounds in foods that decrease the absorption of nutrients), such as phytates and lectins (13).

Although the GI concept may be useful, it has limitations. For example, the GI is based on a 50-g carbohydrate portion, not a food's average serving size. The values are also largely based on tests using single foods. The blood glucose response to high-GI foods may be blunted when combined with low-GI foods in the same meal. However, the GI can be applied to mixed meals by taking a weighted mean of the GI of the carbohydrate-rich foods that make up the meal (13).

Some practitioners suggest that manipulating the GI of foods and meals may enhance carbohydrate availability and improve athletic performance. For example, low-GI carbohydrate-rich foods may be recommended before exercise to promote sustained carbohydrate availability. Moderate- to high-GI carbohydrate foods may be recommended during exercise to promote carbohydrate oxidation and after exercise to promote glycogen repletion.

GI may be useful in sports by helping to fine-tune food choices. However, additional studies are warranted. For example, several companies are marketing energy bars that are reduced in carbohydrate content. One marketing strategy is to offer a snack food that is purported to result in a lower insulin response compared with high-GI foods. A recent study examined the blood glucose and insulin responses to consuming low-, moderate-, or high-carbohydrate energy bars. The results indicated that although substitution of other macro-nutrients for carbohydrate reduces the glycemic response, the insulin response was not uniformly reduced, and, in fact, was actually increased for some bars when compared with white bread (15).

Perhaps more useful than GI is the concept of glycemic load (GL), which considers both GI and the amount of carbohydrate consumed (GL = GI [expressed as a decimal] multiplied by dietary carbohydrate content in grams) (14). Because the carbohydrate content in an actual serving size is considered, the GL of a food is almost always less than its corresponding GI. Although using the GI to choose an individual food may be helpful in certain situations, GL provides an overview of the daily diet and can be used to compare day-to-day intake.

In summary, GI is one factor that may be considered in providing guidance for carbohydrate and food intake before, during, and after exercise. However, other features of foods deserve consideration as well, such as the food's nutritional content and the practical issues of palatability, portability, cost, gastric comfort, and ease of preparation. Because food choices are specific to the individual athlete and exercise situation, athletes need to know their nutritional goals and learn how to choose foods and fluids to help them achieve those goals (13).

Communicating Carbohydrate Recommendations

Nutrition guidelines for the public usually express goals for carbohydrate intake as a percentage of total energy intake. For example, most professional health organizations in the United States recommend 55% to 60% of energy intake from carbohydrate. Although this general guideline may be appropriate for sedentary people, it is not always appropriate for athletes (6,8).

The absolute quantity of carbohydrate, rather than the percentage of energy from carbohydrate, is important for optimal glycogen synthesis and exercise performance. A recommendation to consume 5 to 7 g carbohydrate/kg/day is user-friendly and takes into consideration the athlete's body weight. It is relatively easy for an athlete to determine the carbohydrate content of meals and snacks to achieve a daily carbohydrate goal of 400 g. It takes far more knowledge of nutrition to create a diet plan that provides 60% of energy from carbohydrate. It is also difficult for an athlete to visualize meals and snacks that meet this recommendation.

Another problem with using percentages is that the athlete's energy and carbohydrate requirements are not always matched. Athletes who have large muscle masses and heavy training regimens generally have very high energy requirements and can meet their carbohydrate needs with a lower percentage of energy from carbohydrate. When an athlete consumes 4,000 to 5,000 kcal/day, even a diet providing 50% of energy from carbohydrate will supply 500 to 600 g carbohydrate/day. This translates into 7 to 8 g carbohydrate/kg for a

70-kg athlete, which should be adequate to maintain muscle glycogen stores from day to day (6,8).

Conversely, when a 60-kg athlete consumes less than 2,000 kcal/day, even a diet providing 60% of energy from carbohydrate (4 to 5 g/kg/day) is unlikely to provide sufficient carbohydrate to maintain optimal carbohydrate stores for daily training. This situation is particularly common in female athletes who restrict energy intake to achieve or maintain a low body weight or percentage of body fat (6,8).

Analyzing an athlete's diet based on the percentage of energy derived from carbohydrate can also lead to questionable interpretations of research data. Lamb et al (16) compared the performance of swimmers who consumed either a moderate-carbohydrate diet (43% of energy) or high-carbohydrate diet (80% of energy) for 9 days. There were no significant differences in swim times or ratings of perceived exertion at interval distances ranging from 50 to 3,000 meters. Due to the swimmers' high energy intake of 4,675 kcal, even the moderate-carbohydrate group consumed 502 g carbohydrate/day, compared with 935 g/day in the high-carbohydrate group. This study has been used to support the misleading claim that a diet containing 40% carbohydrate is as effective as a diet containing 80% carbohydrate, without recognizing that both groups of swimmers consumed more than 500 g carbohydrate. The moderate carbohydrate intake met the fuel needs of the swimmers because energy intake was high.

A study by Tarnopolsky et al (17) comparing carbohydrate loading regimens in men and women can also be misinterpreted if percentage of energy from carbohydrate is utilized to explain the study's findings. The male and female subjects consumed 75% of energy from carbohydrate for four days prior to an exercise trial to fatigue. The men consumed more total energy (3,290 kcal) and 617 g carbohydrate/day, whereas the women consumed less total energy (1,973 kcal) and only 370 g carbohydrate/day. Only the men experienced significant increases in muscle glycogen storage (41%) and endurance performance (45%). The authors concluded that men, but not women, benefit from carbohydrate loading (16). A more plausible explanation, however, was that the women did not consume adequate carbohydrate or energy to experience increases in muscle glycogen storage and endurance performance.

For all the reasons outlined above, it is more reliable and practical to recommend that athletes consume an absolute quantity of carbohydrate (5 to 10 g/kg/day) rather than a relative percent of energy from carbohydrate (55% to 60%). Also, attention must be paid to achieving energy balance and to adequacy of protein and fat intake, especially over time. For example, a carbohydrate recommendation of 10/g/kg would be too high to allow for adequate protein and fat intake in an athlete with low body weight (eg, 50 kg) who needs to consume only 2,000 to 2,500 kcal/day. Thus, carbohydrate recommendations need to be made within the context of energy balance and adequacy of other macronutrients.

Muscle Glycogen Supercompensation

Muscle glycogen depletion is a well-recognized limitation to endurance performance. Greater than normal pre-exercise muscle glycogen stores increase exercise time to exhaustion (2) and enable athletes to maintain their pace for a longer period during time trials that exceed 90 minutes (18). Muscle glycogen supercompensation (carbohydrate loading) can nearly double muscle glycogen concentrations from normal values of 80 to 120 mmol/kg wet weight to values of about 200 mmol/kg wet weight (18). The greater the athlete's pre-exercise muscle glycogen content, the greater the endurance potential.

Carbohydrate loading will help only athletes engaged in intense, continuous endurance exercise lasting longer than 90 minutes. Above-normal muscle glycogen stores will not enable athletes to exercise harder during shorter duration exercise (eg, 5- and 10-km runs) and may harm performance due to the associated stiffness and heaviness. Although some body builders use carbohydrate loading to increase muscle size and enhance appearance, Balon et al (19) reported no increase in the girths of seven muscle groups following a carbohydrate-loading regimen in resistance-trained bodybuilders.

Endurance training promotes muscle glycogen supercompensation by increasing the activity of glycogen synthase—an enzyme responsible for glycogen storage. The athlete must be endurance-trained or the regimen will not be effective. Because glycogen stores are specific to the muscle groups used, the exercise to deplete the stores must be the same as the athlete's competitive event. Some athletes note a feeling of stiffness and heaviness associated with the increased glycogen storage (additional water is stored with glycogen) but these sensations dissipate with exercise.

The first carbohydrate-loading regimen utilized a bout of glycogen-depleting exercise followed by 3 days of a high-carbohydrate diet. This soon evolved into the classic 6-day regimen, which began with a bout of glycogen-depleting exercise 6 days before competition. The athlete consumed a low-carbohydrate, high-fat diet for the next 3 days and continued exercising. On the 3 days before competition, the athlete consumed a high-carbohydrate diet and rested to promote muscle glycogen supercompensation (2).

The bout of glycogen-depleting exercise in the 3-day regimen and the low-carbohydrate diet in the 6-day regimen often interfered with the training taper for competition and proved to be too cumbersome for many athletes. As a result, Sherman et al (20) developed a revised 6-day carbohydrate-loading protocol that addressed those concerns and provided muscle glycogen levels comparable to the classical 3- and 6-day regimens. This modified regimen required the athlete to taper training on consecutive days after a bout of glycogen-depleting exercise 6 days before competition. The athlete consumed a normal mixed diet on the first 3 days followed by a high-carbohydrate diet the 3 days before competition. Carbohydrate-loading guidelines are listed in Table 2.1

All three carbohydrate-loading regimens share the drawback that glycogen storage occurs relatively slowly—2 to 6 days are required to attain increased muscle glycogen lev-

TABLE 2.1   Carbohydrate Loading Guidelines

Day	Training (70% of VO_{2max})	Carbohydrate g/kg
1	90 min	5
2	40 min	5
3	40 min	5
4	20 min	10
5	20 min	10
6	Rest	10
7	Competition	

els. This poses a problem for athletes who do not want to alter their normal training before competition.

Fairchild et al (21) evaluated whether 1 day of a high carbohydrate intake after a short bout of high-intensity exercise would result in above-normal levels of muscle glycogen. The authors hypothesized that because all muscle-fiber types are recruited during high-intensity exercise, muscle glycogen supercompensation should take place in all muscle fibers. Furthermore, higher rates of muscle glycogen synthesis have been reported in individuals recovering from a short bout of near-maximal exercise compared with prolonged exercise of moderate intensity. Although the study was limited to seven endurance-trained males, it holds promise that greater-than-normal muscle glycogen stores can be built up within only 24 hours by consuming approximately 10.3 g/kg body weight after a 3-minute bout of high-intensity exercise (20).

If these results are corroborated by future studies, the "new and improved carbohydrate-loading" should result in better compliance compared with other regimens. This newest carbohydrate-loading protocol is faster than other regimens and seems to provide muscle glycogen levels comparable with these regimens. The primary advantage of this rapid regimen is that the diet and exercise strategies required to carbohydrate-load can be initiated 24 hours before competition with minimal disruption to training and pre-event preparation.

High-carbohydrate Liquid Supplements

Athletes who train heavily and have difficulty eating enough food to consume adequate carbohydrate and energy can consider using a commercial, high-carbohydrate liquid supplement (10). Most products are 18% to 24% carbohydrate and contain glucose polymers (maltodextrins) to reduce the solution's osmolality and potential for gastrointestinal distress. If the athlete has no difficulty eating enough conventional food, these products offer only the advantage of convenience.

High-carbohydrate supplements do not replace regular food but help supply supplemental energy, carbohydrate, and liquid during heavy training or carbohydrate loading. Compared with conventional high-carbohydrate foods, high-carbohydrate liquid supplements usually do not have fiber and produce a low stool residue.

High-carbohydrate supplements can be consumed before or after exercise (eg, with meals or between meals). Although ultraendurance athletes may also use them during exercise to obtain energy and carbohydrate, these products are too concentrated in carbohydrate to double for use as a fluid-replacement beverage.

Carbohydrate Before Exercise

Based primarily on the results of one study, athletes have been cautioned not to eat high-glycemic carbohydrates (bread, potato, sports drinks, and many breakfast cereals) in the hour prior to exercise. This admonition was based on research conducted by Foster et al (22) in the late 1970s indicating that consuming 75 g glucose 30 minutes before exercise reduced endurance by causing accelerated muscle glycogen depletion and hypoglycemia. The high blood insulin levels induced by the pre-exercise carbohydrate feeding were blamed for this chain of events. However, subsequent studies contradicted Foster's early findings (23,24). From the results of these and other recent studies, it seems that the blood glucose reductions that may occur during the first 20 minutes of exercise after carbohydrate ingestion is self-correcting during exercise and is not associated with performance decrements.

Thomas et al (25) first sparked interest in the use of the GI in sport by manipulating the glycemic response to pre-exercise meals. In theory, low-GI foods (beans, milk, and pasta) provide a slow and sustained release of glucose to the blood, without an accompanying insulin surge. A 1991 study by Thomas et al (25) reported that the consumption of 1 g carbohydrate/kg from a low-GI food (lentils) 1 hour prior to cycling at 67% of VO_{2max} increased endurance compared with an equal amount of carbohydrate from a high-GI food (potatoes). The lentils promoted lower postprandial blood glucose and insulin responses and more stable blood glucose levels during exercise compared with the potatoes.

Results from subsequent research studies are mixed. DeMarco et al (26) found that a low-GI meal also maintained higher blood glucose levels at the end of 2 hours of exercise, which may have improved subsequent maximal effort. But a second study by Thomas et al (27) found that there were no differences in time to exhaustion between the low- and high-GI meals. Sparks et al (28) found no differences in work output when a low-GI food (lentils) and a high-GI food (potatoes) were consumed 45 minutes prior to exercise.

At the present time, there is insufficient evidence to recommend that all athletes consume low-GI foods before exercise (13), but a low-GI pre-exercise meal may be beneficial for athletes for whom consuming carbohydrate during exercise is not practical or possible. The hypoglycemia and hyperinsulinemia following pre-exercise high-GI carbohydrate feedings are transient and will not harm performance unless the athlete reacts negatively to high-GI foods. Athletes should evaluate their responses to both low- and high-GI carbohydrates in training to find what works the best. Athletes who react negatively to high-GI foods can choose from several strategies: consume a low-GI carbohydrate before exercise; consume carbohydrate a few minutes before exercise; or wait until exercising to consume carbohydrate. The exercise-induced increase in the hormones epinephrine, norepinephrine, and growth hormone inhibit the release of insulin and thus counter insulin's effect in reducing blood glucose.

For athletes who have neglected to eat within several hours of exercise, eating and/or drinking an easily digested food or fluid with a moderate to high GI within 5 minutes of exercise may benefit aerobic endurance performance (29). A food or fluid snack containing approximately 50 g of moderate- to high-GI carbohydrate may provide fuel for working muscles and help to maintain normal blood glucose levels during early exercise. Because initiation of exercise will suppress the release of insulin, even a transient hypoglycemia may not occur.

Consuming a high-GI carbohydrate (eg, glucose) immediately before anaerobic exercise, such as sprinting or weightlifting, will not provide athletes with a quick burst of energy, allowing them to exercise harder. Adequate ATP, creatine phosphate, and muscle glycogen is stored for these anaerobic tasks.

The Pre-exercise Meal

Many athletes who train or compete in the morning forgo food prior to exercise. An overnight fast reduces liver glycogen stores and can impair performance, especially if the athlete engages in prolonged endurance exercise that relies heavily on blood glucose.

During exercise, athletes rely primarily on their preexisting glycogen and fat stores. Although the pre-exercise meal does not contribute immediate energy for exercise, it provides energy when the athlete exercises hard for 1 hour or longer. The pre-exercise meal also prevents athletes from feeling hungry (which may impair performance) and increases blood glucose to provide energy for the exercising muscles.

Consuming carbohydrate 2 to 4 hours before morning exercise helps to restore suboptimal liver glycogen stores and aids endurance in events that rely heavily on blood glucose. Nuefer et al (30) found that endurance performance was also improved when a mixed meal (cereal, bread, milk, and fruit juice) supplying 200 g carbohydrate was consumed 4 hours before exercise.

The ideal pre-exercise meal is carbohydrate-rich, palatable, and well-tolerated. Including some low-GI foods may be beneficial in promoting a sustained release of glucose into the bloodstream. Research by Sherman et al (24,31) suggests that the pre-exercise meal contain 1.0 to 4.5 g carbohydrate/kg, consumed 1 to 4 hours before exercise. To avoid potential gastrointestinal distress when blood is diverted from the gut to the exercising muscles, the carbohydrate and calorie content of the meal should be reduced the closer to exercise the meal is consumed. For example, a carbohydrate feeding of 1 g/kg is appropriate 1 hour before exercise, whereas 4.5 g/kg can be consumed 4 hours before exercise. Recommendations for carbohydrate intake prior to exercise are summarized in Box 2.2.

Many commercially formulated liquid meals satisfy the requirements for pre-exercise food—they are high in carbohydrate, palatable, and provide both energy and fluid. Liquid meals can often be consumed closer to competition than regular meals due to their shorter gastric emptying time. This may help to avoid precompetition nausea for those athletes who are tense and have an associated delay in gastric emptying. Some products were initially designed for hospital patients (eg, Sustacal, Mead Johnson, Evansville, IN, and Ensure, Abbott Laboratories, Abbott Park, IL), whereas others have been specifically created for and marketed to the athlete (eg, Gatorade Nutrition Shake, Gatorade, Chicago IL, and Nutrament and Boost, Novartis Medical Nutrition, Fremont, MI).

Liquid meals produce a low stool residue, thereby minimizing immediate weight gain after the meal. This is especially advantageous for athletes who need to "make weight."

BOX 2.2   Recommended Carbohydrate Intake Prior to Exercise

- Athletes should experiment with low-, medium-, and high-glycemic index foods during training.
- Consider both amount and timing of carbohydrate intake. General recommendations are as follows:

Carbohydrate, g/kg	Timing Prior to Exercise, hours
1.0	1
2.0	2
3.0	3
4.0–4.5	4

They are convenient fuel for athletes competing in day-long competitions, tournaments, and multiple events (eg, triathlons). During heavy training when energy requirements are substantially increased, liquid meals also can be used for nutritional supplementation because they supply a significant amount of energy and contribute to satiety.

Carbohydrate Intake During Exercise

Carbohydrate feedings during exercise lasting at least 1 hour enable athletes to exercise longer and sprint harder at the end of exercise. Coyle et al (32,33) have demonstrated that consuming carbohydrate during cycling exercise at 70% of VO_{2max} can delay fatigue by 30 to 60 minutes. The carbohydrate feedings maintained blood glucose at higher levels, thereby increasing the utilization of blood glucose for energy. Carbohydrate feedings during endurance exercise maintain blood glucose levels at a time when muscle glycogen stores are diminished. Thus, carbohydrate oxidation (and, therefore, ATP production) can continue at a high rate and endurance is enhanced. The maximal rate of exogenous carbohydrate oxidation during moderate-intensity exercise is approximately 1 g/minute (1).

Running performances with and without carbohydrate feedings have also been evaluated (34,35). During a 40-km run in the heat, Millard-Stafford et al (34) found that a carbohydrate feeding (55 g/hour) increased blood glucose levels and enabled runners to finish the last 5 km significantly faster compared with those who ran without carbohydrate. In a treadmill run at 80% of VO_{2max}, Wilber and Moffatt (35) found that the run time when fed carbohydrate (35 g/hour) was 23 minutes longer (115 minutes) compared with the run without carbohydrate (92 minutes).

Carbohydrate feedings may also improve performance in stop-and-go sports (eg, football, basketball, soccer, tennis, and intermittent high-intensity cycling) that require repeated bouts of high-intensity, short-duration effort (36–38). Nicholas et al (36) examined the effects of a 6.9% carbohydrate-electrolyte drink on performance during intermittent, high-intensity shuttle running designed to replicate the activity pattern of stop-and-go sports. The players who consumed carbohydrate rather than a placebo were able to run significantly longer (2 minutes) during the performance trial compared with the placebo (8.9 minutes vs 6.7 minutes). In a later study, Nicholas et al (37) evaluated the effect of carbohydrate feedings on muscle glycogen utilization during intermittent, high-intensity shuttle running. This study established that muscle glycogen utilization was reduced by 22% after ingestion of a carbohydrate-electrolyte drink that provided 51 g carbohydrate/hour.

Davis et al (38) evaluated the effect of carbohydrate feedings on performance during intermittent, high-intensity cycling. The mean time to fatigue in the carbohydrate trial was 89 minutes (21 sprints) compared with 58 minutes (14 sprints) for the placebo. The results of these three studies suggest that the benefits of carbohydrate feedings are not limited to prolonged endurance exercise. Carbohydrate feedings improve performance in stop-and-go sports by selectively sparing glycogen in type II muscle fibers, increasing glycogen resynthesis in type II muscle fibers during rest or low-intensity periods, or a combination of both (37).

The performance benefits of a pre-exercise carbohydrate feeding seem to be additive to those of consuming carbohydrate during exercise. In a study by Wright et al (39), cyclists who received carbohydrate both 3 hours before exercise and during exercise were able to exercise longer (289 minutes) than when receiving carbohydrate either only before exercise (236 minutes) or during exercise (266 minutes). This study indicates that utilizing carbohydrate feedings before and during exercise improved performance more than either feeding alone. However, the improvement in performance with the pre-exercise carbohydrate feedings was less than when smaller quantities of carbohydrate were consumed during exercise. Thus, to obtain a continuous supply of glucose, endurance athletes and those engaged in high-intensity intermittent exercise, such as repeated bouts of interval training, should consume carbohydrate during exercise.

Carbohydrate's primary role in fluid replacement drinks is to maintain blood glucose concentration and enhance carbohydrate oxidation (1,40). Carbohydrate feedings enhance performance during exercise lasting 1 hour or longer, especially when muscle glycogen stores are low. In fact, carbohydrate ingestion and fluid replacement independently improve performance, and their beneficial effects are additive.

Below et al (41) evaluated the effects of fluid and carbohydrate ingestion, alone or in combination, during 1 hour of intense cycling exercise. In the four trials, the subjects ingested either 1,330 mL water (which replaced 79% of sweat loss), 1,330 mL fluid with 79 g carbohydrate, 200 mL water (which replaced 13% of sweat losses), or 200 mL fluid with 79 g carbohydrate. When a large volume of fluid or 79 g carbohydrate was ingested individually, each improved performance by approximately 6% compared with the placebo trial. When both the large volume of fluid and carbohydrate were combined, performance was improved by 12%.

It is recommended that athletes take in 30 to 60 g (120 to 240 kcal) of carbohydrate every hour to improve endurance performance (42). This amount can be obtained through either carbohydrate-rich foods or fluids. Although it makes sense that athletes should consume carbohydrate sources that are rapidly digested and absorbed to promote carbohydrate oxidation, the glycemic response to carbohydrate feedings during exercise has not been systematically studied. However, most athletes choose carbohydrate-rich foods (sports bars and gels) and fluids (sports drinks) that would be classified as having a moderate to high GI (13). Recommendations for carbohydrate intake during exercise are summarized in Box 2.3.

Liquid vs Solid Carbohydrate

The benefits of consuming beverages containing carbohydrate during exercise are well-established. However, endurance athletes often consume high-carbohydrate foods such as energy bars, fig bars, cookies, and fruit. Solid food empties from the stomach more slowly

---

Box 2.3   Recommended Carbohydrate Intake During Exercise

- Carbohydrate intake during exercise improves endurance performance as well as performance in stop-and-go sports.
- General recommendation is 30 to 60 g carbohydrate every hour as food and/or fluid.
- Most athletes choose medium- to high-glycemic index foods.

than liquids, and the protein and fat found in many high-carbohydrate foods can further delay gastric emptying. Despite this, liquid and solid carbohydrate feedings are equally effective in increasing blood glucose and improving performance (43,44).

Liquid and solid carbohydrate each hold certain advantages for the athlete (45). Sport drinks and other liquids encourage the consumption of water needed to maintain hydration during exercise. However, compared with liquids, high-carbohydrate foods, energy bars, and gels can be easily carried by the athlete during exercise and provide both variety and satiety.

Drinking 6 to 12 oz (150 to 350 mL) of a sport drink containing 4% to 8% carbohydrate every 15 to 20 minutes can provide the proper amount of carbohydrate (2,37). For example, drinking 24 oz each hour of a sport drink that contains 6% carbohydrate provides 42 g carbohydrate. Drinking the same quantity each hour of a sport drink containing 8% carbohydrate provides 57 g carbohydrate. Eating one banana (30 g), one sport bar (47 g), two gels (about 50 g) or three large graham crackers (66 g) every hour also supplies an adequate amount of carbohydrate.

Fructose During Exercise

Some athletes take fructose tablets during exercise. Because fructose has a lower GI (it causes a lower blood glucose and insulin response) than glucose, athletes may mistakenly believe that fructose is a superior energy source.

Murray et al (46) compared the physiological, sensory, and exercise performance responses to the ingestion of 6% glucose, 6% sucrose, and 6% fructose solutions during cycling exercise. As expected, blood insulin levels were lower with fructose. However, fructose was associated with more gastrointestinal distress, higher perceived exertion ratings, and higher serum cortisol levels (indicating greater physiological stress) than glucose or sucrose. Cycling performance times were also significantly better with sucrose and glucose than with fructose.

The lower blood glucose levels associated with fructose ingestion may explain why fructose does not improve performance. Fructose metabolism occurs primarily in the liver, where it is converted to liver glycogen. Fructose probably cannot be converted to glucose and released fast enough to provide adequate energy for the exercising muscles. In contrast, blood glucose is maintained or increased by feedings of glucose, sucrose, or glucose polymers. These have been shown to enhance performance and are the predominant carbohydrates in sport drinks. The greater incidence of gastrointestinal distress (bloating, cramping, and diarrhea) often reported with high fructose intakes may be due to the slower intestinal absorption of fructose compared with glucose.

Several popular commercial sport drinks contain fructose as one of several carbohydrate ingredients. In these situations, fructose may provide flavor and enhance intestinal absorption. Research by Shi et al (47) indicated that water absorption is enhanced when rehydration solutions combine two to three different transportable carbohydrate substrates (glucose, sucrose, fructose, or maltodextrins) as opposed to solutions containing only one transportable carbohydrate substrate. The addition of a second or third carbohydrate substrate seems to activate additional mechanisms for intestinal solute transport and involve transport by separate pathways that are noncompetitive. Thus, water and carbohydrate absorption may be optimized by including fructose as one of two or more carbohydrates in a 4% to 8% rehydration solution.

Carbohydrate After Exercise

The restoration of muscle and liver glycogen stores is important for recovery after strenuous training (48–50). An adequate intake of carbohydrate and energy will optimize muscle glycogen storage during consecutive days of hard workouts, whereas delaying carbohydrate intake after exercise may reduce muscle glycogen storage and impair recovery. Rapid repletion of muscle glycogen is beneficial for athletes who train hard several times per day (they get more out of their later workouts) and crucial for athletes in events like the Tour de France (they do not have 24 hours to replenish muscle glycogen stores).

Athletes who exercise hard for more than 90 minutes/day should consume 1.5 g carbohydrate/kg immediately after exercise, followed by an additional feeding of 1.5 g carbohydrate/kg 2 hours later (50). Athletes who are not hungry right after exercising may prefer a high-carbohydrate drink (eg, sport drink, fruit juice, or a commercial high carbohydrate beverage) immediately after exercise, which will also promote rehydration. The second feeding can be a high-carbohydrate meal. Recommendations for carbohydrate intake after exercise are summarized in Box 2.4.

Consuming carbohydrate shortly after exercise enhances the rate of muscle glycogen synthesis. Ivy et al (48) evaluated glycogen repletion following 2 hours of hard cycling exercise that depleted muscle glycogen. When 2 g carbohydrate per kg was consumed immediately after exercise, muscle glycogen synthesis was 15.4 mmol/kg 2 hours after exercise. When the same carbohydrate feeding was delayed for 2 hours, muscle glycogen synthesis was reduced by 66% to 5.0 mmol/kg 2 hours after exercise. By 4 hours after exercise, total muscle glycogen synthesis for the delayed feeding was still 45% less (13.2 mmol/kg) than for the feeding given immediately after exercise (24.0 mmol/kg).

There are several reasons that glycogen repletion occurs faster after exercise: the blood flow to the muscles is much greater immediately after exercise; the muscle cell is more likely to take up glucose; and the muscle cells are more sensitive to the effects of insulin during this time period, which promotes glycogen synthesis. Providing liquid or solid carbohydrate with equal carbohydrate contents after exercise produces similar rates of glycogen repletion. Reed et al (49) found no difference in muscle glycogen storage rates between the liquid and solid feedings at 2 hours postexercise or at 4 hours postexercise.

Glucose and sucrose are twice as effective as fructose in restoring muscle glycogen after exercise (51). Most fructose is converted to liver glycogen, whereas glucose seems to bypass the liver and is stored as muscle glycogen. The type of carbohydrate consumed

---

Box 2.4   Recommended Carbohydrate Intake After Exercise

After hard exercise > 90 minutes:

- 1.5 g carbohydrate/kg immediately after exercise
- Additional 1.5 g carbohydrate/kg 2 hours later

The addition of a small amount of protein may stimulate muscle protein synthesis but does not enhance muscle glycogen synthesis.

(simple vs complex) does not seem to influence glycogen repletion after exercise. Roberts et al (52) compared simple and complex carbohydrate intake during both glycogen-depleted and nondepleted states. The researchers found that significant increases in muscle glycogen could be achieved with a diet high in simple or complex carbohydrates.

The most rapid increase in muscle glycogen content during the first 24 hours of recovery may be achieved by consuming foods with a high GI. Burke et al (53) investigated the effect of GI on muscle glycogen repletion after exercise and found that the increase in muscle glycogen content after 24 hours was greater with the high-GI diet (106 mmol/kg) than with the low-GI diet (71.5 mmol/kg). Although a high-GI diet may be beneficial, it is important to recognize that the total amount of carbohydrate consumed is the most important consideration for glycogen repletion. A daily carbohydrate intake of 7 to 10 g/kg is recommended for glycogen restoration for athletes engaged in heavy training for 2 to 3 hours a day (13).

Athletes may have impaired muscle glycogen synthesis following unaccustomed exercise that results in muscle damage and delayed-onset muscle soreness. The muscular responses to such damaging exercise seem to decrease both the rate of muscle glycogen synthesis and the total muscle glycogen content (54). Although a diet providing 8 to 10 g carbohydrate/kg will usually replace muscle glycogen stores within 24 hours, the damaging effects of unaccustomed exercise significantly delay muscle glycogen repletion. Also, Sherman (54) notes that even the normalization of muscle glycogen stores does not guarantee normal muscle function after unaccustomed exercise.

Adding Protein to Postexercise Carbohydrate Feedings

Some practitioners recommend adding protein to the postexercise carbohydrate feeding to enhance glycogen repletion. In 1992, Zawadzki et al (55) reported that adding protein to a carbohydrate drink produced higher muscle glycogen synthesis rates after exercise than the carbohydrate drink alone. However, the two drinks used in the study were not isocaloric, so the interpretation of the results was problematic. It was not until 2000 that other researchers tried to establish whether the improved recovery observed by Zawadzki was the result of additional protein or additional energy.

Several studies have examined the addition of protein to carbohydrate feedings after exercise (56–59). Although adding protein to carbohydrate does not enhance muscle glycogen storage (56–59), ingesting small amounts of protein shortly before or after exercise may stimulate muscle protein synthesis (60). Consuming protein alone or in combination with carbohydrate improves net protein balance in muscle. In the presence of carbohydrate, it seems that only small amounts of essential amino acids (6 g) are needed for this positive effect (60). This amount of amino acids can easily be obtained by consuming protein-rich foods after exercise. For example, a sandwich with lean meat or chicken and a glass of low-fat milk would provide sufficient protein and carbohydrate for the early recovery period.

Summary

Carbohydrate is the predominant fuel for most sports, especially those activities that demand sustained moderate- to high-intensity activity and those that demand repeated bouts of moderate- to high-intensity activity. The demand for high power output in these activities is met by reliance on carbohydrate as a predominant supplier of ATP. Because the depletion of endogenous carbohydrate stores (muscle and liver glycogen and blood glucose) can impair athletic performance, athletes should strive to optimize their body carbohydrate stores before, during, and after exercise.

In general, an intake of 5 to 7 g carbohydrate/kg/day is recommended for general training needs and 7 to 10 g carbohydrate/kg/day is recommended for endurance athletes. Ultra-endurance athletes' carbohydrate needs may exceed 10 g/kg/day. One to 4 hours prior to exercise, athletes should consume 1 to 4 g carbohydrate/kg to "top off" muscle and liver glycogen stores. During stop-and-go and endurance exercise lasting 1 hour or longer, athletes should consume 30 to 60 g carbohydrate/hour to maintain blood glucose levels and carbohydrate oxidation. To optimize glycogen repletion after exercise lasting 90 minutes or longer, athletes should consume 1.5 g carbohydrate/kg within 30 minutes, followed by an additional feeding of 1.5 g carbohydrate/kg 2 hours later. Although adding protein to the recovery feeding does not improve glycogen restoration, protein does provide amino acids for the building and repair of muscle tissue. These general recommendations may be modified to meet the demands of the athlete's specific sport, unique needs, and preferences.

References

1. Jacobs KA, Sherman WM. The efficacy of carbohydrate supplementation and chronic high carbohydrate diets for improving endurance performance. *Int J Sport Nutr*. 1999;9:92–115.
2. Bergstrom J, Hermansen L, Saltin B. Diet, muscle glycogen, and physical performance. *Acta Physiol Scand*. 1967;71:140–150.
3. Costill DL, Sherman WM, Fink WJ, Maresh C, Whitten M, Miller JM. The role of dietary carbohydrate in muscle glycogen resynthesis after strenuous running. *Am J Clin Nutr*. 1981;34:1831–1836.
4. Fallowfield JL, Williams C. Carbohydrate intake and recovery from prolonged exercise. *Int J Sport Nutr*. 1993;3:150–164.
5. Costill DL, Bowers R, Branam G, Sparks K. Muscle glycogen utilization during prolonged exercise on successive days. *J Appl Physiol*. 1971;31:834–838.
6. Position of the American Dietetic Association, Dietitians of Canada, and the American College of Sports Medicine: Nutrition and Athletic Performance. *J Am Diet Assoc*. 2000;100:1543–1556.
7. Walberg-Rankin J. Dietary carbohydrate as an ergogenic aid for prolonged and brief competitions in sport. *Int J Sport Nutr*. 1995;5(suppl):S13-S28.
8. Burke LM, Cox GR, Cummings NK, Desbrow B. Guidelines for daily carbohydrate intake: do athletes achieve them? *Sports Med*. 2001;31:267–299.
9. Saris WHM, van Erp-Baart MA, Brouns F, Westerterp KR, ten Hoor F. Study of food intake and energy expenditure during extreme sustained exercise: the Tour de France. *Int J Sport Med*. 1989;10(suppl):S26-S31.
10. Brouns F, Saris WHM, Stroecken J, Beckers E, Thijssen R, Rehrer NJ, ten Hoor F. Eating, drinking, and cycling: a controlled Tour de France simulation study, Part I. *Int J Sport Med*. 1989;10(suppl):S32-S40.
11. Brouns F, Saris WHM, Stroecken J, Beckers E, Thijssen R, Rehrer NJ, ten Hoor F. Eating, drinking, and cycling: a controlled Tour de France simulation study, Part II. Effect of diet manipulation. *Int J Sport Med*. 1989;10(suppl):S41-S48.

12. Costill DL, Flynn MJ, Kirwan JP, Houmard JA, Mitchell JB, Thomas R, Park SH. Effect of repeated days of intensified training on muscle glycogen and swimming performance. *Med Sci Sports Exerc*. 1988;20:249–254.

13. Burke LM, Collier GR, Hargreaves M. The glycemic index—a new tool in sport nutrition? *Int J Sport Nutr*. 1998;8:401–415.

14. Foster-Powell K, Holt SH, Brand Miller JC. International tables of glycemic index and glycemic load values: 2002. *Am J Clin Nutr*. 2002;76:5–56.

15. Hertzler SR, Kim Y. Glycemic and insulinemic responses to energy bars of differing macronutrient composition in healthy adults. *Med Sci Monit*. 2003;9:CR84–CR90.

16. Lamb DR, Rinehardt KF, Bartels RL, Sherman WM, Snook JT. Dietary carbohydrate and intensity of interval swim training. *Am J Clin Nutr*. 1990;52:1058–1063.

17. Tarnopolsky MA, Atkinson SA, Phillips SM, MacDougall JD. Carbohydrate loading and metabolism during exercise in men and women. *J Appl Physiol*. 1995;78:1360–1368.

18. Karlsson J, Saltin, B. Diet, muscle glycogen, and endurance performance. *J Appl Physiol*. 1971;31:203–206.

19. Balon TW, Horowitz JF, Fitzsimmons KM. Effects of carbohydrate loading and weight-lifting on muscle girth. *Int J Sport Nutr*. 1992;2:328–334.

20. Sherman WM, Costill DL, Fink WJ, Miller JM. The effect of exercise and diet manipulation on muscle glycogen and its subsequent use during performance. *Int J Sport Med*. 1981;2:114–118.

21. Fairchild TJ, Fletcher S, Steele P, Goodman C, Dawson B, Fournier PA. Rapid carbohydrate loading after a short bout of near maximal-intensity exercise. *Med Sci Sport Exerc*. 2002; 34:980–986.

22. Foster C, Costill DL, Fink WJ. Effects of pre-exercise feedings on endurance performance. *Med Sci Sport Exerc*. 1979;11:1–5.

23. Hargreaves M, Costill DL, Fink WJ, King DS, Fielding RA. Effects of pre-exercise carbohydrate feedings on endurance cycling performance. *Med Sci Sports Exerc*. 1987;19:33–36.

24. Sherman WM, Peden MC, Wright DA. Carbohydrate feedings 1 hour before exercise improves cycling performance. *Am J Clin Nutr*. 1991;54:866–870.

25. Thomas DE, Brotherhood JR, Brand JC. Carbohydrate feeding before exercise: effect of glycemic index. *Int J Sport Med*. 1991;12:180–186.

26. DeMarco HM, Sucher KP, Cisar CJ, Butterfield GE. Pre-exercise carbohydrate meals: application of glycemic index. *Med Sci Sport Exerc*. 1999;31:164–170.

27. Thomas DE, Brotherhood JR, Miller JB. Plasma glucose levels after prolonged strenuous exercise correlate inversely with glycemic response to food consumed before exercise. *Int J Sport Nutr*. 1994;4:361–373.

28. Sparks MJ, Selig SS, Febbraio MA. Pre-exercise carbohydrate ingestion: effect of the glycemic index on endurance exercise performance. *Med Sci Sport Exerc*. 1998;30:844–849.

29. Anantaraman R, Carimines AA, Gaesser GA, Weltman A. Effects of carbohydrate supplementation on performance during 1 hour of high-intensity exercise. *Int J Sport Med*. 1995;16: 461–465.

30. Nuefer PD, Costill DL, Flynn MG, Kirwan JP, Mitchell JB, Houmard J. Improvements in exercise performance: effects of carbohydrate feedings and diet. *J Appl Physiol*. 1987;62:983–988.

31. Sherman WM, Brodowicz G, Wright DA, Allen WK, Simonsen J, Dernbach A. Effects of 4 hour pre-exercise carbohydrate feedings on cycling performance. *Med Sci Sports Exerc*. 1989;12:598–604.

32. Coyle EF, Hagberg JM, Hurley BF, Martin WH, Ehsani AA, Holloszy JO. Carbohydrate feeding during prolonged strenuous exercise can delay fatigue. *J Appl Physiol*. 1983;55:230–235.

33. Coyle EF, Coggan AR, Hemmert WK, Ivy JL. Muscle glycogen utilization during prolonged strenuous exercise when fed carbohydrate. *J Appl Physiol*. 1986;61:165–172.

34. Millard-Stafford ML, Sparling PB, Rosskopf LB, Hinson BT, Dicarlo LJ. Carbohydrate-electrolyte replacement improves distance running performance in the heat. *Med Sci Sports Exerc*. 1992;24:934–940.

35. Wilber RL, Moffatt RJ. Influence of carbohydrate ingestion on blood glucose and performance in runners. *Int J Sport Nutr*. 1994;2:317–327.

36. Nicholas CW, Williams C, Lakomy HK, Phillips G, Nowitz A. Influence of ingesting a carbohydrate-electrolyte solution on endurance capacity during intermittent, high-intensity shuttle running. *J Sport Sci*. 1995;13:283–290.

37. Nicholas CW, Tsintzas K, Boobis L, Williams C. Carbohydrate-electrolyte ingestion during intermittent high-intensity running. *Med Sci Sport Exerc*. 1999;31:1280–1286.

38. Davis JM, Jackson DA, Broadwell MS, Queary JL, Lambert CL. Carbohydrate drinks delay fatigue during intermittent high intensity cycling in active men and women. *Int J Sport Nutr*. 1997;7:261–273.

39. Wright DA, Sherman WM, Dernbach AR. Carbohydrate feedings before, during, or in combination improves cycling performance. *J Appl Physiol*. 1991;71:1082–1088.

40. National Athletic Trainers' Association Position Statement: Fluid replacement for athletes. *J Athl Train*. 2000;35:212–214.

41. Below PR, Mora-Rodriguez R, Gonzalez-Alonso J, Coyle EF. Fluid and carbohydrate ingestion independently improve performance during 1 hour of intense exercise. *Med Sci Sports Exerc*. 1995;27:200–210.

42. Coyle EF, Montain SJ. Benefits of fluid replacement with carbohydrate during exercise. *Med Sci Sports Exerc*. 1992;24(9 Suppl):S324–330.

43. Lugo M, Sherman WM, Wimer GS, Garleb K. Metabolic responses when different forms of carbohydrate energy are consumed during cycling. *Int J Sport Nutr*. 1993;3:398–407.

44. Robergs RA, McMinn SB, Mermier C, Leabetter G, Ruby B, Quinn C. Blood glucose and glucoregulatory hormone responses to solid and liquid carbohydrate ingestion during exercise. *Int J Sport Nutr*. 1998;8:70–83.

45. Coleman E. Update on carbohydrate: solid versus liquid. *Int J Sport Nutr*. 1994;4:80–88.

46. Murray R, Paul GL, Seifert JG, Eddy DE, Halby GA. The effects of glucose, fructose, and sucrose ingestion during exercise. *Med Sci Sports Exerc*. 1989;21:275–282.

47. Shi X, Summers RW, Schedl HP, Flanagan SW, Chang R, Gisofi CV. Effects of carbohydrate type and concentration and solution osmolality on water absorption. *Med Sci Sport Exerc*. 1995;27:1607–1615.

48. Ivy JL, Katz AL, Cutler CL, Sherman WM, Coyle EF. Muscle glycogen synthesis after exercise: effect of time of carbohydrate ingestion. *J Appl Physiol*. 1988;6:1480–1485.

49. Reed MJ, Broznick JT, Lee MC, Ivy JL. Muscle glycogen storage postexercise: effect of mode of carbohydrate administration. *J Appl Physiol*. 1989;75:1019–1023.

50. Ivy JL, Lee MC, Broznick JT, Reed MJ. Muscle glycogen storage after different amounts of carbohydrate ingestion. *J Appl Physiol*. 1988;65:2018–2023.

51. Blom PCS, Hostmark AT, Vaage O, Kardel KR, Maehlum S. Effect of different post-exercise sugar diets on the rate of muscle glycogen synthesis. *Med Sci Sports Exerc*. 1987;19:471–496.

52. Roberts KM, Noble EG, Hayden DB, Taylor AW. Simple and complex carbohydrate-rich diets and muscle glycogen content of marathon runners. *Eur J Appl Physiol*. 1988;57:70–74.

53. Burke LM, Collier GR, Hargreaves M. Muscle glycogen storage after prolonged exercise: effect of glycemic index. *J Appl Physiol*. 1993;75:1019–1023.

54. Sherman WM. Recovery from endurance exercise. *Med Sci Sports Exerc*. 1992;24(9 Suppl):S336-S339.

55. Zawadzki K, Yaspelkis B, Ivy J. Carbohydrate-protein complex increases the rate of muscle glycogen storage after exercise. *J Appl Physiol*. 1992;72:1854–1859.

56. Van Loon L, Saris W, Kruijshoop M, Wagenmakers A. Maximizing postexercise muscle glycogen synthesis: carbohydrate supplementation and the application of amino acid or protein hydrolysate mixtures. *Am J Clin Nutr*. 2000;72:106–111.

57. Jentjens R, van Loon L, Mann C, Wagenmakers AJ, Jeukendrup AE. Additional protein and amino acids to carbohydrates does not enhance postexercise muscle glycogen synthesis. *J Appl Physiol*. 2001;91:839–846.

58. Van Hall G, Shirreffs S, Calbet J. Muscle glycogen resynthesis during recovery from cycle exercise: no effect of additional protein ingestion. *J Appl Physiol*. 2000;88:1631–1636.

59. Carrithers J, Williamson D, Gallagher P, Godard MP, Schulze KE, Trappe SW. Effects of postexercise carbohydrate-protein feedings on muscle glycogen restoration. *J Appl Physiol*. 2000;88:1976–1982.

60. Tipton K, Wolfe R. Exercise, protein metabolism, and muscle growth. *Int J Sports Nutr Exerc Metab*. 2001;11:109–128.

Chapter 3

PROTEIN AND EXERCISE

Martin J. Gibala, PhD, and Krista R. Howarth, MSc*

Introduction

The effect of exercise on protein and amino acid metabolism is an enormous topic that cannot be adequately reviewed in a single volume, let alone a relatively brief chapter of the present length. Consider that there are 20 important amino acids in the human body involved in a wide array of physiological processes, including protein turnover (ie, synthesis and breakdown), intermediary metabolism, membrane transport, acid-base regulation, and immune function (1). Moreover, exercise induces acute and chronic alterations in numerous tissues that take part in protein metabolism, including skeletal muscle, the gut, liver, kidneys, and cardiovascular system.

This chapter does not attempt to review all aspects of protein and amino acid metabolism that are affected by the stress of exercise. Rather, the focus is primarily on skeletal muscle, and the goal is to highlight recent experimental findings that are relevant to athletes and individuals who work with them. Included is discussion of the impact of physical activity on dietary protein requirements, and the effect of exercise on whole-body and skeletal muscle protein turnover and amino acid intermediary metabolism. In the final section, the potential for protein or amino acid ingestion to alter the muscle adaptive response during recovery from exercise is addressed. The interested reader is also referred to several other thorough reviews that have recently been published (2–6), and especially the excellent comprehensive volume by Rennie (1).

Dietary Protein Requirements

Assessment of Dietary Protein Requirements

At the most basic level, the requirement for protein in the diet reflects the need to offset protein losses to maintain nitrogen homeostasis in the body. Proteins are constantly being

*Work cited from the authors' laboratory, the Exercise Metabolism Research Group at McMaster University, was supported by the Natural Sciences and Engineering Research Council of Canada.

synthesized and degraded through the process of protein turnover, which creates a continuous flow of amino acids into and out of the body's free amino acid pool (refer to Figure 3.1). Although the majority of amino acids that are released through protein breakdown are "recycled" or reincorporated back into protein, a small proportion are oxidized (consumed for energy) or otherwise lost and therefore must be replaced.

The traditional method used to assess protein requirements is the nitrogen balance technique. Essentially, this involves the determination of all sources of nitrogen entering and exiting the body over a period of time while the person consumes a known amount of protein. The major source of nitrogen intake is through the diet (or intravenous infusion in patients), whereas nitrogen is lost mainly through the urine, feces, sweat, and other miscellaneous routes including hair and skin. If nitrogen balance is positive, this indicates protein gain, whereas negative nitrogen balance indicates protein loss. The nitrogen balance method usually involves having people consume varying amounts of protein, and a regression analysis of protein intake vs nitrogen balance is done to identify the protein intake required for zero balance. One standard deviation is typically added to the mean to derive the protein intake that will place 97% of the population at zero nitrogen balance (7).

As with any method, there are limitations to the nitrogen balance technique, and researchers have recognized that it is not suitable for determining optimal protein intakes. For example, Tarnopolsky (7) noted that a resistance-trained athlete might maintain nitrogen balance by decreasing muscle protein synthesis, but this would certainly not be bene-

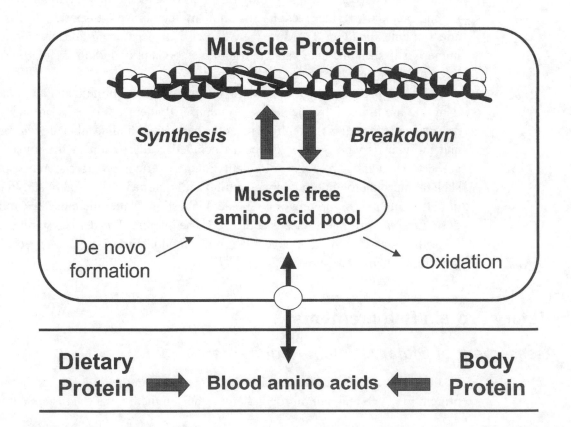

FIGURE 3.1 General overview of protein turnover and factors that influence the free amino acid pool in skeletal muscle.

ficial for physiological function or performance. Investigators have also suggested that stable isotope tracers could be used to evaluate the protein status of an individual (8). A detailed discussion of the methods used to assess dietary protein requirements is beyond the scope of this chapter, but the interested reader is referred to an excellent review of current controversies by Millward (9).

Does Physical Activity Alter Protein Requirements?

The current Dietary Reference Intake (DRI) for protein is 0.8 g/kg/day (0.36 g/lb/day) for individuals older than 18 years of age, irrespective of physical activity status. However, as discussed later in this chapter, data suggest that both strength and endurance athletes may have increased protein requirements as compared with their sedentary counterparts. Indeed, a recent joint position statement endorsed by the American College of Sports Medicine (ACSM), American Dietetic Association (ADA), and Dietitians of Canada (DC) (10) concluded that protein requirements are higher in very active individuals. The position of ACSM, ADA, and DC was that endurance athletes should consume 1.2 to 1.4 g/kg/day (0.55 to 0.64 g/lb/day), whereas resistance-trained athletes may need as much as 1.6 to 1.7 g/kg/day (0.73 to 0.77 g/lb/day). Table 3.1 (11) provides an example of theoretical daily energy and protein requirements for an average sedentary individual and endurance or strength athlete based on the ACSM/ADA/DC position statement (10).

Protein Requirements of Endurance Athletes

Estimates based on stable isotope tracer methods suggest that amino acid oxidation accounts for approximately 2% to 6% of total energy expenditure during endurance exercise (7,12). The energy contribution from amino acid oxidation may be higher under certain conditions,

TABLE 3.1   Daily Energy and Protein Requirements for a 70-kg (154-lb) Man

Type	Energy, kcal/d	Protein g/kg/d (g/lb/d)	g/d	% of Daily Energy*
Sedentary[a]	2800	0.8 (0.36)	56	8
Endurance[b]	3800	1.2–1.4 (0.55–0.64)	84–98	9–10
Strength[c]	3200	1.6–1.7 (0.73–0.77)	112–119	14–15

*Note that protein intake expressed as "% of Daily Energy" is valid only if total energy intake is sufficient—ie, as recommended under "Energy, kcal/d."

[a,b,c] Theoretical values are based on American College of Sports Medicine/American Dietetic Association/Dietitians of Canada Joint Position Statement (10) and assume (a) a resting energy expenditure equivalent to 40 kcal/kg (18 kcal/lb); (b) a male runner who runs 10 miles per day at a pace of 6 minutes/mile with an energy expenditure of running of 0.25 kcal/min/kg of body weight (0.11 kcal/min/lb); and (c) a cost of 6 kcal/kg/day (2.7 kcal/lb/day) for heavy resistance training.

Source: Adapted with permission. Gibala M. Protein and amino acid supplements: do they work? Sports Sci Exchange. 2002;15(4 Suppl):S1.

such as when carbohydrate availability is limited (7,12); however, the dominant substrates catabolized for energy during exercise are carbohydrates and lipids.

Despite the relatively minor contribution from amino acids to total energy expenditure during exercise, endurance athletes may have an increased requirement for protein due to very high training volumes and thus chronically elevated rates of amino acid oxidation. Data supporting a higher daily protein requirement for endurance athletes have been provided by several studies that showed athletes were in negative nitrogen balance when they consumed protein at or near the current DRI (13–16). Both Phillips (12) and Tarnopolsky (7) have performed regression analyses using data from several studies where nitrogen balance could be determined with accuracy. The calculated protein intake for zero nitrogen balance, after extrapolating to include a 95% confidence interval, was 1.11 (12) and 1.16 g/kg/day (7). Regarding maximum values, Tarnopolsky (7) suggested that the highest protein requirements that are likely to be needed by elite endurance athletes are in the range of 1.5 to 1.7 g/kg/day; however, protein deficiency is not a concern in these athletes due to their very high habitual energy intakes.

Protein Requirements of Strength Athletes

Resistance-trained athletes may also have an increased need for protein due to transient, chronic increases in net muscle protein synthesis that are stimulated by habitual training. However, the increased requirement is smaller than most strength athletes would probably believe, and is more than offset by the amount of protein typically consumed by these individuals (7,12). For example, a nitrogen balance study conducted by Tarnopolsky et al (16) reported that bodybuilders needed only 1.12 times more protein than their sedentary counterparts to maintain nitrogen balance. Another investigation by the same group (17), which used both nitrogen balance and stable isotopic tracer methods, concluded that strength athletes could maintain positive nitrogen balance on a diet that provided 1.40 g/kg/day. Phillips (12) and Tarnopolsky (7) have also performed regression analyses using data from several studies conducted on strength athletes. The calculated protein intake for zero nitrogen balance, after extrapolating to include a 95% confidence interval, was 1.35 (12) and 1.38 g/kg/day (7). These data concur with theoretical calculations made by Phillips (12), who estimated that a 100-kg person who wanted to gain 10 kg of pure muscle (not merely body mass) during 1 year of training would require a maximum protein intake of 1.41 g/kg/day to cover all bodily needs and also accommodate this impressive degree of growth.

It should also be noted that the need for increased protein may be higher during the initial phase of training (ie, first 3 to 6 months) when gains in muscle hypertrophy are most pronounced (7). Finally, data suggest that protein efficiency increases with training, which means that trained individuals may actually require less protein on a per mass basis (5,12).

Is There an Optimal Protein Intake For Athletes?

From a practical perspective, the scientific controversy regarding the effect of physical activity on minimum daily protein requirements is moot because the vast majority of athletes consume protein far in excess of any increased dietary requirement (5,7,12). Some athletes may need to monitor their food choices carefully (eg, vegetarians or those engaged in sports with weight categories), but very few individuals are at risk of protein deficiency provided that energy intake is sufficient to maintain body weight and sound nutrition practices are followed, (eg, as outlined in the ACSM/ADA/DC Joint Position Statement [10]). In that regard, the significance of total energy intake and training status should be mentioned in any discussion about protein requirements. Studies by Butterfield and others have highlighted: (*a*) the importance of sufficient energy intake to maintain and/or increase lean body mass; and (*b*) the likelihood that chronic exercise training may actually increase protein utilization and thus decrease protein requirements (18,19).

It should also be emphasized, however, that traditional methods for assessing protein status have focused primarily on minimum needs to maintain nitrogen homeostasis, and no guidelines have been developed for optimal protein intakes. Wolfe (20) has made a theoretical case for protein supplementation in active individuals, given that amino acid ingestion stimulates muscle transport and there is a direct link between amino acid inward transport and muscle protein synthesis (see later in this chapter). For example, the theoretical optimal protein intake for a bodybuilder would be the minimal intake of each individual amino acid that would support maximal muscle mass accretion while minimizing fat deposition. At present, it is not practical or feasible to discern optimal protein intakes for a given individual or specific type of athlete.

Protein Turnover and the Effect of Exercise

Protein turnover refers to the simultaneous yet independently regulated processes of protein synthesis and degradation, which ultimately control net protein accretion or loss within various tissue compartments. It is now well-established that acute exercise can induce profound changes in protein turnover—either during exercise or during recovery. However, the magnitude of change depends on the type, intensity, and duration of contractile activity, as well as the nutritional and training state of the individual (1,2,5).

The following section summarizes the effect of exercise on whole-body and skeletal muscle protein turnover in humans. The skeletal muscle response is broadly subdivided into aerobic (ie, endurance) and resistive-type (ie, weightlifting), given the divergent adaptations induced by chronic training with these two types of exercise.

Methodological Considerations

A significant limitation that has hindered human research progress in the area of exercise and protein turnover has been the experimental methods, which have ranged from relatively simple determinations of compounds in urine to invasive and technically complex measurements of isotopically enriched stable amino acid tracers in tissue samples. Rennie et al (21) noted that issues related to methodology are critically important to those who use the techniques, but often confuse those who simply want to understand the physiology. A detailed discussion of methodological issues is beyond the scope of this chapter but the interested reader is referred to excellent reviews by Rennie (22) and Wagenmakers (23), which critically examine the use of stable isotope tracers for the investigation of muscle protein and amino acid metabolism in humans.

Whole-Body Protein Turnover

Protein Synthesis

The effect of aerobic exercise on protein synthesis in humans has most commonly been studied at the whole-body level in the postabsorptive state, after ingestion or infusion of a trace amount of amino acid. The most common method has been to use $[1-^{13}C]$leucine and measuring $^{13}CO_2$ production in expired breath (24–29), although other stable (eg, $[^{15}N]$glycine) and radioactive (eg, $[1-^{14}C]$leucine) tracers have also been used (23). The first investigations that used the $[1-^{13}C]$leucine method reported that whole-body protein synthesis was decreased during several hours of mild exercise at an intensity of 50% of maximum oxygen consumption (VO_{2max}) or higher (28,29). The method has been refined over the years and subsequent studies have confirmed that whole-body protein synthesis is reduced during prolonged aerobic exercise in humans (24,26), although this finding is not entirely consistent (27). One study measured whole-body protein synthesis during a 60-minute bout of intermittent, circuit-type weightlifting exercise and observed no acute effect during or 2 hours after the bout (30).

Protein Breakdown

It has proved difficult to discern whether whole-body protein breakdown changes during exercise in humans, due to the inherent difficulty in making such measurements as well as lack of agreement regarding the interpretation of results (1). For example, using one method that is based on the rate of leucine appearance into the plasma pool, various groups of investigators have reported an increase in whole-body protein degradation during exercise (27–29), no change (31), and even a decrease (25). The equivocal data may be attributable, in part, to the fact that individual tissues/proteins respond differently to the stress of exercise, and there may be alterations in the interorgan handling of amino acids. A broad inference based on the animal literature is that contractile activity of sufficient intensity or duration increases the rate of protein degradation in liver, gut, and noncontractile muscle, but the rate of contractile protein breakdown is suppressed (1).

Skeletal Muscle Protein Synthesis

Aerobic/Endurance Exercise

Only one study has attempted to measure changes in muscle protein synthesis during prolonged aerobic exercise, and the two studies that examined the postexercise period have yielded equivocal results. Carraro et al (32) measured mixed muscle protein fractional synthetic rate during 4 hours of treadmill walking and observed a slight, nonsignificant decrease at the end of exercise compared with rest (which was determined on a separate day). These authors also reported a 26% increase in vastus lateralis muscle protein synthesis during recovery in the same group of subjects, whereas Tipton et al (33) reported a nonsignificant 42% increase in the deltoid muscle of young women after a 90-minute interval swim workout.

Resistive Exercise

Given the brief, intense efforts that are characteristic of resistance exercise, investigations of this type have examined the protein synthetic response during the postexercise period.

An acute increase in muscle protein synthesis during recovery from heavy resistance exercise (to approximately 50% to 125% higher than baseline values) has repeatedly been observed (34–37) although not in all studies (33). (A typical exercise protocol used in these types of studies consisted of 8 to 12 sets of arm curl [biceps biopsy sampling] or leg extension/leg press actions [vastus lateralis sampling], using 6 to 12 repetitions per set at an intensity equivalent to approximately 80% of 1-repetition maximum.) The duration of the increase in muscle protein synthesis has not been resolved, but it may persist for up to 48 hours, depending on the training state of the individual (36).

Skeletal Muscle Protein Breakdown

Aerobic/Endurance Exercise

There have been no direct measurements of skeletal muscle protein breakdown during aerobic exercise in humans (ie, using isotopically labeled amino acids) and thus it has not been possible to precisely quantify changes in net muscle protein balance. However, based on studies that have quantified the exchange of various amino acids across working human muscle, it seems that the rate of myofibrillar protein breakdown is either unchanged or reduced during aerobic exercise, whereas the rate of noncontractile protein breakdown is increased (28,38,39).

Resistance Exercise

It has been recognized for some time that muscle protein breakdown must also be increased after resistance exercise; otherwise the measured acute increases in muscle protein synthesis would stimulate muscle growth to a much larger extent than what is known to occur after several months of resistance training. However, only recently with the development of new stable isotope techniques has it become possible to discern changes in muscle breakdown rate after resistance exercise. Studies have indicated that leg muscle protein breakdown rate was increased over rest levels for up to 24 hours after a bout of heavy resistance exercise (24,37). In addition, although the relative increase in muscle protein breakdown is smaller than the increase in protein synthesis after an acute bout of exercise (36,37), the absolute rate of protein breakdown is higher such that muscle protein net balance remains negative (ie, catabolic) if subjects remain fasted. However, this response can be modified by nutrient ingestion—such that net protein balance becomes positive (ie, anabolic)—as discussed further later in this chapter.

The Effect of Physical Training on Protein Turnover

Aerobic/Endurance Exercise

The effect of aerobic training on skeletal muscle protein turnover has not been determined in humans, although two studies that examined whole-body changes during exercise using the leucine tracer technique reported no major effect of training. McKenzie et al (26) studied the same group of men and women before and after an 8-week aerobic training program. Whole-body protein synthesis and degradation was less during exercise compared with rest in both groups across all trials, but there was no effect of training per se during exercise at the same absolute or relative work intensities. Similarly, Lamont et al (25) reported that whole-body leucine kinetics during exercise were similar in trained vs untrained individuals when the two groups were studied at the same relative work intensity.

Resistance Exercise

Phillips et al (40) recently described the effect of an 8-week resistance training program on muscle protein turnover at rest and after an acute bout of exercise in the fed state. Muscle protein fractional synthesis rate and fractional breakdown rate were both higher at rest after training, and training attenuated the acute exercise-induced increase in mixed muscle protein synthesis (40). These data supported the results from an earlier cross-sectional study by the same group (37) that showed trained individuals display approximately 50% smaller increases in muscle protein synthesis and breakdown after an acute bout of resistance exercise at the same relative workload. In support of these findings, the only two studies that did not detect a significant increase in muscle protein synthesis after an acute bout of resistance exercise were conducted using trained individuals (33,41), suggesting that the subjects may have already adapted to the exercise stimulus.

Intermediary Metabolism of Amino Acids during Exercise

The Free Amino Acid Pool

The free amino acid pool is comprised of the amino acids present in plasma and intra- and extracellular spaces and represents the small fraction of body protein that actively participates in various metabolic reactions. The body of a 70-kg individual contains approximately 200 g of free amino acids, and about half of this is located within skeletal muscle (6). Although small relative to the total amount in body protein, there is a continuous exchange of amino acids between the free pool and other protein compartments (ie, protein turnover), and the overall size can be affected by factors such as exercise or feeding, which alter the flux of amino acids into and out of the free pool.

Intermediary Metabolism of Amino Acids in Skeletal Muscle

The metabolism of amino acids in skeletal muscle is limited in comparison to other tissues such as the liver, gut, and kidney. For the sake of this chapter, six amino acids seem to play a significant role in skeletal muscle intermediary metabolism: glutamate, alanine, glutamine, and the branched-chain amino acids (BCAA) isoleucine, leucine, and valine (1,6). Glutamate plays a central role in numerous transamination reactions and plays a key role in the deamination of the BCAA, which are the main amino acids oxidized for energy in skeletal muscle. Glutamate is also involved in the formation of both alanine and glutamine, which serve to safely transport amino groups from muscle and are important gluconeogenic precursors.

The Effect of Exercise on Muscle Free Amino Acid Metabolism

Only two amino acids show significant changes in concentration in human skeletal muscle during most types of exercise: glutamate and alanine. Glutamate decreases by less than

50% within the first few minutes of strenuous exercise, and there is a reciprocal increase in alanine (1,5,6). Muscle BCAA remain unchanged during exercise, but it is generally accepted that the rate of BCAA oxidation is increased, as evidenced by an increased uptake from the circulation, increased activation of the enzyme that irreversibly catabolizes BCAA, and increased production of $^{13}CO_2$ in breath from infused ^{13}C-leucine (1,5,6,26,28,38). In regards to amino acid exchange, there is an increased muscle uptake of glutamate and larger efflux of alanine and glutamine (1,6). Alanine release predominates during the initial minutes of exercise, but glutamine is the major amino acid released during prolonged exercise (6).

Muscle Amino Acids as a Source of Energy

The contribution of amino acid oxidation to total energy expenditure is negligible during short-term exercise, regardless of intensity, and likely accounts for between 3% and 6% of the total ATP supplied during prolonged exercise in humans (7,12,15). There are conditions during which the energy contribution from amino acids may be slightly higher—for example, when carbohydrate stores are low (42). However, the dominant substrates catabolized for energy during all forms of exercise are carbohydrates and lipids. Despite this relatively minor role of amino acids in terms of substrate supply, the intermediary metabolism of amino acids impacts on other important energy-producing pathways, including the tricarboxylic acid (TCA) cycle.

Interaction of Amino Acids with the TCA Cycle During Exercise

The TCA cycle occupies a central role in aerobic metabolism and functions to generate reducing equivalents from the catabolism of mainly carbohydrates and fats as part of the process of oxidative phosphorylation. It is now well-accepted that the initial exercise-induced changes in glutamate and alanine serve to increase the total concentration of intermediates within the TCA cycle (TCAI), and it has been suggested that this expansion of the TCAI pool is important for aerobic energy provision (6,43). Thus, alterations in amino acid metabolism have been proposed to play a regulatory role in oxidative metabolism (6). Recent studies, however, have questioned this hypothesis and showed that a decrease in the total concentration of muscle TCAI during exercise did not adversely affect aerobic energy provision or exercise performance (44–46).

Muscle Adaptation During Recovery from Exercise: Role of Protein or Amino Acid Ingestion

There has been considerable interest recently in the potential for protein or amino acid ingestion to alter the muscle adaptive response during recovery. Two areas that have received particular attention involve possible alterations in the rates of (*a*) muscle glycogen resynthesis after prolonged aerobic exercise, and (*b*) muscle protein turnover after resistance exercise.

Muscle Glycogen Resynthesis after Prolonged Exercise: Effect of Protein Ingestion

Muscle glycogen is the predominant fuel catabolized for energy during heavy exercise, and the ability to rapidly replenish glycogen stores during recovery is an important concern for athletes, especially those who partake in exercise bouts of long duration or more than once per day. It is well-established that carbohydrate ingestion markedly accelerates muscle glycogen resynthesis after exercise (47). However, recent studies have addressed the possibility that consuming protein or specific amino acids along with carbohydrate may augment this response. Investigations have focused on the initial few hours after exercise because it has been shown that the addition of protein and fat to a recovery diet does not alter muscle glycogen resynthesis over 24 hours, provided that carbohydrate intake is sufficient (48).

Zawadzki et al (49) were the first to demonstrate an additive effect of protein on muscle glycogen restoration: glycogen resynthesis was 38% higher after 4 hours of recovery in trained cyclists when they ingested 41 g of a whey protein mixture in addition to 112 g carbohydrate immediately and 2 hours after a 2-hour exercise bout. The stimulatory effect of added protein was attributed to an increased rate of insulin secretion and presumably higher rate of muscle glucose uptake as compared to when carbohydrate was consumed alone. However, a potential confounding factor in that study was that subjects consumed approximately 41% more energy during the protein-supplemented trial, and the authors acknowledged that "addition of protein to a carbohydrate supplement may be beneficial only when an inadequate CHO [carbohydrate] source is used" (49). Indeed, although the rate of carbohydrate ingestion (approximately 0.8 g/kg/hour) was more than the 0.5 g/kg/hour that was suggested to be optimal when supplements are administered at 2-hour intervals postexercise (47), considerably higher glycogen resynthesis rates have been reported when carbohydrate is ingested more frequently and/or at a higher rate during recovery (50–53).

In contrast to the findings of Zawadzki et al (49), several recent studies reported no effect of protein supplementation on muscle glycogen resynthesis after exercise when total energy intake was kept constant (52–54) or when protein was added to a carbohydrate supplementation protocol that provided energy at a rate higher than 0.8 g/kg/hour and/or at more frequent intervals (50,51). For example, van Loon et al (52) studied trained cyclists who rode for 90 minutes and then ingested one of three solutions every 30 minute in random order: (*a*) carbohydrate at a rate of 0.8 g/kg/hour, (*b*) the same amount of carbohydrate plus 0.4 g/kg/hour of a protein hydrolysate solution, or (*c*) carbohydrate at a rate of 1.2 g/kg/hour. After 5 hours of recovery, there was no difference in the rate of muscle glycogen resynthesis between the latter two trials, suggesting that protein added to a carbohydrate supplement was no more effective than additional carbohydrate when the total energy intake was kept constant.

In response to the "unequal energy" criticism of their group's earlier paper (49), Ivy et al (55) reported that a carbohydrate-protein supplement was more effective for the rapid replenishment of glycogen after exercise than a carbohydrate supplement of equal energy content, but the effect could not be explained by differences in the plasma insulin response. The practical implications of the work by Ivy et al (55) are debatable because the timing and dose of carbohydrate administered were similar to that provided by Zawadzki et al (49), and others have shown that this protocol is less than optimal for achieving peak rates of muscle glycogen resynthesis (50,51).

Thus, it seems that protein ingestion per se or via augmented insulin secretion does not enhance the rate of muscle glycogen resynthesis when carbohydrate is consumed in sufficient quantities—ie, 1.2 g or more carbohydrate per kg per hour in 15- to 30-minute intervals, during the first 3 to 5 hours of recovery from prolonged exercise (see Figure 3.2) (56). However, from a basic science perspective, the results of Ivy et al (55) are consistent with studies showing that specific amino acids such as glutamine (57) and possibly arginine (58) may influence postexercise glycogen resynthesis to a surprising extent, particularly in the absence of carbohydrate intake.

In addition, protein added to a recovery drink may confer other benefits, including the repair and synthesis of muscle proteins after endurance exercise (59). For example, Levenhagen et al (59) showed that the additional intake of 10 g protein with 8 g carbohydrate and 3 g fat stimulated net leg and whole-body protein accretion during recovery, as opposed to net losses when the same nutrients without protein were provided. Thus, it would seem prudent for endurance athletes to consume a recovery beverage that contains sufficient carbohydrate to replenish muscle glycogen stores and also protein to repair muscle protein (irrespective of whether this macronutrient augments glycogen resynthesis during the immediate postexercise period). Further studies are warranted to determine the optimal recovery beverage composition, but any nutritional strategy that provides carbohydrate at a rate of approximately 1.2 g/kg/hour and protein at a rate of 0.1 to 0.2 g/kg/hour will likely be beneficial. As a practical recommendation, the nutritional composition of low-fat chocolate milk would

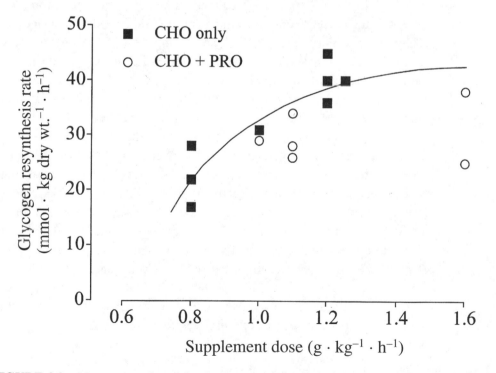

FIGURE 3.2 Mean rates of muscle glycogen resynthesis during recovery from prolonged exercise when subjects were fed carbohydrate (CHO) or CHO + protein (PRO). Data are from references 48–52. There seems to be no additional benefit of protein or amino acid ingestion on glycogen resynthesis when CHO is consumed at a rate of ≥ 1.2 g/kg/hour in 15- to 30-minute intervals. Reprinted with permission from Gibala M. Dietary protein, amino acid supplements and recovery from exercise. *Sports Sci Exchange.* 2002:15:2.

seem to make this product a relatively inexpensive, readily accessible, and highly effective recovery drink for endurance athletes.

Muscle Protein Turnover after Resistance Exercise: Effect of Amino Acid Ingestion

Rates of synthesis and breakdown of mixed proteins in muscle are acutely increased after intense resistance exercise, but as previously discussed the net balance of muscle protein is negative (ie, breakdown exceeds synthesis) if subjects remain fasted (36,37). However, amino acid ingestion can modify this response, as first shown by Tipton et al (60), who had subjects consume 40 g of either mixed or essential amino acids in small doses during approximately 4.5 hours of recovery from heavy resistance exercise. Amino acid ingestion increased net leg muscle protein synthesis compared with a placebo drink, and whereas net balance was negative during the placebo condition, this changed to positive after amino acid ingestion (60).

It seems that a surprisingly small dose of essential amino acids can markedly stimulate muscle protein anabolism during recovery. For example, Rasmussen et al (61) showed that, when compared with placebo (artificial sweetener), 6 g essential amino acids plus 35 g sucrose promoted a transient net increase in muscle protein balance during the hour immediately after beverage ingestion. Børsheim et al (62) found that ingesting 6 g essential amino acids (without carbohydrate) during recovery produced a transient net increase in muscle protein balance that was comparable to that observed by Rasmussen et al (61). Finally, Tipton et al (63) proposed that amino acid ingestion before exercise is even more effective than a postexercise supplement to stimulate muscle anabolism during recovery. They reported that protein net balance during the first hour of recovery was significantly higher when subjects ingested an amino acid/carbohydrate supplement immediately before, as compared with immediately after, a bout of heavy resistance leg exercise.

It is clear that ingestion of a relatively small dose of essential amino acids (approximately 0.1 g/kg)—with or without carbohydrate—either immediately before or during the initial few hours after acute resistance exercise elicits a small transient increase in skeletal muscle net protein balance. The stimulatory effect of resistance exercise plus amino acids seems to be a saturable process, and there is no evidence to suggest that consuming massive doses of amino acids is effective to further increase muscle protein anabolism. However, given that the "anabolic boost" after amino acid ingestion is transient and returns to basal levels within 1 to 2 hours, ingesting repeated small doses of essential amino acids during recovery may be an effective strategy to optimize the muscle protein response (64). Tipton and colleagues recently showed that the acute anabolic response of muscle to resistance exercise and amino acid ingestion reflects the 24-hour response (65). However, it remains to be determined whether these changes persist during several months of training and lead to accelerated rates of muscle protein accretion.

Postexercise Protein Ingestion and Adaptations to Chronic Resistance Training

Esmarck and coworkers (66) reported that "early" intake of an oral protein supplement during recovery was essential for the development of skeletal muscle hypertrophy in elderly men in response to chronic heavy resistance training. Subjects ingested a supplement containing 10 g protein, 7 g carbohydrate, and 3 g fat either immediately (P0) or 2 hours (P2) after each workout during a 12-week resistance training program. One of the most notable findings was that thigh muscle fiber cross-sectional area increased in the P0 group, whereas no significant changes occurred in the P2 group.

The suggestion that immediate postexercise protein intake is crucial for the development of muscle hypertrophy seems at odds with the findings by Rasmussen and colleagues (61), who reported large, acute increases in muscle protein net balance (ie, anabolism) when subjects delayed consumption of a carbohydrate-protein supplement until either 1 hour or 3 hours after a bout of heavy resistance exercise. Direct comparisons between studies are hampered by the disparate age of the subjects studied (ie, old vs young), and the difficulty in extrapolating acute postexercise changes to adaptations that occur after several months of training. It remains to be determined whether younger individuals respond in a similar manner, or if protein ingestion before exercise would further accelerate muscle protein accretion during habitual training, as implied by the acute recovery data reported by Tipton et al (65). It is also possible that elderly individuals may have an altered muscle protein response to nutrient provision after resistance exercise as compared with younger individuals (67). For example, Volpi and coworkers (67) concluded that the response of muscle protein anabolism to hyperaminoacidemia with endogenous hyperinsulinemia is impaired in healthy elderly subjects due to the unresponsiveness of protein synthesis.

Protein Ingestion after Resistance Exercise: Does the Type of Protein Matter?

Despite the often extraordinary claims made in magazines advertisements and on the Internet, few data are available to evaluate whether specific types of protein (eg, whey vs casein vs soy) consumed after resistance exercise promote greater gains in muscle mass. Recent work from Phillips' laboratory, which has appeared in abstract form (68,69), showed that net muscle protein anabolism was acutely increased during the first few hours of recovery when healthy young subjects ingested milk protein as compared with an isonitrogenous soy protein beverage after resistance exercise (68). However, the same group of researchers reported no difference in the amount of lean muscle gained by a group of young subjects who received a milk protein supplement as compared with an isonitrogenous soy protein supplement during a 12-week resistance training program (69). Similarly, in another training study, Haub et al (70) reported that the increases in muscle strength and size in response to a 12-week resistance training program were not influenced by the predominant source of protein (ie, beef-containing vs lacto-ovo-vegetarian diet) consumed by older men with adequate total protein intake. At present, there is little evidence to suggest that the predominant source of dietary protein markedly affects resistance training–induced gains in muscle mass; however, additional work in warranted in this area.

Summary

Exercise induces profound changes in whole-body and skeletal muscle protein turnover and amino acid metabolism. Habitually active individuals may have daily protein requirements that exceed the current DRI, typically in the range of 1.2 to 1.7 g/kg body weight. However, the vast majority of athletes consume sufficient protein to cover any increased need. Recent evidence clearly shows that nutrient provision can acutely modify the muscle metabolic response during recovery from strenuous exercise. The bulk of evidence suggests that protein ingestion does not enhance muscle glycogen resynthesis after prolonged aerobic exercise, provided that carbohydrate is consumed in sufficient quantities and at an optimal rate (approximately 1.2 g/kg/hour). However, the ingestion of relatively small doses of protein (approximately 0.1–0.2 g/kg/hour) can clearly enhance net muscle protein anabolism during recovery from both endurance and resistive-type exercise. On a per unit basis, essential amino acids seem superior to nonessential amino acids, at least with respect to muscle recovery after weightlifting exercise.

An important issue that remains to be resolved is the precise physiological significance of the marked, transient increases in muscle protein net balance that occur in response to acute supplementation, and whether ingestion of specific nutritional formulations is more effective than simply ingesting food that contains protein and carbohydrate after exercise. There is a need for long-term studies designed to elucidate the time course and magnitude of change in muscle protein metabolism over several weeks and months of training (both aerobic and resistive-type), as well as the potential impact of specific nutritional manipulations on muscle protein status. Although easy to recommend in theory, practical constraints—with respect to cost of such studies and the difficulty of precisely controlling all of the various factors involved—hamper ambitious projects of this sort.

References

1. Rennie MJ. Influence of exercise on protein and amino acid metabolism. In: Terjung R, ed. *Handbook of Physiology*. New York, NY: Oxford University Press; 1996:995–1035.
2. Tipton KD, Wolfe RR. Protein and amino acids for athletes. *J Sports Sci*. 2004;22:65–79.
3. Rennie MJ, Wackerhage H, Spangenburg EE, Booth FW. Control of the size of human muscle mass. *Annu Rev Physiol*. 2004;66:799–828.
4. Lemon PWR. Effects of exercise on protein metabolism. In: Maughan RJ, ed. *Nutrition in Sport*. Oxford, UK: Blackwell Science; 2000:133–152.
5. Rennie MJ, Tipton KD. Protein and amino acid metabolism during and after exercise and the effects of nutrition. *Annu Rev Physiol*. 2000;20:457–483.
6. Wagenmakers AJM. Muscle amino acid metabolism at rest and during exercise: role in human physiology and metabolism. In: Holloszy JO, ed. *Exercise and Sports Science Reviews*. Vol. 26. Baltimore, Md: Williams and Wilkins; 1998:287–314.
7. Tarnopolsky MA. Protein metabolism in strength and endurance activities. In: Lamb DR, Murray R, eds. *Perspectives in Exercise Science and Sports Medicine. Volume 12: The Metabolic Basis of Performance in Exercise and Sport*. Carmel, Ind: Cooper Publishing Group; 1999:125–164.
8. Young VR, Bier DM. A kinetic approach to the determination of human amino acid requirements. *Nutr Rev*. 1987;45:289–298.
9. Millward DJ. Protein and amino acid requirements of adults: current controversies. *Can J Appl Physiol*. 2001;26(suppl):S130-S140.
10. American College of Sports Medicine, American Dietetic Association, Dietitians of Canada. Joint position statement: nutrition and athletic performance. *Med Sci Sports Exerc*. 2000;32: 2130–2145.

11. Gibala M. Protein and amino acid supplements: do they work? *Sports Sci Exchange.* 2002;15(4 Suppl):S1.

12. Phillips SM. Assessment of protein status in athletes. In: Driskell JA, Wolinsky I, eds. *Nutritional Assessment of Athletes.* Boca Raton, Fla: CRC Press; 2002:283–316.

13. Friedman JE, Lemon PW. Effect of chronic endurance exercise on retention of dietary protein. *Int J Sports Med.* 1989;10:118–123.

14. Meredith CN, Zackin MJ, Frontera WR, Evans WJ. Dietary protein requirements and body protein metabolism in endurance-trained men. *J Appl Physiol.* 1989;66:2850–2856.

15. Phillips SM, Atkinson SA, Tarnopolsky MA, MacDougall JD. Gender differences in leucine kinetics and nitrogen balance in endurance athletes. *J Appl Physiol.* 1993;75:2134–2141.

16. Tarnopolsky MA, MacDougall JD, Atkinson SA. Influence of protein intake and training status on nitrogen balance and lean body mass. *J Appl Physiol.* 1988;64:187–193.

17. Tarnopolsky MA, Atkinson SA, MacDougall JD, Chesley A, Phillips S, Schwarcz HP. Evaluation of protein requirements for trained strength athletes. *J Appl Physiol.* 1992;73:1986–1995.

18. Butterfield GE. Whole-body protein utilization in humans. *Med Sci Sports Exerc.* 1987;19: S157-S165.

19. Butterfield GE, Calloway DH. Physical activity improves protein utilization in young men. *Br J Nutr.* 1984;51:171–184.

20. Wolfe RR. Protein supplements and exercise. *Am J Clin Nutr.* 2000;72(2 Suppl):551S-557S.

21. Rennie MJ, Bowtell JL, Millward DJ. Physical activity and protein metabolism. In: Bouchard C, Shepherd RJ, Stephens T, eds. *Physical Activity, Fitness and Health. International Consensus Statements.* Champaign, Ill: Human Kinetics; 1994:432–450.

22. Rennie MJ. An introduction to the use of tracers in nutrition and metabolism. *Proc Nutr Soc.* 1999;58:935–944.

23. Wagenmakers AJM. Tracers to investigate protein and amino acid metabolism in human subjects. *Proc Nutr Soc.* 1999;58:987–1000.

24. Bowtell JL, Leese GP, Smith K, Watt PW, Nevill A, Rooyackers O, Wagenmakers AJM, Rennie MJ. Modulation of whole body protein metabolism, during and after exercise, by variation in dietary protein. *J Appl Physiol.* 1998;85:1744–1752.

25. Lamont LS, McCullough AJ, Kalhan S. Comparison of leucine kinetics in endurance-trained and sedentary humans. *J Appl Physiol.* 1999;86:320–325.

26. McKenzie S, Phillips SM, Carter SL, Lowther S, Gibala MJ, Tarnopolsky MA. Endurance exercise training attenuates leucine oxidation and BCOAD activity during exercise in humans. *Am J Physiol Endocrinol Metab.* 2000;278:E580-E587.

27. Phillips SM, Atkinson SA, Tarnopolsky MA, MacDougall JD. Gender differences in leucine kinetics and nitrogen balance in endurance athletes. *J Appl Physiol.* 1993;75:2134–2141.

28. Rennie MJ, Edwards RH, Krywawych S, Davies CT, Halliday D, Waterlow JC, Millward DJ. Effect of exercise on protein turnover in man. *Clin Sci.* 1981;61:627–639.

29. Wolfe RR, Goodenough RD, Wolfe MH, Royle GT, Nadel ER. Isotopic analysis of leucine and urea metabolism in exercising humans. *J Appl Physiol.* 1982;52:458–466.

30. Tarnopolsky MA, Atkinson SA, MacDougall JD, Senor BB, Lemon PWR, Schwarcz H. Whole body leucine metabolism during and after resistance exercise in fed humans. *Med Sci Sports Exerc.* 1991;23:326–333.

31. Evans WJ, Fisher EC, Hoerr RA, Young VR. Protein metabolism and endurance exercise. *Phys Sportsmed.* 1983;11:63–72.

32. Carraro F, Stuart CA, Hartl WH, Rosenblatt J, Wolfe RR. Effect of exercise and recovery on muscle protein synthesis in human subjects. *Am J Physiol Endocrinol Metab.* 1990;259: E470–E476.

33. Tipton KD, Ferrando AA, Williams BD, Wolfe RR. Muscle protein metabolism in female swimmers after a combination of resistance and endurance exercise. *J Appl Physiol.* 1996;81:2034–2038.

34. Biolo G, Maggi SP, Williams BD, Tipton K, Wolfe RR. Increased rates of muscle protein turnover and amino acid transport following resistance exercise in humans. *Am J Physiol Endocrinol Metab.* 1995;268:E514-E520.

35. Chesley A, MacDougall JD, Tarnopolsky MA, Atkinson SA, Smith K. Changes in human muscle protein synthesis after resistance exercise. *J Appl Physiol.* 1992;73:1383–1388.

36. Phillips SM, Tipton KD, Aarsland AA, Cortiella JC, Wolf SP, Wolfe RR. Mixed muscle protein synthesis and breakdown after resistance exercise in humans. *Am J Physiol Endocrinol Metab.* 1997;273:E99–E107.

37. Phillips SM, Tipton KD, Ferrando AA, Wolfe RR. Resistance training reduces the acute exercise-induced increase in muscle protein turnover. *Am J Physiol Endocrinol Metab.* 1999;276: E118–E124.

38. MacLean DA, Graham TE, Saltin B. Branched-chain amino acids augment ammonia metabolism while attenuating protein breakdown during exercise. *Am J Physiol Endocrinol Metab.* 1994;267:E1010–E1022.

39. van Hall G, Saltin B, Wagenmakers AJM. Muscle protein degradation and amino acid metabolism during prolonged knee-extensor exercise in humans. *Clin Sci.* 1999;97:557–567.

40. Phillips SM, Parise G, Roy BD, Tipton KD, Wolfe RR, Tarnopolsky MA. Resistance-training-induced adaptations in skeletal muscle protein turnover in the fed state. *Can J Physiol Pharmacol.* 2002;80:1045–1053.

41. Roy BD, Tarnopolsky MA, MacDougall JD, Fowles J, Yarasheski KE. Effect of glucose supplement timing on protein metabolism after resistance training. *J Appl Physiol.* 1997;82: 1882–1888.

42. Lemon PWR, Mullen JP. The effect of initial muscle glycogen levels on protein catabolism during exercise. *J Appl Physiol.* 1980;48:624–629.

43. Sahlin K, Katz A, Broberg S. Tricarboxylic acid cycle intermediates in human muscle during prolonged exercise. *Am J Physiol Cell Physiol.* 1990;259:C834–C841.

44. Howarth KR, LeBlanc PJ, Heigenhauser GJF, Gibala MJ. Effect of endurance training on muscle TCA cycle metabolism during exercise in humans. *J Appl Physiol.* 2004;97:579–584.

45. Dawson KD, Howarth KR, Tarnopolsky MA, Wong ND, Gibala MJ. Short-term training attenuates muscle TCA cycle expansion during exercise in women. *J Appl Physiol.* 2003;95:999–1004.

46. Gibala MJ, González-Alonso J, Saltin B. Dissociation between muscle TCA cycle pool size and aerobic energy provision during prolonged exercise in humans. *J Physiol.* 2002;545:705–713.

47. Ivy JL. Glycogen resynthesis after exercise: effect of carbohydrate intake. *Int J Sports Med.* 1998;19(Suppl 2):S142–S145.

48. Burke LM, Collier GR, Beasley SK, Davis PG, Fricker PA, Heeley P, Welder K, Hargreaves M. Effect of coingestion of fat and protein with carbohydrate feedings on muscle glycogen storage. *J Appl Physiol.* 1995;78:2187–2192.

49. Zawadzki KM, Yaspelkis BB, Ivy JL. Carbohydrate-protein complex increases the rate of muscle glycogen storage after exercise. *J Appl Physiol.* 1992;72:1854–1859.

50. Jentjens RL, van Loon LJ, Mann CH, Wagenmakers AJ, Jeukendrup AE. Addition of protein and amino acids to carbohydrates does not enhance postexercise muscle glycogen resynthesis. *J Appl Physiol.* 2001;91:839–846.

51. van Hall G, Shirreffs SM, Calbet JAL. Muscle glycogen resynthesis during recovery from cycle exercise: no effect of additional protein ingestion. *J Appl Physiol.* 2000;88:1631–1636.

52. van Loon LC, Saris WH, Kruijshoop M, Wagenmakers AJ. Maximizing postexercise muscle glycogen synthesis: carbohydrate supplementation and the application of amino acid or protein hydrolysate mixtures. *Am J Clin Nutr.* 2000;72:106–111.

53. Carrithers JA, Williamson DL, Gallagher PM, Godard MP, Schulze KE, Trappe SW. Effects of postexercise carbohydrate-protein feedings on muscle glycogen restoration. *J Appl Physiol.* 2000;88:1976–1982.

54. Tarnopolsky MA, Bosman M, MacDonald JR, Vanderputte D, Martin J, Roy BD. Postexercise protein-carbohydrate and carbohydrate supplements increase muscle glycogen in men and women. *J Appl Physiol.* 1997;83:1877–1883.

55. Ivy JL, Goforth HW Jr, Damon BM, McCauley TR, Parsons EC, Price TB. Early postexercise muscle glycogen recovery is enhanced with a carbohydrate-protein supplement. *J Appl Physiol.* 2002;93:839–846.

56. Gibala M. Dietary protein, amino acid supplements and recovery from exercise. *Sports Sci Exchange.* 2002;15:2.

57. Varnier M., Leese GP, Thompson J, Rennie MJ. Stimulatory effect of glutamine on glycogen accumulation in human skeletal muscle. *Am J Physiol Endocrinol Metab.* 1995;269:E309–E315.

58. Yaspelkis BB, Ivy JL. The effect of carbohydrate-arginine supplement on postexercise carbohydrate metabolism. *Int J Sports Nutr.* 1999;9:241–250.

59. Levenhagen DK, Carr C, Carlson MG, Maron DJ, Borel MJ, Flakoll PJ. Postexercise protein intake enhances whole-body and leg protein accretion in humans. *Med Sci Sports Exerc.* 2002;34:828–837.

60. Tipton KD, Ferrando AA, Phillips SM, Doyle D, Wolfe RR. Postexercise net protein synthesis in human muscle from orally administered amino acids. *Am J Physiol Endocrinol Metab.* 1999;276:E628–E634.

61. Rasmussen BB, Tipton KD, Miller SL, Wolf SE, Wolfe RR. An oral essential amino acid-carbohydrate supplement enhances muscle protein anabolism after resistance exercise. *J Appl Physiol.* 2000;88:386–392.

62. Børsheim E, Tipton KD, Wolf SE, Wolfe RR. Essential amino acids and muscle protein recovery from resistance exercise. *Am J Physiol Endocrinol Metab.* 2002;283:E648–E657.

63. Tipton KD, Rasumussen BB, Miller SL, Wolf SE, Owens-Stovall SK, Petrini BE, Wolfe RR. Timing of amino acid-carbohydrate ingestion alters anabolic response of muscle to resistance exercise. *Am J Physiol Endocrinol Metab.* 2001;281:E197–E206.

64. Miller SL, Tipton KD, Chinkes DL, Wolf SE, Wolfe RR. Independent and combined effects of amino acids and glucose after resistance exercise. *Med Sci Sports Exerc.* 2003;35:449–455.

65. Tipton KD, Børsheim E, Wolf SE, Sanford AP, Wolfe RR. Acute response of net muscle protein balance reflects 24 h balance following exercise and amino acid ingestion. *Am J Physiol Endocrinol Metab.* 2003;284:E76-E89.

66. Esmarck B, Andersen JL, Olsen S, Richter EA, Mizuno M, Kjær M. Timing of postexercise protein intake is important for muscle hypertrophy with resistance training in elderly humans. *J Physiol.* 2001;535:301–311.

67. Volpi E, Mittendorfer B, Rasmussen BB, Wolfe RR. The response of muscle protein anabolism to combined hyperaminoacidemia and glucose-induced hyperinsulinemia is impaired in the elderly. *J Clin Endocrinol Metab.* 2000;85:4481–4490.

68. Wilkinson S, MacDonald J, MacDonald M, Tarnopolsky M, Phillips S. Milk proteins promote a greater net protein balance than soy proteins following resistance exercise. *FASEB J.* 2004;18:Abstract 7548.

69. Hartman JW, Bruinsma D, Fullerton A, Perco JG, Lawrence R, Tang JE, Wilkinson SB, Phillips SM. The effect of differing post exercise macronutrient consumption on resistance training-induced adaptations in novices. *Med Sci Sports Exerc.* 2004;36(suppl):S41.

70. Haub MD, Wells AM, Tarnopolsky MA, Campbell WW. Effect of protein source on resistive-training-induced changes in body composition and muscle size in older men. *Am J Clin Nutr.* 2002;76:511 517.

Chapter 4

DIETARY FAT AND EXERCISE

Satya S. Jonnalagadda, PhD, RD

Definition and Type

Lipids are important components of plant, animal, and microbial cell membranes. They are marginally soluble in water and greatly soluble in organic solvents such as chloroform or acetone. There are two major groups of lipids, which include open-chained and closed-ringed molecules. The open-chain lipid compounds include fatty acids, triacylglycerols, sphingolipids, phospholipids, and glycolipids. The second major group of lipids consists of closed-ringed compounds, namely steroids. The main one in this group is cholesterol, which is an important precursor for the synthesis of steroid hormones, bile acids, and vitamin D.

Fat is a major energy source, which helps meet daily energy demands. It also provides energy when other sources are unavailable, such as during starvation or illness or when cells are unable to utilize other energy sources, as is the case with diabetes mellitus. Fat stores also help maintain body temperature and protect body organs from trauma. Additionally, fat aids in the delivery and absorption of fat-soluble vitamins and carotenoids, contributes to the sensory appeal of foods (taste and palatability), and influences the texture of foods. Its high energy density contributes to the satiety value of foods. Fatty acids also function in cell signaling and alter the expression of specific genes involved in lipid and carbohydrate metabolism. Thus, fatty acids serve as regulators of adipogenesis, inflammation, insulin action, and neurological functions.

Fatty Acids

Fatty acids are the simplest lipids and consist of hydrocarbon chains (see Figure 4.1). Fatty acids are a component of the more complex lipids and provide most of the energy in dietary fat. The common dietary fatty acids and the major contributors of these fatty acids are listed in Table 4.1 (1).

Fatty acids are classified based on the number of carbons in the molecule (chain length). Fatty acids may be saturated (SFA) (ie, no double bond), and include lauric (C12:0), myristic (C14:0), palmitic (C16:0), and stearic (C18:0) acids. SFAs can be synthesized in the body and are not only a source of energy, but are also structural components

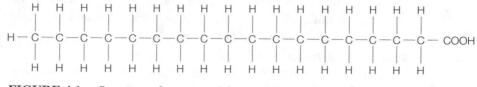

FIGURE 4.1.   Structure of a saturated fatty acid.

TABLE 4.1   Types and Sources of Fatty Acids

Fatty Acid Class	Fatty Acid	Common Abbreviation	Examples of Major Contributors to Intake
Saturated	Lauric acid	C12:0	Coconut oil
	Myristic acid	C14:0	Butterfat, coconut oil
	Palmitic acid	C16:0	Palm oil
	Stearic acid	C18:0	Cocoa butter
Monounsaturated	Oleic acid	C18:1 *cis* n-9*	Olive oil
	Elaidic acid	C18:1 *trans* n-9	Butterfat
Polyunsaturated	Linoleic acid	C18:2 n-6	Most vegetable oils (eg, safflower oil, corn oil)
	Arachidonic acid	C20:4 n-6	Lard, meats
	Linolenic acid	C18:3 n-3	Soybean oil, canola oil
	Eicosapentaenoic acid	C20:5 n-3	Fish oils, shellfish
	Docosahexaenoic acid	C22:6 n-3	Fish oils, shellfish

*Indicates position of double bond counting from the methyl end.
Source: Adapted with permission from Jonnalagadda SS, Mustad VA, Yu S, Etherton RD, Kris-Etherton PM. Effects of individual fatty acids on chronic disease. *Nutr Today.* 1996;31:90–106.

of cell membranes and are associated with the normal functioning of certain proteins. Monounsaturated fatty acids (MUFA), such as oleic acid (C18:1 n-9), contain one double bond. MUFA are also important components of membrane structural lipids, especially the myelin sheath (2).

Polyunsaturated fatty acids (PUFA) contain more than one double bond. Some of these PUFA, namely linoleic and alpha-linolenic acid, cannot be synthesized in the body and are therefore considered essential fatty acids. These essential fatty acids are used for the synthesis of other long-chain PUFA, which play a major role in the synthesis of eicosanoids. Eicosanoids are a family of compounds that are derived from C-20 polyunsaturated fatty acids and include prostaglandins (PG), thromboxanes (TX), and leukotrienes (LT). Based on the C-20 PUFA from which they are derived, there are different subgroups of these compounds. Eicosanoids have hormonal functions, but unlike other hormones they only affect the cells in which they are produced. They regulate cellular functions and play crucial roles in a variety of physiological and pathophysiological processes, including regulation of smooth muscle contractility and various immune and inflammatory functions. Prostaglandins and thromboxanes play an important role in blood pressure regulation, blood platelet aggregation, and diuresis. Combinations of prostaglandins and thromboxanes have antagonistic effects, which enable maintenance of normal physiological functions. Leukotrienes have an effect on contraction of the respiratory, vascular, and intestinal smooth muscles, and have been implicated as mediators in inflammatory reactions, hypersensitivities, asthma attacks, and myocardial infarctions.

The unsaturated fatty acids are also classified according to the position of the first double bond, ie, n-9 (omega-9), n-3 (omega-3), n-6 (omega-6), counted from the methyl end (see Figures 4.2A, 4.2B, 4.2C). Linoleic acid (C18:2, n-6) is a precursor of arachidonic acid, a substrate for eicosanoid production (PGI_2, TXA_2, LTB_4), a component of membrane structural lipids, regulator of gene expression, and important in cell signaling pathways (2). n-6 PUFA also play a critical role in normal epithelial cell function. Deficiency of linoleic acid results in scaly dermatitis, reduced growth, hematological disturbances, and reduced immune response. Alpha-linolenic acid (C18:3, n-3) is a precursor for the long-chained PUFA, namely, eicosapentaenoic acid (EPA) and docosahexaenoic acid (DHA). EPA is a substrate for eicosanoid synthesis (PGI_3, TXA_3 and LTB_5), which has beneficial effects in preventing coronary heart disease, arrhythmias, and thrombosis. Alpha-linolenic acid also plays an important structural role as a component of membrane lipids, mainly in the nervous tissue and retina.

The double bonds present in the unsaturated fatty acids (UFA) exist in the *cis* or *trans* configuration (see Figure 4.3), which determine the properties of these UFA. *Cis* MUFA, such as oleic acid, have one double bond with hydrogen atoms present on the same side of the double bond, causing the fatty acid to bend and providing more fluidity in the hydrocarbon chain. *Trans* fatty acids are unsaturated fatty acids with hydrogen atoms present on either side of the double bond, resulting in an extension of the fatty acid carbon chain similar to SFA, and thus reducing the fluidity of these hydrocarbon chains. Although naturally

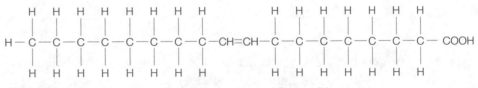

FIGURE 4.2A.   Structure of a monounsaturated fatty acid.

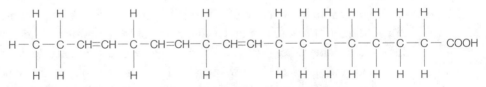

FIGURE 4.2B.   Structure of a polyunsaturated n-3 fatty acid.

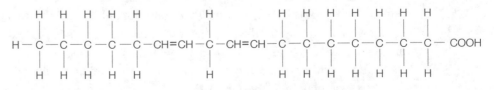

FIGURE 4.2C.   Structure of a polyunsaturated n-6 fatty acid.

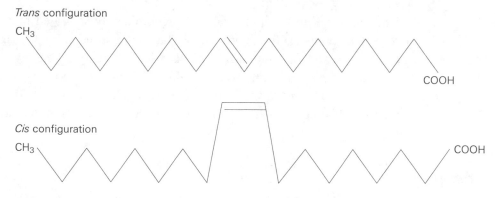

Trans configuration

CH₃

COOH

Cis configuration

CH₃

COOH

FIGURE 4.3.   *Trans* and *cis* configuration of double bonds.

present in a few foods such as beef and other dairy products, the majority of the *trans* fatty acids in the diet are obtained through the use of partially hydrogenated vegetable oils, which are commonly used in making margarine and baked, processed, and other prepared products. Hydrogenation is a process used to harden oils.

Conjugated linoleic acid (CLA) encompasses a group of isomers of linoleic acid in which the *trans* and *cis* double bonds are conjugated, (ie, the double bonds occur without an intervening carbon atom). Two of these isomers, *cis*-9, *trans*-11 and *trans*-10, *cis*-12, contain biological activity. Current evidence, although limited and not very strong, suggests that these isomers may decrease the uptake of lipids by adipocytes and inhibit atherogenesis and carcinogenesis. CLA is naturally present in dairy products and ruminant meats. Currently there are no known requirements for *trans* fatty acids and CLA with respect to specific body functions (2).

The type of fatty acid can influence the physical properties of the fat, its digestion, absorption, metabolism, utilization, and consequently overall health. The major sources of total fat in the US food supply include: meat, poultry, and fish (30%); grain products (25%); milk and milk products (18%); fats and oils, mainly as table spreads and salad dressing (11%); vegetables (9%); and other foods (7%) (3–5). Additionally, meat, poultry, fish, eggs, and dairy products are the major contributors of SFA in the diet. Grain products, such as yeast breads, cakes, and cookies, make considerable contributions to the intake of MUFA and PUFA. Fish and shellfish are the main sources of long-chain PUFA.

Triacylglycerols

Dietary fats and oils are made up of triacylglycerols (TAG), in which three fatty acids are esterified to a glycerol backbone (see Figure 4.4). Fats and oils are comprised of many different fatty acids present in proportions that are unique to the respective fat or oil. Fat from

CH_2O—*FATTY ACID*
|
CHO—*FATTY ACID*
|
CH_2O—*FATTY ACID*

FIGURE 4.4.   Structure of triacylglycerol.

land animals (butter, tallow, lard) is predominantly saturated fat, which remains solid at room temperature. On the other hand, fat from marine animals is predominantly made up of PUFA, mainly n-3 fatty acids, and are liquid in nature. Vegetable oils, such as corn, safflower, soybean, and sunflower, contain PUFA, mainly linoleic acid (n-6). Olive oil, canola oil, pecans, almonds, and avocados predominantly contain MUFA. Oils from tropical plants such as coconut and palm predominantly contain saturated fats and are solid at room temperature.

Phospholipids

Phospholipids contain one glycerol molecule that is esterified with two fatty acids, a phosphate group, and either inositol, choline, serine, or ethanolamine. Phospholipids are amphiphatic in nature, ie, both hydrophobic and hydrophilic. They are primarily located in the cell membrane, providing structural integrity to the cell, and are gatekeepers of the cellular content. Phospholipids are the backbone of the cell membrane and are a source of physiologically active compounds such as arachiodonic acid, which is needed for the synthesis of eicosanoids.

Dietary Recommendations and Fat Consumption in the United States

Dietary Reference Intakes

Dietary Reference Intakes (DRIs) are reference values, established by the National Academy of Sciences, that are quantitative estimates of nutrient intakes and include the Recommended Dietary Allowances (RDAs), Adequate Intakes (AIs), Estimated Average Requirements (EARs), and Tolerable Upper Intake Levels (ULs) (1) (see Appendix A). RDAs, AIs, and EARs have not been established for total fat, saturated fat, monounsaturated fat, or cholesterol. Likewise, *trans* fatty acids are not essential, have been observed to increase blood cholesterol levels, and provide no known benefit to human health. It is therefore recommended that the intake of SFA, *trans* fatty acids, and cholesterol be minimized and individuals follow the dietary guidelines while consuming a nutritionally adequate diet. Because linoleic acid is an essential fatty acid, the AI is 17 g/day for men and 12 g/day for women. The AI for alpha-linolenic acid, another essential n-3 fatty acid, is 1.6 g/day for men and 1.1 g/day for women. A dietary intake ratio of linoleic acid to linolenic acid of 5:1 to 10:1 has been recommended for adults (2).

Based on the existing evidence of the role of dietary fat in chronic disease and the need to provide essential nutrients, Acceptable Macronutrient Distribution Ranges (AMDR) were established for total fat. AMDR is defined as a range of intakes for a particular energy source that is associated with reduced risk of chronic diseases while providing adequate intakes of essential nutrients (2). The AMDR for total fat is 20% to 35% of energy for all adults. This intake of total fat will facilitate adequate intakes of other essential nutrients. The AMDR for linoleic acid is set at 5% to 10% of daily energy needs and 0.6% to 1.2% for linolenic acid.

Dietary Fat Intake Patterns of the General Population

Several national surveys determined that the total fat consumption as a percentage of total energy of the general population decreased in the past two decades from 36.9% (men) and 36.15% (women) to 32.8% for both men and women (3,6–9). Additionally, percent energy from SFA decreased from 13.5% to 10.9% for men and from 13% to 11% for women (7). However, these reductions in the percentage of energy from total fat and saturated fat are attributed to an increase in total energy intake, rather than an actual decline in total amount fat intake. The median total fat intake was 65 to 100 g/day for men and 48 to 63 g/day for women, representing 32% to 34% of total energy (7–9). The SFA intake provided 11% to 12% of total energy in the diets of adults and 12.2% to 13.9% of total energy for children and adolescents (7–9). The MUFA intake contributed 13.6% to 14.3% of total energy intake (7–9). The n-6 PUFA intake contributed 5% to 7% of total energy intake, mainly in the form of linoleic acid (85% to 90%) (7–9). The n-3 PUFA intake contributed approximately 0.7% of total energy intake. The *trans* fatty acid intake ranged from 1.5% to 2.2 % of total energy intake (7–9). The mean cholesterol intake was 256 mg/day (7–9).

Dietary Fat Intake Patterns of Athletes

The dietary fat intake patterns of athletes vary considerably depending on the sport, training, and performance level of the athlete. In general, elite endurance athletes, such as runners and cyclists, have been observed to consume training diets that meet the dietary fat guidelines. Distance runners have been reported to consume between 27% to 35% of energy as fat, while professional cyclists, such as those competing in the Tour de France, were observed to consume approximately 27% of their total energy as fat (10). Likewise, rowers, basketball players, and nordic skiers were reported to consume diets that contained 30% to 40% of energy as fat (11). On the other hand, for athletes participating in sports in which appearance plays a major factor in performance, such as gymnastics and figure skating, the dietary fat intake has been reported to range from 15% to 31% (12,13).

Dietary Fat Recommendations for Athletes

It is the position of the American Dietetic Association that athletes should not restrict their dietary fat intake because there is no performance benefit of very-low-fat diets (< 15% total energy intake) compared with moderate-fat diets (20% to 25% total energy intake) (14). Dietary fat intake should be individualized to the athlete's physical activity level, energy expenditure, growth stage, nutritional needs, and food preferences.

Consequences of a Low-fat Diet in Athletes

Athletes sometimes consume diets with less than 20% of energy from fat in an effort to improve appearance and/or increase competitiveness by reducing body weight or body fat (15). Additionally, athletes, especially endurance athletes, tend to increase their dietary carbohydrate intake at the expense of dietary fat to increase their body glycogen stores. In either case, the resulting low-fat diets may not meet the energy demands for growth and development in the young athlete and the energy needs for endurance performance (10,15). By following low-fat diets for prolonged periods of time, athletes could develop deficiencies of essential fatty acids and fat-soluble vitamins (2,10,14). Intakes of micronutrients such as calcium, iron, and zinc may also be compromised. In female athletes these very-low-fat diets (< 15% of energy) can contribute to menstrual dysfunctions (15). Similarly, in male athletes, low serum testosterone levels are observed with the intake of low-fat diets, which in turn can influence their reproductive functions (15). Very-low-fat diets can result in inadequate dietary intake of fat-soluble vitamins, especially vitamins E and D, which play important roles in maintaining the antioxidant system and bone health, respectively. Therefore, the consumption of very-low-fat diets by athletes is generally not recommended (14).

Metabolism of Fat During Exercise

Fat, along with carbohydrate, is oxidized to supply energy to the exercising muscle. The extent to which these sources contribute to energy expenditure depends on the duration and intensity of exercise. Intramuscular triacylglycerol stores are important energy sources for the contracting muscle. Endurance (> 90 minutes) athletes typically train at 65% to 75% maximum oxygen consumption (VO_{2max}) and are limited by the carbohydrate reserves in the body (16,17). After 15 to 20 minutes of endurance exercise, oxidation of fat deposits (lipolysis) is stimulated and glycerol and free fatty acids are released (see Figure 4.5) (18). During high exercise intensities, a shift in energy supply from fat to carbohydrate is observed, especially at 70% to 80% VO_{2max}, suggesting that there might be limitations to the use of fatty acid oxidation as a means of energy to the exercising muscle. Abernethy et al (19) suggest this shift may be a result of the increased lactate production that inhibits fatty acid supply, the higher oxygen requirement associated with fatty acid oxidation, and/or the limitations of the carnitine transport system. A detailed discussion of the aerobic system and substrate oxidation can be found in Chapter 1.

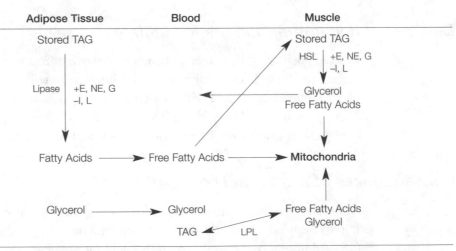

HSL = Hormone sensitive lipase; LPL = lipoprotein lipase; E = epinephrine; NE = norepinephrine; I = insulin; G = glucagon; L = lactate; TAG = triacylglycerol.

FIGURE 4.5.   Fatty acid metabolism. From Sherman WM, Leenders N. Fat loading: the next magic bullet? *Int J Sport Nutr.* 1995;5(suppl):S2, figure 1. Copyright © 1995 by Human Kinetics. Adapted with permission from Human Kinetics (Champaign, IL).

Although fatty acid oxidation during endurance exercise yields more energy when compared with carbohydrate, fatty acids require more oxygen for oxidation than carbohydrates do (77% more oxygen), thereby putting greater stress on the cardiovascular system. However, because of the limited carbohydrate storage capacity, high-intensity exercise performance can be impaired with glycogen depletion. Therefore, several interventions have been examined to spare muscle carbohydrate and increase fatty acid oxidation during endurance exercise (20). These include training, medium-chain triacylglycerol feedings, and high-fat diets, which are discussed later in this chapter. Oral fat emulsion and fat infusions are not recommended. Supplements such as L-carnitine, caffeine, and ephedrine are discussed in Chapter 7.

Training

The trained muscles generally have high muscle lipoprotein lipase, muscle lipase, fatty acid acyl CoA synthetase and reductase, carnitine acyl transferase, and 3-hydroxyl acyl CoA dehydrogenase activities, all of which can enhance fatty acid oxidation. Additionally, trained muscles store more intracellular fat, which can also enhance fatty acid supply and oxidation during exercise, thereby conserving carbohydrate stores during endurance exercise.

Medium Chain Triacylglycerol Ingestion

Medium chain triacylglycerols (MCTs) contain fatty acids that have 6 to 12 carbon atoms. Most MCTs are rapidly absorbed and enter the portal circulation. There is a great deal of literature indicating that approximately 50% of the C-12 MCTs are incorporated into chylomicrons and enter the circulation via the lymphatics as does most dietary fat. However, the majority of MCTs enter the portal circulation without the benefit of chylomicron formation. In the muscle, these medium-chain fatty acids are rapidly taken up by the mitochondria because they do not require the carnitine transport system and can be oxidized faster than long-chain triacylglycerols. However, studies examining the effect of MCT ingestion on exercise performance have been equivocal and the available data do not show a glycogen-sparing effect or improvement in endurance performance. In addition, MCT ingestion may cause severe gastrointestinal distress (21–24). MCTs are further discussed in Chapter 7.

Fat Adaptation, Fat Loading Diets

A carbohydrate-sparing effect of dietary fat has been suggested with aerobic training, implying an increase in oxidation of fat and a decrease in oxidation of carbohydrates (16–18,25–28). This reduction in carbohydrate oxidation can enhance endurance performance with greater reliance on fat for energy. Therefore, it has been hypothesized that increasing dietary fat intake might increase fatty acid oxidation, spare carbohydrate, and improve performance. However, current evidence does not support this hypothesis (16,17,25).

Infusion of a TAG emulsion or ingestion of SFA did not influence work capacity, exercise performance, or muscle glycogen levels during exercise (28–30). Some researchers have used fasting in an attempt to increase fatty acid oxidation and spare carbohydrate during exercise. Although fasting seems to increase fatty acid availability for oxidation during exercise, it does not improve overall exercise performance (31).

Additionally, studies have examined the influence of low-carbohydrate, high-fat diets (> 70% energy) on exercise performance and muscle glycogen stores. However, these dietary manipulations have not shown any consistent effects on muscle glycogen stores, exercise capacity, or performance (25,28). At the present time, the effectiveness of short-term (1 to 3 days) dietary manipulations, such as fat loading, has yet to be proven beneficial in enhancing performance (16–18). Burke (25) observed significant reductions in rate of carbohydrate oxidation during exercise while fat oxidation rate doubled among trained cyclists and triathletes consuming a high-fat, low-carbohydrate diet for 5 days. No improvement in cycling performance was observed. On the other hand, long-term (> 7 days) adaptation to fat-rich diets could potentially induce skeletal-muscle adaptations, metabolism, and/or morphological changes, which in turn could influence exercise performance (26). Lambert et al (32) observed that the consumption of a 76% fat diet vs a 74% carbohydrate diet for 14 days did not impair maximal power output and time to exhaustion in endurance-trained cyclists. However, muscle glycogen stores were two-fold less on the high-fat diet compared with the high-carbohydrate diet, thus making it difficult to interpret the influence of this dietary manipulation on endurance performance.

Similarly, Helge et al (27) observed a 9% increase in VO_{2max} in untrained male subjects fed a high-fat diet (62% of energy) or a high-carbohydrate diet (65% of energy) with training for 4 weeks. Endurance time to exhaustion was increased with both dietary treatments. This suggests that adaptation to a high-fat diet in combination with training for up to 4 weeks, exercising at submaximal workloads, does not seem to impair endurance performance. Conversely, consumption of a high-fat diet for 7 weeks was associated with a reduction in time to exhaustion compared with the high-carbohydrate diet group, suggesting that the duration of this high-fat dietary intake may have an impact on exercise performance (33).

The adaptation to dietary fat could be associated with up-regulation of fatty acid oxidation enzymes. A strong association has been demonstrated between 3-hydroxyacyl CoA dehydrogenase activity and fatty acid uptake and oxidation in humans (34) and may also be associated with an increase in fatty acid binding protein in the cytosol and plasma membrane. Despite this adaptation, training-induced increases in endurance performance with a high-fat diet is not comparable to that observed with a high-carbohydrate diet. The existing scientific evidence does not support the recommendation for these diets. Additionally, the long-term adverse effects of high fat intake on the cardiovascular system are well established and, therefore, this practice should be viewed with caution if being used by athletes to improve performance. A detailed discussion of aerobic training and substrate oxidation can be found in Chapter 1.

Summary

Dietary lipids have important physiological roles in the body, and obtaining adequate amounts is essential. However, excessive consumption of saturated fats and cholesterol can increase risk of cardiovascular disease and other chronic diseases. Additionally, the current obesity epidemic is attributed in large part to the increased total energy intake and total fat intake and decreased physical activity. Therefore, it is prudent to advocate moderation in total fat intake (20% to 35% of total energy) and limited saturated fat intake (10% of energy or less). Given the functional role of fat in the body and the utilization of fat energy during exercise, especially endurance activities, athletes should be strongly discouraged from consuming diets with less than 15% of energy from fat. Additionally, the well-established role of linoleic acid and linolenic acid in synthesis of eicosanoids, which regulate numerous physiological process such as blood pressure, blood flow regulation, blood clotting, inflammation, and bronchiole air flow, makes it imperative that athletes ensure adequate intake of these essential fatty acids by consuming at least 3% to 5% of dietary fat from food sources such as fish and plant oils.

References

1. Jonnalagadda SS, Mustad VA, Yu S, Etherton RD, Kris-Etherton PM. Effects of individual fatty acids on chronic disease. *Nutr Today.* 1996;31:90–106.
2. Institute of Medicine. *Dietary Reference Intakes for Energy, Carbohydrate, Fiber, Fat, Fatty Acids, Cholesterol, Protein and Amino Acids (Macronutrients).* Washington, DC: National Academy Press; 2002. Available at: http://www.nap.edu. Accessed December 30, 2003.
3. Jonnalagadda SS, Egan SK, Heimbach JT, Harris SS, Kris-Etherton PM. Fatty acid consumption pattern of Americans: 1987–1988 USDA Nationwide Food Consumption Survey. *Nutr Res.* 1995;15:1767–1781.
4. Ernst ND. Fatty acid composition of present day diets. In: Nelson GJ, ed. *Health Effects of Dietary Fatty Acids.* Champaign, Ill: American Oil Chemists Society; 1991:1–11.
5. Borrud LG, Tippett KS, Mickle SJ. Food sources of fat in USDA's Continuing Survey of Food Intakes by Individuals 1989–91. Food Surveys Research Group, Beltsville Human Nutrition Research Center, Agricultural Research Center, US Department of Agriculture. Available at: http://www.barc.usda.gov/bhnrc/foodsurvey/eatout95.html. Accessed December 3, 2003.
6. Food Surveys Research Group. What we eat in America. Continuing Survey of Food Intake of Individuals 1994–1996, 1998. Beltsville Human Nutrition Research Center, Agricultural Research Center, US Department of Agriculture. Available at: http://www.barc.usda.gov/bhnrc/foodsurvey.home.htm. Accessed December 3, 2003.
7. Wright JD, Kennedy-Stephenson J, Wang CY, McDowell MA, Johnson CL. Trends in intake of energy and macronutrients: United States, 1971–2000. *MMWR.* 2004;53:80–82.
8. Wilson JW, Enns CW, Goldman JD, Tippett KS, Mickle SJ, Cleveland LE, Chahil PS. Data tables: combined results from USDA's 1994 and 1995 Continuing Survey of Food Intakes by Individuals and 1994 and 1995 Diet and Health Knowledge Survey. 1997. ARS Food Surveys Research Group. Available at: http://www.barc.usda.gov/bhnrc/foodsurvey/pdf/Tbchts95.pdf. Accessed November 3, 2004.
9. McDowell MA, Briefel RR, Alaimo K, Bischof AM, Caughman CR, Carroll MD, Loria CM, Johnson CL. Energy and macronutrient intakes of persons ages 2 months and over in the United States: Third National Health and Nutrition Examination Survey, Phase I, 1988–91. *Adv Data.* 1994;Oct 24(255):1–24.
10. Williams C. Dietary macro- and micronutrient requirements of endurance athletes. *Proc Nutr Soc.* 1998;57:1–8.
11. Burke LM. Nutrition for the female athlete. In: Krummel DA, Kris-Etherton PM, eds. *Nutrition in Women's Health.* Gaithersburg, Md: Aspen Publishers; 1996:263–298.
12. Jonnalagadda SS, Benardot D, Nelson M. Energy and nutrient intakes of the United States national women's artistic gymnastics team. *Int J Sport Nutr.* 1998;8:331–344.
13. Ziegler PJ, Khoo CS, Kris-Etherton PM, Jonnalagadda SS, Sherr B, Nelson JA. Nutritional status of nationally ranked junior US figure skaters. *J Am Diet Assoc.* 1998;98:809–811.

14. American Dietetic Association. Position of the American Dietetic Association, Dietitians of Canada, and the American College of Sports Medicine: nutrition and athletic performance. *J Am Diet Assoc.* 2000;100:1543–1556.

15. Brownell KD, Steen SN, Wilmore JH. Weight regulation practices in athletes: analysis of metabolic and health effects. *Med Sci Sports Exerc.* 1987;18:546–556.

16. Hargreaves M, Hawley JA, Jeukendrup A. Pre-exercise carbohydrate and fat ingestion: effects on metabolism and performance. *J Sports Sci.* 2004;22:31–38.

17. Burke LM, Kiens B, Ivy JL. Carbohydrates and fat for training and recovery. *J Sports Sci.* 2004;22:15–30.

18. Sherman WM, Leenders N. Fat loading: the next magic bullet? *Int J Sport Nutr.* 1995;5(Suppl): S1–S12.

19. Abernethy PJ, Thayer R, Taylor AW. Acute and chronic responses of skeletal muscle to endurance and sprint exercise. *Sports Med.* 1990;10:365–389.

20. Brouns F, van der Vusse GJ. Utilization of lipids during exercise in human subjects: metabolic and dietary constraints. *Br J Nutr.* 1998;79:117–128.

21. Jeukendrup AE, Saris WHM, Schrauwen P, Brouns F, Wagenmakers AJM. Metabolic availability of medium-chain triglycerides coingested with carbohydrates during prolonged exercise. *J Appl Physiol.* 1995;79:756–762.

22. Jeukendrup AE, Saris WHM, Brouns F, Halliday D, Wagenmakers AJM. Effects of carbohydrate (CHO) and fat supplements on CHO metabolism during prolonged exercise. *Metabolism.* 1996;45:915–921.

23. Jeukendrup AE, Saris WHM, Van Diesen R, Brouns F, Wagenmakers AJM. Effect of endogenous carbohydrate availability on oral medium-chain triglyceride oxidation during prolonged exercise. *J Appl Physiol.* 1996;80:949–954.

24. Jeukendrup AE, Thielen JJ, Wagenmakers AJ, Brouns F, Saris WH. Effect of medium-chain tri-acylglycerol and carbohydrate ingestion on substrate utilization and subsequent cycling performance. *Am J Clin Nutr.* 1998;67:397–404.

25. Burke L. Fat adaptation and glycogen restoration for prolonged cycling-recent studies from the Australian Institute of Sport. *Aust J Nutr Diet.* 2001;58(Suppl 1):S23–S27.

26. Kiens B, Helge JW. Effect of high-fat diets on exercise performance. *Proc Nutr Soc.* 1998;57:73–75.

27. Helge JW, Wulff B, Kiens B. Impact of a fat-rich diet on endurance in man: role of the dietary period. *Med Sci Sports Exerc.* 1998;30:456–461.

28. Dyck DJ, Putman CT, Heigenhauser GJF, Hultman E, Spriet LL. Regulation of fat-carbohydrate interaction in skeletal muscle during intense aerobic cycling. *Am J Physiol.* 1993;265:E852–E859.

29. Vukovich MD, Costill DL, Hickey MS, Trappe SW, Cole KJ, Fink WJ. Effect of fat emulsion infusion and fat feeding on muscle glycogen utilization during cycle exercise. *J Appl Physiol.* 1993;75:1513–1518.

30. Hargreaves M, Kiens B, Richter EA. Effect of increasing plasma free fatty acid concentrations on muscle metabolism in exercising men. *J Appl Physiol.* 1991;70:194–201.

31. Loy SF, Conlee RK, Winder WW, Nelson AG, Arnall DA, Fisher AG. Effects of a 24-hour fast on cycling endurance time at two different intensities. *J Appl Physiol.* 1986;61:654–659.

32. Lambert EV, Speechly DP, Dennis SC, Noaks TD. Enhanced endurance in trained cyclists during moderate intensity exercise following 2 weeks adaptation to a high fat diet. *Eur J Appl Physiol Occup Physiol.* 1994;69:287–293.

33. Helge JW, Richter EA, Kiens B. Interaction of training and diet on metabolism and endurance during exercise in man. *J Physiol.* 1996;492:293–306.

34. Kiens B. Effect of endurance training on fatty acid metabolism: local adaptations. *Med Sci Sports Exerc.* 1997;29:640–645.

Chapter 5

VITAMINS, MINERALS, AND EXERCISE

Stella Lucia Volpe, PhD, RD, FACSM

Introduction

Vitamins and minerals are necessary for many metabolic processes in the body, as well as to support growth and development (1). Vitamins and minerals are also required in a number of reactions involved with exercise and physical activity, such as energy, carbohydrate, fat and protein metabolism, oxygen transfer and delivery, and tissue repair (1).

The vitamin and mineral needs of individuals who are physically active have always been a subject of debate. Some reports state that those who exercise require more vitamins and minerals than their sedentary counterparts, but other studies do not report greater micronutrient requirements. The intensity, duration, and frequency of the physical activity, as well as the overall energy and nutrient intakes of the individual, all have an impact on whether micronutrients are required in greater amounts (1–3). The purpose of this chapter is to review the vitamin and mineral needs of individuals who are physically active.

Dietary Reference Intakes

Recommendations for all known vitamins and some essential minerals for healthy, moderately active people were updated between 1997 and 2004 (4–7). These recommendations are known as the Dietary Reference Intakes (DRIs) (see Appendix A). Adequate Intake (AI), Recommended Dietary Allowance (RDA), Estimated Average Requirement (EAR), and Tolerable Upper Intake Level (UL) are all under the DRI heading. The RDA is the dietary intake level that is adequate for approximately 98% of healthy people. The AI is an estimated value that is used when an RDA cannot be determined. The EAR is a value used to approximate the nutrient needs of half of the healthy people in a group (8). The UL is the highest amount of a nutrient most individuals can consume without adverse effects (8).

In general, if energy intakes are adequate, the vitamin and mineral needs of physically active individuals are similar to healthy, moderately active individuals. Thus, the use of the DRI is appropriate. Some athletes may have increased requirements due to excessive losses of nutrients in sweat and urine, and supplementation may be needed. Because many individuals who are physically active choose to supplement with vitamins and minerals, the UL allows for practitioners to give guidelines to these individuals to prevent adverse reactions from excess consumption. Additional information about multivitamin and mineral and antioxidant supplements is in Chapter 7.

There are limitations to the research. Mixed results make it difficult for practitioners to give definitive advice to their clients. The limitations include: (a) small numbers of subjects, most of whom have been male; (b) differences in type of exercise performed and/or levels of training and fitness; (c) lack of strong longitudinal data; (d) differences in assessment methodology or study design; and (e) various types and amounts of supplementation.

For all vitamins and minerals, an assessment of dietary intake is required, especially because many athletes may consume the correct amount of nutrients but not enough energy, which could result in suboptimal exercise performance. Clark et al (9) assessed the pre- and postseason intakes of macro- and micronutrients in female soccer players and found that, despite meeting energy requirements (but not carbohydrate needs), intakes of the micronutrients vitamin E, folate, copper, and magnesium were marginal (< 75% of the DRI).

In an effort to assess if supplementation would affect performance, Telford et al (10) supplemented 82 male and female athletes from different sports with either a vitamin-mineral supplement or a placebo for 7 to 8 months. All athletes in the study consumed diets that met the recommended daily intakes of vitamins and minerals. Although Telford et al reported that vitamin-mineral supplementation did not improve performance in any of the sport-specific variables measured, they did report improved jumping ability in female basketball players. Certainly, the area of supplementation and athletic performance needs to be further studied; however, it seems that individuals who consume adequate intakes of vitamins and minerals from food do not benefit from supplementation.

Water-Soluble Vitamins

Vitamins are classified by their solubility within the body. The water-soluble vitamins, which do not require fat for their absorption, include vitamin B-6, vitamin B-12, folate, thiamin, riboflavin, niacin, pantothenic acid, biotin, and choline. Table 5.1 lists the water-soluble vitamin needs for the athlete.

Vitamin B-6

There are three major forms of vitamin B-6: pyridoxine (PN), pyridoxal (PL), and pyridoxamine (PM). The active coenzyme forms of vitamin B-6 are pyridoxal 5'-phosphate (PLP) and pyridoxamine 5'-phosphate (PMP) (11). Vitamin B-6 is involved in approximately 100 metabolic reactions, including those of gluconeogenesis, niacin synthesis, and lipid metabolism (11).

Some researchers have reported that vitamin B-6 metabolism is affected by exercise and that poor vitamin B-6 status can impair exercise performance (12). It was once thought that exercise caused transient changes in vitamin B-6 status; however, more recent research may indicate differently (13,14). A study in rats suggests that exercise itself caused a retention of vitamin B-6 by decreased excretion, and this occurred even when intake of vitamin B-6 was restricted (15). Although conducted in rats, this study demonstrates an adaptive mechanism

TABLE 5.1   Water-Soluble Vitamin Needs for Athletes

Vitamin	Effect of Exercise on Requirements	Recommended Intake* for Athletes	Food Sources	Comments
Vitamin B-6	Exercise does not cause transient changes in B-6 status.	DRI	Liver, chicken, bananas, potatoes, spinach	
Vitamin B-12	Exercise does not seem to increase needs.	DRI; vegan athletes may need to supplement	Fish, milk and milk products, eggs, meat, poultry, fortified breakfast cereals	
Folate	Exercise does not seem to increase needs.	DRI	Leafy greens (eg, spinach, turnip greens), dry beans, peas, fortified cereals, grain products, strawberries	
Thiamin	Exercise does not seem to increase needs.	DRI	Wheat germ, brewer's yeast, oysters, beef liver, peanuts, green peas, raisins, collard greens	Ergogenic effects are equivocal; positive effects are not strong.
Riboflavin	Exercise does not seem to increase needs.	DRI	Organ meats, milk, cheese, oily fish, eggs, dark leafy green vegetables	
Niacin	Exercise does not seem to increase needs.	DRI	Beef, pork, chicken, wheat flour, eggs, milk	Does not seem to have ergogenic effects; more research is needed.
Pantothenic acid	Not enough information.	DRI	Eggs, whole grain cereals, meat	
Biotin	Not enough information.	DRI	Kidney, liver, eggs, dried mixed fruit	
Vitamin C	Increased intakes may prevent upper respiratory tract infections.	At least the DRI; ultra-endurance athletes need more than the DRI, but below the UL	Brussels sprouts, broccoli, chili and sweet peppers (red and green), kiwi, oranges, papaya, guava.	Strong antioxidant properties reported for endurance and ultraendurance athletes.
Choline	Exercise does not seem to increase needs.	DRI	Liver, egg yolks, peanuts, cauliflower, soybeans, grape juice, and cabbage	Does not seem to have an ergogenic effect; more research required.

Abbreviations: DRI, Dietary Reference Intake; UL, Tolerable Upper Intake level.
*See Appendix A for DRI tables.

that could occur as a result of exercise; however, over time this mechanism may not be sufficient for maintaining vitamin B-6 status if intake continues to be less than adequate levels.

Considering the research conducted to date, it seems that individuals who exercise do not have increased needs for vitamin B-6. However, if deficiencies exist, it may be necessary to supplement with vitamin B-6 at the level of the DRI. Dietary sources of vitamin B-6 can be found in Table 5.1.

Vitamin B-12 and Folate

Vitamin B-12 (cyanocobalamin) and folate (folic acid) are both necessary for DNA synthesis (16,17) and are interrelated in their synthesis and metabolism. Both vitamins are required for normal erythrocyte synthesis; it is this function by which these two vitamins may have an effect on exercise (18).

There is no evidence to suggest that exercise increases the need for either of these vitamins. Inadequate intakes of both vitamins can lead to megaloblastic anemia. The adequate intake of vitamin B-12 is of special concern in vegan athletes because vitamin B-12 is almost exclusively found in animal products (19,20). Vegetarians who consume dairy products and/or eggs are likely to have adequate intakes of vitamin B-12, but vegan athletes need to regularly consume vitamin B-12–fortified foods or may need to supplement (18,20). More information about vitamin B-12 and vegetarian athletes can be found in Chapter 16.

Although injections of vitamin B-12 are used clinically for individuals diagnosed with megaloblastic anemia, oral supplementation is sufficient if a frank anemia has not been diagnosed. A multivitamin and mineral supplement, including 500 to 1,000 mg vitamin C may decrease vitamin B-12 bioavailability from food and may also lead to vitamin B-12 deficiency (21,22). Because vitamin B-12 is secreted daily into the bile and then reabsorbed, it takes approximately 20 years for healthy people to show signs of deficiency (20). However, vitamin B-12 deficiency can be masked by high folate intake; thus, if a vitamin B-12 deficiency is suspected, an assessment of dietary intake will be necessary, especially if the biochemical tests are negative for a B-12 deficiency.

Athletes who consume adequate vitamin B-12 and folate in their diets are probably not at risk for vitamin B-12 or folate deficiencies. Nonetheless, vitamin B-12 or folate deficiencies can lead to increased serum homocysteine levels, which is a risk factor for cardiovascular disease (23), pointing to the need for individuals who exercise to be concerned not only about nutrition and performance but also about overall health. Hermann et al (14) assessed homocysteine, vitamin B-12, and folate serum concentrations in swimmers after high-volume and high-intensity swim training and during 5 days of recovery. Homocysteine levels were increased during both types of training as well as during recovery. Vitamin B-12 levels were unchanged during either type of training, but showed a decrease during the recovery phase, indicating a delayed response to the training. Folate levels, however, decreased during training, but blood levels returned to normal by the end of the recovery periods. Because vitamin B-12 and folate are metabolically interrelated, the changes in one and not the other at different times of exercise and recovery may indicate an adaptive response by each to "protect" the other. At the present time, it is difficult to determine if the increase in homocysteine levels could persist with training or if they are transient; however, it is important for individuals who exercise to consume adequate levels of vitamin B-12 and folate. Dietary sources of folate and vitamin B-12 can be found in Table 5.1.

Thiamin

Thiamin participates in several energy-producing reactions as part of thiamin diphosphate (TDP) (also known as thiamin pyrophosphate [TPP]), including the citric acid cycle, branched-chain amino acid (BCAA) catabolism, and the pentose phosphate pathway (24). For example, thiamin is required for the conversion of pyruvate to acetyl-CoA during carbohydrate metabolism. This conversion is essential for the aerobic metabolism of glucose, and exercise performance and health will be impaired if this conversion does not occur (1). Thus, it is imperative that individuals who exercise consume the proper amount of both thiamin and carbohydrates.

There seems to be a strong correlation between high carbohydrate intakes, physical activity, and thiamin requirements (24). This may be a concern for individuals who exercise because carbohydrates are typically needed in the highest amounts in the diet; however, there has not been clear evidence indicating that individuals who exercise require more thiamin in their diets than sedentary individuals. Nonetheless, it is prudent to recommend that individuals who exercise obtain at least the DRI for thiamin to prevent depletion.

To date, the studies that have been published have had equivocal outcomes of the effects of thiamin supplementation on exercise performance. In three studies, including two with cycle ergometry (25–27), supplementation with thiamin derivatives did not enhance exercise performance. However, Suzuki and Itokawa (28) reported that supplementation with 100 mg/day of thiamin significantly decreased fatigue during cycle ergometry. In a study conducted on the effects of thiamin, riboflavin, and vitamin B-6 depletion on exercise performance, van der Beek and colleagues (29) found no adverse effects on exercise performance.

More research is required to determine if thiamin requirements are greater in individuals who exercise. Thiamin requirements may parallel the intensity, duration, and frequency of exercise. Because so little research has been conducted, practitioners should not recommend thiamin intakes more than the DRI for physically active individuals unless a thiamin deficiency has been determined. Dietary sources of thiamin are listed in Table 5.1.

Riboflavin

Riboflavin is involved in several key metabolic reactions that are important during exercise: glycolysis, the citric acid cycle, and the electron transport chain (30). Riboflavin is the precursor in the synthesis of the flavin coenzymes, flavin mononucleotide (FMN), and flavin-adenine dinucleotide (FAD), which assist in oxidation reduction reactions by acting as 1- and 2-electron transfers (30). Riboflavin status may be altered in individuals who are initiating an exercise program (30); however, it is unclear if it is a transient or long-term effect of exercise. Human studies of longer duration are necessary to evaluate the long-term effects of exercise on riboflavin status (30).

It seems that individuals who are physically active and consume adequate amounts of dietary riboflavin are not at risk for depletion of riboflavin and, thus, do not require levels more than the DRI (30). Dietary sources of riboflavin are listed in Table 5.1.

Niacin

Niacin is a family of molecules that include both nicotinic acid and nicotinamide (30). The coenzyme forms of niacin are nicotinamide adenine dinucleotide (NAD) and NAD phosphate (NADP). Both are involved in glycolysis, the pentose pathway, the citric acid cycle, lipid synthesis, and the electron transport chain (30). Nicotinic acid is often prescribed and used in pharmacological doses to reduce serum cholesterol and C-reactive protein levels (30,31). It seems that pharmacological doses of nicotinic acid may augment the use of carbohydrate as a substrate during exercise by decreasing the availability of free fatty acids

(30). Despite this strong connection to exercise metabolism, no solid data presently exist to support increased niacin supplementation for individuals who exercise (30).

Furthermore, pharmacologic doses of niacin can result in a "niacin rush," whereby individuals have greater blood flow throughout their bodies, notably reddening in the face and extreme itching. Athletes may take high doses of niacin with the thought that "more is better." However, taking too much niacin, as with taking too much of any vitamin or mineral, can be detrimental to health and exercise performance because vitamins and minerals can compete with one another in the body and affect metabolism of other nutrients. Because of niacin's role in vasodilation, several researchers have studied the effect of niacin supplementation on thermoregulation and reported mixed results, likely due to differences in methodology (32,33).

It is important that individuals who exercise obtain the DRI for niacin to ensure adequate intake and prevent alterations in fuel utilization that could possibly impair performance. Dietary sources of niacin are listed in Table 5.1.

Pantothenic Acid

Pantothenic acid, whose biologically active forms are coenzyme A (CoA) and acyl carrier protein, is involved in acyl group transfers such as the acylation of amino acids (34,35). Pantothenic acid coenzymes are also involved in lipid synthesis and metabolism and oxidation of pyruvate and alpha ketoglutarate (35). Acetyl CoA is an important intermediate in fat, carbohydrate, and protein metabolism (35). To date, only a few studies have examined the effects of pantothenic acid supplementation on exercise performance (35,36) and there have been no recent human studies (37). Definite conclusions cannot be made; however, it would be prudent to suggest that athletes consume the DRI for pantothenic acid. Dietary sources include sunflower seeds, mushrooms, peanuts, brewer's yeast, yogurt, and broccoli (1).

Biotin

Biotin is an essential cofactor in four mitochondrial carboxylases (one carboxylase is in both the mitochondria and cytosol) (38). These carboxylase-dependent reactions are involved in energy metabolism; thus, biotin deficiency could potentially result in impaired exercise performance. To date, no studies have been conducted on the role of biotin on exercise performance or biotin requirements for individuals who are physically active. Controlled, well-designed studies are needed to establish whether biotin is needed in larger amounts by individuals who exercise.

Good dietary sources of biotin include peanut butter, boiled eggs, toasted wheat germ, egg noodles, Swiss cheese, and cauliflower (1). It is hypothesized that biotin is synthesized by bacteria in the gastrointestinal tract of mammals; however, there are no published reports proving that this actually occurs (38).

Vitamin C

Vitamin C, also referred to as ascorbic acid, ascorbate, or ascorbate monoanion (39), is involved in the maintenance of collagen synthesis, oxidation of fatty acids, and formation of neurotransmitters. It is also an antioxidant (39,40). It has been fairly well-documented that vitamin C protects against oxidative stress in endurance and ultraendurance athletes, especially preventing upper respiratory tract infections (URTI) (41). It should also be mentioned here that although aerobic exercise increases oxidative stress, it also results in an increase in the enzymatic and nonenzymatic antioxidants as an adaptation to training. Vitamin C levels in the blood can be increased up to 24 hours after exercise; thus, one must be cautious when blood measurements of vitamin C are used as assessment parameters in research studies (42–44) because they may not be truly reflective of status.

Tauler et al (45) reported that high vitamin C intake positively influenced the response of neutrophils and lymphocytes to oxidative stress induced by exercise (duathlon competition), increasing the neutrophil activation. Robson et al (46) also reported a significantly greater neutrophil oxidative burst following exercise after only 7 days of supplementing athletes with an antioxidant combination of 18 mg beta carotene, 900 mg vitamin C, and 90 mg vitamin E. The positive response could not be solely attributed to vitamin C. However, it could be speculated that vitamin C had the greatest impact of the three antioxidant vitamins because it was given at such a high dose. It has been reported that higher plasma vitamin C levels were associated with greater skeletal muscle strength in individuals older than 65 years (47).

Vitamin C is often supplemented in very high doses in the hope that it may prevent colds. Although it has been the belief that supplementation with vitamin C in high doses (≥ 1 g/day) may reduce the severity and duration of colds, more recent research has not shown this to be true (48,49).

Individuals who consistently exercise (at any level) may require at least 100 mg/day of vitamin C to maintain normal vitamin C status and protect the body from oxidative damage caused by exercise (40). This level may easily be consumed in food. Individuals who are competing in ultraendurance events may require up to 500 mg/day or more of vitamin C (40) consumed as supplements. Nonetheless, athletes should not exceed the UL for vitamin C. Dietary sources of vitamin C can be found in Table 5.1.

Choline

Choline is a vitamin-like compound required for the synthesis of all cell membranes (50). It can be synthesized from the amino acid methionine (51). Choline is also involved in carnitine and very-low-density lipoprotein cholesterol (VLDL-C) synthesis (50,52). It has been suggested that choline may affect nerve transmission, improve strength, and expedite the loss of body fat (51).

Overt choline deficiencies have not been reported in humans (53). Although there have been reports that plasma choline concentrations significantly decrease after long-distance swimming, running, and triathlons (54,55), not all researchers observe this same decrease (56). Deuster et al (57) found that although choline supplementation significantly increased plasma choline concentrations, supplementation did not affect physical or cognitive performance after exhaustive physical activity.

There is insufficient research to suggest that athletes need more than the DRI for choline. Beef liver, peanuts, peanut butter, iceberg lettuce, cauliflower, and whole-wheat bread are some of the highest sources of choline. Potatoes, grape juice, tomatoes, bananas, and cucumbers are also good sources (50) (see Table 5.1). Consuming a wide variety of foods will likely provide sufficient amounts and there is no evidence to support choline supplementation.

Fat-Soluble Vitamins

The fat-soluble vitamins include vitamins A, D, E, and K. Aside from vitamin E, data about the other fat-soluble vitamins and exercise are not as abundant as for other micronutrients. Table 5.2 depicts the fat-soluble vitamin needs for the athlete.

Vitamin A

Vitamin A, which is considered a subset of the retinoids, is a fat-soluble vitamin well known for the role it plays in the visual cycle (58). Other important functions of vitamin A include its role in cellular differentiation, reproduction, fetal development, bone formation, and gestation (58,59), and as an antioxidant. Plants can synthesize carotenoids that can serve as precursors of vitamin A; however, humans and other animals convert carotenoids to retinol or acquire preformed vitamin A from animal foods or supplements (58). Assessment of vitamin A intake in individuals who are physically active has shown varied results;

TABLE 5.2   Fat-Soluble Vitamin Needs for Athletes

Vitamin	Effect of Exercise on Requirements	Recommended Intake* for Athletes	Food Sources	Comments
Vitamin A	Exercise may increase needs; results equivocal. Beta carotene may be better than preformed vitamin A, but not definitive.	DRI, but not more than the UL	Carrots, broccoli, tomatoes	Beta carotene supplements are not recommended.
Vitamin D	Exercise does not seem to increase needs.	DRI, but not more than the UL	Oily fish, liver, eggs, fortified foods such as margarine, breakfast cereals, bread, milk, and powdered milk	Higher levels may be needed in the winter if living in northern states (to prevent bone loss).
Vitamin E	Exercise may increase needs.	DRI, but not more than the UL	Plant oils (eg, soybean, corn, olive oils), nuts, seeds, wheat germ	Strong antioxidant effects in endurance athletes, and older athletes.
Vitamin K	Exercise does not seem to increase needs.	DRI, but not more than the UL	Leafy green vegetables (eg, spinach, turnip greens), cabbage, green tea, alfalfa, oats, cauliflower	Increased needs may be needed for bone formation.

Abbreviations: DRI, Dietary Reference Intake; UL, Tolerable Upper Intake Level.
*See Appendix A for DRI tables.

however, some of these assessments are faulty in that they did not necessarily specify the source of vitamin A (plant vs animal) (59). Individuals with low fruit and vegetable consumption will typically have lower beta carotene intakes than those with high fruit and vegetable consumption.

Although preformed vitamin A is a well-known antioxidant, beta carotene is a weak antioxidant and may be a pro-oxidant. It is known that beta carotene quenches singlet oxygen but there are limited data to suggest in vivo antioxidant activity in humans (60). It seems that derivatives of beta carotene may manifest in the lungs and arterial blood, possibly encouraging tumor growth, especially in smokers and individuals exposed to second-hand smoke and automobile fumes (60). Thus, individuals who exercise, and especially those who exercise in cities where there are greater numbers of automobiles, would be wise not to supplement with beta carotene.

A 2003 study found decreased blood levels of beta carotene in well-trained professional cyclists after a cycling stage, but this was not found in amateur cyclists (61). Perhaps this is a preventative response for trained endurance athletes. Nonetheless, vitamin A supplementation for 60 days (in combination with vitamin C and E supplementation) was shown to be effective in decreasing the oxidative response after a 45-minute bout of cycling at 70% of maximum oxygen consumption (VO_{2max}) in untrained, healthy individuals (62). As with other studies that combined antioxidant vitamins, it is difficult to determine if any one vitamin had a greater effect than another.

Athletes are encouraged to consume fruits and vegetables containing beta carotene but supplementation is not recommended. Because vitamin A is a fat-soluble vitamin and stored in the body, athletes should not exceed the UL. It has been reported that excessive intakes of vitamin A may lead to reduced bone-mineral density and increased risk for hip fractures (63). Although this was a cross-sectional study, it underscores the fact that levels more than the UL can have detrimental effects on the body. Table 5.2 lists some dietary sources of vitamin A.

Vitamin D

Vitamin D is considered both a hormone and a vitamin (64). Its roles in maintaining calcium homeostasis and in bone remodeling are well-established. Vitamin D can be obtained from foods as well as from sunlight because 7-dehydrocholesterol is converted to pre–vitamin D_3 in the skin (64). Conversion of vitamin D to its more active forms begins in the liver, then in the kidney where the 1-alpha-hydroxylase adds another hydroxyl group to the first position on 25-hydroxyvitamin D. This results in 1,25-dihydroxyvitamin D_3 [1,25-$(OH)_2$ D_3], also known as calcitriol, the most active form of vitamin D (64). The effects of calcitriol on calcium metabolism are discussed in more detail in the section on calcium.

To date, very little research has been conducted on the effects of physical activity on vitamin D requirements and the effects of vitamin D on exercise performance (65). However, there have been reports that weightlifting may increase serum calcitriol and serum Gla-protein (an indicator of bone formation) levels that may result in enhanced bone accretion (66). Bell et al (66) reported changes in serum calcitriol levels without observing changes in serum calcium, phosphate, or magnesium levels. Furthermore, there is evidence that 1,25-$(OH)_2$ D_3 may affect muscle function because receptors for 1,25-$(OH)_2$ D_3 have been found in cultured human muscle cells (67,68). However, 6 months of daily supplementation with

0.50 μg 1–25 dihydroxyvitamin D_3 did not improve muscle strength in ambulatory men and women older than age 69 (69). Vitamin D supplementation by itself does not improve performance in older adults. More research is needed to determine if vitamin D combined with calcium supplements is beneficial for athletic performance (70).

Athletes who may be consuming fewer or inadequate kilocalories should be evaluated for vitamin D status because long-term negative effects on calcium homeostasis and bone mineral density may occur. Furthermore, individuals who live at or north of 42 degrees latitude (eg, the northern states and Canada) may require more vitamin D during the winter months to prevent increases in parathyroid hormone secretion and decreased bone mineral density (71,72).

The best dietary sources of vitamin D include fatty fish and fortified foods such as milk, breakfast cereals (1), and orange juice (also see Table 5.2). Exposure to only 15 minutes of sunlight per day in light-skinned individuals, and 30 minutes per day in dark-skinned individuals, will also result in sufficient amounts of vitamin D, but not all individuals obtain this amount of sunlight per day because of confinement to the indoors, geographic location, and/or use of sunscreen. Older individuals may be less able to convert vitamin D (73).

Vitamin E

Vitamin E refers to a family of eight related compounds known as the tocopherols and the tocotrienols (74). Like vitamin A, vitamin E is well-known for its antioxidant function in the prevention of free radical damage to cell membranes (74). Vitamin E also plays a role in immune function (74).

Cesari et al (47) reported that plasma alpha tocopherol was significantly correlated with knee extension strength and the summary physical performance score, whereas plasma gamma tocopherol was associated only with knee extension strength in individuals older than 65 years. Bryant et al (75) assessed different levels and combinations of antioxidant supplements in seven trained male cyclists (approximately 22 years of age), who participated in four separate supplementation phases. They ingested two capsules per day containing the following treatments: placebo (placebo plus placebo); vitamin C (1 g/day plus placebo); vitamins C and E (1 g/day vitamin C plus 200 IU vitamin E); and vitamin E (400 IU vitamin E plus placebo). Researchers found that the vitamin E treatment was more effective than vitamin C alone or vitamin C and E together. Plasma malondialdehyde (MDA) concentrations, a general measure of oxidative damage, were lowest with vitamin E supplementation. Others have reported decreased serum creatine kinase levels, a measure of muscle damage, in marathoners supplemented with vitamins E and C (76).

Although vitamin E may be protective during endurance exercise, a persistent question has been whether vitamin E supplementation has any effect on resistance performance. Avery and colleagues (77) assessed the effects of 1,200 IU/day of vitamin E vs a placebo on the recovery responses to repeated bouts of resistance training. There were no significant differences between the vitamin E-supplemented group and the placebo group in muscle soreness, exercise performance, or plasma MDA concentrations. In an earlier study, McBride et al (78) assessed whether resistance training would increase free radical production and whether supplemental vitamin E would affect free radical production. Twelve men who were recreational weight trainers were supplemented with 1,200 IU/day of vitamin E (RRR-d-alpha-tocopherol succinate) or a placebo for 2 weeks. Both the placebo- and vitamin E–supplemented groups showed increases in plasma creatine kinase and MDA levels pre- to postexercise; however, vitamin E diminished the increase in these variables postexercise, thus decreasing muscle membrane disruption (78).

To date, data on the vitamin E status of athletes have been sparse. However, those who have assessed dietary intakes have reported that in female figure skaters and female heptathletes, dietary intake of vitamin E tended to be less than other nutrients, and less than what the athletes may need (79,80). Vitamin E supplementation does not seem to be effective as an ergogenic aid (81). Although vitamin E has been shown to sequester free radicals in exercising individuals by decreasing membrane disruption (78), there have not been reports indicating that supplemental vitamin E improves exercise performance. Nonetheless, vitamin E's role in prevention of oxidative damage due to exercise may be significant, and more long-term research is needed to assess its effects. Dietary sources of vitamin E are listed in Table 5.2.

Vitamin K

Vitamin K, a group of three related substances, is a fat-soluble vitamin. Phylloquinone or phytonadione (vitamin K_1) is found in plants (82). Menaquinone (MK), once referred to as vitamin K_2, is produced by bacteria in the intestines, supplying an undetermined amount of the daily requirement of vitamin K (83). Menadione (K_3) is the synthetic form of vitamin K (82).

All vitamin K variants are fat-soluble and stable to heat. Alkalis, strong acids, radiation, and oxidizing agents can destroy vitamin K. It is absorbed from the upper small intestine with the help of bile or bile salts and pancreatic juices, and then carried to the liver for the synthesis of prothrombin, a key blood-clotting factor (84).

Vitamin K is necessary for normal blood clotting. It is required for the posttranslational modification of prothrombin and other proteins (eg, factors IX, VII, and X) involved in blood coagulation by carboxylating glutamate residues (85). Vitamin K is necessary for conversion of prothrombin to thrombin with the aid of potassium and calcium. Thrombin is the important factor needed for the conversion of fibrinogen to the active fibrin clot (84). Coumarin acts as an anticoagulant by preventing conversion of vitamin K to its active form, thus preventing carboxylation of the glutamate residues. Coumarin, or synthetic dicumarol, is used medically primarily as an oral anticoagulant to decrease functional prothrombin (85). The salicylates, such as aspirin, often taken by patients who have had a myocardial infarction, increase the need for vitamin K (86).

Vitamin K is known to influence bone metabolism by facilitating the synthesis of osteocalcin, also known as bone Gla protein (BGP) (87). Bone contains proteins with vitamin K–dependent gamma carboxyglutamate residues (82). Impaired vitamin K metabolism is associated with undercarboxylation of the noncollagenous bone-matrix protein osteocalcin (which contains gamma carboxyglutamate residues) (88). If osteocalcin is not in its fully carboxylated state, normal bone formation will be impaired (88).

Because strenuous exercise can lead to decreased bone mineral density, Craciun et al (89) assessed 1 month of vitamin K supplementation (10 mg/day) on various bone markers before and after supplementation. At baseline, athletes not using oral contraceptives were biochemically vitamin K–deficient. In all subjects, vitamin K supplementation was associated with an increased calcium-binding capacity of osteocalcin. In the low-estrogen group, vitamin K supplementation increased bone formation by 15% to 20%, with a concomitant decrease of 20% to 25% in bone resorption markers. Because vitamin K may not be absorbed as efficiently as once thought, its role in the prevention of bone loss has become more apparent. Further research may establish a need for increased intake of vitamin K in athletes, especially female athletes.

An average diet will usually provide at least 75 to 150 µg/day of total vitamin K, which is the suggested minimum, although 300 to 750 µg/day may be optimal (90). Absorption of vitamin K may vary from person to person, but is estimated to be 20% to 60% of total intake (90). Vitamin K toxicity rarely occurs from natural sources (vitamin K_1 or MK), but toxic side effects from the synthetic vitamin K used in medical treatment are possible (91). Vitamin K deficiency is more common than previously thought. Western diets high in sugar and processed foods, intakes of vitamins A and E more than the ULs, and antibiotics may contribute to a decrease in intestinal bacterial function, resulting in a decrease in the production and/or metabolism of vitamin K (92). The best dietary sources of vitamin K include green leafy vegetables, liver, broccoli, peas, and green beans (1) (also see Table 5.2).

Major Minerals

Minerals are equally as important as vitamins in exercise metabolism. They play varied roles, with some having a greater impact on performance than others. Minerals are classified as either major or trace minerals. The major minerals include calcium, phosphorus, magnesium, sulfur, potassium, sodium, and chloride (1). Table 5.3 lists the major mineral needs for the athlete.

Calcium

Calcium, a well-studied mineral, is the fifth most common element in the human body (93,94). Ninety-nine percent of calcium exists in the bones and teeth, with the remaining 1% distributed in extracellular fluids, intracellular structures, cell membranes, and various soft tissues (93,95,96). The major functions of calcium include bone metabolism, blood coagulation, neuromuscular excitability, cellular adhesiveness, transmission of nerve impulses, maintenance and functionality of cell membranes, and activation of enzymatic reactions and hormonal secretions.

Calcium Homeostasis
The level of calcium in the serum is tightly managed within a range of 2.2 to 2.5 mmol/L (divide mmol/L by 0.2495 to convert to mg/dL) by parathyroid hormone (PTH), vitamin D, and calcitonin (93,95–97). When serum calcium levels decrease to less than the normal range, PTH responds by increasing the synthesis of calcitriol in the kidney (95,96). Calcitriol increases calcium reabsorption in the kidneys, calcium absorption in the intestines, and osteoclastic activity in the bone (releasing calcium into circulation) (93,95,96). When serum calcium levels are more than normal values, the hormone calcitonin increases renal excretion of calcium, decreases calcium absorption in the intestines, and increases osteoblastic activity (93,95,96).

TABLE 5.3   Major Mineral Needs for Athletes

Mineral	Effect of Exercise on Requirements	Recommended Intake* for Athletes	Food Sources	Comments
Calcium	Individuals who consistently exercise in the heat may have greater requirements.	DRI, but not more than the UL (those who exercise in the heat should take above the DRI, but less than the UL — base on dietary intake).	Milk, cheese, yogurt, tofu processed with calcium, kale, almonds, collard greens, spinach, canned salmon with bones, bok choy, soy milk fortified with calcium	Higher calcium intakes may also be related to fat loss—important for athletes in sports with weight limitations.
Phosphorus	Exercise does not seem to increase needs.	DRI	Milk, cheese, yogurt, nuts, oatmeal, sardines, asparagus	Phosphate loading has not been researched enough; may be more harmful than helpful.
Magnesium	Exercise does not seem to increase needs; however, those exercising in hot environments may require more.	DRI	Peanuts, tofu, broccoli, spinach, Swiss chard, tomato paste, nuts, seeds	No ergogenic effects established.
Sulfur	Exercise does not seem to increase needs.	DRI	Garlic, legumes, nuts, seeds, red meat, eggs, asparagus	
Potassium	Exercise does not seem to increase needs; however, individuals with a high sweat rate may need more.	DRI	Oranges, bananas, tomatoes, sardines, flounder, salmon, potatoes, beans, blackstrap molasses	No ergogenic effects observed at this time.
Sodium	Exercise typically results in increased needs, especially for those who exercise in the heat.	DRI; base on sweat loss	Luncheon and cured meats, processed cheese, most prepared foods	
Chloride	Same as sodium	DRI (same as sodium—DRI is established as sodium chloride)	Similar to foods with high sodium levels, because most are as sodium chloride, also found in salt substitutes as potassium chloride	

Abbreviations: DRI, Dietary Reference Intake; UL, Tolerable Upper Intake level.
*See Appendix A for DRI tables.

Average Calcium Intakes

Calcium intakes are typically less in females than in males. Teenage girls and adult women tend to consume less calcium than teenage and adult males. Master women athletes (older than 50 years) consume approximately 79% of the recommended intake (98).

Individuals who are physically active should strive to consume at least the DRI for calcium. If an individual has high sweat rates or exercises in hot conditions, more calcium than the DRI may be needed. Bergeron et al (99) reported a mean loss of 0.9 mmol/L in women athletes who exercised for 90 minutes in the heat. A lack of studies makes it is difficult to determine how much more calcium athletes should consume; however, consuming more than the DRI but less than the UL for calcium should be safe for most athletes, especially those who consistently exercise in the heat or sweat heavily.

Calcium has been studied for its possible effects on decreasing body weight (100). This could be of significant value, especially to athletes in sports in which body weight is a concern (eg, wrestlers, jockeys, gymnasts, figure skaters, lightweight rowers). It has been reported that a higher calcium intake is inversely related to body weight. For example, Skinner et al (101) reported that calcium intake was negatively related to body fat in growing children.

Some of the first studies on calcium and weight loss were conducted in animals. Lower fat pad mass and body weight gains were also reported in transgenic mice fed either a diet with calcium carbonate (1.2% calcium), or a diet with nonfat dry milk (1.2% or 2.4% calcium) than mice fed a control diet (102). The mice on all three calcium diets had significantly less weight gain and fat pad mass than the control group; however, the effect was greater in the 2.4% calcium group (derived from nonfat dry milk). In addition, Melanson et al (103) reported that higher acute calcium intake is associated with higher rates of whole-body fat oxidation in humans. They also found that total calcium intake was a more important predictor of fat oxidation than calcium intake from dairy sources alone. Nonetheless, increased calcium intake was not correlated with decreased body weight in 100 pre- and postmenopausal women who were given 1,000 mg/day of supplemental calcium (104).

Despite the mixed results of studies on calcium and body weight and the fact that other variables in the diet affect body weight, it would be prudent to encourage increased calcium consumption because increased calcium intakes have been shown to increase bone mineral density. Calcium from low-fat dairy sources will also provide an individual with vitamin D, protein, and possibly fluids. Increased low-fat dairy consumption will also hopefully offset the great increase in soda consumption that has occurred over the past 10 years. An excellent review article of calcium and body weight was written by Barr in 2003 (105).

Various sources of calcium are listed in Table 5.3. Dairy sources have the highest bioavailable form of calcium. If an individual is not consuming enough dietary calcium, supplementation with calcium citrate or calcium carbonate is recommended. Individuals should avoid calcium supplements containing bone meal, oyster shell, and shark cartilage due to the increased lead content in these supplements, which can be toxic (1). Calcium supplements are best absorbed if taken in doses of 500 mg or less and when taken between meals. In older individuals who may suffer from achlorhydria, calcium carbonate is better absorbed with meals (1). Because calcium citrate does not require gastric acid for optimal absorption, it is considered the best calcium supplement for older women (106).

Factors Affecting Calcium Absorption

Certain factors can inhibit or enhance calcium absorption. High-protein and high-sodium diets have been shown to result in increased urinary calcium excretion in postmenopausal women (107). Although high-sodium diets have been well-documented to increase urinary calcium excretion, lower-protein and not high-protein diets may actually reduce intestinal calcium absorption. Kerstetter et al (108) reported that dietary protein intakes of 0.8 g/kg or less per day have been associated with a reduction in intestinal calcium absorption, which can cause secondary hyperparathyroidism. Although phosphorus can reduce urinary calcium loss, high levels of phosphorus may lead to hyperparathyroidism and result in bone loss (1). Fiber and caffeine have small effects on calcium loss; a cup of brewed coffee results in a 3.5 mg loss of calcium (94). Phytates, however, greatly decrease calcium absorption and oxalates greatly reduce calcium bioavailability (1,94). Conversely, vitamin D, lactose, glucose, a healthy digestive system, and higher dietary requirements (eg, pregnancy) all enhance calcium absorption (1). Thus, it is important to convey the need for a well-balanced, varied diet for optimal absorption of calcium.

Phosphorus

Phosphorous is the second most abundant mineral in the body, with approximately 85% of total body phosphorous in bone, mainly as hydroxyapatite crystals (93,109). Phosphate is important in bone mineralization in both animals and humans (109). Even in the presence of a high amount of calcitriol, rickets can result from a phosphate deficiency in humans (109). Although phosphorous is required for bone growth, excessive amounts of phosphorous may actually harm the skeleton, especially when accompanied by a low calcium intake (109). Excessive phosphorus intakes have been negatively correlated with radial bone mineral density (110).

High phosphorous intakes reduce serum calcium levels, especially when calcium intake is low, because phosphorous carries calcium with it into soft tissues (96,109). The resulting hypocalcemia activates PTH secretion, which results in increased bone loss (resorption) to maintain serum calcium homeostasis (109). High phosphorous intakes can also decrease active vitamin D production, further reducing calcium absorption and producing secondary hyperparathyroidism (109). Because of its ubiquitous nature, phosphorus intakes are usually more than recommended intakes (4).

Because most individuals consume enough phosphorus in their diets, overconsumption is usually the concern. A special concern is the amount of soft drinks that individuals consume because many contain high amounts of phosphate and, in children and teenagers, these beverages often replace milk. Several studies reported that the greater the consumption of carbonated beverages, especially cola beverages, the greater the risk of fracture (111–113). This association was stronger in women and girls. These results may have important health implications due to the 300% increase in carbonated beverage consumption combined with a decrease in milk consumption over the past several decades (111).

Another way that individuals who exercise, especially competitive athletes, may consume excessive phosphorus is via "phosphate-loading." Phosphate-loading is thought to decrease the buildup of hydrogen ions that increase during exercise and negatively affect energy production (114). Research on phosphate-loading as an ergogenic aid has shown equivocal results (114). Bremner et al (115) reported a 30% increase in plasma inorganic phosphate levels with a 25% increase in erythrocyte 2,3-bisphosphoglycerate (2,3-BPG) levels after 7 days of phosphate-loading in healthy subjects. They concluded that phosphate loading increased both plasma and erythrocyte phosphate pools, but that the increase in erythrocyte 2,3-BPG was probably a result of the increase in cell inorganic phosphate. These researchers did not assess phosphate-loading on exercise performance. The long-term negative consequences of phosphate-loading on bone-mineral density have not been documented and should be considered before an athlete considers this practice. Furthermore, there has been limited research in this area, and thus the risk-benefit ratio of loading with phosphate has not been established.

Phosphorus content is highest in protein foods. Table 5.3 lists some food sources of phosphorus.

Magnesium

Approximately 60% to 65% of the body's magnesium is present in bone, 27% is in muscle, 6% to 7% is in other cells, and 1% is in extracellular fluid (116). Magnesium plays an important role in several metabolic processes required for exercise, such as mitochondrial function; protein, lipid, and carbohydrate synthesis; energy-delivering processes; and neuromuscular coordination (117,118).

Urinary and sweat magnesium excretion may be exacerbated in individuals who exercise, especially in hot, humid conditions (119). A female tennis player who suffered from hypomagnesemia was supplemented with 500 mg/day of magnesium gluconate, which dissipated her muscle spasms (120). If individuals are consuming inadequate energy and are exercising intensely on a daily basis, especially in the heat, they may lose a large amount of magnesium through sweat (1,9). Mineral sweat loss is typically assessed by using sweat patches placed on different part of the body (because different parts of the body sweat at different rates). Once collected, magnesium can be assessed through specific instruments that assess mineral status, such as atomic absorption spectrophotometry, inductively coupled mass spectrometry, and thermal ionization spectrophotometry. Clinical signs of magnesium deficiency, such as muscle spasms, should be monitored. Nevertheless, hypomagnesemia during exercise is the exception rather than the norm. For example, Kuru et al (121) reported unchanged tissue magnesium levels in older rats that underwent a 1-year swimming program. Table 5.3 lists some food sources of magnesium.

Sulfur

Sulfur is present in the body in a nonionic form and is a constituent of some vitamins (eg, thiamin and biotin), amino acids (eg, methionine and cysteine), and proteins (1). Sulfur also assists with acid-base balance (1). If protein needs are met, sulfur is not required in the diet because it is present in protein foods (1).

Because sulfur is part of a number of proteins, the small body of research on its effects on exercise performance is limited to sulfur-containing amino acids. It has been established that dietary sulfur-containing amino acids affect glutathione synthesis; however, their acute effect under conditions of oxidative stress, such as exercise, is not understood. Mariotti et al (122) fed rats different types of protein or glucose 1 hour prior to a 2-hour run on a treadmill. They found that cysteine from dietary proteins displayed a dose-dependent and short-term stimulatory effect on liver glutathione during exercise, but did not immediately benefit whole-body glutathione homeostasis. At this point, increased sulfur intake does not seem warranted. Individuals consuming the proper amount of complete protein in their diets will be consuming adequate sulfur. Vegans can combine grains and legumes to obtain all of the essential amino acids. Sulfur is present in protein-rich foods (1). (See Table 5.3 for more dietary sources of sulfur).

Potassium

One of the three major electrolytes, potassium is the major intracellular cation (123,124). Total body potassium is about 3,000 to 4,000 mmol (1 g potassium = 25 mmol) (124). The two major roles of potassium in the body are maintaining intracellular ionic strength and maintaining transmembrane ionic potential (123).

An increase in extracellular potassium concentrations in human skeletal muscle may actually play a significant role in development of fatigue during intense exercise (125). Nielsen and colleagues (125) found that intense intermittent training reduced the accretion of potassium in human skeletal muscle interstitium during exercise, which may have been through a reuptake of potassium due to greater activity of the sodium-potassium-ATPase pumps in the muscle. This decreased potassium accretion in the muscle was associated with delayed fatigue during intense exercise. Thus, another response to intense training is the reduction of potassium accumulation in the skeletal muscle. Millard-Stafford et al (126) found that female runners had a greater increase in serum potassium concentrations than did male runners following a simulated 40-km road race in a hot, humid environment. Therefore, it seems that serum potassium shifts into the extracellular space during and immediately after exercise; this shift may occur to a greater extent in more trained individuals. However, this shift seems to be transient because most researchers report a return to baseline in extracellular serum potassium concentrations at 1 hour or more after exercise (125,126).

If an individual becomes hyperkalemic or hypokalemic, cells may become nonfunctional (124). Thus, if the observed shift in potassium after exercise is not transient, serious consequences may occur. However, because potassium is ubiquitous in foods, individuals who exercise may not require more in their diets than they already consume. Furthermore, individuals who exercise at lower levels (eg, walking, gardening, recreational jogging) probably do not experience significant shifts in serum potassium concentrations. Table 5.3 lists some food sources of potassium.

Sodium and Chloride

Sodium and chloride are the most abundant cation and anion, respectively, in extracellular fluid (127) and assist in nerve transmission (1). In these respects they are important in exercise.

The need for proper hydration and electrolyte replacement before, during, and after exercise has been well-established (128,129). Sweat sodium is often measured during and after exercise to assess sodium changes. In a study of 14 women, sweat sodium was increased after 60 minutes of cycling in dry heat, and the amount of sodium in the sweat was greater in the winter than in the summer (130). Millard-Stafford (126) reported that females had higher serum sodium concentrations than males following a 40-km run. Stachenfeld et al (131) reported similar results in sodium concentrations in their female subjects 120 minutes after cycling. As with potassium, this increase in serum sodium concentration seems to be transient. Nonetheless, it seems that increased dietary sodium is warranted in individuals who exercise, especially if they are exercising in hot, humid conditions. Increased sodium is required to maintain fluid balance and prevent cramping. The increase in dietary sodium may be met by either consuming higher sodium foods or by adding salt to foods. Because sodium also increases urinary calcium excretion, a balance between sodium and calcium intake is required. See Chapter 6 for a detailed discussion on fluids, electrolytes, and exercise.

Physically active individuals typically consume more dietary sodium than nonactive individuals do, and some researchers have wondered if sodium could be ergogenic. Jain et al (132) assessed whether 0.5 g/kg body weight of sodium citrate (not sodium chloride) would have an ergogenic effect on oxygen debt and exercise endurance in untrained, healthy men. They reported a decrease in oxygen debt postexercise and an increase in high-intensity exercise performance (on a bicycle ergometer). It is not known what effect sodium citrate supplementation would have on trained athletes.

Physically active individuals should consume varied, balanced diets that include the proper amount of sodium for maintenance of hydration and performance. Specific sodium recommendations for athletes, including those who are salt sweaters, can be found in Chapter 6. Table 5.3 lists some food sources of sodium and chloride. Foods high in sodium are typically high in salt (sodium chloride), and therefore are also high in chloride.

Trace Minerals

As stated earlier, minerals play an important role in energy metabolism, making them important for exercise. The trace minerals include iron, zinc, copper, selenium, iodide, fluoride, chromium, manganese, molybdenum, boron, and vanadium (1). Table 5.4 lists trace mineral needs for the athlete.

Iron

Total body iron constitutes approximately 5.0 mg/kg body weight in men and 3.8 mg/kg in women (133). Iron is utilized for many functions related to exercise, such as hemoglobin and myoglobin synthesis (134), as well as incorporation into mitochondrial cytochromes and nonheme iron compounds (135). Some iron-dependent enzymes (ie, nicotinamide adenine dinucleotide and succinate dehydrogenase) are involved in oxidative metabolism (135,136).

The incidence of iron-deficiency anemia among athletes and nonathletes alike is only approximately 5% to 6% (137,138). However, some have reported that as many as 60% of female athletes may have some degree of iron deficiency (139), with ranges of 30% and 50%, especially among female athletes and male and female athletes who participate in endurance sports (137,140–143). There have been decreases in hemoglobin levels, but not other iron indexes, in college-age males and females who participated in 12 weeks of weight training (144).

Because female athletes do not typically consume proper amounts of dietary iron (as a result of lower energy consumption and/or reduction in meat content of the diet), coupled with iron losses in sweat, gastrointestinal bleeding, myoglobinuria from myofibrillar stress, hemoglobinuria due to intravascular hemolysis, and menstruation (145–148), health and optimal exercise performance may be compromised. Decreased exercise performance is related not only to anemia and a decreased aerobic capacity, but also to tissue iron depletion and diminished exercise endurance (149). Dietary iron-deficiency anemia negatively

TABLE 5.4   Trace Mineral Needs for Athletes

Mineral	Effect of Exercise on Requirements	Recommended Intake* for Athletes	Food Sources	Comments
Iron	Exercise may increase requirements if a person becomes iron depleted or iron-deficient anemic.	DRI, but may need more if iron depleted or iron deficient-anemic.	Clams, red meat, oysters, egg yolks, salmon, tofu, raisins, whole grains	May have an ergogenic effect if the athlete is iron depleted or iron-deficient anemic.
Zinc	Exercise does not seem to increase needs; however, transient losses are often observed.	DRI, but not more than the UL.	Oysters, red meat, poultry, fish, wheat germ, fortified cereals	May have ergogenic effects, but not definitive and mostly animal studies; may impact thyroid hormone function if zinc-deficient.
Copper	Exercise does not seem to increase needs.	DRI	Red meat, fish, soy products, mushrooms, sweet potatoes	
Selenium	Despite antioxidant properties, exercise does not seem to increase needs.	DRI, but not more than the UL.	Fish, meat, poultry, cereal, grains, mushrooms, asparagus	More research is needed.
Iodide	Exercise does not seem to increase needs.	DRI	Eggs, milk, strawberries, mozzarella cheese, cantaloupe	
Fluoride	Exercise does not seem to increase needs.	DRI	Fluoridated water, fish, tea	
Chromium	Exercise does not seem to increase needs, though more research is required due to transient losses seen.	DRI	Broccoli, potatoes, grape juice, turkey ham, waffles, orange juice, beef	Was thought to increase muscle mass, but research has consistently shown that it does not; may have a positive impact in individuals with type 2 diabetes.
Manganese	Exercise does not seem to increase needs.	DRI	Liver, kidneys, wheat germ, legumes, nuts, black tea	
Molybdenum	Exercise does not seem to increase needs.	DRI	Peas, leafy green vegetables (eg, spinach, broccoli), cauliflower	
Boron	Exercise does not seem to increase needs.	DRI	Apples, pears, grapes, leafy green vegetables, nuts	Despite research on its possible effects on bone and muscle, boron does not seem to have ergogenic effects.
Vanadium	Exercise does not seem to increase needs.	DRI	Mushrooms, shellfish, black pepper, parsley, dill weed, grains, grain products	May have a positive impact in individuals with type 2 diabetes.

Abbreviations: DRI, Dietary Reference Intake; UL, Tolerable Upper Intake Level.
*See Appendix A for DRI tables.

impacts the oxidative production of adenosine triphosphate in skeletal muscle, as well as the capacity for prolonged exercise (150,151). There have been reports that iron-depleted women have decreased VO_{2max} as a result of decreased iron storage (152).

Other studies have reported alterations in metabolic rate, thyroid hormone status, and thermoregulation with iron depletion and iron-deficiency anemia (153–156), although some researchers have not observed these alterations (157). Mild iron-deficiency anemia has also been shown to negatively affect psychomotor development and intellectual performance (158) as well as immune function (159).

Iron Supplementation

For individuals who are diagnosed with iron-deficiency anemia, iron supplementation is the most prudent way to increase iron stores and prevent adverse physiological effects (160). Ferrous sulfate is the least expensive and most widely used form of iron supplementation (160,161). For adults diagnosed with iron-deficiency anemia, a daily dose of at least 60 mg elemental iron taken between meals is recommended (160).

Supplementation may also be warranted for athletes with iron depletion (low serum ferritin levels) without iron-deficiency anemia (162). For example, Hinton and colleagues (163) assessed time to complete a 15-km cycle ergometry test in 42 women with iron depletion. Half received 100 mg ferrous sulfate, while the other half received a placebo for 6 weeks. At baseline, there were no differences between the groups in serum ferritin status or in their 15-km time. The iron supplementation increased serum ferritin concentrations in the supplemented group, while subsequently decreasing their 15-km cycle ergometry time. These results suggest that iron depletion may impair aerobic exercise performance, and thus practitioners need to be prudent to assess for iron depletion as well as iron-deficiency anemia.

Factors Affecting Iron Absorption

As with calcium, several factors inhibit or enhance iron absorption. Factors that inhibit iron absorption include phytates; oxalates; tannins in tea and coffee; adequate iron stores; excessive intake of other minerals such as zinc, calcium, and manganese; reduced gastric acid production; and certain antacids.

Factors that enhance iron absorption include heme iron, meat protein factor, ascorbic acid, low iron stores, normal gastric acid secretion, and a high demand for red blood cells, such as occurs with blood loss, exercise training, and especially at high altitude and during pregnancy (1).

Consuming vitamin C–containing foods or beverages with meals and consuming tea or coffee at least an hour before or after a meal rather than with a meal will augment dietary iron absorption. These suggestions should be strongly recommended even if a person who has iron-deficiency anemia is taking iron supplements (1). Table 5.4 lists some dietary sources of iron.

Zinc

Zinc exists in all organs, tissues, fluids, and secretions. Approximately 60% of total body zinc is present in muscle, 29% in bone, and 1% in the gastrointestinal tract, skin, kidney, brain, lung, and prostate (164). Zinc plays a role in more than 300 metabolic reactions in the body (1). Alkaline phosphatase, carbonic anhydrase, and zinc-copper superoxide dismutase are just a few of the zinc metalloenzymes (1). Low zinc status can also impair immune function (159), which can be detrimental to exercise performance as well as overall health.

Many individuals in the United States, including athletes, do not consume the recommended amount of zinc (165,166). It has been reported that approximately 50% of female distance runners consume less than the recommended amount of zinc (167). Some researchers have reported zinc intakes in female and male collegiate swimmers greater than 70% of recommended intakes (168). It seems that when dietary zinc intakes are sufficient, zinc status is not negatively affected by exercise training (169).

The studies conducted on zinc and exercise also show a transient effect of exercise on zinc status. Zinc status has been shown to directly affect basal metabolic rate, thyroid hormone levels, and protein utilization (170), which can have a negative effect on exercise performance and health. Impairments in thyroid hormone metabolism and resting metabolic rate may not only lead to impaired exercise performance, but may lead to difficulty in weight loss for those individuals who may be trying to lose weight.

Baltaci et al (171) assessed the effects of zinc supplementation and zinc deficiency on rats that performed an acute swimming exercise. They reported that zinc-deficient rats had lower glycogen stores than the rats supplemented with zinc. This same group of researchers also reported greater MDA concentrations in zinc-deficient rats compared with rats supplemented with zinc, which were all placed on a swimming program of 30 minutes per day for 4 weeks (172). These findings, although in rats, demonstrate zinc's important role in exercise performance and overall health.

Therefore, consumption of a varied diet with adequate amounts of zinc should be emphasized. Table 5.4 includes some dietary sources of zinc.

Copper

Approximately 50 to 120 mg copper is found in the human body (173). Some of the functions of copper include enhancing iron absorption (via metalloenzyme ceruloplasmin), forming collagen and elastin, participating in the electron transport chain (cytochrome C oxidase), and acting as an antioxidant (zinc-copper superoxide dismutase) (1,173).

Deficiencies of copper are unlikely, but because copper plays a role in red blood cell maturation, anemia can develop with copper deficiency (1,173). Gropper et al (174) surveyed 70 female collegiate athletes and found that intakes (including supplementation) ranged from 41% to 118% of the recommended intakes for copper. They reported that athletes across all sports had normal copper status (as measured by serum copper and ceruloplasmin levels). Toxicity symptoms of copper include vomiting (1,173).

Because the copper content of food is greatly affected by soil conditions, it is rarely listed in computer databases. Some good dietary sources of copper are organ meats (eg, liver), seafood (eg, oysters), cocoa, mushrooms, various nuts, seeds (eg, sunflower seeds), and whole-grain breads and cereals (1). (Also see Table 5.4.)

Selenium

Selenium is well-known for its role as an antioxidant in the body (metalloenzyme glutathione peroxidase) (1). Selenium also functions in normal thyroid hormone metabolism (1).

Limited data are available about whether individuals who exercise require more selenium than sedentary individuals. Because of the increased oxidation with exercise, it seems that more selenium in the diet would be necessary for individuals who are physically active. In a double-blind study, Tessier et al (175) placed 12 men on 180 μg selenomethionine and 12 men on a placebo for 10 weeks and reported that endurance training enhanced the antioxidant potential of glutathione peroxidase, but the selenium supplementation had no effect on performance.

It has also been reported that a combination of 150 μg selenium, combined with 2,000 IU retinol, 120 mg ascorbic acid, and 30 IU alpha tocopherol increased total plasma antioxidant status after exercise (176). However, because little data are available and excess selenium is toxic, individuals who exercise should consume no more than the DRI for selenium and never exceed the UL.

Like copper, the selenium content of food can vary greatly with the soil content. Good sources of selenium include fish, shellfish, meat, eggs, and milk (1). (Also see Table 5.4.)

Iodide

The thyroid hormones are synthesized from iodide and tyrosine (1). Thus, iodide is required for normal metabolic rate.

No data on iodide requirements for individuals who are physically active have been reported. Nonetheless, inadequate intake of iodide may have an impact on performance because of its role in thyroid hormone synthesis. Iodide is mainly found in saltwater fish, molasses, iodized salt, and seafood (1). (Also see Table 5.4.)

Fluoride

Fluoride's main function is to maintain teeth and bone health (1). It has long been known that fluoride in adequate amounts in the water can prevent tooth decay (1,177). Fluoride is important to bone health because it stimulates bone growth (osteoblasts), increases trabecular bone formation, and increases vertebral bone mineral density (178).

To date, studies are lacking on the fluoride requirements for individuals who exercise. Most research on fluoride has been conducted to assess its effect on bone mineral density and prevention of osteoporosis. Because of fluoride's important role in bone metabolism, more studies with fluoride and female athletes are warranted.

Dietary sources of fluoride are limited to tea, seaweed, seafood, and, in some communities, naturally fluoridated water or fluoridated public water systems (1). (Also see Table 5.4.)

Chromium

Chromium is a well-studied mineral. Chromium potentiates the action of insulin and thus influences carbohydrate, lipid, and protein metabolism (179). Chromium may also have antiatherogenic effects by reducing serum cholesterol levels (180), but these reports have not been well-documented. Supplement manufacturers have marketed chromium as a way to increase lean body mass and decrease body weight. However, a number of researchers have shown that chromium does not increase lean body mass or decrease body weight (181–183).

Urinary chromium excretion has been reported to be more on the days that individuals exercise compared with days they do not exercise (184,185). Increased chromium excretion coupled with inadequate dietary intake suggests that individuals who exercise need more chromium in their diets; however, it has not been established that individuals who exercise require more than the DRI for chromium. Whether chromium may enhance muscle mass and/or decrease body weight has not been established (183,186,187), despite reports in the popular press. More information about chromium picolinate supplements can be found in Chapter 7. Dietary sources of chromium include whole grains, organ meats, beer, egg yolks, mushrooms, and nuts (1). (Also see Table 5.4.)

Manganese

Manganese plays a role in antioxidant activity in the body because it is part of superoxide dismutase (1). Manganese also plays a role in carbohydrate metabolism and bone metabolism (1).

There are no data about whether individuals who exercise require more manganese in their diets or if it contributes as an ergogenic aid. Dietary sources of manganese include whole grains, leafy vegetables, nuts, beans, and tea (1). (Also see Table 5.4.)

Molybdenum

Molybdenum interacts with copper and iron. Excessive intakes of molybdenum may inhibit copper absorption (1). Molybdenum also plays a role in glucocorticoid metabolism (131).

There are no data about molybdenum requirements for individuals who are physically active. Beans, nuts, whole grains, milk, and milk products are all good dietary sources of molybdenum (1). (Also see Table 5.4.)

Boron

Presently, boron has not been found to be essential for humans but may play a role in bone metabolism by its interactions with calcitriol, estradiol, testosterone, magnesium, and calcium (188–191). Many athletes believe that boron will increase lean body mass and increase bone mineral density, but research studies have not shown boron to have these effects (190,192).

To date, most of the research on boron has been limited to its effect on bone-mineral density and lean body mass (189,190). Whether individuals who exercise require more boron in their diets has not been established. Dietary sources of boron include fruits and vegetables as well as nuts and beans (1). (Also see Table 5.4.)

Vanadium

Like chromium, vanadium has been shown to potentiate the effects of insulin (193). In addition, supplements of vanadium, as vanadyl sulfate, have been theorized to increase lean body mass, but these anabolic effects have not been reported in research studies (193). No reports of increased needs or ergogenic effects of vanadium have been documented. Supplementation with vanadium is not warranted.

Vanadyl sulfate supplements are discussed in Chapter 7. Dietary sources of vanadium include grains, mushrooms, and shellfish (1). (Also see Table 5.4.)

Summary

Overall, the vitamin and mineral needs of individuals who are physically active are similar to the requirements for all healthy individuals. If dietary intakes are adequate (ie, the individual is meeting 70% or more of the DRI for nutrients), supplementation is unnecessary. However, sweat and urinary losses may require some individuals to consume higher amounts of some micronutrients, quantities that can be obtained with a varied diet of properly selected foods. Supplementation may be necessary when intake is inadequate. Care must be taken so that individuals do not exceed the UL, which could impair both exercise performance and health.

Special attention must be given to individuals who are physically active to assess their micronutrient needs. In assessing these individuals, consider the following: frequency, intensity, duration, and type(s) of physical activity; environment (hot or cold) in which exercise is performed; gender; and dietary intakes and food preferences. It is particularly important to assess usual dietary intakes of calcium and iron in female athletes.

Proper assessment will assist the professional in helping individuals who are physically active consume adequate amounts of micronutrients for optimal health and performance. In particular, athletes should be encouraged to consume adequate total energy. If they do so, they will typically consume adequate vitamins and minerals, as well. Encouraging those who exercise to consume sufficient fruits and vegetables will also help to ensure they will obtain the adequate amounts of vitamins and minerals needed for overall health and optimal performance.

A general summary of all the vitamins and minerals discussed in this chapter, including the effect of exercise on their requirements, recommended intakes for athletes, general food sources, and possible ergogenic effects, can be found in Tables 5.1 through 5.4. These tables can act as a quick reference guide for dietetics professionals.

References

1. Wardlaw GM. *Perspectives in Nutrition*. 4th ed. Boston, Mass: WCB McGraw-Hill; 1999.
2. Burke L, Heeley P. Dietary supplements and nutritional ergogenic aids in sport. In: Burke L, Deakin V, eds. *Clinical Sports Nutrition*. Sydney, Australia: McGraw-Hill Book Co; 1994:227–284.
3. Kimura N, Fukuwatari T, Sasaki R, Hayakawa F, Shibata K. Vitamin intake in Japanese women college students. *J Nutr Sci Vitaminol*. 2003:49:149–155.
4. Institute of Medicine. *Dietary Reference Intakes for Calcium, Phosphorus, Magnesium, Vitamin D, and Fluoride*. Washington, DC: National Academy Press, 1997.
5. Institute of Medicine. *Dietary Reference Intakes for Thiamin, Riboflavin, Niacin, Vitamin B6, Folate, Vitamin B12, Pantothenic Acid, Biotin, and Choline*. Washington, DC: National Academy Press; 1998.
6. Institute of Medicine. *Dietary Reference Intakes for Vitamin C, Vitamin E, Selenium, and Carotenoids*. Washington, DC: National Academy Press; 2000.
7. Institute of Medicine. *Dietary Reference Intakes for Vitamin A, Vitamin K, Arsenic, Boron, Chromium, Copper, Iodine, Iron, Manganese, Molybdenum, Nickel, Silicon, Vanadium, and Zinc*. Washington, DC: National Academy Press; 2000.
8. Yates AA, Schlicker SA, Suitor CW. Dietary reference intakes: the new basis for recommendations for calcium and related nutrients, B vitamins, and choline. *J Am Diet Assoc*. 1998;98:699–706.

9. Clark M, Reed DB, Crouse SF, Armstrong RB. Pre- and post-season dietary intake, body composition, and performance indices of NCAA division I female soccer players. *Int J Sport Nutr Exerc Metab.* 2003;13:303–319.

10. Telford RD, Catchpole EA, Deakin V, Hahn AG, Plank AW. The effect of 7 to 8 months of vitamin/mineral supplementation on athletic performance. *Int J Sport Nutr.* 1992;2:135–153.

11. Leklem JE. Vitamin B-6. In: Ziegler EE, Filer LJ Jr, eds. *Present Knowledge in Nutrition.* 7th ed. Washington, DC: ILSI Press; 1996:174–183.

12. Sampson DA. Vitamin B-6. In: Wolinsky I, Driskell JA, eds. *Sports Nutrition.* Boca Raton, Fla: CRC Press; 1997:75–84.

13. Crozier PG, Cordain L, Sampson DA. Exercise-induced changes in plasma vitamin B-6 concentrations do not vary with exercise intensity. *Am J Clin Nutr.* 1994;60:552–558.

14. Herrmann M, Wilkinson J, Schorr H, Obeid R, Georg T, Urhausen A, Scharhag J, Kindermann W, Herrmann W. Comparison of the influence of volume-oriented training and high-intensity interval training on serum homocysteine and its cofactors in young, healthy swimmers. *Clin Chem Lab Med.* 2003;41:1525–1531.

15. Okada M, Goda H, Kondo Y, Murakami Y, Shibuya M. Effect of exercise on the metabolism of vitamin B6 and some PLP-dependent enzymes in young rats fed a restricted vitamin B6 diet. *J Nutr Sci Vitaminol.* 2001;47:116–121.

16. Herbert V. Vitamin B-12. In: Ziegler EE, Filer LJ Jr, eds. *Present Knowledge in Nutrition.* 7th ed. Washington, DC: ILSI Press; 1996:191–205.

17. Selhub J, Rosenberg IH. Folic acid. In: Ziegler EE, Filer LJ Jr, eds. *Present Knowledge in Nutrition.* 7th ed. Washington, DC: ILSI Press; 1996:206–219.

18. McMartin K. Folate and vitamin B-12. In: Wolinsky I, Driskell JA, eds. *Sports Nutrition.* Boca Raton, Fla: CRC Press; 1997:75–84.

19. American Dietetic Association. Position paper on vegetarian diets (technical support paper). *J Am Diet Assoc.* 1988;88:352–355.

20. Frail H. Special needs: the vegetarian athlete. In: Burke L, Deakin V, eds. *Clinical Sports Nutrition.* Sydney, Australia: McGraw-Hill Book Co; 1994:365–378.

21. Herbert V. Vitamin C supplements and disease: counterpoint (editorial). *J Am Coll Nutr.* 1995;14:112–113.

22. Herbert V. Folic acid and vitamin B12. In: Rothfield B, ed. *Nuclear Medicine In Vitro.* Philadelphia, Pa: JB Lippincott; 1983:337–354.

23. Green R, Jacobsen DW. Clinical implications of hyperhomocysteinemia. In: Bailey LB, ed. *Folate in Health and Disease.* New York, NY: Marcel Dekker; 1995:75–122.

24. Peifer JJ. Thiamin. In: Wolinsky I, Driskell JA, eds. *Sports Nutrition.* Boca Raton, Fla: CRC Press; 1997:47–55.

25. Webster MJ, Scheett TP, Doyle MR, Branz M. The effect of a thiamin derivative on exercise performance. *Eur J Appl Physiol Occup Physiol.* 1997;75:520–524.

26. Doyle MR, Webster MJ, Erdmann LD. Allithiamine ingestion does not enhance isokinetic parameters of muscle performance. *Int J Sport Nutr.* 1997;7:39–47.

27. Webster MJ. Physiological and performance responses to supplementation with thiamin and pantothenic acid derivatives. *Eur J Appl Physiol Occup Physiol.* 1998;77:486–491.

28. Suzuki M, Itokawa Y. Effects of thiamine supplementation on exercise-induced fatigue. *Metab Brain Dis.* 1996;11:95–106.

29. van der Beek EJ, van Dokkum W, Wedel M, Schrijver J, van den Berg H. Thiamin, riboflavin and vitamin B6: impact of restricted intake on physical performance in man. *J Am Coll Nutr.* 1994;13:629–640.

30. Lewis RD. Riboflavin and niacin. In: Wolinsky I, Driskell JA, eds. *Sports Nutrition.* Boca Raton, Fla: CRC Press; 1997:57–73.

31. Backes JM, Howard PA, Moriarty PM. Role of C-reactive protein in cardiovascular disease. *Ann Pharmacother.* 2004;38:110–118.

32. Murray R, Bartoli WP, Eddy DE, Horn MK. Physiological and performance responses to nicotinic-acid ingestion during exercise. *Med Sci Sports Exerc.* 1995;27:1057–1062.

33. Stephenson LA, Kolka MA. Increased skin blood flow and enhanced sensible heat loss in humans after nicotinic acid ingestion. *J Therm Biol.* 1995;20:409.

34. Plesofsky-Vig N. Pantothenic acid. In: Ziegler EE, Filer LJ Jr, eds. *Present Knowledge in Nutrition.* 7th ed. Washington, DC: ILSI Press; 1996:236–244.

35. Thomas EA. Pantothenic acid and biotin. In: Wolinsky I, Driskell JA, eds. *Sports Nutrition.* Boca Raton, Fla: CRC Press; 1997:97–100.

36. Smith CM, Narrow CM, Kendrick ZV, Steffen C. The effect of pantothenate deficiency in mice on their metabolic response to fast and exercise. *Metabolism.* 1987;36:115–121.

37. Nice C, Reeves AG, Brinck-Johnsen T, Noll W. The effects of pantothenic acid supplementation on human exercise capacity. *J Sports Med Phys Fitness.* 1984;24:26–29.

38. Mock DM. Biotin. In: Ziegler EE, Filer LJ Jr, eds. *Present Knowledge in Nutrition.* 7th ed. Washington, DC: ILSI Press; 1996:220–235.

39. Levine M, Rumsey S, Wang Y, Park J, Kwon O, Xu W, Amano N. Vitamin C. In: Ziegler EE, Filer LJ Jr, eds. *Present Knowledge in Nutrition.* 7th ed. Washington, DC: ILSI Press; 1996:146–159.

40. Keith RE. Ascorbic acid. In: Wolinsky I, Driskell JA, eds. *Sports Nutrition.* Boca Raton, Fla: CRC Press; 1997:29–45.

41. Evans W. Vitamin E, vitamin C, and exercise. *Am J Clin Nutr.* 2000:72(suppl):647S–652S.

42. Duthie GG, Robertson JD, Maughan RJ, Morrice PC. Blood antioxidant status and erythrocyte lipid peroxidation following distance running. *Arch Biochem Biophys.* 1990;282:78–83.

43. Fishbaine B, Butterfield G. Ascorbic acid status of running and sedentary men. *Int J Vitam Nutr Res.* 1984;54:273.

44. Gleeson M, Robertson JD, Maughan RJ. Influence of exercise on ascorbic acid status in man. *Clin Sci.* 1987;73:501–505.

45. Tauler P, Aguilo A, Gimeno I, Noguera A, Agusti A, Tur JA, Pons A. Differential response of lymphocytes and neutrophils to high intensity physical activity and to vitamin C diet supplementation. *Free Radic Res.* 2003;37:931–938.

46. Robson PJ, Bouic PJ, Myburgh KH. Antioxidant supplementation enhances neutrophil oxidative burst in trained runners following prolonged exercise. *Int J Sport Nutr Exerc Metab.* 2003;13:369–381.

47. Cesari M, Pahor M, Bartali B, Cherubini A, Penninx BW, Williams GR, Atkinson H, Martin A, Guralnik JM, Ferrucci L. Antioxidants and physical performance in elderly persons: The Invecchiare in Chianti (InChianti) study. *Am J Clin Nutr.* 2004;79:289–294.

48. Audera C, Patulny RV, Sander BH, Douglas RM. Mega-dose vitamin C in treatment of the common cold: a randomized controlled trial. *Med J Aust.* 2001;175:359–362.

49. Douglas RM, Chalker EB, Treacy B. Vitamin C for preventing and treating the common cold. *Cochrane Database Syst Rev.* 2000;2:CD000980.

50. Zeisel SH. Choline. In: Shils ME, Olson JA, Shike M, eds. *Modern Nutrition in Health and Disease.* 8th ed. Philadelphia, Pa: Lea & Febiger; 1994:449–458.

51. Burke ER. Nutritional ergogenic aids. In: Berning JR, Steen SN, eds. *Nutrition for Sport & Exercise.* 2nd ed. Gaithersburg, Md: Aspen Publishers; 1998:119–142.

52. McChrisley B. Other substances in foods. In: Wolinsky I, Driskell JA, eds. *Sports Nutrition.* Boca Raton, Fla: CRC Press; 1997:205–219.

53. Kanter MM, Williams MH. Antioxidants, carnitine, and choline as putative ergogenic aids. *Int J Sport Nutr.* 1995;5(suppl):S120–S131.

54. Sandage BW, Sabounjian LA, White R, et al. Choline citrate may enhance athletic performance. *Physiologist.* 1992;35:236a.

55. Von Allworden HN, Horn S, Kahl J, Feldheim W. The influence of lecithin on plasma choline concentrations in triathletes and adolescent runners during exercise. *Eur J Appl Physiol.* 1993;67:87–91.

56. Spector SA, Jackman MR, Sabounjian LA, Sakkas C, Landers DM, Willis WT. Effect of choline supplementation on fatigue in trained cyclists. *Med Sci Sports Exerc.* 1995;27:668–673.

57. Deuster PA, Singh A, Coll R, Hyde DE, Becker WJ. Choline Ingestion does not modify physical or cognitive performance. *Mil Med.* 2002;167:1020–1025.

58. Olson JA. Vitamin A, retinoids, and carotenoids. In: Shils ME, Olson JA, Shike M, eds. *Modern Nutrition in Health and Disease.* 8th ed. Philadelphia, Pa: Lea & Febiger; 1994:287–307.

59. Stacewicz-Sapuntzakis M. Vitamin A and carotenoids. In: Wolinsky I, Driskell JA, eds. *Sports Nutrition.* Boca Raton, Fla: CRC Press; 1997:101–109.

60. Omenn GS. An assessment of the scientific basis for attempting to define the Dietary Reference Intake for beta carotene. *J Am Diet Assoc.* 1998;98:1406–1409.

61. Aguilo A, Tauler P, Pilar Guix M, Villa G, Cordova A, Tur JA, Pons A. Effect of exercise intensity and training on antioxidants and cholesterol profile in cyclists. *J Nutr Biochem.* 2003;14: 319–325.

62. Vassilakopoulos T, Karatza MH, Katsaounou P, Kollintza A, Zakynthinos S, Roussos C. Antioxidants attenuate the plasma cytokine response to exercise in humans. *J Appl Physiol.* 2003;94:1025–1032.

63. Melhus H, Michaelsson K, Kindmark A, Bergstrom R, Holmberg L, Mallmin H, Wolk A, Ljunghall S. Excessive dietary intake of vitamin A is associated with reduced bone mineral density and increased risk for hip fracture. *Ann Intern Med.* 1998;129:770–778.

64. Norman AW. Vitamin D. In: Ziegler EE, Filer LJ Jr, eds. *Present Knowledge in Nutrition.* 7th ed. Washington, DC: ILSI Press; 1996:120–129.

65. Lewis NM, Frederick AM. Vitamins D and K. In: Wolinsky I, Driskell JA, eds. *Sports Nutrition.* Boca Raton, Fla: CRC Press; 1997:111–117.

66. Bell NH, Godsen RN, Henry DP, Shary J, Epstein S. The effects of muscle-building exercise on vitamin D and mineral metabolism. *J Bone Miner Res.* 1988;3:369–373.

67. Simpson R, Thomas G, Arnold A. 1,25 dihydroxyvitamin D receptors in skeletal and heart muscle. *J Biol Chem.* 1985;260:8882–8884.

68. Costa E, Blau H, Feldman D. 1,25(OH)$_2$-D$_3$ receptors and humoral responses in cloned human skeletal muscle cells. *Endocrinology.* 1986;119:2214–2217.

69. Grady D, Halloran B, Cummings S, Leveille S, Wells L, Black D, Byl N. 1,25-dihydroxyvitamin D$_3$ and muscle strength in the elderly: a randomized controlled trial. *J Clin Endocrin Metab.* 1991;73:1111–1117.

70. Latham NK, Anderson CS, Reid IR. Effects of vitamin D supplementation on strength, physical performance, and falls in older persons: a systematic review. *J Am Geriatr Soc.* 2003;51: 1219–1226.

71. Krall EA, Sahyoun N, Tannenbaum S, Dallal GE, Dawson-Hughes B. Effect of vitamin D intake on seasonal variations in parathyroid hormone secretion in postmenopausal women. *N Engl J Med.* 1989;321:1777–1783.

72. Dawson-Hughes B, Dallal GE, Krall EA, Harris S, Sokoll LJ, Falconer G. Effects of vitamin D supplementation on wintertime and overall bone loss in healthy postmenopausal women. *Ann Intern Med.* 1991;115:505–512.

73. Simon J, Leboff M, Wright J, Glowacki J. Fractures in the elderly and vitamin D. *J Nutr Health Aging.* 2002;6:406–412.

74. Sokol RJ. Vitamin E. In: Ziegler EE, Filer LJ Jr, eds. *Present Knowledge in Nutrition.* 7th ed. Washington, DC: ILSI Press; 1996:130–136.

75. Bryant RJ, Ryder J, Martino P, Kim J, Craig BW. Effects of vitamin E and C supplementation either alone or in combination on exercise-induced lipid peroxidation in trained cyclists. *J Strength Cond Res.* 2003;17:792–800.

76. Rokitzi L, Logemann E, Sagredos AN, Murphy M, Wetzel-Roth W, Keul J. Lipid peroxidation and antioxidant vitamins under extreme endurance stress. *Acta Physiol Scand.* 1994;154: 149–154.

77. Avery NG, Kaiser JL, Sharman MJ, Scheett TP, Barnes DM, Gomez AL, Kraemer WJ, Volek JS. Effects of vitamin E supplementation on recovery from repeated bouts of resistance exercise. *J Strength Cond Res.* 2003;17:801–809.

78. McBride JM, Kraemer WJ, Triplett-McBride T, Sebastianelli W. Effect of resistance exercise on free radical production. *Med Sci Sports Exerc.* 1998;30:67–72.

79. Mullins VA, Houtkooper LB, Howell WH, Going SB, Brown CH. Nutritional status of U.S. elite female heptathletes during training. *Int J Sport Nutr Exerc Metab.* 2001;11:299–314.

80. Ziegler PJ, Nelson JA, Jonnalagadda SS. Nutritional and physiological status of U.S. national figure skaters. *Int J Sport Nutr.* 1999;9:345–360.

81. Meydani M, Fielding RA, Fotouhi N. Vitamin E. In: Wolinsky I, Driskell JA, eds. *Sports Nutrition.* Boca Raton, Fla: CRC Press; 1997:119–135.

82. Suttie JW. Vitamin K. In: DeLuca HF, ed. *The Fat Soluble Vitamins.* London, England: Plenum Press; 1978.

83. Binkley NC, Suttie JW. Vitamin K nutrition and osteoporosis. *J Nutr.* 1995;125:1812–1821.

84. Tortora G, Grabowski S. In: Tortora GJ, Grabowski SR. *Principles of Anatomy and Physiology.* 8th ed. New York, NY: John Wiley & Sons; 1996:569.

85. Brown WH, Foote CS. Vitamin K, blood clotting, and basicity. In: Brown WH, Foote CS, eds. *Organic Chemistry.* 2nd ed. Orlando, Fla: Saunders College Publishing; 1998:635,1026.

86. Mayers PA. Structure and function of the lipid-soluble vitamins. In: Murray RK, Granner DK, Mayers PA, Rodwell VW, eds. *Biochemistry.* Sydney, Australia: Prentice-Hall International; 1990.

87. Kanai T, Takagi T, Masuhiro K, Nakamura M, Iwata M, Saji F. Serum vitamin K level and bone mineral density in post-menopausal women. *Int J Gynecol Obstetr.* 1997;56:25–30.

88. Philip WJ, Martin JC, Richardson JM, Reid DM, Webster J, Douglas AS. Decreased axial and peripheral bone density in patients taking long-term warfarin. *QJM.* 1995;88:635–640.

89. Craciun AM, Wolf J, Knapen MH, Brouns F, Vermeer C. Improved bone metabolism in female elite athletes after vitamin K supplementation. *Int J Sports Med.* 1998;19:479–484.

90. Booth SL, Suttie JW. Dietary intake and adequacy of vitamin K. *J Nutr.* 1998;128:785–788.

91. Shearer MJ, Bach A, Kohlmeier M. Chemical, nutritional sources, tissue distribution, and metabolism of vitamin K with specific reference to bone health. *J Nutr.* 1996;126(4 Suppl): 1181S–1186S.

92. Olson RE. Vitamin K. In: Shils ME, Olson JA, Shike M, eds. *Modern Nutrition in Health and Disease.* 8th ed. Philadelphia, Pa: Lea & Febiger; 1994:342–358.

93. Arnaud CD, Sanchez SD. Calcium and phosphorus. In: Ziegler EE, Filer LJ Jr, eds. *Present Knowledge in Nutrition.* 7th ed. Washington, DC: ILSI Press; 1996:245–255.

94. Heaney RP. Osteoporosis. In: Krummel DA, Kris-Etherton PM, eds. *Nutrition in Women's Health.* Gaithersburg, Md: Aspen Publishers; 1996:418–439.

95. Allen LH, Wood RJ. Calcium and phosphorous. In: Shils ME, Olson JA, Shike M, eds. *Modern Nutrition in Health and Disease.* 8th ed. Philadelphia, Pa: Lea & Febiger; 1994:144–163.

96. Clarkson PM, Haymes EM. Exercise and mineral status of athletes: calcium, magnesium, phosphorus, and iron. *Med Sci Sports Exerc.* 1995;27:831–843.

97. Zeman FJ, Ney DM. *Applications in Medical Nutrition Therapy.* 2nd ed. Upper Saddle River, NJ: Prentice Hall; 1996.

98. Beshgetoor D, Nichols JF. Dietary intake and supplement use in female master cyclists and runners. *Int J Sport Nutr Exerc Metab.* 2003;13:166–172.

99. Bergeron MF, Volpe SL, Gelinas Y. Cutaneous calcium losses during exercise in the heat: a regional sweat patch estimation technique [abstract]. *Clin Chem.* 1998;44(suppl):A167.

100. Moyad MA. The potential benefits of dietary and/or supplemental calcium and vitamin D. *Urol Oncol.* 2003;21:384–391.

101. Skinner JD, Bounds W, Carruth BR, Zeigler P. Longitudinal calcium intake is negatively related to children's body fat indexes. *J Am Diet Assoc.* 2003;103:1626–1631.

102. Zemel MB, Shi H, Greer B, Dirienzo D, Zemel PC. Regulation of adiposity by dietary calcium. *FASEB J.* 2000;14:1132–1138.

103. Melanson EL, Sharp TA, Schneider J, Donahoo WT, Grunwald GK, Hill JO. Relation between calcium intake and fat oxidation in adult humans. *Int J Obes Relat Metab Disord.* 2003;27:196–203.

104. Shapses SA, Heshka S, Heymsfield SB. Effect of calcium supplementation on weight and fat loss in women. *J Clin Endocrinol Metab.* 2004;89:632–637.

105. Barr SI. Increased dairy product or calcium intake: is body weight or composition affected in humans? *J Nutr.* 2003;133(suppl):245S–248S.

106. Dawson-Hughes B, Dallal GE, Krall EA, Sadowski L, Sahyoun N, Tennenbaum S. A controlled trial of the effect of calcium supplementation on bone density in postmenopausal women. *N Engl J Med.* 1990;323:878–883.

107. Harrington M, Bennett T, Jakobsen J, Ovesen L, Brot C, Flynn A, Cashman KD. The effect of a high-protein, high-sodium diet on calcium and bone metabolism in postmenopausal women and its interaction with vitamin D receptor genotype. *Br J Nutr.* 2004;91:41–51.

108. Kerstetter JE, O'Brien KO, Insogna KL. Dietary protein, calcium metabolism, and skeletal homeostasis revisited. *Am J Clin Nutr.* 2003;78(3 Suppl):584S–592S.

109. US Dept Health and Human Services. *The Surgeon General's Report on Nutrition and Health.* Rocklin, Calif: Prima Publishing and Communications; 1988.

110. Metz JA, Anderson JJ, Gallagher PN Jr. Intakes of calcium, phosphorus, and protein, and physical activity level are related to radial bone mass in young adult women. *Am J Clin Nutr.* 1993;58:537–542.

111. Wyshak G, Frisch RE, Albright TE, Albright NL, Schiff I, Witschi J. Nonalcoholic carbonated beverage consumption and bone fractures among former college athletes. *J Orthopaedic Res.* 1989;7:91–99.

112. Wyshak G. Teenaged girls, carbonated beverage consumption, and bone fractures. *Arch Pediatr Adolesc Med.* 2000;154:610–613.

113. Wyshak G, Frisch RE. Carbonated beverages, dietary calcium, the dietary calcium/phosphorus ratio, and bone fractures in girls and boys. *J Adolesc Health.* 1994;15:210–215.

114. Horswill CA. Effects of bicarbonate, citrate, and phosphate loading on performance. *Int J Sport Nutr.* 1995;5(suppl):S111–S119.

115. Bremner K, Bubb WA, Kemp GJ, Trenell MI, Thompson CH. The effect of phosphate loading on erythrocyte 2,3-bisphosphoglycerate levels. *Clin Chim Acta.* 2002;323:111–114.

116. Shils ME. Magnesium. In: Ziegler EE, Filer LJ Jr, eds. *Present Knowledge in Nutrition.* 7th ed. Washington, DC: ILSI Press; 1996:256–264.

117. Haymes EM, Clarkson PC. Minerals and trace minerals. In: Berning JR, Steen SN, eds. *Nutrition for Sport & Exercise.* 2nd ed. Gaithersburg, Md: Aspen Publishers; 1998:77–107.

118. Konig D, Weinstock C, Keul J, Northoff H, Berg A. Zinc, iron, and magnesium status in athletes: influence on the regulation of exercise-induced stress and immune function. *Exerc Immunol Rev.* 1998;4:2–21.

119. McDonald R, Keen CL. Iron, zinc and magnesium nutrition and athletic performance. *Sports Med.* 1988;5:171–184.

120. Liu L, Borowski G, Rose LI. Hypomagnesemia in a tennis player. *Phys Sportsmed.* 1983;11:79–80.

121. Kuru O, Senturk MK, Gunduz F, Aktekin B, Aktekin MR. Effect of long-term swimming exercise on zinc, magnesium, and copper distribution in aged rats. *Biol Trace Elem Res.* 2003;93:105–112.

122. Mariotti F, Simbelie KL, Makarios-Lahham L, Huneau JF, Laplaize B, Tome D, Even PC. Acute ingestion of dietary proteins improves post-exercise liver glutathione in rats in a dose-dependent relationship with their cysteine content. *J Nutr.* 2004;134:128–131.

123. Oh MS. Water, electrolyte, and acid-base balance. In: Shils ME, Olson JA, Shike M, eds. *Modern Nutrition in Health and Disease.* 8th ed. Philadelphia, Pa: Lea & Febiger; 1994:112–143.

124. Luft FC. Potassium and its regulation. In: Ziegler EE, Filer LJ Jr, eds. *Present Knowledge in Nutrition.* 7th ed. Washington, DC: ILSI Press; 1996:272–276.

125. Nielsen JJ, Mohr M, Klarskov C, Kristensen M, Krustrup P, Juel C, Bangsbo J. Effects of high-intensity intermittent training on potassium kinetics and performance in human skeletal muscle. *J Physiol.* 2004;554:857–870.

126. Millard-Stafford M, Sparling PB, Rosskopf LB, Snow TK, DiCarlo LJ, Hinson BT. Fluid intake in male and female runners during a 4-km field run in the heat. *J Sports Sci.* 1995;13:257–263.

127. Luft FC. Salt, water, and extracellular volume regulation. In: Ziegler EE, Filer LJ Jr, eds. *Present Knowledge in Nutrition.* 7th ed. Washington, DC: ILSI Press; 1996:265–271.

128. Shirreffs SM, Armstrong LE, Cheuvront SN. Fluid and electrolyte needs for preparation and recovery from training and competition. *J Sports Sci.* 2004;22:57–63.

129. Coyle EF. Fluid and fuel intake during exercise. *J Sports Sci.* 2004;22:39–55.

130. Keatisuwan W, Ohnaka T, Tochihara Y. Physiological responses of women during exercise under dry-heat condition in winter and summer. *Appl Human Sci.* 1996;15:169–176.

131. Stachenfeld NS, Gleim GW, Zabetakis PM, Nicholas JA. Fluid balance and renal response following dehydrating exercise in well-trained men and women. *Eur J Appl Physiol.* 1996;72:469–477.

132. Jain P, Jain P, Tandon HC, Babbar R. Effect of sodium citrate ingestion on oxygen debt and exercise endurance during supramaximal exercise. *Indian J Med Res.* 2003;118:42–46.

133. Huebers H, Finch CA. Transferrin: physiologic behavior and clinical implications. *Blood.* 1984;64:763–767.

134. Finch CA, Lenfant L. Oxygen transport in men. *N Engl J Med.* 1972;286:407–410.

135. Dallman PR. Tissue effects of iron deficiency. In: Jacobs A, Worwood M, eds. *Iron in Biochemistry and Medicine.* London, England: Academic Press; 1974:437–476.

136. Dallman PR. Biochemical basis for the manifestations of iron deficiency. *Annu Rev Nutr.* 1986;6:13–40.

137. Balaban EP, Cox JV, Snell P, Vaughan RH, Frenkel EP. The frequency of anemia and iron deficiency in the runner. *Med Sci Sports Exerc.* 1989;21:643–648.

138. Fogelholm GM, Himberg JJ, Alopaeus K, Gref CG, Laakso JT, Lehto JJ, Mussalo-Rauhamaa H. Dietary and biochemical indices of nutritional status in male athletes and controls. *J Am Coll Nutr.* 1992;11:181–191.

139. Cowell BS, Rosenbloom CA, Skinner R, Summers SH. Policies on screening female athletes for iron deficiency in NCAA division I-A institutions. *Int J Sport Nutr Exerc Metab.* 2003;13:277–285.

140. Brown RT, McIntosh SM, Seabolt VR, Daniel WA. Iron status of adolescent female athletes. *J Adolesc Health Care.* 1985;6:349–352.

141. Parr RB, Bachman LA, Moss RA. Iron deficiency in female athletes. *Phys Sportsmed.* 1984;12:81–86.

142. Plowman SA, McSwegin PC. The effects of iron supplementation on female cross-country runners. *J Sports Med.* 1981;21:407–416.

143. Schena F, Pattini A, Mantovanelli S. Iron status in athletes involved in endurance and in preva- lently anaerobic sports. In: Kies C, Driskell JA, eds. *Sports Nutrition: Minerals and Elec- trolytes.* Philadelphia, Pa: CRC Press; 1995:65–79.

144. Deruisseau KC, Roberts LM, Kushnick MR, Evans AM, Austin K, Haymes EM. Iron status of young males and females performing weight-training exercise. *Med Sci Sports Exerc.* 2004;36: 241–248.

145. Bank WJ. Myoglobinuria in marathon runners: possible relationship to carbohydrate and lipid metabolism. *Ann N Y Acad Sci.* 1977;301:942–950.

146. Ben BT, Motley CP. Myoglobinemia and endurance exercise: a study on 25 participants in a triathlon competition. *Am J Sports Med.* 1984;12:113–118.

147. Miller BJ, Pate RR, Burgess W. Foot impact force and intravascular hemolysis during distance running. *Int J Sports Med.* 1988;9:56–60.

148. Nickerson HJ, Holubets MC, Weiler BR, Haas RG, Schwartz S, Ellefson ME. Causes of iron deficiency in adolescent athletes. *J Pediatr.* 1989;114:657–663.

149. Viteri FE, Torun B. Anemia and physical work capacity. *Clin Hematol.* 1974;3:609–626.

150. Finch CA, Miller LR, Inamdar A, Person R, Seiler K, Mackler B. Iron deficiency in the rat: physiological and biochemical studies of muscle dysfunction. *J Clin Invest.* 1976;58:447–453.

151. McLane JA, Fell RD, McKay RH, Winder WW, Brown EB, Holloszy JO. Physiological and biochemical effects of iron deficiency on rat skeletal muscle function. *Am J Physiol.* 1981;241: C47–C54.

152. Zhu YI, Haas JD. Iron depletion without anemia and physical performance in young women. *Am J Clin Nutr.* 1997;66:334–341.

153. Martinez-Torres C, Cubeddu L, Dillmann E, Brengelmann GL, Leets I, Layrisse M, Johnson DG, Finch C. Effect of exposure to low temperature on normal and iron-deficient subjects. *J Physiol.* 1984;246:R380–R383.

154. Beard JL, Borel MJ, Derr J. Impaired thermoregulation and thyroid function in iron-deficiency anemia. *Am J Clin Nutr.* 1990;52:13–19.

155. Beard J, Tobin B, Green W. Evidence for thyroid hormone deficiency in iron-deficient anemic rats. *J Nutr.* 1989;119:772–778.

156. Rosenzweig PH, Volpe SL. Iron, thermoregulation, and metabolic rate. *Crit Rev Food Sci Nutr.* 1999;39:131–148.

157. Harris Rosenzweig P, Volpe SL. Effect of iron supplementation on thyroid hormone levels and resting metabolic rate in two college female athletes: a case study. *Int J Sport Nutr Exerc Metab.* 2000;10:434–443.

158. Lozoff B. Behavioral alterations in iron deficiency. *Advances Pediatr.* 1988;35:331–359.

159. Gleeson M, Nieman DC, Pedersen BK. Exercise, nutrition and immune function. *J Sports Sci.* 2004;22:115–125.

160. Yip R, Dallman PR. Iron. In: Ziegler EE, Filer LJ Jr, eds. *Present Knowledge in Nutrition.* 7th ed. Washington, DC: ILSI Press; 1996:277–292.

161. Solvell L. Oral iron therapy: side effects. In: Hallberg L, ed. *Iron Deficiency: Pathogenesis, Clinical Aspects, Therapy.* London, England: Academic Press; 1970:573–583.

162. Nielsen P, Nachtigall D. Iron supplementation in athletes. *Sports Med.* 1998;26:207–216.

163. Hinton PS, Giordano C, Brownlie T, Haas JD. Iron supplementation improves endurance after training in iron-depleted, nonanemic women. *J Appl Physiol.* 2000:88:1103–1111.

164. Cunnane SC. *Zinc: Clinical and Biochemical Significance.* Boca Raton, Fla: CRC Press; 1988.

165. Ganapathy S, Volpe SL. Zinc, exercise, and thyroid hormone function. *Crit Rev Food Sci Nutr.* 1999;39:369–390.

166. Micheletti A, Rossi R, Rufini S. Zinc status in athletes: relation to diet and exercise. *Sports Med.* 2001;31:577–582.

167. Deuster PA, Day BA, Singh A, Douglass L, Moser-Veillon PB. Zinc status of highly trained women runners and untrained women. *Am J Clin Nutr.* 1989;49:1295–1301.

168. Lukaski HC, Siders WA, Hoverson BS, Gallagher SK. Iron, copper, magnesium and zinc status as predictors of swimming performance. *Int J Sports Med.* 1996;17:534–540.

169. Lukaski HC, Hoverson BS, Gallagher SK, Bolonchuk WW. Physical training and copper, iron, and zinc status of swimmers. *Am J Clin Nutr.* 1990;51:1093–1099.

170. Wada L, King J. Effect of low zinc intakes on basal metabolic rate, thyroid hormones and protein utilization in adult men. *J Nutr.* 1986;48:1045–1053.

171. Baltaci AK, Ozyurek K, Mogulkoc R, Kurtoglu E, Ozkan Y, Celik I. Effects of zinc deficiency and supplementation on the glycogen contents of liver and plasma lactate and leptin levels of rats performing acute exercise. *Biol Trace Elem Res.* 2003;96:227–236.

172. Ozturk A, Baltaci AK, Mogulkoc R, Oztekin E, Sivrikaya A, Kurtoglu E, Kul A. Effects of zinc deficiency and supplementation on malondialdehyde and glutathione levels in blood and tissues of rats performing swimming exercise. *Biol Trace Elem Res.* 2003;94:157–166.

173. O'Dell BL. Copper. In: Brown ML, ed. *Sports Nutrition.* 6th ed. Washington, DC: International Life Sciences Institute-Nutrition Foundation; 1990:261–273.

174. Gropper SS, Sorrels LM, Blessing D. Copper status of collegiate female athletes involved in different sports. *Int J Sport Nutr Exerc Metab.* 2003;13:343–357.

175. Tessier F, Margaritis I, Richard M-J, Moynot C, Marconnet P. Selenium and training effects on the glutathione system and aerobic performance. *Med Sci Sports Exerc.* 1995;27:390–396.

176. Margaritis I, Palazzetti S, Rousseau AS, Richard MJ, Favier A. Antioxidant supplementation and tapering exercise improve exercise-induced antioxidant response. *J Am Coll Nutr.* 2003; 22:147–156.

177. Phipps KR. Fluoride. In: Ziegler EE, Filer LJ Jr, eds. *Present Knowledge in Nutrition.* 7th ed. Washington, DC: ILSI Press; 1996:329–333.

178. Phipps KP. Fluoride and bone health. *J Public Health Dent.* 1995;55:53–56.

179. Nielsen FH. Chromium. In: Shils ME, Olson JA, Shike M, eds. *Modern Nutrition in Health and Disease.* 8th ed. Philadelphia, Pa: Lea & Febiger; 1994:264–268.

180. McCarty MF. Up-regulation of intracellular signalling pathways may play a central pathogenic role in hypertension, atherogenesis, insulin resistance, and cancer promotion—the "PKC syndrome." *Med Hypotheses.* 1996;46:191–221.

181. Hallmark MA, Reynolds TH, Desouza CA, Dotson CO, Anderson AA, Rogers MA. Effect of chromium and resistive training on muscle strength and body composition. *Med Sci Sports Exerc.* 1996;28:139–144.

182. Lukaski HC, Bolonchuk WW, Siders WA, Miline DB. Chromium supplementation and resistance training: effects on body composition, strength, and trace element status of men. *Am J Clin Nutr.* 1996;63:954–965.

183. Volpe SL, Huang HW, Larpadisorn K, Lesser II. Effect of chromium supplementation and exercise on body composition, resting metabolic rate and selected biochemical parameters in moderately obese women following an exercise program. *J Am Coll Nutr.* 2001;20:293–306.

184. Anderson RA, Polansky MM, Bryden NA. Strenuous running: acute effects on chromium, copper, zinc, and selected clinical variables in urine and serum of male runners. *Biol Trace Elem Res.* 1984;6:327–336.

185. Anderson RA, Bryden NA, Polansky MM, Deuster PA. Exercise effects on chromium excretion of trained and untrained men consuming a constant diet. *J Appl Physiol.* 1988;64:249–252.

186. Campbell WW, Joseph LJ, Anderson RA, Davey SL, Hinton J, Evans WJ. Effects of resistive training and chromium picolinate on body composition and skeletal muscle size in older women. *Int J Sport Nutr Exerc Metab.* 2002;12:125–135.

187. Kobla HV, Volpe SL. Chromium, exercise, and body composition. *Crit Rev Food Sci Nutr.* 2000;40:291–308.

188. Nielsen FH. Other trace elements. In: Ziegler EE, Filer LJ Jr, eds. *Present Knowledge in Nutrition.* 7th ed. Washington, DC: ILSI Press; 1996:353–377.

189. Meacham SL, Taper LJ, Volpe SL. The effect of boron supplementation on blood and urinary calcium, magnesium, phosphorus, and urinary boron in female athletes. *Am J Clin Nutr.* 1995; 61:341–345.

190. Volpe SL, Taper LJ, Meacham SL. The effect of boron supplementation on bone mineral density and hormonal status in college female athletes. *Med Exerc Nutr Health.* 1993;2:323–330.

191. Volpe SL, Taper LJ, Meacham SL. The relationship between boron and magnesium status, and bone mineral density: a review. *Magnes Res.* 1993;6:291–296.

192. Ferrando AA, Green NR. The effect of boron supplementation on lean body mass, plasma testosterone levels, and strength in male bodybuilders. *Int J Sport Nutr.* 1993;3:140–149.

193. Bucci L. Dietary supplements as ergogenic aids. In: Wolinsky I, ed. *Nutrition in Exercise and Sport.* 3rd ed. Boca Raton, Fla: CRC Press LLC; 1998:315–368.

Chapter 6

FLUID, ELECTROLYTES, AND EXERCISE

Bob Murray, PhD, FACSM

Maintaining adequate hydration during physical activity is one of the most important nutritional practices for optimizing performance and protecting health and well-being. Even a slight amount of dehydration (eg, 1% loss of body weight, which is 1.5 lb [0.7 kg] in a 150-lb [68-kg] athlete) can adversely affect the body's ability to cope with physical activity, particularly when that activity occurs in a warm environment. Greater dehydration (eg, >1% loss of body weight) is known to impair performance. The physiological consequences of dehydration are comprehensively reviewed in the scientific literature (for selected reviews, see references 1–4), but when educating coaches and athletes, the emphasis is better placed on the physiological and performance benefits of staying well-hydrated (5–7).

This chapter focuses on the practical relevance of ingesting adequate amounts of fluid and electrolytes before, during, and after physical activity to replace sweat losses. The information in this chapter is gleaned from decades of research on the physiological and performance-related responses to changes in hydration status. In addition, numerous position stands on the topic of hydration and exercise have been published by a variety of professional organizations (8–16), and the key points from those documents are also included in this chapter.

For individuals who engage in vigorous physical activity or who spend considerable time in warm environments, water and electrolyte losses can be prodigious and can have a large impact on daily fluid and electrolyte needs (17,18). For that reason, it is important to have a fundamental understanding of daily fluid and electrolyte balance.

Daily Fluid and Electrolyte Balance

Control of Fluid Balance

At rest in thermoneutral conditions (thermoneutral refers to environmental temperatures and activity levels that do not provoke sweating), body fluid balance is maintained at ± 0.2% of total body weight (19), a very narrow tolerance befitting the critical importance of hydration status on physiological function, even in nonexercise conditions. Under thermoneutral, sedentary conditions, the daily intake of fluid usually matches or exceeds the volume of fluid that is lost in urine, feces, and sweat; through respiration; and via transcutaneous water loss. Maintaining fluid balance requires the constant integration of input from hypothalamic osmoreceptors (to gauge the osmolality of the blood) and vascular baroreceptors (to gauge the pressure within major vessels) so that fluid intake matches or modestly exceeds fluid loss. In this regard, the combination of thirst-driven and spontaneous drinking is such that fluid balance is normally maintained in most people over the course of a day. Interestingly, thirst-driven fluid intake accounts for only a small percentage of daily fluid intake; most fluid is spontaneously consumed with meals or snacks during the day and not directly in response to being thirsty (20).

When sweating occurs, body fluid balance is regulated by mechanisms that reduce urinary water and sodium excretion and stimulate thirst. Sweat loss is accompanied by a decrease in plasma volume and an increase in plasma osmolality (because more water than salt is lost in sweat, the sodium and chloride concentrations in plasma increase). These changes are sensed by vascular pressure receptors (these baroreceptors respond to a drop in blood volume) and hypothalamic osmoreceptors, which respond to an increase in plasma sodium. In response to dehydration, integrated input from baroreceptors and osmoreceptors results in an increase in vasopressin (antidiuretic hormone) release from the pituitary gland and in renin release from the kidneys. These hormones, including angiotensin II and aldosterone, which result from an increase in plasma renin activity, increase water and sodium retention by the kidneys and provoke an increase in thirst (21).

During the course of a day, ingesting adequate water and electrolytes in foods and beverages eventually restores plasma volume and osmolality to normal levels and, whenever excess fluid is ingested, water balance is restored by the kidneys (ie, excess fluid is excreted) (22). However, for physically active people, body fluid balance is often compromised because the human thirst mechanism is an imprecise gauge of immediate fluid needs and because it is sometimes difficult to ingest enough fluid to offset the large volume of sweat that can be lost during physical activity.

Daily Fluid Needs

Many people are confused by the oft-repeated recommendation that they should consume eight, 8-ounce glasses of water per day to maintain proper hydration (23). Although the genesis of this advice is a matter of debate, it is interesting that eight, 8-ounce servings amounts to 2 liters (approximately 2 quarts), the volume that has been cited as the daily fluid requirement for sedentary adults (24). In point of fact, there is no one fluid-intake recommendation that will suffice for everyone because of the wide disparity in daily fluid needs created by body size, physical activity, and environmental conditions (25). Two liters per day might be too much fluid for a small, elderly individual living in an assisted-care facility, but for a physically active person, 2 liters might represent the fluid needs of just 1 hour of activity. The 2004 Dietary Reference Intake recommendations for water and electrolytes (26) identify the Adequate Intake (AI) for water to be 3.7 liters/day in males (130 oz/day; the equivalent of 16 cups/day of fluid) and 2.7 liters/day for females (95 oz/day; about 12 cups/day) (26). The AI is an estimate of the daily nutrient intake that is assumed to be adequate. In other words, there is a low probability of inadequacy if sedentary males and females ingest between 2.7 to 3.7 liters/day of fluid.

The 12 cups of fluid that represent the AI for water intake in adult females does not mean that women should literally drink at least 12 cups of water each day. Rather, it means that a total of 12 cups of fluid from all sources will meet the hydration needs of most adult females. This important distinction should be stressed when educating and counseling people about their hydration needs. Regardless of the extent of daily water needs, water can be supplied by a variety of foods and fluids such as fruits and vegetables, milk, soft drinks, fruit juices, sport drinks, water, fruit, coffee, tea, and soup. Approximately 20% of daily water needs comes from water found in food, and the remaining 80% is provided by fluids ingested during the day (26). In brief, the prevailing scientific consensus is that sedentary individuals living in temperate environments can rely on the combination of thirst and spontaneous drinking to successfully maintain daily fluid balance, whereas physically active people and those living in warm environments often find it difficult to keep pace with their daily fluid needs.

Between 45% and 75% of body weight is water, a value that varies inversely with fat mass (26). Regardless of the volume of total body water, maintenance of fluid balance in physically active people can be an ongoing challenge. Fluid is constantly lost from the body by way of the kidneys (urine), gastrointestinal tract (feces), respiratory tract, and skin (the latter two routes represent insensible water loss), and periodically lost from the eccrine sweat glands during exercise and heat exposure (2,19,24). (Eccrine sweat glands are responsible for secreting sweat onto the skin in response to physical activity and heat stress. Apocrine glands are found in the armpits and are not part of the thermoregulatory response.)

The total volume of fluid lost from the body on a daily basis is determined by the environmental conditions, the size (and surface area) of the individual, the individual's metabolic rate, physical activity and sweat loss, the composition of the diet, and the volume of excreted fluids. Insensible water loss via the skin is relatively constant (see Table 6.1) (24), but water loss via the respiratory tract is affected by the ambient temperature, relative humidity, and ventilatory volume. Inhaled air is humidified during its passage through the respiratory tract, and, as a result, exhaled air has a relative humidity of 100%. Inhaling warm, humid air reduces insensible water loss because the inhaled air already contains substantial water vapor. As indicated in Table 6.1, athletes and workers experience more insensible water losses via the respiratory tract merely because of the overall increase in breathing that accompanies exercise. The air inhaled during cold-weather activity contains relatively little water vapor, so as it is warmed and humidified during its transit through the respiratory tract, additional water loss occurs. For this reason, during cold-weather activity, especially when conducted at altitude, transcutaneous and respiratory water loss can be quite high, at times exceeding 1 liter/day (27).

What is the absolute minimum water needed for a sedentary individual? That value is difficult to accurately discern, but it is likely to be no less than 1 liter/day. The reasoning for this is that minimum urine flow is approximately 500 mL/day, transcutaneous water loss is approximately 400 mL/day, and respiratory loss is a minimum of 200 mL/day. Keep in mind that this minimum value would apply only to someone who was completely sedentary for the entire day in a temperate environment. It is thought that the water requirement in most minimally active adults ranges between 3 to 4 liters/day due to the transcutaneous, respiratory, and urinary water loss that accompanies normal daily living (23,26).

When individuals work, train, and compete in warm environments, their daily water needs can be considerably larger and might increase to more than 10 liters/day (28). For example, an athlete who trains 2 hours each day can easily lose an additional 4 liters of

TABLE 6.1   Typical Daily Fluid Losses (mL) for a 70-kg Athlete

	Normal Weather (68°F/20°C)	Warm Weather (85°F/29°C)	Exercise in Warm Weather (85°F/29°C)
Insensible loss			
Skin	350	350	350
Respiratory tract	350	250	650
Urine	1400	1200	500
Feces	100	100	100
Sweat	100	1400	5000
TOTAL	**2300**	**3300**	**6600**

Note: Daily fluid loss varies widely among athletes and can exceed 10 liters/day under some circumstances.
Source: Adapted from Guyton AC, Hall JE. *Textbook of Medical Physiology.* 10th ed. Philadelphia, Pa: WB Saunders Co; 2000, with permission from Elsevier. Copyright © 2000, Elsevier, Inc.

body fluid, resulting in a daily fluid requirement in excess of 7 to 8 liters. Many people are active more than 2 hours each day, further increasing their fluid needs. Such losses can strain the capacity of the fluid regulatory system such that thirst becomes an inadequate stimulus for fluid intake and, coupled with inadequate opportunities for spontaneous drinking, persistent dehydration (hypohydration) results.

To put these volumes of fluid loss in perspective, consider that the body of a 60-kg (132-lb) individual contains approximately 36 kg water (60% of body weight). If that person remains sedentary in a moderate environment, daily fluid requirements will be approximately 3 liters or 8.3% of total body water ($3 \div 36 \times 100$). In other words, every 12 days that person's body water will completely turn over. Now consider an 80-kg (176-lb) football player who sweats profusely during two-a-day practices in the heat of August. That individual's water needs might be 10 liters/day, representing about 20% of his total body water. If such large volumes seem unreasonably high, consider that most athletes will lose between 1 and 2 liters of sweat per hour of exercise, and some people are capable of sweating more than 3 liters/hour (3).

Urine production is reduced during physical activity as the kidneys attempt to conserve water and sodium to offset losses due to sweating. When fluid intake is limited and dehydration occurs, the kidneys are capable of concentrating the urine to four to five times the concentration of blood. However, some renal fluid loss (approximately 500 mL/day) is obligatory for waste removal. Daily urine losses in some athletes and workers tend to be less than in sedentary individuals, a trend that is exacerbated by warm weather as the body strives to conserve fluid. However, most athletes consume large volumes of fluid during the day and actually produce more urine than their sedentary counterparts. Reduced urine volume in physically active individuals usually indicates inadequate fluid intake. In general, urine volumes tend to be 800 to 1,500 mL/day in sedentary individuals, but can exceed 4 liters/day in physically active individuals who ingest large volumes of fluid.

What impact does the composition of the diet have on daily water needs? The simple answer to this question is that in sedentary individuals, the water required to excrete urea from protein (amino acid) degradation and to excrete excess electrolyte intake can represent a meaningful increase in daily water needs. However, for physically active people who already have an increased water requirement, the effect of diet is usually quite small. For example, to excrete the urea produced from the degradation of 100 g protein would require approximately 700 mL water to be excreted from the body. How much water is contributed by the oxidation of macronutrients? This volume is also relatively small, approximately 130 mL/1,000 kcal (29), and is relatively inconsequential for those individuals consuming more than 2 liters of fluid per day.

Control of Electrolyte Balance

The concentrations of electrolytes across cell membranes must be tightly regulated to assure proper function of cells throughout the body. In the case of cardiac muscle, for example, an electrolyte imbalance such as hyperkalemia can have fatal consequences if plasma potassium concentration increases just a few mmol/liter. For this reason, the kidneys are well-equipped to maintain electrolyte balance by conserving or excreting minerals such as sodium, chloride, potassium, calcium, and magnesium. Although an "appetite" for sodium chloride does exist in humans (30), there is little evidence to suggest that the intake of other minerals is governed in a similar way. In most individuals, when dietary energy intake is adequate, mineral intake is usually in excess of mineral needs, assuring positive mineral balance. However, repeated days of profuse sweating can result in substantial electrolyte loss, especially sodium and chloride, the two minerals found in greatest concentrations in sweat. When dietary mineral intake is not sufficient to compensate for such large losses, severe muscle cramping (31) and hyponatremia (32) might result.

Daily Electrolyte Needs

Electrolytes are lost in urine and sweat. Some athletes, soldiers, and workers lose large volumes of sweat on a daily basis (eg, 4 to 10 liters or more) and that loss is accompanied by a similarly large electrolyte loss. As shown in Table 6.2, the concentrations of potassium, magnesium, and calcium in sweat are low and relatively constant compared with the higher, more variable concentrations of sodium and chloride in sweat. The fact that sodium concentration in sweat varies widely among individuals means that some people will be prone to large sodium deficits whereas others will not. Increased risk of heat-related problems, hyponatremia, and muscle cramps has been linked to large sodium chloride losses in sweat (31–33). Increased salt intake mitigates severe whole-body muscle cramping that seem to result from chronic sodium deficits caused by large sweat losses. However, increased salt intake is not helpful in cramps of other origin. Some people mistakenly believe that potassium loss is what causes muscle cramps and suggest eating oranges and bananas to replace the potassium lost in sweat. However, potassium loss is not the culprit. Potassium is lost in sweat (28), but the concentration of potassium in sweat (usually less than 10 mmol/liter) is far less than that of sodium (20 to more than 100 mmol/liter).

For some individuals, the amount of sodium chloride lost in sweat is not trivial. Consider, for example, a football player who practices for 5 hours/day, during which time he loses 8 liters of sweat (1.6 liters/hour). If his sweat contains 50 mmol Na^+/liter, his total sodium loss will be 9,200 mg sodium (ie, 23 g NaCl). This sodium loss, which does not include the 50 to 200 mmol (1,150 to 4,600 mg) of sodium that is typically lost in urine, makes it apparent that physically active people often require a large salt intake to replace losses in sweat. The 2004 Dietary Reference Intake recommendations (26) indicate that

TABLE 6.2   Mineral (Electrolyte) Losses in Sweat

Mineral	Concentration in Sweat, mmol/L (mg/L)	AI Values, mg/d	Possible AI Lost in Sweat, %/L
Sodium	20–80 (460–1840)	1300	35–140
Chloride	20–80 (710–2840)	1300	35–140
Potassium	4–10 (160–390)	4700	3–8
Magnesium	0–1.5 (0–36)	240–420	0–15
Calcium	0–3 (0–120)	1000–1300	0–12

Abbreviation: AI, Adequate Intake.

Americans and Canadians should restrict their daily sodium intake to only 1.5 g/day (3.8 g salt per day), with a Tolerable Upper Intake Level for salt of 5.8 g/day (2.3 g sodium per day)

The basis of this recommendation is that a reduction in dietary sodium intake can blunt the age-related increase in blood pressure. Clearly, these stringent dietary recommendations are inadequate for athletes, fitness enthusiasts, and workers who lose considerably more salt in their sweat. However, this discrepancy is recognized in the DRI report: "This AI does not apply to highly active individuals . . . who lose large amounts of sweat on a daily basis" (26).

Human sweat contains small amounts of dozens of organic and inorganic substances (eg, amino acids, urea, lactic acid, calcium, magnesium, iron), some of which are minerals. Even when sweat losses are large, it is unlikely that minerals such as magnesium, iron, and calcium will be lost in sufficient quantities in sweat to provoke a mineral imbalance in most people. However, there may be some individuals for whom such losses could constitute an additional dietary challenge, as might be the case with sweat calcium losses in physically active females (see Table 6.2). For example, a female athlete who loses 3 liters of sweat in a day could lose up to 120 to 360 mg calcium. Although this amount of calcium can be easily replaced by consuming a cup of milk, sweat calcium loss does increase the dietary calcium needs of active males and females.

Position Stands on Fluid and Electrolyte Replacement

There are at least nine position stands published by a variety of professional organizations that address fluid and electrolyte replacement before, during, and after physical activity (8–16). Table 6.3 provides a summary of the key recommendations from those documents. As can quickly be seen by scanning Table 6.3, the recommendations do vary and they have evolved over time, although the differences among the recommendations are relatively small and the central intent of each is to assure that physically active individuals remain well-hydrated. The general consensus is that proper hydration practices help reduce the risk of dehydration and heat illness, maintain cardiovascular function, and improve performance during vigorous physical activity.

Fluid and Electrolyte Replacement Before Exercise

Adequate hydration before physical activity helps assure optimal physiological and performance responses. In fact, laboratory subjects who ingest fluid in the hour before

TABLE 6.3   Recommendations for Fluid and Electrolyte Replacement When Exercising

Position Stand	Before Exercise	During Exercise	After Exercise	Electrolyte Replacement
American College of Sports Medicine (1985) (8)	No recommendation.	Runners should consume 100–200 mL (3–6 oz) at each aid station.	No recommendation.	No recommendation.
American College of Sports Medicine (1996) (10)	No recommendation.	Runners should replace sweat losses or consume 150–300 mL (5.3–10.5 oz) every 15 minutes.	No recommendation.	Provide water and carbohydrate-electrolyte beverages in equal volumes at aid stations.
American College of Sports Medicine (1996) (9)	Drink ~500 mL (~17 oz) about 2 h before exercise.	Start drinking early and at regular intervals in an attempt to consume fluids at a rate sufficient to replace all of the water lost through sweating.	No recommendation.	For exercise lasting > 1 hour, include 0.5–0.7 g of sodium per liter of fluid to enhance palatability, promote fluid retention, and reduce the risk of hyponatremia.
National Athletic Trainers Association (2000) (11)	Consume approximately 500–600 mL (17–20 oz) of water or sport drink 2–3 h before exercise and 200–300 mL (7–10 oz) 10–20 min before exercise.	Fluid replacement should approximate sweat and urine losses, with the goal of keeping weight loss < 2% body mass. Example: 200–300 mL (7–10 oz) every 10–20 min, but individualized recommendations should be followed.	To ensure hydration within 4–6 h after exercise, drink about 25%-50% more than existing weight loss.	Adding a modest amount of salt (0.3–0.7 g/L) is acceptable to stimulate thirst, increase voluntary fluid intake, and decrease the risk of hyponatremia.
American Academy of Pediatrics (2000) (12)	Before prolonged physical activity, the child should be well-hydrated.	Periodic drinking should be enforced, even if a child is not thirsty. Example: for a child weighing 40 kg (88 lb), drink 150 mL of water or a flavored, salted beverage every 20 min.	No recommendation.	Make water or a flavored, salted beverage available for active children.
American Dietetic Association, Dietitians of Canada, and the American College of Sports Medicine (2000) (13)	2 h before exercise, drink 400–600 mL (14–22 oz).	Ingest 150–350 mL (6–12 oz) every 15–20 minutes, depending on tolerance.	Drink ≥ 450–675 mL (16–24 oz) for every pound (0.5 kg) of body weight lost during exercise.	Sodium in amounts between 0.5–0.7 g/L is recommended during exercise lasting > 1 h because it may enhance palatability and the drive to drink, therefore increasing the amount of fluid consumed. Athletes can also rehydrate in conjunction with a sodium-containing meal.

continues

TABLE 6.3 Recommendations for Fluid and Electrolyte Replacement When Exercising (continued)

Position Stand	Before Exercise	During Exercise	After Exercise	Electrolyte Replacement
International Marathon Medical Directors Association-Association of International Marathons (2002) (14)	No recommendation.	Runners should drink as needed between 400–800 mL/h, depending on race speed and environmental conditions.	No recommendation.	No recommendation.
Inter-Association Task Force on Exertional Heat Illnesses (2003) (15)	Athletes should begin exercise properly hydrated.	Fluid intake should nearly approximate fluid losses. Individualized recommendations must be followed.	No recommendation.	Hydrating with a sport drink containing carbohydrates and electrolytes before and during exercise is optimal to replace losses and provide energy. Replacing lost sodium after exercise is best achieved by consuming food, in combination with a rehydration beverage.
USA Track and Field (2003) (16)	Consume approximately 500–600 mL (17–20 oz) of water or sport drink 2–3 h before exercise and 300–360 mL (10–12 oz) 0–10 min before exercise.	During the race drink no more than 1 cup (8–10 oz) every 15–20 min.	Drink about 25% more than sweat losses to ensure optimal hydration 4–6 h after the event.	Addition of modest amounts of sodium (0.5–0.7 g/L) can offset sodium lost in sweat and may minimize medical events associated with electrolyte imbalances (eg, muscle cramps, hyponatremia).

exercise exhibit lower core temperatures and heart rates during exercise than when no fluid is ingested (33–35).

Clearly, athletes who enter competition in a dehydrated state are at a competitive disadvantage (4). For example, in a study by Armstrong et al (36), subjects performed runs of 5,000 meters (approximately 19 minutes) and 10,000 meters (approximately 40 minutes) in either a normally hydrated or dehydrated condition. When dehydrated by approximately 2% of body weight (by a diuretic given prior to exercise), their running speeds decreased significantly (by 6% to 7%) in both events. To make matters worse, exercise in the heat exacerbates the performance-impairing effects of dehydration (37).

When people live and are physically active in warm environments, voluntary fluid intake is often insufficient to meet fluid needs, as verified by a study conducted with soccer players in Puerto Rico (38). The athletes were studied during 2 weeks of training. When the players were allowed to drink fluids throughout the day as they wished (average intake = 2.7 liters/day), their total body water at the end of 1 week was approximately 1.1 liters less than when they were mandated to drink 4.6 liters of fluid per day. In other words, their voluntary fluid consumption did not match their fluid losses, causing them to enter training and competition already dehydrated.

How do individuals know when they are adequately hydrated? This simple question continues to perplex scientists and clinicians because there is no one method that can accurately and reliably determine adequate hydration status. Measuring plasma osmolality is one method that is often used in laboratory settings to assess hydration status, but a blood draw and expensive equipment are required. The specific gravity of urine from the first void after awaking in the morning can provide useful information about hydration status, but some equipment is needed (eg, a refractometer or hydrometer), although the cost of such equipment is reasonable (eg, less than $200).

Noting the color and volume of urine is practical way to help physically active people subjectively assess their hydration status. Darkly colored urine of relatively small volume is an indication of dehydration, a signal to ingest more fluid prior to activity. Monitoring urine output is a common recommendation in occupational settings such as the mining industry in which the workers are constantly exposed to conditions of high heat and humidity. In brief, in addition to measuring body weight after awakening, the use of some measure of urine concentration (eg, specific gravity, osmolality, or color) will often allow for the detection of dehydration. Monitoring urine color is the easiest way to estimate hydration status because dark-yellow urine is usually consistent with dehydration. However, the intake of B vitamin supplements, specifically riboflavin, can cause brightly colored urine even when an individual is well-hydrated.

It has been hypothesized that ingesting a glycerol solution before physical activity in the heat might confer cardiovascular and thermoregulatory advantages. In fact, ingesting glycerol solutions prior to exercise does result in a reduction in urine production and in the temporary retention of fluid (34,35). Glycerol-induced hyperhydration is accompanied by weight gain that is proportional to the amount of water retained (usually approximately 0.5 to 1 kg). Fluid retention occurs because after glycerol molecules are absorbed and distributed throughout the body water (with the exception of the aqueous-humor and the cerebral-spinal fluid compartments) their presence provokes a transient increase in osmolality, prompting a temporary decrease in urine production. As glycerol molecules are removed from the body water in the subsequent hours, plasma osmolality decreases, urine production increases, and the excess water is excreted.

There are several reasons why it is unwise to recommend glycerol-induced hydration to athletes:

1. Athletes pay a metabolic cost for carrying extra body weight.
2. There is no compelling evidence that glycerol-induced hyperhydration results in a physiological benefit (35).
3. The side effects of ingesting glycerol can range from mild sensations of bloating and lightheadedness to more severe symptoms of headaches, dizziness, and nausea (39).
4. Glycerol-induced hyperhydration can cause blood sodium levels to decrease (40), possibly predisposing to hyponatremia.

As noted in Table 6.3, there are several somewhat similar recommendations for fluid intake before exercise (when heavy sweating is anticipated), but a general recommendation is this: Drink approximately 7 mL/kg body weight (about 1 oz/10 lb body weight) of water or sport drink 2 hours before exercise. This will allow ample time for excess fluid to be excreted or for additional fluid to be consumed. If profuse sweating is expected, as would be the case with a vigorous workout in a warm environment, drink an additional 3 to 4 mL/kg body weight (0.6 oz/10 lb body weight) within 20 minutes before exercise. For example, a 70-kg (154-lb) individual would ingest 500 mL (about 16 oz) of fluid 2 hours before exercise and an additional 200 to 300 mL (7 to 10 oz) within 20 minutes before exercise. There is no need to drink large volumes of fluid before exercise. In fact, doing so can lead to gastrointestinal discomfort and an increased risk of hyponatremia, a dangerously low blood sodium level that can be prompted by excessive fluid intake.

There is currently no recommendation regarding electrolyte intake before physical activity, although some football players, tennis players, endurance athletes, and workers have learned to stave off muscle cramps and reduce the risk of hyponatremia by consuming salty food or drink prior to exercise. Individuals who excrete large volumes of salty sweat (skin and clothing caked in the white residue of salt after exercise) are advised to take steps to assure adequate salt intake throughout the day (32). Some endurance athletes rely on salt tablets to help assure adequate sodium replacement during long training sessions and competition. If used judiciously and taken with ample fluid, salt tablets can be an acceptable way to replace sodium. However, the risk is that insufficient fluid is ingested with the tablets. This would cause a concentrated saline solution to be introduced into the small intestine and that would cause water to pass from the bloodstream into the intestinal lumen to dilute the saline. To prevent such an occurrence, a tablet that contains 180 mg sodium should be consumed with at least 8 oz (240 mL) of water or sports drink. Salty foods such as pretzels, tomato juice, and soup can also serve as additional sources of sodium.

Fluid and Electrolyte Replacement During Exercise

Recent research has shown that cardiovascular, thermoregulatory, and performance responses are optimized by replacing sweat loss during exercise (see Table 6.4) (7,41,42). These and many other research findings are reflected in the various recommendations for fluid and electrolyte intake during exercise.

TABLE 6.4 Beneficial Responses to Adequate Fluid Intake During Exercise

Characteristic	Response
Heart rate	Lower
Stroke volume	Higher
Cardiac output	Higher
Skin blood flow	Higher
Core temperature	Lower
Perceived exertion	Lower
Performance	Better

Source: Data are from references 7 and 42.

For example, the American College of Sports Medicine recommends: "During exercise, athletes should start drinking early and at regular intervals in an attempt to consume fluids at a rate sufficient to replace all the water lost through sweating, or consume the maximal amount that can be tolerated" (9). This recommendation clearly states that the goal of fluid intake during exercise is to prevent dehydration, but recognizes that goal might be difficult to attain under some circumstances. In many instances, voluntary fluid intake alone will be insufficient to fully replace sweat loss during physical activity. For that reason, it is essential that athletes and workers who sweat profusely follow a prescribed regimen to guide the frequency and volume of their fluid intake. Under ideal circumstances, this requires that each individual's sweat rate is known. Sweat rate is easily assessed by recording body weight before and after activity: weight loss indicates inadequate drinking, while weight gain indicates excessive drinking (see Figure 6.1) (43). Also under ideal circumstances, specific individual recommendations are made regarding fluid intake during activity (see Figure 6.2; Box 6.1). Beginning activity with a comfortable volume of fluid already in the stomach, followed by additional fluid intake at 10- to 30-minute intervals (depending on sweat rate), will help assure a rapid gastric emptying rate by maintaining a large gastric volume, an important driver of gastric emptying (44).

Why is thirst an imprecise regulator of fluid needs during exercise? There are at least three reasons. The first is that there are usually many distractions during physical activity, so thirst signals can easily be missed or disregarded. The second reason is that fluid is often not readily available, so even if thirst is perceived, it might not be convenient to act on it. The third reason is rooted in the physiology of the thirst mechanism. Consider that the plasma osmolality of a well-hydrated (euhydrated) person is 285 mOsm/kg (some would argue that 280 mOsm/kg is the correct value, but for this example, we will use 285). The thirst threshold is the plasma osmolality above which thirst is triggered and this is thought to be 293 mOsm/kg (this varies among people, but usually falls within 290 to 295 mOsm/kg). A simple calculation using total body water (TBW) shows the amount of fluid that has to be lost from the body before thirst is stimulated: $TBW - [(TBW \times 285)/293]$. For example, if TBW is 36 liters (as it would be for a 60-kg [132-lb] person), then 1 liter of water must first be lost from the body for thirst to be initiated: $36 - [(36 \times 285)/293] = 1$ liter. This is the scientific rationale for the admonition that by the time thirst is perceived, some dehydration has already occurred.

Not surprisingly, most humans prefer—and drink more of—beverages that are flavored and sweetened (41). This is an important consideration in preventing dehydration because any step that can be taken to increase voluntary fluid intake will help reduce the risk of health problems associated with dehydration and heat stress. In addition to having palatable beverages available for athletes to drink (45), it is also important for athletes to record body weights before and after vigorous physical activity as a way to assess the effectiveness of fluid intake and as a reminder of the importance of drinking adequate amounts (46).

When performance is a key consideration in a workout or competition, a sport drink has documented advantages over plain water. Carbohydrate is an important component of a fluid-replacement beverage because it improves palatability by conferring sweetness, provides a source of fuel for active muscles, and stimulates fluid absorption from the intestine (28). The performance benefits of carbohydrate feeding during physical activity are covered in more detail in other chapters. Although it is clear that carbohydrate feeding benefits performance (2,10,16,30), more carbohydrate in a beverage is not necessarily better.

FIGURE 6.1. Calculating sweat rates. Reproduced with permission from Murray R. Fluid replacement: the American College of Sports Medicine position stand. *Sports Sci Exch* 1996;9(63):6.

Drinking fluid during exercise to keep pace with sweat loss goes a long way toward helping fitness enthusiasts, athletes, and workers feel good and work hard. Because sweat rates can vary widely, it is important to be aware of how much sweat is lost during physical activity. Knowing how much fluid is typically lost through an hour of activity becomes a goal for fluid replacement. Here are some simple steps to take to determine hourly sweat rate. In the example given below, Kelly K. should drink about 1 liter (32 oz) of fluid during each hour of activity to remain well hydrated.

A	B	C	D	E	F	G	H	I	J
		Body Weight							
Name	**Date**	**Before Exercise**	**After Exercise**	**Δ BW** (C − D)	**Drink Volume**	**Urine Volume***	**Sweat Loss** (E + F − G)	**Exercise Time**	**Sweat Rate** (H/I)
Kelly K.	9/15	61.7 kg	60.3 kg	1400 g	420 mL	90 mL	1730 mL	90 min	19 mL/min
		(lb/2.2)	(lb/2.2)	(kg × 1000)	(oz × 30)	(oz × 30)	(oz × 30)	1.5 h	1153 mL/h
		kg	kg	g	mL	mL	mL	min	mL/min
		(lb/2.2)	(lb/2.2)	(kg × 1000)	(oz × 30)	(oz × 30)	(oz × 30)	h	mL/h
		kg	kg	g	mL	mL	mL	min	mL/min
		(lb/2.2)	(lb/2.2)	(kg × 1000)	(oz × 30)	(oz × 30)	(oz × 30)	h	mL/h
		kg	kg	g	mL	mL	mL	min	mL/min
		(lb/2.2)	(lb/2.2)	(kg × 1000)	(oz × 30)	(oz × 30)	(oz × 30)	h	mL/h

Abbreviation: Δ BW, change in body weight.

*Weight of urine should be subtracted *if urine was excreted prior to postexercise body weight.*

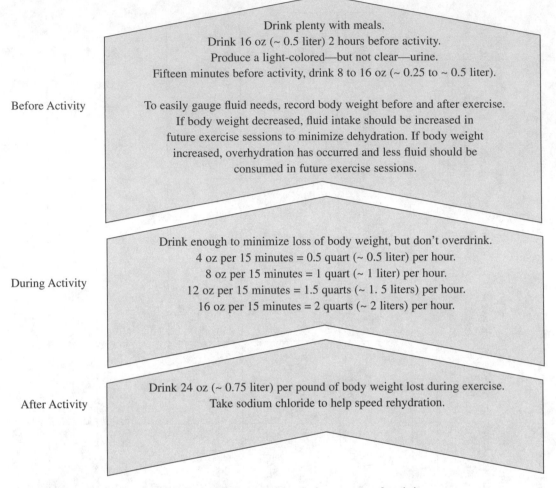

FIGURE 6.2.   Recommendations for fluid intake during stages of activity.

Research has demonstrated that ingesting drinks containing more than 14 g carbohydrate per 8-ounce serving (ie, a 6% carbohydrate solution) will decrease the rate of gastric emptying (47) and fluid absorption (48).

Table 6.3 includes recommendations about sodium intake during exercise as a way to improve beverage palatability, promote rehydration, and reduce the risk of hyponatremia and severe muscle cramps. Electrolyte intake becomes important whenever sweat loss is high (eg, more than 4 liters/day), as commonly occurs during two-a-day practices and prolonged training and competition. Sweat contains more sodium and chloride than other minerals and although sodium content of sweat is normally substantially less than the plasma value (plasma = 138 to 142 mmol/liter; sweat = 20 to 80 mmol/liter), large sweat losses can result in considerable salt loss (refer to Table 6.2). Normally, sodium deficits are uncommon among athletes and military personnel (49), in large part because a normal diet often provides more than enough salt to replace that lost in sweat.

However, persistent sodium losses can present problems, as illustrated by Bergeron (50) in a case study of a nationally ranked tennis player who suffered from frequent muscle cramps. A high sweat rate (2.5 liters/hour) coupled with a higher-than-normal sweat

Box 6.1   Tips for Encouraging Drinking Before, During, and Following Physical Activity

- Take fluid with you. Wear a bottle belt or fluid pack; take along a cooler full of drinks.
- Know the warning signs of dehydration (unusual fatigue, lightheadedness, headache, dark urine, dry mouth).
- Know where to find fluid (water fountains, stores, etc).
- Drink early and often, but don't overdrink.
- Keep a comfortably full stomach during activity.
- Better hydration means better performance.
- One medium mouthful of fluid = about 1 oz.
- Practice drinking during training.
- Stop to drink if that's what it takes to assure adequate intake. You will more than make up the time by staying well-hydrated.
- Grab 2 cups of fluid at each aid station.
- During a road race, pinch the top of the drink cup to form a spout that will make drinking easier.
- Always carry money to buy drinks.
- Put more in your stomach than on your head. Pouring water over your head does *nothing* to lower body temperature.
- Freeze fluid bottles overnight to allow the drink to stay cold longer.
- Complete rehydration requires full replacement of fluid *and* sodium losses.
- Have a variety of beverage flavors to choose from.
- Chart your body weight before and after activity.
- Drink by schedule—not by thirst.
- Prehydrate to produce a light-colored urine.
- Plan for fluid intake during competition.
- Train yourself to drink more during exercise.
- Start activity with a belly full of fluid.
- You can carry fluid with you during a road race by folding the top of the cup over, keeping the fluid from spilling over.
- After activity, drink 24 oz for every pound of weight lost during activity.

Box 6.2   Tips to Encourage Fluid Intake

- Educate coaches, trainers, supervisors, parents, and athletes about the benefits of proper hydration.
- Create educational posters, flyers, brochures, or presentations.
- Have palatable fluids readily available.
- Establish individualized fluid replacement regimens.
- Compare pre- and post-exercise weights.

sodium concentration (90 mmol/liter) predisposed the player to severe cramping. The cramps were eliminated when the player increased his daily dietary intake of sodium chloride from less than10 g/day to 15 to 20 g/day, relied on a sport drink during practices and games, and increased his daily fluid intake to assure adequate hydration.

It is also important to understand that ingesting sodium chloride in a beverage consumed during physical activity not only helps ensure adequate fluid intake (51) but also stimulates more complete rehydration after activity (52). Both of these responses reflect the critical role that sodium plays in maintaining the osmotic drive to drink and in providing an osmotic stimulus to retain fluid in the extracellular space (ie, in the plasma and interstitial fluid compartments).

The sodium content of a fluid-replacement beverage does not directly affect the rate of fluid absorption (53). This is because the amount of sodium that can be included in a beverage is small compared with the amount of sodium that can be provided from the bloodstream. Whenever fluid is ingested, sodium diffuses from plasma into the gut, driven by an osmotic gradient that strongly favors sodium influx. In brief, sodium chloride is an important constituent of a properly formulated sport drink because it improves beverage palatability, helps maintain the osmotic drive for drinking, reduces the amount of sodium that the blood has to supply to the intestine prior to fluid absorption, helps maintain plasma volume during exercise, and serves as the primary osmotic impetus for restoring extracellular fluid volume after exercise (51,52,54).

A good example of the effect that beverage composition has on voluntary fluid intake is demonstrated by the work of Wilk and Bar-Or (55). Preadolescent boys (ages 9 to 12 years) completed 3 hours of intermittent exercise in the heat, during which time they could drink one of three beverages ad libitum. The boys completed this protocol on three occasions. The beverages tested included water, a sport drink, and a placebo (a flavored, artificially sweetened replica of the sport drink). The boys drank almost twice as much sport drink as they did water, whereas consumption of the placebo fell in between. Flavoring and sweetness increased voluntary fluid intake (more intake with placebo vs water), and the presence of sodium chloride in the sport drink further increased consumption (ie, the subjects drank more sport drink than placebo).

These results are consistent with the physiology of the thirst mechanism. In humans the sensation of thirst is a function of changes in plasma sodium concentration (plasma osmolality) and of changes in blood volume (30). Drinking plain water removes the osmotic drive to drink (by quickly diluting the sodium concentration of the blood) and reduces the volume-dependent drive (by partially restoring blood volume), causing the premature satiation of thirst. Unfortunately, the resulting decrease in fluid intake occurs before adequate fluid has been ingested. As the Wilk and Bar-Or research demonstrated, the osmotic drive for drinking can be maintained by the presence of low levels of sodium chloride in a beverage, resulting in greater fluid intake (55). This application of basic physiology is nothing new. For centuries, bartenders have known that salty foods and snacks help sustain fluid intake among their patrons.

Some individuals mistakenly interpret the current recommendations for fluid intake to mean that dehydration is to be avoided at all costs and that there is no such thing as drinking too much fluid. Unfortunately, this is not true. Excessive water intake, even at rest, can result in life-threatening hyponatremia. Ingesting too much water, beer, or other low-sodium fluid can quickly dilute the plasma sodium concentration. When this occurs, the osmotic balance across the blood-brain barrier is disrupted and water quickly enters the brain, causing swelling that can lead to seizures, coma, and even death (33). In similar fashion, excessive drinking during prolonged exercise can also result in hyponatremia. For that reason, physically active individuals should be counseled to limit their fluid intake to no more than is needed to minimize dehydration and to ingest sodium in food or drink during prolonged exercise (eg, > 2 hours) (see Box 6.3) (56).

Fluid and Electrolyte Replacement After Exercise

On those occasions when a fluid deficit (ie, dehydration) exists after physical activity, it is often important to rehydrate quickly. An afternoon of working in the yard, two-a-day football practices, a day-long sports tournament, and 8 hours of manual labor are all examples of activities in which dehydration (more precisely referred to in this instance as *hypohydration*) is likely. Fluid and electrolyte intake after physical activity is a critical factor in helping people recover quickly—both physically and mentally. Maughan et al (52) concluded that ingesting plain water is ineffective at restoring euhydration because water absorption causes plasma osmolality to decrease, suppressing thirst and increasing urine output. When sodium is provided in fluids or foods, the osmotic drive to drink is maintained (51,52,57), and urine production is decreased.

Plain water is a good thirst quencher, but not an effective rehydrator. Only when water is ingested in combination with foods that contain sodium, chloride, and other minerals will sufficient water be retained to promote complete rehydration. Low-fat foods and beverages containing ample sodium include tomato juice, baked potato chips, pretzels, pickles, and crackers. These can be consumed as snacks on days when large sweat sodium losses are expected.

Maughan et al (52) also emphasized the importance of ingesting fluid in excess of the deficit in body weight to account for obligatory urine losses. In other words, the advice normally given athletes—"drink a pint [454 mL] of fluid for every pound [454 g] of body weight deficit"—must be amended to "drink *at least* a pint of fluid for every pound of body weight deficit." More precise recommendations for how much fluid athletes should ingest to assure rapid and complete rehydration will evolve from future research; existing data indicate that ingestion of 150% of weight loss is required to achieve normal hydration within 6 hours after exercise (54).

Finally, when rapid rehydration is the goal, consumption of alcoholic beverages is contraindicated because of alcohol's diuretic properties. Caffeine is, by comparison, a much milder diuretic and in those who regularly ingest caffeine might not be much of a diuretic at all (25). The 2004 DRI recommendations conclude that, "While consumption of beverages containing caffeine and alcohol have been shown in some studies to have diuretic effects, available information indicates that this may be transient in nature, and that such beverages can contribute to total water intake and thus can be used in meeting recommendations for dietary intake of total water" (26). However, when rapid rehydration is required, athletes should rely on noncaffeinated and nonalcoholic beverages. Education efforts with athletes should reflect the fact that many individuals will choose to consume alcoholic and caffeinated beverages. For those who do drink coffee, colas, beer, and similar beverages, the best advice is to do so in moderation, avoiding such drinks prior to and in the first few hours following physical activity.

Box 6.3   Drinking Dos and Don'ts

Dehydration is the most common performance-sapping mistake, but it's also the most preventable. Here are some guidelines to help physically active people stay well-hydrated.

DO	DON'T
Do start exercise well-hydrated. • When heavy sweating is expected, drink 2–3 cups (475–700 mL; ~7 mL/kg body weight or ~1 oz/10 lb body weight) of fluid 2–3 hours before exercise to allow excess fluid to be lost as urine. About 30 minutes before exercise, drink 5–10 oz (150–300 mL; ~3–4 mL/kg body weight or ~0.6 oz/10 lb body weight). There is no benefit to hyperhydration, so don't drink excessively.	*Don't* rely solely on water. • Drinking only water keeps you from replacing the electrolytes lost in sweat and from ingesting performance-boosting carbohydrates that help you exercise longer and stronger. And excessive water drinking can lead to dangerous electrolyte disturbances.
Do weigh yourself. • The best way to determine if you'd had enough to drink during a workout is to check to see how much weight you've lost. Minimal weight loss (eg, < 1 lb; ~0.5 kg) means that you've done a good job staying hydrated. Remember that weight loss during an exercise session is water loss, not fat loss, and must be replaced.	*Don't* over-drink. • Water is definitely a good thing, but you *can* get too much of a good thing. Drinking large amounts of fluid is not only unnecessary, but can be downright dangerous. Bloated stomach, puffy fingers and ankles, a bad headache, and confusion are warning signs of hyponatremia.
Do drink during exercise. • Most athletes find it helpful to drink every 10 to 20 minutes during a workout. People who sweat heavily can benefit from drinking more often (eg, every 10 minutes) whereas individuals who sweat lightly should drink less often (every 20+ minutes).	*Don't* gain weight during exercise. • If you weigh more after exercise than you did before, that means that you drank more than you needed. Be sure to cut back the next time so that no weight is gained.
Do ingest sodium during exercise. • The best time to begin replacing the sodium lost in sweat is during exercise. That's one reason why a good sport drink is better than plain water. Sodium intake of 1 g per hour is recommended during prolonged exercise where heavy sweat loss is expected.	*Don't* restrict salt in your diet. • Ample salt (sodium chloride) in the diet is essential to replace the salt lost in sweat. Because athletes sweat a lot, their need for salt is often much more than for nonathletes.

continues

Box 6.3 **Drinking Dos and Don'ts** (continued)	
DO	**DON'T**
Do follow your own plan. • Everyone sweats differently, so every athlete should have a drinking plan tailored to his or her individual needs.	*Don't* use dehydration to lose weight. • Restricting fluid intake during exercise impairs performance and increases the risk of heat-related problems. Dehydration should be kept to a minimum by following an individualized fluid-replacement plan.
Do drink plenty during meals. • If you weren't able to drink enough during practice to keep from losing weight, be sure to drink enough before the next practice. Mealtime is the best time to do that because of the ease of drinking and the sodium that comes along with food. When rapid rehydration is required, drink 50% more than the existing fluid deficit. (eg, if a 2-lb [~1-kg] fluid deficit exists, drink 48 oz [1,500 mL] of fluid to get caught up).	*Don't* delay drinking during exercise. • Stick to a drinking schedule so that you avoid dehydration early in exercise. Once dehydrated, it's next to impossible to catch up to what your body needs because dehydration actually slows the speed at which fluid exits the stomach.

Source: Adapted with permission from Murray R, Stofan J, Eichner ER. Hyponatremia in athletes. *Sports Sci Exch.* 2003;16(1):1–6.

Fluid and Electrolyte Balance at Environmental Extremes

The environment has a major impact on fluid and electrolyte balance (58). Exposure to extreme heat, high humidity, prolonged cold, water immersion, altitude, and reduced gravity increases the need for water and electrolytes to match the increased losses that occur in those circumstances (59). For example, in extreme dry heat, combined water loss from sweating, respiration, and transcutaneous routes can increase water and salt needs to high levels, often exceeding 10 liters and 20 g, respectively. Although respiratory water loss is minimal during exposure to wet heat, sweating is profuse as the body struggles to lose heat through the evaporation of sweat from the skin. This can be particularly troublesome for unacclimatized individuals exposed to high humidity; the inability of the sweat glands to respond maximally to environmental heat and humidity imposes a limit on both thermal comfort and the physiological capacity to sustain even mild exercise. During physical activity in cold environments, respiratory water loss increases due to the low humidity and increased ventilatory rate, and it is also possible for sweat rates to exceed 1 liter/hour due to the warm, humid microenvironment created underneath the clothing. Being immersed in water increases urine production because the increase in plasma volume that accompanies immersion triggers high-pressure baroreceptors. Competitive swimmers can sweat during tough workouts whenever internal body temperature exceeds the sweat threshold. Physical activity at altitude provokes the same responses as does activity in the cold, with additional challenges to hydration posed by an altitude-induced reduction in food and fluid intake and increased urinary water and salt loss. Astronauts who spend days in zero-gravity conditions lose considerable water and salt as a result of the inevitable diuresis that occurs. All of these conditions promote fluid loss and increase the risk of dehydration.

Water is constantly lost from the body with each water-saturated breath, with the seeping of water through the skin, with the obligatory production of urine and feces, in substantial volumes in sweat, and, when ill, through emesis and diarrhea. Fortunately, the combination of thirst and spontaneous drinking does a good job of matching fluid intake to losses so that progressive, chronic dehydration is usually not an issue, even for the elderly. However, for any individual who sweats profusely day after day, adequate water and salt replacement can pose a considerable challenge that can only be met by following practical yet scientifically founded recommendations for fluid and electrolyte intake.

Summary

The human body relies on an adequate volume of body water for all physiological and biochemical processes, so it should be no surprise that dehydration can adversely affect the health and performance of athletes and nonathletes. For that reason, it is essential that physically active people ingest ample fluids throughout the day to replace what is lost in sweat and urine. Approximately two hours before a physical activity during which heavy sweating is expected, drink approximately 7 mL/kg body weight (~1 oz/10 lb body weight) of water or sport drink. During exercise, the goal is to drink enough to minimize weight loss (ie, minimize dehydration). Light sweaters require only modest volumes of fluid intake (eg, < 750 mL/hour [24 oz/hour]), whereas heavy sweaters may have to ingest in excess of 1.5 liters/hour (~50 oz/hour) to minimize dehydration. To fully restore hydration status after exercise, it is necessary to ingest 150% of the existing fluid deficit. For example, if the fluid deficit is 2 lb (0.9 kg), 48 oz (1.4 liters) of fluid should be consumed. For those who exercise only once per day, fluid deficits are usually corrected during the course of normal eating and drinking. Those who train more than once each day or who sweat throughout the day (eg, workers and soldiers) have to adopt a more aggressive fluid replacement plan, along with adequate salt intake, to avoid chronic dehydration.

References

1. Murray R. Nutrition for the marathon and other endurance sports: environmental stress and dehydration. *Med Sci Sports Exerc.* 1992;24(suppl):S319–S323.
2. Sawka MN. Body fluid responses and dehydration during exercise and heat stress. In: Pandolf KB, Sawka MN, Gonzalez RR, eds. *Human Performance Physiology and Environmental Medicine at Terrestrial Extremes.* Indianapolis, Ind: Benchmark Press; 1988:227–266.
3. Sawka MN, Pandolf KB. Effects of body water loss on physiological function and exercise performance. In: Gisolfi CV, Lamb DR, eds. *Perspectives in Exercise Science and Sports Medicine: Fluid Homeostasis During Exercise.* Indianapolis, Ind: Benchmark Press; 1990:1–38.
4. Sawka MN. Physiological consequences of dehydration: exercise performance and thermoregulation. *Med Sci Sports Exerc.* 1992;24:657–670.

5. Below PR, Coyle EF. Fluid and carbohydrate ingestion individually benefit intense exercise lasting one hour. *Med Sci Sports Exerc.* 1995;27:200–210.

6. Coyle EF, Montain SJ. Benefits of fluid replacement with carbohydrate during exercise. *Med Sci Sports Exerc.* 1992;24(suppl):S324–S330.

7. Montain SJ, Coyle EF. The influence of graded dehydration on hyperthermia and cardiovascular drift during exercise. *J Appl Physiol.* 1992;73:1340–1350.

8. American College of Sports Medicine. Position stand on the prevention of thermal injuries during distance running. *Med Sci Sports Exerc.* 1985;17:ix–xiv.

9. American College of Sports Medicine. Position stand on exercise and fluid replacement. *Med Sci Sports Exerc.* 1996;28:i–vii.

10. American College of Sports Medicine. Position stand on heat and cold illnesses during distance running. *Med Sci Sports Exerc.* 1996;38:i–x.

11. National Athletic Trainers' Association. Position statement: fluid replacement for athletes. *J Athl Train.* 2000;35:212–224.

12. American Academy of Pediatrics. Climatic heat stress and the exercising child and adolescent. *Pediatrics.* 2000;106:158–159.

13. American Dietetic Association. Position of the American Dietetic Association, Dietitians of Canada, and the American College of Sports Medicine: nutrition and athletic performance. *J Am Diet Assoc.* 2000;100:1543–1556.

14. Noakes T. Fluid replacement during marathon running. *Clin J Sports Med.* 2003;13:309–318.

15. Inter-Association Task Force. Exertional heat illness consensus statement. *NATA News.* 2003; 6:24–29.

16. Casa D. Proper hydration for distance running: identifying individual fluid needs. A USA Track and Field advisory. April 2003. Available at: http://www.usatf.org/groups/Coaches/library/hydration/ProperHydrationForDistanceRunning.pdf. Accessed November 3, 2004.

17. Coyle EF, Montain SJ. Carbohydrate and fluid ingestion during exercise: are there trade-offs? *Med Sci Sports Exerc.* 1992;24:671–678.

18. Gisolfi CV, Duchman SD. Guidelines for optimal replacement beverages for different athletic events. *Med Sci Sports Exerc.* 1992;24:679–687.

19. Greenleaf JE. Problem: thirst, drinking behavior, and involuntary dehydration. *Med Sci Sports Exerc.* 1992;24:645–656.

20. Phillips PA, Rolls BJ, Ledingham ML, Morton JJ. Body fluid changes, thirst and drinking in man during free access to water. *Physiol Behav.* 1984;33:357–363.

21. Wade CE, Freund BJ. Hormonal control of blood flow during and following exercise. In: Gisolfi CV, Lamb DR, eds. *Perspectives in Exercise Science and Sports Medicine: Fluid Homeostasis During Exercise.* Indianapolis, Ind: Benchmark Press; 1990:3:207–246.

22. Booth DA. Influences on human fluid consumption. In: Ramsay DJ, Booth DA, eds. *Thirst: Physiological and Psychological Aspects.* London, England: Springer-Verlag; 1991:56.

23. Valtin H. "Drink at least eight glasses of water a day?" Really? Is there scientific evidence for "8 x 8"? *Am J Physiol Regul Integr Comp Physiol.* 2002;283:R993–R1004.

24. Guyton AC, Hall JE. *Textbook of Medical Physiology.* 10th ed. Philadelphia, Pa: WB Saunders Co; 2000.

25. Grandjean AC, Reimers KJ, Buyckx ME. Hydration: issues for the 21st century. *Nutr Rev.* 2003;61:261–271.

26. Institute of Medicine. *Dietary Reference Intakes for Water, Potassium, Sodium, Chloride, and Sulfate.* Washington, DC: National Academies Press; 2004. Available at: http://www.nap.edu. Accessed February 18, 2005.

27. Ladell WS. Water and salt (sodium chloride) intakes. In: Edholm O, Bacharach A, eds. *The Physiology of Human Survival.* New York: Academic Press. 1965;235–299.

28. Maughan RJ, Shirreffs SM, Galloway DR, Leiper JB. Dehydration and fluid replacement in sport and exercise. *Sports Exerc Inj.* 1995;1:148–153.

29. Hoyt RW, Honig A. Environmental influences on body fluid balance during exercise: altitude. In: Buskirk ER, Puhl SM. *Body Fluid Balance.* Boca Raton, Fla: CRC Press; 1996;186.

30. Hubbard RW, Szlyk PC, Armstrong LE. Influence of thirst and fluid palatability on fluid ingestion during exercise. In: Gisolfi CV, Lamb DR, eds. *Perspectives in Exercise Science and Sports Medicine: Fluid Homeostasis During Exercise.* Vol 3. Indianapolis, Ind: Benchmark Press; 1990:39–96.

31. Bauman A. The epidemiology of heat stroke and associated thermoregulatory disorders. In: Sutton JR, Thompson MW, Torode ME, eds. *Exercise and Thermoregulation.* Sydney, Australia: University of Sydney; 1995:203–208.

32. Bergeron MF. Heat cramps: fluid and electrolyte challenges during tennis in the heat. *J Sci Med Sport.* 2003;6:19–27.

33. Montain SJ, Sawka MN, Wenger CB. Hyponatremia associated with exercise: risk factors and pathogenesis. *Exerc Sports Sci Rev.* 2001;3:113–117.

34. Riedesel ML, Allen DY, Peake GT, Al-Qattan K. Hyperhydration with glycerol solutions. *J Appl Physiol.* 1987;63:2262–2268.

35. Latzka WA, Sawka MN, Montain SJ, Skrinar GS, Fielding RA, Matott RP, Pandolf KB. Hyperhydration: tolerance and cardiovascular effects during uncompensable exercise-heat stress. *J Appl Physiol.* 1998;84:1858–1864.

36. Armstrong LE, Costill DL, Fink WJ. Influence of diuretic-induced dehydration on competitive running performance. *Med Sci Sports Exerc.* 1985;17:456–461.

37. Sawka MN, Francesconi RP, Young AJ, Pandolf KB. Influence of hydration level and body fluids on exercise performance in the heat. *JAMA.* 1984;252:1165–1169.

38. Rico-Sanz J, Frontera WA, Rivera MA, Rivera-Brown A, Mole PA, Meredith CN. Effects of hyperhydration on total body water, temperature regulation and performance of elite young soccer players in a warm climate. *Int J Sports Med.* 1995;17:85–91.

39. Murray R, Eddy DE, Paul GL, Seifert JG, Halaby GA. Physiological responses to glycerol ingestion during exercise. *J Appl Physiol.* 1991;71:144–149.

40. Freund BJ, Montain SJ, Young AJ, Sawka MN, DeLuca JP, Pandolf KB, Valeri CR. Glycerol hyperhydration: hormonal, renal, and vascular fluid responses. *J. Appl Physiol.* 1995;79:2069–2077.

41. Greenleaf JE, Castle BL. Exercise temperature regulation in man during hypohydration and hyperthermia. *J Appl Physiol.* 1971;30:847–853.

42. Walsh RM, Noakes TD, Hawley JA, Dennis SC. Impaired high-intensity cycling performance time at low levels of dehydration. *Int J Sports Med.* 1994;15:392–398.

43. Murray R. Fluid replacement: the American College of Sports Medicine position stand. *Sports Sci Exch.* 1996;9(63):6.

44. Maughan RJ. Gastric emptying during exercise. *Sports Sci Exch.* 1993;6(5):1–6.

45. Greenleaf JE. Environmental issues that influence intake of replacement beverages. In: Marriott BM, ed. *Fluid Replacement and Heat Stress.* Washington, DC: National Academy Press; 1991;XV:1–30.

46. Broad E. Fluid requirements of team sport players. *Sports Coach.* 1996(Summer):20–23.

47. Horswill CA. Effective fluid replacement. *Int J Sport Nutr.* 1988;8:175–195.

48. Ryan AJ, Lambert GP, Shi X, Chang RT, Summers RW, Gisolfi CV. Effect of hypohydration on gastric emptying and intestinal absorption during exercise. *J Appl Physiol.* 1998;84:1581–1588.

49. Armstrong LE, Costill DL, Fink WJ. Changes in body water and electrolytes during heat acclimation: effects of dietary sodium. *Aviat Space Environ Med.* 1987;58:143–148.

50. Bergeron MF. Heat cramps during tennis: a case report. *Int J Sport Nutr.* 1996;6:62–68.

51. Nose H, Mack GW, Shi X, Nadel ER. Role of osmolality and plasma volume during rehydration in humans. *J Appl Physiol.* 1988;65:325–331.

52. Maughan RJ, Shirreffs SM, Leiper JB. Rehydration and recovery after exercise. *Sport Sci Exch.* 1996;9(62):1–5.

53. Gisolfi CV, Summers RW, Schedl HP, Bleiler TL. Effect of sodium concentration in a carbohydrate-electrolyte solution on intestinal absorption. *Med Sci Sports Exerc.* 1995;27:1414–1420.

54. Shirreffs SM, Taylor AJ, Leiper JB, Maughan RJ. Post-exercise rehydration in man: effects of volume consumed and drink sodium content. *Med Sci Sports Exerc.* 1996;28:1260–1271.

55. Wilk B, Bar-Or O. Effect of drink flavor and NaCl on voluntary drinking and hydration in boys exercising in the heat. *J Appl Physiol.* 1996;80:1112–1117.

56. Murray R, Stofan J, Eichner ER. Hyponatremia in athletes. *Sports Sci Exch.* 2003;16(1):1–6.

57. Gonzalez-Alonso J, Heaps CL, Coyle EF. Rehydration after exercise with common beverages and water. *Int J Sports Med.* 1992;13:399–406.

58. Piantodosi CA. *The Biology of Human Survival.* New York, NY: Oxford University Press; 2003.

59. Shirreffs SM, Maughan RJ. Whole body sweat collection in humans: an improved method with preliminary data on electrolyte content. *J Appl Physiol.* 1997;82:336–341.

Chapter 7

DIETARY SUPPLEMENTS AND ERGOGENIC AIDS

Marie Dunford, PhD, RD, and Michael Smith, RD

Introduction

Athletes spend millions of dollars on dietary supplements each year for the purpose of improving performance or health. Although some dietary supplements may be beneficial, others may actually impair performance and health. Particularly important to trained athletes are those substances known as ergogenic aids. An ergogenic aid is any substance or strategy that improves athletic performance by improving the production of energy.

The legal definition for the term *dietary supplement* is as follows: "A dietary supplement is a vitamin, mineral, herb, botanical, amino acid, metabolite, constituent, extract, or a combination of any of these ingredients" (1). Such a broad definition puts supplements with different structures, functions, or safety profiles in the same category. Prior to the 1994 Dietary Supplement Health and Education Act (DSHEA), botanicals and herbals were considered neither food nor drugs, but DSHEA currently classifies them as dietary supplements (1).

In the United States, dietary supplements are regulated under DSHEA, which establishes legal definitions and label guidelines (1). The act does not ensure safety, effectiveness, or quality of dietary supplements. It is the responsibility of the consumer to understand and judge those attributes. It is critical for athletes, parents, coaches, trainers, sports dietitians, exercise physiologists, physicians, and anyone else involved in sports medicine to learn about dietary supplements and address this ever-changing aspect of athletics.

DSHEA establishes label guidelines. The Supplements Facts label uses a format similar to the Nutrition Facts label found on food. The label is an important source of information about suggested serving size, type, and quantity of ingredients and percent Daily Values (if established). Health claims, but not therapeutic claims, may also be found on the labels. Therapeutic claims involve the diagnosis, treatment, or prevention of disease. The Food and Drug Administration (FDA) requires the following statement to appear on the label: "This product is not intended to diagnose, treat, cure, or prevent any disease."

However, it is often difficult for consumers to understand the difference between health claims (eg, calcium builds strong bones) and therapeutic claims (eg, calcium restores lost bone).

The FDA Task Force on Consumer Health Information for Better Nutrition (2) proposes a new system for evaluating health claims. Using an evidence-based model, the strength of the scientific evidence is considered and grades of "A," "B," "C," or "D" are awarded. The highest grade, "A," is also known as an "unqualified" health claim. "A" indicates that a large number of rigorous scientific studies support the claim. "B," "C," and "D" are "qualified" health claims and carry disclaimers. "B" signifies that scientific evidence is good but not conclusive whereas "C" indicates that results are mixed and therefore inconclusive. "D" appears when there is little scientific evidence to support a label claim. The goal is to provide science-based health information to help consumers judge the effectiveness of dietary supplements.

Athletes use dietary supplements for a variety of reasons, including to improve performance, delay fatigue, change body composition, and improve health (3). Supplement use among athletes is high. It is estimated that approximately 60% of all elite athletes use one or more dietary supplements (4). Nearly 45% of collegiate athletes use dietary supplements, most often multivitamin/mineral supplements and creatine (5,6). Adolescent athletes, who are influenced by professional athletes, use supplements less often, but usage rates may be as high as 30% (7). Clearly, athletes are regular users of dietary supplements and they need up-to-date, reliable information.

The two critical questions regarding any supplement are always the same: is it safe and is it effective? In most cases, these questions are not easily answered "yes" or "no." Athletes may need more detailed information about safety and effectiveness and need to consider the risk-benefit ratio. It is imperative that consumers understand that safety, effectiveness, and potency of dietary supplements are not comparable to over-the-counter medications or prescription drugs.

The active ingredient(s) in a dietary supplement can vary tremendously, especially in herbal products. In 2000, before ephedrine-containing dietary supplements were banned by the FDA, Gurley et al (8) found that the ephedrine alkaloid content of half of the 20 dietary supplements studied varied by more than 20% when compared with the amount listed on the label. One product had no active ingredient, one contained more than 150%, and five contained norpseudoephedrine, a controlled substance (drug). Athletes need to be aware that dietary supplements sometimes contain banned substances, and athletes are subject to disqualification even if they were unaware that the supplement contained a banned substance.

Practitioners who simply dismiss the use of dietary supplements may lose credibility with athletes. When working with athletes, it is important to understand their goals. For elite athletes, competitions are won by slim margins, and dietary supplements could make a performance difference. Practitioners and athletes must seriously discuss if, and how much of, a supplement would be safe and effective. Athletes should be aware that a substance may be regulated or banned by a particular governing body. Advertisements often quote research studies, sometimes out of context, and the practitioner should explain to the athlete the physiological mechanisms, the effects of training, the potential side effects, and the conditions of use.

Recommendations should be evidence-based and consider each person's unique genetic profile as well as individual differences and preferences. It is the professional's role to provide as much unbiased information as possible to the athlete considering supplementation and it is appropriate to express concerns about safety. It is unethical to suggest that the information is unbiased if the athlete's supplement purchase would mean monetary gain for the person giving the information. In other words, anyone selling a supplement is not an unbiased source of information.

The use of dietary supplements is an ever-changing and ever-challenging aspect of sports nutrition. Sports dietitians should be open-minded skeptics. Safety and effectiveness are paramount. Dietary supplements must be considered in the context of dietary intake because some of the ingredients found in supplements are also found in food. However, many supplements, in particular herbals and botanicals, are not found in common foods. Education is key as athletes consider dietary supplement use in the broad context of their health and performance goals.

Commonly Used Supplements

The number of new products introduced to the market is dizzying. Sports dietitians must constantly update their knowledge base. Coverage of all of the available supplements would be impossible, but this chapter does cover those that athletes commonly use and ask about. They are listed here in alphabetical order.

Androstenedione

Androstenedione is an anabolic steroid used to increase blood testosterone. It received widespread media attention when professional baseball player Mark McGwire admitted use during his homerun record-setting season in 1998. This admission influenced use in others, including adolescents, and drove up the sale of androstenedione (9).

Androstenedione, androstenediol and, to a lesser extent, dehydroepiandrosterone (DHEA) are often referred to as *prohormones*. The human body potentially converts oral androstenedione into testosterone with the possible anabolic benefits of enhanced lean body mass and sexual performance (10), increased strength, altered mood, and decreased body fat (11).

One study showed that sublingual androstenedione supplementation increased free testosterone (12). This same trial also showed an increase in estradiol, a female sex hormone. Studies conducted with resistance-trained men over an 8-week period showed no effect on muscle size, strength, or body composition (13,14).

A 2001 study showed no acute adverse effects from androstenedione or androstenediol (15). Chronic use provokes concerns about an increase in estrogen, which can increase prostate cancer risk. Androstenedione may decrease high-density lipoprotein cholesterol, thus increasing risk of cardiovascular disease (11). The FDA, in a white paper released in March 2004, listed more than 25 potential androgenic and estrogenic effects (16). This review of the scientific literature prompted the FDA to crack down on dietary supplements containing androstenedione. Letters were sent to 23 companies that manufactured, marketed, or distributed androstenedione-containing dietary supplements, asking them to stop distributing such supplements. The FDA considers such supplements to be adulterated, and therefore illegal to market. Most sports governing bodies list androstenedione as a banned substance, including Major League Baseball.

Amino Acids

See Protein Supplements.

Antioxidants

See Multivitamin and Mineral Supplements.

Beta-Hydroxy-Beta-Methylbutyrate (HMB)

See HMB.

Branched-Chain Amino Acids (BCAA)

The branched-chain amino acids (BCAA), named for their chemical structure, are leucine, isoleucine, and valine. During prolonged endurance exercise when glycogen stores are low, skeletal muscle can metabolize these amino acids for energy. BCAA also compete with tryptophan, an amino acid associated with mental fatigue, and are involved in the immune system [17].

In theory, greater availability of BCAA late in prolonged exercise could provide a much needed fuel source. Higher blood levels of BCAA in the presence of tryptophan could help to delay fatigue. However, supplemental BCAA have not been shown to delay fatigue or improve endurance performance in elite athletes [17].

Although the trials are small, some positive effects have been reported in studies that examined immune response [18,19]. Immunosuppression in endurance-trained athletes, such as triathletes, may be a result of decreased glutamine levels. BCAA supplementation reverses the decline in glutamine because BCAA are metabolized to glutamine in skeletal muscle. The role BCAA supplements may play in supporting immune function is an active area of research. Supplemental BCAA, often consumed 5 to 20 g/day in divided doses, seems to be safe. (See also Glutamine section of this chapter.)

Caffeine

Caffeine is used as an ergogenic aid to improve endurance performance as well as to delay fatigue and enhance fat loss. There have been a considerable number of studies and review articles [20–22], and the consensus opinion is that caffeine may be an effective ergogenic aid. Contrary to what was believed in the past, although caffeine may enhance free fatty acid mobilization during endurance exercise, fat oxidation is not significantly increased, nor is muscle glycogen spared. The ergogenic benefit of caffeine use may be more closely related to its role as a central nervous system stimulant resulting in a heightened sense of awareness and a decreased perception of effort.

Some strength athletes use caffeine for the purpose of activating muscle fibers. Caffeine may have an effect on recruitment of muscle for exercise by reducing the motor unit recruitment threshold and enhancing nerve conduction velocity. It may also have a direct effect on muscle by altering calcium release kinetics by the sarcoplasmic reticulum.

Although caffeine is touted as a "fat burner," there is no evidence to support that caffeine alone has a significant effect on fat or weight loss. Caffeine does potentiate the effect of ephedrine, which is used for weight loss. More information about caffeine and ephedrine together is found under the Ephedra section.

To achieve the desired ergogenic effect, users must have a significant amount of caffeine in their blood. An effective dose for endurance athletes seems to be 5 to 6 mg/kg body weight. For the 110-pound (50-kg) person, the recommended dose would be 250 to 300 mg caffeine. This amount of caffeine could be consumed in a variety of ways, including the consumption of strongly brewed coffee (8 oz = 85 mg), caffeine-containing soft drinks (12 oz = 36 mg), or caffeine-containing pills (1 tablet = 100 mg). The latter are used because they contain a standardized concentrated dose.

Caffeine is legally and socially acceptable throughout the world, but at certain levels is considered a controlled/restricted substance. For a National Collegiate Athletic Association (NCAA) athlete, urinary caffeine levels exceeding 15µg/mL would subject the athlete to disqualification. Such levels would be very difficult to reach via food intake (ie, the equivalent of 17 caffeine-containing soft drinks) and the equivalent amount of caffeine-containing tablets would likely impair performance in other ways (ie, shaking, rapid heartbeat, etc). However, some athletes have achieved this level and were disqualified. The International Olympic Committee (IOC) moved caffeine from its Prohibited List to its Monitoring Programme in 2004. This allows athletes to take common cold remedies containing caffeine and drink caffeinated drinks without risk of disqualification. The IOC will monitor this change to determine its effects.

Caffeine is considered safe to use by most adults although it is has several known adverse effects. Blood pressure is increased both at rest and during exercise, heart rate is increased, gastrointestinal distress can occur, and insomnia may result. The adverse effects are more likely to occur in those people who are caffeine-naïve. For routine users, caffeine is addictive and sudden withdrawal results in severe headaches. Caffeine does not seem to cause dehydration or electrolyte imbalance (23).

Carnitine

Carnitine is essential in the human body to transport fatty acids into the mitochondria to be used for energy. It is found in the diet and can be synthesized in the body from the amino acid lysine. Deficiencies have been seen, but typically not in healthy adults (24). Because carnitine is used in fat oxidation, claims for supplemental carnitine include decreased muscle pain and increased weight loss, endurance, cardiovascular function, and strength.

Carnitine supplementation is known to normalize long-chain fatty acid metabolism in carnitine-deficient individuals (25), but the benefits to healthy people are questionable. A study of 36 overweight women supplementing with carnitine combined with regular exercise showed no difference in weight loss or endurance (26). Two studies with healthy subjects concluded that carnitine supplementation increased fat oxidation (25,27). Increased fat oxidation always raises questions about a potential role as a fat loss agent, but more studies are needed. A study of 10 healthy active men supplementing carnitine for 3 weeks showed significant improvement in recovery from high-repetition squat exercises (28).

Carnitine is sold in pill or liquid form. Most study protocols use an oral dose of 2 to 4 g/day (25–29), which is the typical recommended dose by manufacturers. Carnitine supplementation seems to be safe at recommended doses. At the present time, studies are mixed, with some showing promise and others showing no effect.

Chondroitin Sulfate

See Glucosamine/Chondroitin Sulfate.

Chromium (Chromium Picolinate)

Chromium is an essential mineral that augments the action of insulin. It seems to enhance insulin sensitivity by increasing the number of insulin receptors, thus improving glucose utilization (30). Enhanced insulin sensitivity could also promote the uptake of amino acids into muscle cells and stimulate protein synthesis. These biological functions make chromium supplements attractive to athletes who want to increase muscle mass and decrease body fat.

Chromium is found in a variety of foods, such as beef, poultry, eggs, nuts, whole grains, and wheat germ. The Dietary Reference Intake (DRI) for adults ranges from 20 to 35 µg/day, depending on age and gender. Mean daily dietary intake by adults is approximately 25 µg for females and 33 µg for males. Athletes who consume sufficient energy and a variety of foods would not likely be deficient. No Tolerable Upper Intake Level (UL) has been established (31).

Chromium is a popular supplement and is usually found as chromium picolinate. The picolinate makes the compound extremely stable and this stability results in much greater gastrointestinal absorption of supplemental chromium than food-based chromium (32). There is concern that chromium picolinate supplements can result in an increase in free radical production and other forms, such as chromium chloride, are now becoming more popular (33). Chromium supplementation of 50 to 200 µg/day seems to be safe. Higher intakes may decrease iron absorption. Accumulated chromium in the body can damage DNA (34).

Supplemental chromium's initial popularity was based on animal and initial human studies that reported an increase in muscle mass and a decrease in body fat. The changes were statistically significant but considered small: approximately 1.8-kg (4-lb) increase in muscle mass and approximately 3.4-kg (7.5-lb) decrease in body fat. Later studies, with stricter methodology including better measurements of body composition, did not replicate the initial results (35,36). Most studies use 200 to 400 µg supplemental chromium per day.

Supplemental chromium is also advertised as a weight loss aid for obese individuals. Volpe et al (37) found no change in body composition or resting metabolic rate in moderately obese women who consumed 400 µg chromium picolinate per day and participated in a 3-month exercise program. A meta-analysis of randomized, double-blind, placebo-controlled studies of body weight found that chromium picolinate supplements produced a small effect on weight loss, with questionable clinical significance (38). At the present time, the evidence does not support the effectiveness of chromium supplements for increasing muscle mass or reducing body fat in a meaningful way. The potential to cause oxidative damage is a risk associated with chromium picolinate supplementation.

Conjugated linoleic acid

Conjugated linoleic acid (CLA) is an isomer of the essential fatty acid linoleic acid (39) and part of a group of polyunsaturated fatty acids found in lamb, beef, and dairy products (40). Claims for supplemental CLA include weight loss, fat loss, gains in muscle mass and strength, and improved health related to heart disease and other chronic diseases.

Studies in animals have shown CLA to be beneficial in decreasing body fat, carcinogenesis, atherosclerosis, and catabolism while improving lipoprotein metabolism, insulin sensitivity, bone density, and immunity (40–44). Studies in humans show mixed results. It seems that the effect of CLA in humans is less than that seen in studies of mice (45).

Significant positive results of CLA supplementation in humans include decreased body fat (46,47), improvement of triglycerides and very-low-density lipoprotein cholesterol (39), and an increased resting metabolic rate (48). One of the studies reporting a decrease in body fat consisted of healthy subjects exercising 90 minutes, 3 days per week (47).

However, several studies (41–44,49) showed no improvements, including a 28-day study that included 23 resistance-trained men. No significant changes in the following were shown: body weight, body mass index (BMI), lipoprotein concentrations, insulin sensitivity, blood glucose, fatty acid and glycerol metabolism, immunity, appetite, fat-free mass, fat mass, percent body fat, energy expenditure, fat oxidation, bone mass, strength, or catabolism.

The typical dose administered in these studies was 3 to 4 g CLA per day, usually taken in three divided doses with meals (39,41–49). These studies were done over a 4- to 8-week period and no long-term studies have been reported. Although some studies have shown CLA supplementation to be beneficial in humans, more research is needed. There have not been any studies reporting adverse effects of CLA supplementation.

Creatine

Creatine is a nitrogen-containing compound found in meat and fish in small amounts. It is used in the body as a source of muscle energy in the form of phosphocreatine. Supplemental creatine may increase storage of phosphocreatine, regulate phosphocreatine increases during exercise, and increase ATP production secondary to increased hydrogen ion buffering (50). The potential ergogenic effect of creatine supplementation may be increased strength, endurance, and muscle gains.

Creatine is the most widely used nutritional supplement among athletes, including adolescents (5–7,51). It is sold in powder, pill, and liquid forms and in protein bars. A survey of more than 1,000 high school football players showed that 30% of 12th graders used creatine. The greatest perceived benefit among this group was enhanced recovery (7). A survey of 10 to 18 year olds showed that 8.8% of boys use creatine to increase athletic performance and improve appearance (52). It is important to note that creatine studies are conducted in adults and the safety and efficacy in children and adolescents is not known.

There is a large body of scientific research reporting the effects of creatine supplementation in active people. Positive results include increased body mass (53–56), increased lean mass (53,55–58), strength gains (51,53,55,57–62), enhanced recovery, and increased endurance (53,55–57). A meta-analysis (53) and a review by Volek and Rawson (63) help form a broad picture of the effects of creatine.

Branch (53) conducted a meta-analysis of 100 studies published in peer-reviewed journals. With short-term creatine supplementation, there is a small but significant increase in lean body mass with repeated high-intensity, short-duration (< 30 seconds) exercise bouts. Creatine supplementation may help the athlete maintain or sustain force output for a longer period of time, thus completing more repetitions. One explanation for creatine's effects is that such an extra training stimulus over time may lead to greater strength or power gains. The evidence does not support a positive effect of creatine on running or swimming performance.

Volek and Rawson (63) report that most studies of creatine show an ergogenic effect for a variety of athletes and a performance effect for weight lifters. The studies are generally conducted under laboratory conditions so it is debatable if the ergogenic effect results in increased performance for most athletes. In the case of runners, the weight gain that accompanies creatine supplementation could have a detrimental effect on performance.

Creatine supplementation, which increases intracellular water in the muscle, seems to stimulate muscle glycogen, thus enhancing glycogen storage. Increases in intracellular water also influence protein metabolism. More studies are needed to determine if creatine supplementation has a direct effect on muscle protein synthesis or breakdown (63).

The safety of creatine supplementation has been debated, but research suggests that creatine supplementation is safe. Although widely reported in the press that creatine supplementation results in dehydration, there are no scientific studies to support that statement. Studies show no adverse effects in any areas including renal and hepatic function, hormone levels, lipids, or sperm count and mobility (64–67). A study of 23 NCAA Division II football players found no long-term detrimental effects on kidney or liver function (65).

Supplemental creatine is consumed as creatine monohydrate. The usual dose is 3 to 5 g/day. Some athletes use a short-term loading period—up to 20 to 25 g/day for 5 to 7 days—but the initial "loading" dose has not been shown to be more beneficial. The typical dose in research studies is about 20 g/day for the first 5 days, and 5 to 10 g/day thereafter. Some complaints of minor side effects such as gastrointestinal disturbances and cramps have been reported (67,68).

Whereas some athletes respond to creatine supplements with significant increases in muscle creatine levels, others are nonresponders. This is likely explained by the amount of creatine in the muscle prior to supplementation. Insulin is known to play a role in creatine transport into muscle. More research is needed to determine whether carbohydrate and/or protein intake could influence creatine uptake in skeletal muscle (63).

Dehydroepiandrosterone

Dehydroepiandrosterone (DHEA) is a precursor to testosterone and estrogen but it is considered a weak androgen (69). The biochemical link to testosterone has made it a popular prohormone among athletes. The hope is that the prohormones—androstenedione, androstenediol, and DHEA—will elevate blood testosterone levels, which in turn will increase muscle mass. Masters' athletes have expressed an interest in DHEA because it diminishes substantially with age; in fact, it is one of the steepest hormonal decreases in humans (70). DHEA supplements are often advertised as being "a fountain of youth."

Studies suggest there is no evidence that DHEA, the weakest of the three androgens, has an anabolic effect or can enhance athletic performance (71). Its specific biological role in older adults has not yet been determined. The decrease in DHEA is probably due to a decrease in the number of cells that produce it and supplementation in older adults does increase blood DHEA concentrations. The effect of such supplementation on older adults and masters athletes is not known because of a lack of controlled clinical trials (68).

Issues of safety have been discussed. Before the passage of the Dietary Health and Supplement Education Act in 1994, DHEA was a prescription drug. In the United States, it is now available over the counter and in dietary supplements; in other countries it remains a controlled substance due to abuse potential. The effects of high doses or long-term use are not known. Because of its unknown safety profile and lack of proven effectiveness, DHEA supplementation for athletes is not recommended at this time (70).

Dihydroxyacetone (DHA)

See Pyruvate and Dihydroxyacetone (DHA).

Ephedra (Ephedrine-Containing Supplements)

No dietary supplement has been as controversial as ephedra. In April 2004, the FDA banned sales of dietary supplements containing ephedra. This ban was based on the FDA ruling that dietary supplements containing ephedrine alkaloids present an unreasonable risk of illness or injury (72). In April 2005, a federal judge struck down the ban, but the court's order only applied to low-dose (10 mg or less) ephedra-containing supplements. The FDA has appealed the decision. The ban remains in place for any higher dose dietary supplements. States (eg, California, Illinois) may ban the sale of ephedra-containing supplements. These state laws are not affected by the federal court's 2005 decision. Ephedrine is also found in over-the-counter medications. These products are not affected by the FDA ban.

Even the terminology has caused confusion. *Ephedra, ephedrine alkaloids,* and *ephedrine* are different terms, although they are frequently used interchangeably. Scientifically, *ephedra* refers to a genus of plants. Some species in this genus contain *ephedrine alkaloids* in the stems and branches. One of the ephedrine alkaloids is *ephedrine.* Although there is a scientific distinction, in common usage ephedra refers to any dietary supplement that contains ephedrine alkaloids.

Ma huang, a traditional Chinese herbal medicine, is extracted from the species *Ephedra sinica* Stapf and contains six different ephedrine alkaloids. Of the six, the main active ingredient is ephedrine. Ephedrine can also be synthesized in the laboratory. Ma huang has been used for centuries to treat asthma and nasal congestion. In the United States, ephedrine is added to over-the-counter medications for the same purposes. But ephedrine use in athletes has more often been related to weight loss, increased energy, and enhanced performance. So the critical questions are whether ephedrine-containing supplements are safe and effective for these purposes.

In some respects, ephedra is the poster child for the Dietary Supplement Health and Education Act (DSHEA) of 1994. At the time that the act was passed, many health professionals thought that herbal medicines, which prior to this act were considered neither a food nor drug, were inappropriately categorized as dietary supplements. Their concern was that some herbal products were being used as medications, and as such, dose was an important issue. The FDA shared these concerns.

What made the ephedra issue more contentious was that experts did not agree on what dose was safe. The FDA proposed that not more than 8 mg of ephedrine alkaloids be used in a 6-hour period *and* not more than 24 mg in a 24-hour period. Usage should not exceed 7 days (73). However, another group of scientists suggested that a single dose should not exceed 30 mg ephedrine alkaloids and that up to 90 mg in a 24-hour period is safe, and that usage should not exceed 6 months (74). Such differing dose recommendations make it confusing for both consumers and health professionals.

Within a few years after the passage of the DSHEA, the FDA became increasingly concerned about the safety of ephedrine. By 1997, half of the adverse event reports (AERs) that consumers telephoned in to a hotline involved ephedrine. The adverse events reported included known side effects such as headache, increased heart rate, increased blood pressure, and insomnia. The AERs also included deaths to otherwise healthy middle-aged and young adults, which alarmed the FDA.

The adverse events reports are hard to interpret. Data collected from self-reports lack scientific rigor. Many of the AERs do not contain information about dose, even though dose is a critical factor. Some consumers may have used these supplements despite the manufacturers' warnings. Most warn against use by those with a history of heart disease, diabetes, or high blood pressure, or by pregnant or lactating women.

The safety of ephedrine-containing dietary supplements has been hotly debated. Shekelle et al (75) reviewed 16,000 AERs and found that 21 were serious events: two deaths, nine strokes, four heart attacks, one seizure, and five psychiatric problems. In these cases, ephedrine was believed to be the sole contributor, but there was not enough evidence to establish a cause and effect relationship. In addition to the 21 serious adverse effects, 10 other cases involved ephedrine as a contributing (but not sole) factor. Based on this and other evidence, the FDA concluded that ephedrine-containing dietary supplements presented an unreasonable safety risk.

"Significant or unreasonable risk of illness or injury" (72) is the basis for the ban on ephedrine-containing dietary supplements. Proponents of the ban point to documented deaths and serious cardiovascular and psychiatric events. They believe that the risk-benefit ratio meets the "unreasonable risk" portion of the FDA criterion. Opponents of the ban counter that the risk is very small. The federal court's 2005 decision to overturn the ban was based on the fact that the FDA did not have sufficient scientific evidence to show that a daily dose of 10 mg or less presented an unreasonable risk. In 1999, approximately 3 million people purchased ephedrine-containing dietary supplements and consumed an estimated 3 billion "servings." The risk of a serious adverse event is estimated to be less than 1 in 1,000 and opponents point out that a cause-and-effect relationship has not been established. They argue that the deaths, while tragic, do not represent a significant risk (76).

Of particular importance to athletes is the risk associated with using ephedrine before strenuous workouts in the heat. In 2001 the National Football League (NFL) banned ephedra after the death of lineman Korey Stringer, who collapsed and died from heatstroke. Practice was held in hot and humid conditions (approximating 110°F on the heat index) and his body temperature upon hospital admission was reported to have been 108.8°F. Toxicological tests were not conducted on autopsy, but an ephedrine-containing dietary supplement was found in his locker.

In 2003, major league pitching prospect Steve Bechler, age 23, also suffered heatstroke while training in hot and humid conditions. His body temperature rose to 108°F. In this case, the coroner cited the use of ephedrine as a cause of death. In Belcher's case, there seems to have been several contributing circumstances, including a history of borderline hypertension and liver abnormalities and a restriction of both food and fluid in the previous 24 hours in an effort to lose weight.

Another safety issue is quality control. In 2000, Gurley et al (8) published a study of the ephedrine alkaloid content of 20 dietary supplements. The content of 10 of the products varied by more than 20% when compared with the amount listed on the label. One product contained more than 150% of the amount listed on the label and one had no active ingredient. Five contained norpseudoephedrine, a controlled substance (drug). "Spiked" products are especially problematic because most athletes are subject to testing for banned substances (77).

In addition to safety, effectiveness must be considered. Regarding weight loss, most study protocols use ephedrine and caffeine in combination because caffeine is known to enhance the effect of ephedrine. Studies report that the use of ephedrine and caffeine by obese people can produce a short-term weight loss of 8 to 9 pounds. Studies to date have not been conducted for longer than 6 months, so it is unknown what the long-term effect might be or the effect of discontinuing the ephedrine and caffeine. It is also not known if an ephedrine-induced short-term weight loss has long-term health benefits (75).

Most athletes are not obese, but they may use ephedrine-containing dietary supplements before and during training camp to lose weight that was gained in the off-season. There have been no studies to date in athletes who use this combination for short-term weight loss.

Results of studies using ephedrine and caffeine as a performance enhancer have been mixed (75,78–83). In two trials using cycle ergometers (78,79), ephedrine and caffeine significantly increased time to exhaustion. Military subjects ran 3.2 km with 11 kg of gear, and individuals in the ephedrine-caffeine trial recorded faster times than those in the control group (80). No effect of ephedrine and caffeine was reported in a trial of treadmill walking (81). In a study of 13 weight-trained males, ephedrine increased the number of repetitions completed in the first set of circuit training but not subsequent sets. The effect seems to be a result of the ephedrine, not the caffeine (82). More research is needed to clearly determine the role that ephedrine and caffeine play in enhancing anaerobic and aerobic performance.

Some athletes claim that ephedrine- and caffeine-containing dietary supplements give them "more energy." This is likely due to the stimulant effect of these compounds, which can mask fatigue. It is known that some brands are "spiked" with norpseudoephedrine and such drugs are stimulatory. With the current ban on high-dose ephedrine, there is concern that bitter orange (citrus aurantium) or similar compounds will become a substitute herbal stimulant source in some dietary supplements. Bitter orange contains synephrine, which is considered a drug (84).

Glucosamine/Chondroitin Sulfate

Glucosamine and chondroitin are sold as dietary supplements to reduce joint pain and improve function. They are used as an alternative therapy for osteoarthritis (OA). Glucosamine is an amino sugar that may help form and repair cartilage. Chondroitin is part of a protein that aids in elasticity of cartilage. The mechanism of action is unknown, but glucosamine and chondroitin may stimulate cartilage protein synthesis or inhibit breakdown. The body manufactures glucosamine and chondroitin and the amount produced is not associated with dietary intake (85).

Early studies were promising, but they were also controversial because they lacked scientific rigor. More recent studies of the efficacy of glucosamine and chondroitin are positive (86–90). One study found that 12 weeks of glucosamine provided pain relief and improved function in patients with prior cartilage injury and/or OA (86). A 3-year study showed that glucosamine improved joint structure and symptoms over placebo (87). This study compared glucosamine and ibuprofen, a nonsteroidal anti-inflammatory drug (NSAID) for treatment of joint pain. The authors concluded that glucosamine significantly decreased pain with fewer adverse effects than NSAIDs. In a 3-year study of post-menopausal women with OA of the knee, glucosamine supplements delayed the progression of the OA (90).

The typical recommended dose of glucosamine and chondroitin is the same as what has been used in studies—1,500 to 2,000 mg/day and 1,200 mg/day, respectively, for 6 to 8 weeks. It is recommended that they be used for a minimum of 6 to 8 weeks. However, if improvement does not occur after 8 weeks of continuous use, it is not likely it will help. Minimal adverse effects have been reported, especially compared with frequent use of NSAIDs. Chondroitin may act as a blood-thinning agent and should not be used in individuals already taking a blood-thinning medication (91).

Although glucosamine has also been theorized to increase blood sugar, a 2003 study showed that glucosamine supplementation had no effect on glucose metabolism in subjects with type 2 diabetes (92).

Glutamine

Glutamine is a nonessential amino acid under normal conditions, but a conditionally essential amino acid under physiological stress where glutamine is a fuel source for immune system cells. Plasma glutamine in endurance athletes can be decreased after strenuous exercise. Supplemental glutamine is theorized to be beneficial for decreasing exercise-induced stress (93).

Study results have been mixed and it is hard to draw conclusions at this time (94–99). Castell (94) reports a decrease in the incidence of infections in endurance athletes who supplement with glutamine. A review by Nieman (95) concluded that glutamine supplementation is not an effective countermeasure for immunologic stress, and Hiscock and Pedersen (98) indicate no role in decreasing exercise-induced immunosuppression.

Claims related to glutamine supplementation in weight training include improved recovery, decreased muscle catabolism, and muscle gain. Research studies have not been favorable to such claims. Four studies showed no changes in immune function (97), muscle performance, body composition, protein degradation (96), leg or bench press, or any weight-lifting performance (98,99).

Recommendations made by manufacturers range from 5 to 10 g/day to more than 20 g/day. Because glutamine is found in the amino acid profile of dietary proteins, no specific DRI or Recommended Dietary Allowance has been established. No studies have shown adverse effects of glutamine supplementation. It is known that some endurance athletes consume diets low or marginal in protein, and increasing protein intake, and therefore glutamine intake, would likely be beneficial. Claims have been made that glutamine supplements sold as peptides are better absorbed than free-form glutamine, but no studies to date support this claim.

HMB

Beta-hydroxy-beta-methylbutyrate (HMB) is a metabolite of the amino acid leucine. This branched-chain amino acid has been known to be anticatabolic in nature. Therefore, HMB is promoted to enhance lean body mass and to increase strength gains. Taken as a supplement, HMB theoretically minimizes the protein breakdown that follows intense exercise, but the mechanism by which it works is unknown (100).

The results of research studies have been mixed. A meta-analysis of hundreds of supplements showed that HMB is one of the few that confers benefits (57). Studies in support of supplemental HMB suggest that it significantly increases lean body mass (101–103) and strength (101,103,104) and minimizes muscle damage (104,105). Other studies have shown that HMB supplementation does not affect aerobic or anaerobic ability (106–108) or body composition (107,108). This includes a study of Oklahoma State University football players that combined strenuous exercise with 3 g HMB per day for 4 weeks. No significant changes in strength or body composition over placebo were observed (107). A 2004 study in elderly women showed positive effects in strength, functionality, body composition, and protein metabolism (109).

HMB supplements seem to be safe (110,111). Subjects who consumed 3 g HMB per day for 6 to 8 weeks showed no adverse effects on lipid profiles or hepatic, renal, or immune function. The recommended dose is 3 g/day in three 1-g doses. There is no evidence that larger doses will be beneficial (111). Further research is needed to determine the long-term safety profile of HMB.

L-Carnitine

See Carnitine.

Medium-Chain Triglycerides

Medium-chain triglycerides (MCT) contain fatty acids with 6 to 10 carbon atoms. MCT are quickly emptied from the stomach, rapidly absorbed via the portal vein and easily transported into the mitochondria. These features give MCT distinct advantages over long-chain triglycerides as a readily available energy source (112).

As the intensity of exercise increases, the body shifts its fuel usage from fat to carbohydrate. One of the adaptations the body makes to endurance training is the increased ability to oxidize fat during moderate- to high-intensity exercise (112). Athletes have looked at many methods to increase fat availability and oxidation in an effort to spare glycogen and prolong performance. The ingestion of supplemental MCT oil is one such method (113).

Several studies of well-trained endurance cyclists have reported that the ingestion of MCT oil does not enhance endurance performance (114–116). The MCT oil did not significantly alter fat oxidation during exercise and did not spare muscle glycogen. There seems to be no ergogenic benefit for endurance athletes. MCT is cleverly advertised to body builders as "the oil for the well-tuned human machine." However, there have been no research studies of MCT use in strength athletes and no plausible theory for how such a supplement would enhance performance.

Kern et al (117) posed questions about the safety of MCT supplementation. In a 2-week study of male endurance runners, the ingestion of 30 g MCT oil twice per day resulted in altered blood lipids. Total cholesterol, low-density lipoprotein cholesterol, and triacylglycerol were increased, although none exceeded established desirable ranges. Because there seems to be no performance benefit, these increases in blood lipids further support the case against recommending MCT supplements for athletes.

Multivitamin and Mineral Supplements

Multivitamin and mineral supplements are among the most popular dietary supplements consumed by athletes. Nearly 45% of collegiate athletes use dietary supplements, most often multivitamin/mineral supplements and creatine (6). They represent an easy, convenient, and fairly inexpensive way to obtain nutrients that are lacking in the diet. Because athletes have busy schedules, they often perceive a one-a-day type multivitamin and mineral supplement to be an "insurance policy."

A comprehensive review of vitamins and minerals is found in Chapter 5. There is no scientific evidence at this time that all athletes should consume a daily multivitamin and mineral supplement. With the inclusion of energy bars, cereal, and other highly fortified products in the diet, many athletes may already be consuming the equivalent of a multivitamin and mineral supplement. However, athletes who chronically restrict energy or who are recovering from eating disorders are generally deficient in one or more nutrients. They would benefit from supplementation, as would those who are pregnant or lactating.

Fortunately, there are good tools to help determine if dietary deficiencies may be present. Computerized nutrient analysis compares self-reported intake with the current recommendations. The UL is helpful in determining if total intake from food and supplements is potentially harmful. Thorough nutritional assessment is necessary before multivitamin and mineral supplements are recommended to individual athletes.

The routine use of multivitamin supplements by the general population for the prevention of cancer or cardiovascular disease is controversial. The US Preventive Services Task Force (118) recommends against it, whereas other respected scientists recommend the routine use of multivitamin (not mineral) supplements (119). The controversy is a result of different interpretations of the research studies.

Antioxidant Vitamin Supplements (Vitamins C and E)

Vitamins C and E are powerful antioxidants that work in conjunction with each other and glutathione to guard against oxidative stress. Endurance athletes are subject to great oxidative stress and there have long been questions about whether such athletes need more vitamins C and E, especially in the form of supplements (120–125). Whereas strenuous aerobic exercise has the potential to produce more tissue-damaging reactive oxygen species (free radicals), a positive result of aerobic training is a buildup of the body's natural defenses against free radicals, the enzymatic and nonenzymatic antioxidants (121). At the present time, athletes do not seem to have a greater need than the DRI for vitamin C (120).

Peake (120) reports that except for those who chronically restrict energy, athletes tend to consume more dietary vitamin C than the general population and meet the DRI. There is no universal recommendation for vitamin C supplements for endurance athletes (123) although individual elite athletes do monitor their vitamin C status and may choose to supplement (124). Research studies often use a daily 500-mg vitamin C supplement in their study protocols. Such a dose, in addition to that consumed through food, would likely result in a vitamin C intake that would not exceed the UL of 2,000 mg. Higher doses of vitamin C supplements (eg, > 2,000 mg/day) may result in diarrhea (122).

Recurring upper respiratory tract infections and colds are the bane of endurance athletes (strenuous endurance exercise may be immunosuppressive), and athletes may be quick to use vitamin C supplements. The effectiveness of such supplements on the incidence and prevalence of the common cold has been well-studied in the general population over the past 20 years. Vitamin C does not seem to prevent colds, but it does seem to modestly reduce the duration of a cold (126). Once the cold begins and until symptoms disappear, recommendations for supplemental vitamin C range from 250 to 1,000 mg/day, with some evidence to support the higher doses (126). Supplemental vitamin C is likely effective because of its mild antihistamine effect. This constitutes the use of vitamin C as a disease treatment and in this respect should be evaluated like an over-the-counter cold medication.

Scientists do not fully agree about the role supplemental vitamin E in preventing oxidative damage. Clarkson and Thompson (125) suggest that supplemental vitamin E does not enhance performance, but that it may protect against chronic oxidative damage, which could help delay the onset of degenerative diseases such as heart disease. Takanami et al (127) are convinced that supplemental vitamin E is beneficial and suggest that all endurance athletes use 100 to 200 mg/day. Note that these levels are not obtainable through diet alone. Vitamin E has a very low toxicity and the UL is 1,000 mg (122).

The DRI for vitamin E for adults is 15 mg (122). This level can be obtained through diet alone if excellent food sources are chosen, such as vegetable oils, nuts and seeds. One concern is that endurance athletes tend to follow a low-fat diet and/or have low vitamin E intake, in which case supplemental vitamin E may be beneficial.

Protein (Including Whey Protein and Essential Amino Acid Supplements)

In general, athletes engaged in training need between 1.2 and 1.7 g protein/kg body weight/day. Many athletes report intakes more than this level (128); body builders sometimes report intakes as high as 2.5 to 3.5 g/kg/day. Protein supplement advertisements may claim that adequate protein intake cannot be achieved through diet alone, that protein powders are better quality than protein found in food, and that individuals cannot consume too much protein. Protein supplements may be sold as "time-released" or "night-time" proteins with the claim that such supplements reduce the catabolic process during sleep. To date, studies do not support these claims.

Many factors contribute to protein needs, including overall energy intake; carbohydrate availability; protein quality; exercise intensity, duration, and time; training history; gender; age; and timing of intake (128). Once protein needs are met, the overall energy content of the diet affects body composition more than any other variable (129). Each athlete must be individually assessed to determine estimated protein need. Most male strength athletes, with the exception of those who have weight class restrictions (eg, wrestlers), consume adequate protein from food. Thus, the protein needs of athletes can be achieved without supplementation (128). Some athletes believe protein supplements are necessary and others find protein supplements more convenient than eating food proteins.

Purported benefits of protein supplements include increased muscle mass, strength, and recovery. In a 2001 survey, approximately 50% of freshman football players believed that protein supplementation was necessary to increase muscle growth and development (6). A meta-analysis that evaluated all trials relating to protein supplementation with resistance training for 2 or more days per week for 3 weeks between 1967 and 2001 showed no change in lean weight gain or strength (57). However, some studies have shown that protein supplementation in combination with resistance training significantly increased lean tissue mass over placebo (129,130).

Protein supplements contain a variety of proteins, including whey, casein, and soy. Whey has always been a popular source because of its high biological value. Other benefits may include solubility, immune system influence, and antioxidant properties. Whey and casein are milk proteins. Whey is the liquid portion of coagulated milk, whereas casein is found in the curds (semisolid portion). During processing, the whey proteins are concentrated and the fat and lactose are removed. Whey protein isolate is lactose-free whereas whey powder and whey protein concentrate can contain substantial amounts of lactose (131).

Because whey has greater solubility than casein, the amino acids found in whey enter the bloodstream faster. In one study (130), whey-supplemented subjects had a small increase in lean tissue mass (~2 kg) when compared with subjects who consumed a placebo. Those who supplemented with whey and creatine had the greatest increase in lean tissue mass (~4 kg). However, some performance measures were not greater when compared with placebo. Studies now underway should help to clarify whey protein's influence.

Protein supplements seem to be safe for athletes without latent or known kidney or liver disease. It does not seem that excessive protein intake by athletes harm healthy kidneys (132). Those who consume high levels of protein should monitor their health and follow up with a physician if problems occur. From a practical perspective, daily protein intakes exceeding 2.5 g/kg body weight put athletes at risk for dehydration, low carbohydrate intake, excessive energy intake, and increased excretion of urinary calcium. Athletes should consider protein intake, including supplementation, in the context of their total energy, macronutrient, and fluid needs. The bottom line is that protein supplements are neither more nor less effective than food proteins. For healthy athletes, protein supplements are generally considered safe.

Athletes who are focused on their protein intake often consider individual amino acid supplements. These include essential amino acid (EAA) combinations, HMB, branched-chain amino acids (BCAA), and glutamine. Studies have not shown a performance benefit for EAA supplements (17). HMB, BCAA, and glutamine are covered elsewhere in this chapter. Although theories exist about the optimal amounts or combinations of EAAs and athletic performance, guidelines have not been developed for "optimal" protein intake. As explained in Chapter 3, the recommended protein intake for athletes is based primarily on maintaining nitrogen balance, not on attaining maximum muscle mass.

Pyruvate and Dihydroxyacetone

Pyruvate is the end product of glycolysis, a cellular energy process that takes place outside of the mitochondria. Once transported into the mitochondria, pyruvate can be converted to acetyl-CoA. Dihydroxyacetone (DHA) is also produced during glycolysis. Both are 3-carbon compounds; thus, they are referred to as trioses, but pyruvate is the more popular and well-known supplement. Pyruvate supplements are probably safe for adults, although minor side effects, such as gas or diarrhea, have been reported (133).

It has been suggested that pyruvate supplements can increase aerobic endurance and decrease body fat. Body builders in particular have been interested in the fat-reducing effects. Pyruvate is often advertised as a weight-loss aid to both athletes and sedentary individuals. Although studies in the early 1990s were promising, those promises have not been realized with more recent studies.

In 1990 Stanko et al (134,135) published two studies suggesting that endurance capacity could be enhanced with pyruvate and DHA supplementation. The studies were conducted in untrained males, so their application to athletes was immediately questioned. High levels of pyruvate (> 20 g/day) were used and there were adverse gastrointestinal effects, such as gas and nausea, from the high doses. This raised further questions about the feasibility of pyruvate supplementation.

A 2000 study (136) cast doubt on previous research results, which had not been replicated by the original researchers or others. The 2000 study found that aerobic performance was not improved in trained, recreational athletes. In fact, blood pyruvate concentrations were not even increased with 7 g supplemental pyruvate. All subjects complained of increased gastrointestinal effects as the dose was increased, and some subjects could not complete the study because of these adverse effects. There is no evidence that pyruvate supplements are an effective ergogenic aid.

Pyruvate supplementation is also linked to weight loss claims. Animal studies suggested a possible mechanism. The results of two studies by Stanko et al (137,138) are widely cited as evidence that pyruvate supplements reduce body weight and body fat in humans. These studies were conducted in morbidly obese inactive women in a metabolic ward, and energy intake was restricted to 500 or 1,000 kcal/day. Additionally, study doses of pyruvate were more than 20 g/day. Although there were small but statistically significant weight and fat losses in these subjects when living in a metabolic ward, the conditions under which the studies were conducted limit any application of the results to active, free-living people.

Pyruvate is expensive to produce and most supplements contain approximately 1 g per tablet. The usual dose sold is unlikely to increase blood pyruvate levels. Even at the more than 20-g levels used in research studies, there is no evidence to suggest that pyruvate supplements will improve performance or result in weight or fat loss in athletes or other active people.

Ribose

Ribose is a 5-carbon sugar. Most sugars found in food, such as glucose and fructose, are 6-carbon sugars. Thus, little ribose is obtained from dietary sources but cells can easily synthesize ribose, which is needed for ATP synthesis. The theoretical question posed is whether ribose supplementation could increase ATP production and improve high-intensity exercise performance.

Studies have not been able to demonstrate that ribose supplementation (5 g/day for 5 days) positively affects anaerobic capacity or alters the body's metabolic response to exercise. Such supplements, although they seem to be safe, are not effective in improving high-intensity exercise performance (139).

Vanadium (Vanadyl Sulfate)

Vanadium is a trace element that is essential for animals and may be essential for humans, although the latter has not yet been established. Daily dietary intake is approximately 10 to 30 µg, with a total body pool of approximately 100 to 200 µg. Supplemental vanadium is usually sold as vanadyl sulfate or a similar compound because of enhanced bioavailability (140). The UL has been established at 1.8 mg for adults (31).

Studies in rats and in humans with type 2 diabetes have shown that supplemental vanadyl sulfate has insulin-mimetic properties. Effects include increased hepatic and muscle insulin sensitivity, augmented glucose uptake, and a stimulation of glycogen synthesis (141,142). These properties, all of which could be beneficial to athletes, have resulted in increased popularity of this supplement among active people. However, the effects demonstrated in studies with subjects with type 2 diabetes have not been replicated in humans without diabetes (140). At this time, vanadium supplements are not recommended to athletes without type 2 diabetes because there is no evidence of a beneficial insulin-mimicking effect.

The evidence for the use of vanadyl sulfate with those with type 2 diabetes is promising . A 2003 review (143) notes at least five studies have reported improved insulin sensitivity and increased glucose uptake. However, these studies were nonrandomized trials, and results from randomized clinical trials are needed. It should be noted that the doses used in research studies exceed levels that would be possible through food intake alone. Therefore, it seems that the effect of vanadium supplements is pharmacological. Athletes with diabetes should be counseled to regard the use of vanadyl supplements as a medication even though they are legally sold as dietary supplements.

Summary

Table 7.1 summarizes the safety and effectiveness of the dietary supplements discussed in this chapter. Because the body of scientific literature is always changing, practitioners must continually update their knowledge. Even with the large number of questionable supplements flooding the market, it is important to consider the possibility of an athlete benefiting from a particular supplement because athletes will always be looking for a competitive edge. There are some supplements that are safe but not effective. There also may be some supplements that are effective but not safe, and these pose serious risk-benefit questions that ultimately can only be answered by the athlete. For those select few dietary supplements determined to be safe and effective, it still remains crucial that the practitioner assesses the individual athlete's needs and goals, and educate accordingly.

TABLE 7.1   Safety and Effectiveness of Selected Dietary Supplements and Ergogenic Aids

Supplement	Safety (at recommended doses)	Effectiveness
Androstenedione	Safety concerns about chronic use.	Not effective.
BCAA	Seems to be safe.	Not effective to delay fatigue; some promising studies related to immune system support.
Caffeine	Seems to be safe, although known adverse effects may affect performance.	Effective as a central nervous system stimulant.
Carnitine	Seems to be safe.	Effectiveness is unknown because study results are mixed.
Chromium (chromium picolinate)	Safety concerns about chronic use.	Not effective for increasing muscle mass or decreasing body fat.

continues

TABLE 7.1 Safety and Effectiveness of Selected Dietary Supplements and Ergogenic Aids (continued)

Supplement	Safety (at recommended doses)	Effectiveness
CLA	Seems to be safe.	Effectiveness is unknown because study results are mixed.
Creatine	Seems to be safe.	Effective for increasing lean body mass in athletes performing repeated high intensity, short duration (< 30 seconds) exercise bouts. Performance benefit in weight lifters.
DHEA	Safety concerns about acute high doses and chronic use.	Not effective.
Ephedrine	Safety concerns hotly debated. Banned by the FDA due to significant safety risks. Ban on low-dose (≤ 10 mg) supplements overturned by federal court.	Effective as a central nervous system stimulant. With caffeine, effective for short-term, 8- to 9-lb weight loss in obese people. Effectiveness as a performance enhancer is unknown because study results are mixed.
Glucosamine/ Chondroitin sulfate	Seems to be safe.	Effective in some individuals.
Glutamine	Seems to be safe.	Effectiveness is unknown because study results are mixed.
HMB	Seems to be safe.	Effectiveness is unknown because study results are mixed.
MCT	Safety concerns about acute and chronic use.	Not effective.
Multivitamin and mineral supplements	Safety concerns about doses that, in conjunction with diet, would exceed the UL.	Effective to reverse nutrient deficiencies. Recommended for pregnant and lactating women. Daily multivitamin supplements are recommended by some as effective to prevent chronic disease in adults.
Protein	Seems safe for those without latent or known kidney or liver disease.	No more or less effective than food proteins.
Pyruvate	Seems to be safe.	Not effective.
Ribose	Seems to be safe.	Not effective.
Vanadium (vanadyl sulfate)	Seems to be safe.	Not effective as a performance enhancer. May be effective in type 2 diabetes as a pharmacological agent.

Abbreviations: BCAA, branched-chain amino acid; CLA, conjugated linoleic acid; DHEA, dehydroepiandrosterone; FDA, Food and Drug Administration; HMB, beta-hydroxy-beta-methylbutyrate; MCT, medium-chain triglycerides; UL, Tolerable Upper Intake Level.

References

1. Food and Drug Administration. 1994 Dietary Supplement Health and Education Act (DSHEA). Available at: http://www.cfsan.fda.gov/~dms/dietsupp.html. Accessed January 12, 2004.
2. Food and Drug Administration Task Force on Consumer Health Information for Better Nutrition. 2003. Available at: http://www.cfsan.fda.gov/~dms/nuttftoc.html. Accessed January 12, 2004.
3. Haskell WL, Kiernan M. Methodologic issues in measuring physical activity and physical fitness when evaluating the role of dietary supplements for physically active people. *Am J Clin Nutr.* 2000;72(2 Suppl):541S–550S.

4. Schroder H, Navarro E, Mora J, Seco J, Torregrosa JM, Tramullas A. The type, amount, frequency and timing of dietary supplement use by elite players in the First Spanish Basketball League. *J Sports Sci.* 2002;20:353–358.

5. Greenwood M, Farris J, Kreider R, Greenwood L, Byars A. Creatine supplementation patterns and perceived effects in select division I collegiate athletes. *Clin J Sport Med.* 2000;10: 191–194.

6. Jonnalagadda SS, Rosenbloom CA, Skinner R. Dietary practices, attitudes, and physiological status of collegiate freshman football players. *J Strength Cond Res.* 2001;15:507–513.

7. McGuire TA, Sullivan JC, Bernhardt DT. Creatine supplementation in high school football players. *Clin J Sport Med.* 2001;11:247–253.

8. Gurley BJ, Gardner SF, Hubbard MA. Content versus label claims in ephedra-containing dietary supplements. *Am J Health Syst Pharm.* 2000;57:963–969.

9. Brown WJ, Basil MD, Bocarnea MC. The influence of famous athletes on health beliefs and practices: Mark McGwire, child abuse prevention, and Androstenedione. *J Health Commun.* 2003;8:41–57.

10. Yesalis CE, Bahrke MS. Anabolic-androgenic steroids and related substances. *Curr Sport Med Rep.* 2002;1:246–252.

11. Broeder CE. Oral andro-related prohormone supplementation: do the potential risks outweigh the benefits? *Can J Appl Physiol.* 2003;28:102–116.

12. Brown GA, Martini ER, Roberts BS, Vukovich MD, King DS. Acute hormonal response to sublingual androstenediol intake in young men. *J Appl Physiol.* 2002;92:142–146.

13. Van Gammeren D, Falk D, Antonio J. Effects of norandrostenedione and norandrostenediol in resistance-trained men. *Nutrition.* 2002;18:734–737.

14. Van Gammeren D, Falk D, Antonio J. The effects of supplementation with 19-nor-4-androstene-3,17-dione and 19-nor-4-androstene-3,17-diol on body composition and athletic performance in previously weight-trained male athletes. *Eur J Appl Physiol.* 2001;84:426–431.

15. Colker CM, Antonio J, Kalman D. The metabolism of orally ingested 19-nor-4-androstene-3,17-dione and 19-nor-4-androstene-3,17-diol in healthy, resistance-trained men. *J Strength Cond Res.* 2001;15:144–147.

16. Food and Drug Administration. FDA White Paper: health effects of androstenedione. Released March 11, 2004. Available at: http://www.fda.gov/oc/whitepapers/andro.html. Accessed August 23, 2004.

17. Wagenmakers AJ. Amino acid supplements to improve athletic performance. *Curr Opin Clin Nutr Metab Care.* 1999;2:539–544.

18. Bassit RA, Sawada LA, Bacurau RF, Navarro F, Costa Rosa LF. The effect of BCAA supplementation upon the immune response of triathletes. *Med Sci Sports Exerc.* 2000;32:1214–1219.

19. Bassit RA, Sawada LA, Bacurau RF, Navarro F, Martins E Jr, Santos RV, Caperuto EC, Rogeri P, Costa Rosa LF. Branched-chain amino acid supplementation and the immune response of long-distance athletes. *Nutrition.* 2002;18:376–379.

20. Paluska SA. Caffeine and exercise. *Curr Sports Med Rep.* 2003;2:213–219.

21. Graham TE. Caffeine, coffee and ephedrine: impact on exercise performance and metabolism. *Can J Appl Physiol.* 2001;26(suppl):S103–S119.

22. Spriet LL. Caffeine and performance. *Int J Sport Nutr.* 1995;5(suppl):S84–S99.

23. Armstrong LE. Caffeine, body fluid-electrolyte balance, and exercise performance. *Int J Sport Nutr Exerc Metab.* 2002;12:189–206.

24. Mahan KL, Escott-Stump S, eds. *Krause's Food, Nutrition and Diet Therapy.* 11th ed. Philadelphia, Pa: WB Saunders Co; 2004.

25. Muller DM, Seim H, Kiess W, Loster H, Richter T. Effects of oral L-carnitine supplementation on in vivo long-chain fatty acid oxidation in healthy adults. *Metabolism.* 2002;51:1389–1391.

26. Villani RG, Gannon J, Self M, Rich PA. L-Carnitine supplementation combined with aerobic training does not promote weight loss in moderately obese women. *Int J Sport Nutr Exerc Metab.* 2000;10:199–207.

27. Cha YS, Choi SK, Suh H, Lee SN, Cho D, Li K. Effects of carnitine coingested caffeine on carnitine metabolism and endurance capacity in athletes. *J Nutr Sci Vitaminol.* 2001;47: 378–384.

28. Volek JS, Kraemer WJ, Rubin MR, Gomez AL, Ratamess NA, Gaynor P. L-Carnitine L-tartrate supplementation favorably affects markers of recovery from exercise stress. *Am J Physiol Endocrinol Metab.* 2002;282:474–482.

29. Rubin MR, Volek JS, Gomez AL, Ratamess NA, French DN, Sharman MJ, Kraemer WJ. Safety measures of L-carnitine L-tartrate supplementation in healthy men. *J Strength Cond Res.* 2001;15:486–490.

30. Speich M, Pineau A, Ballereau F. Minerals, trace elements and related biological variables in athletes and during physical activity. *Clin Chim Acta.* 2001;312:1–11.

31. Institute of Medicine. *Dietary Reference Intakes for Vitamin A, Vitamin K, Arsenic, Boron, Chromium, Copper, Iodine, Iron, Manganese, Molybdenum, Nickel, Silicon, Vanadium, and Zinc.* Washington, DC: National Academy Press; 2001.

32. Vincent J. The biochemistry of chromium. *J Nutr.* 2000;130:715–718.

33. Vincent JB. The potential value and toxicity of chromium picolinate as a nutritional supplement, weight loss agent and muscle development agent. *Sports Med.* 2003;33:213–230.

34. Lukaski HC. Magnesium, zinc, and chromium nutriture and physical activity. *Am J Clin Nutr.* 2000;72(2 Suppl):585S–593S.

35. Lukaski H. Chromium as a supplement. *Annu Rev Nutr.* 1999;19:279–302.

36. Campbell WW, Joseph LJ, Anderson RA, Davey SL, Hinton J, Evans WJ. Effects of resistive training and chromium picolinate on body composition and skeletal muscle size in older women. *Int J Sport Nutr Exerc Metab.* 2002;12:125–135.

37. Volpe SL, Huang HW, Larpadisorn K, Lesser II. Effect of chromium supplementation and exercise on body composition, resting metabolic rate and selected biochemical parameters in moderately obese women following an exercise program. *J Am Coll Nutr.* 2001;20:293–306.

38. Pittler MH, Stevinson C, Ernst E. Chromium picolinate for reducing body weight: meta-analysis of randomized trials. *Int J Obes Relat Metab Disord.* 2003;27:522–529.

39. Noone EJ, Roche HM, Nugent AP, Gibney MJ. The effect of dietary supplementation using isomeric blends of conjugated linoleic acid on lipid metabolism in healthy human subjects. *Br J Nutr.* 2002;88:243–251.

40. Belury MA. Dietary conjugated linoleic acid in health: physiological effects and mechanisms of action. *Annu Rev Nutr.* 2002;22:505–531.

41. Zambell KL, Horn WF, Keim NL. Conjugated linoleic acid supplementation in humans: effects on fatty acid and glycerol kinetics. *Lipids.* 2001;36:767–772.

42. Medina EA, Horn WF, Keim NL, Havel PJ, Benito P, Kelley DS, Nelson GJ, Erickson KL. Conjugated linoleic acid supplementation in humans: effects on circulating leptin concentrations and appetite. *Lipids.* 2000;35:783–788.

43. Zambell KL, Keim NL, Van Loan MD, Gale B, Benito P, Kelley DS, Nelson GJ. Conjugated linoleic acid supplementation in humans: effects on body composition and energy expenditure. *Lipids.* 2000;35:777–782.

44. Kreider RB, Ferreira MP, Greenwood M, Wilson M, Almada AL. Effects of conjugated linoleic acid supplementation during resistance training on body composition, bone density, strength, and selected hematological markers. *J Strength Cond Res.* 2002;16:325–334.

45. Terpstra AH. Effect of conjugated linoleic acid on body composition and plasma lipids in humans: an overview of the literature. *Am J Clin Nutr.* 2004;79:352–361.

46. Smedman A, Vessby B. Conjugated linoleic acid supplementation in humans-metabolic effects. *Lipids.* 2001;36:773–781.

47. Thom E, Wadstein J, Gudmundsen O. Conjugated linoleic acid reduces body fat in healthy exercising humans. *J Int Med Res.* 2002;29:392–396.

48. Kamphuis MM, Lejeune MP, Sarin WH, Westerterp-Plantenga MS. The effect of conjugated linoleic acid supplementation after weight loss on body weight regain, body composition, and resting metabolic rate in overweight subjects. *Int J Obes Relat Metab Disord.* 2003;27: 840–847.

49. Kelley DS, Taylor PC, Rudolph IL, Benito P, Nelson GJ, Mackey BE, Erickson KL. Dietary conjugated linoleic acid did not alter immune status in young healthy women. *Lipids.* 2000;35:1065–1071.

50. Lemon PW. Dietary creatine supplementation and exercise performance: why inconsistent results? *Can J Appl Physiol.* 2002;27:663–681.

51. Dempsey RL, Mazzone MF, Meurer LN. Does oral creatine supplementation improve strength? A meta-analysis. *J Fam Pract.* 2002;51:945–951.

52. Metzl JD, Small E, Levine SR, Gershel JC. Creatine use among young athletes. *Pediatrics.* 2001;108:421–425.

53. Branch JD. Effect of creatine supplementation on body composition and performance: a meta-analysis. *Int J Sport Nutr Exerc Metab.* 2003;13:198–226.

54. Cox G, Mujika I, Tumilty D, Burke L. Acute creatine supplementation and performance during a field test simulating match play in elite female soccer players. *Int J Sport Nutr Exerc Metab.* 2002;12:33–46.

55. Arciero PJ, Hannibal NS, Nindl BC, Gentile CL, Hamed J, Vukovich MD. Comparison of creatine ingestion and resistance training on energy expenditure and limb blood flow. *Metabolism.* 2001;50:1429–1434.

56. Volek JS, Duncan ND, Mazzetti SA, Putukian M, Gomez AL, Kraemer WJ. No effect of heavy resistance training and creatine supplementation on blood lipids. *Int J Sport Nutr Exerc Metab.* 2000;10:144–156.

57. Nissen SL, Sharp RL. Effect of dietary supplements on lean mass and strength gains with resistance exercise: a meta-analysis. *J Appl Physiol.* 2003;94:651–659.

58. Chrusch MJ, Chilibeck PD, Chad KE, Davidson KS, Burke DG. Creatine supplementation combined with resistance training in older men. *Med Sci Sports Exerc.* 2001;33:2111–2117.

59. Chwalbinska-Moneta J. Effect of creatine supplementation on aerobic performance and anaerobic capacity in elite rowers in the course of endurance training. *Int J Sport Nutr Exerc Metab.* 2003;13:173–183.

60. Warber JP, Tharion WJ, Patton JF, Champagne CM, Mitotti P, Lieberman HR. The effect of creatine monohydrate supplementation on obstacle course and multiple bench press performance. *J Strength Cond Res.* 2002;16:500–508.

61. Wilder N, Gilders R, Hagerman F, Deivert RG. The effects of a 10-week, periodized, off-season resistance-training program and creatine supplementation among collegiate football players. *J Strength Cond Res.* 2002;16:343–352.

62. Izquierdo M, Ibanez J, Gonzalez-Badillo JJ, Gorostiaga EM. Effects of creatine supplementation on muscle power, endurance and sprint performance. *Med Sci Sports Exerc.* 2002;34: 332–343.

63. Volek JS, Rawson ES. Scientific basis and practical aspects of creatine supplementation for athletes. *Nutrition.* 2004;20:609–614.

64. Crowe MJ, O'Connor DM, Lukins JE. The effects of beta-hydroxy-beta-methylbutyrate (HMB) and HMB/creatine supplementation on indices of health in highly trained athletes. *Int J Sport Nutr Exerc Metab.* 2003;13:184–197.

65. Mayhew DL, Mayhew JL, Ware JS. Effects of long-term creatine supplementation on liver and kidney functions in American college football players. *Int J Sport Nutr Exerc Metab.* 2002;12:453–460.

66. Schilling BK, Stone MH, Utter A, Kearney JT, Johnson M, Coglianese R, Smith L, O'Bryant HS, Fry AC, Starks M, Keith R, Stone ME. Creatine supplementation and health variables: a retrospective study. *Med Sci Sports Exerc.* 2001;33:183–188.

67. Poortmans JR, Francaux M. Adverse effects of creatine supplementation: fact or fiction? *Sports Med.* 2000;30:155–170.

68. Smith J, Dahm DL. Creatine use among a select population of high school athletes. *Mayo Clin Proc.* 2000;75:1257–1263.

69. Murray R, Mayes PA, Rodwell VW and Granner DK, eds. *Harper's Illustrated Biochemistry.* 26th ed. New York, NY: McGraw-Hill; 2003.

70. Hornsby, PJ. DHEA: a biologist's perspective. *J Am Geriat Soc.* 1997;45:1395–1401.

71. Corrigan B. DHEA and sport. *Clin J Sport Med.* 2002;12:236–241.

72. Food and Drug Administration. 2004. Final Rule Declaring Dietary Supplements Containing Ephedrine Alkaloids Adulterated Because They Present an Unreasonable Risk. Available at: http://www.fda.gov/oc/initiatives/ephedra/february2004/finalsummary.html. Accessed May 17, 2004.

73. Food and Drug Administration. 2000. Safety of Dietary Supplements Containing Ephedrine Alkaloids. (Transcript of a public meeting held August 8–9, 2000.) Available at: http://www.fda.gov. Accessed January 12, 2004.

74. CANTOX Health Services International. Safety Assessment and Determination of a Tolerable Upper Limit of Ephedra; 2000. Available at: http://www.crnusa.org. Accessed January 12, 2004.

75. Shekelle PG, Hardy ML, Morton SC, Maglione M, Mojica WA, Suttorp MJ, Rhodes SL, Jungvig L, Gagne J. Efficacy and safety of ephedra and ephedrine for weight loss and athletic performance: a meta-analysis. *JAMA.* 2003;289:1537–1545.

76. Food and Drug Administration. Evidence on the safety and effectiveness of ephedra: implications for regulation. 2003. Available at: http://www.fda.gov/bbs/topics/NEWS/ephedra/whitepaper.html. Accessed January 12, 2004.

77. Baylis A, Cameron-Smith D, Burke LM. Inadvertent doping through supplement use by athletes: assessment and management of the risk in Australia. *Int J Sport Nutr Exerc Metab.* 2001;11:365–383.

78. Bell DG, Jacobs I, Zamecnik J. Effects of caffeine, ephedrine and their combination on time to exhaustion during high-intensity exercise. *Eur J Appl Physiol Occup Physiol.* 1998;77:427–433.

79. Bell DG, Jacobs I, McLellan TM, Zamecnik J. Reducing the dose of combined caffeine and ephedrine preserves the ergogenic effect. *Aviat Space Environ Med.* 2000;71:415–419.

80. Bell DG, Jacobs I. Combined caffeine and ephedrine ingestion improves run times of Canadian Forces Warrior Test. *Aviat Space Environ Med.* 1999;70:325–329.

81. Bell DG, Jacobs I, McLellan TM, Miyazaki M, Sabiston CM. Thermal regulation in the heat during exercise after caffeine and ephedrine ingestion. *Aviat Space Environ Med.* 1999;70:583–588.

82. Jacobs I, Pasternak H, Bell DG. Effects of ephedrine, caffeine, and their combination on muscular endurance. *Med Sci Sports Exerc.* 2003;35:987–994.

83. Bell DG, Jacobs I, Ellerington K. Effect of caffeine and ephedrine ingestion on anaerobic exercise performance. *Med Sci Sports Exerc.* 2001;33:1399–1403.

84. Marcus DM, Grollman AP. Ephedra-free is not danger-free. *Science.* 2003;301:1669–1671.

85. Delafuente JC. Glucosamine in the treatment of osteoarthritis. *Rheum Dis Clin North Am.* 2000;26:1–11.

86. Braham R, Dawson B, Goodman C. The effect of glucosamine supplementation on people experienced regular knee pain. *Br J Sports Med.* 2003;37:45–49.

87. Matheson AJ, Perry CM. Glucosamine: a review of its use in the management of osteoarthritis. *Drugs Aging.* 2003;20:1041–1060.

88. McAlindon TE, LaValley MP, Gulin JP, Felson DT. Glucosamine and chondroitin for treatment of osteoarthritis: a systemic quality assessment and meta-analysis. *JAMA*. 2000;283:1469–1475.

89. Reginster JY, Deroisy R, Rovati LC, Lee RL, Lejeune E, Bruyere O, Giacovelli G, Henrotin Y, Dacre JE, Gossett C. Long-term effects of glucosamine sulphate on osteoarthritis progression: a randomised, placebo-controlled trial. *Lancet*. 2001;357:251–256.

90. Bruyere O, Pavelka K, Rovati LC, Deroisy R, Olejarova M, Gatterova J, Giacovelli G, Reginster JY. Glucosamine sulfate reduces osteoarthritis progression in postmenopausal women with knee osteoarthritis: evidence from two 3-year studies. *Menopause*. 2004;11:138–143.

91. The Arthritis Foundation. Alternative Therapies: Glucosamine and Chondroitin Sulfate. Available at: http://arthritis.org/conditions/alttherapies/glucosamine.asp. Accessed January 12, 2004.

92. Scroggie DA, Albright A, Harris MD. The effect of glucosamine-chondroitin supplementation on glycosylated hemoglobin levels in patients with type 2 diabetes mellitus: a placebo-controlled, double-blinded, randomized clinical trial. *Arch Intern Med*. 2003;163:1587–1590.

93. Krzywkowski K, Peterson EW, Ostrowski K, Link-Amster H, Boza J, Halkjaer-Kristensen J, Pedersen BK. Effect of glutamine and protein supplementation on exercise induced decreases in salivary IgA. *J Appl Physiol*. 2001;91:832–838.

94. Castell LM. Can glutamine modify the apparent immunodepression observed after prolonged, exhaustive exercise? *Nutrition*. 2002;18:371–375.

95. Nieman DC. Exercise immunology: nutritional countermeasures. *Can J Appl Physiol*. 2001;26(Suppl):S36-S44.

96. Candow DG, Chilibeck PD, Burke DG, Davidson KS, Smith-Palmer T. Effect of glutamine supplementation combined with resistance training in young adults. *Eur J Appl Physiol*. 2001;86:142–149.

97. Gleeson M, Bishop NC. Special feature for the Olympics: effects of exercise on the immune system: modification of immune responses to exercise by carbohydrate, glutamine and antioxidant supplements. *Immunol Cell Biol*. 2000;78:554–561.

98. Hiscock N, Pedersen BK. Exercise-induced immunodepression-plasma glutamine is not the link. *J Appl Physiol*. 2002;93:813–822.

99. Antonio J, Sanders MS, Kalman D, Woodgate D, Street C. The effects of high-dose glutamine ingestion on weightlifting performance. *J Strength Cond Res*. 2002;16:157–160.

100. Slater GJ, Jenkins D. Beta-hydroxy-beta-methylbutyrate (HMB) supplementation and the promotion of muscle growth and strength. *Sports Med*. 2000;30:105–116.

101. Jowko E, Ostaszewski P, Jank M, Sacharuk J, Zieniewicz A, Wilczak J, Nissen S. Creatine and beta-hydroxy-beta-methylbutyrate (HMB) additively increase lean body mass and muscle strength during a weight-training program. *Nutrition*. 2001;17:558–566.

102. Vukovich MD, Stubbs NB, Bohlken RM. Body composition in 70-year-old adults responds to dietary beta-hydroxy-beta-methylbutyrate similarly to that of young adults. *J Nutr*. 2001;131:2049–2052.

103. Gallagher PM, Carrithers JA, Godard MP, Schulze KE, Trappe SW. Beta-hydroxy-beta-methylbutyrate ingestion, part I: effects on strength and fat free mass. *Med Sci Sports Exerc*. 2000;32:2109–2115.

104. Panton LB, Rathmacher JA, Baier S, Nissen S. Nutritional supplementation of the leucine metabolite beta-hydroxy-beta-methylbutrate (HMB) during resistance training. *Nutrition*. 2000;16:734–739.

105. Knitter AE, Panton L, Rathmacher JA, Petersen A, Sharp R. Effects of beta-hydroxy-beta-methylbutyrate on muscle damage after a prolonged run. *J Appl Physiol*. 2000;89:1340–1344.

106. O'Connor DM, Crowe MJ. Effects of beta-hydroxy-beta-methylbutyrate and creatine monohydrate supplementation on the aerobic and anaerobic capacity of highly trained athletes. *J Sports Med Phys Fitness*. 2003;43:64–68.

107. Ransone J, Neighbors K, Lefavi R, Chromiak J. The effect of beta-hydroxy-beta-methyl-butyrate on muscular strength and body composition in collegiate football players. *J Strength Cond Res.* 2003;17:34–39.

108. Slater G, Jenkins D, Logan P, Lee H, Vukovich M, Rathmacher JA, Hahn AG. Beta-hydroxy-beta-methylbutyrate (HMB) supplementation does not affect changes in strength or body composition during resistance training in trained men. *Int J Sport Nutr Exerc Metab.* 2001;11:384–396.

109. Flakoll P, Sharp R, Baier S, Levenhagen D, Carr C, Nissen S. Effect of beta-hydroxy-beta-methylbutyrate, arginine, and lysine supplementation on strength, functionality, body composition, and protein metabolism in elderly women. *Nutrition.* 2004;20:445–451.

110. Crowe MJ, O'Connor DM, Lukins JE. The effects of beta-hydroxy-beta-methylbutyrate (HMB) and HMB/creatine supplementation on indices of health in highly trained athletes. *Int J Sport Nutr Exerc Metab.* 2003;13:184–197.

111. Gallagher PM, Carrithers JA, Godard MP, Schulze KE, Trappe SW. Beta-hydroxy-beta-methylbutyrate ingestion, part II: effects on hematology, hepatic and renal function. *Med Sci Sports Exerc.* 2000;32:2116–2119.

112. Horowitz JF, Klein S. Lipid metabolism during endurance exercise. *Am J Clin Nutr.* 2000;72(2 Suppl):558S–563S.

113. Hawley JA. Effect of increased fat availability on metabolism and exercise capacity. *Med Sci Sports Exerc.* 2002;34:1485–1491.

114. Angus DJ, Hargreaves M, Dancey J, Febbraio MA. Effect of carbohydrate or carbohydrate plus medium-chain triglyceride ingestion on cycling time trial performance. *J Appl Physiol.* 2000;88:113–119.

115. Horowitz JF, Mora-Rodriguez R, Byerley LO, Coyle EF. Preexercise medium-chain triglyceride ingestion does not alter muscle glycogen use during exercise. *J Appl Physiol.* 2000;88:219–225.

116. Goedecke JH, Elmer-English R, Dennis SC, Schloss I, Noakes TD, Lambert EV. Effects of medium-chain triaclyglycerol ingested with carbohydrate on metabolism and exercise performance. *Int J Sport Nutr.* 1999;9:35–47.

117. Kern M, Lagomarcino ND, Misell LM, Schuster VV. The effect of medium-chain triacylglycerols on the blood lipid profile of male endurance runners. *J Nutr Biochem.* 2000;11:288–292.

118. US Preventive Services Task Force. Routine vitamin supplementation to prevent cancer and cardiovascular disease: recommendations and rationale. *Ann Intern Med.* 2003;139:51–55.

119. Fletcher RH, Fairfield KM. Vitamins for chronic disease prevention in adults: clinical applications. *JAMA.* 2002;287:3127–3129.

120. Peake JM. Vitamin C: effects of exercise and requirements with training. *Int J Sport Nutr Exerc Metab.* 2003;13:125–151.

121. Powers SK, Lennon SL. Analysis of cellular responses to free radicals: focus on exercise and skeletal muscle. *Proc Nutr Soc.* 1999;58:1025–1033.

122. Institute of Medicine. *Dietary Reference Intakes for Vitamin C, Vitamin E, Selenium, and Carotenoids.* Washington, DC: National Academy Press; 2000.

123. Evans WJ. Vitamin E, vitamin C, and exercise. *Am J Clin Nutr.* 2000;72(2 Suppl):647S–652S.

124. Sen CK. Antioxidants in exercise nutrition. *Sports Med.* 2001;31:891–908.

125. Clarkson PM, Thompson H. Antioxidants: what role do they play in physical activity and health? *Am J Clin Nutr.* 2000;72(2 Suppl):637S–646S.

126. Douglas RM, Chalker EB, Treacy B. Vitamin C for preventing and treating the common cold. *Cochrane Database Syst Rev.* 2000;(2):CD000980.

127. Takanami Y, Iwane H, Kawai Y, Shimomitsu T. Vitamin E supplementation and endurance exercise: are there benefits? *Sports Med.* 2000;29:73–83.

128. Lemon PW. Beyond the zone: protein needs of active individuals. *J Am Coll Nutr.* 2000;19:513–521.

129. Rozenek R, Ward P, Long S, Garhammer J. Effects of high-calorie supplements on body composition and muscular strength following resistance training. *J Sports Med Phys Fitness.* 2002;42:340–347.

130. Burke DG, Chilibeck PD, Davidson KS, Candow DG, Farthing J, Smith-Palmer T. The effect of whey protein supplementation with and without creatine monohydrate combined with resistance training on lean tissue mass and muscle strength. *Int J Sport Nutr Exerc Metab.* 2001;11:349–364.

131. Geiser M. The wonders of whey. *NSCA's Performance Training J.* 2003;2:13–15.

132. Poortmanns JR and Dellalieux O. Do regular high protein diets have potential health risks on kidney function in athletes? *Int J Sport Nutr Exerc Metab.* 2000;10:28–38.

133. Sukala WR. Pyruvate: beyond the marketing hype. *Int J Sport Nutr.* 1998;8:241–249.

134. Stanko RT, Robertson RJ, Spina RJ, Reilly JJ Jr, Greenawalt KD, Goss FL. Enhancement of arm exercise endurance capacity with dihydroxyacetone and pyruvate. *J Appl Physiol.* 1990; 68:119–124.

135. Stanko RT, Robertson RJ, Galbreath RW, Reilly JJ Jr, Greenawalt KD, Goss FL. Enhanced leg exercise endurance with a high-carbohydrate diet and dihydroxyacetone and pyruvate. *J Appl Physiol.* 1990;69:1651–1656.

136. Morrison MA, Spriet LL, Dyck DJ. Pyruvate ingestion for 7 days does not improve aerobic performance in well-trained individuals. *J Appl Physiol.* 2000;89:549–556.

137. Stanko RT, Tietze DL, Arch JE. Body composition, energy utilization, and nitrogen metabolism with a 4.25-MJ/d low-energy diet supplemented with pyruvate. *Am J Clin Nutr.* 1992;56: 630–635.

138. Stanko RT, Tietze DL, Arch JE. Body composition, energy utilization, and nitrogen metabolism with a severely restricted diet supplemented with dihydroxyacetone and pyruvate. *Am J Clin Nutr.* 1992;55:771–776.

139. Kreider RB, Melton C, Greenwood M, Rasmussen C, Lundberg J, Earnest C, Almada A. Effects of oral D-ribose supplementation on anaerobic capacity and selected metabolic markers in healthy males. *Int J Sport Nutr Exerc Metab.* 2003;13:76–86.

140. Jentjens RL, Jeukendrup AE. Effect of acute and short-term administration of vanadyl sulphate on insulin sensitivity in healthy active humans. *Int J Sport Nutr Exerc Metab.* 2002;12:470–479.

141. Verma S, Cam MC, McNeill JH. Nutritional factors that can favorably influence the glucose/insulin system: vanadium. *J Am Coll Nutr.* 1998;17:11–18.

142. Cusi K, Cukier S, DeFronzo RA, Torres M, Puchulu FM, Redondo JC. Vanadyl sulfate improves hepatic and muscle insulin sensitivity in type 2 diabetes. *J Clin Endocrinol Metab.* 2001;86:1410–1417.

143. Yeh GY, Eisenberg DM, Kaptchuk TJ, Phillips RS. Systematic review of herbs and dietary supplements for glycemic control in diabetes. *Diabetes Care.* 2003;26:1277–1294.

Section 2

Sports Nutrition Screening and Assessment

General sports nutrition recommendations need to be tailored to each athlete, and part of that process involves screening and assessment. This section begins with health screening and dietary assessment, standard practice for sports dietitians. Chapter 9 reviews fitness assessment whereas Chapter 10 provides a detailed review of assessment of body size and composition. Athletes frequently ask questions about calories and weight, and many sports dietitians will work closely with athletes who wish to change energy balance, body composition, and/or weight.

Chapter 8

HEALTH SCREENING AND DIETARY ASSESSMENT

Melinda M. Manore, PhD, RD, and Katherine A. Beals, PhD, RD, FACSM

Introduction

Prior to beginning a fitness program, it is recommended that individuals undergo a health screening and, when appropriate, a complete medical evaluation. Health screening can help identify medical risks and their nutritional relationships and is the first step in planning an appropriate and safe exercise and nutrition program. A complete medical evaluation should include measurements that lead to a better understanding of general health, level of physical fitness, and nutritional status. Although nutrition professionals may only be directly involved with the dietary assessment portions of health screenings and medical evaluations, they should have a general understanding of all the components. This chapter will describe uses and components of health screening, medical evaluation, and dietary assessment.

Health Screening

To optimize safety during exercise participation and to develop an effective exercise prescription that can improve fitness, an initial health screening is recommended (1). A primary care physician typically does the initial health screening. For high school or collegiate athletes, the health screening is usually done as part of the sport pre-participation physical examination. In the health club or fitness setting, the health screening is usually done as part of the fitness orientation and, in some cases, may require a complete medical examination and physician clearance prior to participation. The purposes of a health screening include the following (1):

- Identification and exclusion of individuals with medical contraindications to exercise

- Identification of individuals at increased risk for disease because of age, symptoms, or risk factors that indicate a need for further medical evaluation and exercise testing before starting an exercise program
- Identification of individuals with clinically significant disease who should participate in a medically supervised exercise program
- Identification of individuals with other special needs

The health screening procedure or tool used should be valid, cost-effective, and time-efficient (2). The procedure can range from a self-administered questionnaire to more sophisticated diagnostic tests (1). The American College of Sports Medicine (ACSM) recommends that the minimal standard for entry into moderate physical activity be completion of the Physical Activity Readiness Questionnaire (PAR-Q) (3). The PAR-Q focuses primarily on symptoms that might suggest cardiovascular disease, although it is also useful in identifying musculoskeletal problems that might necessitate modification in the exercise program (2). If an individual has a positive response to the PAR-Q, it is recommended that they complete the Physical Activity Readiness Medical Examination (PARmed-X) Questionnaire (3) and be evaluated by a physician.

Using information from the health screening and the guidelines and risk stratification categories established by the ACSM, health professionals can identify clients who might face health risks from an exercise program. ACSM uses three categories of risk stratification (1):

1. *Low risk:* An individual is young (age < 45 years for men, < 55 years for women) and has no more than one risk factor for coronary artery disease (CAD) (eg, family history, smoking, hypertension, hypercholesterolemia, impaired fasting glucose, obesity, sedentary lifestyle).
2. *Moderate risk:* An individual is older (men ≥ 45 years of age; women ≥ 55 years of age) and has two or more risk factors for CAD.
3. *High risk:* An individual with one or more signs/symptoms for CAD or known cardiovascular, pulmonary, or metabolic disease.

Components of Health Screening

The extent to which medical evaluation is necessary prior to exercise participation largely depends on the assessment of risk as determined by the health screen and risk stratification (1). The medical evaluation may include any or all of the following: medical history and physical examination, including an evaluation of general systems, blood pressure, blood lipids, pulmonary function, and dietary history.

Medical History

Active individuals are generally healthier and have fewer chronic disease-related issues than their sedentary counterparts; nevertheless, health professionals should obtain a complete medical history, including both past and current medical events. The medical history should be comprehensive enough to give the health professional a good understanding of the individual's risk of developing an illness or injury. Finally, the medical history should include the review of any past physical examinations if available. The medical history should address the following areas (1), with specific attention give to medical issues that occur more frequently in active individuals.

- Medical diagnoses of disease (eg, cardiovascular or pulmonary disease, hypertension, diabetes, anemia, osteoporosis, emotional disorders, eating disorders) or risk factors for disease (eg, abnormal blood lipids and lipoproteins, edema). A brief outline of the types of blood assessment parameters that might be included on a basic biochemical chemistry profile are given in Box 8.1.
- History of symptoms of heart disease (eg, lightheadedness, dizziness, shortness of breath; rapid heart beats or palpitations), especially if associated with physical activity, eating a large meal, or emotional upset.
- Recent illnesses, hospitalizations, or surgical procedures.
- Orthopedic problems such as arthritis, joint swelling, stiffness, or soreness.
- Medication use and drug allergies; drug habits—including caffeine, alcohol, tobacco, or recreational drugs.
- Menstrual history—including age of menarche, typical cycle length, and any episodes of menstrual dysfunction (ie, amenorrhea, oligomenorrhea, anovulation, shortened luteal phase). If amenorrhea is present, check for pregnancy and other primary causes.
- Exercise and work history (eg, habitual physical activity; type of work).
- Family health history of cardiac, pulmonary, or metabolic disease, stroke, or sudden death.

Physical Examination

A licensed physician, nurse practitioner, or physician's assistant should conduct the physical examination. Vital signs (ie, temperature, pulse rate and regularity, blood pressure, respiration), head-to-toe inspection, resting 12-lead electrocardiogram (ECG) and stress test (if indicated), heart sounds, anthropometric measurements, biochemical data, tests of neurological function (including reflexes), and physical fitness evaluation are all components of the physical examination (1). The frequency and depth with which an individual should have a physical examination depends on medical history, age, and physical condition.

Pre-participation Examinations for Athletes

Prior to participating in an organized sport at the high school or college level, athletes customarily undergo a physical examination, called the pre-participation examination. The examination is conducted to (a) assess the athlete's general health; (b) identify existing physical, cardiorespiratory, or musculoskeletal problems that may limit participation or predispose the athlete to injury; (c) recommend preventive measures to optimize health; and (d) provide legal clearance for sports participation (4,5). For many adolescent athletes, this may be the only routine health assessment they receive.

The pre-participation examination should be conducted 6 weeks before the athlete begins a competitive season. This allows time to evaluate and treat problems identified during the examination and rehabilitate any residual injuries prior to the start of the season (6).

Box 8.1   General Blood Biochemical Assessment Parameters

Lipids:
- Total cholesterol
- Low-density lipoprotein (LDL) cholesterol
- High-density lipoprotein (HDL) cholesterol
- Total triglycerides

Electrolytes/Liver Function:
- Sodium
- Potassium
- Chloride
- Bicarbonate
- Phosphorus
- Calcium
- Blood urea nitrogen (BUN)
- Uric acid
- Creatinine (Creat)
- BUN-to-Creat ratio
- Serum glutamic-oxaloacetate transaminase (SGOT) or aspartate transaminiase (AST)
- Lactate dehydrogenase (LDH)
- Serum glutamic-pyruvate transaminase (SGPT) or alanine transaminase (ALT)
- Alkaline phosphatase

Protein:
- Albumin (A)
- Total protein
- Globulin (G)
- A-to-G ratio

Glucose
Iron Profile:
- Serum iron
- Ferritin
- Iron-binding capacity
- Hemoglobin
- Hematocrit

Although the frequency of the pre-participation examination will depend on the state, school system, and collegiate policies, ideally it should be done as frequently as necessary to assure the health of the athlete.

The components of the pre-participation examination are similar to those for the health screening and medical evaluation of the adult exercise participant outlined earlier in this chapter. The examination should include an in-depth medical and diet history, with an additional focus on previously sustained sports-related injuries. For female athletes, an in-depth menstrual history and assessment of current menstrual status are a necessity (7). In addition, for all female athletes, health professionals should screen for patterns of disordered eating and/or pathogenic weight-control behaviors, and obtain an in-depth history of stress fractures (indicative of potential bone-mineral density deficiencies). In-depth information about disordered eating and eating disorders is found in Chapter 17.

Dietary Assessment

Assessment of nutritional status is an integral part of health screening because it can identify nutritional risks and serve as a starting point for developing a dietary regimen or nutrition plan. The primary goal of dietary assessment is to achieve the most accurate description of the typical food and nutrient intake of an individual or group. Therefore, the dietary assessment method used must be valid, reliable, and appropriate for the individual or population being studied. Dietary assessment involves not only collecting the food intake information but also analyzing and evaluating the data. Selecting the appropriate dietary intake tool can also increase the accuracy of the overall assessment. Factors to consider when selecting a dietary intake tool include the objectives of the assessment, the individual or group being assessed, the dietary information of interest (ie, energy, specific nutrients, food groups, dietary patterns), the time frame involved, cost, and the interviewer's qualifications and experience (8).

Collection of the food intake data is only one part of dietary assessment. Once the diet data have been collected, they must be analyzed for nutrient content and subsequently evaluated, which typically entails comparing the data to nutrient standards or goals. Dietary intake data are generally analyzed for nutrient content using computerized nutrient-analysis programs (9). To avoid introducing additional error into the diet-assessment technique, care should be taken in the selection and use of these computer programs.

Analysis of dietary intake involves comparing actual intake to recommended intakes or dietary strategies. Although a variety of dietary standards or references are available for evaluating nutrient intake, those most commonly used are the latest Dietary Reference Intakes (DRIs) established by the Institute of Medicine (10,11). Research on the nutrient needs of athletes has also produced dietary recommendations by sport and nutrition organizations. For example, the American Dietetic Association has a Position Stand on Nutrition and Athletic Performance (12) and the International Olympic Committee (IOC) recently published an IOC Consensus on Sport Nutrition 2003 (13).

Components of Dietary Assessment

Table 8.1 summarizes the currently available methods for obtaining dietary intake information along with the strengths and weaknesses of each (8). These methods can be broadly classified as retrospective, prospective, or some combination of the two.

Diet History

The diet history usually involves a one-on-one interview with the client to obtain current and past diet and activity information. This information can then be used to estimate energy intake and nutrient requirements. For the physically active individual, diet history data can

TABLE 8.1   Strengths and Limitations of Diet Assessment Methods

Method and Description	Strengths	Weaknesses/Limitations
24-hour recall • Interview prompts respondent to recall and describe all foods and beverages consumed over the past 24 hours, usually starting with the meal immediately preceding the interview. • Food models and measuring cups and spoons are used to get a rough estimate of portion sizes. • May be done face-to-face or via telephone.	• Easy to administer. • Respondent burden is low. • Time required to administer is short. • Bias introduced by record-keeping is avoided. • Inexpensive. • Useful in clinical situations. • More objective than dietary history. • Does not alter usual diets. • Good reliability between interviewers. • Serial 24-hour recalls can provide estimates of usual intakes of individuals. • Data obtained can be repeated with reasonable accuracy.	• Does not provide adequate quantitative data on nutrient intakes. • Individual diets vary daily so that a single day's intake may not be representative of habitual intake. • An experienced interviewer is required. • Relies heavily on memory. • Desire to please the interviewer may result in inaccurate intakes. • Data may not accurately reflect nutrient intakes for populations because of variations in food consumption from day to day. • May be tendency to overreport intake at low levels and underreport intake of high levels, leading to a "flat slope syndrome" with reports of group intakes.
Food frequency questionnaire • Respondent records or describes usual intakes as a list of different foods and the frequency of consumption per day, week, or month, over a period of several months or a year. • The number and type of food items vary depending on the purpose of the assessment.	• Easy to standardize. • Does not require highly trained interviewers, and some types may be self-administered. • Inexpensive. • Easy and quick to administer. • No observer bias. • Good at describing food intake patterns for diet and meal planning. • Can be used for large population studies. • Useful when purpose is to study associations of a specific food or small number of foods and diseases (eg, alcohol and birth defects). • Specific information about nutrient intakes may be obtained if food sources of nutrients are limited to a few sources. • Can be analyzed rapidly for nutrients or food groups using a computer. • Foods can be ranked in relation to intakes of certain food items or groups of foods. • Does not alter usual diets.	• Does not provide adequate data to determine quantitative nutrient intake. • Incomplete responses may be given. • Response rates may be lower if questionnaire is self-administered. • Lists compiled for general population are not useful for obtaining information about groups with different eating patterns (eg, vegetarians or those on special ethnic or therapeutic diets). • Estimation of total consumption is difficult to obtain because not all foods can be included in the lists; thus, underestimation can occur. • Respondent burden increases as number of items queried increases. • Analysis is difficult without the use of computers. • Reliability is lower for individual foods than for groups of foods. • Foods differ in extent to which they are overreported or underreported (errors are not random). • Amount and frequency with which a food is consumed influence errors in estimation; staples and large quantities are better estimated than accessories or items eaten less frequently. • Each questionnaire requires validation. • Translation of food groups to nutrient intakes requires many assumptions.

continues

TABLE 8.1   Strengths and Limitations of Diet Assessment Methods (continued)

Method and Description	Strengths	Weaknesses/Limitations
Semiquantitative food frequency questionnaire • Similar to a food frequency questionnaire. • Portion sizes are specified as standardized portion size or choice (of a range of sizes). • Foods are chosen to encompass the most frequently consumed foods as well as the most common source of nutrients. • The major sources of nutrients for a given population should be included for the questionnaire to be valid.	• Inexpensive and rapid to administer. • May be self-administered. • Usual diets are not altered. • On some versions, precoding and direct data entry to computer are available to speed analysis. • Can rank or categorize individuals by rank of nutrient intakes rather than measuring group means. • Correlations between this and other methods are satisfactory for food items and targeted nutrients when groups are the focus of analysis. • Sufficiently simple to obtain dietary information on large epidemiological studies that would not otherwise be possible with other methods. • Can provide useful information on intake of a wide variety of nutrients. • Respondent burden varies.	• Good for the general population but not necessarily for specific groups. • Culture-specific (ie, assessment of intake in a culturally distinct group requires the creation and validation of another instrument). • Not validated for individual dietary assessments. • Questionnaires available for adults cannot be used for children. • Must be constantly updated. • Specific nutrient intakes, rather than all nutrient intakes or food constituents, are measured. • Not yet validated for individuals who eat modified or unusual diets. • Ability to monitor short-term changes in food intake (weeks or months) is unknown. • Correlations for individual nutrient intakes obtained with semiquantitative food frequency questionnaires are poor when compared with diet histories and food records in household measures. • May be reliable but invalid in some cases. • May reflect "core diets" of a week's duration. • Default codes with estimated variables may influence the results unduly.
Burke-type dietary history • Respondent orally reports all foods and beverages consumed on a usual day, then the interviewer progresses to questions about frequency and amount of consumption of the foods. • Often the respondent provides additional documentation of several days' intakes in the form of food diaries. • Food models, crosschecks on food consumption, careful probing, and other techniques are frequently used. • Respondent records all foods and beverages consumed in a food diary, including estimated portion sizes, at the time of consumption for several days or only at specified times.	• Provides a more complete and detailed description of both qualitative and quantitative aspects of food intake than do food records, 24-hour recalls, or food frequency questionnaires. • Eliminates individual day-to day variations. • Takes into consideration seasonal variations in diet. • Good for longitudinal studies. • Does not alter usual diets. • Provides good description of usual intakes. • Provides some data on previous diet before beginning prospective studies. • What is eaten is recorded (or should be recorded) at the time of consumption; thus, errors of recall are less than with retrospective methods.	• Highly trained interviewers required to administer dietary histories. • Highly dependent on subject's memory. • Difficult to standardize because of considerable variability among and within interviewers. • Diet histories overestimate intakes compared with food records collected over the same period because of bigger portion sizes and greater frequencies reported. • Does not account for missed meals or snacks. • Costs of analysis are high because records must be checked, coded, and entered appropriately. • Time frame actually used by subject for reporting intake history is uncertain, probably no longer than a few weeks. • Validity must be established in each study. • Food intake may be altered during reporting periods. • Respondent burden is great.

continues

TABLE 8.1 Strengths and Limitations of Diet Assessment Methods (continued)

Method and Description	Strengths	Weaknesses/Limitations
	• Respondent can be instructed in advance to reduce recording errors.	• Individual must be literate and physically able to write. • If respondent does not record intakes on assigned days, records may not accurately represent dietary habits. • Difficult to estimate portion size. • Underreporting is common. • Number of sampled days must be sufficient to provide usual intakes. • Records must be checked and coded in a standardized way. • Measured food intakes are more valid than records. • Costs of coding and analysis are high. • Requires competency in recording food items and quantities. • Number of days surveyed depends on the nutrient being studied. • The very act of recording may change what is eaten.
Weighed food diary • Similar to a food record except that the individual weighs all food and drink consumed on a scale rather than simply estimating portion sizes. All food is recorded at the time it is eaten.	• Increased accuracy of portion sizes over food diaries (where errors are substantial, up to 40% for foods and 25% for nutrients)	• Expensive and time-consuming. • May restrict choice of food. • Subjects must be highly motivated. • Requires reliable equipment (eg, calibrated, operable scales). • Other disadvantages similar to those of a food diary.
Telephone record • Instead of personal face-to-face interviews, telephones are used to report food intakes as soon as they have occurred.	• Some anonymity is maintained. • Validity is good. • Respondent burden is low. • Respondent acceptance is good. • Effect of forgetting is minimum. • Outreach is greater. • May be easier to carry out after face-to-face interview and instruction.	• Assumption is made that portion sizes reported are actually taken. • Validation studies are incomplete.
Photographic or videotape records • Individual photographs or videotapes all foods to be eaten at a standard distance.	• Validity is good.	• Problems with estimating portion sizes and identifying some foods from photographs. • Food waste may not be taken into account, leading to overestimation. • Obtrusive. • Respondent burden is high.

continues

TABLE 8.1　Strengths and Limitations of Diet Assessment Methods (continued)

Method and Description	Strengths	Weaknesses/Limitations
Electronic records (food recording electronic device [FRED]) • Respondent records food intake on a specially programmed electronic recording device (hand-held computer or small tape recorder).	• Preliminary validations are good. • Decreased respondent burden. • Eliminates time for coding and data entry, and associated errors occurring at those stages.	• Requires considerable instruction and training. • Special food groups must be constructed for population to be studied. • Portion size estimates are often imprecise.
Duplicate portion collection and analysis • A duplicate portion of the foods and beverages consumed by an individual is collected. Foods are then chemically analyzed to obtain a direct nutrient analysis.	• Highly accurate in metabolic research. • Duplicate portion permits direct chemical analysis. • Helpful for validating other methods for constituents on which food consumption data are incomplete. • Good for individuals consuming unusual foods. • Can be used with patients who cannot write.	• Intakes may be altered. • High respondent burden. • Expensive, time-consuming, and messy. • Differences between duplicate portions and weighed records are large (7% for energy, larger discrepancies for other nutrients).
Measured intakes and outputs • Applicable to confined individuals, usually in institutions. • All foods entering and leaving the room are measured. The differences between them are assumed to be equivalent to what the respondents ate.	• Low respondent burden. • Assessment can be accomplished without the individual knowing about it. • Good for individuals incapable of writing or remembering.	• Others in the room may have eaten the individual's food. • Individual may have hidden or thrown away food (eg, clients with anorexia nervosa). • Staff may forget to deliver or collect the food.
Direct observation by video recording • Video cameras are used to monitor the individual's food intake over a certain period. • Videotapes may then be reviewed and intakes recorded accordingly.	• Low respondent burden. • Measures usual and habitual food intake. • Highly accurate. • Details may be observed. • Individual may or may not know he or she is being observed.	• High initial cost. • Not good for large studies. • May have technical problems (eg, angle of camera, low-quality picture detail). • Intakes may be altered if individual is aware of observation.
Direct observation by trained observer • In controlled, highly supervised environments, intakes may be directly watched by trained observers who use any of the methods mentioned above. Sometimes the observation is covert.	• Low respondent burden. • Overt or covert observation is possible. • Precise measurements may be obtained.	• Obtrusive. • Expensive and time-consuming for observer. • Not ideal for large studies. • Intakes may be altered, especially if person is aware of observation. • Details may be overlooked.

Source: Adapted with permission from Dwyer JT. Dietary assessment. In: Shils ME, Olson JA, Shike M, ed. *Modern Nutrition in Health and Disease.* 9th ed. Philadelphia, Pa: Lea & Febiger; 1998:937–957.

be gathered through the medical chart, interview, or both. It is especially important that information be obtained on the type, duration, and intensity of activity that the individual is, or will be, engaged in. This information assists the health professional in assessing any dietary or nutrient issues relevant to a given activity. The following diet history interview format has been adapted for use with physically active individuals, with an emphasis on understanding the eating and food environment and the typical exercise routine:

- *Weight:* Current weight, usual weight, weight goal for sport, recent weight loss or gain, percent body fat, goal body fat, and frequency of dieting for weight loss, methods used to control weight in the past or currently.
- *Appetite and intake:* Appetite changes and factors affecting appetite/intake such as training routine, activity level, anorexia, stress, allergies, medications, chewing/swallowing problems (bulimia, oral health), and gastrointestinal problems (gastritis, laxative abuse, constipation).
- *Eating patterns:* Typical patterns (weekdays/weekends); primary eating place (dorm, home, cafeteria, training table); primary food shopper at home; dietary restrictions (understanding of and compliance with these restrictions); frequency of eating out; effect of training, precompetition, competition, and travel on typical eating patterns; ethnicity of diet.
- *Food preferences and dietary practices:* Food likes and dislikes; any food restrictions due to dietary practices or beliefs (ie, vegetarianism, religious dietary practices, food allergies, and food intolerances, such as lactose intolerance).
- *Estimation of typical energy and nutrient intake:* Compare intake with the DRIs and recommendations made for active individuals (12,13). Food intake information may be obtained from a 24-hour recall, food frequency questionnaire (FFQ), and/or food diary.
- *Psychosocial data:* Economic status, occupation, educational level, living and cooking arrangements, and mental status.
- *Medication and/or supplement use:* Current use of medications and supplements, including amounts and reason for use (14). Drug-nutrient or nutrient-nutrient interactions may necessitate special dietary consideration. Consider effect of medication on physical performance and eating habits.
- *Other:* Age; gender; types of physical activity and amount (minutes per day, miles per week) engaged in during competition, training, and nontraining periods; fitness level (maximum oxygen consumption [VO_{2max}]; strength tests; and flexibility).

Methods for Collecting Dietary Intake Data

Retrospective Methods

Retrospective methods involve looking back at, or recalling, dietary intake over a specified time period. Consequently, these methods rely heavily on memory and, thus, are limited by the individual's ability to remember dietary intake in the near or more distant past. Nonetheless, with a skilled interviewer the data generated can approximate or even equal that derived from prospective methods (8). The most commonly used retrospective methods include the 24-hour recall and FFQ.

24-Hour Recall

The 24-hour recall is the easiest and fastest method available for assessing food and nutrient intake. This method requires that a client recall in detail all the foods and beverages consumed during the previous 24 hours. Knowing the preparation methods, the brand names of foods and beverages, and any vitamin-mineral supplements is critical to a thorough evaluation. In addition to the limitations listed in Table 8.1, a major limitation of the 24-hour recall is the tendency for some clients to minimize food choices they perceive to be less healthful or acceptable and to overstate those they perceive to be more healthful or acceptable.

The success of the 24-hour recall depends in large part on the client's memory, motivation to respond accurately, and ability to convey precise information. The accuracy of a 24-hour recall can be improved by a skilled interviewer's use of probing questions, measuring devices, and food models to help the client remember the types and amounts of foods consumed (8).

A single 24-hour recall is most appropriately used for estimating the nutrient intake of a group or population, as opposed to assessing the usual food and nutrient intake of an individual (8,15). If the 24-hour recall is to be used for estimating individual food intakes, the US Committee on Food Consumption Patterns recommends that a minimum of four 24-hour recalls be collected over a 1-year period (16).

Food Frequency Questionnaire

An FFQ is designed to provide descriptive information about an individual's usual dietary intake. The information collected can then be used to assess food patterns and preferences that may not be evident from a food recall or diet record. For best results the FFQ should be brief, requiring less than 30 minutes for administration and completion (17). As with the 24-hour recall, a major limitation of the FFQ is that it relies heavily on memory and, thus, may not be appropriate for use with very young children or with individuals who have poor memories. Additionally, although FFQs are good for describing dietary patterns of populations, they are more limited in their ability to provide quantitative information about specific nutrient intakes of individuals. However, if only a single nutrient is of interest, it may be possible to estimate intake of that particular nutrient with a comprehensive FFQ.

Some researchers have developed a picture approach to the FFQ. In this method a color picture or black-and-white line drawing of the food is shown. The subjects then identify the foods they eat and sort them into categories based on frequency of consumption (eg, daily, once per week, never, etc). Portion sizes can also be reviewed because the pictures indicate standard portion sizes (17).

The FFQ can be designed to provide either qualitative or semiquantitative information about a client's typical food intake (8,18). Questionnaires that provide qualitative data (ie, list only typical foods consumed) are most useful for obtaining general, descriptive information about an individual's dietary patterns or for comparing consumption of certain foods before and after nutrition intervention (17). Semiquantitative FFQs not only list typical foods consumed, but also attempt to quantify the usual intake of these foods. This type of questionnaire allows the assessment of specific nutrient intakes in addition to dietary patterns. Selective FFQs can also be created to inquire about specific nutrient concerns such as fat, carbohydrate, and cholesterol.

Because the aim of the FFQ is to assess the frequency with which certain food items or food groups are consumed during a specified period, it is important that the questionnaire be designed and tested specifically for the population and nutrient being measured. For example, Rockett et al (19) have recently tested and validated a youth and adolescent FFQ, and Coates and Monteilh (20) have published a FFQ for minority populations. For general assessment of adult populations, the most frequently used FFQs are those adapted from the original Block et al (21) questionnaire and those adapted from the FFQ developed by Willett and colleagues (22) at Harvard.

Prospective Methods

Prospective methods of collecting dietary intake data involve recording food intake at the time the food is eaten or shortly thereafter. The most commonly used prospective methods are food records or diaries. Other techniques that are applicable in certain situations are: collection of duplicate portions of all food eaten; observations of intakes and food wastes; and photographic, videotaped, and electronic microcomputer records of consumption. Because prospective methods are less dependent on memory, they tend to be more accurate than the retrospective methods. Nonetheless, they have limitations. The very act of recording intake tends to influence food choices and nutrient intakes, or may otherwise lead the respondent to alter intake during the recording period (8,15).

Food Records

A food record is a list of all foods consumed, including a description of food preparation methods and brand names used, during a specified time period (typically 3 to 7 days). To predict nutrient content accurately, it is best if the foods consumed are weighed or measured. However, it is most common for consumed foods to be recorded by common portion sizes expressed in common household measuring units. Depending on the reasons for recording food intake, more in-depth information about eating habits, such as time, place, feelings, and behaviors associated with eating, can also be included on a food record. When the records are completed, the nutrient contribution from each food is determined and average nutrient intake for the time period being monitored can be calculated.

Determining the number of days that food intake should be recorded to give an accurate and reliable estimate of typical dietary intake has been addressed by several researchers. Schlundt (23) determined that, for most purposes, diet records collected for 3 to 4 days will provide accurate estimates of nutrient intake; however, both reliability and accuracy tend to increase with each additional day up to 7 days. For most nutrients, there is little advantage to measuring intakes beyond 2 or 3 weeks because increases in recording duration generally produce an increase in respondent burden.

The accuracy of a food record relies heavily on the client's cooperation and skill in recording foods consumed. Underreporting of food intake remains a substantial problem that can severely compromise the accuracy of the dietary analysis (24,25). Research indicates that certain individuals are more prone to underreporting energy intake, including women and those who are older, overweight, or trying to lose weight (24). Knowing who is likely to underreport food intake will allow the nutrition professional to take extra precautions when selecting and administering the food intake protocol and analyzing the record. The accuracy of the food record may be increased if the client is given adequate incentive and proper instructions. Specific guidelines for keeping records should be included in the instruction sheet given to the client and also be reviewed verbally.

Combination Methods

Another, perhaps more comprehensive, approach to obtaining a representative estimate of food intake by an individual or group is to combine two or more dietary intake methods. Using a combination of dietary assessment methods not only provides a more complete picture of an individual's typical dietary habits and nutrient intake, but also may increase the accuracy of the assessment because the shortcomings of one method may be counterbalanced by the strengths of another (8). For example, the National Health and Nutrition Examination Survey uses a combination of a 24-hour recall and FFQ.

Validity of Dietary Intake Methods

The validity of dietary intake methods, particularly 24-hour recalls and food records, has been difficult to determine, at least without the use of direct observation, which is time-consuming, costly, and largely unrealistic. However, with the development of various biochemical markers, most notably doubly-labeled water, it is now possible to assess the validity of different dietary intake methods (26). Doubly-labeled water allows for the estimation of energy expenditure in free-living humans. Under conditions of weight maintenance, energy intake is equal to energy expenditure. Thus, if energy expenditure is measured, the validity of reports of energy intake can be assessed. Similarly, protein (nitrogen) intake can be checked against crude nitrogen balance.

Nutrient Analysis Programs

Currently, computerized diet analysis is the most popular and widely used method for analyzing dietary intake information. When properly applied, this method is considered the most efficient, accurate, and timely means available for analyzing the nutrient content of consumed foods (9).

Interpreting the Dietary Data

Once dietary intake information has been collected and analyzed, it must be evaluated. This generally entails comparing nutrient intakes to accepted standards to make the information more meaningful to the client and to help set the groundwork for formulating dietary goals.

Several methods are used for dietary evaluation. A simple and quick method is to compare dietary intake to the federal government's Dietary Guidelines for Americans (27) and determine whether any major food groups are completely omitted from the individual's diet or are consumed infrequently. Because no single food can provide all of the nutrients needed, the diet must also be checked for variety within each food group. In general, a monotonous diet will increase the risk of poor nutritional status. In addition, because foods within each group vary in their fat and sodium content, the frequency of consumption of foods high in fat and/or sodium within each group should also be checked. Finally, if an individual consistently consumes foods high in simple sugars and/or fats, fat and energy intake may be high, even though he or she is eating a variety of other foods (17). It is generally assumed that if adequate energy and a variety of foods are consumed from each food group, micronutrient intake will be adequate.

References

1. American College of Sports Medicine. *ACSM's Guidelines for Exercise Testing and Prescription*. 6th ed. Philadelphia, Pa: Lippincott, Williams and Wilkins; 2000.

2. American College of Sports Medicine and American Heart Association. ACSM and AHA joint position statement: recommendations for cardiovascular screening, staffing, and emergency policies at health/fitness facilities. *Med Sci Sports Exerc.* 1998;30:1009–1017.

3. Canadian Society for Exercise Physiology. *Physical Activity Readiness (PAR-Q) Questionnaire and You.* Gloucester, Canada: Canadian Society for Exercise Physiology; 1994:1–2. Available at: http://www.csep.ca/pdfs/par-q.pdf. Accessed November 4, 2004.

4. Cantwell JD. Pre-participation physical evaluation: getting to the heart of the matter. *Med Sci Sports Exerc.* 1998;30(10 Suppl):S341–S344.

5. Peltz JE, Haskell WL, Matheson GO. A comprehensive and cost-effective preparticipation exam implemented on the World Wide Web. *Med Sci Sports Exerc.* 1999;31:1727–1740.

6. Myers A, Sickles T. Preparticipation sports examination. *Primary Care.* 1998;25:225–236.

7. Johnson MD. Tailoring the preparticipation exam to female athletes. *Phys Sportsmed.* 1992;20:61–72.

8. Dwyer JT. Dietary assessment. In: Shils ME, Olson JA, Shike M, eds. *Modern Nutrition in Health and Disease.* 9th ed. Philadelphia, Pa: Lea & Febiger; 1998:937–957.

9. Lee RD, Nieman DC, Rainwater M. Comparison of eight microcomputer dietary analysis programs with the USDA nutrient data base for standard reference. *J Am Diet Assoc.* 1995;95:858–867.

10. Institute of Medicine. *Dietary Reference Intakes for Calcium, Phosphorous, Magnesium, Vitamin D, and Fluoride.* Washington, DC: National Academy Press; 1997. Available at: http://www.nap.edu. Accessed November 4, 2004.

11. Institute of Medicine. *Dietary Reference Intakes for Thiamin, Riboflavin, Niacin, Vitamin B-6, Folate, Vitamin B-12, Pantothenic Acid, Biotin, and Choline.* Washington, DC: National Academy Press; 1998. Available at: http://www.nap.edu. Accessed November 4, 2004.

12. Manore M, Barr S, Butterfield G; American Dietetic Association. Position of the American Dietetic Association, Dietitians of Canada, and the American College of Sports Medicine: nutrition and athletic performance. *J Am Diet Assoc.* 2000;100:1543–1556.

13. Burke LM. The IOC Consensus on Sport Nutrition 2003: new guidelines for nutrition for athletes. *Int J Sport Nutr Exerc Metab.* 2004;13:549–552.

14. United States Olympic Committee. *Guidelines on Dietary Supplements.* 2001. Available at: http://www.usolympicteam.com/eduation/sports_med/guide1.pdf. Accessed June 14, 2004.

15. Lee RD, Nieman DC. *Nutritional Assessment.* 3rd ed. Boston, Mass: McGraw Hill; 2003.

16. Gibson RS. *Principles of Nutritional Assessment.* New York, NY: Oxford University Press; 1990.

17. Cade J, Thompson R, Burley V, Warm D. Development, validation and utilization of food-frequency questionnaires—a review. *Public Health Nutr.* 2002;5:567–587.

18. Dwyer JT, Coleman KA. Insights into dietary recall from a longitudinal study: accuracy over four decades. *Am J Clin Nutr.* 1997;65(4 Suppl):1153S–1158S.

19. Rockett HR, Breitenbach M, Frazier AL, Witschi J, Wolf AM, Field AE, Colditz GA. Validation of a youth/adolescent food frequency questionnaire. *Prev Med.* 1997;26:808–816.

20. Coates RJ, Monteilh CP. Assessments of food-frequency questionnaires in minority populations. *Am J Clin Nutr.* 1997;65(4 Suppl):1108S–1115S.

21. Block G, Hartman AM, Dresser CM, Carroll MD, Gannon J, Gardner L. A data-based approach to diet questionnaire design and testing. *Am J Epidemiol.* 1986;124:453–469.

22. Willett WC, Renyolds RD, Cottrell-Hoehner S, Sampson L, Browne ML. Validation of a semi-quantitative food-frequency questionnaire: comparison with a 1-year diet record. *J Am Diet Assoc.* 1987;87:43–47.

23. Schlundt EG. Accuracy and reliability of nutrient intake estimates. *J Nutr.* 1988;118: 1432–1435.

24. Livingstone MBE, Black AE. Markers of the validity of reported energy intake. *J Nutr.* 2003;133(Suppl 3):895S-920S.

25. Becker W, Welten D. Under-reporting in dietary surveys: implications for development of food-based dietary guidelines. *Public Health Nutr.* 2000;4:683–687.

26. Champagne CM, Bray GA, Kurtz AA, Monteiro JB, Tucker E, Volaufova J, Delany JP. Energy intake and energy expenditure: a controlled study comparing dietitians and non-dietitians. *J Am Diet Assoc.* 2002;102:1428–1432.

27. US Departments of Health and Human Services and Agriculture. Dietary Guidelines for Americans. 2005. Available at: http://www.healthierus.gov/dietaryguidelines. Accessed April 29, 2005.

Chapter 9

PHYSICAL FITNESS ASSESSMENT AND PRESCRIPTION

CATHRYN R. DOOLY, PhD, FACSM, AND KATHERINE A. BEALS, PhD, RD, FACSM

Introduction

The term *physical fitness* has many connotations and, thus, may be defined in several ways. Until recently, definitions have focused largely on proficiencies or elements relating to athletic performance but not necessarily health. However, because evidence supports a positive relationship between health and physical activity, health-related definitions of physical fitness are more prevalent (1–3). The primary concept that underlies health-related fitness is that improvement in any of the fitness components is associated with a lower risk for chronic diseases and functional disabilities (4–6). The components of health-related fitness typically include body composition, cardiorespiratory endurance, muscular strength and endurance, and flexibility.

The measurement of physical fitness is an important component of any preventive or rehabilitative exercise program and serves several purposes (4):

- Provides a basis for developing an exercise prescription
- Allows for collection of baseline and follow-up data for evaluation of progress
- Motivates participants by establishing reasonable and attainable fitness goals
- Educates participants about the concepts of physical fitness and health
- Allows for stratification of participants based on risk for disease (ie, risk stratification)

A sound, well-conducted physical fitness test should be valid, reliable, relatively inexpensive, and easy to administer. Additionally, the test should yield results that can be directly and appropriately compared with normative data (4).

Fitness Assessment Components

A comprehensive fitness assessment should include at least one test to measure each of the components of fitness: body composition, cardiorespiratory endurance, muscular strength and endurance, and flexibility. How the testing session is organized can be very important, especially if multiple tests are being administered (4). If all of the components are assessed during a single session, body composition measures should be taken first, followed (in order) by tests of cardiorespiratory endurance, muscular strength and endurance, and flexibility. Testing cardiorespiratory endurance after assessing muscular strength and endurance, which elevates heart rate, may lead to an underestimation of an individual's cardiorespiratory endurance, especially if submaximal tests are used (4). Similarly, assessing body composition after cardiorespiratory endurance or muscular strength and endurance may lead to inaccuracies in body composition assessment. If the testing protocol involves assessing resting measures (eg, heart rate, blood pressure, and blood lipids), such measures should be taken before any fitness testing begins (4).

Body Composition

It is well-known that excessive body fat can be harmful to health. Body composition assessment allows for the determination of the relative fat mass and lean body mass to total body weight. A variety of methods for measuring body composition are currently available; however, specialized equipment and training limits the accessibility and practicality of several of these methods. This section will briefly describe the most commonly used field techniques for assessing body composition and their interpretation relative to the health/fitness assessment. For a more detailed account of body composition assessment, including laboratory techniques, refer to Chapter 10 and the *Resource Manual for Guidelines for Exercise Testing and Prescription* (7).

Hydrostatic Weighing

Underwater or hydrostatic weighing (HW) is one of the most common laboratory methods for estimating body composition and has recently been made available for the field setting with the introduction of mobile tanks. HW provides a reasonably accurate estimate for body density, but several potential sources of error must be considered, including residual lung volume, gastrointestinal tract gas, and bone density (8). Residual lung volume (RLV), or the volume of air that remains in the lung after a maximal forced expiration, can be large and must be accounted for. When RLV is measured, the precision of HW is quite good; however, measurement error increases significantly when the RLV is estimated (8). Similarly, the estimation of the volume of gas in the gastrointestinal tract can introduce error as can variation in estimates of bone density (8).

Of course, the method will only be accurate if the individual being assessed can successfully complete the test. Because hydrostatic weighing requires an individual to be submerged underwater (after expelling all his or her air) for an extended period of time (several seconds), it is likely to be uncomfortable, anxiety-provoking, and difficult for many people to do. Finally, hydrostatic weighing requires expensive, complex equipment (computer, electronic load cell, tank, filter, and warming unit), and the procedure is somewhat tedious and time-consuming, rendering it largely impractical as a field method for assessing body composition. (9).

Air Displacement Plethysmography

Air displacement plethysmography (ADP), also known as the BOD POD (Life Measurement Instruments, Concord, CA), uses air displacement and pressure-volume relationships rather than water displacement to estimate body volume (10). ADP has several advantages over hydrostatic weighing. It is reasonably portable and relatively easy to operate, measurement time is only 5 to 10 minutes, only minimal skill is required by the technician administering the test, and it may be better able to accommodate special populations such as young children, obese individuals, the elderly, or individuals with disabilities (10). Although ADP has been reported to have similar predictive accuracy and validity as HW, several factors related to the client, testing conditions, and percent body fat conversion formulas may be reason for the measurement error of ADP.

Anthropometry

Anthropometry includes measures such as height, weight, limb and torso circumferences, and skinfold thickness. Anthropometric measurements can be used in equations to either directly predict percent fat or indirectly predict whole-body density that can then be used to estimate percent fat (10). Although the equipment used for anthropometry is much less expensive than HW or ADP, accurate assessment relies more heavily on the knowledge and skill of the individual administering the assessment. Thus, proper training in the technique is imperative.

Skinfolds

Measuring skinfolds is one of the most commonly used anthropometric methods for estimating body fat percentage. This method is based on the assumption that the thickness of the subcutaneous adipose tissue is proportional to the total amount of body fat mass, and the sites selected for measurement represent the average thickness of the subcutaneous adipose tissue. The accuracy and reliability of percentage of fat estimated from skinfolds depend on the technician's skill, type of skinfold caliper used, and the prediction equation used to estimate body fatness (10). If administered correctly, body composition determined from skinfold measurements correlates well ($r = 0.80$) with body composition as assessed by HW (4).

Body Mass Index

Body mass index (BMI) is used to assess weight relative to height and provides an acceptable approximation of total body fat in population-based studies. In addition, BMI demonstrates a strong positive correlation with morbidity and mortality; thus, it provides a direct indication of health status and disease risk (11). Calculating BMI is simple, quick, and inexpensive (BMI = weight in kg/height in m^2). The major limitations of BMI are that it does not provide information about regional body fat distribution and it is difficult to project changes in actual body fat loss to BMI changes (4). In addition, although BMI is positively correlated with body fat in obese individuals, it does not accurately reflect body fat percentage of those with normal or low BMI. Also, BMI has been routinely shown to overestimate body fat in individuals who are very muscular (eg, athletes or highly active individuals) and underestimate body fat in those who have lost muscle mass (eg, people who are ill or elderly) (11).

Waist-to-Hip Ratio

Individuals with high amounts of fat in the abdominal region, especially visceral abdominal fat, are at increased risk for premature death and several chronic diseases, including hypertension, type 2 diabetes, hyperlipidemia, and coronary artery disease (12,13). The waist-to-hip ratio (WHR) is a simple method for determining an individual's body fat pattern or the relative ratio of abdominal to gluteal-femoral body fat (14). Ratios of more than 0.90 for men and more than 0.80 for women place the individual at significantly increased risk of disease (14).

It has recently been suggested that a combination of BMI, waist circumference, and risk factors for disease be used to assess whether a person is overweight and to evaluate the need for weight loss (11). The National Heart, Lung, and Blood Institute's *Clinical Guidelines on the Identification, Evaluation, and Treatment of Overweight in Adults* (11) defines overweight as a BMI of 25 to 29.9 and obesity as a BMI more than 30. A waist circumference more than 40 inches in men and more than 35 inches in women signifies an increased risk for obesity-related diseases in individuals with a BMI of 25 to 34.8 (11).

Bioelectrical Impedance Analysis

Bioelectrical impedance analysis (BIA) is a simple, quick, and noninvasive method for estimating FFM or total body water in community and clinical settings. This method involves passing a small electric current through the body and measuring the resistance encountered. The technique is based on the assumption that tissues that are high in water content (eg, muscle) will conduct electrical currents with less resistance or "impedance" than those with little water (eg, adipose). An advantage of the BIA method is that it does not require a high degree of technical skill to administer. Nonetheless, body composition estimates from BIA are generally less accurate and require more assumptions than those obtained from accurate skinfold measurements (4,15). A major limitation of BIA is that it is greatly affected by state of hydration. Moreover, BIA has been shown to consistently overestimate percent body fat in very lean individuals and underestimate percent body fat in obese individuals (10,15).

Near-Infrared Interactance

Near-infrared interactance (NIR) was originally developed for agricultural use to measure the fat content of meat and grains (10) and has become a commonly used method for estimating body fat percentage in field and clinical settings. It is based on the principle of light absorption and reflection using near-infrared spectroscopy to provide information about the chemical composition of the body (4). In general, the instrument can be used to estimate fatness over the biceps area of the body but does not provide accurate estimates of whole-body composition (10).

Selecting and Interpreting Body Composition Measurement Techniques

Although validity is the most important factor to consider when choosing a body composition technique (ie, has the technique been validated on the population of which the client is a member), availability most often governs choice. Space and budget limitations generally preclude the use of hydrostatic weighing. Indeed, the most common field techniques for measuring body composition (skinfolds, BIA, and near infra-red interactance [NRI]) can be wrought with error as was documented in the previous paragraphs (and detailed in Chapter 10). Nonetheless, they can still provide valuable information for the client seeking to improve his or her health and fitness if used correctly.

It is recommended that a client's body composition measurements not be compared against some arbitrary standard or used to define an exact level of optimal body fat (16).

Rather, the initial body composition assessment should be used to establish a baseline and subsequent measures used to track the success of alterations in dietary and activity patterns. Given this approach, it is essential that the technique used for subsequent measurements be identical to that used to establish the baseline measurement.

Finally, the health professional conducting the assessment needs to make sure the client fully understands the error inherent in the method and the impact that this error has on the interpretation of his or her body composition measurement. For example, interpretation of a ± 3% to 5% standard error means that a given body composition estimate will typically differ from the client's true value by ± 3% to 5%. Thus, a body composition estimate of 20% implies that the client's true body composition could be as high as 23% to 25%, or as low as 15% to 17%, in most cases.

Cardiorespiratory Endurance

Cardiorespiratory endurance is defined as the ability to perform large-muscle, dynamic, moderate- to high-intensity exercise for prolonged periods and is considered one of the most important components of physical fitness (4,17). Every fitness assessment should include a test of cardiorespiratory fitness at rest and during exercise.

Resting Evaluation

A resting evaluation of cardiorespiratory function should be taken prior to exercise testing and should include the following (17):

- Heart rate
- Supine, sitting, and standing blood pressure
- 12-lead electrocardiogram (ECG)

Heart Rate

The resting heart rate (RHR) is the heart rate measured when an individual is resting but not sleeping. It can be measured in a seated or supine position via auscultation (using a stethoscope), radial or carotid palpitation, or ECG recordings (17). Regardless of the method used, the client should rest 5 to 10 minutes in either the supine or seated position prior to taking the measurement. The average RHR for men and women is 60 to 80 beats per minute (bpm). RHRs as low as 28 to 48 bpm have been reported for highly conditioned endurance athletes, whereas poorly trained, sedentary individuals may have an RHR of 100 bpm (17). Caution should be taken in using RHR as a measure of cardiorespiratory fitness because it is a highly variable measure that fluctuates easily due to such factors as environmental temperatures, anxiety, stress, caffeine, time of day, and body position. A low RHR may indicate a pathologically diseased heart (18).

Another valuable heart rate measure in the assessment of cardiorespiratory fitness is maximum heart rate (MHR). MHR is the highest heart rate that an individual can achieve and can be determined directly via a graded exercise test (ie, when a client is brought to total exhaustion) or indirectly by subtracting age in years from 220 (ie, MHR = 220 – age [in years]) The direct measurement of MHR is preferred because individuals of the same sex and age have heart rates that vary greatly (19,20). Because this formula provides only an estimate of MHR, caution is advised when using it to develop a fitness program. For example, a 45-year-old individual may have a true heart rate of 145 to 205 bpm, rather than the estimated 175 bpm. However, two thirds of the population at this age would have MHRs of 165 to 185 bpm. Although heart rate will increase in direct proportion to the intensity of exercise, MHR changes little with training.

Blood Pressure

Blood pressure is a measure of the force or pressure exerted by the blood on the arteries. The highest pressure or systolic blood pressure reflects the pressure in the arteries during systole of the heart when myocardial contraction forces a large volume of blood into the arteries; diastolic blood pressure reflects the lowest pressure in the arteries during diastole or the resting phase of the cardiac cycle. Blood pressure should be taken in the supine, sitting, and standing position prior to exercise testing. More detailed information about procedures for obtaining proper blood pressure measurement is found in variety of excellent sources (17). According to the most recent report of the Joint National Committee on Prevention, Detection, Evaluation, and Treatment of High Blood Pressure (21), optimal blood pressure is defined as a systolic blood pressure of less than 120 mm Hg and a diastolic pressure of less than 80 mm Hg. A systolic blood pressure in the range of 120 to 139 mm Hg or a diastolic pressure of 80 to 89 mm Hg is indicative of "prehypertension," and hypertension is indicated if the systolic blood pressure is greater than 140 mm Hg or the diastolic pressure is greater than 90 mm Hg. More detailed information about blood pressure is found in Chapter 20.

12-lead ECG

The ECG is a composite record of the electrical events of the heart during the cardiac cycle. As the heart depolarizes (contracts) and repolarizes (relaxes) during contraction, an electrical signal spreads to the tissues surrounding the heart. Electrodes placed on opposite sides of the heart transmit the electrical signal to an ECG recorder. The ECG can be used to detect such contraindications to exercise testing as evidence of previous myocardial infarction, ischemic ST segment changes, conduction defects, and left ventricular hypertrophy (17). The reading and interpretation of ECGs require a high degree of skill and should be undertaken only by a qualified exercise specialist or physician (17).

Exercise Evaluation

The graded exercise test (GXT) is a frequently used technique to assess a client's cardiorespiratory fitness and exercise capacity prior to starting an exercise program. A GXT is also commonly used in the detection, treatment, and rehabilitation of cardiovascular disease. A variety of GXT protocols (maximal and submaximal) and modalities (bike, treadmill, bench-step, walk/run) have been developed for assessing cardiorespiratory fitness. The choice of the most appropriate protocol or modality depends on several factors. These include the client's age, fitness level, known health problems, risk factors for heart disease, and fitness goals, as well as the availability of equipment and qualifications/skill level of the health professional administering the test (9). For an in-depth review of cardiorespiratory fitness and testing modalities, consult the American College of Sports Medicine's *Guidelines for Exercise Testing and Prescription,* 6th edition (4), and the *Resource Manual for Guidelines for Exercise Testing and Prescription* (7).

The traditionally accepted criterion measure of cardiorespiratory fitness derived from an exercise evaluation is maximum oxygen consumption (VO_{2max}) (4). In healthy individuals, oxygen consumption increases as work load increases until a plateau is reached. This threshold is referred to as VO_{2max}. Thus, VO_{2max} is the greatest rate of oxygen consumption attained during exercise and is usually expressed in liters per minute (absolute) or milliliters per kilogram of body weight per minute (relative to body weight). Measurement of VO_{2max} involves direct analysis of expired air samples collected while the subject performs exercise of progressing intensity (22).

Maximum oxygen consumption is often assessed in athletes to predict performance, with direct measurement of VO_{2max} preferred over estimation. In general, the higher the VO_{2max} value obtained, the greater the client's potential for sustaining high-intensity aerobic work (23). However, other factors also contribute to an individual's exercise performance, including motivation, state of training, and nutritional status (24).

Percentage of VO_{2max} utilized during exercise is the amount of oxygen consumed relative to VO_{2max}. This percentage is useful for determining how stressful the exercise is with respect to one's maximum capacity. Percentage of VO_{2max} is calculated by dividing the oxygen consumption (VO_2) during exercise by the VO_{2max} and multiplying by 100:

$$\% \, VO_{2max} = (VO_2 \text{ during exercise}/VO_{2max}) \times 100$$

Although VO_{2max} seems to be significantly influenced by genetics, chronic endurance training has been shown to increase VO_{2max} in the range of 10% to 30% and can improve the ability to utilize a higher percentage of VO_{2max} without lactic acid accumulation (19,23,25).

Whereas VO_{2max} is the most commonly used measure of cardiorespiratory endurance, other related measures are frequently provided during exercise testing. Thus, nutrition professionals should be familiar with the terminology.

Power

By definition, power is work produced per unit of time and can be expressed as force (*f*) times distance (*d*) divided by time (*t*):

$$\text{Power} = (f \times d)/t$$

Power, therefore, is a combination of both speed and strength, and refers to the rate at which one performs work (26). Simple anaerobic tests for power consist of running up a flight of stairs (Margaria Stair-Climb Test) or timing a 50-yard dash with a 15-yard running start (26). Tests such as the Wingate Anaerobic Bicycle Test and the vertical leap test have been developed to measure peak anaerobic power, mean power, and rate of fatigue by using a predetermined force to produce a supramaximal effort (26).

Anaerobic Threshold (AT) and Lactate Threshold (LT)

The point at which blood lactic acid rises systematically during a graded exercise test is termed the lactate or anaerobic threshold. As exercise intensity increases, blood levels of lactic acid begin to increase systematically in an exponential pattern. This occurs at approximately 50% to 60% of VO_{2max} in untrained subjects, and at approximately 65% to 80% VO_{2max} in trained subjects. When used in combination with other physiological measurements (eg, VO_{2max}), the LT can be a useful predictor of success in distance running.

Coaches and athletes can also use LT as a guideline in planning the level of exercise intensity for optimizing endurance training programs (9). This can be done by using the corresponding heart rate at which AT or LT occurs. Based on the corresponding heart rates, different programs with varying heart rate zones can be created. This is more specific than using age.

Regular exercisers may perceive LT as the exercise intensity at which breathing and talking become somewhat difficult. In most individuals the onset of blood lactic acid accumulation is a marker for determining the upper end of the intensity range for aerobic exercise programs (9). Fitness programs emphasizing aerobic exercise are ideal if exercise intensity decreases to less than the LT, at a pace at which the individual is able to carry on a conversation (called the conversational pace), to prevent the rapid accumulation of lactic acid, which usually causes discomfort and necessitates an earlier termination of the exercise.

Metabolic Equivalents

Metabolic equivalents (METs) are often used to measure the workload at various stages of a graded exercise test as well as to prescribe the intensity of the exercise. One MET is equal to the resting oxygen consumption of the average human and equals 3.5 mL/kg/min or approximately 1 kcal/kg/hr of oxygen consumed. The following formula can be used to determine the MET level for a particular exercise (4):

$$\text{METs} = \text{Oxygen required for exercise/Oxygen required at rest}$$
$$\text{Where: Oxygen required at rest equals 3.5 mL/kg/min.}$$

Healthy, sedentary people can usually exercise up to 10 to 12 METs, and well-conditioned athletes often exercise above 15 METs (26). See Appendix C for more information on METs.

Exercise Testing Protocols

Mode of Testing

Commonly used modes of exercise testing include treadmill walking or running and stationary cycling. Arm crank ergometry is useful for individuals with paraplegia or who have limited use of their lower extremities. Bench or step tests are frequently used in the health/fitness industry where time, equipment, and qualified personnel may be limited. In addition, a variety of running and walking field tests have been developed for mass fitness testing. Two of the most widely used running tests are the Cooper 12-minute run and the 1.5-mile run test for time (4). The most common walking test is the 1-mile Rockport Fitness Walking Test. For more information on the administration and interpretation of these tests, see *Resource Manual for Guidelines for Exercise Testing and Prescription* (7).

Maximal vs Submaximal Exercise Testing

VO_{2max} can be directly measured during maximal exercise testing by direct analysis of expired gases or estimated from a submaximal exercise test (27). The decision to select a maximal or submaximal exercise test depends on the reasons for the test, the type of subject to be tested, and the availability of the appropriate equipment and personnel (27). Direct measurement of expired gases during maximal-effort exercise yields the most accurate determination of VO_{2max}; however, it is costly (in terms of equipment), requires specially trained personnel, and tends to be time-consuming (4). Thus, direct measurement of VO_{2max} is generally reserved for the research or clinical setting, whereas the vast majority of health/fitness facilities utilize submaximal tests to estimate VO_{2max} and assess cardiorespiratory fitness.

The basic aim of submaximal exercise testing is to determine the relationship between a subject's heart rate response and his or her VO_2 during progressive exercise, and then to use that relationship to predict VO_{2max} (4). To accurately determine this relationship, heart rate and VO_2 need to be measured at two or more submaximal exercise intensities.

Any of the GXT (graded exercise test) protocols can be used for submaximal or maximal testing. The only difference is the criteria for stopping the test. All tests should be terminated if any of the abnormal responses listed in Box 9.1 (4) occur. In the absence of abnormal responses, the submaximal test is usually terminated when the client or participant reaches a predetermined heart rate (typically 85% of predicted maximum heart rate reserve). A test is considered maximal when the following criteria are met:

- Failure of heart rate to increase with additional increases in exercise intensity
- Leveling off of the VO_2 (< 150 ml/kg/min between final two workloads)
- Postexercise blood lactate of > 8 mmol/liter
- Respiratory exchange ratio (RER) > 1.15
- Volitional exhaustion
- Rating of perceived exertion (RPE) > 17

Note that clients or participants will meet some or all of these criteria. Good judgment on the part of the exercise physiologist in using the various objective and subjective indicators listed above will help confirm that maximal effort has been elicited during the GXT. Also note that elderly people, children, and individuals who have had cardiac events may demonstrate an RER > 1.15 because RER tends to vary with age and fitness status (4).

Use of Subjective Rating Scales

A valuable parameter for determining exercise intensity and monitoring individual tolerance to an exercise load is a subjective measure of effort level known formally as the *rating of perceived exertion* (RPE) (4,28). RPE is frequently used when conducting a GXT and has been shown to be significantly and positively correlated with measured exercise heart rates and calculated oxygen consumption (4). The original RPE scale developed by Borg (29) was based on a scale of 6 to 20 (roughly based on resting to maximal heart rate (ie, 60 to 200 bpm) (9). A revised and simplified scale of 0 to 10 has been developed, which is easier for most individuals to understand or interpret and, thus, provides the tester with more valid information to further direct the GXT (30). Although both scales account for the linear increase in VO_2 and heart rate during exercise, the revised scale also considers the nonlinear responses of variables such as blood lactic acid accumulation and ventilation (see Table 9.1). It has been found that a cardiorespiratory training effect and the threshold for blood lactate accumulation are achieved at a rating of "somewhat hard" or "hard," which corresponds to a rating of 13 to 16 on the original scale or 6 to 8 on the revised scale (4,29).

Some drawbacks to using the RPE scale are that some people are unable to provide a reliable or valid rating, regardless of the scaling method used. A small percentage of adults may have difficulty in understanding the scale and how it corresponds to physical exertion. If an individual does not know what a 15 on the 6 to 20 scale feels like, then he or she

---

Box 9.1   Contraindications to Exercise Testing

Absolute
- A recent significant change in the resting ECG suggesting significant ischemia, recent myocardial infarction (within 2 days), or other acute cardiac event
- Unstable angina
- Uncontrolled cardiac arrhythmias causing symptoms or hemodynamic compromise
- Severe symptomatic aortic stenosis
- Uncontrolled symptomatic heart failure
- Acute pulmonary embolus or pulmonary infarction
- Acute myocarditis or pericarditis
- Suspected or known dissecting aneurysm
- Acute infections

Relative
- Left main coronary stenosis
- Moderate stenotic valvular heart disease
- Electrolyte abnormalities (eg, hypokalemia, hypomagnesemia)
- Severe arterial hypertension (ie, systolic blood pressure of > 200 mm Hg and/or a diastolic blood pressure of > 110 mm Hg) at rest
- Tachyarrhythmias or bradyarrhythmias
- Hypertrophic cardiomyopathy and other forms of outflow tract obstruction
- Neuromuscular, musculoskeletal, or rheumatoid disorders that are exacerbated by exercise
- High-degree atrioventricular block
- Ventricular aneurysm
- Uncontrolled metabolic disease (eg, diabetes, thyrotoxicosis, or myxedema)
- Chronic infectious disease (eg, mononucleosis, hepatitis, AIDS)

Source: Reprinted with permission. American College of Sports Medicine. *Guidelines for Exercise Testing and Prescription.* 6th ed. Baltimore, Md: Lippincott Williams & Wilkins; 2000.

---

would not be able to provide a valid corresponding number. Additionally, individuals limited in intelligence, mathematical ability, or verbal skills may also respond poorly to the usage of the RPE scale (4).

GXT Guidelines, Measures, and Termination Criteria

Healthy young individuals (men ≤ 45 years of age and women ≤ 55 years of age) can usually begin a moderate or vigorous exercise program without a GXT (4). Older individuals (men ≥ 45 years of age and women ≥ 55 years of age) can begin a moderate exercise program without a GXT; however, they should undergo a complete medical evaluation including a GXT prior to starting a vigorous exercise program (4). In addition, all individuals, regardless of age, who demonstrate signs or symptoms suggestive of cardiopulmonary disease or have known cardiac, pulmonary, or metabolic disease should have a complete medical exam and clinical GXT (with a physician present) prior to exercise participation (4).

TABLE 9.1 Original and Revised Scales for Ratings of Perceived Exertion (RPE)

Original Scale	Revised Scale
6	0 Nothing at all
7 Very, very light	0.5 Very, very weak
8	1 Very weak
9 Very light	2 Weak
10	3 Moderate
11 Fairly light	4 Somewhat strong
12	5 Strong
13 Somewhat hard	6
14	7 Very strong
15 Hard	8
16	9
17 Very hard	10 Very, very strong
18	Maximal
19 Very, very hard	
20	

Source: Reprinted with permission. American College of Sports Medicine. *Guidelines for Exercise Testing and Prescription.* 6th ed. Baltimore, Md: Lippincott Williams & Wilkins; 2000.

As previously described, a resting (pre-exercise) heart rate (HR) and BP should be obtained during the period immediately preceding the GXT. Additionally, HR, BP, and RPE should be obtained at regular intervals during the GXT (typically every 3 minutes or at least once during each stage of the test). During the recovery period (ie, approximately 3 to 5 minutes of low-intensity exercise), HR and BP measures should continue to be taken at 1- to 2-minute intervals (4,9).

The criteria for test termination depend on the testing protocol used. That is, a maximal test is terminated when oxygen uptake plateaus and does not increase with a further increase in workload or the subject reaches volitional exhaustion (17) whereas submaximal testing often uses predetermined criteria for termination, typically 85% of predicted maximal heart rate reserve (max HRR) (ie, [max HRR – RHR] × 0.85). Occasionally, however, the test should be terminated prior to the aforementioned endpoints, the primary reason being that the client or participant wants to stop. The indications for terminating a GXT are outlined in Box 9.1. For more specific termination criteria, consult ACSM's *Guidelines for Exercise Testing and Prescription* (4).

When the graded exercise test is completed, the following information should be included in the laboratory report (25):

- Pre-exercise HR and blood pressure
- Maximum exercise level achieved and the energy cost of the maximum workload

- HR and blood pressure at each stage of the test
- HR and blood pressure during recovery
- ECG abnormalities noted on the pre-exercise recording, at any test stage, and during recovery
- Any symptoms that occurred during the testing period, and the test stage at which they started
- Reason for termination of the test (eg, target achieved, symptoms, volitional exhaustion, ECG findings)
- Test interpretations, including risks and the likelihood of disease, and any relevant findings and their significance

This information can then be used in client education and exercise prescription.

Muscular Strength and Endurance

Muscular strength and endurance are important components of both physical fitness and overall health. Development and maintenance of muscular strength and endurance help to preserve functional capacity and attenuate the loss of FFM and bone density that often accompanies advancing age (31). In addition, because skeletal muscle is more metabolically active than fat tissue, development of muscle mass via strength training will cause a corresponding increase in resting metabolic rate, which is an important factor in the prevention and management of obesity (31). Finally, improvements in muscular strength and endurance can improve personal appearance and self-esteem (4).

Muscular strength is generally defined as the maximum amount of force that can be exerted by a muscle, whereas muscular endurance is the ability of a muscle to exert a force repeatedly over a period of time (9). Because of the interrelationship between muscular strength and endurance, an increase in one of these components usually results in some degree of improvement in the other. The assessment of muscular strength and endurance has been reviewed in-depth elsewhere (9,31,32) and thus will be addressed only briefly here.

Muscular Strength

Static or isometric muscle strength is demonstrated when a muscle is activated and develops tension, yet no visible movement at the joint occurs (33). An example would be holding a weight stationary. Isometric strength can be conveniently measured using a variety of devices, including cable tensiometers and handgrip dynamometers (33). Unfortunately, measures of isometric strength are specific both to the muscle group and joint angle involved in testing and, therefore, their utility in assessing overall muscular strength is limited.

Exercise that involves movement of body parts is called dynamic exercise. Two types of muscle actions occur with dynamic exercise: concentric and eccentric. Muscular shortening with movement of a body part is concentric. Muscular lengthening with movement of a body part is eccentric. Dynamic strength measures provide a more comprehensive test of muscular strength and involve movement of the body or an external load. The most common measures of dynamic strength involve various 1-repetition maximum (1-RM) weightlifting tests, defined as the heaviest weight that can be lifted only once. Isokinetic strength testing involves the assessment of muscle tension generated throughout a range of joint motion at a constant angular velocity. Equipment that allows control of the speed of joint rotation (degrees/second) as well as adjustment to test movement around various joints (eg, knee, hip, shoulder, elbow) is available from several commercial sources; however, it is extremely expensive compared with other strength-testing modalities (4,31).

Muscular Endurance

Simple field tests such as the 60-second sit-up test or the maximum number of push-ups that can be performed without rest may be used to evaluate the endurance of the abdominal muscle groups and upper body muscles, respectively (4,31). Methods of administration and age- and gender-specific percentile norms for these tests have been published (32). Resistance training and isokinetic equipment can also be adapted to measure muscular endurance by selecting an appropriate submaximal level of resistance and measuring the number of repetitions or duration of static contraction before fatigue (4). For example, the YMCA bench press test (32) involves performing standardized repetitions at a rate of 60 bpm. The rhythm is timed by a metronome, with each click representing a movement either up (lifting phase) or down (lowering phase). Women lift a 35-lb barbell, and men lift an 80-lb barbell. The test is terminated when an individual is no longer able to reach full extension of the elbows, or the individual breaks the rhythm and cannot keep pace with the metronome. The individual's score equals the number of successful repetitions.

Flexibility

Flexibility is defined as the maximum ability to move a joint through a range of motion. It is characterized by the range of motion that occurs at a single joint, or the total range of motion within a series of joints. A number of specific variables influence flexibility, including distensibility (expansion) of the joint capsule, muscle temperature, age, gender, physical activity status, muscle hypertrophy, excess body fat, and muscle viscosity. Additionally, compliance ("tightness") of various other tissues, such as ligaments and tendons, affects the range of motion (ROM) (4,34). Having functional ROM at all joints of the musculoskeletal system is desirable to ensure efficient body movement. In addition, increasing evidence suggests that improving flexibility can enhance muscular performance and, perhaps, aid in the prevention and treatment of musculoskeletal injuries (34).

The assessment of flexibility has been reviewed in detail by Fredette (34) and Corbin (35). In general, assessment of flexibility is not complicated and can be done with minimal equipment (tape and measuring stick) and cost. The most common flexibility test used for mass screening is the "sit-and-reach" (trunk flexion) test (4).

Exercise Prescription

Recent prospective epidemiological studies support the belief that a physically active lifestyle and a moderate to high level of cardiorespiratory fitness independently reduce the risk for some chronic diseases such as coronary artery disease, obesity, hypertension, colon cancer, type 2 diabetes, and osteoporosis (4). Most of this epidemiological evidence was based on single assessments of physical activity; however, recent studies (5,36) indicate that increases in physical activity or fitness in initially sedentary adults support the premise that regular activity increases longevity.

The fundamental objective of exercise prescription is the successful integration of exercise principles with behavioral techniques to promote long-term program compliance and the attainment of personal fitness goals. A comprehensive exercise prescription should include the appropriate mode(s), intensity, duration, frequency, and progression of physical activity (4). These five components apply regardless of the client's age, functional capacity, or risk factors for disease; however, each should be adjusted to meet the individual's needs, goals, motivation, and initial fitness level.

Prior to giving the client an exercise prescription, the health professional should obtain information on his or her medical history, current health, and fitness (36). Even though a GXT is not required for all individuals prior to beginning an exercise program, the exercise prescription should be developed with careful consideration of the individual's health status, including risk factor profile and medications currently being taken (37).

Aerobic Exercise

Aerobic activity should be a major part of the exercise prescription because of its association with cardiovascular fitness (ie, VO_{2max} and prevention of cardiovascular disease) (2,5,38,39). The most common aerobic activities are walking, jogging, cycling, swimming, stepping, rowing, aerobic dancing, or some combination of these. Clearly, this wide range of activities provides ample individual variability in terms of skill level and enjoyment factors that are paramount to exercise program compliance and desired outcomes (4). The ACSM provides the following exercise recommendations for improving cardiorespiratory fitness (4,24,25):

- Frequency of training: 3 to 5 days per week
- Intensity of training: 55%/65% to 90% of maximum HR or 40%/50% to 85% of maximum oxygen uptake reserve ($VO_{2reserve}$) of maximum HRR. The lower intensity values (ie, 40% to 49% of VO_2 or HRR and 55% to 64% of maximum HR) are most applicable to individuals who are very unfit.
- Duration of training: 20 to 60 minutes of continuous or intermittent (minimum of 10-minute bouts accumulated throughout the day) aerobic activity. Duration is highly dependent on the intensity of the activity; thus, lower-intensity exercise should be conducted over a longer period of time (> 30 minutes), and higher-intensity exercise can be conducted over a slightly shorter time period (> 20 minutes).

These recommendations, particularly those regarding the intensity of exercise, are necessary for individuals wishing to improve their VO_{2max}. However, it should be stressed that research has shown that exercise of lower intensity may promote significant health benefits and decrease one's risk of chronic disease (5,40). Moreover, because of the potential hazards and adherence problems associated with high-intensity activity, moderate-intensity activity of longer duration and greater frequency is probably more appropriate for adults not training for athletic competition (25).

Resistance Training

Resistance training should also be an integral part of any adult fitness program. The resistance training prescription should include exercises for all major muscle groups, be progressive in nature, and be of sufficient intensity to enhance muscular strength and endurance and maintain FFM and bone density (41). One set (8 to 12 repetitions) of 8 to 10 exercises that condition the major muscle groups performed 2 to 3 days per week is the general recommendation. However, multiple-set regimens and/or varying numbers of repetitions performed with more frequency may provide greater and/or more specific (ie, muscular strength vs muscular endurance) benefits (41).

Flexibility

Flexibility exercises sufficient to develop and maintain optimal range of motion should also be incorporated into the overall fitness program (24,34). A well-rounded stretching program should include exercises for all the major muscle/tendon groups. At least four repetitions per muscle/tendon group should be performed at a minimum of 2 to 3 days per week (24).

Motivating Clients to Become and Stay Active

An effective physical activity program should include methods to maintain client motivation and prevent relapse to their more sedentary, and potentially unhealthy, habits. Strategies aimed at making exercise more enjoyable should be emphasized and periodic follow-ups for fitness assessment, positive reinforcement, and permanent lifestyle change should be encouraged (24).

References

1. *Surgeon General's Report on Physical Activity and Health.* Washington, DC: US Dept of Agriculture Health and Human Services; 1988. DHHS (PHS) publication 88–50210.
2. Pate RR, Pratt M, Blair SN, Haskell WL, Marcera CA, Bouchard C. Physical activity and public health: a recommendation from the Centers for Disease Control and Prevention and the American College of Sports Medicine. *JAMA.* 1995;273:402–407.
3. National Institutes of Health Consensus Development Conference. *Physical Activity and Cardiovascular Health.* Rockville, Md: National Institutes of Health; 1996.
4. American College of Sports Medicine. *Guidelines for Exercise Testing and Prescription.* 6th ed. Baltimore, Md: Lippincott Williams & Wilkins; 2000.
5. Blair SN, Kohl HW III, Barlow CE, Paffenbarger RS Jr, Gibbons LW, Marcera CA. Changes in physical fitness and all-cause mortality. *JAMA.* 1995;273:1093–1098.
6. Bouchard C, Shephard RJ, Stephens T, eds. *Physical Activity, Fitness, and Health: International Proceedings and Consensus Statement.* Champaign, Ill: Human Kinetics; 1994.
7. Darcy P, ed. *Resource Manual for Guidelines for Exercise Testing and Prescription.* 4th ed. Baltimore, Md: Lippincott Williams & Wilkins; 2001.
8. Going SB. Densitomitry. In: Roche AF, Heymsfield SB, Lohman TG, eds. *Human Body Composition.* Champaign, Ill: Human Kinetics; 1996:1–24.
9. Howley ET, Franks BD. *Health Fitness Instructor's Handbook.* 4th ed. Champaign, Ill: Human Kinetics; 2003.
10. Lohman TG, Houtkooper L, Going SB. Body fat measurement goes high-tech: not all are created equal. *ACSM's Health Fitness J.* 1997;1:30–35.
11. National Heart, Lung, and Blood Institute. *Clinical Guidelines on the Identification, Evaluation, and Treatment of Overweight and Obesity in Adults.* Bethesda, Md: National Heart, Lung, and Blood Institute; 1998.

12. Bjorntorp P. Abdominal fat distribution and disease: an overview of epidemiological data. *Ann Med.* 1992;24:15–28.

13. Walton C, Lees B, Crook D, Worthington M, Godsland IF, Stevenson JC. Body fat distribution, rather than overall adiposity, influences serum lipids and lipoproteins in healthy men independently of age. *Am J Med.* 1995;99:459–464.

14. Bray GA. Pathophysiology of obesity. *Am J Clin Nutr.* 1992;55(2 Suppl):488S–494S.

15. Baumgartner RN. Electrical impedance and total body electrical conductivity. In: Roche AF, Heymsfield SB, Lohman TG, eds. *Human Body Composition.* Champaign, Ill: Human Kinetics; 1996:79–108.

16. Manore MM, Thompson J. *Sport Nutrition for Health and Performance.* Champaign, Ill: Human Kinetics; 2000.

17. Heyward V. *Advanced Fitness Assessment and Exercise Prescription.* 4th ed. Champaign, Ill: Human Kinetics; 2002.

18. McArdle WD, Katch FL, Katch VL. *Exercise Physiology, Energy, Nutrition, and Human Performance.* 5th ed. Baltimore, Md: Lippincott Williams & Wilkins; 2001.

19. Astrand PO, Rodahl K, Dahl HA, Stomme SB. *Textbook of Work Physiology.* 4th ed. Champaign, Ill: Human Kinetics; 2003.

20. National Heart, Lung, and Blood Institute. *The Fifth Report of the Joint Committee on Detection, Evaluation, and Treatment of High Blood Pressure.* Bethesda, Md: National Institutes of Health; 1995.

21. National Heart, Lung and Blood Institute. *The Seventh Report of the Joint National Committee on Prevention, Detection, Evaluation, and Treatment of High Blood Pressure.* Bethesda, Md: National Institutes of Health; 2003.

22. Franklin BA, Roitman JL. Cardiorespiratory adaptations to exercise. In: Darcy P, ed. *Resource Manual for Guidelines for Exercise Testing and Prescription.* 4th ed. Baltimore, Md: Lippincott Williams & Wilkins; 2001:160–163.

23. Franklin BA. Normal cardiorespiratory responses to acute aerobic exercise. In: Darcy P, ed. *Resource Manual for Guidelines for Exercise Testing and Prescription.* 4th ed. Baltimore, Md: Lippincott Williams & Wilkins; 2001:141–149.

24. American College of Sports Medicine. Position stand: the recommended quantity and quality of exercise for developing and maintaining cardiorespiratory and muscular fitness, and flexibility in healthy adults. *Med Sci Sports Exerc.* 1998;30:975–991.

25. McConnell TR. Cardiorespiratory assessment of apparently health populations. In: Darcy P, ed. *Resource Manual for Guidelines for Exercise Testing and Prescription.* 4th ed. Baltimore, Md: Lippincott Williams & Wilkins; 2001:361–366.

26. Graves JE, Pollock ML, Bryant CX. Assessment of muscular strength and endurance. In: Darcy P, ed. *Resource Manual for Guidelines for Exercise Testing and Prescription.* 4th ed. Baltimore, Md: Lippincott Williams & Wilkins; 2001:376–380.

27. Carton RL, Rhodes EC. A critical review of the literature on ratings scales for perceived exertion. *Sports Med.* 1985;2:198–222.

28. Borg G. Perceived exertion as an indicator of somatic stress. *Scand J Rehabil Med.* 1970; 2:92–98.

29. Borg G. Psychophysical bases of perceived exertion. *Med Sci Sports Exerc.* 1982;14:377–381.

30. Nieman DC. *Fitness and Your Health.* Palo Alto, Calif: Bull Publishing Co; 1993.

31. Skinner JS, Oja P. Laboratory and field tests for assessing health-related fitness. In: Bouchard C, Shephard RJ, Stephens T, eds. *Physical Activity, Fitness, and Health: International Proceedings and Consensus Statement.* Champaign, Ill: Human Kinetics; 1994:160–179.

32. Golding LA, ed. *YMCA Fitness Testing and Assessment Manual.* 4th ed. Champaign, Ill: Human Kinetics; 2000.

33. Fleck SJ, Kraemer WJ. *Designing Resistance Training Programs*. Champaign, Ill: Human Kinetics; 2004.

34. Fredette DM. Exercise Recommendations for Flexibility and Range of Motion. In: Darcy P, ed. *Resource Manual for Guidelines for Exercise Testing and Prescription*. 4th ed. Baltimore, Md: Lippincott Williams & Wilkins; 2001:468–477.

35. Corbin C. Flexibility. *Clin Sports Med*. 1984;3:101–117.

36. Paffenbarger RS, Kampert JB, Lee IM. Changes in physical activity and other lifeway patterns influencing longevity. *Med Sci Sports Exerc*. 1994;26:857–865.

37. Gordon NF. Pre-participation health appraisal in the non-medical setting. In: Darcy P, ed. *Resource Manual for Guidelines for Exercise Testing and Prescription*. 4th ed. Baltimore, Md: Lippincott Williams & Wilkins; 2001:355–360.

38. Holly RG, Shaffrath JD. Cardiorespiratory endurance. In: Darcy P, ed. *Resource Manual for Guidelines for Exercise Testing and Prescription*. 4th ed. Baltimore, Md: Lippincott Williams & Wilkins; 2001:449–459.

39. Lee CD, Blair SN, Jackson AS. Cardiorespiratory fitness, body composition, and all-cause cardiovascular mortality in men. *Am J Clin Nutr*. 1996;68:373–380.

40. Shephard RJ. How much physical activity is needed for good health? *Int J Sports Med*. 1999;20:23–27.

41. Bryant CX, Peterson JA, Graves JE. Muscular strength and endurance. In: Darcy P, ed. *Resource Manual for Guidelines for Exercise Testing and Prescription*. 4th ed. Baltimore, Md: Lippincott Williams & Wilkins; 2001:460–467.

Chapter 10

ASSESSMENT OF BODY SIZE AND COMPOSITION

CHRISTOPHER M. MODLESKY, PhD

Introduction

The body is an elaborate structure consisting of many components that change with growth, development, physical activity, and aging. Monitoring these changes assists health professionals in their assessment of nutritional status, physical fitness, and disease risk. Specifically, measurement of body size allows health professionals to track the changes in the physical dimensions of the body, whereas measurement of body composition allows them to track changes in the body's fat and fat-free components. Excess body weight, especially body fat, often reflects high energy intake, reduced levels of physical activity, or a combination thereof, and can contribute to poor physical performance. Adiposity is also believed to increase disease risk because it is positively associated with cardiovascular disease, diabetes mellitus, and other chronic diseases (1). Extremely low body weight and low body fat reflect disease states associated with undernutrition, such as anorexia nervosa and diseases associated with poor musculoskeletal status, such as osteoporosis. The purposes of this chapter are to: (*a*) review the application of body size and body composition measurement in adults, and (*b*) describe the most common and the most accurate measurement techniques.

Assessment of Body Size

With respect to physical performance, there are advantages and disadvantages associated with being a particular body size, which are evident in different sports. Taller people tend to be successful in sports in which reaching a level high above the ground is required, such as basketball and volleyball. Shorter people have an advantage in sports that require rotation of the body around an axis, such as gymnastics. Within team sports a particular position may dictate a size advantage. In football a large body mass is advantageous to offensive linemen, giving them the size and power to move players in their path. Conversely, wide receivers tend to be much lighter and to have a lower percentage of body fat than lineman, allowing them to run at great speeds.

With the exception of very low body weight, disease risk increases with body weight at a given height (2). This adverse relationship between body weight and disease has led to the search for an ideal or desirable body weight.

Height-Weight Tables

Insurance companies initially developed height-weight tables to provide, for given heights, gross weight ranges associated with the greatest longevity and lowest mortality rate (3). Although they are widely used, these tables have been scrutinized because the data collection procedures were flawed and the sample used to create the tables was not representative of the general population (4,5). Moreover, a weight for height gives no insight into a person's body composition or body fat distribution (5). In some instances, healthy individuals who are highly muscular might be considered overweight and at risk for disease, whereas individuals with a high proportion of body fat but a body weight in the desirable range would be considered at low risk for disease. Despite their flaws, height-weight tables may be useful if used in conjunction with other markers of disease risk—such as diet, blood lipid profile, and waist circumference—to identify individuals at risk for chronic disease.

Body Mass Index

Body mass index (BMI) is a measure of body size (based on height and weight) that is used to assess disease risk (see Appendix B). In people with a BMI more than 20, morbidity increases as BMI increases (2). In contrast, a very low BMI (< 18.5) is associated with undernutrition, anemia, menstrual irregularities, and a higher risk for skeletal fracture (6). Furthermore, a very low BMI may be a sign that someone suffers from anorexia nervosa. Similar to height-weight tables, there are several versions of BMI that are commonly used. The most widely accepted BMI is the Quetelet Index in which weight (kg) is divided by height squared (m^2). BMI can also be calculated as follows:

$$BMI = [weight\ (lb)/height\ (in)^2] \times 704.5$$

BMI is used more frequently than height-weight tables to assess disease risk in the general population because it

- Is moderately correlated with body fat percentage ($r = 0.58$) (7)
- Is readily used for comparisons among men, women, children, and individuals of different heights
- Reflects health status, with high and very low values associated with health detriments

However, similar to height-weight tables, BMI is insensitive to varying degrees of fat mass, fat-free mass, and fat distribution (3). This can be a particular problem in athletes. For example, a very large, physically fit male athlete measuring 76 inches (1.93 meters) in height and weighing 250 lb (113.6 kg) with a lean body (< 15% fat) has a BMI of 30.5. Such a value would be considered overweight or obese by any BMI recommendations currently available. On the other hand, a sedentary woman with a poor diet, measuring

65 inches (1.65 meters) in height, and weighing 140 lb (63.4 kg), with a high percentage of body fat (40%) by any standard would have an optimal BMI of 23.4.

Several BMI ranges have been proposed to identify healthy and at-risk individuals (8,9). However, some factors, such as age and race, make it difficult to define a desirable BMI range. Some studies suggest the recommended BMI ranges should increase with age (10–12) and should be higher in African-Americans than in whites (13,14). After a careful review of the scientific literature, the National Heart, Lung, and Blood Institute (NHLBI) Obesity Education Initiative Expert Panel on the Identification, Evaluation, and Treatment of Overweight and Obesity in Adults (2) has recommended the following BMI ranges:

- Underweight: < 18.5
- Normal: 18.5–24.9
- Overweight: 25.0–29.9
- Class I obesity: 30.0–34.9
- Class II obesity: 35–39.9
- Extreme obesity: ≥ 40

Moreover, the panel recommended that BMI should not be used alone, but instead evaluated in conjunction with other markers such as fat distribution, when assessing health risk and making weight loss or weight gain recommendations (2).

Waist Circumference and Waist-to-Hip Ratio

Fat distribution has been identified as an important marker of disease risk (15,16). For instance, individuals exhibiting a larger proportion of fat in the upper half of the body (android obesity or apple shape) are at greater risk for health complications than individuals having a larger proportion of fat in the lower half (gynoid obesity or pear shape). More specifically, deep abdominal (visceral) fat is a strong independent predictor of disease (15,16). Diseases associated with android obesity include hypertension, hypercholesterolemia, diabetes, cardiovascular disease, metabolic syndrome, and gallbladder disease (17,18), with women also having a greater risk for oligomenorrhea (8) and breast cancer (9).

One of the easiest ways to assess upper-body fat distribution and obesity type is to measure waist circumference. The girth of the abdomen is highly correlated ($r = 0.77$ to 0.87) with deep abdominal fat measured using computed tomography, an expensive technique that provides precise measurement of deep and subcutaneous adipose tissue (15,16). Another approach is to combine waist circumference with hip circumference to calculate waist-to-hip ratio. A higher waist-to-hip ratio reflects android obesity and is associated with greater disease risk. Risk increases steeply when waist-to-hip ratio is more than 0.95 in men or 0.80 in women (19). However, because waist circumference provides a better measure of deep abdominal fat than waist-to-hip ratio (15,16), measurement of waist circumference is preferred when assessing risk of disease (2,16).

Federal Clinical Guidelines

The NHLBI released guidelines for the identification, evaluation, and treatment of overweight and obesity in adults (2). These guidelines were developed based on a careful assessment of the obesity-related scientific literature. Assessment of overweight and obesity involves three important components: BMI, waist circumference, and risk factors for diseases and conditions associated with obesity. Considering all three components, rather than a single component, provides more definitive information about a person's disease risk. All individuals 18 years of age and older with a BMI of 25 or more are considered at risk for several chronic diseases. Treatment is recommended for individuals who are classified as overweight (BMI = 25–29.9) or obese (BMI ≥ 30) who have two or more risk factors (see Box 10.1) (2,20). Treatment is also recommended for men with a waist circumference more than 40 inches (102 cm) and women with a waist circumference more than 35 inches (88 cm). Because waist circumference cutpoints lose their predictive power in clients with

---

Box 10.1   Risk Factors to Consider Before Recommending Obesity Treatment

Disease Conditions
- Established coronary disease
- Other atherosclerotic diseases (peripheral artery disease, abdominal aortic aneurysm, symptomatic carotid artery disease)
- Type 2 diabetes mellitus
- Sleep apnea

Other Obesity-Related Diseases
- Gynecological abnormalities
- Osteoarthritis
- Gallstones and their complications
- Stress incontinence

Cardiovascular Risk Factors
- Cigarette smoking
- Hypertension (systolic blood pressure ≥ 140 mm Hg or diastolic blood pressure ≥ 90 mm Hg, or patient is taking antihypertensive agents)
- High-risk low-density lipoprotein cholesterol (≥ 160 mg/dL)
- Low high-density lipoprotein cholesterol (< 40 mg/dL)*
- Impaired fasting glucose (110 to 125 mg/dL)
- Family history of premature coronary heart disease (definite myocardial infarction or sudden death in father or other male first-degree relative ≤ 55 years of age, or in mother or other female first-degree relative ≤ 65 years of age)
- Age (men ≥ 45 years; women ≥ 55 years or postmenopausal)

Other Risk Factors
- Physical inactivity
- High serum triglycerides (> 200 mg/dL)

Source: Adapted from National Heart, Lung and Blood Institute. *Clinical Guidelines on the Identification, Evaluation, and Treatment of Overweight and Obesity in Adults: The Evidence Report.* Bethesda, MD: National Institutes of Health; 1998. Data marked with * are from the National Heart, Lung, and Blood Institute. *Third Report of the National Cholesterol Education Program (NCEP) Expert Panel on Detection, Evaluation, and Treatment of High Blood Cholesterol in Adults (Adult Treatment Panel III).* Bethesda, Md: National Heart, Lung and Blood Institute; 2001.

a BMI of 35 or more, the latter guidelines are appropriate only for those with a BMI ranging from 25 to 34.9 (2).

Although overweight and obesity have received substantial attention, being underweight (BMI < 18.5) is also a considerable problem. Athletes involved in sports that have an aesthetic component (21) or athletes involved in endurance sports that require translocation of the body are most susceptible to weight-restriction practices and low body weight (22). Although low body weight is associated with optimal health and may enhance performance in certain sports, a body weight that is too low is associated with nutritional deficiency, menstrual irregularities (ie, amenorrhea), anemia, and low bone mass (22,23). Osteopenia, an early stage of osteoporosis, is fairly prevalent in athletes involved in sports with a marked emphasis on body weight (24,25). Hence, avoiding very low body weight (BMI < 18.5) is a reasonable recommendation.

Body Size Measurement Techniques

Standing Height

Standing height is one of the most fundamental physical measures used to quantify body size. In addition to being used in combination with body weight to screen for disease risk, it is used to detect growth deficiencies in children and skeletal diseases, such as osteoporosis, that lead to a significant reduction in standing height in the elderly.

Equipment

A stadiometer (a vertical measurement board or rod with a horizontal headpiece) may be used to measure standing height following this procedure (26):

1. The client is measured while standing on a flat horizontal surface that is at a right angle to the stadiometer.
2. The client should wear as little clothing as possible to facilitate optimal body position, and should be barefoot or wearing thin socks.
3. The head, upper back (or shoulder blades), buttocks, and heels should be positioned against the vertical board or rod of the stadiometer. If a reasonable natural stance cannot be maintained while these body parts are touching the vertical board, the person can be positioned so that only the buttocks and heels or head are touching the board.
4. Weight should be distributed evenly on both feet with heels together, arms to the side, palms facing the thighs, legs straight, and the head in the Frankfort Horizontal Plane (ie, looking straight ahead).
5. Before measurement, a deep breath should be taken and held until the headpiece is pressed against the head (enough to compress the hair) and measurement is attained.
6. Measurement should be made to the nearest 0.1 cm or 0.125 inch while viewing the measure at eye level to the headboard.

Measuring height using a tape measure against the wall is not recommended. If it is done, a wall that is free of a baseboard and not in contact with a carpeted floor should be chosen (26).

Recumbent Length

Recumbent length is measured in those unable to stand without assistance, such as babies or individuals that are disabled or bedridden.

Equipment

A recumbent length table (see Figure 10.1) may be used to measure recumbent length following this procedure (26):

1. The client lies supine on the recumbent length table.
2. The body is positioned so that the top of the head touches the vertical headboard attached to the table and the center line of the body matches up with the center line of the table.
3. One measurer stands behind the end of the table with the vertical board and holds the head of the person being measured in the Frankfort plane, perpendicular to the plane of the table.
4. The shoulders and hips are at right angles to the long axis of the body, while the shoulders and buttocks are flat against the table.
5. A second measurer places one hand on the knees of the client to ensure the legs are flat against the table and uses the other hand to press the movable board against the heels of the feet.
6. Length is recorded to the nearest 0.1 cm or 0.125 inch.

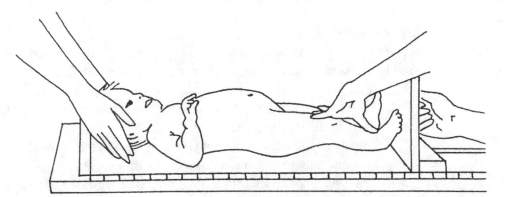

FIGURE 10.1. Measurement of recumbent length. Reprinted with permission from Gordon CC, Chumlea WC, Roche AF. Stature, recumbent length, and weight. In: Lohman TG, Roche AF, Martorell R, eds. *Anthropometric Standardization Reference Manual.* Champaign, Ill: Human Kinetics; 1988:3–8.

Body Weight

Body weight is another fundamental physical measurement used to quantify body size. Periodic measurement of body weight is important because extremes are associated with nutritional, metabolic, and cardiovascular disorders. Body weight is also used to estimate energy expenditure and body composition.

Equipment

A beam balance scale with movable weights may be used to measure body weight following this procedure (26):

1. The scale should be on a hard, flat, horizontal surface.
2. Before measurement, the scale should be calibrated to zero.
3. It is important to calibrate the scale monthly or quarterly, and whenever the scale is moved. Measurement accuracy can be verified using standard weights.
4. Ideally, weight should be measured before consumption of the first meal and after the bladder has been emptied.
5. When being measured, the client should wear as little clothing as possible.
6. The client should stand still over the center of the scale platform with weight evenly distributed between both feet.
7. Weight is determined to the nearest 0.5 lb or 0.2 kg using the movable beam. Body weight in pounds divided by 2.2 yields weight in kilograms (1 kg = 2.2 lb).

A calibrated digital scale can also be used to assess body weight.

If the person being measured cannot stand without assistance, a beam chair scale or a bed scale can be used. When measuring an infant, a leveled pan scale with a pan at least 100 cm in length is recommended (26).

Body Circumference

Body circumference measurements are used to estimate muscularity (27), fat patterning (28), nutritional status, changes in the physical dimensions of a child during growth, and changes in adults during weight-loss or weight-gain programs. When combined with measurements of skinfold thickness, circumference measurements can also estimate adipose tissue and the underlying muscle and bone (29).

Equipment

A flexible but inelastic tape measure may be used to measure body circumference following this procedure (28):

1. The zero end of the tape measure is held in one hand while the other end of the tape is held in the other hand.
2. The areas being measured should be free of clothing or covered by as little clothing as possible.
3. All circumference measurements, other than the head and neck, should be taken with the plane of the tape around the body part perpendicular to the long axis of the segment being measured.
4. When measuring the head the tape should compress the hair and the soft tissue of the scalp. For all circumference measurements other than the head, the tape should be snug but not tight enough to compress the soft tissue.
5. Measurements should be recorded to the nearest 0.1 cm or 0.125 inch.

Locations for circumference measurements of the head, neck, mid-upper arm, wrist, chest, waist, hips, and thigh are found in Figures 10.2 through 10.11.

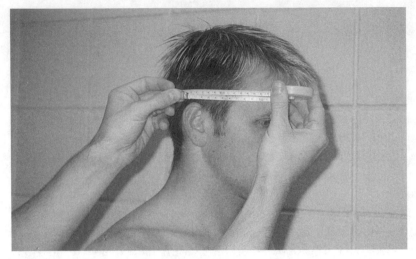

FIGURE 10.2. Head circumference is taken just above the eyebrows and posteriorly so that maximum circumference is measured.

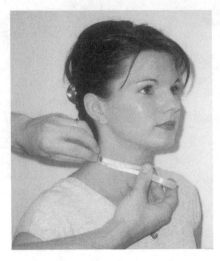

FIGURE 10.3. Neck circumference is measured just below the laryngeal prominence (Adam's apple) with the head in the Frankfort Horizontal Plane (looking straight ahead).

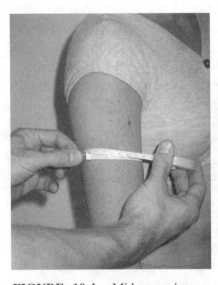

FIGURE 10.4. Mid-arm circumference of the upper-arm is measured midway between the acromion process of the scapula and the olecranon process of the ulna.

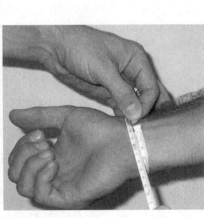

FIGURE 10.5. Wrist circumference is measured just distal to the styloid processes of the radius and ulna.

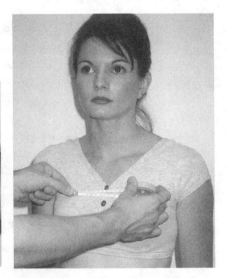

FIGURE 10.6. Chest circumference is measured horizontally at the 4th costosternal joints (at the level of the 6th ribs), after normal expiration.

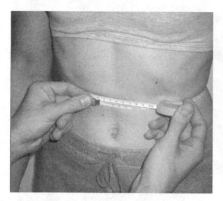

FIGURE 10.7. Waist circumference is measured just above the uppermost border of the iliac crests (ie, hip bones).

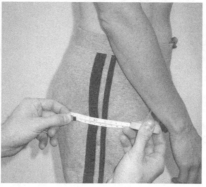

FIGURE 10.8. Hip (buttocks) circumference is measured over the maximal circumference of the buttocks.

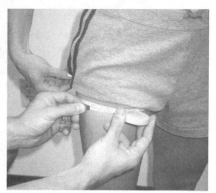

FIGURE 10.9. Proximal thigh circumference is measured horizontally, just distal to the gluteal fold.

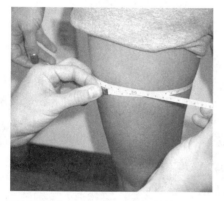

FIGURE 10.10. Mid-thigh circumference is measured midway between the inguinal crease and the proximal border of the patella.

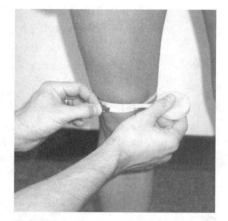

FIGURE 10.11. Distal thigh circumference is measured just proximal to the femoral epicondyles.

Body Breadth

Body breadth measurements are useful in the determination of body type and frame size (29). Somatotyping is one body-typing technique in which body breadths, along with circumference measures, are used to categorize individuals into three distinct categories (27):

1. Endomorphy: relative fatness and leanness
2. Mesomorphy: relative musculoskeletal development per unit of height
3. Ectomorphy: relative linearity

Specific somatotypes associated with athletic success have been identified for some, but not all, sports. For instance, a higher degree of endomorphy has been linked to lower performance scores in elite female gymnasts (30) and moderately trained distance runners

(31). Unfortunately, there are no somatotype guidelines for specific athletic groups. On the other hand, assessing frame size can help determine a desirable weight for a given height and can help determine appropriate lean weight gains in athletes and in malnourished individuals. Frame size can be categorized using Table 10.1, which was developed based on the first and second National Health and Nutrition Examination Survey data sets (32).

Procedure

A standard anthropometer, sliding caliper, or spreading caliper may be used to measure body breadths following this procedure (29):

1. The client being measured should wear as little clothing as possible to facilitate identification of measurement sites.
2. Using the tips of the fingers, identify the bony landmarks of the area to be measured.
3. Using both hands, hold the anthropometer or caliper so that the tips of the index fingers are adjacent to the projecting blades.
4. Position the blades of the anthropometer or sliding caliper at the bony landmarks.
5. Apply enough pressure to the blades so that the underlying skin, fat, and muscle contribute minimally to the measurement.
6. Measurements are made to the nearest 0.1 cm or 0.125 inch.

To minimize experimenter bias, measurements should be made sequentially, such that all sites are measured once and then the sequence is repeated until a minimum of three measurements are made at each site. The mean measurement at each site is recorded.

TABLE 10.1 Frame Size by Elbow Breadth (cm) of US Male and Female Adults*

| Age, y | Frame Size | | |
	Small	Medium	Large
Males			
18–24	≤ 6.6	> 6.6 and < 7.7	≥ 7.7
25–34	≤ 6.7	> 6.7 and < 7.9	≥ 7.9
35–44	≤ 6.7	> 6.7 and < 8.0	≥ 8.0
45–54	≤ 6.7	> 6.7 and < 8.1	≥ 8.1
55–64	≤ 6.7	> 6.7 and < 8.1	≥ 8.1
65–74	≤ 6.7	> 6.7 and < 8.1	≥ 8.1
Females			
18–24	≤ 5.6	> 5.6 and < 6.5	≥ 6.5
25–34	≤ 5.7	> 5.7 and < 6.8	≥ 6.8
35–44	≤ 5.7	> 5.7 and < 7.1	≥ 7.1
45–54	≤ 5.7	> 5.7 and < 7.2	≥ 7.2
55–64	≤ 5.8	> 5.8 and < 7.2	≥ 7.2
65–74	≤ 5.8	> 5.8 and < 7.2	≥ 7.2

*Derived from NHANES I and II combined data sets.
Source: Reprinted from Frisancho R. New standards of weight and body composition by frame size and height for assessment of nutritional status of adults and the elderly. *Am J Clin Nutr.* 1984;40:806–819. Reproduced with permission by the *American Journal of Clinical Nutrition.* Copyright © Am J Clin Nutr. American Society for Clinical Nutrition.

Proper measurement of the elbow and ankle breadth is demonstrated in Figures 10.12 and 10.13. Elbow breadth, regarded as the best marker of frame size, can also be measured using a Frameter (5) (see Figure 10.14) (29).

Assessment of Body Composition

Although height-weight and BMI charts are used to determine appropriate weights and to assess disease risk, they are not sensitive to differences in body composition (5,33). Body composition is more closely tied to disease risk than anthropometric measurements (33), with a higher body fat percentage related to increased risk of metabolic and cardiovascular diseases (34).

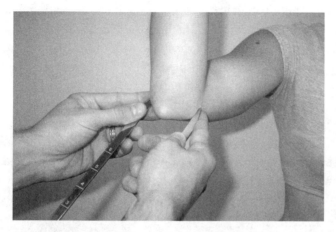

FIGURE 10.12.   Measurement of elbow breadth using a standard anthropometer. The measurement is taken at the epicondyles of the humerus.

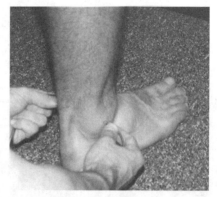

FIGURE 10.13. Measurement of ankle breadth, using a spreading caliper, taken at the maximum distance between the most medial extension of the medial malleolus and the most lateral extension of the lateral malleolus in the same horizontal plane.

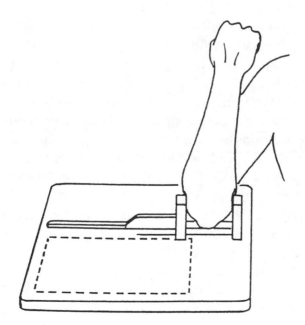

FIGURE 10.14. Elbow breadth measured using a Frameter. Reprinted with permission from Lohman TG, Roche AF, Martorell R, eds. *Anthropometric Standardization Reference Manual.* Champaign, Ill: Human Kinetics; 1988.

Body Composition and Disease Risk

Many of the adverse conditions associated with obesity are linked to excess amounts of total body fatness, but the actual contribution of body fatness to disease risk has yet to be determined. Our poor understanding of this complex issue is attributed to a paucity of large, prospective, epidemiological randomized studies that use the most accurate techniques to assess body composition (33). Further, causal associations with chronic diseases likely take years to detect, making it unclear whether changes in body composition precede or follow the onset of disease (33).

Because of the uncertainty surrounding the role of total body fatness in disease risk, the development of standards has been difficult. According to Lohman (35), the mean body fat percentage is 15% in men and 25% in women. Body fat values of 10% to 22% in men and 20% to 32% in women are generally considered satisfactory (35). However, the data supporting these values have not been clearly defined, such as for BMI and waist circumference cutpoints described in the *Clinical Guidelines on the Identification, Evaluation, and Treatment of Overweight and Obesity in Adults* (2). Furthermore, the most accessible methods used to assess body fat are generally limited. Until more research examining the relationship between body composition and disease risk is conducted, the use of body fat percentage as a marker of disease risk should be viewed with caution.

Growing evidence suggests the distribution rather than the absolute amount of fat in the body is more predictive of disease risk, with a higher concentration of fat in the intraabdominal region associated with a higher risk for metabolic and cardiovascular diseases (36). Moreover, a higher concentration of fat within and around skeletal muscle is an independent predictor of type 2 diabetes (37,38). Although it is important to assess the distribution of body fat, the most accurate methods (ie, magnetic resonance imaging and computed tomography) are expensive, have limited availability, and require tedious processing procedures.

Body Composition and Performance

Body composition is related to athletic performance, especially in sports that require translocation of the body horizontally (ie, running) or vertically (ie, jumping) (39,40). Excess body fat is detrimental because it adds to the load carried by the body (ie, body mass) without contributing to the body's force-producing capacity. Furthermore, a greater metabolic cost is incurred, limiting prolonged performance (41–42).

Specific body composition recommendations for athletes have yet to be determined, although ranges for different sports have been published (43). Because each athlete probably has a fat percentage and body weight at which he or she performs best, it may be more appropriate to use the ranges as a guide but identify specific levels of fat and fat-free mass that are optimal for a particular athlete.

Body composition can also be used to monitor the health of an athlete and to track compositional changes following weight loss or gain during training. Often, when an athlete is trying to lose weight during a training program that incorporates resistance training, body weight may not change but an increase in fat-free mass and a decrease in fat mass are likely. Unless body composition is accurately assessed, these positive changes may go unnoticed. Even if body composition is assessed, small changes may go unnoticed using the most widely available techniques (44,45), and large changes may be detected but the degree of change inaccurate (46,47).

Body composition differs from one athlete to another. Some athletes believe that extremely low levels of body fat are necessary for success in their sport. On the contrary, very low body fat levels can have deleterious effects on health and physical performance. Minimum levels have not been clearly defined for most sports, but body fat percentages less than 5% in men and less than 12% in women are generally not recommended (43). In 1996 the American College of Sports Medicine (ACSM) released a position statement on weight loss in wrestlers (48). It recommended that males 16 years of age and younger with a body fat less than 7% and those older than 16 years of age with a body fat less than 5% receive medical clearance before they compete. According to ACSM, body fat levels less than 12% to 14% are not recommended in female wrestlers (48).

When considering minimum body fat percentage values, it is important to note that error is associated with all methods of assessment. Under the best conditions, most methods have an error of 3% to 4% body mass (34,49). Therefore, a body fat percentage may actually be less or more than reported. For example, a body fat of 13% may actually be 9% to 10% or even less, which is a dangerously low level in females. The margin of error associated with body composition assessment techniques must be explained to athletes. To account for the error and to safeguard against reaching a body fat percentage that is too low, a more conservative approach would be to raise the lower limit a few percentage points. For example, instead of a lower limit of 5% fat, a limit of 8% would be a safer recommendation.

Body Composition Measurement Techniques

The composition of the human body can be described using several different classification systems, such as those based on body tissue (muscle, adipose, nervous, connective, etc) and chemical (fat, water, protein, mineral, etc) makeup. Methods that produce the most accurate measures of tissue or chemical composition tend to have poor accessibility, a high expense, and extensive processing procedures. Methods that are more accessible, inexpensive, and require little analysis time are generally less accurate. The following section reviews some of the different methods used to assess body composition, including their advantages and disadvantages.

Criterion Methods of Body Composition

Providing the most accurate estimates of human body components are criterion (or gold standard) methods of body composition assessment, against which other methods are compared. Three techniques regarded as criterion methods of body composition assessment are magnetic resonance imaging (MRI), computed tomography (CT), and multicomponent models.

Magnetic Resonance Imaging and Computed Tomography

MRI and CT are radiographic techniques used to estimate whole-body and regional adipose, muscle, bone, and nervous tissue (50). Magnetic resonance is based on the interaction among nuclei of hydrogen atoms, which are abundant in all biological tissues, and the magnetic fields generated and controlled by MRI instrumentation (51). CT uses x-ray to produce images of the different tissues in the body. Although both techniques have been shown to provide accurate and reliable estimates of body composition (52), their high expense, limited availability, and tedious processing procedures, as well as the high radiation exposure associated with CT, limits their use to research and clinical studies.

Multicomponent Models

There are basically two types of multicomponent models: (*a*) elaborate models based on in vivo measurement of the elemental constituents within the body, using in vivo neutron activation analysis (IVNAA); and (*b*) simpler, less expensive chemical models based on the in vivo measurement of water and/or mineral (bone) and body density.

Although IVNAA is the most accurate body composition technique, yielding measurements of body fat percentage within 1% body mass (53), its extreme expense and radiation exposure limit its use and availability. The simpler chemical multicomponent models are slightly less accurate than the IVNAA model, but they are acceptable criterion methods. The four-component chemical model, in which body water, mineral, and density are assessed, measures body fat percentage within 1.5% body mass (53). Although a three-component model, in which body water and density are assessed, involves measurement of one less body component than the four-component model (ie, body mineral is not measured), the loss in accuracy is minimal (54,55). Three- and four-component models are frequently used by scientists to accurately assess body composition and to validate simpler, more accessible body composition techniques. Percent fat equations based on the three- and four-component models are presented in Table 10.2 (55–58).

Despite the advances with multicomponent models, a paucity of studies have used them to assess the accuracy of the simpler, less expensive, and more accessible body composition techniques (55,59–63). The accuracy of the simpler techniques will remain limited until they are validated against the criterion methods.

Dual-energy X-ray Absorptiometry

Dual-energy x-ray absorptiometry (DXA), derived from single and dual photon absorptiometry, was originally developed to assess the bone mineral content and areal density. The technology is based on the x-ray energy attenuation properties of bone mineral and soft

TABLE 10.2 Percent Body Fat Equations Based on Two-, Three-, and Four-Component Models

No. of Components (Source)	Equation
2—body density (Siri [56])	% Body fat = $(495/D_b) - 450$
2—body density (Brozek et al [57])	% Body fat = $(457/D_b) - 414.2$
2—body water	% Body fat = $[\{1 - [\text{water (kg)/weight (kg)}]\}/0.73] \times 100$
3 (Modlesky et al [55])	% Body fat = $[(2.1176/D_b) - (0.78W) - 1.35] \times 100$
4 (Lohman [58])	% Body fat = $[(2.747/D_b) - (0.714W) + (1.146M) - 2.0503] \times 100$

Abbreviations: D_b, body density (g/cm³); M, mineral fraction of body mass; W, water fraction of body mass.

tissue (64). X-ray energy transmitted through the client is attenuated (lost) in proportion to the material's composition and thickness, and thickness of the components within the material. Bone mineral, because it has a much higher density, attenuates an x-ray beam to a greater degree than soft tissue. Similarly, soft tissue is differentiated into fat and fat-free tissue based on their different attenuation properties. Measurements are made while the client is lying supine on the DXA table. Low dose x-rays are passed through the client in the posterior to anterior position. Older pencil-beam systems pass a thin x-ray beam through the body side to side, traveling head to toe in 0.6- to 1.0-cm increments (65). Pencil-beam instruments usually scan the body in 12 to 15 minutes. Newer fan-beam systems pass an x-ray beam across a larger area and, thus, can scan the entire body in as little as 2½ minutes. Most total body scans require between 2½ to 15 minutes, depending on the instrumentation. Up to 30 minutes may be required with larger subjects when they are scanned on older pencil-beam instruments and a slower scan mode is used.

Accuracy

Compared with a four-component model, the accuracy of body fat assessment from DXA seems to be as good as or slightly better than hydrodensitometry in college-aged athletes and nonathletes (less than ± 3% body fat percentage points) (66), but it is questionable in children (59,60) (unless child-specific software is used [67]) and in the elderly (59,61).

Advantages

DXA is a fairly quick, comfortable, and noninvasive procedure that has good accuracy for assessing body fat in athletes and in the general population. It provides measurements of three body components (bone mineral, fat-free soft tissue, and fat masses) vs two components from most other methods (fat and fat-free masses). Moreover, it provides regional estimates of body composition (arms, legs, head, and trunk).

Disadvantages

Although the cost of a single DXA scan is somewhat reasonable (approximately $200), the cost of a DXA system is very expensive, ranging in price between $50,000 and $175,000. Furthermore, many states require a licensed x-ray technician or technician with a limited scope x-ray license and appropriate medical supervision to perform the tests. In addition to these major limitations, the instrument is not portable or mobile.

Hydrodensitometry (Underwater Weighing)

This densitometric technique for body composition assessment relies on a two-component model, in which the body is divided into fat and fat-free components. Assuming the density of the fat component (~ 0.9 g/cm^3), fat-free component (~ 1.1 g/cm^3), and the total body are known, the contribution of each component to the total can be calculated. The assumed density of fat is derived from 20 subcutaneous and abdominal adipose tissue samples taken from three men and two women (68), whereas the density of the fat-free component is based on the dissection of animals (69,70), three male human cadavers (57), and the assumed densities of fat, mineral, protein, and water (56). Researchers and clinicians can determine body density by dividing body weight measured on land by body volume measured using underwater weighing (ie, water displacement) or plethysmography (ie, air displacement) techniques. Based on these assumptions and the measurement of total body density, percentage body fat can be calculated using equations developed by Siri (56) or Brozek et al (57) found in Table 10.2. Percentage body fat equations based on more advanced three- and four-component models are also reported in Table 10.2 (55,58).

Until recently, underwater weighing was considered one of the gold standard techniques of body composition assessment against which all other methods were compared. Although measurements of body composition have become more sophisticated with multiple body components (ie water, mineral, protein, and fat) or body tissues (ie, muscle, adipose, and bone) being examined, underwater weighing alone is an acceptable method of body composition assessment. The technique is based on Archimedes's principle that a body immersed in a fluid is acted on by a buoyancy force equal to the volume of the fluid displaced (71). Because fat is less dense than fat-free tissue, a greater proportion of body fat will cause a person to be more buoyant (float) and weigh less in the water. Conversely, a greater proportion of fat-free tissue will cause the person to be less buoyant (sink) and weigh more in the water. This contrast is demonstrated in Figure 10.15 (72). The clients are

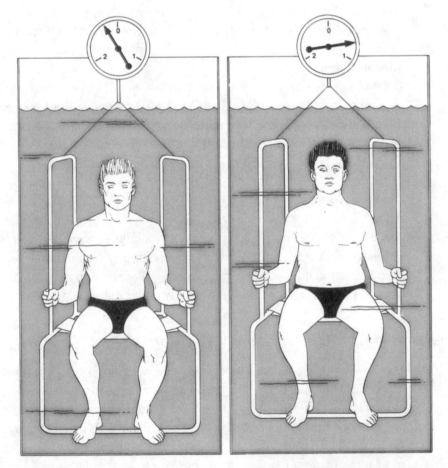

FIGURE 10.15.   Underwater weighing of two men who have the same height and weight but different degrees of density and fatness. The man on the left has a greater body density and lower percentage body fat. Reprinted from Powers SK, Howley HT. *Exercise Physiology: Theory and Application to Fitness and Performance.* Dubuque, Iowa: William C. Brown Publishers; 1990, with permission from McGraw Hill Companies. All rights reserved.

the same height and weight, but the client on the left has a higher body density and a lower percentage body fat.

Equipment

The following equipment is needed for hydrodensitometry:

1. Underwater weighing tank, pool, or hot tub 4 to 5 feet deep.
2. 9-kg Chatillion autopsy scale or a digital scale with 10-g increments. (A 15-kg scale with 25-g increments may be necessary for very obese subjects.)
3. Overhead beam or diving board from which the scale can hang.
4. Chair (32 inches wide with a back height of 24 inches) made from 3/4- to 1-inch plastic pipe with holes drilled in the pipe to avoid air entrapment and a belt secured to the chair to keep the individual in the chair while submerged under water. This is especially important for obese subjects. Because the density of fat is less than the density of water, subjects with a high body fat percentage will have a tendency to float in the water.
5. Weights to give the chair a minimum weight in the water of 3 kg (4 to 6 kg with the obese).
6. Thermometer to record the temperature of the water during measurement.

Procedure

The procedure for hydrodensitometry is as follows (73):

1. The chair, weights, and belt secured to the chair hang from the scale into the tank.
2. The water in the tank should be filtered, chlorinated, 89° to 95° F (~32° to 35° C), and range from shoulder to chin height when the client is sitting in the chair.
3. When placed in the water, the weight of the chair minus the weight of the client should be at least 3 kg. A higher weight (4 to 6 kg) may be required for obese people. These weights can be obtained by adding weights to the chair.
4. Hydrodensitometry should be done after a 2- to 3-hour fast of food and drink. Foods that can cause an excess amount of intestinal gas should be avoided approximately 12 hours before the measurement.
5. After a bowel movement and urinary void (if necessary), the person is weighed on land while wearing only a bathing suit.
6. The client enters the tank of water and submerges up to the chin without touching the chair. The weight of the chair, any attached weights, and the belt that is secured to the chair is then recorded.
7. The person is instructed to sit in the chair that is suspended from the scale and to secure himself or herself to the chair via the belt. The feet should be positioned on the front bar of the chair, which serves as a foot rest.
8. Just as a maximal exhalation is being completed, full submersion under the water is accomplished by slowly leaning forward. Upon submersion, the person must remain still in the chair with feet on the foot rest and hands on the side rails of the chair.
9. While the client is underwater, the measurer should keep one hand on the scale to steady it and observe the weight of the person underwater to the nearest 10 g.

10. The test should be repeated 10 times and the final three trials averaged (73).
11. During each trial, temperature of the water should be recorded.
12. The density of the water during measurement can be determined using Table 10.3 (74,75).
13. Because some air remains in the lungs after forced exhalation, the residual lung volume of air (RLV, in liters) must be measured or estimated (measurement is preferred). The RLV can be measured using nitrogen washout, oxygen dilution, or helium dilution techniques before, after, or during the underwater weighing procedure. Measurement during the procedure is preferred. Residual lung volume can be estimated using the following equations (76):

$$RLV_{males} = (0.017 \times Age) + (0.06858 \times Ht) - 3.447$$

$$RLV_{females} = (0.009 \times Age) + (0.08128 \times Ht) - 3.9$$

Where: Age = age in years and Ht = height in inches

14. Body density (D_b) is calculated using the following equation:

$$D_B = \frac{W_A}{\dfrac{(W_A - W_w)}{D_W} - (RLV + GV)}$$

Where: W_A = weight in air (kg); W_w = weight of the person, chair, belt, and weights in the water (kg) minus the weight of the chair, belt, and weights recorded in step 11 (kg); D_w = density of the water at the time of measurement (kg/L); GV = an estimate of gastrointestinal volume during underwater weighing (assumed to be 0.1 liter).

15. Body fat percentage is calculated using the Siri (56) or Brozek et al (57) equation (see Table 10.2), which yield almost identical estimates of percentage body fat (ie, within 1% body fat), except in individuals who are obese (ie, % fat > 30%) and very lean (ie, % fat < 5%).

TABLE 10.3 Water Density at Different Temperatures

Water Temperature, °Celsius	Water Density, g/cm³
28	0.996264
29	0.995976
30	0.995678
31	0.995372
32	0.995057
33	0.994734
34	0.994403
35	0.994063

Source: Data are from references 74 and 75.

Accuracy

The accuracy of percentage body fat from underwater weighing is approximately ± 4% in the general population (56) and ± 2.7% in the population from which the Siri and Brozek et al equations were developed (young white males) (77). Thus, in the general population, a 20% estimate of fat from underwater weighing typically varies between 16% and 24%.

Advantages

Underwater weighing is an established technique for assessing body composition and it has good accuracy.

Disadvantages

The equations typically used to estimate percentage fat from body density yield reasonably accurate measurements, especially in young white males. However, the density of the fat-free mass can stray markedly in population groups other than young white males and result in larger error. For instance, a lower density of the fat-free mass has been reported in men with extreme muscularity (55,78). Other equations have been proposed for African Americans (79) and women (34); however, there is evidence that the Siri and Brozek et al equations are appropriate for these groups (78,80,81).

Air Displacement Plethysmography

Air displacement plethysmography is another technique used to assess body composition by body density. The BOD POD Body Composition System (Life Measurement Instruments, Concord, CA), a recently developed air-displacement plethysmograph, seems to have overcome many of the problems experienced with its predecessors. The BOD POD determines body volume from air displacement and body fat percentage is calculated using the Siri (56) or Brozek et al (57) equations (see Table 10.2).

Accuracy

Fields et al recently evaluated the accuracy of body composition estimates from the BOD POD (82). Although the few studies that compared body composition estimates from the BOD POD with estimates from a four-component model suggest the BOD POD underestimates percentage body fat by 2% to 3% in adults and children, the authors concluded that the BOD POD provides valid and reliable estimates of body composition in the general population. More research is needed to more accurately assess the validity of body composition estimates from the BOD POD.

Advantages

Assessment of body composition via the BOD POD is comfortable and involves very little stress (no submersion in water or pinching is required). Moreover, the procedure is fairly quick, requiring only approximately 10 minutes.

Disadvantages

The cost of a single body composition assessment using the BOD POD is reasonable (between $20 and $100), but the cost of a system is expensive, ranging between $22,000 and $37,000. It also lacks portability, requiring a small space to house the chamber and other system components.

Hydrometry

Hydrometry is another technique for body composition assessment. Until recently, it was considered a gold standard in body composition assessment. This technique involves a two-component model in which water is assumed to represent approximately 73% of the body's fat-free component. Thus, a higher measure of body water indicates a higher amount of fat-free tissue. Total body water is measured by the dilution of a known quantity of nonmetabolizable tracer (eg, deuterium oxide). A lower concentration of tracer after ingestion and equilibration (~ 3 to 4 hours) reflects a higher amount of body water and vice versa. Tracer concentration can be assessed in a variety of body fluids such as blood, urine, and saliva.

Accuracy

The accuracy associated with hydrometry is similar to that of underwater weighing (approximately ± 4% in the general population and ± 2.7% in groups in which body fat is assessed using an equation developed specifically for that population).

Advantages

The advantage of using body water to assess body composition is that it provides a good measure of body fatness in the general population. Body water is primarily used in research settings in combination with other body measures using a multicomponent approach to assessing body composition.

Disadvantages

The disadvantages of hydrometry are the tedious analysis procedures and exposure to body fluids. Furthermore, because the water concentration of the fat-free component may vary from the assumed 73%, population-specific equations should be developed for groups with different concentrations of water in the fat-free component (58).

Bioelectrical Impedance Analysis

Bioelectrical impedance analysis (BIA) is commonly used to assess body composition in field settings. The technique is based on the conductive and dielectric properties of different tissues within the body at different frequencies. Tissues that contain large amounts of fluid and electrolytes, such as blood, have high conductivity, whereas fat, bone, and lungs have high resistance or are dielectric (83,84). A small alternating current that is passed through the body flows predominantly through tissue with higher conductivities. BIA determines the resistance to flow (impedance) of the current as it passes through the body.

Procedure

A bioelectrical impedance analyzer and the tetrapolar (ie, four-electrode) technique used to assess body composition are described here (83,84):

1. The subject must remove shoes, socks, and metallic jewelry.
2. Measurement occurs while the client is lying supine on a flat surface that is non-conductive, such as a bed or cot free of metal framing. It is recommended that the measurement is taken after the client is lying supine for 10 minutes to allow for fluid shifts that occur after one moves from the standing position to the supine position (85). Measurement in individuals restricted to bed rest for several hours may lead to errors of 1.0 to 1.5 liters in estimated body water (86).
3. The client's head should be flat or supported by a thin pillow.
4. The arms are abducted slightly so they do not touch the trunk.
5. Legs are separated so that the ankles are at least 20 cm apart and the thighs are not touching.
6. The client and analyzer should be at least 50 cm from metallic objects and electronic equipment.
7. The skin at each site is cleaned with alcohol before application of the electrodes.
8. Placement of electrodes is demonstrated in Figure 10.16. Electrodes are attached to the wrist (midway between the styloid processes), hand (at least 5 cm distal to the wrist electrode), ankle (midway between the malleoli), and foot (at least 5 cm distal to the ankle electrode).
9. The source cable (black) is attached to the electrodes on the hand and foot. The source cable introduces the current to the client.
10. The sensing cable (red) is attached to the electrodes on the wrist and ankle.
11. An excitation current ranging from 500 to 800 μA at a frequency of 50 kHz is transmitted by the electrolytes within body fluids and impeded by the resistive tissues.
12. The electrical impedance of the tissues provides an estimate of total body water, from which fat-free and fat components are determined.

Accuracy

The standard error estimate for body water from BIA is typically less than 2 liters (84). Although body fat estimates from BIA can vary by as much as 10% of body mass due to

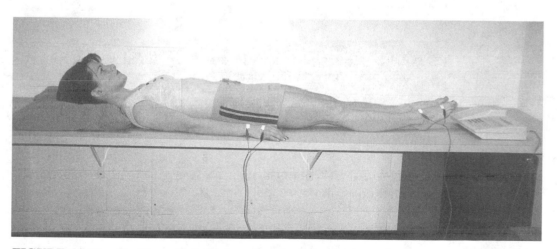

FIGURE 10.16. Position of electrodes when assessing body composition using bioelectrical impedance analysis.

differences in instrumentation and methodologies, most prediction errors for young adults are 5% or less. It is generally recommended that population-specific equations be used to reduce potential error associated with the BIA technique. Although population-specific equations are available (75), very few population-specific equations have been validated against the most recently accepted criterion techniques. Population-specific equations that have been validated using multicomponent models are reported in Box 10.2 (34,87).

In addition to the technique described in this chapter, body composition can be estimated using lower body or upper body regional versions of the BIA. The lower body instrument requires the client to stand on a platform, and the upper body instrument requires the client to hold a handgrip attached to the instrument. A recent study by Lukaski and Siders (88) suggests that the lower and upper body instruments need considerable improvement because they yield overestimates of percentage body fat when compared with estimates from DXA. More research examining the accuracy of body composition measures from BIA vs measures from multicomponent models are needed.

Advantages

The advantages of using BIA to assess body composition are its convenience, ease of use, precise measurement, and relatively low expense. The regional versions can be purchased for as little as $50.

Disadvantages

The disadvantages of BIA are its limited accuracy in the severely obese, its inability to accurately assess short-term changes in body composition, and the lack of validation studies using populations other than white European and North American non-Hispanic white subjects (84). Furthermore, the accuracy of body fat assessment may be compromised in very muscular athletes with disproportionately high concentrations of water in the fat-free mass; amputees; and those suffering from unilateral hemiparesis, edema, or tissue atrophy (84). Another disadvantage is that few population-specific equations have been validated using a criterion method of body composition assessment.

Box 10.2   Equations to Estimate Body Composition from Bioelectrical Impedance Analysis in Elderly Men and Women

Males: FFM = $-$ 10.68 + 0.65 Height^2/Resistance + 0.26 Weight +0.02 Resistance

Females: FFM = $-$ 9.53 + 0.69 Height^2/Resistance +0.17 Weight +0.02 Resistance

Where: FFM = fat-free mass measured in kg; Height is measured in cm; Resistance is measured in ohms; Weight is measured in kg.

Source: Formulas are from reference 87.

Skinfold Thickness

Skinfold thickness measurement is one of the most commonly used field methods for assessing body composition. The method is based on the assumptions that subcutaneous fat represents a certain proportion of the total body fat, and total subcutaneous fat can be accurately determined by measuring skinfold thickness at a few specific sites on the body.

Procedure

Skinfold calipers that apply a constant pressure of 10 g/mm^2 are often used. Harpenden (Baty International, West Sussex, UK) and Lange (Beta Technology Inc, Santa Cruz, CA) calipers are preferred. The following procedure is used (89):

1. Using anatomical landmarks and a tape measure when necessary, carefully identify the site to be measured.
2. Those with little experience may mark the site with a black felt pen.
3. Common skinfold measurement sites include the chest (Figure 10.17), abdomen (Figure 10.18), thigh (Figure 10.19), triceps (Figure 10.20), suprailium (Figure 10.21), and subscapula (Figure 10.22).
4. The skinfold is grabbed and elevated by the thumb and index finger of the left hand. The amount of tissue being grabbed must form a fold with sides being approximately parallel.
5. Hold skinfold calipers in the right hand, with the heads perpendicular to the site being measured and the dial facing up. After opening the caliper arms with pressure, the caliper heads are applied to the fold and pressure is gradually released. The heads should be applied where the sides of the fold are parallel, approximately midway between the body site where the skinfold originates and the crest of the skinfold.
6. Read the dial to the nearest 1 mm approximately 4 seconds after the caliper has been applied to the site. Waiting longer to observe the measurement causes smaller readings because fluids are forced from the tissues at the site.
7. After the measurement is read the calipers should be opened and then removed from the site.
8. A minimum of two measurements should be taken for each site. If the first two measurements vary by more than 1 mm, additional measurements should be taken until consistency is established. A minimum of 15 seconds should be allowed between measurements. It is recommended that all sites are measured before the second set of measurements is made.
9. In the obese, it may be necessary to grab the skinfold with two hands while a partner measures the skinfold thickness. If the fold is too thick to apply the calipers, an alternative body composition method is necessary.
10. Sites should not be measured when the skin is moist (to avoid grabbing excess skin and increasing skinfold measures), or immediately after exercise (because body fluid shifts may increase the skinfold size).
11. When all sites have been measured, adult body fat percentage can be determined using Tables 10.4 and 10.5 (90), derived using skinfold equations developed by Jackson et al (91,92).

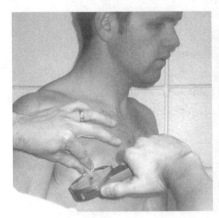

FIGURE 10.17. Chest skinfold measured with the long axis of the fold directed to the nipple.

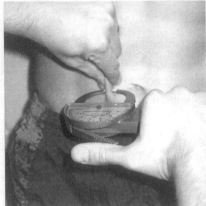

FIGURE 10.18. Abdomen skinfold measured immediately lateral of the umbilicus.

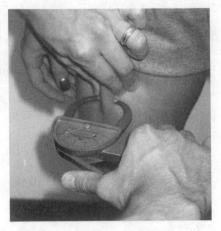

FIGURE 10.19. Mid-thigh skinfold measured midway between the inguinal crease and the proximal border of the patella.

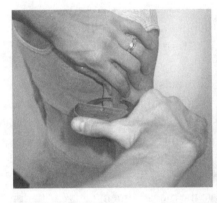

FIGURE 10.20. Triceps skinfold measured on the midline posterior surface of the arm over the triceps muscle, at the midpoint between the acromion process of the scapula and the olecranon process of the ulna.

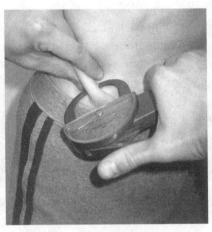

FIGURE 10.21. Suprailiac skinfold measured on the midaxillary line just superior to the iliac crest.

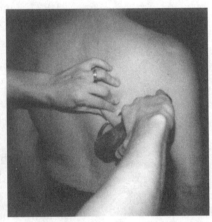

FIGURE 10.22. Subscapular skinfold measured at an approximately 45-degree angle just inferior to the inferior angle of the scapula.

Accuracy

Several factors can influence the accuracy of body fat estimates from skinfolds, such as the equation used to calculate body fat percentage. When population-specific equations are used, the accuracy of skinfold estimates of percentage body fat is generally 3% to 4% body weight (77). Population-specific equations can be found in other publications (75). Unfortunately, few studies have examined the applicability of different skinfold equations using a criterion method. A recent study that used a four-component model as a criterion method (93) suggested skinfolds provide accurate estimates of body fat in collegiate wrestlers when the following equation, published by Lohman (77), is used (p. 203):

TABLE 10.4   Percent Fat Estimate for Men: Sum of Chest, Abdomen, and Thigh Skinfolds

Sum of Skinfolds, mm	Age to Last Year								
	Under 22	23–27	28–32	33–37	38–42	43–47	48–52	53–57	Over 57
8–10	1.3	1.8	2.3	2.9	3.4	3.9	4.5	5.0	5.5
11–13	2.2	2.8	3.3	3.9	4.4	4.9	5.5	6.0	6.5
14–16	3.2	3.8	4.3	4.8	5.4	5.9	6.4	7.0	7.5
17–19	4.2	4.7	5.3	5.8	6.3	6.9	7.4	8.0	8.5
20–22	5.1	5.7	6.2	6.8	7.3	7.9	8.4	8.9	9.5
23–25	6.1	6.6	7.2	7.7	8.3	8.8	9.4	9.9	10.5
26–28	7.0	7.6	8.1	8.7	9.2	9.8	10.3	10.9	11.4
29–31	8.0	8.5	9.1	9.6	10.2	10.7	11.3	11.8	12.4
32–34	8.9	9.4	10.0	10.5	11.1	11.6	12.2	12.8	13.3
35–37	9.8	10.4	10.9	11.5	12.0	12.6	13.1	13.7	14.3
38–40	10.7	11.3	11.8	12.4	12.9	13.5	14.1	14.6	15.2
41–43	11.6	12.2	12.7	13.3	13.8	14.4	15.0	15.5	16.1
44–46	12.5	13.1	13.6	14.2	14.7	15.3	15.9	16.4	17.0
47–49	13.4	13.9	14.5	15.1	15.6	16.2	16.8	17.3	17.9
50–52	14.3	14.8	15.4	15.9	16.5	17.1	17.6	18.2	18.8
53–55	15.1	15.7	16.2	16.8	17.4	17.9	18.5	19.1	19.7
56–58	16.0	16.5	17.1	17.7	18.2	18.8	19.4	20.0	20.5
59–61	16.9	17.4	17.9	18.5	19.1	19.7	20.2	20.8	21.4
62–64	17.6	18.2	18.8	19.4	19.9	20.5	21.1	21.7	22.2
65–67	18.5	19.0	19.6	20.2	20.8	21.3	21.9	22.5	23.1
68–70	19.3	19.9	20.4	21.0	21.6	22.2	22.7	23.3	23.9
71–73	20.1	20.7	21.2	21.8	22.4	23.0	23.6	24.1	24.7
74–76	20.9	21.5	22.0	22.6	23.2	23.8	24.4	25.0	25.5
77–79	21.7	22.2	22.8	23.4	24.0	24.6	25.2	25.8	26.3
80–82	22.4	23.0	23.6	24.2	24.8	25.4	25.9	26.5	27.1
83–85	23.2	23.8	24.4	25.0	25.5	26.1	26.7	27.3	27.9
86–88	24.0	24.5	25.1	25.7	26.3	26.9	27.5	28.1	28.7
89–91	24.7	25.3	25.9	26.5	27.1	27.6	28.2	28.8	29.4
92–94	25.4	26.0	26.6	27.2	27.8	28.4	29.0	29.6	30.2
95–97	26.1	26.7	27.3	27.9	28.5	29.1	29.7	30.3	30.9
98–100	26.9	27.4	28.0	28.6	29.2	29.8	30.4	31.0	31.6
101–103	27.5	28.1	28.7	29.3	29.9	30.5	31.1	31.7	32.3
104–106	28.2	28.8	29.4	30.0	30.6	31.2	31.8	32.4	33.0
107–109	28.9	29.5	30.1	30.7	31.3	31.9	32.5	33.1	33.7
110–112	29.6	30.2	30.8	31.4	32.0	32.6	33.2	33.8	34.4
113–115	30.2	30.8	31.4	32.0	32.6	33.2	33.8	34.5	35.1
116–118	30.9	31.5	32.1	32.7	33.3	33.9	34.5	35.1	35.7
119–121	31.5	32.1	32.7	33.3	33.9	34.5	35.1	35.7	36.4
122–124	32.1	32.7	33.3	33.9	34.5	35.1	35.8	36.4	37.0
125–127	32.7	33.3	33.9	34.5	35.1	35.8	36.4	37.0	37.6

Source: Table 5 (Percent Fat Estimate for Men) reproduced with permission from Jackson AS, Pollock ML: Practical assessment of body composition. *Phys Sportsmed.* 1985;13(5):85. © 2004 The McGraw Hill Companies. All rights reserved.

TABLE 10.5   Percent Fat Estimate for Women: Sum of Triceps, Suprailium, and Thigh Skinfolds

Sum of Skinfolds, mm	Age to Last Year								
	Under 22	23–27	28–32	33–37	38–42	43–47	48–52	53–57	Over 57
23–25	9.7	9.9	10.2	10.4	10.7	10.9	11.2	11.4	11.7
26–28	11.0	11.2	11.5	11.7	12.0	12.3	12.5	12.7	13.0
29–31	12.3	12.5	12.8	13.0	13.3	13.5	13.8	14.0	14.3
32–34	13.6	13.8	14.0	14.3	14.5	14.8	15.0	15.3	15.5
35–37	14.8	15.0	15.3	15.5	15.8	16.0	16.3	16.5	16.8
38–40	16.0	16.3	16.5	16.7	17.0	17.2	17.5	17.7	18.0
41–43	17.2	17.4	17.7	17.9	18.2	18.4	18.7	18.9	19.2
44–46	18.3	18.6	18.8	19.1	19.3	19.6	19.8	20.1	20.3
47–49	19.5	19.7	20.0	20.2	20.5	20.7	21.0	21.2	21.5
50–52	20.6	20.8	21.1	21.3	21.6	21.8	22.1	22.3	22.6
53–55	21.7	21.9	22.1	22.4	22.6	22.9	23.1	23.4	23.6
56–58	22.7	23.0	23.2	23.4	23.7	23.9	24.2	24.4	24.7
59–61	23.7	24.0	24.2	24.5	24.7	25.0	25.2	25.5	25.7
62–64	24.7	25.0	25.2	25.5	25.7	26.0	26.7	26.4	26.7
65–67	25.7	25.9	26.2	26.4	26.7	26.9	27.2	27.4	27.7
68–70	26.6	26.9	27.1	27.4	27.6	27.9	28.1	28.4	28.6
71–73	27.5	27.8	28.0	28.3	28.5	28.8	29.0	29.3	29.5
74–76	28.4	28.7	28.9	29.2	29.4	29.7	29.9	30.2	30.4
77–79	29.3	29.5	29.8	30.0	30.3	30.5	30.8	31.0	31.3
80–82	30.1	30.4	30.6	30.9	31.1	31.4	31.6	31.9	32.1
83–85	30.9	31.2	31.4	31.7	31.9	32.2	32.4	32.7	32.9
86–88	31.7	32.0	32.2	32.5	32.7	32.9	33.2	33.4	33.7
89–91	32.5	32.7	33.0	33.2	33.5	33.7	33.9	34.2	34.4
92–94	33.2	33.4	33.7	33.9	34.2	34.4	34.7	34.9	35.2
95–97	33.9	34.1	34.4	34.6	34.9	35.1	35.4	35.6	35.9
98–100	34.6	34.8	35.1	35.3	35.5	35.8	36.0	36.3	36.5
101–103	35.3	35.4	35.7	35.9	36.2	36.4	36.7	36.9	37.2
104–106	35.8	36.1	36.3	36.6	36.8	37.1	37.3	37.5	37.8
107–109	36.4	36.7	36.9	37.1	37.4	37.6	37.9	38.1	38.4
110–112	37.0	37.2	37.5	37.7	38.0	38.2	38.5	38.7	38.9
113–115	37.5	37.8	38.0	38.2	38.5	38.7	39.0	39.2	39.5
116–118	38.0	38.3	38.5	38.8	39.0	39.3	39.5	39.7	40.0
119–121	38.5	38.7	39.0	39.2	39.5	39.7	40.0	40.2	40.5
122–124	39.0	39.2	39.4	39.7	39.9	40.2	40.4	40.7	40.9
125–127	39.4	39.6	39.9	40.1	40.4	40.6	40.9	41.1	41.4
128–130	39.8	40.0	40.3	40.5	40.8	41.0	41.3	41.5	41.8

Source: Table 6 (Percent Fat Estimate for Women) reproduced with permission from Jackson AS, Pollock ML: Practical assessment of body composition. *Phys Sportsmed.* 1985;13(5):86. © 2004 The McGraw Hill Companies. All rights reserved.

$$D_b = 1.0982[0.000815 \, (SFT + SFS + SFA)] + [0.00000084 \, (SFT + SFS + SFA)^2]$$

Where: SFT, SFS and SFA represent skinfold thickness of the thigh, subscapula and abdomen, respectively.

On the other hand, equations developed specifically for boys and girls (94) have been found to yield percentage fat estimates 3.5% less than estimates from a four-component model (67).

Another factor that can affect body fat estimates is the technician measuring skinfold thickness. Lohman et al (95) found that up to 17% of the variability in skinfold thickness measurement can be attributed to the technician, even if the technician is trained. The type of caliper can also have a substantial effect on body fat estimates. For instance, the inexpensive Adipometer caliper yields mean estimates of body fat that are similar to the expensive Harpenden caliper (95,96). Conversely, the expensive Lange caliper has been found to give body fat estimates 3.5 percentage points higher than the Harpenden caliper (95). The discrepancy between investigators and calipers is greater for the abdomen, suprailiac, and thigh than for the subscapula and triceps.

Advantages

Some advantages of using skinfolds to assess body composition include low expense, little space required to store the equipment, quick measurement, and reasonably accurate estimates of percentage body fat.

Disadvantages

Disadvantages of using skinfold calipers are the considerable effect on accuracy of the technician measuring skinfold thickness, the caliper used, and the equation used for body fat estimates. Although population-specific equations are available, few equations have been validated using a criterion method of body composition assessment.

Near Infrared Interactance

Near infrared interactance (NIR) is based on the principles of light absorption and reflection. The method was originally developed to determine the amount of protein, water, and fat in agriculture products, which are assumed to have different bands of light absorption (97). The commercially available portable NIR device produced by Futrex, Inc (Gaithersburg, MD) uses a light probe with a silicon detector, two near-infrared diodes that emit light at a wavelength of 940 nm, and two near-infrared diodes that emit light at a wavelength of 950 nm. At a measurement site, typically the bicep, the intensity of light or optical density emitted at the different wavelengths is determined. The machine estimates body fat using the optical density at the two different wavelengths, body weight, height, gender, and activity level.

Assessment of the accuracy of NIR, using underwater weighing as the criterion, has yielded conflicting results. Although a few studies suggest that NIR has reasonable accuracy (98), others suggest its use is problematic in children and adolescents (99), women (100), the obese (101,102), and collegiate football players (103). Discrepancies have also been found when different models of the instrument were used (104). Furthermore, the ability of NIR to detect changes in fat and fat-free mass has not been determined. In conclusion, NIR may be a promising method for assessing body composition, but research to date suggests that further development of this technology is needed before it can be used with confidence.

Summary

The methods for assessing body size are straightforward and firmly established. Several methods have been developed for assessing body composition. The use of the most accurate methods (ie, CT, MRI, and multicomponent models) are restricted by their expense, processing procedures, and limited availability. Although less expensive methods are available, their accuracy is limited, especially when the outcome is dependent on age, sex, and race. Age-, sex-, and race-specific equations have been developed, but studies assessing their validity against a criterion method are generally lacking. General tips that will aid in obtaining accurate measures of body composition are presented in Box 10.3.

Federal guidelines (2) have been developed to identify those at risk for disease using simple anthropometric measurements. Although assessment of body composition would likely aid in the assessment of the individual's disease risk, appropriate guidelines are needed. A useful application of body composition assessment would be to track change during a training program; however, large changes are probably needed before they are detected. Even then, the accuracy of the change is limited in the non-criterion methods. The limitations of body composition assessment methods must be recognized when used in the field.

Box 10.3   Tips for Measuring Body Composition

- Clients should not exercise several hours before measurement.
- For many measurement techniques, clients should be adequately hydrated before measurement.
- Measurements that are included in the assessment, such as height and weight, should be performed as precisely and accurately as possible.
- When assessing changes in body composition, the same technician should perform the assessment using the same technique and instrumentation.
- Error associated with many methods of body composition assessment can be substantially reduced if performed by a trained and experienced technician.
- Clients need to be educated about accuracy limitations because they often think body fat percentage numbers are as accurate as scale weights. Most methods for estimating body fat have an accuracy of 3% to 4% or more under the best circumstances.
- Use population-specific equations to determine body fat when appropriate, especially equations that have been validated against a multicomponent model.

References

1. Bray GA. Complications of obesity. *Ann Intern Med.* 1985;103:1052–1062.
2. National Heart, Lung, and Blood Institute. *Clinical Guidelines on the Identification, Evaluation, and Treatment of Overweight and Obesity in Adults: The Evidence Report.* Bethesda, Md: National Institutes of Health; 1998.
3. Robinett-Weiss N, Hixson ML, Keir B, Sieberg J. The metropolitan height-weight tables: perspectives for use. *J Am Diet Assoc.* 1984;84:1480–1481.
4. Knapp TR. A methodological critique of the "ideal weight" concept. *JAMA.* 1983;250:506–510.
5. Frisancho RF. Nutritional anthropometry. *J Am Diet Assoc.* 1988;88:553–555.
6. van der Voort DJ, Geusens PP, Dinant GJ. Risk factors for osteoporosis related to their outcome: fractures. *Osteoporos Int.* 2001;12:630–638.
7. Revicki DA, Israel RG. Relationship between body mass indices and measures of body adiposity. *Am J Public Health.* 1986;76:992–994.
8. Rimm AA, Hartz AJ, Fischer ME. A weight shape index for assessing risk of disease in 44,820 women. *J Clin Epidemiol.* 1988;41:459–465.
9. Shapira DV, Kumar NB, Lyman GH, Cox CE. Abdominal obesity and breast cancer risk. *Ann Intern Med.* 1990;112:182–186.
10. Andres R, Elahi D, Tobin JD, Muller DC, Brant L. Impact of age on weight goals. *Ann Intern Med.* 1985;103:1030–1033.
11. Sichieri R, Everhart JE, Hubbard VS. Relative weight classifications in the assessment of underweight and overweight in the United States. *Int J Obes Relat Metab Disord.* 1992;16:303–312.
12. Lew EA, Garfinkel L. Variations in mortality by weight among 750,000 men and women. *J Chronic Dis.* 1979;32:563–576.
13. Wienpahl J, Ragland DR, Sidney S. Body mass index and 15-year mortality in a cohort of black men and women. *J Clin Epidemiol.* 1990;43:949–960.
14. Durazo-Arvizu R, Cooper RS, Luke A, Prewitt TE, Liao Y, McGee DL. Relative weight and mortality in U.S. blacks and whites: findings from representative national population samples. *Ann Epidemiol.* 1997;7:383–395.
15. Despres JP, Prud'homme D, Pouliot MC, Tremblay A, Bouchard C. Estimation of deep abdominal adipose-tissue accumulation from simple anthropometric measurements in men. *Am J Clin Nutr.* 1991;54:471–477.
16. Pouliot MC, Despres JP, Lemieux S, Moorjani S, Bouchard C, Tremblay A, Nadeau A, Lupien PJ. Waist circumference and abdominal sagittal diameter: best simple anthropometric indexes of abdominal visceral adipose tissue accumulation and related cardiovascular risk in men and women. *Am J Cardiol.* 1994;73:460–468.
17. Larsson B, Svardsunn K, Welin L, Wilhelmsen L, Bjorntorp P, Tibblin G. Abdominal adipose tissue distribution, obesity, and risk of cardiovascular disease and death: 13 year follow up of participants in the study of men born in 1913. *BMJ.* 1984;288:1401–1404.
18. Wannamethee G, Shaper AG. Body weight and mortality in middle aged British men: impact of smoking. *BMJ.* 1989;299:1497–1502.
19. Ducimetiere RP, Cambien F, Avons P, Jacqueson A. Relationships between adiposity measurements and the incidence of coronary heart disease in a middle-aged male population: the Paris Prospective Study I. In: Vague J, Bjorntorp P, GuyGrand M, Rebuffe-Scrive M, Vague P, eds. *Metabolic Complications of Human Obesities.* Amsterdam, The Netherlands: Elsevier; 1985:31–38.
20. National Heart, Lung, and Blood Institute. *Third Report of the National Cholesterol Education Program (NCEP) Expert Panel on Detection, Evaluation, and Treatment of High Blood Cholesterol in Adults (Adult Treatment Panel III).* Bethesda, Md: National Heart, Lung and Blood Institute; 2001.

21. Byrne S, McLean N. Elite athletes: effects of the pressure to be thin. *J Sci Med Sport.* 2002;5:80–94.

22. Otis CL, Drinkwater B, Johnson M, Loucks A, Wilmore J. American College of Sports Medicine position stand. The Female Athlete Triad [see comments]. *Med Sci Sports Exerc.* 1997; 29:i–ix.

23. Coin A, Sergi G, Beninca P, Lupoli L, Cinti G, Ferrara L, Benedetti G, Tomasi G, Pisent C, Enzi G. Bone mineral density and body composition in underweight and normal elderly subjects. *Osteoporos Int.* 2000;11:1043–1050.

24. Bennell KL, Malcolm SA, Wark JD, Brukner PD. Skeletal effects of menstrual disturbances in athletes. *Scand J Med Sci Sports.* 1997;71:261–273.

25. Khan KM, Liu-Ambrose T, Sran MM, Ashe MC, Donaldson MG, Wark JD. New criteria for female athlete triad syndrome? As osteoporosis is rare, should osteopenia be among the criteria for defining the female athlete triad syndrome? *Br J Sports Med.* 2002;36:10–13.

26. Gordon CC, Chumlea WC, Roche AF. Stature, recumbent length, and weight. In: Lohman TG, Roche AF, Martorell R, eds. *Anthropometric Standardization Reference Manual.* Champaign, Ill: Human Kinetics; 1988:3–8.

27. Carter JEL, Heath BH. *Somatotyping: Development and Applications.* Cambridge, England: Cambridge University Press; 1990.

28. Callaway CW, Chumlea WC, Bouchard C, Himes JH, Lohman TG, Martin AD, Mitchell CD Mueller WH, Roche A, Seefeldt VD. Circumferences. In: Lohman TG, Roche AF, Martorell R, eds. *Anthropometric Standardization Reference Manual.* Champaign, Ill: Human Kinetics; 1988:39–54.

29. Wilmore JH, Frisancho RA, Gordon CC, Himes JH, Martin AD, Martorell R, Seefeldt VD. Body breadth equipment and measurement techniques. In: Lohman TG, Roche AF, Martorell R, eds. *Anthropometric Standardization Reference Manual.* Champaign, Ill: Human Kinetics; 1988:27–38.

30. Claessens AL, Lefevre J, Beunen G, Malina RM. The contribution of anthropometric characteristics to performance scores in elite female gymnasts. *J Sports Med Phys Fitness.* 1999;39: 355–360.

31. Berg K, Latin RW, Coffey C. Relationship of somatotype and physical characteristics to distance running performance in middle age runners. *J Sports Med Phys Fitness.* 1998;38: 253–257.

32. Frisancho R. New standards of weight and body composition by frame size and height for assessment of nutritional status of adults and the elderly. *Am J Clin Nutr.* 1984;40:806–819.

33. Baumgartner RN, Heymsfield SB, Roche AF. Human body composition and the epidemiology of chronic disease. *Obesity Res.* 1995;3:73–95.

34. Lohman TG. *Advances in Body Composition Assessment.* Champaign, Ill: Human Kinetics; 1992.

35. Lohman TG. Body composition methodology in sports medicine. *Phys Sportsmed.* 1982; 10:47–58.

36. Bjorntorp P. "Portal" adipose tissue as a generator of risk factors for cardiovascular disease and diabetes. *Arteriosclerosis.* 1990;10:493–496.

37. Goodpaster BH, Thaete FL, Kelley DE. Thigh adipose tissue distribution is associated with insulin resistance in obesity and in type 2 diabetes mellitus. *Am J Clin Nutr.* 2000;71:885–892.

38. Goodpaster BH, Thaete FL, Simoneau JA, Kelley DE. Subcutaneous abdominal fat and thigh muscle composition predict insulin sensitivity independently of visceral fat. *Diabetes.* 1997;46: 1579–1585.

39. Beunen G, Malina RM, Ostyn M, Renson R, Simons J, Van Gerven D. Fatness, growth, and motor fitness of Belgian boys 12 through 20 years of age. *Hum Biol.* 1983;55:599–613.

40. Cureton KJ, Sparling PB, Evans BW, Johnson SM, Kong UD, Purvis JW. Effect of experimental alterations in excess weight on aerobic capacity and distance running performance. *Med Sci Sports Exerc.* 1978;15:218–223.

41. Cureton KJ, Sparling PB. Distance running performance and metabolic responses to running in men and women with excess weight experimentally equated. *Med Sci Sports Exerc.* 1980;12: 288–294.

42. Buskirk ER, Taylor HL. Maximal oxygen intake and its relation to body composition, with special reference to chronic physical activity and obesity. *J Appl Physiol.* 1957;11:72–78.

43. Houtkooper LB, Going SB. Body composition: how should it be measured? Does it affect performance? *Sports Sci Exch.* 1994;7(5).

44. Evans EM, Saunders MJ, Spano MA, Arngrimsson SA, Lewis RD, Cureton KJ. Body composition changes with diet and exercise in obese women: a comparison of estimates from clinical methods and four-component model. *Am J Clin Nutr.* 1999;70:5–12.

45. Evans EM, Saunders MJ, Spano MA, Arngrimsson SA, Lewis RD, Cureton KJ. Effects of diet and exercise on the density and composition of the fat-free mass in obese women. *Med Sci Sports Exerc.* 1999;31:1778–1787.

46. Fogelholm GM, Sievanen HT, van Marken Lichtenbelt WD, Westerterp KR. Assessment of fat-mass loss during weight reduction in obese women. *Metabolism.* 1997;46:968–975.

47. Albu J, Smolowitz J, Lichtman S, Heymsfield SB, Wang J, Pierson RN Jr, Pi-Sunyer FX. Composition of weight loss in severely obese women: a new look at old methods. *Metabolism.* 1992;41:1068–1074.

48. American College of Sports Medicine. ACSM position stand on weight loss in wrestlers. *Med Sci Sports Exerc.* 1996;28:ix–xii.

49. Lukaski HC. Methods for the assessment of human body composition: traditional and new. *Am J Clin Nutr.* 1987;46:537–556.

50. Ross R, Goodpaster B, Kelley D, Boada F. Magnetic resonance imaging in human body composition research. From quantitative to qualitative tissue measurement. *Ann N Y Acad Sci.* 2000;904:12–17.

51. Ross R. Magnetic resonance imaging provides new insights into the characterization of adipose and lean tissue distribution. *Can J Physiol Pharmacol.* 1996;74:778–785.

52. Mitsiopoulos N, Baumgartner RN, Heymsfield SB, Lyons W, Gallagher D, Ross R. Cadaver validation of skeletal muscle measurement by magnetic resonance imaging and computerized tomography. *J Appl Physiol.* 1998;85:115–122.

53. Heymsfield SB, Lichtman S, Baumgartner RN, Wang J, Kamen Y, Aliprantis A, Pierson RN Jr. Body composition of humans: comparison of two improved four-component models that differ in expense, technical complexity, and radiation exposure. *Am J Clin Nutr.* 1990;52:52–58.

54. Withers RT, LaForgia J, Pillans RK, Shipp NJ, Chatterton BE, Schultz CG, Leaney F. Comparisons of two-, three-, and four-compartment models of body composition analysis in men and women. *J Appl Physiol.* 1998;85:238–245.

55. Modlesky CM, Cureton KJ, Lewis RD, Prior BM, Sloniger MA, Rowe DA. Density of the fat-free mass and estimates of body composition in male weight trainers. *J Appl Physiol.* 1996;80: 2085–2096.

56. Siri WE. Body composition from fluid spaces and density: analysis of methods. In: Brozek J, Henschel A, eds. *Techniques for Measuring Body Composition.* Washington, DC: National Academy of Sciences National Research Council; 1961:223–244.

57. Brozek J, Grande F, Anderson JT, Keys A. Densitometric analysis of body composition: revision of some quantitative assumptions. *Ann N Y Acad Sci.* 1963;110:113–140.

58. Lohman TG. Applicability of body composition techniques and constant for children and youths. In: Pandolf K, ed. *Exercise and Sports Science Reviews.* 14th ed. New York, NY: Macmillian; 1986:325–357.

59. Bergsma-Kadijk JA, Baumeister B, Deurenberg P. Measurement of body fat in young and elderly women: comparison between a four-compartment model and widely used reference methods. *Br J Nutr.* 1996;75:649–657.

60. Roemmich JN, Clark PA, Weltman A, Rogol AD. Alterations in growth and body composition during puberty. I. Comparing multicompartment body composition models. *J Appl Physiol.* 1997;83:927–935.

61. Clasey JL, Hartman ML, Kanaley J, Wideman L, Teates CD, Bouchard C, Weltman A. Body composition by DEXA in older adults: accuracy and influence of scan mode. *Med Sci Sports Exerc.* 1997;29:560–567.

62. Cote KD, Adams WC. Effect of bone density on body composition estimates in young adult black and white women. *Med Sci Sports Exerc.* 1993;25:290–296.

63. Ortiz O, Russell M, Daley TL, Baumgartner RN, Waki M, Lichtman S, Wang J, Pierson RN Jr, Heymsfield SB. Differences in skeletal muscle and bone mineral mass between black and white females and their relevance to estimates of body composition. *Am J Clin Nutr.* 1992;55:8–13.

64. Lukaski HC. Soft tissue composition and bone mineral status: evaluation by dual energy x-ray absorptiometry. *J Nutr.* 1993;123:438–443.

65. Lohman TG. Dual-energy X-ray absorptiometry. In: Roche AF, Heymsfield SB, Lohman TG, eds. *Human Body Composition.* Champaign, Ill: Human Kinetics; 1996:63–78.

66. Prior BM, Cureton KJ, Modlesky CM, Evans EM, Sloniger MA, Saunders M, Lewis RD. In vivo validation of whole-body composition estimates from dual-energy X-ray absorptiometry. *J Appl Physiol.* 1997;83:623–630.

67. Wells JCK, Fuller NJ, Dewit O, Fewtrell MS, Elia M, Cole TJ. Four-component model of body composition in children: density and hydration of fat-free mass and comparison with simpler models. *Am J Clin Nutr.* 1999;69:904–912.

68. Fidanza F, Keys A, Anderson JT. Density of body fat in man and other mammals. *J Appl Physiol.* 1953;6:252–256.

69. Morales MF, Rathbun EN, Smith RE, Pace N. Theoretical considerations regarding the major body tissue components, with suggestions for application to man. *J Biol Chem.* 1945;158: 677–684.

70. Rathbun EN, Pace N. The determination of total body fat by means of the body specific gravity. *J Biol Chem.* 1945;158:667–676.

71. Behnke AR. Comment of the determination of whole body density and a resume of body composition data. In: Brozek J, Henschel A, eds. *Techniques for Measuring Body Composition.* Washington, DC: National Academy of Sciences National Research Council; 1961:118–133.

72. Powers SK, Howley HT. *Exercise Physiology: Theory and Application to Fitness and Performance.* Dubuque, Iowa: William C. Brown Publishers; 1990.

73. Going SB. Densitometry. In: Roche AF, Heymsfield SB, Lohman TG, eds. *Human Body Composition.* 3rd ed. Champaign, Ill: Human Kinetics; 1996:3–23.

74. *Handbook of Physical Chemistry.* Cleveland, Ohio: Chemical Rubber Company; 1967.

75. Heyward VH, Stolarczyk LM. *Applied Body Composition Assessment.* Champaign, Ill: Human Kinetics; 1996.

76. Goldman HI, Becklake MR. Respiratory function tests; normal values at median altitudes and the prediction of normal results. *Am Rev Tuberc.* 1959;79:457–467.

77. Lohman TG. Skinfolds and body density and their relation to body fatness: a review. *Hum Biol.* 1981;53:181–225.

78. Prior BM, Modlesky CM, Evans EM, Sloniger MA, Saunders MJ, Lewis RD, Cureton KJ. Muscularity and the density of the fat-free mass in athletes. *J Appl Physiol.* 2001;90:1523–1531.

79. Schutte JE, Townsend EJ, Hugg J, Shoup RF, Malina RM, Blomqvist CG. Density of lean body mass is greater in blacks than in whites. *J Appl Physiol.* 1984;56:1647–1649.

80. Millard-Stafford ML, Collins MA, Modlesky CM, Snow TK, Rosskopf LB. Effect of race and resistance training status on the density of fat-free mass and percent fat estimates. *J Appl Physiol.* 2001;91:1259–1268.

81. Visser M, Gallagher D, Deurenberg P, Wang J, Pierson RN Jr, Heymsfield SB. Density of fat-free body mass: relationship with race, age, and level of body fatness. *Am J Physiol.* 1997;272:E781-E787.

82. Fields DA, Goran MI, McCrory MA. Body-composition assessment via air-displacement plethysmography in adults and children: a review. *Am J Clin Nutr.* 2002;75:453–467.

83. Baumgartner RN. Electrical impedance and total body electrical conductivity. In: Roche AF, Heymsfield SB, Lohman TG, eds. *Human Body Composition.* Champaign, Ill: Human Kinetics; 1996:79–107.

84. Bioelectrical impedance analysis in body composition measurement. *NIH Technol Assess Statement.* 1996;(Dec 12–14):1–35.

85. Ellis KJ, Bell SJ, Chertow GM, Chumlea WC, Knox TA, Kotler DF, Lukaski HC, Schoeller DA. Bioelectrical impedance methods in clinical research: a follow-up to the NIH Technology Assessment Conference. *Nutrition.* 1999;15:874–880.

86. Kushner RF, Gudivaka R, Schoeller DA. Clinical characteristics influencing bioelectrical impedance analysis measurements. *Am J Clin Nutr.* 1996;64(suppl):423S-427S.

87. Sun SS, Chumlea WC, Heymsfield SB, Lukaski HC, Schoeller D, Friedl K, Kuczmarski RJ, Flegal KM, Johnson CL, Hubbard VS. Development of bioelectrical impedance analysis prediction equations for body composition with the use of a multicomponent model for use in epidemiologic surveys. *Am J Clin Nutr.* 2003;77:331–340.

88. Lukaski HC, Siders WA. Validity and accuracy of regional bioelectrical impedance devices to determine whole-body fatness. *Nutrition.* 2003;19:851–857.

89. Harrison GC, Buskirk ER, Carter JEL, Johnston FE, Lohman TG, Pollack ML, Roche AF, Wilmore J. Skinfold thicknesses and measurement technique. In: Lohman TG, Roche AF, Martorell R, eds. *Anthropometric Standardization Reference Manual.* Champaign, Ill: Human Kinetics; 1988:55–70.

90. Jackson AS, Pollock ML. Practical assessment of body composition. *Phys Sportsmed.* 1985;13:76–90.

91. Jackson AS, Pollock ML. Generalized equations for predicting body density of men. *Br J Nutr.* 1978;40:497–504.

92. Jackson AS, Pollock ML, Ward A. Generalized equations for predicting body density of women. *Med Sci Sports Exerc.* 1980;12:175–182.

93. Clark RR, Bartok C, Sullivan JC, Schoeller DA. Minimum weight prediction methods cross-validated by the four-component model. *Med Sci Sports Exerc.* 2004;36:639–647.

94. Slaughter MH, Lohman TG, Boileau RA, Horswill CA, Stillman RJ, Van Loan MD, Bemben DA. Skinfold equations for estimation of body fatness in children and youth. *Hum Biol.* 1988;60:709–723.

95. Lohman TG, Pollock ML, Slaughter MH, Brandon L, Boileau RA. Methodological factors and the prediction of body fat in female athletes. *Med Sci Sports Exerc.* 1984;16:92–96.

96. Léger LA, Lambert J, Martin P. Validity of plastic caliper measurements. *Hum Biol.* 1982;54:667–675.

97. Lanza E. Determination of moisture, protein, fat and calories in raw pork and beef by near infrared spectroscopy. *J Food Sci.* 1983;48:471–474.

98. Nielsen DH, Cassady SL, Wacker LM, Wessels AK, Wheelock BJ, Oppliger RA. Validation of Futrex 5000 near-infrared spectrophotometer analyzer for assessment of body composition. *J Orthop Sports Phys Ther.* 1992;16:281–287.

99. Cassady SL, Nielsen DH, Janz KF, Wu Y, Cook JS, Hansen JR. Validity of near infrared body composition analysis in children and adolescents. *Med Sci Sports Exerc.* 1993;25:1185–1191.

100. Eaton AW, Israel RG, O'Brien KF, Hortobagyi T, McCammon MR. Comparison of four methods to assess body composition in women. *Eur J Clin Nutr.* 1993;47:353–360.

101. Heyward VH, Cook KL, Hicks VL, Jenkins KA, Quatrochi JA, Wilson WL. Predictive accuracy of three field methods for estimating relative body fatness of nonobese and obese women. *Int J Sport Nutr.* 1992;2:75–86.

102. Wilmore KM, McBride PJ, Wilmore JH. Comparison of bioelectric impedance and near-infrared interactance for body composition assessment in a population of self-perceived overweight adults. *Int J Obes Relat Metab Disord.* 1994;18:375–381.

103. Houmard JA, Israel RG, McCammon MR, O'Brien KF, Omer J, Zamora BS. Validity of a near-infrared device for estimating body composition in a college football team. *J Appl Sport Sci Res.* 1991;5:53–59.

104. Smith DB, Johnson GO, Stout JR, Housh TJ, Housh DJ, Evetovich TK. Validity of near-infrared interactance for estimating relative body fat in female high school gymnasts. *Int J Sports Med.* 1997;18:531–537.

Chapter 11

ENERGY BALANCE AND WEIGHT MANAGEMENT

Leah Moore Thomas, MS, RD

Introduction

Body weight and body composition are common concerns among athletes of all levels and abilities. Athletes frequently ask about these topics, which can be difficult to address. Typical goals of athletes include increasing lean body mass, losing body fat, or maintaining current weight as physical training increases. These goals are usually appropriate and may be essential to achieve and maintain optimal performance.

Evidence from various sports settings and age groups has demonstrated a relationship between fat mass and physical performance. In activities that involve movement of the body either vertically (eg, jumping), horizontally (eg, running), or rotationally around the body's axis (eg, diving and gymnastics), excess body fat can be detrimental to performance because it adds non-force-producing mass to the body, thus reducing speed and acceleration (1–4). In addition, excess body fat increases the metabolic cost of these physical activities and is associated with reduced aerobic capacity and endurance performance (4). A high power-to-weight ratio is important in sports where power, speed, and agility are critical, such as certain positions in football.

Long-distance swimming may be an exception. Distance swimmers may benefit from somewhat higher levels of body fat due to its contribution to thermal insulation and buoyancy (5). In general, however, physical activities that involve movement of the total body are more efficient mechanically and metabolically at lower levels of body fat. Conversely, high levels of total body mass may be advantageous in physical activities where athletes are required to overcome the inertia of another body (eg, sumo wrestlers or football lineman) or an external object (eg, weightlifters or discuss throwers).

Methods for measuring body composition and their limitations are described in Chapter 10. This chapter focuses on energy balance and body weight. Body composition distinguishes between fat-free mass and fat mass, whereas body weight does not. Body weight goals may or may not reflect appropriate body composition goals. Erroneous information or pressure from coaches, strength coaches, trainers, teammates, peers, or oneself may influence athletes to strive for body weights that may be detrimental to both athletic performance and overall health (6). In sports in which weight is a participation criterion, such as boxing, lightweight rowing, or wrestling, athletes may be encouraged to change body weight to meet weight class specifications.

Additionally, when working with athletes, it is important for the practitioner to encourage health screening to identify medical conditions, such as diabetes, hypertension, or hypercholesterolemia. Optimal performance and health over the long-term will depend on the early identification and management of these conditions.

The role of the sports dietitian is to help the athlete identify appropriate body weight and body composition goals. Consideration must be given to volume and intensity of training prior to competition, during the competitive season, and during the off-season or post-competition period. Athletes who wish to make substantial changes to body composition and body weight will benefit from nutrition counseling, which outlines a comprehensive plan to modify energy intake and meet nutrient needs. Many athletes, even elite athletes who are relatively weight-stable, will seek to fine-tune body composition and therefore body weight. For athletes who wish to lose body fat, sports dietitians can help them achieve their goals by modifying energy intake in a way that does not negatively impact health or performance. Before modification of energy intake can begin, it is necessary to determine energy needs.

Determining Energy Needs

Determining energy needs is extremely important when working with individuals on a sound nutrition plan, whether adjusting an athlete's diet or guiding a sedentary individual. Body weight remains stable when energy intake is equal to energy expenditure; therefore, manipulating body weight in the ultimate desired direction is based on knowing what the individual's basic energy needs are. Body structures and systems operate with an adequate supply of energy. Any time the body is in a state of change, such as growth/development, strenuous exercise, or illness, additional energy is needed to accommodate these changes. It is important to understand all of the factors that may affect energy demands so that need can be more accurately assessed.

An estimate of total daily energy expenditure (TDEE) is comprised of the following (7–10):

1. Resting metabolic rate (RMR), which generally accounts for 60% to 70% of TDEE
2. Thermic effect of food (TEF), which generally accounts for 5% to 10% of TDEE
3. Thermic effect of exercise (TEE), which generally accounts for 25% to 35% of TDEE

Resting Metabolic Rate

RMR is the amount of energy the body requires for normal function in a resting state. There are several factors that can affect RMR, including total body weight, fat-free mass, age, gender, and genetics. Lean body mass (LBM) is the greatest determinant of the RMR, accounting for up to 75% to 80%. Athletes generally have more LBM than sedentary individuals of the same weight, due to physical training (9,11).

Some researchers have found that trained individuals who regularly participate in aerobic exercise have RMRs 3% to 16% higher than untrained individuals. The reasons are unknown but may include regular aerobic training, acute exercise, and energy flux. It is known that energy expenditure increases during exercise and does not return to baseline values immediately after the activity; however, the magnitude and duration of this postexercise energy expenditure is controversial. Exercise duration and intensity may play an important role in the increase of RMR (7,12). Although this is still debated, most researchers agree that those who engage in aerobic exercise on a daily basis demonstrate long-term maintenance of LBM, which has the greatest impact on RMR (9).

There is a significant increase in RMR that persists for hours (or even days) after very intense or very long exercise sessions (8,13). However, it is important to note both the intensity and the duration because an exercise bout of 30 to 60 minutes of moderate intensity (50% to 65% of maximum oxygen consumption [VO_{2max}]) does not seem to significantly increase RMR for any appreciable length of time after the exercise ends. High-intensity exercise (such as racing a 1,500-meter swim or a 10-km road race) and exercise that is longer in duration show more significant increases in the continued increase of the metabolic rate (8,13).

Energy flux refers to the amount of energy expended each day compared to the energy consumed each day. Many athletes, particularly males, are in a state of high total energy flux because they have high daily energy expenditures (4,000 to 5,000 kcal) and they have to consume many calories to stay in energy balance. This high total energy flux has been shown to increase RMR in some athletes.

Calorimetry

Calorimetry is the measurement of a subject's energy expenditure. Laboratory methods, such as indirect calorimetry, can help determine energy requirements by measuring the rate of oxygen consumption and carbon dioxide gas production. The measurement of respiratory gas exchange through the use of metabolic carts provides one method for measuring RMR. These carts are computerized and automated so their use is fairly simple and minimal training is required for proper use (14). Such systems work well in a laboratory setting, but, due to their size, they are not easily portable.

Smaller, handheld calorimeters are also available. These may prove to be an appropriate alternative to metabolic carts, but further validation studies are needed. RMR is calculated by measuring oxygen uptake and ventilation amount based on a fixed resting respiratory quotient (RQ). Using a fixed RQ leaves more room for error due to human variation, but this error may be minimal because fluctuations in RQ are extremely small. Because there is more fluctuation due to variations in respiration, allowing sufficient measuring time will reduce error. Because the handheld calorimeter is a relatively new device, additional research on its reliability and validity is needed, but some initial data support the validity of this device (15).

Prediction Equations

There are numerous formulas for estimating RMR, some of which are more valid than others (see Table 11.1) (11,16). These prediction equations use measurements of an individual's weight, height, fat-free mass, and/or age to estimate RMR. Historically, these equations were used as standards to determine if an individual's measured RMR was within normal range. Presently, these equations are most often used in a clinical setting to

TABLE 11.1 Prediction Equations

Equation	Males	Females
Shofield	$48W - 0.11H + 3670$	$34W + 0.06H + 3530$
Harris-Benedict	$(66 + 13.8W + 5H - 6.8A) \times 4.18$	$(655 + 9.5W + 1.9H - 4.7A) \times 4.18$
Cunningham	$500 + 22FFM$	$500 + 22FFM$
Mifflin	$5 + 10W + 6.25H - 5A$	$-161 + 10W + 6.25H - 5A$

Abbreviations: A, age in years; FFM, fat-free mass in kg; H, height in cm; W, weight in kg.
Source: Data are from references 11 and 16.

predict needs instead of taking direct measurements (16). These equations may be useful in other situations, such as when working with athletes, as long as factors such as body composition are considered.

Despite the well-documented differences in RMR between athletes and sedentary individuals, specific prediction equations have not been developed for elite or recreational athletes. Among the published formulas, research shows that most equations significantly underestimate RMR in both males and females (16). Both the Schofield and the Harris-Benedict equations result in only slight underestimations in females and overestimations in males. The Mifflin equation has been identified as producing more accurate predictions than the Harris-Benedict equation in obese and nonobese adults (16). The Cunningham equation, due to its consideration of fat-free mass, is considered one of the better prediction equations for use with athletes (11).

In 2002, the Dietary Reference Intakes (DRIs) established Estimated Energy Requirements (EERs) at four levels of energy expenditure (see Appendix A). One category is described as an "active" physical activity level, although it may be too low for many athletes. The EERs represent dietary energy intakes that will promote energy balance in healthy adults. EER is calculated with the use of prediction equations. As always, there is individual variability, some of which is accounted for within the prediction equations. However, there is not an established Recommended Dietary Allowance (RDA) or Tolerable Upper Intake Level (UL) for energy because intakes that are more than an individual's EER should result in weight gain, which may be undesirable and possibly harmful (17).

Thermic Effect of Food

The thermic effect of food (TEF) is the increase in metabolic activity due to the consumption and digestion of food. TEF is most often expressed as a percentage of the absolute increase in calories over the total caloric make-up of the meal. The composition of the meal plays an important role in this metabolic change. Each macronutrient is metabolized differently, making the metabolic cost different. The cost of digesting and metabolizing protein is greatest, approximately 25% of its energy content. The cost for carbohydrate is approximately 10% whereas the cost for fat is 3%. When a mixed meal, containing varying amounts of carbohydrate, protein, and fat, is consumed, the metabolic cost is approximately 8%. As previously noted, TEF makes up only a small portion of total daily energy expenditure. However, over time, this effect can add up. Over the course of a year, a 1%

decrease in TEF would result in approximately 9,125 fewer kcal expended in someone who is neither overweight nor underweight (8).

Although it has been observed that TEF varies from person to person, it is not completely clear why the variation exists. Despite the difficulty in analyzing studies comparing TEF between lean and obese individuals, it is clear that obese subjects have a lower TEF than lean subjects. One theory suggests that insulin resistance in overweight and obese individuals might explain this observation (8).

Thermic Effect of Exercise

The thermic effect of exercise (TEE) is the component of total daily energy expenditure that varies most among individuals and that an individual can influence most. Although TEE may only contribute 25% to 35% of expended energy, the number of calories may be as high as 2,000 kcal/day for an endurance athlete. Sedentary individuals may only expend 300 kcal/day through physical activity. Unlike RMR, which is proportional to lean body mass, TEE is based on total body weight. In other words, it takes twice as much energy for a 300-lb person to walk the same speed and distance as a 150-lb person (8).

Estimating the Cost of Physical Activity

Estimating the amount of energy needed to support physical activity or athletic training is essential to estimate total daily energy expenditure. Communicating with coaches, strength coaches, and trainers and observing training sessions are crucial to understanding an athlete's training regimen. Once the activities of training are determined, an estimate of energy expenditure can be made using metabolic equivalents (METs) (see Appendix C). METs are used by exercise physiologists to estimate the metabolic cost (or oxygen used) during physical activity. At rest, the body uses approximately 3.5 mL of oxygen/kg/min or 1 kcal/kg/hr. This resting metabolic cost is referred to as 1.0 MET. Based on this initial value, activities can be assigned various MET levels according to their intensity. For example, an activity that is rated 2.0 MET requires twice the oxygen (7.0 mL oxygen/kg/min or 2 kcal/kg/hr) that rest requires. A 10 MET activity requires 10 times the oxygen or 10 kcal/kg/hr. Table 11.2 (18) lists various activities and their metabolic equivalents.

Additionally, charts have been created that simplify the calculations by providing the estimated energy cost of various activities per minute for various body weights. Any simplification of the calculations, such as rounding off numbers, will reduce the accuracy of the results. Estimating the intensity or duration of exercise also introduces error. All of these methods are estimations based on scientific studies. Box 11.1 illustrates one method of estimating the energy needs of an athlete.

Establishing Appropriate Goals

Establishing appropriate body weight goals can sometimes be a challenging task. What is considered healthy and appropriate by the sports dietitian may not be the same as that of the athlete, coach, or trainer. All measures are subject to error, and standards established

TABLE 11.2 Selected Activities and MET

Activity	MET
Very high-intensity, short duration	
Weight lifting (free, nautilus, or universal-type), light or moderate effort	3.0
Track and field, throwers	4.0
Track and field, jumpers	6.0
Intermittent high-intensity	
Tennis (doubles)	6.0
Racquetball, casual game	7.0
Tennis (singles), basketball or volleyball	8.0
Soccer or rugby	10.0
Endurance	
Bicycling, stationary, 100 watts, light effort	5.5
Rowing, stationary, 100 watts, moderate effort	7.0
Swimming, laps, freestyle, slow, moderate to light effort	7.0
Skiing, cross-country, 4.0–4.9 mph, moderate speed and effort	8.0
Running, 5 mph (12 min/mile)	8.0
Bicycling, 12–13.9 mph, leisure, moderate effort	8.0
Rowing, stationary, 150 watts, vigorous effort	8.5
Swimming, laps, freestyle, fast, vigorous effort	10.0
Bicycling, 14–15.9 mph, racing or leisure, vigorous effort	10.0
Running, 8 mph (7.5 min/mile)	13.5
Running, 10.9 mph (5.5 min/mile)	18.0
Weight- and body-focused	
Gymnastics, general	4.0
Wrestling	6.0
Low endurance, precision skill	
Golf, walking and carrying clubs	4.5
Softball or baseball, fast or slow pitch	5.0
Miscellaneous activities	
Walking, less than 2.0 mph, strolling	2.0
Walking, 3.0 mph, level, moderate pace	3.3
Walking, 4.0 mph, level, very brisk pace	5.0
Aerobics, low impact	5.0
Aerobics, high impact	7.0

Source: Data are from reference 18.

for the general population are not perfect. It is important to be familiar with the various methods of assessing weight status and health and to know the limitations of each.

Body Mass Index

BMI is a nationally recognized screening tool used to assess weight status and classify obesity. However, there are several limitations that make it inappropriate for use with athletic populations (19). The BMI is an indirect measurement of body fat and is only moderately correlated with percentage body fat ($r = 0.58$). To illustrate this point, consider JM, a 27-year-old

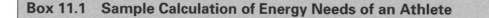

Box 11.1   Sample Calculation of Energy Needs of an Athlete

21-year-old male collegiate soccer player
Height: 5 feet 10 inches (70 inches × 2.54 = 177.8 cm)
Weight: 165 lb (165/2.2 = 75 kg)
One day's activities: 1.5 h soccer, 15.5 h very light activity, 7 h rest

1. Use Mifflin equation to calculate resting metabolic rate (RMR), where W = weight in kg, H = height in cm, and A = age in years:

$$RMR = 5 + 10W + 6.25H - 5A$$

$$RMR = 5 + 10(75) + 6.25(177.8) - 5(21)$$

$$RMR = 1{,}761.25 \approx 1{,}760 \text{ kcal}$$

2. Estimate 24-h activity using activity factors (rest, 1.0; very light, 1.5; light, 2.5; moderate, 5.0; heavy, 7.0):

Rest:	7 h × 1.0 = 7.0
Very light:	15.5 h × 1.5 = 23.25
Heavy:	1.5 h × 7.0 = 10.5
Average activity factor:	(7.0 + 23.25 + 10.5)/24 h = 40.75/24 = 1.7

3. Estimate energy needs:

$$RMR \times \text{Average activity factor} = \text{Energy needs}$$

$$1{,}760 \times 1.7 = 2{,}992 \text{ kcal/d}$$

man, who weighs 325 lb and stands 6 feet 4 inches tall. His BMI of 39.6 falls just below the cutoff for Class III obesity. However, JM's percentage of body fat is approximately 20% and he is a successful NFL football player. Using only BMI, he would be classified as morbidly obese (19). For many athletes, there is a mismatch between BMI and body fat.

Body Fat

Body composition is a better marker for assessing health and fitness and can aid in establishing more appropriate weight goals for athletes. Although this method is better than using BMI, it is still not perfect. Consideration must be given to other influences such as genetic predisposition, age, and gender. These factors cannot be changed and will inevitably have an effect on body composition (20,21).

Because performance largely depends on the athlete's ability to sustain power and overcome resistance, it can be directly influenced by body composition. Less fat mass means less resistance; more lean mass means more power (20). Research has demonstrated a strong negative correlation between sports performance and percentage body fat for most sports (22). However, the percentage of body fat appropriate for a particular athlete must be individually determined. Some athletes have an understanding of this concept, but others may not. Misinformed athletes may try to attain an inappropriate percentage of body fat based on the body composition of a successful individual in their sport. A firm understanding of body composition and body weight, how each relates to optimal fitness and performance, and what is considered healthy is vital when working with athletes, coaches, and trainers. In one survey, 92% of coaches and athletic trainers (who play influential roles in their athletes' lives) rated body composition as important (6).

Unlike BMI, there is no universally accepted set of body fat standards. Various fitness organizations have established reference ranges for percentage of body fat. Not all of these variations are based on research nor do they take into account the morphology of athletes vs sedentary individuals. Exercise and conditioning programs result in the development of specific muscle groups and physical fitness is associated with not just the quantity of fat but also its distribution (23).

In addition, there are several different methods of assessing body fat percentages, each of which has a margin of error. This is important to remember when assessing and discussing body composition with individuals. It is also important to remember that adult standards should not be applied to children or adolescents.

Separate "health" and "physically active" standards have been developed for adults and may become useful when working with a varied clientele (see Table 11.3) (24). *Health Standards* refer to the body fat percentage that is considered healthy because it does not independently increase risk for health problems such as high blood pressure, diabetes, or heart disease. Men and women younger than age 55 years who have a body fat percentage of more than 22% and 35%, respectively, may increase their risk for these health problems. Other factors, such as nutrient intake, physical activity, stress, and lifestyle choices, can also increase or decrease this risk. *Physically Active Standards* refer to a percentage of body fat that reflects more physical training. A greater percentage of muscle mass along with a lower percentage of fat mass has been shown to have the following advantages to athletes:

- Greater strength (pound for pound), which is beneficial in weight-class sports such as wrestling, rowing, and boxing,
- Increased speed and/or endurance, which is beneficial in sports like distance running, road cycling, jumping events, and activities that require rotation around an axis, such as diving and gymnastics,
- Greater aesthetic appeal, which is critical in sports such as figure skating, gymnastics, dance, diving, and bodybuilding. In these sports, appearance can be an important consideration in score.

No standards for athletes in specific sports have been established. However, several researchers have reported typical percentage body fat levels for men and women in various sports (20). While these typical ranges may be helpful as a general guideline, it is imperative that athletes and those who work with them recognize that the percentage body fat that is consistent with optimal performance must reflect the individual athlete's genetic predisposition.

Although less body fat is desirable in athletes and has demonstrated performance benefits, health problems can result by having too little body fat. Both men and women need a certain amount of body fat to insulate vital organs, regulate body temperature, and ensure an adequate production of sex hormones. The actual percentage that is considered at risk

TABLE 11.3 Health and Physical Activity Standards for Body Fat Percentages

		Body Fat, %	
Standard Type	Age, y	Women	Men
Health*	< 55	20–35	8–22
	> 55	25–38	10–25
Physical activity[†]	< 55	16–28	5–15
	> 55	20–33	7–18

*Defined as the body fat percentage that is considered healthy because it does not independently increase risk for health problems such as high blood pressure, diabetes, or heart disease.
[†]For individuals who engage in substantial physical training.
Source: Data are from reference 24.

for being too low may vary slightly among individuals; however, Heyward and Wagner (24) give a definition of at-risk of less than 5% for males and less than 12% for females. In either gender, if body fat gets too low, athletic performance is jeopardized and health problems can result.

The level of body fat that is considered unsafe can vary from person to person. In particular, women who restrict energy intake and/or exercise excessively run the risk of developing characteristics of the female athlete triad. This condition is characterized by an energy imbalance, often secondary to disordered eating or an eating disorder, amenorrhea, and osteoporosis. It is unclear if extremely low body fat is the cause of very low estrogen levels that result in amenorrhea in these women, or if other behaviors contribute more to the problem. Psychological, emotional, and physiological stress can result in neuroendocrine changes. Research indicates that restrictive dietary habits resulting in an energy imbalance may be the primary culprit (25).

It is clear that a firm understanding of weight, body composition, sport-specific goals and expectations, and long-term health is necessary when working with physically active individuals. All of these factors are important to consider when determining energy and micronutrient needs.

Recommended Macronutrient Distribution

After total energy needs are established and an appropriate body weight goal has been identified, the next step is to determine how to meet energy and nutrient needs. Carbohydrates, proteins, and fats all contribute to the caloric value of a meal plan, as does alcohol. The contributions that should be made by these macronutrients vary depending on the athlete's training and competition schedule. Reviewing the athlete's performance goals, and factors that influence them, such as general health, body weight, intensity, duration, and frequency of training and food preferences, will help establish the proportions of energy from each macronutrient.

Recommendations for carbohydrate, protein, and fat for athletes are described in detail in Chapters 2, 3, and 4. In general, athletes are advised to consume 5 to 10 g carbohydrate per kg body weight per day. At a minimum, all athletes should consume 5 g/kg/day; however, some athletes, particularly male endurance athletes, need 8 to 10 g/kg/day (26). Recommended protein intakes range from 1.2 to 1.7 g/kg/day. Fat recommendations for athletes are 20% to 25% of total energy as fat, assuming that energy intake is adequate. The recommended fat intake for athletes is often 1 g/kg/day. These general recommendations must be fine-tuned to meet the demands of the athlete's training and performance goals (27).

Weight Maintenance

Maintaining optimal weight can be a challenge for some individuals. Athletes may face unwanted weight gain or loss. Either situation can often be prevented by paying close attention to dietary habits. It may be helpful for the athlete to focus on a time when weight was stable in the past and recall how that weight was achieved. When developing meal plans or when educating an athlete about energy intake, attention should also be paid to energy intake throughout the day. Smaller, more frequent meals have been the method of choice over recent years to control total daily energy intake. It is usually best to spread energy intake throughout the day to prevent an energy deficient or an energy excess (20).

Nutrition periodization is an important concept to consider when working with athletes and is covered in detail in Chapter 24. The nutrition needs of athletes change as training changes over the course of the year. An athlete goes through different phases of training, with changes in volume and intensity in order to peak for competition. As volume and intensity change, energy and macronutrient needs also change. During the off-season or during rehabilitation of an injury, energy intake and distribution may need to be reevaluated to match the current volume and intensity of training or to aid in rehabilitation and recovery. This practice is aimed to reduce any unwanted weight (fat) gain and to help the athlete reenter training and/or competition as smoothly as possible.

Weight Reduction

If weight reduction is appropriate, a state of negative energy balance must be achieved and maintained over a period of time. Thus, the amount of energy consumed must be less than the amount of energy expended. Because the energy content of 1 pound of fat is approximately 3,500 kcal, in theory, to lose 1 pound of fat per week, a 500-kcal deficit per day (via increased exercise and/or reduced food intake) must be created and maintained over time. However, the actual rate of weight loss varies among individuals.

Sports dietitians and athletes must be cautious about the timing and severity of weight-loss attempts so as not to jeopardize performance. Weight-loss strategies are most appropriate during the off-season or the postcompetition period. Weight loss may also be a goal early in the season, when the volume and intensity of training is lower. Weight loss during a competitive season, especially if it is rapid and involves severe restriction, may compromise performance. However, with careful planning and appropriate meal scheduling, a healthy and appropriate weight can be achieved during the athlete's competitive season. In some cases, athletes may find that as the season progresses and training becomes more intense and focused, a goal weight and body composition can be achieved without extra effort. This would indicate that current eating patterns may be appropriate for the type and amount of training.

Assuming that weight loss is appropriate, a goal weight needs to be established based on a healthy body composition and the volume of training. For example, consider a 210-lb male baseball player who has a body fat of 17% but would like his body fat to be 11%, as it was a year ago. As shown in Box 11.2, a weight loss of 12 lb of body fat (with minimal loss of lean mass) would result in a goal weight of approximately 198 lb and approximately 11% body fat.

To assist the athlete in weight reduction, the steps presented in the following sections may be helpful.

Identify an Appropriate Weight Range

Use body composition as a guide to establish an appropriate goal for weight loss. Consider the athlete's past and present weight and body composition, the demands of training, the demands of the sport, and gender.

Evaluate Current Dietary and Exercise Practices

Instruct the athlete to record several days of food and fluid intake and analyze the athlete's current dietary practices and energy intake:

- Are meals being skipped?
- How many meals and snacks does the athlete consume?
- Where does the athlete usually eat (home, work, school, restaurants, especially fast-food restaurants)?
- Does the athlete cook and if so, what kinds of foods are prepared?
- Are the foods consumed generally nutrient-dense?
- Does the athlete eat a variety of foods and might there be any nutrient deficiencies?
- How frequently does the athlete consume sports-type food products (sport drinks, energy bars, etc)?

Box 11.2   Sample Calculations of Body Fat Loss

210-lb male baseball player
Body fat: 17%
Body fat goal: 11%

1. **Current fat mass:**
   210 lb × 0.17 = 35.7 lb fat mass

2. **Fat loss:**
   35.7 lb − 12 lb = 23.7 lb

3. **Weight loss:**
   210 lb − 12 lb = 198 lb

4. **Percentage Body Fat:**
   23.7 lb/198 lb = 0.11 = 11%

- Does the athlete use dietary supplements?
- What types of foods and fluids are consumed before, during, or after exercise?

Establish Energy and Macronutrient Requirements

Using the recommendations for carbohydrate (5 to 10 g/kg), protein (1.2 to 1.7 g/kg), and fat (approximately 1 g/kg) and the athlete's goal weight, establish energy requirements and macronutrient needs to promote gradual weight (body fat) loss. Because minimum carbohydrate and protein needs must be met to support training and maintain muscle mass, weight-loss diets are often low in fat (and devoid of alcohol). For athletes not already engaged in high-volume training, aerobic exercise may be added to training to increase energy expenditure. Athletes may also increase their nontraining activities (such as parking in the outer lots on campus and walking from there) as a way of expending more energy.

Devise a Dietary Plan for Achieving Goals Based on Established Needs

The plan must reflect the athlete's food preferences, food availability, and daily schedule (class, work, training, etc). Based on the analysis of food records, the changes needed to achieve a negative energy balance may be apparent. The athlete may need to make major changes in food selection or intake patterns to achieve weight loss, but in some cases only small adjustments may be necessary.

Educate the Athlete, Review the Dietary Plan, and Monitor Status

The athlete must be involved in the analysis, decision-making, and planning activities. It is important that the athlete understand the approach taken, how needs were determined, and the meal plan itself. Educating the athlete without providing an overwhelming amount of information is important. Reviewing the meal plan promotes understanding and also allows the athlete to ask questions. Weight and body composition status should be monitored on a regular basis and the plan should be evaluated. Evaluation will help identify any adjustments that might need to be made in energy or macronutrient intake. If performance or health is impaired, changes must be made immediately. Because weight loss is likely to be slow, progress must be monitored over time (weeks or months).

Monitor Changes in Menstruation

Monitoring of menstrual function is recommended. If irregular menstruation is observed, it may be that energy intake is not sufficient, in which cases changes must be made in the plan. Irregular or absent menstruation is one component of the female athlete triad and a red flag not to be ignored (see Chapter 18).

Weight Gain

Gaining body weight requires a consistent excess energy intake. Many athletes desire to gain lean weight or muscle mass. However, there are cases in which body fat percentage might be too low, making it desirable and appropriate to gain body fat.

When the athlete's goal is to gain lean weight, the excess energy intake must be combined with a resistance training program. Ideally, the added energy intake would come from all three macronutrients. However, it is common for strength athletes who want to build muscle mass to consume only excess protein, through both foods and supplements.

Scientific evidence indicates that protein levels more than 1.7 to 1.8 g/kg result in oxidation of the excess amino acids (28). In other words, a higher than recommended protein intake does not result in greater muscle gain, even with an intense resistance training program. Therefore, it is important to increase both dietary carbohydrates and protein as well as consume an adequate amount of fat to create an energy excess.

As is the case with weight reduction, five steps are necessary to establish a nutrition plan: (a) identify an appropriate weight goal; (b) evaluate current dietary and exercise practices; (c) establish energy and macronutrient requirements; (d) devise a dietary plan for achieving goals based on established needs; and (e) educate the athlete, review the dietary plan, and monitor status. In the case of weight gain, consider the following tips:

- Encourage the athlete to eat at least three meals per day, plus snacks.
- Include energy-dense foods. Foods that are high in fat tend to be high in calories. There are a variety of energy bars and shakes that are calorie-dense and can be added to meals or used as snacks.
- Focus on foods that contain mono- and polyunsaturated fats, such as nuts, seeds, avocados, and vegetable oils. These foods are energy-dense but contain heart-healthy fats. High-calorie spreads, such as nut butters, guacamole, or olive tapenades are recommended.
- Replace the energy expended during practices, workouts, or competitions as quickly as possible.
- Check for macronutrient balance.
- Choose calorie-containing beverages rather than noncaloric liquids such as water, coffee, or tea.

Practical Approaches to Counseling: Promoting Success

The responsibilities of a sports dietitian include assessing body weight and body composition, determining the demands of the athlete's sport, establishing appropriate goals, and helping the athlete design a nutrition plan to accomplish those goals. It is important to involve the athlete in the assessment and decision-making processes to facilitate understanding of the plan and to encourage compliance. It will be necessary to monitor, evaluate, and, possibly, revise the plan. Communication among the athlete, sports dietitian, and the coaching and training staffs is vital to success.

Summary

Aiding athletes in the management of body weight and body composition is critical. Establishing appropriate goals and then a dietary plan to help them accomplish these goals is important for achieving optimal performance and health. A firm understanding of energy needs and energy balance is crucial to develop a dietary plan that meets the needs of the athlete without creating excesses or deficits. Realistic goals accompanied by an individualized plan, along with communication on a regular basis, promote greater success.

References

1. Boileau RA, Lohman TG. The measurement of human physique and its effect on physical performance. *Orthop Clin North Am.* 1977;8:563–581.
2. Malina RM. Physique and body composition: effects on performance and effects on training, semistarvation, and overtraining. In: Brownell KD, Rodin J, Wilmore JH, eds. *Eating, Body Weight, and Performance in Athletes.* Philadelphia, Pa: Lea & Febiger; 1992:94–114.
3. Pate RR, Slentz CA, Katz DP. Relationship between skinfold thickness and performance of health related fitness test items. *Res Q Exerc Sport.* 1989;60:183–189.
4. Houtkooper LB. Body composition assessment and its relationship to athletic performance. In: Berning JF, Steen SN, eds. *Nutrition for Sport & Exercise.* Gaithersburg, Md: Aspen Publishers; 1998:155–166.
5. Walberg-Rankin J. Changing body weights and composition in athletes. In: Lamb DR, Murray R, eds. *Exercise, Nutrition, and Weight Control.* Carmel, Ind: Cooper Publishing; 1998:199–236. Perspectives in Exercise Science and Sports Medicine series; vol 11.
6. Rockwell MS, Nickols-Richardson SM, Thye FW. Nutrition knowledge, opinions, and practices of coaches and athletic trainers at a division I university. *Int J Sport Nutr.* 2001;11:174–185.
7. Melby CL, Commerford SR, Hill JO. Exercise, macronutrient balance, and weight control. In: Lamb DR, Murray R, eds. In: Lamb DR, Murray R, eds. *Exercise, Nutrition, and Weight Control.* Carmel, Ind: Cooper Publishing; 1998:1–60. Perspectives in Exercise Science and Sports Medicine series; vol 11.
8. Bouchard C. Genetic factors and body weight regulation. In: Dalton S, ed. *Overweight and Weight Management: The Health Professional's Guide to Understanding and Practice.* Gaithersburg, Md: Aspen Publishers, Inc; 1997:161–186.
9. LaForgia J, Withers RT, Williams AD, Murch BJ, Chatterton BE, Schultz CG, Leaney F. Effect of 3 weeks of detraining on the resting metabolic rate of and body composition of trained males. *Eur J Clin Nutr.* 1999;53:126–134.
10. van der Ploeg GE, Withers RT. Predicting the resting metabolic rate of 300 60-year-old Australian males. *Eur J Clin Nutr.* 2002;56:701–708.
11. De Lorenzo A, Taglliabue A, Andreoli A, Testolin G, Comelli M, Deurenberg P. Measured and predicted resting metabolic rate in Italian males and females, aged 18–59 y. *Eur J Clin Nutr.* 2001;55:208–214.
12. Potteiger JA, Koch AJ, Kuphai KE, Fisher DH. Effects of intermittent and continuous exercise on energy expenditure, substrate utilization, and RMR in women. *Clin Exerc Phys.* 2001;3:137–143.
13. Manore MM. The overweight athlete. In: Maughan RJ, ed. *The Encyclopaedia of Sports Medicine: Nutrition in Sport, Vol II.* Oxford, England: Blackwell Science Ltd; 2000:469–483.
14. Macfarlane DJ. Automated metabolic gas analysis systems. *Sports Med.* 2001;31:841–861.
15. Igawa S, Sakamaki M, Miyazaki M. Examination of the reliability of the portable calorimeter. *Clin Exp Pharm Phys.* 2002;29(suppl):S13–S15.
16. Frankenfield DC, Rowe WA, Smith JS, Cooney RN. Validation of several established equations for resting metabolic rate in obese and nonobese people. *J Am Diet Assoc.* 2003;103;1152–1159.
17. Institute of Medicine. *Dietary Reference Intakes for Energy, Carbohydrates, Fiber, Fat, Protein and Amino Acids (Macronutrients).* Washington, DC: National Academy Press; 2002. Available at: http:www.nap.edu. Accessed July 27, 2004.
18. Ainsworth BE. The compendium of physical activities tracking guide. January 2002. Prevention Research Center, Norman J. Arnold School of Public Health, University of South Carolina. Available at: http://prevention.sph.sc.edu/tools/docs/documents_compendium.pdf. Accessed February 18, 2005.

19. Prentice AM, Jebb SA. Beyond body mass index. *Obesity Rev.* 2001;2:141–147.

20. Benardot D. *Nutrition For Serious Athletes*. Champaign, Ill: Human Kinetics; 2000.

21. Cattrysse E, Zinzen E, Caboor D, Duquet W, Van Roy P, Clarys JP. Anthropometric fractionation of body mass: Matiegka revisited. *J Sports Sci.* 2002;20:717–723.

22. Brownell KD, Steen SN, Wilmore JH. Weight regulation practices in athletes: analysis of metabolic and health effects. *Med Sci Sports Exerc.* 1987;19:546–556.

23. Stewart AD, Hannan WJ. Prediction of fat and fat-free mass in male athletes using duel X-ray absorptiometry as the reference method. *J Sports Sci.* 2000;18:263–274.

24. Heyward VH, Wagner DR. *Applied Body Composition Assessment*. Champaign, Ill: Human Kinetics; 2004.

25. Zanker CL, Cooke CB, Truscott JG, Oldroyd B, Jacobs HS. Annual changes of bone density over 12 years in an amenorrheic athlete. *Med Sci Sports Exerc.* 2004;36:137–142.

26. Burks LM, Cox GR, Culmmings NK, Desbrow B. Guidelines for daily carbohydrate intake: do athletes achieve them? *Sports Med.* 2001;31:267–299.

27. Position of the American Dietetic Association, Dietitians of Canada, and the American College of Sports Medicine: nutrition and athletic performance. *J Am Diet Assoc.* 2000;100:1543–1556.

28. Tipton KD, Wolfe RR. Protein and amino acids for athletes. *J Sports Sci.* 2004;22:65–79.

Section 3

Sports Nutrition Across the Life Cycle

From early in childhood to late in life, many people engage in sports or physical activity. Some are looking to improve performance as they move through amateur competition and become professional athletes. Others have no professional aspirations but wish to maintain or improve their fitness and performance, some across the course of their entire life. The first four chapters of this section examine sports nutrition primarily through the filter of age—child, adolescent, college, and masters athletes. Although none of these stages are strictly defined by age or ability, they are convenient classifications. Working with elite athletes is the dream of many sports dietitians, and that chapter draws on both the scientific literature and the author's personal experience.

Several factors influence training and performance, such as age, health status, changes in physiology, presence of chronic disease, and individual eating preferences and behaviors. Individual chapters in this section cover a variety of conditions and disease states: vegetarianism, disordered eating, pregnancy, diabetes, and cardiovascular disease.

Chapter 12

CHILD AND ADOLESCENT ATHLETES

Diane L. Habash, PhD, RD*

Introduction

Organized youth sports are more prevalent now than ever with an estimated 30 million to 40 million youth participating in some capacity (1). Women and children have been allowed sports opportunities only within the last 50 years (1–4). Ironically, despite increased sports participation, pediatric obesity is increasing. This dichotomy provides ample justification for the work of sports dietitians and for education of all individuals involved with youth sports.

To add dimension to this challenge, for the past 20 years there has been increasing emphasis on year-round training and sport specialization in youth. Although sports nutrition research has increased, there is still much to learn about the effects of training on the child and adolescent (5–7). Few school athletic departments and youth sports associations have the finances to use sports dietitians on a routine basis. In fact, if nutrition information is provided, coaches and trainers often communicate it. Aspiring sports dietitians should be aware of these situations and should volunteer to talk with the various and diverse audiences (coaches, trainers, teachers, parents/guardians, and athletes). Volunteering is a way for sports dietitians to help improve nutrition among children and adolescents for sports as well as for life (7,8).

This chapter provides information for the sports dietitian who is counseling elementary, middle, and high school athletes. References to sophisticated and in-depth reviews are offered throughout the text, but perhaps the most helpful suggestion for counseling these athletes is to know your audience. These are the formative years for youth, who will often do almost anything to excel. Also, there is likely more diversity of behavior and food and taste preferences in this population compared with adult athletes, so sports dietitians should be prepared to offer a variety of suggestions.

*The author wishes to acknowledge Angela Illing and Kristen Brogan Habash for assistance in manuscript preparation and NIH Grant M01RR00034.

Child and Adolescent Differences from Adults

The lure of professional sports begins early, as demonstrated by the many Olympic-caliber athletes who are teenagers (4). Strict training regimens require years of physical conditioning and skill development. Regardless of the level of athleticism and the hours of training, it is important to note that "children are not mini-adults" (9). Following are some key differences between the adult and child body. See additional reviews for more in-depth information (9–13).

- Until adulthood is attained and depending on age, genetics, diet, and physical training, the bones of children are more porous and cartilaginous. Epiphyseal (growth) plates are susceptible to damage from excessive use (for instance, distance running) or high-impact sports (eg, gymnastics). Severe injuries can occur in sports in which the bones protecting vital organs such as the heart can be compressed from crushing impacts (such as baseball, soccer, and football). (4,6,12,14).

- Compared with adults, cardiac stroke volume is lower, heart and respiration rates as well as oxygen consumption per kilogram of body weight are higher, and anaerobic capability is lower in children (11). In effect, children are not as capable of utilizing glycogen and working in an anaerobic capacity as adults are, but they may recover faster after exercise. Additionally, there is controversy about the response to endurance training in prepubertal compared with mid- and post-pubertal stages (11,15) when aerobic endurance increases more easily during pre- and postpuberty. Also, males may be more likely to demonstrate training effects in absolute aerobic power across all pubertal stages than females, who may reach absolute aerobic power and may not continue to increase power across all stages of puberty (note, however, that aerobic trainability in young females has not bee well studied) (11). Overall, young athletes are not as efficient at movement as adults, resulting in a relative increase in energy expenditure per kilogram of body weight (16).

- Muscle tissue in children contains more water than adult muscle (79% vs 74%, respectively) (17,18). Although this sounds beneficial, thermoregulation at younger ages during activity in temperate climates requires more attention to good hydration practices. Based on body mass comparison, children produce more body heat, sweat less, and are not as quick to acclimatize to heat as adults are (19).

- Among children and adolescents, growth is not always predictable or even linear within individuals, and energy requirements are not stable like those of adults. In addition, some growing athletes may find that some types of athletic maneuvers, which at one time seemed simple (tumbling), will become more difficult with growth. These aspects of physical performance do not apply to the adult body, which has fairly stable metabolism, energy requirements, and movement efficiency (20).

- Body structure of children and size characteristics can provide a challenge when using training equipment that adults use (ie, weight-lifting machines), and the sense of balance such as that required for using free weights may not be adequate in youth (9).

- Children and adolescents are still in the process of learning about themselves. Mental and emotional health is maturing during this part of the life cycle, and despite the determination to please coaches, trainers, and parents, children cannot be expected to have the emotional competencies of an adult. In addition, a child's reaction to the brutal demands of elite training may be immature and can impact performance and lifestyle behaviors (9–11,13).

- Children and adolescents do not have the same knowledge base as adults and may require explanations and definitions for nutrition concepts such as carbohydrate, glycogen, protein, antioxidants, amino acids, nutrient functions, and other concepts. They may need help identifying specific foods that contain the various nutrients.
- Finally (and simply), children and to some extent adolescents depend on adults for their supply of food.

For many reasons, there is limited research about child and adolescent athletes (11). To understand the impact of nutrition on performance during these life stages, some extrapolation must come from adult comparisons.

Growth and Development

Many people, including athletes, parents, coaches, and trainers, may not completely understand the normal growth patterns of childhood and adolescence. Growth varies among individuals and is influenced by factors such as genetics, growth hormones, adequacy of nutrient and energy intake, and total energy expenditure. Without guidance, athletes (and others) can have unrealistic expectations about many aspects of their growth, performance, and body in general. This may be especially true because youth often accept the media's portrayal of athletes as their unrealistic gold standard, especially when it comes to body shape, size, and weight. This occurs at young ages. In fact, in one study, 25% of the boys and 33% of the girls reported a desire to lose weight, and 17% and 24%, respectively, were actually dieting (21). In a more recent prospective study of almost 15,000 girls and boys between the ages of 9 and 14 years, dieting to control body weight was not effective, and those with dieting behaviors were actually more likely to gain weight regardless of body mass index (BMI) and Tanner stage (22).

Growth Charts and Body Weight

Yearly growth evaluations using the standardized percentile charts as noted in Figures 12.1 and 12.2 (height, weight, age, and BMI) from the National Center for Health Statistics (23) are helpful when demonstrating growth patterns. Current NCHS charts have increased the upper age limit to 20 years of age and have replaced age-specific height and weight tables with age-specific BMI percentiles. This change is more realistic, although it includes a small potential for error when interpreting BMI without some assessment of muscle mass and bone density. Children with a BMI more than the 85th percentile are considered overweight, and those with a BMI more than the 95th percentile are overfat.

Childhood
Although children in the first several years of life may experience individualized growth spurts, there is often a consistent and predictable pattern of growth experienced from 2 years of age until near the start of puberty (approximately 8 to 13 years of age in girls and 9.5 to 13.5 years of age in boys) (13,24). On average, children grow approximately 5 to 6 cm (2 to 3 inches) and gain 2 to 3 kg (4 to 7 lb) per year (13,24).

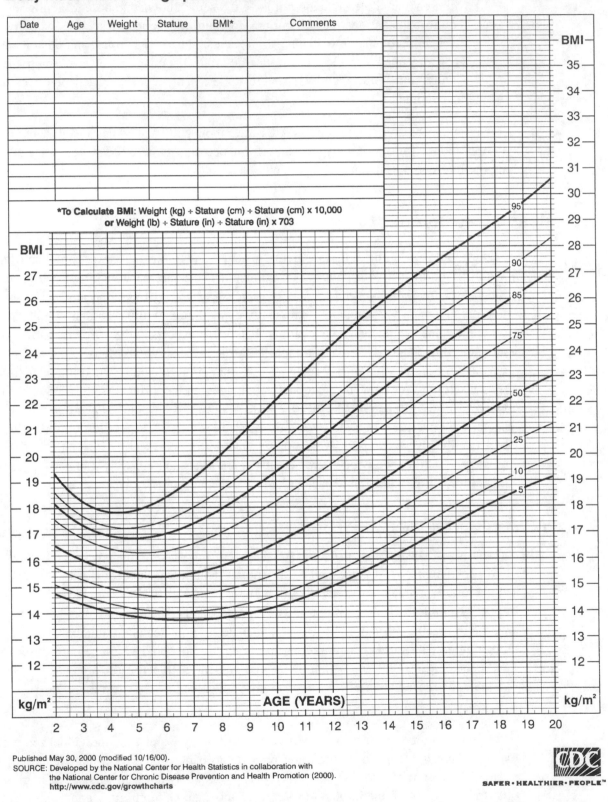

2 to 20 years: Boys
Body mass index-for-age percentiles

NAME _____

RECORD # _____

Date	Age	Weight	Stature	BMI*	Comments

*To Calculate BMI: Weight (kg) ÷ Stature (cm) ÷ Stature (cm) x 10,000
or Weight (lb) ÷ Stature (in) ÷ Stature (in) x 703

BMI

95
90
85
75
50
25
10
5

AGE (YEARS)

kg/m²

Published May 30, 2000 (modified 10/16/00).
SOURCE: Developed by the National Center for Health Statistics in collaboration with
the National Center for Chronic Disease Prevention and Health Promotion (2000).
http://www.cdc.gov/growthcharts

CDC
SAFER • HEALTHIER • PEOPLE™

FIGURE 12.1. Centers for Disease Control and Prevention growth chart: 2 to 20 years: boys. Body mass index-for-age percentiles. Available at: http://www.cdc.gov/growthcharts. Accessed November 9, 2004.

2 to 20 years: Girls
Body mass index-for-age percentiles

NAME _____

RECORD # _____

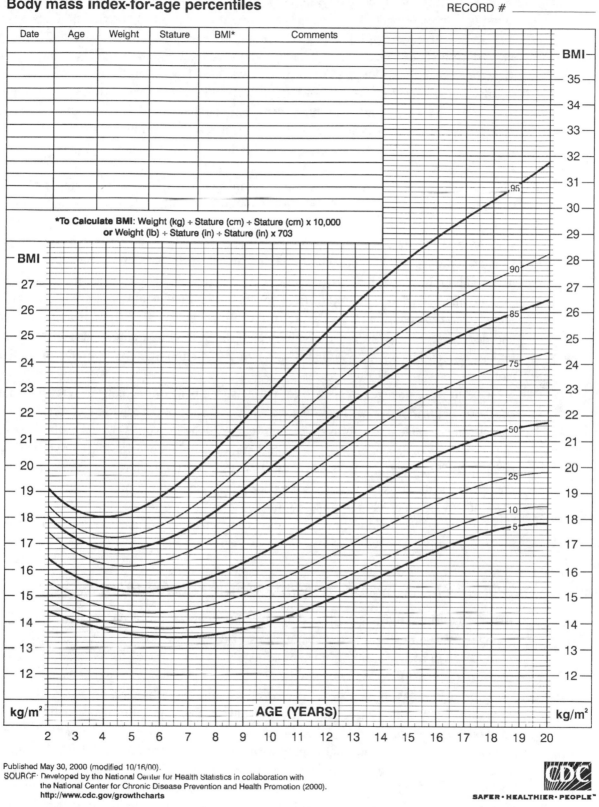

Date	Age	Weight	Stature	BMI*	Comments

*To Calculate BMI: Weight (kg) ÷ Stature (cm) ÷ Stature (cm) x 10,000
or Weight (lb) ÷ Stature (in) ÷ Stature (in) x 703

Published May 30, 2000 (modified 10/16/00).
SOURCE: Developed by the National Center for Health Statistics in collaboration with
the National Center for Chronic Disease Prevention and Health Promotion (2000).
http://www.cdc.gov/growthcharts

CDC

SAFER · HEALTHIER · PEOPLE™

FIGURE 12.2. Centers for Disease Control and Prevention growth chart: 2 to 20 years: girls. Body mass index-for-age percentiles. Available at: http://www.cdc.gov/growthcharts. Accessed November 9, 2004.

There is limited information about the effect of excessive training on growth in child athletes because sport specificity, body typing, and self-induced energy deficits are confounding variables that have not been adequately studied (9,11). Current literature does not support the assertion that high levels of training will decrease growth potential (11) especially during adolescence, although delays in growth and sexual maturity are documented in gymnasts, dancers, long-distance runners (25), and wrestlers (26). In fact, a 3-year prospective annual measurement of elite athletes ages 8 to 16 years in England (in gymnastics, tennis, soccer, and swimming) demonstrated that the athletes remained consistent in their growth percentiles and were comparable to a control group (27).

Adolescence

Adolescence is a period of rapid yet unpredictable growth. On average, during puberty (ie, the period of complete sexual development and maturation), girls grow 25 cm (10 in) and 24 kg (53 lb) and boys grow 28 cm (11 in) and 32 kg (70 lb) (28). The growth pattern and velocity may be related to those of the parents and can be influenced by many factors, such as energy balance (10,11,28). During early puberty, girls develop sooner than boys and may be taller than boys at the same chronologic age. Puberty is crucial for the development of bone mass and can have implications for long-term bone health because nearly 40% of bone is laid down during this period (29). The initial gender disparity in lean mass growth and deposition is soon compensated by male growth in height and muscle mass. In fact, males may continue to grow well into their mid-20s; an important piece of information that can influence sport performance.

Due to these changes in growth (or perhaps lack of), some young athletes may begin sports specialization sooner than others or may switch sports altogether as a result. There can be considerable pressure in sports involving weight classifications (wrestling, jockeying), appearance (dance, diving, gymnastics, figure skating, cheerleading), or speed (cross-country running/track) to control body weight. (See Weight Control Practices later in this chapter.) For these reasons, body composition assessments are now being considered in some statewide school systems and minimum weight standards are being adapted for some sports (eg, wrestling). Education about growth should be part of the curriculum for coaches and trainers.

Body Composition and Appropriate Methods for Youth Athletes

As a body grows and matures to adulthood, the composition of the fat-free mass (FFM) changes. Water content decreases from 79% to 74% and the bone mineral content becomes more dense FFM, increasing from approximately 3.7% in infancy to 7% in adulthood (30). Because the densities of fat and lean tissues are not as constant as that of an adult, and with the great variations in age, stage of growth, gender, and ethnicity, precision in the estimation of body composition becomes difficult. This is especially true when using field methods that are not as well validated as the more sophisticated but less practical methods of hydrodensitometry and dual energy x-ray absorptiometry (DXA) (9,10,31). Because most sports dietitians have limited access to these more sophisticated assessment methods, the recommended field methods and equations (31,32) for youth include Slaughter et al (33) when using skinfolds and Houtkooper et al (34) when using bioimpedance, as demonstrated in Box 12.1 (30,31). Extensive reviews of body composition methods are available (31,32).

Box 12.1 Equations for Field Measures of Body Composition in African Americans and White Americans, 8–17 Years of Age

1. Skinfold Equations

Boys: % BF = 0.735 ($\sum$2SKF) + 1.0
$\qquad$ R^2 = 0.77; SEE = 3.8% BF

Girls: % BF = 0.610 ($\sum$2SKF) + 5.1
$\qquad$ R^2 = 0.77; SEE = 3.8% BF

Where: BF = body fat; ($\sum$2SKF) = sum of tricep and calf skinfold (SKF), for African American and white American boys and girls aged 8–17 years, and using the Harpendon calipers.
$\qquad$ If body fat is elevated, replace tricep with subscapular skinfold as follows:

Boys: % BF = 0.783 ($\sum$2SKF) + 1.6
$\qquad$ R^2 = 0.77; SEE = 3.8% BF

Girls: % BF = 0.546 ($\sum$2SKF) + 9.7
$\qquad$ R^2 = 0.77; SEE = 3.8% BF

Where: SKF = Tricep + Subscapular skinfolds

2. Bioimpedance Equation

FFM = 0.61(Ht^2/R) + 0.25(BW) + 1.31

Where: FFM = fat free mass (kg); Ht = height (cm); R = resistance; and BW = body weight (kg) using RJL 101 Bioimpedance Analyzer (RJL Systems, Inc, Clinton Township, MI).

Source: Data are from references 30 and 31.

Standards for evaluating body composition in children and teens are listed in Table 12.1 (29,31). These standards are susceptible to errors involved in obtaining the measurement as well as in the interpretation. Although pediatric obesity is of increasing concern, it is important, when counseling an individual, to move the focus from the body fat of the child to a plan for incorporating an adequate balance of dietary intake and energy expenditure (24,28,31). Preoccupation with body weight has been shown to promote disordered eating and difficulties with body image. An additional note of importance is that male and female bodies are similarly fat in childhood (24) and only in later puberty do they begin to move to their adult levels of body fat (28).

Body Image and Psychosocial Aspects

Youth athletes most at risk for body image disorders and disordered eating are involved in sports with aesthetic or appearance requirements such as gymnastics, figure skating, and

TABLE 12.1   Standards for Percent Body Fat in Children Ages 6–17 Years

Gender	Not Recommended	Low	Mid	Upper	Obesity
Male	< 5	5–10	11–25	26–31	> 31
Female	< 12	12–15	16–30	31–36	> 31

Source: Data are from references 29 and 31.

ballet, or in sports in which low fat mass is beneficial such as wrestling, rowing, and distance running. Despite the notion that image and eating disorders may be most prevalent in athletes of these sports, recent research suggests that these disorders are just as prevalent in sedentary youth (35,36). However, self-esteem education, as tested in a school program for 11- to 14-year-olds, can significantly decrease risks of these image disorders even at 1 year after intervention (37).

The prevailing thought that disorders of body image and eating behaviors are minimal in young males has also been disputed by recent research that indicates, for select sports, that boys find the same pressure to attain a "beautiful body" as girls (38,39). In general, boys want to have a bigger, more muscular and "cut" physique whereas girls prefer to be smaller and leaner. Girls who participated in aesthetic sports between ages 5 and 7 years reported an increased incidence of weight concerns at age 7 (40). The impact and impression of body weight is significant early in training, which reinforces the importance of positive approaches and consistent education by the adults surrounding each athlete (35–42).

Interestingly, even without disordered body images, athletes are consistently dieting (42). Many dietitians are now beginning to incorporate size acceptance into their counseling and educational practices with people and athletes of all ages. Their message, a suggested topic for review when working with these age groups, demonstrates the necessity to move the focus and effort from body image to balanced eating and activity and eventually to improving self-esteem without body weight or muscle mass as the sole determination of their success (8,11,43–45).

Nutrition Assessment and Nutrient Recommendations

A review of dietary assessment methods (46) suggests regular review of an athlete's diet, especially if problems are suspected. A typical diet record of several days' length may not be enough to capture nutrient adequacy or food behavior-related problems. Regular assessments would be ideal for naive athletes, especially those who have shown tendencies for disordered eating once they narrow their training to a specific sport for which there is significant competition (35).

Energy

The Dietary Reference Intakes (DRIs) for Estimated Energy Requirements (EERs) in children and adolescents were determined using doubly labeled water methods. (Equations are provided in Box 12.2 [47]). This method provides EER for ages 9 through 18 years, with specifics for gender, height, weight, and four levels of physical activity. An additional mean value of 25 kcal/day was added for energy deposition (or growth).

Several assumptions must be considered regarding these recommendations. First, they assume a level of activity that may be less than that of an elite youth athlete. Second, levels and intensities of physical activity decrease as children reach 18 years of age. Finally, typical physical activity will not deter growth and tissue deposition, which may not be true for some athletes (25).

Specific calculations of energy demands for the sport or activity are difficult to obtain and there are limited data for these energy costs per kilogram body weight in children (47). In fact, Jonnalagadda (46) cites several studies suggesting that reported energy intake of youth athletes significantly underestimated the DRI recommendations, with no performance deficits. Several authors also noted that youth athletes may require more energy for sport activities than do adults due to lower efficiency of movement among youth (16, 46,48).

Table 12.2 contains a portion of the 2002 DRI table giving EERs for average children at ages 9, 14, and 18 years, with calculations for each of the four levels of activity (47). Although more complete data charts are available (47), this limited chart can provide an adequate view of the contrast in energy requirements by gender, age, and physical activity level.

These recommendations as well as others (47–50) present a diverse range of energy intake requirements for adolescents. Females may require approximately 1,700 to 2,800 kcal/day and males may require 2,000 to 3,800 kcal/day. Many authors suggest that energy intake may be underreported, especially in adolescent females (5,46,51), but athletes do

---

Box 12.2   Estimated Energy Requirements (EERs) for Children Ages 9–18 Years

EER = Total Energy Expenditure + Energy for tissue deposition (growth)

Boys: EER = 88.5 – 61.9A + PA (26.7W + 903H) + 25 kcal/day

Girls: EER = 135.3 – 30.8A + PA (10.0W + 934H) + 25 kcal/day

Where: A = age (years); W = weight (kg); H = height (meters); and PA = physical activity factor (defined in terms of minutes walked per day at 2.5 mph).

PA: Sedentary is ≥ 1.0 to < 1.4
    Low active ($\sim$ 120 minutes walking) is ≥ 1.4 to ≤ 1.6
    Active ($\sim$ 230 minutes walking) is ≥ 1.6 to ≤ 1.9
    Very active (400 minutes walking) is ≥ 1.9 to ≤ 2.5

Source: Adapted with permission from Institute of Medicine. *Dietary Reference Intakes for Energy, Carbohydrate, Fiber, Fat, Fatty Acids, Cholesterol, Protein, and Amino acids (Macronutrients).* Washington, DC: National Academy Press; 2002. Available at: http://www.nap.edu/books. Accessed November 9, 2004. Courtesy of National Academy Press, Washington, DC.

TABLE 12.2   Estimated Energy Requirements* for Children

Age, y	Mean Weight, kg	Mean Height, m	BEE, kcal/d	PAL[†]			
				Sedentary	Low Active	Active	Very Active
Boys							
9	28.6	1.34	1187	1530	1787	2043	2359
14	51.0	1.64	1578	2090	2459	2829	3283
18	67.2	1.76	1777	2383	2823	3263	3804
Girls							
9	29.0	1.33	1094	1415	1660	1890	2273
14	49.4	1.60	1337	1718	2036	2334	2831
18	56.2	1.63	1327	1690	2024	2336	2858

Abbreviations: BEE, basal energy expenditure; PAL, physical activity level (kcal/d).

*Estimated energy requirements include kcal for growth.

[†]See Box 12.2 for explanation of physical activity levels.

Source: Adapted with permission from Institute of Medicine. *Dietary Reference Intakes for Energy, Carbohydrate, Fiber, Fat, Fatty Acids, Cholesterol, Protein, and Amino acids (Macronutrients).* Washington, DC: National Academy Press; 2002. Available at: http://www.nap.edu/books. Accessed November 9, 2004. Courtesy of National Academy Press, Washington, DC.

seem to understand that food is fuel (51). One way to demonstrate adequacy and balance in energy intake and other nutrients is to use the approach offered by Bloch and Wheeler (52). This is an excellent practical guide for nutrient content and meal patterns at 1,700, 1,900, 2,200, and 2,800 kcal, including some vegetarian menus. All plans offer three meals and two snacks composed of common foods found in the American diet but without sports bars or beverages. These plans are packed with fruits, vegetables, nuts, dairy, lean meats, and whole grains. In addition, many of the foods suggested are both realistic and healthful food choices for teenagers, such as fast-food grilled chicken, pizza, tacos, and stir-fried vegetables with brown rice.

Protein

The protein DRI for children and adolescents is based on factorial methods and, in the case of adolescents (14 to 18 years of age), adult studies of nitrogen balance were used (47). By using body weight, this method sums the protein needed for maintenance with that for growth. Few studies are available in children and adolescents to estimate additional requirements for exercise training. Regardless of the paucity of data, the Estimated Average Requirement (EAR) remains at or slightly less than 0.8 g/kg/day for all ages with a range of 0.71 to 0.76 g/kg/day (47). The Recommended Dietary Allowance (RDA) is slightly more than 0.8 g/kg/day, ranging from 0.85 g/kg/day in older adolescents to 0.95 g/kg/day in 4- to 13-year-old children, with no differences by gender.

The current DRI suggests that additional protein is needed for exercising adults (47), but others dispute this recommendation (53,54). Regardless, the American public most likely consumes sufficient protein. However, athletes who are dieting, limiting food intake for their sport, or practicing vegetarianism may have inadequate protein intakes. A relatively new theory, and yet unproven in youth, is that inclusion of protein in the recovery meal and perhaps before strength training may be critical for an anabolic effect of protein (55). Additionally, new DRI recommendations regarding lysine content of the diet may be especially pertinent for vegetarian athletes or any athlete restricting food intake.

Iron

The role of iron in normal metabolism and performance, along with indicators of function and status are described in Chapter 5 and in other reviews (56,57). Iron is critical during growth and maturation so it becomes increasingly important during adolescence (58) and when physical performance is included (57,59–62). Although there are limited exercise-related data in youth, the following list contains circumstances that may contribute to low iron stores (nonanemic iron deficiency) or eventual anemia, especially when combined with a rigorous year-round training schedule:

- Increased growth and physical activity demands
- Decreased energy and protein intake (if on self-imposed diet)
- Poor absorptive capacity
- Sports-related hemolysis and blood loss
- Menstruation in females
- Frequent use of nonsteroidal anti-inflammatory agents
- Inconsistent, inadequate, or faddish dietary intake
- Stress of competition
- Heavy sweat loss
- Poor socioeconomic status and food insecurity
- Risky lifestyle practices (laxatives, excessive fasting)
- Medical or family history of bleeding disorders
- Excessive consumption of tea, coffee, or other iron-binding components (56–63)

Adolescents, in general, may be at greater risk of low iron stores (50,56,58). Current research in pubescent and prepubescent athletes training at elevated intensity and duration (for example, 5 to 6 days per week for 2 to 3 hours each day), indicates that iron stores could be challenged by this amount of training (59–61). Although males and females were evaluated, there is limited information about how typical teenage diets affect iron status and function. One study of female athletes with subclinical eating disorders compared with a group of control subjects demonstrated a low plasma ferritin level despite an adequate iron intake (between 17 and 22 mg/day). Much of the iron came from fortified foods with lower bioavailability (fortified cereal, breakfast bars, and snack items) than from heme sources such as meat (64).

Suggestions for discussing the importance of iron and its food sources in this young population (65) include the following:

- A poignant explanation of a major side effect of low blood iron such as fatigue. Most athletes are concerned about keeping their energy levels high for performance. Because low iron levels can directly influence energy for performance, this should be a key educational goal.

- Descriptions of other consequences of low blood iron on how they feel and their performance such as an inability to keep warm, headaches, pallor, sensitivity to light, susceptibility to infections, glossitis, koilonychias, and impaired ability to concentrate.
- Explanation of how iron stores decrease (blood loss, usual loss from gastrointestinal cells, training of long duration and heavy sweating, extra loss with diarrhea and other gastrointestinal disturbances) and that food is necessary to replace these losses.
- Explanation of the best iron-containing foods (heme vs nonheme), foods that can improve iron absorption (vitamin C assists absorption), and foods that deter iron absorption (coffee, tea, calcium supplements, oxalates, phytates, excessive fiber intake). It is also important to point out that snacks often used during competition days such as fortified cereals, dried fruits, and orange juice can assist with iron bioavailability but should not be mainstays of the diet.
- Explanation that a vitamin/mineral supplement may benefit an individual who is training throughout an entire year and has been recommended by the committee establishing the DRI (56), but it should not be the sole source of iron.

In fact, the DRI for iron states that vegetarians may require 1.8 times the requirement for iron (56). The EAR recommended by some experts would be 30% more for regularly exercising individuals and perhaps up to 70% more for some populations of athletes (56). If an athlete is a vegetarian, this can mean between 19 and 25 mg/day for 9- to 13-year-old boys and girls, 26 to 34 mg/day for 14- to 18-year-old boys and 35 to 46 mg/day for girls aged 14 to 18 years (56). Given these estimations, it is easier to understand that low iron stores and iron deficiency can exist in an exercising adolescent population.

Calcium and Vitamin D

Bone health throughout the lifespan relies, to some extent, on calcium intake and physical activity during childhood and adolescence (29). The foundation for getting an adequate dietary intake of calcium is laid by parents during childhood and reinforced during adolescence. Peak calcium accretion and retention is age 14.5 years for boys and age 13 years for girls (66). After the onset of menarche, the calcium absorption efficiency decreases, which suggests that girls should not decrease their intake of calcium (66). The calcium Adequate Intake for boys and girls ages 8 to 18 years is 1,300 mg/day (66).

Compared with iron, calcium's importance for performance may not be as obvious to athletes (67,68). Several studies have noted calcium intakes less than the RDA (5,51). Because adolescent athletes are at great risk for disordered eating and are often driven to excel no matter the cost, a pervading myth they often discuss (and use as an excuse for not getting enough calcium) is that "dairy products are fattening." Among girls, these myths coupled with restrictive eating behaviors can result in the classic "female athlete triad," which includes disordered eating, amenorrhea, and subsequent premature osteoporosis.

Poor vitamin D intake can also contribute to bone-related problems either during puberty or later in life. Low levels of vitamin D intake have been noted in some Finnish female athletes, especially in winter (69). There are many important nutrients to consider in a discussion of bone health. The interaction and importance of other nutrients such as magnesium, phosphorus, potassium, and vitamins A and K should be stressed, especially for athletes restricting food or particular food groups (such as fruits and vegetables). For review, see the DRIs (68).

Water and Hydration Practices

The surface area–to-mass ratio in children is much greater than in adults. This is one of the reasons for greater fluid and energy requirements in youth compared with adults and it is also the cause of greater heat absorption in children. Children also lack adequately functioning sweat glands until well into puberty, which contributes to their inability to sweat and thus to lose heat (19,70,71). Because children do not have some of the physiological advantages of the adult—such as hydration resiliency—it is imperative to keep them hydrated and to assess them for signs of dehydration and heat effects.

The same rule of thumb for hydrating before an event applies to youth athletes, and recent research indicates that in a controlled heat chamber or an experiment outdoors in a temperate climate (70), voluntary dehydration was avoided by young boys who consumed adequate fluid when it was slightly flavored and contained sodium (18 mmol/L) and carbohydrate (6%). These pre-event fluids are similar to sport drinks, which are slightly more diluted than milk or juice. The best or most appropriate concentration of carbohydrate needed for an athlete to begin competition or training in a hydrated state can be individualized. A review of fluid, electrolytes, and exercise is found in Chapter 6.

Two other excellent resources for practical information about hydration (and other sports nutrition information more specific for youth) include Lair and Murdoch (72) and Berning and Steen (13). Both texts have excellent charts, graphs, and other user-friendly tables that are excellent for young athletes and their parents. It is often difficult to get athletes of this age group to drink at all. Lair and Murdoch suggest that coaches get the athletes to work out how many sips it takes to drink a half-cup portion of fluid and then require that number of sips before allowing the athlete to return to their event (72). The following are some guidelines offered by the Gatorade Sports Science Institute and quoted in Lair and Murdoch regarding hydration (also see Table 12.3) (72,73):

- Encourage young athletes to stop at the water fountain and drink between classes at school.
- Teach them to pack a water bottle or sport drink with their practice gear every day.
- Explain that they are dehydrated when they wake in the morning, so drinking as soon as they get up can help them out later in the day with practices after school.
- Encourage them to drink extra fluids at lunch to help prepare for afternoon practices.
- Encourage them to have drinks available on the sidelines that they like to encourage more fluid intake.

Other Nutrients

The many other nutrients important to growth, health, physical activity, and performance are detailed in previous chapters. Reviews of the functions of vitamins, minerals, and other macronutrients are also available (47,56,57,66,74,75). Limited data are available to evaluate these nutrients and their impact on sports performance in youth athletes, though it is

TABLE 12.3 Fluid Guidelines for Young Athletes

| Age, y | *Fluid to Drink, oz* | | | |
	1–2 Hours Before Activity	*15 minutes Before Activity*	*Every 20 Minutes During Constant Activity*	*After Activity*
< 10	4	4	4	16 per lb lost
> 10	8	6	8	16 per lb lost

Source: Adapted with permission from Bar-Or O. Children's responses to exercise in hot climates: implications for performance and health. *Sports Sci Exchange.* 1994;4:1–4.

accumulating (47,56,66). Because growth and physical activity occur simultaneously in these athletes, the most important concepts to convey involve adequacy of the macronutrients as well as balance from all food groups. Many of these issues are addressed in the following section or in other reviews (72,74) on practical aspects of working with this population.

Additional Applied Nutrition Topics

Pre- and Postevent Meals

There is no research in children that suggests they differ from adults in pre- and postevent meal recommendations. The athlete should obtain adequate food to help supply the appropriate fuel for the event and should not feel hungry before or during the event. Children may not need the same volumes of food and fluid as adults, however.

Depending on the age of the child and the circumstances surrounding training vs competition, it is important to plan meals and snacks. For instance, training could be in the early morning or just after the school day or both. Parents are instrumental in providing food for young athletes and the foresight for planning in the case of the adolescent who may have greater resources and be much more independent.

Sports dietitians for these age groups should be armed with lists or charts for the athletes and parents that include these practical issues. For instance, develop a chart of snack foods often available (ie, study their environment, such as school cafeteria menus and vending machine choices, to be most effective in providing good advice) with notes to describe the best nutrient content for pre- vs postevent snacks (ie, list portable, high-carbohydrate snacks and beverages for hydration for preevent and snacks with protein, carbohydrate, and fluid for postevent, if a postevent snack is necessary).

Practical Issues and Meal Patterns

Often there are many seemingly simple practical issues related to food availability, desirability, and consumption that can impact performance. Youth athletes may need to be reminded to bring foods and fluids with them daily so they have options for staying hydrated and nourished. Parents appreciate ideas for the appropriate foods to have available and athletes need to self-study their personal likes/dislikes. Coaches and trainers should allow some time during the training season for educating them about food and fluid's impact on performance (72,74).

When counseling these athletes, a thorough assessment of their behaviors and environment is necessary. For instance, following are some examples of the variety of unplanned circumstances that affect food intake, behaviors, and eventually performance (76):

- A middle school or high school athlete has a mandatory lunch at 10:30 AM and must compete at 4:30 PM without going home; choices from a school vending machine are not appealing and the situation worsens without planning and money.
- An extremely nervous athlete cannot eat the food that Mom packed and has not eaten in the 6 hours prior to the event, or is able to only drink before the game.
- An athlete has a game or practice at 8 AM on Saturday morning, gets out of bed at 7:30 AM.
- An athlete gets home from school and has 20 minutes before getting back in the car to get to practice or game on time.
- The sport involved causes jostling of stomach contents and the athlete is extremely sensitive; he or she must eat 4 hours ahead but has an early meet.
- An athlete exhausted every night; falls asleep doing homework and eating dinner.
- An athlete concerned about body weight refuses to eat breakfast and eats a tossed salad for lunch with diet soda or eats a very limited–carbohydrate diet.
- A track, gymnastics, or swim athlete must compete at 9 AM, 1 PM, and 3 PM.
- A dual-sport athlete has a game on one night and a match the next morning.

These are a few examples of situations a sports dietitian will field when working with youth athletes. There are many others related to personal issues, food sensitivities, sleep habits, supplement use, and fad diets that all warrant education. In most of these cases, this is an opportunity to educate the athlete about the value of carbohydrates and performance, the importance of pre- and postevent foods and fluids, and the significance of eating complete meals (ie, foods from all food groups for a balanced diet). Although busy lifestyles do lead athletes to do more snacking and to eat small frequent meals, it is important to demonstrate that snacking can result in the exclusion of some food groups.

Vegetarianism in Young Athletes

Current research does not suggest that athletic performance is affected positively or negatively with a vegetarian diet. In fact, there is no evidence to substantiate claims that the increased fiber content of a vegetarian diet would decrease the bioavailability of minerals or that the amino acid content will not support training and performance in athletes (77). Evidence suggests that low energy intake, not necessarily due to a vegetarian diet, can increase the risks for inconsistent menses (67).

Sports dietitians working with young athletes should know that these athletes, especially females, may idolize and emulate what they perceive to be the behaviors and practices of the elite athletes in their sport. Regardless of the true practices of that elite athlete, the young athlete may focus on body image and body weight and thus try to control and "correct" their bodies by manipulating diet. They may not understand or practice vegetarianism correctly. Sports dietitians should provide ample education to the athlete and the adults interacting with that athlete (parents, coaches, trainers). Vegetarianism may be a "red flag" for the presence of disordered eating or inappropriate dieting. Addressing an athlete's motivation for becoming vegetarian may support methods of education and counseling that can help deter behaviors of disordered eating.

The 2002 DRIs indicate that diets limited in protein, specifically animal protein, could be insufficient in lysine, especially because the digestibility of vegetable protein is more limiting (47). This is a greater concern for growing children and adolescents. The RDA for lysine for 9- to 18-year-old boys ranges from 43 to 46 mg/kg/day, whereas the RDA for 9- to 18-year-old girls is 40 to 43 mg/kg/day. The best vegetarian sources of lysine include tofu and legumes; foods with lower concentrations include wheat bread, brown rice, peanut butter, almonds, and cornmeal (47).

Female Athlete Triad

In simplest terms, this syndrome is a combination of disordered eating, amenorrhea, and low bone density. In reality, it may not be diagnosed until bone fractures occur. It manifests slowly as intensely training premenopausal females incorporate restrictive and disordered eating into their daily lifestyle, consistently consuming low- or very low–energy diets. Eventually, this restrictive eating and intense training results in amenorrhea, low levels of estrogen, and bone density loss (osteoporosis) (78). See reviews for more information (78–82).

Due to several factors, the actual prevalence of this triad in female athletes is unknown. For example, poor eating behaviors are often disguised; also, a diagnosis of osteoporosis and amenorrhea require, at minimum, the participation of the athlete and some sophisticated tests (81). However, some suggest (81) that the prevalence of this triad is similar to that of amenorrhea in athletes, which is between 3% and 66% (a very wide range, indeed) (83). Although difficult to prove, these dieting behaviors likely begin in childhood; some recent research shows 25% of young girls already claim that they are dieting by age 7 (21).

Because this triad is so closely linked to psychological disturbances of depression, perfectionism, low self-esteem, and excessive behaviors with food and exercise, a cross-section of health care professionals comprise the treatment team. The sports dietitian's role may vary depending on the age of the athlete. Often the sports dietitian, school nurse, or team trainer are the first to hear some of the early symptoms: "fatigue, poor performance, an inability to gain weight with strength training, feeling cold, and extreme mood changes" (45). Repeat visits and establishment of a good rapport with the athlete may make the diagnosis more evident but the important work of education should occur regardless of a diagnosis. According to one expert in the field (45), the following are some important activities for the sports dietitian:

- Assess current food intake and habits of the athlete.
- Estimate appropriate body weight and energy expenditure for activities.
- Show the athlete support and flexibility in new food behaviors.
- Educate the athlete about normal and abnormal eating behaviors and body weights.
- Dispel nutrition and body weight myths as they relate to performance (a very popular myth is that eating meat makes you fat).

- Continue to use age-specific teaching concepts.
- Integrate all of these with a multidisciplinary approach and a team of professionals.

Ergogenic Aids and Dietary Supplements

Despite the many factors that combine to influence young people to "win at all costs," there is little to no scientific evidence for either the efficacy or the safety of performance-enhancing agents and dietary supplements in children and adolescents. In fact, some suggest that health professionals who interact with these athletes should explain the scientific evidence for risks as well as for benefits. This is meant to broaden their understanding and judgment of supplements (84).

Sports dietitians should explain how the physiological mechanism for a particular nutrient or supplement could be exaggerated by sales and marketing slogans. These opportunities for education will help parents/guardians and athletes be more selective consumers of supplements.

Aggressive, elite athletes are risk takers. Their choice and use of performance-enhancing agents is indicative of this trait. Also, and mentioned earlier, youth athletes emulate their idols or what they perceive of their idols' behaviors, which media and advertising campaigns promote. Education of athletes and parents is essential to demonstrate the value of supplements and, most obviously, a balanced diet.

The percentage of young athletes using ergogenic aids and dietary supplements has not been extensively studied; however, the most popular ergogenic aids include creatine, ephedrine, and androstenedione (85). This report along with others (84–88) has noted that approximately 5% of 8th-grade athletes report use of creatine, and 22% to 25% of high school seniors report such use.

Youth are savvy with computer and Internet searching, and some may prefer using this route to gather information about their sports, idols, performance enhancers, and supplements. When a Google search with the key words *sports performance* was completed, more than 8 million hits occurred. This helps to demonstrate the diverse yet potentially suspect information available (88). In Santerre's (85) discussion of ergogenic supplement use in adolescents, he indicated that an insurance company estimated that 1 million adolescents (4%) take one or more ergogenic aid. These numbers may increase despite the lack of minimum manufacturing standards by the Food and Drug Administration (FDA) (89).

Youth athletes and their parents/guardians should be educated about the regulations set up by sports organizations governing colleges and universities and their scholarship programs (89). Numerous college, Olympic, and professional athletes have been sanctioned because banned substances found in their blood were contaminants in vitamin, mineral, or other nutritional supplements. More information on dietary supplements and ergogenic aids can be found in Chapter 7.

Childhood Obesity and Sports Participation

The incidence of childhood overweight and obesity in the United States is becoming a burden for youth and their future health (90). Some label it an epidemic (91). Opportunities to decrease and prevent overweight and obesity require multidisciplinary approach to address dietary intake (92) and physical activity (91–95). Sports dietitians are well-informed of this increasing problem and can provide expert counseling, education, and motivation to these young clients.

Nutrition Education Opportunities

The impressions and dreams of youth are terrific opportunities for teachable moments when educating young athletes about the connection between nutrition and performance. Everyone wants to be the Michael Jordan or Mia Hamm of their sport. Children are eager to please and adolescents are eager to excel. Some athletes are ready to hear the message of nutrition and performance and some are not. It may be necessary to have a variety of educational approaches for the different ages and genders. Questions and ideas that sports dietitians should be prepared to address for all of the audiences involved with youth sports include the following:

- What to eat before, during, and after competition or practice with different food ideas for children vs teens
- The importance of staying hydrated for performance and health, with practical ways to do this
- The risks and benefits of supplements, especially creatine
- The best body weight for a particular sport or by gender
- The best body composition for a particular sport (by position and gender)
- The appropriate use and benefits of sport drinks and bars
- Popular fad diets and their effects on performance and health
- Key concepts for gaining lean muscle mass
- Whether there is an ideal meal or diet to eat for performance

Young people, like the general public, are looking for quick fixes and magic cures. Few want to hear about planning meals or eating foods from all the food groups each day. However, athletes and their parents will appreciate Web sites that are up-to-date and recommended by the sports dietitian (see Appendix F).

Weight-Control Practices

With all of the issues surrounding body weight, obesity, and the athlete's desire for an edge, sports dietitians must be prepared to address popular issues and practices (45,74) to control or decrease body weight. Athletes may do the following:

- Decrease total food intake or delete entire nutrients or foods (fats, carbohydrates, proteins, water, sweets, breakfast foods, or a food they identify as "bad")
- Skip meals
- Practice disordered eating
- Use laxatives, appetite suppressants, caffeine containing products, or herbals advertised to assist in weight loss
- Use fad diets or the combination of fad diets and unhealthful (excessive) exercise regimens
- Wear sweat suits while working out or use saunas
- Increase daily frequency and duration of exercise
- Participate in contests with other athletes to lose weight (76)

- Avoid eating during certain times of the day (eg, after 6 PM)
- Completely fast for 24 hours or more

The physiology of the child and adolescent body, specifically the muscle cell, makes it feasible to lose body water quickly and thus produce weight loss. This relatively quick weight loss can provide a false sense of empowerment for the athlete. In fact, however, striving for rapid weight loss has resulted in fatalities in several wrestlers (94). These kinds of examples are powerful messages and should be discussed.

Suggestions for a more reasonable plan (45,74,76) of weight loss include the following:

- Provide private but open discussions about weight-loss methods and reasonable weight goals.
- Identify short-term vs long-term goals that can be monitored and adjusted over time.
- Reduce portion sizes of foods before totally removing them.
- Identify and help to alter food behaviors and attitudes that might decrease success.
- Agree on the appropriate amount of training and set goals to achieve.
- Learn to understand realistic expectations for all goals being set.
- Consider weight classifications and accept realistic weight expectations.
- Get the athlete to consider evaluating something simple like soda or juice intake for excess energy intake.

Strategies for Educating Athletes, Coaches, Trainers, and Parents

Sports dietitians working with the spectrum of individuals who surround youth athletes will likely need to do some investigative work before speaking with these audiences. Before talking to groups, sports dietitians should ask the people who recruited them why they want a dietitian to speak. Speakers should ask about specific concerns and probe for more information. Questions to ask include the following:

- How many athletes, parents, coaches, trainers will attend?
- What is the age, gender, and socioeconomic status of the audience, especially the athletes?
- Who is responsible for preparing food and feeding (parent, caregiver, sibling)?
- How open are the parents or others to role modeling?
- What are the food resources at the school? (that is, what are the cafeteria menu and vending machine choices, and what are the nearby fast food restaurants?)
- What are the resources for feeding the athletes before, during, and after games?
- Who normally takes care of making food arrangements for the team? Would they consider the speaker a threat if he or she offered suggestions?
- Who are the physical education or health teachers in the school? Do they have any influence on the meals for the athletes?
- What are the procedures for sending informational flyers home with the athletes for family education and nutrition tips? Could these be posted around school?

The speaker should be prepared to make suggestions for vitamin/mineral supplements, sport drinks, sport bars, sport gels, energy drinks, and other supplements, and also be ready to offer information regarding how the athlete will feel when dehydrated, improperly fueled during competition, or when iron stores are low because these are some of the most prevalent effects of a poor diet. The speaker also should take a list of suggestions for meals once he or she knows what the school, parents, trainers, and coaches currently do for offering foods to the athletes. It is helpful to take a few good resources that parents can get in bookstores, on the Internet, or from the dietitian (8,13,49,52,72,74,76,92,96,97).

The speaker should be prepared to dispel some of the myths about nutrition and performance. For example, females may think eating meat or dairy makes them fat and that vegetarian diets are more healthful than other diets, whereas males may think eating meat makes them grow big muscles.

It is important to ask athletes for written lists or e-mail lists with their questions, including the most popular dietary supplements used. Adolescent females will often not ask questions in public and males will ask about building muscle mass and gaining weight. All athletes may have more personal questions that they would rather ask privately. To be most effective, this desire for private contacts needs to be incorporated and should be facilitated by the person who recruits the sports dietitian.

The speaker should also ask for lists of favorite foods by category to encourage the audience to think about foods across the food groups and envision eating some from each of these every day. It can be helpful to inquire about use of the Internet and then direct audience members to quality Web sites to use to assess their diet.

Summary

Child and adolescent athletes are the future of sports. They aspire to high levels of performance and focus on the achievements of elite and professional athletes as goals to surpass. In doing so, the path to these achievements may be enhanced by the guidance of the adults who are involved in their training and performance and who understand nutrition. Because youth athletes are in various stages of growth and development both physically and emotionally, the influence of nutrition is critical. However, children and adolescents are not "mini-adults," and sports nutrition advice for them is not yet fully understood. This chapter examined the differences between youth and adult athletes and provided information as well as application of nutrition advice for common occurrences that youth of all athletic abilities encounter in their pursuit of sports excellence.

References

1. Patel DR, Nelson TL. Sports injuries in adolescents. *Med Clin of North Am.* 2000;84:983–1007.
2. Metzl JD. Expectations of pediatric sport participation among pediatricians, patients, and parents. *Pediatr Clin North Am.* 2002;49:497–504.
3. Martin TJ, Martin JS. Special issues and concerns for the high school- and college-aged athletes. *Pediatr Clin North Am.* 2002;49:533–552.
4. Committee on Sports Medicine and Fitness. Intensive training and sports specialization in young athletes. *Pediatrics.* 2000;106:154–157.
5. Ziegler PJ, Nelson JA, Jonnalagadda SS. Nutritional and physiological status of U.S. national figure skaters. *Int J Sport Nutr.* 1999;9:345–360.
6. Emery HM. Considerations in child and adolescent athletes. *Rheum Dis Clin North Am.* 1996;22:499–513.
7. Stricker PR. Sports training issues for the pediatric athlete. *Pediatr Clin North Am.* 2002;49:793–802.

8. American Dietetic Association. Practice points: translating research into practice. Fueling their engines for the long haul: teaching good nutrition to young athletes. *J Am Diet Assoc.* 1998; 98:418.

9. Guest JE, Lewis NL, Guest JR. Assessment of growth in child athletes. In: Driskell JR, Wolinsky I, eds. *Nutritional Assessments of Athletes.* Boca Raton, Fla: CRC Press; 2002:91–114.

10. Hills A, Parizkova J. Assessment of growth in adolescent athletes. In: Driskell JR, Wolinsky I, eds. *Nutritional Assessments of Athletes.* Boca Raton, Fla: CRC Press; 2002:115–134.

11. Naughton G, Farpour-Lambert NJ, Carlson J, Bradney M, Praagh EV. Physiological issues surrounding the performance of adolescent athletes. *Sports Med.* 2000;30:309–325.

12. American Academy of Pediatrics, Committee on Sports Medicine and Fitness. Medical conditions affecting sports participation. *Pediatrics.* 2001;107:1205–1209.

13. Steen SN. Nutrition for the school-age child athlete. In: Berning JR and Steen SN, eds. *Nutrition for Sport and Exercise.* 2nd ed. Gaithersburg, Md: Aspen Publishers; 1998:217 244.

14. Radelet MA, Lephart SM, Rubinstein EN, Myers JB. Survey of injury rate for children in community sports. *Pediatrics.* 2002;110:1–11.

15. Rowland T. Trainability of the cardiorespiratory system during childhood. *Can J Sports Sci.* 1992;17:259–263.

16. Walker JL, Murray RD, Jackson AS. The energy cost of horizontal walking and running in adolescents. *Med Sci Sports Exerc.* 1999;31:311–322.

17. Lohman TG. Assessment of body composition in children. *Ped Exerc Sci.* 1989;1:19–30.

18. Wells JCK, Fuller NJ, Dewit O, Fewtrell MS, Elia M, Cole RJ. Four-component model of body composition in children: density and hydration of fat-free mass and comparison with simpler models. *Am J Clin Nutr.* 1999;69:904–912.

19. Bar-Or O. Temperature regulation during exercise in children and adolescents. In: Gisolfi CR and Lamb DR, eds. *Youth, Exercise, and Sport.* Indianapolis, Ind: Benchmark; 1989;2:335–362. Perspectives in Exercise Science and Sports Medicine, vol. 2.

20. Rogol AD, Clark PA, Roemmich JN. Growth and pubertal development in children and adolescents: effects of diet and physical activity. *Am J Clin Nutr.* 2000;72(suppl):521S–8S.

21. Robinson TN, Chang JY, Haydel KF, Killen JD. Overweight concerns and body dissatisfaction among third-grade children: the impacts of ethnicity and socioeconomic status. *Pediatrics.* 2000;138:181–185.

22. Field AE, Austin SB, Taylor CB, Malspeis S, Rosner B, Rockett HR, Gillman MW, Colditz GA. Relation between dieting and weight change among preadolescents and adolescents. *Pediatrics.* 2003;112:900–906.

23. National Center for Health Statistics. 2002 BMI-for-Age Growth Charts. Available at: http://www.cdc.gov/nchs/about/major/nhanes/growthcharts/clinical_charts.htm. Accessed July 21, 2004.

24. Orabella M. Nutrition during growth: preschool through preadolescence. In: Mitchell MK, ed. *Nutrition Across the Lifespan.* 2nd ed. Philadelphia, Pa: WB Saunders Co; 2003:271–313.

25. Malina RM. Physical growth and biological maturation of young athletes. *Exerc Sport Sci Rev.* 1994;22:389–433.

26. Roemmich JN, Sinning WE. Weight loss and wrestling training: effects on nutrition, growth, maturation, body composition and strength. *J Appl Physiol.* 1997;82:1751–1759.

27. Baxter-Jones ADG, Helms PJ. Effects of training at a young age: a review of the training of young athletes study. *Pediatr Exerc Sci.* 1996;8:310–327.

28. Mitchell KM. Nutrition during adolescence. In: Mitchell MK, ed. *Nutrition Across the Lifespan.* 2nd ed. Philadelphia, Pa: WB Saunders Co; 2003:341–381.

29. Matkovic V. Calcium intake and peak bone mass. *N Engl J Med.* 1993;327:119–122.

30. Foman SJ, Haschke F, Ziegler EE, Nelson SE. Body composition reference for children from birth to 10 years. *Am J Clin Nutr.* 1982;35:1169–1175.

31. Heyward VH, Wagner DR. Body composition and children. In: Heyward VH and Wagner DR, eds. *Applied Body Composition.* 2nd ed. Champaign, Ill: Human Kinetics; 2004:109–122.

32. Lohman TG, Houtkooper L, Going SB. Body fat measurement goes high-tech: not all created equal. *Am Coll Sports Med Health Fitness J.* 1997;7:30–35.

33. Slaughter MH, Lohman TG, Boileau RA, Horswill CA, Stillman RJ, VanLoan MD, Bemben DA. Skinfold equations for estimation of body fatness in children and youth. *Hum Biol.* 1988;60:709–723.

34. Houtkooper LB, Going SB, Lohman TG, Roche AF, Van Loan M. Bioelectrical impedance estimation of fat-free body mass in children and youth: a cross-validation study. *J Appl Physiol.* 1992;72:366–373.

35. Fulkerson JA, Keel PK, Leon GR, Dorr T. Eating-disordered behaviors and personality characteristics of high school athletes and nonathletes. *Int J Eat Disord.* 1999;26:73–79.

36. Casper RC, Michaels J, Simon K. Body perception and emotional health in athletes: a study of female adolescents involved in aesthetic sports. *World Rev Nutr Diet.* 1997;82:134–147.

37. O'Dea JA, Abraham S. Improving the body image, eating attitudes, and behaviors of young male and female adolescents: a new educational approach that focuses on self-esteem. *Int J Eat Disord.* 2000;28:43–57.

38. Parks PS, Read MH. Adolescent male athletes: body image, diet, and exercise. *Adolescence.* 1997;32:593–602.

39. Daley AJ, Hunter B. Comparison of male and female junior athletes' self perceptions and body image. *Percept Mot Skills.* 2001;93:626–630.

40. Davison DD, Earnest MB, Birch LL. Participation in aesthetic sports and girls' weight concerns at ages 5 and 7 years. *Int J Eat Disord.* 2002;31:312–317.

41. Middleman AB, Vasquez I, Durant RH. Eating patterns, physical activity, and attempts to change weight among adolescents. *J Adolesc Health.* 1998;22:37–42.

42. Ziegler PJ, Khoo CS, Sherr B, Nelson JA, Larson WM, Drewnowski A. Body image and dieting behaviors among elite figure skaters. *Int J Eat Disord.* 1998;24;421–427.

43. Kratina K. Size acceptance in a win-win proposition. *SCAN's Pulse.* 2003;22:1–6.

44. Wann M. Questioning weight prejudice: a good thing to do and good for you? *Healthy Weight J.* 2003;17:12–15.

45. Woolsey MM. Assessment of possible presence of eating disorders. In: Driskell JR, Wolinsky I, eds. *Nutritional Assessments of Athletes.* Boca Raton, Fla: CRC Press; 2002:61–87.

46. Jonnalagadda S. Evaluation of nutrient adequacy of athletes' diets using nutrient intake data. In: Driskell JR, Wolinsky I, eds. *Nutritional Assessments of Athletes.* Boca Raton, Fla: CRC Press; 2002:43–60.

47. Institute of Medicine. *Dietary Reference Intakes for Energy, Carbohydrate, Fiber, Fat, Fatty Acids, Cholesterol, Protein, and Amino acids (Macronutrients).* Washington, DC: National Academy Press; 2002. Available at: http://www.nap.edu/books. Accessed November 9, 2004.

48. Frost G, Dowling J, Dyson K, Bar-Or O. Cocontraction in three age groups of children during treadmill locomotion. *J Electromyogr Kinesiol.* 1997;7:179–186.

49. Steen, SN. Elementary and middle school athletes. In: Rosenbloom C, ed. *Sports Nutrition: A Guide for the Professional Working with Athletes.* 2nd ed. Chicago, Ill: American Dietetics Association; 1999:253–270.

50. Wahl R. Nutrition in the adolescent. *Pediatr Ann.* 1999;28:107–111.

51. Cupisti A, D'Alessandro C, Castrogiovanni S, Barale A, Morelli E. Nutrition knowledge and dietary composition in Italian adolescent female athletes and non-athletes. *Int J Sport Nutr Exerc Metab.* 2002;12:207–219.

52. Bloch TD, Wheeler KB. Dietary examples. A practical approach to feeding athletes. *Clin Sports Med.* 1999;18:703–711.

53. Millward J. Optimal intakes of protein in the human diet. *Proc Nutr Soc.* 1999;58–403-413.

54. Lemon PWR. Effects of exercise on dietary protein requirements. *Int J Sport Nutr.* 1998;8: 426–447.

55. Lemon PW, Berardi JM, Noreen EE. The role of protein and amino acid supplements in the athlete's diet: does type or timing of ingestion matter? *Curr Sports Med Rep.* 2002;1:214–221.

56. Institute of Medicine. *Dietary Reference Intakes for Vitamin A, Vitamin K, Arsenic, Boron, Chromium, Copper, Iodine, Iron, Manganese, Molybdenum, Nickel, Silicon, Vanadium, and Zinc.* Washington, DC: National Academy Press; 2001. Available at: http://www.nap.edu/ books. Accessed November 9, 2004.

57. Lukaski H. Assessment of mineral status of athletes. In: Driskell JR, Wolinsky I, eds. *Nutritional Assessments of Athletes.* Boca Raton, Fla: CRC Press; 2002:350–353.

58. Takala TI, Suominen P, Lehtonen-Veromaa M, Mottonen T, Viikari J, Rajamaki A, Irjala K. Increased serum soluble transferring receptor concentration detects subclinical iron deficiency in healthy adolescent girls. *Clin Chem Lab Med.* 2003;41:203–208.

59. Constantini NW, Eliakim A, Zigel L, Yaaron M, Falk B. Iron status of highly active adolescents: evidence of depleted iron stores in gymnasts. *Int J Sport Nutr Exerc Metab.* 2000;10:62–70.

60. Spodaryk K. Iron metabolism in boys involved in intensive physical training. *Physiol Behav.* 2002;75:201–206.

61. Boyadjiev N, Taralov Z. Red blood cell variables in highly training pubescent athletes: a comparative analysis. *Br J Sports Med.* 2000;34:200–204.

62. Escanero JF, Villaneuva J, Rojo A, Herrera A, DelDiego C, Guerra M. Iron stores in professional athletes throughout the sports season. *Physiol Behav.* 1997;62:811–814.

63. DeRuisseau KC, Cheuvront SN, Haymes EM, Sharp RG. Sweat iron and zinc losses during prolonged exercise. *Int J Sport Nutr Exerc Metab.* 2002;12:428–437.

64. Beals KA, Manore MM. Nutritional status of female athletes with subclinical eating disorders. *J Am Diet Assoc.* 1998;98:19–39.

65. Habash DL. High school athletes. In: Rosenbloom C, ed. *Sports Nutrition: A Guide for the Professional Working with Athletes.* 2nd ed. Chicago, Ill: American Dietetic Association; 1999: 271–282.

66. Institute of Medicine. *Dietary Reference Intakes for Calcium, Phosphorus, Magnesium, Vitamin D, and Fluoride.* Washington, DC: National Academy Press; 1997. Available at: http://www. nap.edu/books. Accessed November 9, 2004.

67. Beals KA, Manore MM. Disorders of the female athlete triad among collegiate athletes. *Int J Sport Nutr Exerc Metab.* 2002;12:281–293.

68. American Academy of Pediatrics, Committee on Sports Medicine and Fitness. Medical concerns in the female athlete. *Pediatrics.* 2000;106:610–613.

69. Lehtonen-Veromaa M, Mottonen T, Irjala K, Karkkainen M, Lamberg-Allardt C, Hakola P, Viikari J. Vitamin D intake is low and hypovitaminosis D common in healthy 9- to 15-year-old Finnish girls. *Eur J Clin Nutr.* 1999;53:746–751.

70. Rivera-Brown AM, Gutierrez R, Gutierrez JC, Frontera WR, Bar-Or O. Drink composition, voluntary drinking, and fluid balance in exercising, trained, heat-acclimatized boys. *J Appl Physiol.* 1999;86:78–84.

71. American Academy of Pediatrics, Committee on Sports Medicine and Fitness. Medical conditions affecting sports participation. *Pediatrics.* 2001;107:1205–1209.

72. Lair C, Murdoch S. What and when to feed a young athlete? In: Lair C, Murdoch S, eds. *Feeding the Young Athlete: Sports Nutrition Made Easy for Players and Parents.* Seattle, Wash: Moonsmile Press; 2002:18–23.

73. Bar-Or O. Children's responses to exercise in hot climates: implications for performance and health. *Sports Sci Exchange.* 1994;4:1–4.

74. Berning JR, Steen SN. *Nutrition for Sport and Exercise.* 2nd ed. Gaithersburg, Md: Aspen Publishers; 1998.

75. McArdle WD, Katch FI, Katch VL. Optimal nutrition for exercise and sport. In: McArdle WD, Katch FI, Katch VL, eds. *Essentials of Exercise Physiology.* 2nd ed. Philadelphia, Pa: Lippincott, Williams and Wilkins; 2000:206–226.

76. Habash DL, Buell J. Eating well while in training and competition. In: *Nutrition: A Communiqué to Health and Education Professionals. Research, Practice, and Application.* 1998;2:6–8.

77. Nieman DC. Physical fitness and vegetarian diets: is there a relation? *Am J Clin Nutr.* 1999;70(3 Suppl):570S-575S.

78. McArdle WD, Katch FI, Katch VL. Micronutrients and water. In: McArdle WD, Katch FI, Katch VL, eds. *Essentials of Exercise Physiology.* 2nd ed. Philadelphia, Pa: Lippincott, Williams and Wilkins; 2000:75–83.

79. Manore MM. Nutritional needs of the female athlete. *Clin Sports Med.* 1999;18:549–563.

80. Beals KA, Brey RA, Bonyou JB. Understanding the female athlete triad: eating disorders, amenorrhea, and osteoporosis. *J School Health.* 1999;69:337–340.

81. Kleposki RW. The female athlete triad: a terrible trio. Implications for primary care. *J Am Acad Nurse Pract.* 2002;14:26–31.

82. Lo BP, Hebert C, McClean A. The female athlete triad. No pain, no gain? *Clin Pediatr.* 2003;42:573–580.

83. Smith A. The female athlete triad: causes, diagnosis, and treatment. *Phys Sport Med.* 1996;24:67–76.

84. Congeni J, Miller S. Supplements and drugs used to enhance athletic performance. *Pediatr Clin North Am.* 2002;49:435–461.

85. Santerre CR. Ephedra: Ergogenic supplements and adolescent athletes. Presentation at: Indiana Association of Family and Consumer Sciences; 2003; Indianapolis, Ind.

86. McGuine RA, Sullivan JC, Bernhardt DA. Creatine supplementation in Wisconsin high school athletes. *Wisc Med J.* 2002;101:25–30.

87. Metzel JD. Strength training and nutritional supplement use in adolescents. *Curr Opin Pediatr.* 1999;11:292–296.

88. Google search engine (key word "sports performance"). Available at: http://www.google.com. Accessed June 14, 2004.

89. Anderson RJ. The wrong stuff. *Training and Conditioning.* 2004 (May/June):13–21.

90. American Academy of Pediatrics. Policy statement: prevention of pediatric overweight and obesity. Organizational principles to guide and define the child health care system and/or improve the health of all children. *Pediatrics.* 2003;112:424–430.

91. Bar-Or O. The juvenile obesity epidemic: is physical activity relevant? *Sports Sci Exch.* 2003;16:1–7.

92. Kosharek SM. *If Your Child Is Overweight: A Guide for Parents.* 2nd ed. Chicago, Ill: American Dietetic Association; 2003.

93. Stephens M. Children, physical activity and public health: another call to action. *Am Fam Physician.* 2002;65:1033–1034.

94. Sirard J, Pate RR. Physical activity assessments in children and adolescents. *Sports Med.* 2001;31:439–454.

95. Fulton JE, McGuire MT, Caspersen CJ, Dietz WH. Interventions for weight loss and weight gain prevention among youth. *Sports Med.* 2001;31:153–165.

96. Carey R. Tips for parents: food and drink for young athletes. *Sports Sci Exchange.* 2000;13(suppl):2.

97. Satter EM. *How to Get Your Kid to Eat . . . But Not Too Much.* Palo Alto, Calif: Bull Publishing; 1987.

Chapter 13

COLLEGE ATHLETES

Christine A. Rosenbloom, PhD, RD, and Rob Skinner, MS, RD, CSCS

Introduction

The National Collegiate Athletic Association (NCAA) reported that 206,573 males and 149,115 females participated in all divisions of NCAA-sponsored sports in 2000–2001 (1). Yet, only a few college athletic programs use the expertise of dietetics professionals as full-time sports dietitians. College athletes who have nutrition concerns frequently consult athletic trainers, strength and conditioning staff, coaches, or other athletes for advice.

The opportunity for dietetics professionals in the college athletic arena is growing. Suzanne Nelson Steen, DrSc, RD, director of Sports Nutrition at the University of Washington, believes nutrition professionals should be an integral part of the collegiate athletic association (personal communication). According to Kristine Clark, PhD, RD, director of Sports Nutrition at Penn State University, "Opportunities for establishing strong sports nutrition positions at major universities are on the horizon" (2). The purpose of this chapter is twofold: to review the published literature on nutrition and college athletes and to describe a comprehensive nutrition program at one NCAA Division IA institution.

Concerns of College Athletes

College athletes are not different from other athletes in wanting to improve performance, increase energy, and alter body composition to increase lean mass and decrease fat mass. This chapter applies to college athletes, but it is important to remember that in the college arena both male and female athletes participate in a wide range of sports, each with specific energy and nutrient demands (for more information on energy and nutrient needs of athletes participating in specific sports, see Chapters 21 to 26). The NCAA sponsors athletes in baseball, basketball, cross country, fencing, field hockey, football, golf, gymnastics, ice hockey, lacrosse, rifle, rowing, skiing, soccer, softball, swimming, tennis, track, volleyball, water polo, and wrestling. In addition, there are nine emerging sports for women: archery, badminton, bowling, rowing, ice hockey, squash, synchronized swimming, team handball, and water polo (an emerging sport is defined as a sport that is intended to provide additional sports opportunities to female-student athletes) (3). College athletes face many challenges that are unique to their sports and to the college environment.

Nutrition Knowledge and Practices

Most college athletes understand that food choices have consequences for body composition, athletic performance, and health, but many arrive at college with limited nutrition knowledge (4–8). Surveys on nutrition knowledge show that college athletes hold many misconceptions about the role of nutrition and performance. For example, many athletes believe that sugar eaten before an event will adversely affect performance, that protein is the main source of energy for working muscles, and that vitamin supplements increase energy and muscle strength (4,5). A study with female collegiate cross-country runners found that although the runners had accurate nutrition knowledge about iron and hydration, their nutrition knowledge about vitamins, minerals, and protein was rated poor (6).

A survey of football players (7) found that they had a high frequency of eating (3.6 times per day) with a high frequency of eating out (4.8 times per week) with fast-food restaurants being the most common restaurants frequented by these athletes. Athletes may be conscious of good food habits, but they may also be tempted by fast food, which is inexpensive and readily available (often in the school's dining hall). Dietitians who work with college athletes report that lack of nutrition education, sleeping through breakfast, improper weight loss and weight gain practices, indiscriminate use of dietary supplements, and disordered eating patterns are the biggest concerns (8).

Even if athletes want to make nutritious food choices, they often lack the domestic skills needed to shop and prepare meals. Although many college dorm rooms have refrigerators, stoves, and microwave ovens, most college athletes are "cooking impaired."

Sources of Nutrition Information

Athletes get nutrition and dietary supplement information from a variety of sources. Froiland et al (9) surveyed athletes at one Midwestern Division I institution and found family members, fellow athletes, strength coaches, and athletic trainers were the most frequently cited sources of nutrition information about dietary supplements. Male athletes were significantly more likely than female athletes to get nutrition information from a store clerk, fellow athletes, friends, coaches, television, or magazines (9). Women were more likely than men to get nutrition information from university classes, nutritionists, or individual sport coaches (5). Zawila et al (6) found that the cross-country athletes who completed a college course on nutrition scored significantly higher in nutrition knowledge than those who had not taken a course. Burns et al (10) surveyed student athletes from eight NCAA Division I schools and found athletic trainers to be the most frequent source of information. Athletic trainers are accessible to athletes on a daily basis, and Rockwell et al (11) found that athletic trainers at one Division I institution responded correctly to 67% of nutrition knowledge questions, indicating that dietetics professionals could complement the nutrition education of athletic trainers.

Sports dietitians have observed that the media are increasingly popular sources of nutrition information, especially about dietary supplements. The media are quick to provide nutrition information to athletes; in particular, the growing number of "muscle" and "fitness" magazines are quick to hype supplementation and unproven diet manipulations as the way to achieve the ideal image. Testimonials about supplements substitute as scientific proof of efficacy, and college athletes may be tempted to follow these recommendations. Magazines are getting more sophisticated in the methods used to present information, frequently citing research in reputable professional journals to back up claims. However, a search of the references finds that much of the cited research is taken out of context, lacks sound methodology, or is conducted in animals, not humans.

Supplement Use

College athletes use dietary supplements to enhance performance, improve body composition, and boost energy levels to gain the competitive edge. Surveys show that more than half of college athletes report taking vitamin and mineral supplements. Of the sports performance supplements on the market, creatine ranks as the number one supplement, with 28% to 41% of all student athletes at NCAA schools using creatine (12,13). (For a review of dietary supplements, see Chapter 7.) A survey of 414 coaches conducted by General Nutrition Center, *Training and Conditioning,* and *Coaching Management* magazines found that 87% thought nutrition supplements were safe for athletes. Also, 92% of the coaches believed that athletes are using more supplements than ever before. Seventy-seven percent of the coaches surveyed said they did their own research on supplements through magazines, newspaper articles, and Web sites (14). The NCAA, commenting on the survey, offered the following suggestions to athletic departments about supplement use (15):

- Develop a supplement use policy based on sound science.
- Enlist the help of the athletic trainer who has more face time with athletes than almost anyone else.
- Make sure no coaches are distributors of supplements.
- Expand education programs beyond scare tactics because scare tactics do not work with athletes.
- Explain to athletes that "natural" and "completely safe" are not the same thing.
- Remind athletes that salespeople are not trained to offer advice on NCAA banned substances.
- Explain that a supplement that lists "related compounds" in the ingredients could contain a banned substance such as ephedra.

Many supplements are sold from Web sites. Commercial Web sites usually sell products and present biased information passed off as "research" to support claims. For example, a search for the word "creatine" conducted in February 2004 on a common search engine found 346,000 Web pages. More than 90% were commercial sites selling dietary supplements.

The NCAA publishes a banned drug class list and updates can be found on the NCAA Web site (16). Athletes and dietitians are urged to check the Web site frequently for updates. Box 13.1 highlights the banned substances that can be found in some of the over-the-counter dietary supplements. The banned substance list also contains the following warning to athletes: "Many nutritional/dietary supplements contain NCAA banned substances. In addition, the US Food and Drug Administration (FDA) does not strictly regulate the supplement

---

Box 13.1   Examples of Substances Banned by the NCAA but Found in Over-the-Counter Dietary Supplements

Stimulants
- Caffeine (if the concentration in the urine exceeds 15 µg/mL)
- Ephedrine (also called *ephedra, ma huang, Chinese ma huang, epitonin,* and *sida cordifolia*)*
- Phenylpropanolamine (PPA)*
- Synephrine (also called *citrus aurantium, zhi shi, bitter orange*)

Anabolic Agents
- Adrostenedione and Androstenediol (also called *andro*)[†]
- Norandrostenedione (also called *norandro*)
- Dehydroepiandrosterone (DHEA)

Abbreviation: NCAA, National Collegiate Athletic Association.
*Products containing ephedra have been banned by the Food and Drug Administration. A federal judge struck down the ban for doses ≤ 10 mg. Products containing PPA were voluntarily withdrawn from the market due to concerns with increasing stroke risk. However, products containing ephedra and PPA are still sold, and these products are not banned in other countries.
[†]In 2004, the Food and Drug Administration sent warning letters to 23 companies selling androstenedione and requested the companies cease and desist sales of andro. However, supplements containing andro are still available for sale through the Internet.
Source: Data are from reference 16.

---

industry; therefore, purity and safety of nutritional/dietary supplements cannot be guaranteed. Impure supplements may lead to a positive NCAA drug test. The use of supplements is at the student-athlete's own risk" (16).

Athletes must be made aware that dietary supplements have caused positive drug tests, with athletes who tested positive losing eligibility. Ignorance that a dietary supplement contained a banned substance is not a defense that will be considered by the NCAA (17). Information about the NCAA drug testing program can be found on the NCAA Web site (16).

Time

College athletes lead busy lives with many demands on their time. They often take heavy class loads, have mandatory study halls, engage in early-morning conditioning workouts, participate in team practices that may include two-a-day workouts, report for team meetings, and participate in media interviews. This demanding schedule leaves little time or opportunity for food preparation and meals (18).

Body Weight and Body Composition

Athletes frequently have an inappropriate perception of their "ideal" weight or desired percentage body fat, which can conflict with good health practices. Many athletes and coaches have misconceptions about appropriate weight, body composition, and weight loss practices, including the common misperception that body composition can predict sports performance (8,19). Athletic trainers rated body weight as very or moderately important (76%

of trainers surveyed [N = 53]) to an athlete's sports performance but viewed body composition as less important (11).

In a college athletic population, there are wide ranges of body composition—from very lean and thin cross-country runners to very big, and sometimes fat, football players. Body composition measurement can be a useful tool for assessing change over time, but it offers only a snapshot of an athlete's fat-free and fat mass when used alone. This is encouraging because body composition cannot predict sports performance, a common misconception among athletes and some coaches (19).

Noel et al (20) measured body composition in Division I football players and compared the results with previously reported data to determine whether the increase in the size of football players during the last decade was accompanied by an increase in fat mass. The researchers found that the offensive and defensive linemen and tight ends had, on average, more than 25% body fat—a level that approaches overweight. They also found that much of the fat was located in the abdomen, increasing the risk for development of diabetes and heart disease. They suggest that the increases in weight in football players must be addressed to minimize fat weight and increase lean weight (20).

Health Risks

A multicenter, cross-sectional study of seven major collegiate institutions in the United States, including 2,298 male and female athletes, found that college athletes are at greater risk for maladaptive lifestyles and risky health behaviors than their nonathletic peers (21). The athletes in the study were less likely to use seatbelts. They rode more often as a passenger in a vehicle driven by a driver under the influence of alcohol or drugs. They also used smokeless tobacco and anabolic steroids more frequently and were more likely to be involved in physical fights than their nonathletic peers. Female athletes reported a higher prevalence of irregular menses, amenorrhea, and stress fractures than female nonathletes (21). Other researchers have found that college athletes consume significantly more alcohol per week and engage in binge drinking more often than nonathletes (22).

Disordered Eating

College athletes are concerned about body composition and performance, and female athletes in particular are often concerned about appearance. Disordered eating is one of the most difficult situations to deal with in college athletics (23). Athletes report that factors contributing to disordered eating include "lack of education by coaches, self-conscious feelings about uniforms, administrative policies of making weight, and constant images from the media that imply fat is bad rather than stressing the importance of good nutrition" (23).

The prevalence of disordered eating in female collegiate athletes is not known, but surveys indicate that approximately 10% of female athletes had significant problems with bulimia or binge eating and 1.1% had anorexia nervosa (24). In a study of 425 female collegiate athletes, Beals and Manore (25) reported that 2.3% had a clinical diagnosis of bulimia and 3.3% had anorexia. They found that 31% of the athletes had menstrual irregularities. They also reported that although the prevalence of clinical eating disorders is low in female athletes, many of these young women are at high risk for the development of eating disorders, menstrual irregularities, and bone injury.

Athletic trainers are frequently the ones to uncover and identify disordered eating, but in a survey of 171 athletic trainers, only 25% of the athletic trainers felt confident in identifying an eating disorder, 38% felt confident about asking an athlete about eating disorders, and 25% worked at an institution that had a policy on handling eating disorders (26). Almost all of the trainers surveyed (93%) believed that more attention needed to be given to preventing eating disorders in female collegiate athletes (26).

Researchers believe that the higher incidence of disordered eating in college athletes is due to a change to a new, unpredictable environment (ie, moving from high school to college), new social roles and codes of conduct, increased pressure for academic and continued athletic excellence, and little adult guidance (27). However, in a study comparing 206 female college athletes with 197 college nonathletes, there was no significant difference in eating disorders between the two groups, despite slightly higher scores in the Eating Attitude Test in the athletes (27). The authors speculated that disordered eating may be more prevalent than previously thought among young women who are not athletes. They also hypothesized that the college athletic environment is more supportive of student athletes and is finding ways to identify disordered eating patterns earlier and offer more academic, educational, and emotional support than in the past (27).

Although the incidence and prevalence of eating disorders in males are low, there is increasing concern that men have a desire for larger, more muscular bodies, and researchers are beginning to address the syndrome called "muscle dysmorphia" (28). This syndrome is described as the opposite of anorexia nervosa because men who exhibit this syndrome never think they are big enough. They desire a perfect body with perfect muscle symmetry, and they believe that they are not sufficiently muscular. Warning signs include excessive exercise (such as long hours of weight training), shunning social or work obligations to spend time in the gym, and avoiding situations where the body might be exposed (such as the beach or swimming pool) (28). Sports dietitians working with collegiate athletes should be aware that disordered eating can occur in male athletes as well as females.

One program that provides useful information for athletes, athletic trainers, coaches, parents, and athletic administrators is the NCAA Nutrition and Performance Web site (29). Each section contains a checklist specific to athletes, trainers, coaches, parents, and administrators on issues to help create a positive body image and peak performance. (See also Chapter 18 for more information on disordered eating.)

Experience at One NCAA Division IA Collegiate Athletic Association

This part of the chapter is not meant to describe all of the programs offered at colleges and universities—indeed, there is scant published information about the types of programs offered at institutions of higher learning. Instead, this section is meant to highlight one program at an NCAA Division IA school. From the information presented, sports dietitians can gain insight into services that they may consider offering on a consultant, part-time, or full-time basis.

In 1988 the Georgia Tech Athletic Association (Georgia Institute of Technology, Atlanta) hired a nutrition consultant to work with a few offensive linemen who had body fat percentages more than 30%. Trainers, coaches, and other athletes soon began requesting nutrition services, and a few years later a full-time nutrition position was created. A three-pronged approach (nutrition screening, team education, and individual counseling) implemented by the sports dietitian is described in the following sections.

Nutrition Services for the Student Athlete

Approximately 400 student athletes playing 17 sports are eligible for nutrition services. The following are nutrition services offered to student athletes:

- Nutrition screening at yearly physicals
- Blood chemistry
- Lipid profiles
- Screening for iron deficiency and iron deficiency anemia
- Body composition using body plethysmography
- Indirect calorimetry using MedGem (HealtheTech, Golden, CO)
- Team seminars
- Individual nutrition counseling
- Diet analysis
- Nutrition education at the training table
- Off-season weight control, weight gain, or weight maintenance plans
- Help with off-campus meal selection
- Cooking demonstrations
- Medical nutrition therapy for specialized problems (eg, injury recovery, diabetes, hypertension)

Nutrition Screening

Services usually begin at yearly physicals, when nutrition screening is conducted. This screening is not meant to be comprehensive. Time is limited as athletes rotate through 15 stations, so the purpose of this screening is to establish nutrition as an integral part of the sports medicine team and to introduce the sports dietitian to freshman and transfer athletes. The screening form is also used to assess supplement use and knowledge of NCAA-banned substances. Data from the screening have been analyzed and published (4,7).

For all athletes, blood is drawn for routine chemical analysis yearly. Lipid profiles are obtained on all athletes, and anemia is assessed for all freshman, all female athletes, and male cross-country athletes. Iron-deficiency anemia screening is evaluated using hemoglobin, hematocrit, serum ferritin, and total iron-binding capacity (TIBC). If serum ferritin levels are less than 20 µg/dL and TIBC is more than 300 to 360 µg/dL, the team physician is notified, and the sports dietitian and physician determine together the most appropriate course of action (30).

All sports medicine teams are urged to develop a policy on screening athletes for iron deficiency. Even though iron deficiency is the most prevalent nutritional deficiency in the United States and the condition has been reported to affect 60% of female athletes, the authors found that screening for iron deficiency at NCAA Division I schools is not a routine procedure, and for those that do screen, there is great variability in diagnostic criteria and treatment (31).

Also during the screening, body composition measurement is obtained by using body plethysmography (ie, BOD POD, Life Measurement Inc, Concord, CA). When screenings were first conducted, the air displacement method of body composition measurement was used on all athletes, but the coach and sports dietitian have more recently decided that it is not necessary, and that it may be harmful to measure body composition in sports in which there is greater concern with disordered eating (eg, cross country, cheerleading). Body composition measurement is not mandatory; decisions to assess body composition are made by the coach and sports dietitian. Occasionally, skinfold measurements are obtained by the sports dietitian at the practice field when use of the BOD POD is not practical.

Team Education

Team nutrition education can take place in a variety of ways, depending on the needs of the coach and the team. For example, one season the men's basketball team wanted five 10-minute mini-lectures to be given after preseason conditioning workouts. In contrast, for women's basketball, a series of eight interactive discussions, similar to focus groups, were held, complete with "homework" assignments that were turned in at each session. The women's cross-country coach wanted the sports dietitian to conduct a seminar on the importance of iron for endurance athletes. The seminar included information such as why iron is important, food sources rich in iron, maximizing iron absorption from plant foods, and how to take iron supplements, if prescribed, to minimize adverse gastrointestinal effects. For the golf team, each athlete's resting metabolic rate was estimated and body composition measured. Each golfer was provided with a booklet containing data for each athlete along with an individualized calorie-level with sample meal plans. For the volleyball team, a "nutrition playbook" was developed to provide comprehensive nutrition materials.

There is no one right way to provide nutrition information to athletes. In the authors' experience, talking to each team's coach, athletic trainer, and strength and conditioning coach helps set the agenda for nutrition education. Asking the athlete what he or she wants to know about nutrition is critically important. By gathering information from all sources, a sound and well-received nutrition education plan can be ensured. To reinforce nutrition education, the sports dietitian is a frequent visitor to team practices to answer questions or discuss nutrition concerns.

Individual Nutrition Counseling

Athletes can obtain individualized diet plans through referral by the team physician, coach, trainer, or strength staff, or by self-referral to the sports dietitian. Typically, a 3-day diet record is obtained and analyzed with a commercial software package. However, for those athletes unwilling to complete 3-day dietary records, 24-hour recalls or "usual" intakes will be evaluated. Nutrient goals are personalized and often differ from the Dietary Reference Intakes (DRIs) because the goals reflect a higher need for some nutrients. For example, daily protein requirements are calculated using 1.6 to 1.7 g/kg body weight for strength athletes and 1.2 to 1.4 g/kg body weight for endurance athletes, instead of the Recommended Dietary Allowance of 0.8 g/kg body weight (32). A personalized nutrition plan is completed, and the goals are reviewed with the athlete. During the nutrition counseling session, proper food selection at the training table, in the dorm room, and in restaurants is emphasized.

Education at the Training Table

Several nutrition education strategies are used in the dining hall. Pie charts are displayed for each food item served, and athletes are taught how to use the information to support their nutrition or body-composition goals. Information is displayed about portion size; calories; percentage of calories from carbohydrate, protein, and fat; and fat grams. Table tents are developed with timely nutrition messages and rotated weekly. In addition, many sports-nutrition handouts are used in team seminars and individual counseling sessions and also displayed at the cafeteria training table.

Nutrition Consultation to Coaches and Sports Medicine Staff

The sports dietitian's biggest ally may be the athletic trainer. The trainer often fulfills several roles, including team nutritionist, and the athletic trainers at this institution were happy to give up the role of nutritionist. At Georgia Tech, nutrition services have been well received and even championed by the athletic trainers. It was the director of sports medicine (a certified athletic trainer) who suggested that nutrition screening be part of the yearly physicals. Kundrat (33) suggests several strategies for fostering the relationship between the sports nutritionist and the athletic trainer.

Others who may welcome the services of a dietitian are strength and conditioning coaches. Georgia Tech coaches were bombarded with requests from salespeople (often well-meaning alumni or former athletes) to use nutritional supplements or products. The sports dietitian provides a scientific evaluation of the supplement and gives a report of the pros and cons with recommendations for use. Trainers and coaches no longer have the burden of evaluating nutritional supplements. Guidelines for evaluating ergogenic aids as well as books about dietary supplements have been published to aid in the process (34,35).

The sports dietitian at this institution also had the lead role in developing a dietary supplement policy. With input from the athletic director, the sports medicine director, and the strength and conditioning coach, a dietary supplement policy was established and implemented. In 2000, the NCAA adopted a new policy preventing college institutions from providing athletes with supplements that enhance weight gain, including many of the most popular nutritional supplements (36,37). Bylaw 16.5.2 (g) states "An institution may provide only non–muscle-building nutritional supplements to a student athlete at any time for the purpose of providing additional calories and electrolytes, provided the supplements do not contain any NCAA banned substances. Permissible non–muscle-building nutritional supplements are identified according to the following classes: carbohydrate/electrolyte drinks, energy bars, carbohydrate boosters, and vitamins and minerals" (36,37). Box 13.2 provides examples of the permissible and nonpermissible nutritional supplements (36,37), but this list should only be used as a guide to understanding the application of the legislation. The list is not exhaustive.

The NCAA defines a non–muscle-building supplement as those that fit into the four specified categories mentioned earlier (carbohydrate/electrolyte drinks, energy bars, carbohydrate boosters, and vitamins and minerals). After the legislation was adopted, member institutions wanted to know how much protein was permitted in an energy bar or carbohydrate booster, so "the 30% protein rule was an additional specification added after the legislations was passed" (personal communication, Mary Wilfert, NCAA Assistant Director of

---

Box 13.2   Permissible and Nonpermissible Nutritional Supplements for NCAA Athletes*

Permissible
- Vitamins and minerals
- Energy bars
- Energy replacement drinks (for example, Ensure, Abbott Laboratories, Abbott Park, IL; Boost, Novartis US, New York, NY)
- Electrolyte replacement drinks (for example, Gatorade, Gatorade Company, Chicago, IL; PowerAde, Coca-Cola Company, Atlanta, GA)
- Non-muscle building supplements that contain less than 30% of energy from protein

Nonpermissible
- Amino acids
- Chrysin
- Chondroitin
- Creatine/creatine-containing compounds
- Ginseng
- Glucosamine
- Glycerol
- HMB
- L-carnitine
- Melatonin
- Pos-2
- Protein powders
- Tribulus
- Supplements that contain more than 30% of energy from protein

Abbreviations: HMB, beta-hydroxy-beta-methylbutyrate; NCAA, National Collegiate Athletic Association.
*Permissible supplements can be purchased by athletic departments for distribution to athletes. Nonpermissible supplements cannot be purchased by athletic departments for distribution to athletes. However, athletes may use supplements from the nonpermissible list if they are not banned substances and do not contain any banned substances.
Source: Data are from references 36 and 37.

Education Outreach). Some supplement makers have devised a line of "collegiate" energy bars and drinks that provide no more than 30% of energy from protein.

The Nutrition Facts or Supplement Facts panel should be used as a guide to determine whether a supplement is permissible. For example, a beverage that contains less than 30% protein is in violation of the NCAA regulation if the drink is made from a protein powder that contains 100% protein and juice, because the protein powder used in the mixture is in the nonpermissible category (personal communication with Mary Wilfert, NCAA Assistant Director of Education and Outreach). Similarly, an energy bar that provides 200 kcal and 20 g protein is not be permissible under the NCAA rules because the product contains 40% protein.

Additionally, "it is not permissible for an NCAA institution or an institutional staff member to sell or arrange the sale of muscle-building supplement to student athletes" (37). Beginning in 2004, all schools must provide the NCAA banned substance list and information about the risks of using dietary supplements to all incoming prospective student athletes at the earliest practical time but no later than July 1 of each calendar year (38). Sports dietitians working with college athletes can find information about dietary supplements from the National Center for Drug Free Sport Web site (39).

The sports dietitian at Georgia Tech helps trainers with pregame meal selection because trainers are responsible for meal selection for away games. The athletic trainer is the person who spends the most time with the athletes and knows what athletes will or will not eat. By reviewing the menus with the sports dietitian, the trainer can choose the most appropriate selections (ie, those appropriate for pregame competition and those that the athlete will eat).

The sports dietitian also plays a role in the recruitment of future athletes. Recruits and their families (especially the recruits' parents) are impressed with the nutrition services offered and appreciate that good tasting, healthful food is provided on campus. A brief presentation by the sports dietitian and a tour of the Nutrition Center are part of the athlete's recruitment visit at Georgia Tech.

Working With the Foodservice Staff

The sports dietitian should work with the foodservice provider and staff to review menus and make recommendations for recipe modification. The philosophy of the Georgia Tech Athletic Association is that athletes should be offered a wide variety of menu items and be educated about the best choices to meet their individual body composition and performance goals. A policy for meals served at the training table was established and includes the following considerations:

- The foodservice director submits a cycle menu to the sports dietitian for review and suggestions.
- The foodservice director provides recipes to the sports dietitian for nutrient analysis and production of pie charts containing nutrition information.
- The salad bar includes a variety of vegetables (eg, spinach, romaine lettuce, grated carrots, mushrooms, green peppers, onions, and canned beans) and reduced-fat and fat-free salad dressings in addition to the full-fat dressings.
- A pasta bar is offered at meals to provide high-carbohydrate food choices and as an alternative to meat-based entrees.
- Nutrient cards are posted for all items to allow the athlete to make a point-of-purchase decision about the nutrient content of the item.

In 1996 the NCAA implemented a one-meal-per-day rule for training tables (38). At Georgia Tech, this means that other students can eat at a special dining facility for athletes for breakfast or dinner, but lunch is reserved exclusively for athletes and staff. Information regarding meals for student athletes can be found in Articles 15 and 16 of the 2003–2004 NCAA Division I Manual. Manuals for Division II and III schools are also available and all can be viewed on the Internet (38).

Future Needs

The following suggestions are made by the sports dietitians associated with Georgia Tech based on their 25 years of collective experience working with college athletes. Four areas need to be considered.

1. Providing opportunities for dietetics students to work in sports nutrition.
2. Documenting the benefits of nutrition interventions through outcome studies.
3. Developing a program for "de-training" the athlete who does not go on to play at the professional level.
4. Developing a network of full-time sports dietitians at colleges and universities to share information.

Students

Dietetics educators frequently say that most of their students want to be sports dietitians. A college athletic association can offer dietetics students a good environment for student placement and internship opportunities that allow them to experience the realities of working with athletes. Students often think that athletes are highly motivated to follow all nutrition advice or that student athletes don't have weight control issues, so the opportunity to see the real-world of sports nutrition is a valuable experience.

Although Georgia Tech does not have an academic nutrition department (it is an engineering school), the sports dietitian has been providing experiences for dietetics students from other local universities that have both dietetic internships and graduate programs in nutrition. Students can provide many services that complement the services provided by a single sports dietitian. Interns at Georgia Tech develop new educational handouts, suggest recipes, make table tents, write newsletter articles, analyze athletes' diets, survey athletes about satisfaction with the training table, and conduct cooking demonstrations. Students who want to work with athletes should have a solid base in life cycle nutrition, medical nutrition therapy, nutrition therapy for management of disordered eating, exercise physiology, business basics, and communication skills (40).

Nutrition Outcomes

The need for documenting sports nutrition outcomes has been described (41). The reasons that athletes seek nutrition counseling should be documented, as well as the effectiveness of nutrition interventions with the entire team. The American Dietetic Association has published the Nutrition Care Process, and sports dietitians can use this process and model to identify quality care for athletes and document the outcomes (42).

A pilot nutrition outcome study was completed with the Georgia Tech men's basketball team, with plans to expand the model to other teams. The goal of the study was to determine whether nutrition interventions resulted in behavior change during the basketball season. The pilot study demonstrated the value of sports nutrition counseling using a team approach (43), although the study was challenging to conduct (it took the complete cooperation of the coaching staff to conduct a research study during the season, and there was no control or comparison group to use in a study design because the school has only one men's basketball team). The study found that basketball players were more aware of practicing appropriate eating strategies after the education sessions and that they found it useful to weigh themselves before and after practice to monitor fluid loss (43).

"De-Training" Programs

Many athletes need to be "de-trained" when their playing days are over. The probability that a college football player will go on to a professional football career is only 2 for every 100 student athletes. For men's basketball the number is 1.3 in 100 (1). Although data are not available to support the observation, the authors note that many college athletes experience an unhealthful weight gain after their college athletic career ends. This is especially true for sports that encourage higher weights, like football. It is not unusual to see an offensive lineman gain weight in the year or two after his playing days end. Millard-Stafford et al (44) noted that overfat college football linemen had significantly higher mean values for systolic blood pressure and triglycerides, and that their food records, obtained during their college years, showed that intakes of fat, sugar, cholesterol, and sodium were higher than the recommended levels. The importance of continued physical activity and sound nutritional practices for life are frequently discussed with athletes. However, a formal program that targets athletes after their eligibility has ended could benefit them for life.

Sports Dietitian Network

There is no formal network of full-time sports dietitians working at the collegiate level, and it is through word of mouth that sports dietitian hear about the work of other sports dietitians at colleges or universities. A formal network would serve multiple purposes: to provide a formal exchange of ideas between dietetics professionals in a unique full-time position; to provide "best practices" to encourage other colleges and universities to hire sports dietitians; and to foster collaborative research on supplement use, effective nutrition education strategies, and outcomes' documentation. Four dietitians who are currently working at universities offer tips for working with college athletes in Box 13.3.

Conclusion

The rewards of providing nutrition education and services to college athletes are many—the chance to see athletes adopt more healthful eating habits, the recognition that hydration and fueling improves performance, and the camaraderie of being a part of the team. Not all college athletes are motivated to change dietary behaviors, however. The opportunity for dietetics professionals to work in the arena is growing—with the thousands of colleges and universities that have athletic programs, there is a role for sports nutrition in every one. Funding a sports dietitian position is frequently cited as a reason for not hiring a dietetics professional at the college level, but as sports dietitians "prove" their worth and publish the results of successes, more colleges might be inclined to find the funds to establish a position.

Box 13.3   Tips for Working with College Athletes

From Kristine Clark, PhD, RD, Director of Sports Nutrition, Center for Sports Medicine, Penn State University, University Park, Pa:

- You must be regarded as an nutrition "expert" in the eyes of athletes and coaches. Therefore, it is important to read and interpret the literature and translate it into practice. You need to inform and educate athletes, coaches, and trainers on specific nutrition issues.
- Set your goal to become an integral part of the sports medicine team—team physicians, athletic trainers, strength and conditioning coaches, physical therapists, and administrators. Provide nutrition handouts and make yourself available for team seminars and recruiting tours.
- Know that you are ultimately a clinical practitioner. Sports nutrition is not a job for the person fresh out of undergraduate school. A graduate degree and work experience are highly regarded by administrators.

From Suzanne Nelson Steen, DSc, RD, Director of Sports Nutrition, Department of Intercollegiate Athletics, University of Washington, Seattle, Wash:

- Support student-athletes during competition, in addition to advising them on nutrition for peak performance. Attend practices and competitions.
- Appreciate nutrition issues from the athlete's perspective. Be a good listener. Creatively tailor advice to the individual for his or her sport.
- Be a team player. Support leadership development and promote scholastic excellence by athletes.

From Michelle S. Rockwell, MS, RD, Sports Nutritionist, University of Florida Athletic Association, Gainesville, Fla:

- Establish yourself as the expert in body composition measurement and weight management counseling. Prioritize health and performance goals over actual weight and body composition. Create a positive nutrition environment that promotes balanced eating and healthy body image.
- Have a solid knowledge of medical nutrition therapy because you will encounter many conditions benefiting from nutrition intervention (for example: diabetes, osteoporosis, sickle cell anemia, iron deficiency anemia, etc.).
- Take a hands-on approach to your job. You are the "food coach" and should be present when athletes are fueling and hydrating such as before and after practices and workouts and during pre-competition and team meals.

From Leah Moore Thomas, MS, RD, Sports Dietitian, Georgia Tech Athletic Association, Atlanta, Ga:

- Familiarize yourself with the athlete's practice, competition, and weight room schedule. Learn what motivates athletes and what turns them off. Use all of this knowledge to relate to them and to show interest in more than just nutrition.
- Be present—both at practice and competition at home and away, if possible—to show your interest and support.
- Open up and let athletes learn about you and the things you do. If you are in training and competition for sport, share that with them.

References

1. NCAA Fact Sheet. Available at: http://www.ncaa.org/about/fact_sheet. Accessed February 26, 2004.
2. Clark KL. Working with college athletes, coaches, and trainers at a major university. *Int J Sport Nutr.* 1994;4:135–141.
3. Rosenberg B. Emerging-sports' idea has yielded championship results. *The NCAA News.* April 26, 2004. Available at: http://www.ncaa.org/news/2004/20040426/awide/4109n07.html. Accessed May 16, 2005.
4. Rosenbloom CA, Jonnalagadda SS, Skinner R. Nutrition knowledge of collegiate athletes in a Division I National Collegiate Athletic Association institution. *J Am Diet Assoc.* 2002;102:418–420.
5. Jacobson BH, Sobonya C, Ransone J. Nutrition practices and knowledge of college varsity athletes: a follow-up. *J Strength Cond Res.* 2001;15:63–68.
6. Zawila LG, Steib CS, Hoogenboom B. The female collegiate cross-country runner: nutritional knowledge and attitudes. *J Athl Train.* 2003;38:67–74.
7. Jonnalagadda SS, Rosenbloom CA, Skinner R. Dietary practices, attitudes, and physiological status of collegiate freshman football players. *J Strength Cond Res.* 2001;15:507–513.
8. Manore MM, Clark K, Berning JR, Engelbert-Fenton K. Roundtable: consulting in sport nutrition. *Int J Sport Nutr.* 1996;6:198–206.
9. Froiland K, Koszewski W, Hingst J, Kopecky L. Nutritional supplement use among college athletes and their sources of information. *Int J Sports Nutr Exerc Metab.* 2004;14:104–120.
10. Burns RD, Schiller R, Merrick MA, Wolf KN. Intercollegiate student athlete use of nutritional supplements and the role of athletic trainers and dietitians in nutrition counseling. *J Am Diet Assoc.* 2004;104:246–249.
11. Rockwell MS, Nickols-Richardson SM, Thye FW. Nutrition knowledge, opinions, and practices of coaches and athletic trainers at a Division I university. *J Sports Nutr Exerc Metab.* 2001;11:174–185.
12. Krumbach CJ, Ellis DR, Driskell JA. A report of vitamin and mineral supplement use among university athletes in a Division I institution. *Int J Sports Nutr.* 1999;9:416–425.
13. Meiggs R. Committee continues to monitor creatine use in sports. *NCAA News.* April 12, 2004.
14. Survey of prep school, high school, and collegiate coaches. GNC Pro Performance. Available at: http://gnc.com. Accessed May 13, 2004.
15. Diligence and education work to help counter the culture. *NCAA News.* June 9, 2003.
16. NCAA Banned-Drug Classes 2003–2004. Available at: http://www.ncaa.org/sports_sciences/drugtesting. Accessed February 28, 2004.
17. Grandjean AC. Dietary supplements and drug testing. *National Strength Cond Assoc.* 2003;25:71.
18. Burke L. Practical issues in nutrition for athletes. *J Sports Sci.* 1995;13(suppl):S83–S90.
19. Manore M, Thompson J. *Sport Nutrition for Health and Performance.* Champaign, Ill: Human Kinetics; 2000.
20. Noel MB, Van Heest JL, Zaneteas P, Rodgers CD. Body composition in Division I football players. *J Strength Cond Res.* 2003;17:228–237.
21. Nativ A, Puffer JC, Green GA. Lifestyles and health risks of collegiate athletes: a multi-center study. *Clin J Sport Med.* 1997;7:262–272.
22. Leichliter JS, Meilman PW, Presley CA, Cashin JR. Alcohol use and related consequences among students with varying levels of involvement in college athletics. *J Am Coll Health.* 1998;46:257–262.
23. Barnes D. SAAC speaks: student-athletes seek nutritional balance. *NCAA News.* April 9, 2001.

24. Johnson C, Powers PS, Dick R. Athletes and eating disorders: the National Collegiate Athletic Association Study. *Int J Eat Disord.* 1999;26:179–188.

25. Beals KA, Manore MM. Disorders of the female athlete triad among collegiate athletes. *Int J Sport Nutr Exerc Metab.* 2002;12:281–292.

26. Vaughan JL, King KA, Cottrell RR. Collegiate athletic trainers' confidence in helping female athletes with eating disorders. *J Athl Train.* 2004;39:71–76.

27. Kirk G, Singh K, Getz H. Risk of eating disorders among female college athletes and nonathletes. *J College Counseling.* 2001;4:122–132.

28. Choi PYL, Pope HG, Olivardia R. Muscle dysmorphia: a new syndrome in weightlifters. *Br J Sports Med.* 2002;36:375–376.

29. NCAA Nutrition and Performance Web site. Available at: http://www1.ncaa.org/membership/ed_outreach/nutrition-performance/index.html. Accessed November 9, 2004.

30. Ashenden MJ, Martin DT, Dobson GP, Mackintosh C, Hahn AG. Serum ferritin and anemia in trained female athletes. *Int J Sport Nutr.* 1998;8:223–229.

31. Cowell BS, Rosenbloom CA, Skinner R, Summers SH. Policies on screening female athletes for iron deficiency in NCAA Division I-A institutions. *Int J Sports Nutr Exerc Metab.* 2003;13:277–285.

32. Lemon PW. Effects of exercise on dietary protein requirement. *Int J Sport Nutr.* 1998;8: 426–447.

33. Kundrat S. Fostering the sports nutritionist-athletic trainer relationship. *SCAN's Pulse.* 1998; 17:7–8.

34. Rosenbloom C, Storlie J. A nutritionist's guide to evaluating ergogenic aids. *SCAN's Pulse.* 1998;17:1–5.

35. Fragakis AS. *The Health Professional's Guide to Popular Dietary Supplements.* 2nd ed. Chicago, Ill: American Dietetic Association; 2003.

36. Legislative assistance. *NCAA News & Features.* April 14, 2003. Available at: http://www.ncaa.org/news/2003.20030414.memoinfo/4008n25.html. Accessed February 28, 2004.

37. Legislative assistance. *NCAA News & Features.* August 14, 2000. Available at: http://www.ncaa.org/news/2000/20000814/active/3717n22.html. Accessed May 16, 2005.

38. *2003–2004 NCAA Division I Manual.* Available at: http://www.ncaa.org. Accessed February 28, 2004.

39. The National Center for Drug-Free Sport Web site. Available at: http://www.drugfreesport.com. Accessed November 9, 2004.

40. Clark N. Identifying the educational needs of aspiring sports nutritionists. *J Am Diet Assoc.* 2000;100:1522–1524.

41. Clark KS. Sports nutrition counseling: documentation of performance. *Top Clin Nutr.* 1999;14:34–40.

42. Lacey K, Pritchett E. Nutrition care process and model: ADA adopts road map to quality care and outcomes management. *J Am Diet Assoc.* 2003;103:1061–1072.

43. Rosenbloom CA, McDonald S, Skinner R. The benefits of sports nutrition counseling: experience with a Division IA NCAA men's basketball team. *Today's Dietitian.* 2002;4:44–48.

44. Millard-Stafford M, Rosskopf LB, Sparling PB. Coronary heart disease: risk profiles of college football players. *Phys Sports Med.* 1989;17:151–163.

Chapter 14

MASTERS ATHLETES

CHRISTINE A. ROSENBLOOM, PHD, RD*

Introduction

What do athletes do when they get older and are no longer competitive in the sport they love? Many of them are taking on a new title—veteran or masters athlete. Events for masters athletes can range from sanctioned events through formal governing bodies such as USA Track and Field to events such as the Huntsman World Senior Games held annually in Utah. In 2002 the World Senior Games hosted more than 6,500 athletes competing in 20 sports, a substantial increase from the 500 athletes who competed in 1985 when the inaugural senior games were held. Almost every city and country in the world—from Auckland, New Zealand, to Vancouver, British Columbia—has an association devoted to masters athlete competitions. It is uncertain how many masters athletes there are worldwide, but in Europe it is estimated that 40,000 athletes are competing as masters (1).

Who Are Masters Athletes?

Many sports have masters divisions defined by the rules of the governing body (eg, USA Track and Field, World Masters Athletics, or National Senior Games Association) or a separate organization designed to meet the needs of retired professional athletes (eg, the Champion's Tour in golf, formerly called the Senior Tour, and the Seniors Tennis Tour). The age at which one becomes a "master" ranges from sport to sport and can be as young as 19 years (swimming) or as old as 50 years (golf). The World Masters Athletics (WMA) organization defines masters athletes as age 35 years for women and age 40 years for men.

Competition is also age-graded, usually in 5-year intervals. The Web site of the International Association of Athletics Federations (IAAF) displays records for masters events in age-graded categories that go as high as 95- to 99-year-olds. The focus of this chapter is on athletes who are 50 years of age or older.

*The author wishes to thank graduate student Michele Bahns for her help in gathering research for this chapter.

Increased Aging Population in the United States

When the 20th century began, the mean life expectancy in the United States was 42 years (2). Today the average person in the United States lives twice as long. The mean life expectancy for a child born in 2001 is 79.8 years for females and 74.4 years for males (3). The mean life expectancy for a woman at age 65 is another 19 years; men who reach age 65 can expect to live another 16 years. By 2030, it is projected there will be about 70 million older Americans, more than twice their number in 2000. By 2040 one of every four Americans will be 65 years of age or older (3).

The number of older people who will be competing at a masters level in athletics is unknown, but growth in masters competitions in recent years suggests increasing numbers in the future. Dychtwald (4) points out that baby boomers (the 79 million individuals born in the United States between 1946 and 1964) are more likely to be active than the generations before them. In 2002, 5.6 million adults age 45 to 54 years belonged to health clubs, accounting for 17% of membership, and 23% of health club members were older than 55 years of age (5).

Benefits of Exercise in Adults

In 1996 the Surgeon General issued *Physical Activity and Health: A Report of the Surgeon General* (6), the first report of its kind. The physical and mental benefits of a physically active lifestyle are summarized in Box 14.1 (6–8). The report concluded that regular physical activity induces higher cardiopulmonary fitness, which decreases overall mortality, reduces risk of coronary heart disease and high blood pressure, reduces the risk of colon cancer, protects against the development of type 2 diabetes mellitus, builds bone mass, increases muscle strength and balance, helps to control body weight, relieves the symptoms of depression and anxiety, and improves mood (6). The report recommended that "all Americans accumulate at least 30 minutes or more of moderate-intensity physical activity on most, or preferably all, days of the week" (6). Although the report did not make age-specific exercise recommendations, it was noted that previously sedentary older adults can achieve and maintain high levels of fitness and improved skeletal muscle function at any age (6). At any age, exercise induces beneficial physiological adaptations that improve functional abilities.

Healthy People 2010 (7) identifies several objectives to increase physical activity in adults. Although not age-specific, these objectives have been used as a framework by local and state governments, as well as professional organizations, to set goals for older adults. One such report, *National Blueprint: Increasing Physical Activity Among Adults Age 50 and Older* (8), suggests many strategies for increasing exercise in older adults and calls for more research to identify seniors who are currently active to help develop interventions for all older adults.

Aging and Exercise

It is common to classify aging based on chronological age, but chronological age is a poor predictor of functional age. Someone may be 50 years old (chronological age) but, due to

---

Box 14.1   Benefits of a Physically Active Lifestyle

Physiological Responses
- Decreased resting blood pressure
- Increased cardiac output
- Increased blood flow to skeletal muscles and skin
- Increased maximal oxygen uptake (VO_{2max})
- Increased components of immune system such as natural killer cells and circulating T-lymphocytes and B-lymphocytes
- Increased bone mass
- Increased high-density lipoprotein cholesterol
- Increased strength and balance

Health Benefits
- Decreased overall mortality
- Decreased risk of cardiovascular disease
- Decreased risk of hypertension
- Decreased risk of thrombosis
- Decreased risk of colon cancer
- Decreased risk of type 2 diabetes mellitus
- Decreased risk of obesity
- Decreased risk of falls and fractures in older adults
- Decreased symptoms of depression and anxiety
- Increased psychological well-being

Source: Data are from references 6–8.

---

a sedentary lifestyle, may have difficulty performing activities of daily living (functional age). A 75-year-old who has been physically active throughout life may have better functional capacity than a much younger person who has not been active. For example, a masters athlete at 65 years of age may outperform a sedentary 25-years-old on measures of maximum oxygen consumption (VO_{2max}), muscle strength, and flexibility (9).

Astrand (10) reviewed both laboratory data and statistics of world records and noted that personal best performances decreased after the age of 30 to 35. At this age range, there is a decrease in maximum aerobic power, even in those athletes who were well-conditioned and trained (10).

Peak performance in a sport depends on the key functional element that is required for success. For example, in sports such as gymnastics for which flexibility is crucial, top athletes are usually in their teens (9). In aerobic sports, competitors usually peak in their mid 20s when training improvements and competition experience help athletes before a decrease in VO_{2max} negates those gains. In sports like golf, the best athletes are generally in their 30s or 40s (9).

Maximum oxygen consumption decreases by approximately 5 mL/kg/min each decade, beginning at age 25 years. Researchers note that it is hard to determine how much of this loss is due to the normal aging process or to the adoption of a more sedentary lifestyle. Athletes who train regularly experience a rate of decrease as they age that is slightly slower than the general population (9). Early research with masters athletes was done cross-sectionally, but recent longitudinal studies have reported that the decrease in VO_{2max} in masters athletes is more than previously believed (11). In a longitudinal study of 42 athletes, Katzel et al (12) found a 22% decrease in VO_{2max} in older endurance athletes during an 8-year period of follow-up. The greatest decrease in VO_{2max} occurred in those athletes who could not maintain a high volume of training, suggesting that the decrease in VO_{2max} is less related to aging but more related to an inactive lifestyle (12). In this study, only 7 athletes (17% of study participants) were still training at high volume at the end of the study. The authors conclude that maintaining a high level of aerobic fitness, even for the highly motivated athlete, becomes more difficult with advancing age (12).

Muscle strength peaks at approximately 25 years of age, plateaus through ages 35 or 40, and then decreases, with 25% loss of peak strength by age 65 (10). The decrease in muscular strength seems to parallel decreases in muscle mass (10). The age-related loss of skeletal muscle mass is called sarcopenia (13). Forty percent of women between ages 55 and 64 years, 45% between 65 and 74 years, and 65% between 75 and 84 years cannot lift 10 lb (13). However, muscle strength can be improved in as little as 10 weeks with resistance training, even in frail nursing-home residents (13).

Research on Masters Athletes

In general, the research on masters athletes shows that participation in competition at the masters level confers physical and psychological benefits (14–19). Shephard et al (14) studied 750 endurance masters athletes during a 7-year period. During the follow-up, only 0.6% had a nonfatal heart attack and 0.6% required coronary bypass surgery. Ninety percent said they were very interested in maintaining good health, 76% considered themselves to be less vulnerable to viral infections than their sedentary peers, and 68% reported their quality of life as much better than their sedentary peers.

There were some former smokers in the group, but most had stopped smoking before they were regular exercisers. Thirty-seven percent of the former smokers reported that exercise helped them with the effects of withdrawal from tobacco. Fifty-nine percent reported getting regular medical checkups, and 88% reported sleeping very well. The authors concluded that participation in masters competition seems to carry real health benefits, but the gains may, in part, reflect an overall healthy lifestyle (14).

Morgan and Costill (15) reported on health behaviors and psychological characteristics of 15 male marathon runners who were first tested in 1969 (N = 8) and again in 1976 (N = 7) with a mean age of 50 years at the time of follow-up. The health behaviors in this sample of men were uniformly positive—all reported moderate use of alcohol, no insomnia, few physical health problems, and good overall mood (15).

Seals et al (16) compared 14 endurance-trained masters athletes with younger endurance athletes and older sedentary men to determine whether the masters athletes had a more favorable lipid profile than younger men or sedentary older men. Diet was not assessed, but alcohol intake was recorded and none of the subjects ingested more than 2 oz of alcohol per day. Total cholesterol (TC) and low-density lipoprotein (LDL) cholesterol were higher in the masters athletes than in the young athletes, and high-density lipoprotein (HDL) cholesterol was significantly higher in the masters athletes than in the other groups (66 mg/dL vs 55 mg/dL in young athletes and 45 mg/dL in older untrained men who were lean). The TC:HDL ratios were lower for both the young and the older groups of athletes compared with the older untrained men. This study showed that the older masters athletes have significantly higher HDL cholesterol levels than their sedentary peers, which may confer a reduced risk for coronary artery disease (16).

A longitudinal study on coronary heart disease (CHD) risk factors in older track athletes was reported by Mengelkoch et al (17). Twenty-one subjects, ages 60 to 92 years, were assessed at three evaluation points (initial, 10-year, and 20-year). Measurements included smoking history, blood pressure, resting electrocardiogram, TC, plasma glucose, body weight, percentage body fat, body mass index (BMI), waist-to-hip ratio (WHR), and VO_{2max}. All CHD risk factors remained low, and even after 20 years all values for variables measured were within normal limits. Thus, in this study, the prevalence of CHD risk factors remained low into old age in masters athletes (17), indicating that regular activity has a favorable effect on physical measurements that impact chronic disease risk.

Giada et al (18) found that a 2-month hiatus from training resulted in a reversal of the favorable lipid profile found in trained cyclists. Thus, like the decreases in VO_{2max} seen with decreased training volume, it seems that continued exercise is necessary to maintain a favorable lipid profile in older athletes.

Seals et al (19) compared endurance-trained masters athletes (mean age of 60 years) with young endurance-trained men (mean age of 26 years) to obtain information about glucose tolerance. Each subject had an oral glucose tolerance test. The masters athletes had a significantly blunted insulin response that was similar to the young athletes. These data suggest the deterioration of glucose tolerance is not an inevitable aging process and that regular vigorous physical activity can prevent the deterioration of glucose tolerance and insulin sensitivity (19).

Currently, there is not abundant research on the benefits of physical activity in masters athletes. Most of the studies involve athletes competing in endurance events (predominantly running and cycling), but it is clear from the research reviewed that people who maintain an active lifestyle reap many physical health benefits. Chronic diseases such as cardiovascular disease, hypertension, and diabetes are rarely seen in masters athletes. Changes considered a "normal" consequence of aging, such as reduced muscle mass and strength, reduced aerobic capacity, bone loss, and deterioration of the insulin response to a glucose challenge, seem to be minimized in masters athletes due to their lifelong habit of physical activity. These athletes might very well "use it and not lose it."

Nutrition Concerns

Energy Intake and Exercise

Although there is evidence to suggest that energy needs decrease with age (approximately one third of the decrease is related to a decrease in basal metabolic rate [BMR] and the remainder to decreases in physical activity [20]), these data do not include individuals who vigorously exercise. Van Pelt et al (21) concluded that resting metabolic rate (RMR) decreases with age even in highly active older men but the decrease is related to age-associated decreases in exercise training and intensity.

The Dietary Reference Intakes (DRIs) for energy and macronutrient intakes established estimated energy requirements (EERs) at four levels of energy expenditure (22). But, even the category of "active" physical activity level, as described by the DRI report may be too low for a masters athlete. Table 14.1 shows EERs for active older adults, which may be used to determine individualized energy needs (22).

Few studies have assessed energy needs of older exercisers. In the studies that have tried to quantify energy needs (23–25), results have shown that energy needs do not differ for masters athletes compared with younger athletes. The main factor predicting energy needs is the volume of exercise, not aging per se. In a review of energy expenditure and aging, Starling (26) concluded that regular participation in physical activity (aerobic activities, primarily running) may attenuate the age-related decrease in RMR for men and women.

Wilmore et al (24) measured RMR in men and women (ages 17 to 63 years) after a 20-week endurance training program and found that RMR was not elevated after the training bout when measured 24 and 72 hours after exercise. The training group had small changes in body composition (less body fat, less fat mass, more fat-free mass) that were statistically significant, as well as an improvement in oxygen consumption. However, these changes did not significantly alter RMR. Although an endurance program will improve body composition, it may not have an effect on RMR in aging athletes.

Even fewer studies have assessed energy needs of masters athletes engaged in strength training. Campbell et al (25) studied the effects of 12 weeks of progressive resistance training on energy balance in sedentary, healthy older adults (eight men and four women, ages 56 to 80 years). At the end of 12 weeks of strength training, muscular strength increased, fat-free mass increased, fat mass decreased, and mean energy intake needed to maintain body weight increased by approximately 15% during the resistance-training program (25).

Studies have reported that exercise training increases the thermic effect of food (TEF) in older subjects. Lundholm et al (27) studied ten active, well-conditioned men (mean age 70 years) participating in aerobic exercise three to five times a week for at least 1 hour. Case controls were used for comparison. Subjects were fed a liquid formula containing 500 kcal (56% carbohydrate, 24% protein, 20% fat) and BMR was measured. Higher oxygen uptake was found in the well-trained men compared with the sedentary controls, and the TEF was significantly increased (~ 56%). The authors concluded that in this study physical activity seemed to have a potentiating effect on TEF in older subjects.

TABLE 14.1   Estimated Energy Requirements for Active Older Adults

Age Group, y	Men, kcal/d	Women, kcal/d
50–59	2757	2186
60–69	2657	2116
70–79	2557	2046
80–89	2457	1976

Source: Data are from reference 22.

Researchers have suggested that exercise increases the response of the sympathetic nervous system, leading to an increase in TEF. Jones et al (28) studied four groups of healthy men (16 young and 11 older sedentary men as controls compared with 9 young and 10 older habitually exercising men) to examine the plasma norepinephrine and epinephrine in the sedentary and active groups. TEF was increased in the exercising men of both age groups, but the activity of the sympathetic nervous system, as measured by catecholamine levels, was unchanged. The authors conclude that while TEF is greater in active men, the difference is not explained by sympathetic nervous activity.

Although scant research exists on energy needs of masters athletes, practitioners can use the same energy equations they use for younger athletes in assessing energy needs. It is important to quantify activity as much as possible because training tends to decrease in older athletes and therefore, based on training volume, energy expenditure might not be as high.

Macronutrients

Carbohydrate should provide the major source of energy in any athlete's diet (29). The DRIs suggest a range of carbohydrate of 45% to 65% to total energy (22). Although no ideal level of carbohydrate consumption has been defined for masters athletes, the guidelines used for younger athletes should be recommended—5 to 7 g/kg/day for general training needs and 7 to 10 g/kg/day for the increased needs of endurance athletes. Flexibility is important in establishing carbohydrate goals, recognizing that individual preferences as well as training and competition schedules may necessitate adjustment of carbohydrate intake.

To meet fuel needs and general nutrition goals, athletes who exercise less than 1 hour per day with moderate-intensity activity or several hours with low-intensity exercise should aim for 5 to 7 g/kg/day. For recovery after exercise, 1.0 to 1.5 g/kg carbohydrate is recommended within an hour of exercise, with the goal of consuming an additional 1 g/kg 2 hours later. This is especially important for those athletes engaged in daily training. Recent studies have suggested that addition of a small amount of protein along with carbohydrate in the recovery period improves stimulation of protein synthesis by increasing amino acid delivery to the muscle (30).

Many masters athletes may be confused about the role of carbohydrate in sport because they are exposed to media messages that promote protein as "good" and carbohydrate as "bad." Athletes who drastically cut carbohydrate intake while increasing protein foods may experience a decline in their performance. Aiming for "quality" carbohydrates (whole grains, fruits, and vegetables) while decreasing refined carbohydrates and sugar-rich foods can be one way to help athletes to consume adequate carbohydrate to meet the demands of training and competition, maintain energy balance, and reduce risk for some chronic diseases.

The debate about protein needs of exercising individuals is not new, but when aging is thrown into the equation it begs the question: What are the dietary protein requirements of masters athletes? Although the question cannot be answered with precision, several researchers have examined protein requirements in active, older people and have concluded that their needs are similar to younger athletes. Both Meredith et al (31) and Campbell et al (32) studied protein requirements of older, active men. Meredith's group conducted a metabolic study of nitrogen balance and found that with adequate energy intake, protein needs were 0.94 g/kg/day ± 0.05 g/kg/day for older subjects (31).

Campbell et al (32) assessed the effect of 12 weeks of strength training in 12 older men and women. The results showed that whole-body protein was significantly changed with strength training, and nitrogen retention was related to the anabolic stimulus of strength training. The efficiency of nitrogen retention was greater when subjects ingested a lower protein intake (0.8 g/kg/day) compared with a higher protein intake (1.62 g/kg/day). This study demonstrates that the anabolic stimulus of strength training enhances nitrogen retention when protein requirements are based on nitrogen balance studies (32). From this study it can be concluded that protein needs seem to be higher in the early phases of strength training, but are not higher when an athlete strength trains on a regular basis.

It is reasonable to assume that the protein needs of masters athletes are similar to younger athletes. It is important to remember that in research studies, energy intake is usually adequate to support protein utilization. Athletes who ingest low-calorie diets, less than recommended carbohydrate intakes, or who are in the beginning stages of endurance- or strength-training programs need more protein than those who get sufficient energy and carbohydrate, or are well trained (33). The current recommendations for daily protein intake for athletes of 1.2 to 1.7 g/kg can be used for the masters athlete. The DRIs suggest a range of protein from 10% to 35% of total energy (22) and with such a wide range for protein recommendations, individual assessment of protein needs is imperative.

The recommended daily intake of fat for athletes is approximately 1 g/kg. Fat intake for older active people does not differ from that of younger people (20). A minimum of 10% of energy from fat ensures adequate intake of essential fatty acids, with 30% to 35% of energy from fat as the upper limit recommended by most professional health organizations (34). The DRIs suggest fat ranges of 20% to 35% of total energy (22).

Micronutrients

Ideal vitamin and mineral requirements for older individuals have yet to be established. The DRIs recognize the increased need for some micronutrients in people older than age 50 (35). The DRI for vitamins D, B-6, B-12, and the mineral calcium are higher for older adults, and the DRI for iron is decreased for older women. Deficiencies in micronutrients can impair exercise tolerance, but little is known about the dietary intakes or requirements of masters athletes.

Only a few studies have looked at nutrient intakes in masters athletes. Nieman et al (36) studied completed 3-day food records from 291 masters men and 56 masters women who participated in the 1987 Los Angeles Marathon. The authors used national survey data from USDA Continuing Survey of Food Intakes by Individuals (CSFII) to compare the masters runners' nutrient intakes. The masters men marathoners averaged 2,526 kcal/day vs 2,426 kcal/day for CSFII data from men; the masters women marathoners averaged 1,868 kcal/day vs 1,602 kcal/day. In this study, the marathoners consumed a greater percentage of their energy from carbohydrate and a smaller percentage of energy from fat compared with data for the general population. Nieman et al found that the women runners had low intakes of vitamin D and zinc compared with the RDA (36).

Chatard and colleagues (37) studied 23 French cyclists, runners, swimmers, walkers, and tennis players, mean age 63 years. Dietary intakes were recorded twice during 3 consecutive weekdays and compared with the French RDA. The athletes consumed a mean of 2,760 kcal/day compared with the RDA of 2,200 kcal/day, 24% more than the recommended energy intake for the general population. Despite the higher energy intakes, the men still had intakes of vitamin D and magnesium that were lower than the French RDA.

A 2003 study (38) of 25 female masters cyclists and runners (mean age 50.4 years) compared supplement users with non–supplement users. Compared to the non-supplementing athletes, those who took dietary supplements consumed significantly more vitamin C (1,042 mg vs 147 mg), vitamin E (268 mg vs 13 mg), calcium (1,000 mg vs 791 mg), and magnesium (601 mg vs 366 mg). When the diets of the athletes who took supplements were analyzed without the supplements, their mean intakes of vitamin D, vitamin E, folic acid, calcium, magnesium, and zinc were less than the DRI.

Although limited studies have shown that masters athletes have increased energy intake, it is often assumed that higher energy intakes will result in improved nutrient intakes. However, that is not always true for all nutrients. Professionals working with masters athletes should pay close attention to vitamins D, E, B-12, folate, riboflavin, pyridoxine, and the minerals calcium, magnesium, and zinc when assessing diet and performance. Masters athletes in age categories older than 60 years may benefit from synthetic forms of vitamins D and B-12 because absorption and utilization of natural forms may be impaired in aging.

Antioxidant supplements are frequently touted to improve performance and help reduce oxidative damage resulting from exercise. If there is a "down" side to exercise it is the production of free radicals produced during periods of strenuous activity. Although the body increases its natural antioxidant defense systems in the face of activity (39), it is not clear if it is sufficient to fight free radical production without additional antioxidants obtained from supplements (40). Increasing antioxidant rich foods in the diet is one way to increase these nutrients, but for vitamin E, a fat-soluble vitamin, it is often difficult to get the DRI of 15 mg without including plant oils, seeds, and nuts. Although the evidence for using antioxidant supplements to combat free radical production is equivocal, using the Tolerable Upper Intake Level (UL) established in the DRIs (2,000 mg of vitamin C and 1,000 mg of vitamin E), can provide guidance for a sports dietitian working with masters athletes (35).

Food and drug interactions should be monitored in masters athletes who have chronic conditions that require the use of medications. For example, use of thiazide diuretics causes urinary losses of sodium, potassium, and magnesium and use of salicylates and nonsteroidal anti-inflammatory drugs (NSAIDs) may cause iron losses. Such losses must be considered when determining dietary needs of older athletes. Nutrient and drug interactions should also be investigated for those masters athletes taking cholesterol-lowering medications and other hypertension drugs, such as angiotensin-converting enzyme inhibitors.

Much remains to be learned about the effect of aging and activity on micronutrient intakes. Blumberg and Meydani (41) point out that there is little evidence to support an ergogenic effect of increased intakes of vitamins or minerals; however, optimal intakes of nutrients show promise to reduce tissue injury resulting from exercise.

Fluids

There are several reasons to be concerned about hydration status in masters athletes. First, older adults have less body water. Body water decreases to about 60% to 70% in older adults, from a high of 80% in infancy (42). Second, thirst sensation decreases with age. Body water regulation relies on thirst to control water intake (42). Third, after the age of 40, renal mass declines with a subsequent decrease in renal blood flow. The ability of the older kidney to concentrate urine decreases, meaning more water is needed to remove waste products (42). In addition, sweat glands change as the skin ages with less sweat produced per gland with aging (43). Normal age-related changes in thirst and fluid requirements, coupled with the increased need for fluids in the exercising individual, make this a topic of paramount concern to masters athletes.

Kenney and Anderson (44) conducted several studies on the effect of exercise in older persons and fluid needs. In 1988 they studied 16 women (8 older women, mean age 56 years; and 8 younger women, mean age 25 years) exercising in hot, dry environments and warm, humid environments. Subjects exercised on a motor-driven treadmill for 2 hours at 35% to 40% VO_{2max} and were not allowed to consume fluids during the trials. Four of the older women were unable to complete either the hot-dry or warm-humid exercise trials. In the warm-humid environment, older women sweat at a rate equal to young women, but in the hot-dry environment the older women sweat less. The authors suggest that older women retain the ability to produce high sweat rates, but the sweat rate may be altered if adequate hydration is not available (44).

Zappe et al (45) studied 12 men (6 active older men, 62 to 70 years, and 6 young men, 17 to 34 years) to assess whether older active men showed an expansion of fluid volume after repeated exercise, as is seen in younger men. Subjects exercised with a cycle ergometer at 50% VO_{2max} for 90 minutes on 4 successive days. No fluids were given during exercise, but 3 mL/kg of sport drinks was given at the end of exercise. During the 4 days of exercise, the older subjects were able to maintain body fluid and electrolyte balance similar to the younger subjects. However, the older subjects did not increase their plasma volume compared with the younger men. The older men had a blunted thirst effect in the face of loss of body water (45).

Kenney (44) notes that older athletes can exercise in hot environments and can tolerate the heat stress as well as younger athletes of similar VO_{2max}, acclimatization state, body size, and composition. However, there are subtle age-related differences in the blood flow to the skin and body fluid balance. Masters athletes who are well conditioned and acclimatized to the heat should not suffer adverse effects associated with normal aging. Kenney believes that the ability to exercise in warm environments is less a function of aging than physiological health and functional capacity (46,47). Box 14.2 (47) gives tips for older athletes exercising in hot or humid conditions.

The "graying" of the population brings challenges and opportunities to athletes. Today, older people run marathons, climb mountains, skydive, swim competitively, and hike the 2,160-mile Appalachian Trail. Consider these feats by masters athletes:

- Eamonn Coghlan, a dominating indoor runner in the mid 1970s and 1980s, was the first man older than 40 to break the 4-minute mile.
- Priscilla Welch, a 58-year-old lifelong marathoner, was recently named the best female masters marathoner in history by *Runner's World*. At age 42 she won the overall women's title at the New York City marathon—the oldest woman to claim that honor.
- Nolan Ryan played major league baseball for 27 seasons and was still hurling his fastball at 95 miles per hour at the age of 45.

> ## Box 14.2   Fluid Tips for Older Athletes in Hot or Humid Conditions
>
> - *Acclimate.* Perform about half of your usual exercise on the first few days of hot weather. Decrease the duration or slow down the pace, then gradually build it back up.
> - *Hydrate.* Drink about 16 oz of fluid 30 to 40 minutes before exercise and at least 8 oz every 15 minutes during exercise. Weigh yourself before and after exercise. After exercise, drink enough fluid to get back to, or near, the pre-exercise weight over a 2-hour period. Eat foods with high water content. Use a sport drink to restore lost electrolytes and keep the drive to drink alive.
> - *Use common sense.* If you are concerned that it is too hot to exercise, it probably is.
> - *Learn about exercise in the heat.* Pay attention to warning signs and symptoms of dehydration, heat exhaustion, and heat stroke.
>
> *Source:* Data are from reference 47.

- Boxer George Foreman, who is now well known for his low-fat grilling techniques, won the world heavy-weight championship 2 months shy of his 46th birthday.

Summary

The evidence is clear that a vigorous lifestyle can be maintained by many older people. Although there is minimal research on the nutritional needs of masters athletes, several conclusions can be drawn. Metabolic rate is driven by lean tissue and physical activity. Older adults who remain physically active have the same needs for energy as an active younger athlete. Energy intake should be adjusted when training volume decreases. Fluid may be the most important nutrient for masters athletes—a programmed schedule of drinking can reduce the risk for dehydration. Carbohydrate, protein, and fat recommendations are the same as for younger athletes, but older adults should pay special attention to vitamin and mineral intakes and a "senior" type multivitamin/mineral supplement may be a good addition to supplement dietary intake. "Senior" formulated vitamin/mineral supplements contain less iron with more vitamins B-12, B-6, and D.

References

1. Grech P. Athletics: pulling down the age barrier. April 22, 2003. Available at: http://www.runnersweb.com. Accessed January 10, 2004.
2. Chernoff R. Demographics of aging. In: Chernoff R, ed. *Geriatric Nutrition: The Health Professional's Handbook.* 2nd ed. Gaithersburg, Md: Aspen Publishers; 1999:1–12.
3. US Department of Health and Human Services. Administration on Aging. *A Profile of Older Americans: 2001.* Available at: http://www.aoa.gov/prof/Statistics/profile/2001/2001profile.pdf. Accessed November 11, 2004.

4. Dychtwald K. Introduction: healthy aging or Tithonius' revenge? In: Dychtwald K, ed. *Healthy Aging: Challenges and Solutions.* Gaithersburg, Md: Aspen Publishers; 1999:1–16.

5. *38 Million Boomers to Be 50+ by 2005: Insights to Help You Tap This Trillion Dollar Market.* New York, NY; FIND/SVP, Inc; 2002.

6. US Dept Health and Human Services. *Physical Activity and Health: A Report of the Surgeon General.* Atlanta, Ga: US Dept Health and Human Services, Centers for Disease Control and Prevention, National Center for Chronic Disease Prevention and Health Promotion; 1996.

7. US Department of Health and Human Services. *Healthy People 2010.* 2nd ed. Washington, DC, US Government Printing Office; 2000.

8. Robert Wood Johnson Foundation. *National Blueprint: Increasing Physical Activity Among Adults Age 50 and Older.* Princeton, New Jersey: Robert Wood Johnson Foundation; 2001. Available at: http://www.rwjf.org/publications/publicationsPdfs/Age50_Blueprint_singlepages.pdf. Accessed November 11, 2004.

9. Shephard RJ. Aging and exercise. In: Fahey TD, ed. *Encyclopedia of Sports Medicine and Science.* Internet Society for Sport Science. Available at: http://www.sportsci.org. Accessed January 10, 2004.

10. Astrand PO. Exercise physiology of the mature athlete. In: Sutton JR, Brock RM, eds. *Sports Medicine for the Mature Athlete.* Indianapolis, Ind: Benchmark Press; 1986:3–13.

11. Wiswell RA, Jaque SV, Marcell TJ, Hawkins SA, Tarpenning KM, Constantino N, Hyslop DM. Maximal aerobic power, lactate threshold, and running performance in master athletes. *Med Sci Sports Exerc.* 2000;32:1165–1170.

12. Katzel LI, Sorkin JD, Fleg JL. A comparison of longitudinal changes in aerobic fitness in older endurance athletes and sedentary men. *J Am Geriatr Soc.* 2001;49:1657–1664.

13. Evans WJ. Effects of aging and exercise on nutrition needs of the elderly. *Nutr Rev.* 1996;54(suppl):S35–S39.

14. Shephard RJ, Kavanagh T, Mertens DJ, Qureshi S, Clark M. Personal health benefits of Masters athletic competition. *Br J Sports Med.* 1995;29:35–40.

15. Morgan WP, Costill DL. Selected psychological characteristics and health behaviors of aging marathon runners: a longitudinal study. *Int J Sports Med.* 1996;17:305–312.

16. Seals DR, Allen WK, Hurley BF, Dalsky GP, Ehsani AA, Hagberg JM. Elevated high-density lipoprotein cholesterol levels in older endurance athletes. *Am J Cardiol.* 1984;54:390–393.

17. Mengelkoch LJ, Pollock ML, Limacher MC, Graves JE, Shireman RB, Riley WJ, Lowenthal DT, Leon AS. Effects of age, physical training, and physical fitness on coronary heart disease risk factors in older track athletes at twenty-year follow-up. *J Am Geriatr Soc.* 1997;45:1446–1453.

18. Giada F, Vigna GB, Vitale E, Baldo-Enzi G, Bertaglia M, Crecca R, Fellin R. Effect of age on the response of blood lipids, body composition, and aerobic power to physical conditioning and deconditioning. *Metabolism.* 1995;44:161–165.

19. Seals DR, Hagberg JM, Allen WK, Dalsky GP, Ehsani AA, Holloszy JO. Glucose tolerance in young and older athletes and sedentary men. *J Appl Physiol.* 1984;56:1521–1525.

20. Carter WJ. Macronutrient requirements for elderly persons. In: Chernoff R, ed. *Geriatric Nutrition: The Health Professional's Handbook.* 2nd ed. Gaithersburg, Md: Aspen Publishers; 1999;13–26.

21. Van Pelt RE, Dinneno FA, Seals DR, Jones PP. Age-related decline in RMR in physically active men: relation to exercise volume and energy intake. *Am J Physiol Endocrinol Metab.* 2001;281:E633–E639.

22. Institute of Medicine. *Dietary Reference Intakes for Energy, Carbohydrates, Fiber, Fat, Protein, and Amino Acids (Macronutrients).* Washington, DC: National Academy Press; 2002. Available at: http://www.nap.edu/books. Accessed July 26, 2004.

23. Bunyard LB, Katzel LI, Busby-Whitehead MJ, Wu Z, Goldberg AP. Energy requirements of middle-aged men are modifiable by physical activity. *Am J Clin Nutr.* 1998;86:1136–1142.

24. Wilmore JH, Stanforth PR, Hudspeth LA, Gagnon J, Daw EW, Leon AS, Rao, DC, Skinner JS, Bouchard C. Alterations in resting metabolic rate as a consequence of 20 wk of endurance training: the HERITAGE Family Study. *Am J Clin Nutr.* 1998;68:66–71.

25. Campbell WW, Crim MC, Young VR, Evan WJ. Increased energy requirements and changes in body composition with resistance training in older adults. *Am J Clin Nutr.* 1994;60:167–175.

26. Starling RD. Energy expenditure and aging: effects of physical activity. *Int J Sport Nutr Exerc Metab.* 2001;11(suppl):S208–S217.

27. Lundholm K, Holm G, Lindmark L, Larrson B, Sjostrom L, Bjorntop P. Thermogenic effect of food in physically well trained elderly men. *Eur J Appl Physiol.* 1986;55:486–492.

28. Jones, PP, Van Pelt RE, Johnson DG, Seals DR. Role of sympathetic neural activation in age- and habitual exercise-related differences in the thermic effect of food. *J Clin Endrocrinol Metab.* 2004;89:5138–5144.

29. Burke LM, Cox GR, Culmmings NK, Desbrow B. Guidelines for daily carbohydrate intake: do athletes need them? *Sports Med.* 2001;31:267–299.

30. Tipton KD, Rasmussen BB, Miller SL, Wolf SE, Owens-Stovall SK, Petrini BE, Wolfe RR. Timing of amino acid-carbohydrate ingestion alters anabolic response of muscle to resistance exercise. *Am J Physiol Endocrinol Metab.* 2001;281:E197–E206.

31. Meredith CN, Zacklin WR, Frontera WR, Evans WJ. Dietary protein requirements and body protein metabolism in endurance-trained men. *J Appl Physiol.* 1989;66:2850–2856.

32. Campbell WW, Crim MC, Young VR, Joseph LJ, Evans WJ. Effects of resistance training and dietary protein intake on protein metabolism in older adults. *Am J Physiol.* 1995;268:E1143–E1153.

33. Lemon PWR. Effects of exercise on dietary protein requirements. *Int J Sport Nutr.* 1998;8: 426–447.

34. Krauss RM, Eckel RH, Howard B, Appel LJ, Daniels SR, Dickelbaum RJ, Erdman JW, Kris-Etherton P, Goldberg IJ, Kotchen TA, Lichtenstein AH, Mitch WE, Mullis R, Robinson K, Wylie-Rosett J, St Jeor S, Suttie J, Tribble DL, Bazzarre T. AHA Dietary Guidelines: Revision 2000: a statement for healthcare professionals from the Nutrition Committee of the American Heart Association. *Circulation.* 2000;102:2296–2311.

35. Food and Nutrition Board. *Dietary Reference Intakes: Recommended Intakes for Individuals.* Washington, DC: National Academy Press; 1998.

36. Nieman DC, Butler JC, Pollett LM, Dietrich, SJ, Lutz RD. Nutrient intake of marathon runners. *J Am Diet Assoc.* 1989;89:1273–1278.

37. Chatard JC, Boutet C, Tourny C, Garcia S, Berthouze S, Guezennee CY. Nutritional status and physical fitness in elderly sportsmen. *Eur J Appl Physiol.* 1998;77:157–163.

38. Beshgetoor D, Nichols JF. Dietary intake and supplement use in female master cyclists and runners. *Int J Sport Nutr Exerc Metab.* 2003;13:166–172.

39. Powers SK, Criswell D, Lawler J, Martin D, Lieu F, Ji L, Herb RA. Rigorous exercise training increases superoxide dismutase activity in ventricular myocardium. *Am J Physiol.* 1998;265: H2094–H2098.

40. Clarkson PM, Thompson HS. Antioxidants: what role do they play in physical activity and health? *Am J Clin Nutr.* 2000;72(2 Suppl):637S–646S.

41. Blumberg JB, Meydani M. The relationship between nutrition and exercise in older adults. In: Lamb DR, Gisolfi CV, Nadal E, eds. *Perspectives in Exercise Science and Sports Medicine: Exercise in Older Adults.* Vol 8. Carmel, Ind: Cooper Publishing Group; 1995:353–394.

42. Chernoff R. Thirst and fluid requirements. *Nutr Rev.* 1994;52(suppl):S3–S5.

43. Kenney WL, Fowler SR, Methylcholine-activated eccrine sweat gland density and output as a function of age. *J Appl Physiol.* 1988;65:1082–1086.

44. Kenney WL, Anderson RK. Responses of older and younger women to exercise in dry and humid heat without fluid replacement. *Med Sci Sports Exerc.* 1988;20:155–160.

45. Zappe DH, Bell GW, Swartzentruber H, Wideman RF, Kenney WL. Age and regulation of fluid and electrolyte balance during repeated exercise sessions. *Am J Physiol.* 1996;270:R71–R79.

46. Kenney WL. Are there special hydration requirements for older individuals engaged in exercise? *Austral J Nutr Diet.* 1996;53(suppl):S43–S44.

47. Kenney WL. The older athlete: exercise in hot environments. *Sports Sci Exch.* 1993;6(3). Available at: http://www.gssiweb.com. Accessed November 11, 2004.

Chapter 15

ELITE ATHLETES

Louise M. Burke, PhD, APD, FACSM

Introduction

The usual working definition of *elite* is "the best" or "the chosen few." In the world of sport, this title is often bestowed on a wide range of athletes based on subjective judgments, rather than any objective criteria of excellence in terms of physiological characteristics or sporting achievement. This chapter addresses the nutritional needs of athletes who have reached the professional, world-class, or Olympic rank in their respective sports. These athletes have special nutritional requirements or challenges as a result of their extreme levels of training and competition, as well as the lifestyle that underpins their sporting involvement.

There are many reasons sports dietitians and sports nutritionists are drawn to work with top athletes, including the following (1):

- These athletes are often operating at the extremes of human nutrition and physiological capacity. It is fascinating to see what the human body can achieve and how it must be fueled to reach this level of operation.
- Elite athletes represent a motivated group of clients who seek and appreciate the nutrition advice that they are offered and usually adhere to recommendations.
- Sports dietitians have the opportunity to work with famous people and in high-profile situations. The work is glamorous and can publicize a private practice.
- Sports dietitians are surrounded by inspired and inspiring people. They become participants in the excitement and emotion of high-level sports competitions.
- The work can provide opportunities to travel.
- Sports nutrition is a precise discipline with tangible benefits. The athlete and the sports dietitian receive short-term rewards and rapid feedback about the success of their nutrition strategies.
- The work draws on the sports dietitian's creativity and ingenuity to find practical strategies to address the athlete's unique nutritional challenges. Finding individualized solutions to these problems is interesting and challenging.

Of course these and other ideas about working with elite athletes are usually just perceptions, and some ideas are ill-founded. For example, many dietetics students are interested in sports nutrition as an alternative to a professional career of weight-loss counseling. Yet, the most common reason for athletes to seek the help of a sports dietitian is to reduce weight or body fat. This chapter will provide an overview of some of the nutritional issues that are important to top level athletes, as well as strategies for the sports dietitian to work successfully with such clients.

The Structure of High-Level Sport—Implications for Nutritional Needs and Practice

There are several characteristics of high-level sports that create special nutritional needs or challenges for the athletes involved. These include the following:

- Heavy training load
- Demanding competition schedule
- Frequent travel
- Unusual environments for training adaptations or competition preparation (heat, altitude)
- The culture of sport: the price and rewards of fame and publicity
- Influence and power of coaches and other personnel involved with the athlete

Although there are clear differences between sports, the elite or professional athlete typically trains 15 to 30 hours each week. Because this usually involves moderate- to high-intensity exercise, the training program typically results in a high energy cost, high carbohydrate needs, and substantial losses of fluids and electrolytes through sweating. Additionally, there is evidence, albeit inconclusive, that training increases daily requirements for other nutrients, including iron (2) and protein (3) (see Section 1 of this book for information on individual nutrients).

It is generally presumed that any increases in nutrient requirements are met within a well-chosen and varied diet that meets the athlete's increased energy needs. However, very few studies have been conducted on the dietary practices of the world's top athletes and much of the available literature fails to address the potential for biased data due to the limitations of dietary survey methodology (4). Even fewer studies have measured indexes of nutritional status among top athletes. Nevertheless, it seems that most elite male athletes at least have the potential to consume diets that meet the present guidelines for sports nutrition. By contrast, elite female athletes are at greater general risk of suboptimal intakes of a range of nutrients due to their apparent restriction of energy intakes and pursuit of fad diets due to concerns about body mass and body fat. Other athletes at risk are those involved in weight controlled or weight-division sports (eg, boxing, wrestling, weightlifting, lightweight rowing, etc) for which preparation for competition often involves severe energy restriction (5).

The competition schedule of the elite athlete usually presents a different set of nutritional and lifestyle challenges to the training situation. In general, athletes organize their training to "peak" for one to three major competitions each year; however, most will compete in several other events each year. Athletes use these minor competitions to practice and fine-tune their strategies for key events, or to provide themselves with a high-quality "training" session for the more important competitions.

In addition, each competition may involve more than one round of events (ie, heats, semifinals, and finals) that ultimately decide the final outcome. Other sports, particularly team sports, can be played in a tournament format with a series of games being undertaken every 24 to 48 hours. In team sports played in a seasonal fixture, the traditional weekly game has now developed into a more demanding competition program at the elite level of competition. In fact, it is not unusual for professional soccer and basketball players to play a match every 2 or 3 days, especially when the player or the team is entered into more than one association or league (6).

During such competition phases, the athlete is usually focused on acute issues of refueling and rehydration—undertaking special eating strategies before, during, and after an event to meet the needs of their event. Travel and other factors that limit food availability can often challenge the athlete to meet immediate nutritional goals, not to mention "the big picture" issues of energy balance, and overall macro- and micronutrient needs. The sports dietitian needs to be creative in helping the athlete achieve strategies such as carbohydrate loading, an optimal pre-event meal, intake during an event, and proactive recovery eating. However, when competition makes up a significant proportion of the elite athlete's life and total eating patterns—for example, professional cyclists who compete approximately 100 days each year and ride in stage races lasting up to 3 weeks in duration (7)—there is a need for competition nutrition strategies to include all dietary goals.

The lifestyle of most top-level athletes is busy and irregular. At entry point into an elite sport, many younger athletes need to juggle training and events around the commitments of high school and college. Because many sports are not wholly "professional" or financially rewarding, some top-class athletes must continue to work part- or full-time in addition to their sporting commitments. Meals and snacks eaten during the day must fit into their lifestyles (eg, work, school, and family commitments). A chaotic or displaced eating pattern may challenge the ability of some athletes to meet the high energy and nutrient requirements associated with dimensional and muscular growth, training, and recovery— in particular, prolonged sessions of high-intensity work or resistance-training programs designed to increase muscle size and strength.

Professional (or otherwise "full-time") athletes generally have the luxury of spreading their training schedule, and other commitments such as medical and testing appointments or team activities, over the day. However, sometimes during periods of multiple daily practices, training camps, or competition travel, the athlete is faced with a busy timetable that interferes with a normal eating schedule. At other times, they are left with a considerable amount of time on their hands during the day. In some situations, eating becomes a form of entertainment, which can lead to nutritional problems such as the intake of unnecessary amounts or inappropriate choices of food. In both situations, it is important for the athlete to have a clear understanding of their nutritional goals and formulate an eating program that can achieve such goals.

Travel plays a major role in the lifestyle of the elite athlete, with most world-class athletes traveling within their own state or country as well as internationally to compete or find specialized training opportunities. Travel disrupts both the athlete's normal eating routine and access to their preferred foods, and also exposes them to different types of food and water hygiene. The elite athlete needs to become an organized traveler, identify the challenges of their intended locations before the trip, and planning to circumvent potential problems. The travel plan may include organizing catering needs and menus before the trip. In addition, supplies of special foods and drinks may be taken on the trip to complement these catering plans or to make up for the absence of key nutrients or favorite foods.

Often, competitions or specialized training protocols occur in physiologically challenging environments such as a hot climate or moderate altitude. For example, the 2008 Summer Olympics will be in very hot weather in Beijing. In such cases, the athlete usually undertakes a period of acclimatization in a similar environment, or in a chamber that can simulate the same characteristics as the competition site. This is done as a final preparation for the competition. However, on other occasions the athlete may choose to train in hot conditions or at a high altitude (or simulated altitude) to gain physiological adaptations that will be applied to a moderate weather or sea-level environment. Nutritional requirements during these specialized periods will reflect both the type of training, ranging from a precompetition taper to a period of intensified training, as well as the additional needs posed by heat or altitude. In each of these environmental conditions, an increase in sweat losses and carbohydrate use may be expected compared with exercise in a control condition (8). As a result, the athlete will need to focus on appropriate carbohydrate and fluid replacement strategies before, during, and after each exercise session, as well as throughout the day. Iron and micronutrient requirements may increase under these conditions.

The elite levels of sport have their own specialized environments, which include not only the physical aspects of club rooms and training and competition venues, but also the culture of each sport. This often means that the athlete is desperate to find dietary short cuts or "magic bullets," becoming an easy target for the unsupported claims made for fad diets, dietary supplements, and other unusual eating strategies. The athlete is not only susceptible, but is often specifically targeted by companies and individuals who recognize the benefits of being associated with a high-profile individual or team.

Many sports provide an insular world where high-level athletes swap ideas and theories with their peers, trainers and coaches, or through material on the Internet and in sports magazines. Sports dietitians need to break into these circles to be aware of the latest trends and ideas. They must also contend with a wide array of other, often influential, sources of nutrition advice directed at the athlete. They may also have to fight for the athlete's time, concentration, or resources—these are often limited and must be shared with other sports science and medical professionals, the media, managers, and the coaching and training staff. On the positive side, most top-level athletes take a professional approach to the preparation for their sport and will make effective use of information and practical advice. The structure of many high-level teams and sporting organizations is to surround their athletes with a group of professionals specializing in sports science/medicine and training/conditioning. It is both efficient and rewarding to be part of such a support network.

Nutritional Issues

Meeting Energy and Fuel Needs Across a Range of Extremes

An athlete's energy intake is of interest for several reasons (9):

- It sets the potential for achieving the athlete's requirements for energy-containing macronutrients (especially protein and carbohydrate), and the food needed to provide vitamins, minerals, and other non–energy-containing dietary compounds required for optimal function and health.

- It assists the manipulation of muscle mass and body fat levels to achieve the specific body composition that is ideal for athletic performance.
- It affects the function of hormonal and immune systems.
- It challenges the practical limits to food intake set by issues such as food availability and gastrointestinal comfort.

The total energy expenditure of each athlete is unique, arising from the contribution of basal metabolic rate, the thermic effects of food, and exercise, and in some cases growth (10). Energy expenditure is increased by high levels of lean body mass, growth (including the desired adaptations to a resistance-training program), and a high volume training program. For some elite athletes these three factors co-exist to create very large energy demands—for example, the male swimmer or rower who faces an increase in training commitment during periods of adolescent growth spurts. Other elite athletes have very large energy requirements due to the extraordinary fuel demands of their competition programs. For example, various studies of cyclists in 2- to 3-week stage races such as the Tour de France or Tour of Spain have reported daily energy requirements and intakes of approximately 24 MJ or 6,000 kcal (11,12).

At such extreme levels of energy demand, the elite athlete is often advised to consume foods and drinks, particularly in the form of carbohydrate and/or protein, at special times or in greater quantities than would be provided in an everyday diet or dictated by their appetite and hunger. The athlete may also need to consume energy during and after exercise when the availability of foods and fluids, or opportunities to consume them, are limited. Practical issues interfering with the achievement of energy intake goals during post-exercise recovery include loss of appetite and fatigue, poor access to suitable foods, and distraction from other activities.

In contrast, other elite athletes have low-moderate energy needs—particularly when they are trying to lose body weight or maintain low levels of body fat, and are involved in a sport in which training, however prolonged, is based on skill rather than energy expenditure, such as gymnastics, archery, or baseball. Such athletes face many practical challenges in satisfying their nutritional goals and appetite with a smaller energy budget. Specialized advice from a sports dietitian is often useful to assist in the achievement of the energy intake challenges faced by individual athletes (see Box 15.1 [9] as well as Chapter 11).

The "Ideal" Body Composition for Optimal Performance

Physical characteristics, including height, limb lengths, total body mass (weight), muscle mass, and body fat can all play a role in the performance of sport. Many elite athletes are subjected to rigid criteria for an "ideal physique," based on the characteristics of other successful competitors. The pressure to conform to such an ideal comes from the athlete's own perfectionism and drive to succeed as well as the influence of coaches, trainers, other athletes, and the media. Although information about the characteristics of other elite athletes is useful, it fails to take into account the considerable variability in the physical characteristics of people, even between individuals in the same sport. It also fails to acknowledge that sometimes it takes many years of training and maturation for an athlete to finally achieve their ideal shape and body composition. Therefore it is dangerous to establish rigid

---

Box 15.1   Guidelines for Achieving High Energy Intakes by Elite Athletes

Meal Spacing
- Use a food diary to identify *actual* intake rather than perceived intake.
- Consume carbohydrate during prolonged exercises to provide fuel and additional energy.
- Eat a carbohydrate and protein snack after exercise to enhance recovery and increase total daily energy intake.

Food Availability
- Shop for food and prepare meals in advance of hectic periods.
- Overcome postexercise fatigue by preparing meals and snacks in advance.
- When traveling, take snacks that can be easily prepared and eaten (eg, cereal and powdered milk, granola and sport bars, liquid meal supplements, and dried fruit and nuts).
- Have snacks and light meals available at home (eg, fruit, fruit smoothies, yogurt and sandwiches).
- Consider specialized products such as sport drinks, gels and bars during exercise and sport bars and liquid meal supplements after exercise. (In most training situations, athletes will need to provide their own products.)

Appetite Management and Gastric Comfort
- Reduce gastric discomfort with small frequent meals.
- Drink liquid meal supplements, flavored milk, fruit smoothies, sport drinks, soft drinks, and juices to provide energy, nutrients, and fluids.
- Choose energy-dense meals and snacks, including sugar-rich foods.
- Avoid excessive intake of high-fiber foods, which may limit total energy intake or lead to gastrointestinal discomfort.
- Appetite-suppression may be overcome with small pieces or easy-to-eat foods that do not require considerable cutting and chewing (eg, fruit, sandwiches served as "finger-foods," or a stir-fry).
- Consider postexercise environmental conditions. Heat and dehydration may be matched by cool and liquid-based choices such as fruit smoothies, yogurt, or ice cream. In cold conditions, warm soup, toasted sandwiches, or pizza may be more appetizing.

Source: Data are from reference 9.

---

prescriptions for individuals, particularly with regard to body weight or body fat levels. A preferable strategy is to use a range of acceptable values for body fat and body weight within each sport, and then monitor the health and performance of individual athletes within this range. Sequential profiling of an athlete can monitor the development of physical characteristics that are associated with good performance for that individual, as well as identify the changes in physique that can be expected over a season or period of specialized training.

A reduction in body mass, particularly through loss of body fat, is a common nutritional goal of elite athletes. There are situations when an athlete is clearly carrying excess body fat and will improve their health and performance by reducing body fat levels. This may occur due to heredity or lifestyle factors, or because the athlete has been in a situation where a sudden change in energy expenditure has occurred without a compensatory change in energy intake—for example, the athlete has failed to reduce energy intake while injured or taking a break from training. Loss of body fat should be achieved through a program based on a sustained and moderate energy deficit, usually no more than 500 kcal deficit daily.

However, in many sports in which a low body mass or body fat level offers distinct advantages to performance, fat loss has become a focus or even obsession. The benefits of leanness can be seen in terms of the energy cost of movement (eg, distance running, cycling), the physics of movement in a tight space or against gravity (eg, gymnastics, diving, cycling uphill) or aesthetics (eg, gymnastics, body building). In many such "weight-conscious" or "body fat-conscious" sports, elite athletes now strive to achieve minimum body fat levels per se, with many trying to reduce their body fat below the level that seems "natural" or "healthy" for them. In the short-term, this may produce an improvement in performance. However, the long-term disadvantages include outcomes related to having very low body-fat stores, as well as the problems associated with unsound weight-loss methods. Excessive training, chronically low intakes of energy and nutrients, and psychological distress are often involved in fat-loss strategies and may cause long-term damage to health, well-being, or performance (13). In recent years, some high-profile athletes have died as an apparent result of unsafe weight-loss techniques, including training while severely restricting energy, dehydration, and the use of ephedrine-containing fat-loss supplements (14).

Do the Results of Studies on Recreational Athletes Apply to Elite Athletes?

Some people think that sports foods and supplements or sports nutrition strategies such as carbohydrate loading are targeted at the elite athlete. It is true that the pressures and rewards for optimal performance are greater at this level and may justify the expense or effort involved in addressing special nutritional needs. However, it is interesting to note that the majority of studies on sports nutrition strategies involve subjects within the spectrum from recreationally active to well-trained. In fact, few intervention studies have involved world-class or elite athletes. This is understandable, of course, because by definition elite athletes are a scarce resource, and it is difficult to arrange a study that does not conflict with their commitments to training and competition (15). However, elite athletes almost certainly have genetic endowment, and acquired traits gained from their training history and training programs that differ from those of subelite athletes. Therefore, because the results of a research study apply with reasonable certainty only to populations that have similar characteristics to the sample involved in the investigation, it is not clear if elite athletes will respond in the same way to strategies that have been tested on subelite or recreational competitors. An elite athlete may benefit from something that has no detectable effect on recreational athletes. Conversely, strategies that enhance the performance of a recreational performer may not benefit the elite athlete.

Dietetics professionals are already familiar with the possibility of individual variability in response to strategies such as caffeine (16) and creatine supplementation (17), although at this stage there is no practical way to distinguish between responders and non-responders or to suspect that training status or genetic characteristics of elite athletes are responsible for differences. Nevertheless, it is possible that certain nutritional strategies "work" by achieving similar benefits to that achieved by a long history or volume of training. Genetics may also play a role in helping an athlete excel in a particular sport. Therefore, in the hands of the elite athlete, a nutritional strategy may have less effect on systems that have already been optimized.

For some treatments, variations in outcomes in the field may be expected because the real-life practices of elite athletes do not conform to the conditions that were used when the nutritional practice was tested in the laboratory. For example, many studies are done with subjects in a fasted state, drinking only water during an exercise session. The results may be different when the same intervention after a carbohydrate-rich meal (18). At other times, elite athletes may choose or be forced by the circumstances of their event not to follow the existing guidelines. For example, world-class marathon runners typically drink at rates of around 200 to 600 mL per hour during races, despite hydration guidelines that promote higher rates of intake to better match sweat losses (19). Because these runners are relatively successful (ie, they are the race winners), it is hard to argue that closer adherence to the guidelines is needed.

In summary, at present there is insufficient information to make different recommendations for elite athletes regarding sports nutrition practice other than to recognize that the rules and conditions of their events may provide logistical challenges to fulfilling the existing guidelines. However, sports scientists are encouraged to conduct research with elite athletes and the real-life conditions under which their sport is played so that recommendations can be fine-tuned.

Evaluating the Benefits of Supplements When Winning Margins Can Be Measured in Decimals

Most scientific investigations of supplements are biased toward rejecting the hypothesis that the product enhances performance. This bias is due to small sample sizes, performance testing protocols with low reliability, and the use of "statistical significance" to decide whether there was a difference between a treatment and a control or placebo condition. In other words, the framework of most intervention studies is sufficient only to detect large differences in performance outcomes. Yet, most competitions in elite sport are decided by millimeters and fractions of seconds, and many high-level athletes would be happy to consider any supplement or nutrition intervention that could enhance their performance by this tiniest of margins.

Hopkins et al (15) have discussed alternative ways to detect worthwhile performance enhancements in elite sports. This paper considers the challenges in finding middle ground between what scientists and athletes consider "significant." An athlete's required improvement is not the small margin between those who place among the top finishers in a race. Instead, the needed improvement is influenced by a factor related to the day-to-day variability in performance in such an event. By modeling the results of various sporting events, Hopkins and colleagues suggest that "worthwhile" changes to the outcome of most events require a performance difference equal to approximately 0.5 to 1 times the variability (coefficient of variation [CV]) of performance for that event, and that across a range of events the CV of performance of top athletes is usually within the range of 0.5% to 5%.

Such a difference is still outside the realm of detection for many of the studies commonly published in scientific journals. Nevertheless, scientists can interpret their results meaningfully by reporting the outcome as a percentage change in a measure of athletic performance and using 95% confidence limits to describe the likely range of the true effect of the treatment on the average athlete represented in the study (15).

When weighing pros and cons of using a supplement, elite athletes must consider:

- Expense of the product
- Likelihood of product yielding performance benefits
- Risks of adverse effects

A recent addition to this list is the risk of a positive drug test, because "inadvertent doping" through supplement use has emerged as a major concern for athletes who participate in sporting competitions governed by an antidoping code. Some supplements and sports foods contain ingredients from the Proscribed Lists of the World Anti-doping Agency or the international federations governing sports, and an athlete may return a positive drug test after unintentionally consuming a banned substance found in such products. Because supplements are often regarded as harmless or as alternatives to drugs, some athletes may not carefully read product labels to check the ingredient list for banned substances. In addition, there is now growing evidence that some supplements or sports foods contain banned substances as undeclared ingredients or contaminants (20). Sports authorities now warn elite athletes to seek expert advice before using supplements.

Strategies for Working with Elite Athletes

A successful practice with elite athletes requires certain types of strategies and personal characteristics of the sports dietitian. The following ideas can help the sports dietitian to develop a rewarding career.

Getting Started

Be prepared to start at the bottom to gain experience. Look for opportunities to start with local teams and athletes rather than expecting to start with a job with a national sporting organization or major professional team.

Use your existing contacts and involvement in sports to develop a knowledge base and experience. Your own sporting experiences can buy credibility with athletes and coaches, and provide an intimate understanding of what it is like to be an athlete.

Find a mentor. Set a professional development program for yourself that includes regular journal reading and conference attendance—stay up to date with both the science and practice of sports nutrition.

Understanding a Sport and Its Special Features

Learn all you can about how a sport influences nutritional needs of players, as well as current nutrition practices and beliefs. Get specific information about training practices, competition programs, and lifestyle patterns—including individual differences between players on a team and between different sports.

Attend training sessions and events to better understand the culture and experiences of athletes, coaches, and other team members. Let the athletes know that you are interested in their activities.

Stay informed about supplements used or promoted within a sport. Follow the Internet, sports magazines, health food shops and supplement stores, and the general talk among players to stay abreast of current ideas and practices.

Be a Team Player

Identify all the people who work with an athlete or team to provide their nutrition ideas or achieve their nutrition practice. This will include people in the organized support structure and in the personal network that each athlete may develop. Be prepared to listen to the approaches and input of these people, and find a niche in which your services and ideas will be appreciated.

Know when to stand your ground (you are the nutrition expert) and when to be flexible (a compromise of your ideas may be necessary for athletes to accept). Look for middle ground. For example, a coach or trainer may insist that the athlete consume branched-chain amino acids after a training session to promote recovery. Rather than debating whether the present literature provides support for benefits of post-exercise supplementation with amino acid supplements, consider setting up recovery snacks for the team including fruit smoothies, flavored yogurt, and cereal/sports bars. Provide educational material showing the coach and athletes that these snacks provide a good source of branched-chain amino acids (similar to amounts found in supplements) as well as carbohydrate and fluid for refueling and rehydration.

Participate (when invited) in all activities of the athlete or team support network, even if these do not directly seem to involve nutrition. Cultivate relationships between other professionals or team support personnel so that they are aware of what you can do, can provide early referrals of athletes for your specialty services, and can support your nutrition plan when you are not present (eg, during team travel).

Be Creative with Nutrition Activities

Create educational resources that target the needs and the interests of your individual athletes and teams. Use innovative ways to provide information rather than relying on standard interview/consultation or lecture formats. Be prepared to put information or activities into "bite-size" chunks or address the issues that are of immediate interest to your athletes rather than following a standard script.

Plan interactive activities—eg, cooking classes, supermarket tours, installation of recovery snacks at a training or competition venue. These activities provide tangible outcomes. Many people learn better through practical activities.

Tips for Survival in a High-Pressure Environment

Be organized and have definite goals for your activities. Set up a contract with the appropriate person (medical director, head coach, athlete) in which the range of services you can provide is discussed and agreed to. Provide feedback or summary information on completed services so that your input is documented and appreciated.

Don't forget to build in ways of assessing and rewarding your own progress and achievement of goals. It is easy to overlook your own performance when all the focus is on the athletes.

Be prepared for the politics of high-level sport. Coaches and medical staff are frequently abandoned by their athletes, often for no fault of their own. Expect that this will happen to you. Be prepared to pick yourself up and develop a new plan.

References

1. Burke LM. *Applied Sports Nutrition.* Champaign, Ill: Human Kinetics, 2006.
2. Deakin V. Iron depletion in athletes. In: Burke L, Deakin V, eds. *Clinical Sports Nutrition.* 2nd ed. Sydney, Australia: McGraw-Hill; 2000:273–311.
3. Tipton KD, Wolfe RR. Protein and amino acids for athletes. *J Sports Sci.* 2004;22:65–79.
4. Burke LM, Cox GR, Cummings NK, Desbrow B. Guidelines for daily CHO intake: do athletes achieve them? *Sports Med.* 2001;31:267–299.
5. Walberg-Rankin J. Making weight in sports. In: Burke L, Deakin V, eds. *Clinical Sports Nutrition.* 2nd ed. Sydney, Australia: McGraw-Hill; 2000:185–209.
6. Reilly T. Football. In: Reilly T, Secher N, Snell P, Williams C, eds. *Physiology of Sports.* London, England: E & FN Spon; 1990:371–426.
7. Mujika I, Padilla S. Physiological and performance characteristics of male professional road cyclists. *Sports Med.* 2001;31:479–487.
8. Febbraio MA. Exercise at climatic extremes. In: Maughan RJ, ed. *Nutrition in Sport.* Oxford, England: Blackwell Science; 2000:497–509.
9. Burke LM. Energy needs of athletes. *Can J Appl Physiol.* 2001;26(Suppl):S202–S219.
10. Manore M, Thompson J. Energy requirements of the athlete: assessment and evidence of energy efficiency. In: In: Burke L, Deakin V, eds. *Clinical Sports Nutrition.* 2nd ed. Sydney, Australia: McGraw-Hill; 2000:124–145.
11. Garcia-Roves PM, Terrados N, Fernandez SF, Patterson AM. Macronutrients intake of top level cyclists during continuous competition—change in feeding pattern. *Int J Sports Med.* 1998;19:61–67.
12. Saris WHM, Van Erp-Baart MA, Brouns F,Westerterp KR, Ten Hoor F. Study on food intake and energy expenditure during extreme sustained exercise: the Tour de France. *Int J Sports Med.* 1989;10(suppl 1): S26–S31.
13. Otis CL, Drinkwater B, Johnson M, Loucks A, Wilmore J. American College of Sports Medicine position stand: the female athlete triad. *Med Sci Sports Exerc.* 1997;29(5):i–ix.
14. Charatan F. Ephedra supplement may have contributed to sportsman's death. *BMJ.* 2003;326:464.
15. Hopkins WG, Hawley JA, Burke LM. Design and analysis of research on sport performance enhancement. *Med Sci Sports Exerc.* 1999;31:472–485.
16. Graham TE, Spriet LL. Performance and metabolic responses to a high caffeine dose during prolonged exercise. *J Appl Physiol.* 1991;71:2292–2298.
17. Greenhaff PL, Bodin K, Soderlund K, Hultman E. Effect of oral creatine supplementation on skeletal phosphocreatine resynthesis. *Am J Physiol.* 1994;266:E725–E730.
18. Burke LM, Claassen A, Hawley JA, Noakes TD. Carbohydrate intake during prolonged cycling minimizes effect of glycemic index of preexercise meal. *J Appl Physiol.* 1998;85:2220–2226.
19. Noakes TD. IMMDA advisory statement of guidelines for fluid replacement during marathon running. *New Studies in Athletics.* 2002;17:15–24.
20. International Olympic Committee. IOC nutritional supplements study points to need for greater quality controls [press release]. April 4, 2002.

Chapter 16

VEGETARIAN ATHLETES

D. Enette Larson-Meyer, PhD, RD, FACSM

Introduction

Many athletes and active individuals are adopting vegetarian diets for health, ecological, religious, spiritual, economical, and ethical reasons. If they contain a variety of plant foods, vegetarian diets—except fruitarian and strict macrobiotic diets—can meet the nutritional requirements for all types of athletes. Vegetarian athletes, like most athletes, may benefit from education about food choices that provide adequate nutrients to promote optimal performance and good health.

This chapter reviews the energy, macronutrient, vitamin, and mineral requirements of the vegetarian athlete and provides tips for meeting nutrition and fluid needs with a vegetarian diet. The chapter also discusses supplements of interest to vegetarian athletes; nutrition recommendations before, during, and after exercise; special concerns of female vegetarian athletes; and tips for professionals working with vegetarian athletes.

Sports Nutrition Considerations: Energy and Macronutrient Requirements

Energy

The energy needs of active individuals vary considerably and depend on the athlete's body size, body composition, gender, training regimen, and activity pattern. Energy expenditure, assessed by doubly labeled water, is shown to vary from approximately 2,600 kcal/day in female swimmers to approximately 8,500 kcal/day in male cyclists participating in the Tour de France bicycle race (1). The energy requirements of smaller or less active individuals may be slightly less.

In clinical practice, an athlete's total daily energy expenditure (TDEE) must be estimated because methods like doubly labeled water are expensive and impractical (see Chapter 11 for estimation methods and Appendix C for estimates of the energy cost of specific physical activities). It should be noted, however, that resting energy expenditure is acutely elevated after exercise due to increased body temperature, circulation, and ventilation, as well as the additional energy cost required for removing lactate and resynthesizing ATP (2). While this increase is generally small, it may amount to an additional 100 to 200 kcal/day, or more, in athletes training or competing for more than 80 to 90 minutes/day (3).

It is reported that athletes who follow vegetarian diets, and especially those following vegan diets, have difficulty meeting energy requirements due to the low energy density of plant-based diets (4). Although this may be true in some cases, nutrition professionals are likely to encounter active vegetarians with a variety of energy needs. Some will need to consume six to eight meals and snacks per day to meet energy needs. Others may require weight loss for health or performance reasons. Various eating plans have been developed for educating individuals who consume vegetarian or vegan diets (5–8). If necessary, these plans can be modified to meet the increased energy needs of athletes by increasing the number of servings recommended. Box 16.1 contains sample menus for a 3,000-kcal vegetarian diet and a 4,600-kcal vegan diet, energy levels that may be required to meet the needs of individuals who exercise regularly.

Carbohydrate

Carbohydrates should make up the bulk of the athlete's diet. Adequate carbohydrate intake optimizes muscle and liver glycogen stores (9–12) and optimizes performance during prolonged, moderate-intensity exercise (eg, distance running and cycling) (13–16) and during intermittent and short-duration, high-intensity exercise (17,18), which includes sprinting performance at the end of an endurance or intermittent bout of exercise (19,20). Thus, for many athletes and active vegetarians, sufficient carbohydrate intake translates into a longer playing (or exercising) time before fatigue and faster sprinting potential at the end of a race or event.

The benefit of carbohydrate consumption, however, may not be limited to maintenance of glycogen stores. Dietary carbohydrate may also be important for maintenance of Krebs cycle intermediates (13) and preservation of the bioenergetic state of exercising muscle (18), factors also related to muscle fatigue.

The carbohydrate needs of active individuals can be easily met on a vegetarian diet, but active individuals at all levels may benefit from education about carbohydrate recommendations and dietary carbohydrate sources. Active vegetarians should strive to consume the carbohydrate intake for athletes of 6 to 10 g/kg/day recommended by the American College of Sports Medicine, the American Dietetic Association and Dietitians of Canada (21). College, elite, or other competitive athletes in heavy training may benefit from a higher carbohydrate intake and should strive for the upper range of close to 8 to 10 g/kg/day. Conversely, smaller female athletes, those participating at a level that demands less training (eg, recreational exercisers), or those attempting to reduce body weight or fat stores may require only 6 to 7 g carbohydrate per kilogram of body weight. In all cases, carbohydrate exchanges and label-reading exercises are often useful and are usually well-received. Knowledge of carbohydrate sources is also useful in planning carbohydrate intake before, during, and after exercise.

Protein

Protein needs of athletes vary according to the type of activity and level of training. Protein needs of active vegetarians who perform light to moderate activity several times per week

Box 16.1   Sample 3,000-kcal Vegetarian Menu and 4,600-kcal Vegan Menu

3,000 kcal	4,600 kcal
Breakfast	**Breakfast**
1 cup raisin bran	1½ cups raisin bran
1 cup fat-free milk	1 cup fortified soy milk
2 slices mixed-grain toast	1½ cups bran flakes cereal with raisins
2 tsp soy margarine	3 slices mixed-grain toast
1 medium banana	3 tsp soy margarine
8 oz fruit juice	1 medium banana
	8 oz fruit juice
Lunch	**Lunch**
Whole-wheat pita stuffed with shredded spinach, sliced tomato, 2 oz feta cheese, 2 Tbsp olive oil	Tofu salad on a 4-oz hoagie roll (1 cup firm tofu, 2 tsp mustard, 2 tsp soy mayonnaise, lettuce, tomato)
1 large apple	1 large apple
2 small oatmeal cookies	3 small oatmeal cookies
	8 oz carrot juice
Snack	**Snack**
Sesame seed bagel	Sesame seed bagel
1 Tbsp peanut butter	1 Tbsp peanut butter
1 Tbsp jam	1 Tbsp jam
	1 cup fortified soy milk
Dinner	**Dinner**
Lentil spaghetti sauce (1 cup cooked lentils, ½ onion, 1½ cups canned tomatoes, 1 Tbsp olive oil)	Lentil spaghetti sauce (1½ cup cooked lentils, ½ onion, 1½ cups canned tomatoes, 1 Tbsp olive oil)
3 oz dry pasta, cooked	4 oz dry pasta, cooked
1 Tbsp parmesan cheese	3 (1-oz) slices french bread dipped in 2 Tbsp olive oil
2 (1-oz) slices french bread dipped in 1 Tbsp olive oil	1½ cups steamed collards
1 cup steamed broccoli	
Snack	**Snack**
1 cup fruit yogurt	1 cup fruit sorbet
	1 oz toasted almonds

Vegetarian menu: 3,066 kcal, 106 g protein, 469 g carbohydrate, 85 g fat (14% protein, 25% fat, 61% carbohydrate), 1,600 mg calcium, 29 mg iron, 14 mg zinc. Vegan menu: 4,626 kcal, 146 g protein, 704 g carbohydrate, 136 g fat (13% protein, 26% fat, 61% carbohydrate), 1,133 mg calcium, 60 mg iron, 15 mg zinc.

Note: Both menus assume grain products are made from enriched flour.

are likely met by the Recommended Dietary Allowance (RDA) of 0.8 g/kg, but protein requirements of athletes who train more heavily may be considerably more than the RDA. The protein recommendation for endurance athletes is 1.2 to 1.4 g/kg/day, and the recommendation for resistance and strength-training athletes may be as much as 1.6 to 1.7 g/kg/day (21). The rationale for the additional protein in endurance and strength training results from increased protein utilization as an auxiliary fuel during exercise and, to a lesser degree, protein deposition during muscle development.

Inadequate intakes of carbohydrate and total energy also increase protein needs. During prolonged endurance activity, athletes with low glycogen stores metabolize twice as much protein as those with adequate stores, primarily due to increased gluconeogenesis (22). Although there is no research to suggest that protein recommendations are different for vegetarian athletes, it has been suggested that vegetarians may need to consume approximately 10% more protein than omnivores to account for the lower digestibility of plant proteins compared with animal proteins (23). Accordingly, the protein requirements of vegetarian athletes (based on the aforementioned recommendations for athletes) would be approximately 1.3 to 1.8 g/kg (21).

Vegetarian athletes can easily achieve adequate protein if their diets are adequate in energy and contain a variety of plant-based protein foods such as nuts, seeds, legumes, and grains. As reviewed by Young and Pellett (24), vegetarians need not be concerned with eating specific combinations of plant proteins in the same meal as was once believed. Research indicates that consuming an assortment of plant foods during the course of a day can provide all essential amino acids and ensure adequate nitrogen retention and utilization in healthy adults (24,25). Emphasizing amino acid balance at each meal is not appropriate because "limiting amino acids" in one meal are buffered by "free amino acid pools" (24) found primarily in skeletal muscle (26). Furthermore, although some plant foods tend to be low in certain amino acids, usual dietary combinations of protein tend to be "complete" (ie, they provide all essential amino acids) (24).

Vegetarian diets generally contain 12.5% of energy from protein, whereas vegan diets contain 11% (6). Therefore, an 80-kg male athlete consuming 3,600 kcal would receive 1.41 g protein per kilogram of body weight from the average vegetarian diet and 1.2 g/kg from the average vegan diet. A 50-kg female gymnast consuming 2,200 kcal would receive 1.38 g/kg from a vegetarian diet and 1.21 g/kg from a vegan diet. Thus, most vegetarian athletes meet the requirements for endurance training without special meal planning. Strength-training athletes (weightlifters, football players, wrestlers) or those with high training volumes or low energy intakes may need to include more protein-rich foods. This is easily accomplished by encouraging the athlete to add between one and three servings of protein-rich vegetarian foods to their regular meals or snacks (eg, soy milk to a fruit snack, lentils to spaghetti sauce, tofu to stir-fry, or garbanzo beans to salad). Table 16.1 provides a list of commercially available protein-rich vegetarian foods.

Fat

Dietary fat should make up the remainder of energy intake after carbohydrate and protein needs are met. The American College of Sports Medicine, the American Dietetic Association, and Dietitians of Canada recommend that the athlete's diet contain approximately

TABLE 16.1   Nutrient Content of Selected Whole and Commercially Available Protein Foods

Food, Serving Size	Protein, g	Fat, g	Carbohydrate, g	Energy, kcal	Calcium, mg	Iron, mg	Zinc, mg
Legumes*							
Black beans, 1 cup	15	0.9	41	227	46	3.6	1.9
Chickpeas, 1 cup	14.5	4	45	270	80	4.7	2.5
Kidney beans, 1 cup	15	0.9	40	225	62	5.2	1.8
Lentils, 1 cup	18	0.8	40	230	38	6.6	2.5
Pinto beans, 1 cup	15	1.1	45	245	79	3.6	1.7
Tempeh, 1 cup	31	18	16	320	184	4.5	1.9
Tofu, firm, 1 cup	20	11	4	176	507	4.1	2.1
Tofu, soft, 1 cup	16	9	4.5	151	275	2.8	1.6
Vegetarian Burger-Style Patties							
Boca Burger, Vegan Original	13	1	6	80	60	1.8	na
Boca Burger All American Flame Grilled	14	4	5	110	100	1.8	na
Gardenburger, Original	6	3	16	110	60	tr	na
Morningstar Farms Spicy Black Bean Burger	11	4.5	16	150	40	1.8	na
Morningstar Farms Better'N Burgers	13	2	6	100	40	1.8	na
Morningstar Farms Grillers	15	6	5	140	40	1.1	na
Yves Veggie Burger	12	4	4	111	na	5.2	7.8
Vegetarian Burger-Style Crumbles							
Boca Meatless Ground Burger, ½ cup	11	0.5	7	70	80	1.4	na
Morningstar Farms Ground Meatless Crumbles, ½ cup	10	0	4	60	20	1.8	na
Morningstar Farms Grillers Burger Style Recipe Crumbles, ⅔ cup	10	2.5	4	80	20	1.8	na
Vegetarian Chicken-Style Patties and Nuggets							
Boca Chik'n Nuggets, 4 nuggets	15	6	17	180	80	1.8	na
Boca Spicy Chik'n Patties	11	6	12	150	60	1.1	na
Morningstar Farms Chik'n Nuggets, 4 nuggets	12	7	18	190	20	2.7	na
Morningstar Farms Buffalo Wings, 5 nuggets	12	9	18	200	20	2.7	na
Morningstar Farms Chik Patties	9	6	16	150	0	1.8	na

continues

TABLE 16.1 Nutrient Content of Selected Whole and Commercially Available Protein Foods (continued)

Food, Serving Size	Protein, g	Fat, g	Carbohydrate, g	Energy, kcal	Calcium, mg	Iron, mg	Zinc, mg
Yves Veggie Chick'n Patties	15	2.8	5.2	107	nr	4.7	4.8
Vegetarian Dogs							
Morningstar Farms Veggie Dog	11	0.5	6	80	0	0.7	na
Yves Tofu Dog	9	0.5	2	47	20	2.9	0.8
Other							
Boca Bratwurst, 1 each	14	7	6	140	40	1.8	na
Morningstar Farms Corn Dogs, 1 each	7	4	22	150	0	1.1	na
Yves Turkey Slices	15	1.7	4.4	85	na	4.3	4.5
Yves Ham Slices	14	0.2	6.0	80	na	4.3	4.5

Abbreviations: na, not available; tr, trace.

Manufacturers: Boca Foods Co, Madison, WI; Gardenburger Authentic Foods Co, Clearfield, UT; Morningstar Farms, Kellogg Co, Battle Creek, MI; Yves Veggie Cuisine, Vancouver, Canada.

*Legumes are cooked, boiled without salt. Tofu is prepared with calcium sulfate.

Source: Legume and tofu nutrient values obtained from the USDA National Nutrient Database for Standard Reference. Available at: http://www.nal.usda.gov/fnic/foodcomp/search/index.html. Other product nutritional information is obtained from food company Web sites or the food label.

20% to 25% of energy from fat to facilitate adequate carbohydrate intake (21). However, the point should be made that athletes with high energy needs can still meet their carbohydrate and protein requirements on a diet that provides 30% to 40% of energy from fat. An athlete's diet should not be too low in fat, however. Fat is important in the athletes' diet because it provides energy and essential fatty acids. Fat is also needed for absorption of fat-soluble vitamins. Recent research suggests that dietary fat may be necessary for maintaining intramyocellular triglyceride (IMTG) stores (27,28), which is an important fuel source during prolonged, moderate-intensity exercise (29,30). Compromised stores, as a result of heavy training and a low-fat dietary regimen, are thought to impair endurance performance (31). Studies to date, however, have not demonstrated that low IMTG is responsible for the reduced performance associated with very-low-fat diets (31,32).

Some vegetarian athletes, particularly endurance-trained groups (runners and triathletes), may consume excessive carbohydrate and inadequate fat. Similarly, although the extremely low-fat vegetarian diet recommended by Ornish et al (< 10% energy from fat) (33) may be beneficial to those with a history of cardiovascular disease (ie, the post-myocardial infarction [MI] recreational athlete) because it may result in regression of coronary atherosclerosis (33–35), such low-fat diets may be too restrictive for athletes during heavy training (as discussed earlier). Incorporating foods high in mono- and polyunsaturated fats (such as nuts and nut butters, seeds, tahini, avocados, olives, olive oil, and sesame oil) may help vegetarian athletes meet energy and nutrient needs and ensure that nutritional status (36) and IMTGs are not compromised (27,32,37). The importance of fat intake should be emphasized and a minimum of two servings of fat per day from fat-rich plant foods is recommended (5). On the other hand, nutritionists can still expect to encounter vegetarian athletes and active individuals with diets that lack carbohydrates and are too rich in saturated fat, mainly from full-fat dairy products or processed foods.

Sports Nutrition Considerations: Minerals and Vitamins

Calcium and Vitamin D

Regular exercise has not been shown to increase calcium requirements. Thus, athletes and active individuals (between ages 19 and 50) should strive for the recommended Dietary Reference Intake of 1,000 mg calcium per day. Those younger than 18 should strive for 1,300 mg/day and those older than 50 should strive for 1,200 mg/day (38). Evidence suggests that amenorrheic athletes (those not experiencing a menstrual cycle for at least 3 months) may require an intake of 1,500 mg/day to retain calcium balance (39). Low calcium intake has been associated with an increased risk of stress fractures (40) and decreased bone density, particularly in amenorrheic athletes (41).

Eumenorrheic athletes can meet calcium requirements by including several servings of dairy products or 8 servings of calcium-containing plant foods per day. Plant foods that are rich in well-absorbable calcium include low-oxalate green leafy vegetables (collard, mustard, and turnip greens), calcium-set tofu, fortified soy and rice milks, textured vegetable protein, tahini, certain legumes, fortified orange juice, almonds, and blackstrap molasses (5). Laboratory studies have determined that the calcium bioavailability of most of these foods is as good as or better than milk, which has a fractional absorption of about 32% (42–44). The exceptions include fortified soymilk, most legumes, nuts, and seeds that have a fractional absorption in the range of 17% to 24%. On the other hand, foods with a high oxalate or phytate content such as spinach, swiss chard, beet greens, and rhubarb are not well-absorbed sources of calcium. In support of the laboratory calcium studies, a recent clinical study demonstrated that eight young vegetarians were able to maintain a similar positive calcium balance and appropriate bone resorption (measured by urinary deoxypyridinoline) when calcium was provided either solely by plant foods or by a diet including dairy products, despite a lower calcium intake on the vegan compared with the lacto-vegetarian diet (843 ± 140 mg vs 1,322 ± 303 mg, respectively) (45).

Although it is certainly possible to maintain calcium balance on a plant-based diet in a Western lifestyle (25,43), many athletes may find it more convenient to use fortified foods or calcium supplements to achieve calcium balance, particularly when amenorrhea is evident. Calcium carbonate and calcium citrate are well-absorbed sources used in supplements, but calcium carbonate is generally less expensive. Recent studies have noted that long-term supplementation with calcium carbonate does not compromise iron status in iron-replete adults (46), but it is preferable to ingest calcium supplements at bedtime rather that with iron-containing meals (47). Because vitamin D is also required for adequate calcium absorption, regulation of serum calcium levels and promotion of bone health, a calcium supplement that also contains vitamin D is advised. Some athletes may be at risk of poor vitamin D status (an unrecognized epidemic) if intake of fortified foods or supplements is low and exposure to the sun is limited (especially in northern climates) (48). Foods that are fortified with vitamin D include cow's milk, some brands of soymilk and rice milk, some breakfast cereals and margarines (25). It should be noted that the form used to fortify cereals is often not vegan (5).

Iron

All athletes, particularly female endurance athletes, are at risk for iron depletion and iron-deficiency anemia (49). Iron loss may be increased in some athletes, particularly high-volume endurance athletes, due to gastrointestinal bleeding (50), heavy sweating (51), hemolysis (52), and/or menstrual blood losses (53). Insufficient iron intake or reduced absorption, however, are the most probable causes of poor iron status. Snyder et al (54) found that female vegetarian runners had a similar iron intake but lower iron status than nonvegetarian runners, a finding that has been well-documented in nonathletes (6,7). Most of the iron in a vegetarian diet is nonheme iron, which has a relatively low absorption rate (2% to 20%) compared with the absorption rate of heme iron (15% to 35%) (55). This may be of significance because low iron stores, even without anemia, have been associated with decreased endurance (56) and lower maximal oxygen uptake (57).

In most cases, vegetarian athletes can achieve adequate iron status without iron supplementation. However, these athletes should be educated about plant sources of iron (see Tables 16.1 and 16.2) and factors that enhance and interfere with nonheme iron absorption (55,58). Substances that inhibit nonheme iron absorption include plant phytates, plant polyphenolics, bran, soy, egg and milk protein, cocoa, coffee, tea (including some herbal teas), and foods with high dietary concentrations of calcium, zinc, and other diva-lent cations. Substances that enhance nonheme iron absorption include ascorbic and other organic acids (citric, malic, lactic, and tartaric acids) and meat, poultry, and fish protein. As an example, an athlete who consumes milk or tea with legumes at a meal could be advised to replace the beverage with citrus fruit juice to enhance the iron absorbed from that meal.

In some cases, active individuals may require supplements to replenish or maintain iron stores. However, iron status (serum ferritin level or serum iron-binding capacity) should be determined before iron supplementation is considered. Reduced hemoglobin, hematocrit, and/or red blood cell levels in athletes are not good indicators of iron status in endurance athletes due to exercise-induced plasma volume expansion (59). Athletes taking iron supplements should have iron status monitored due to the prevalence of hemochro matosis (iron overload) in the United States and the potential association between iron sta-tus and chronic disease (60).

Zinc

Several studies have reported that athletes in heavy training commonly have serum zinc concentrations that are on the low range of or below the recommended level. (61). This finding, coupled with the reportedly low zinc intakes in athletes, has stimulated some con-cern that active individuals may be at risk for compromised zinc status. Manore et al (62), however, has cautioned that apparent changes in serum zinc concentration due to exercise may be transient and that measurement of plasma zinc during heavy training periods may

TABLE 16.2   Iron Content of Selected Vegetarian Foods*

Food	Portion	Iron, mg
Grains and Pasta		
Bread, whole-wheat	1 slice	0.9
Corn Flakes	1 cup	8.1
Cheerios	1 cup	10.3
Oatmeal	1 cup, cooked	1.6
Macaroni, elbow, enriched	1 cup, cooked	2.0
Pasta, enriched	2 oz	0.7
Spaghetti, whole-wheat	1 cup, cooked	1.5
Rice, brown, medium-grain	1 cup, cooked	1.0
Rice, long-grain, enriched	1 cup, cooked	1.9
Fruits		
Apricots	5 halves, dried	0.9
Prunes	¼ cup	0.4
Raisins	¼ cup	0.7
Watermelon	1¼ cup cubed	0.7
Vegetables		
Greens, collard	½ cup, cooked	1.1
Greens, turnip	½ cup, cooked	1.6
Peas	½ cup	1.2
Potato, baked	Medium	2.2
Sweet potato, baked	Medium	1.1
Nuts		
Almonds	1 oz	1.2
Peanuts, dry roasted	1 oz	0.6
Pumpkin seeds	1 oz	4.2
Sunflower seeds	1 oz	1.1

*For iron values of legumes and meat alternatives, refer to Table 16.1.

Source: Values obtained from the USDA National Nutrient Database for Standard Reference. Available at: http:// www.nal.usda.gov/fnic/foodcomp/search/index.html.

not reflect zinc status. Although more research is needed in this area, published studies have found that zinc supplementation does not influence zinc levels during training (62,63) and does not seem to benefit athletic performance (63).

Little is known about the zinc status of vegetarian athletes. Concern has been expressed, nonetheless, about the adequacy of zinc provided by vegetarian diets because the absorption of this mineral from plant foods is somewhat lower than from animal products due to higher phytate concentrations in plant foods (64). Animal protein is also thought to enhance zinc absorption (64). A recent study from the US Department of Agriculture found that nonathletic women consuming a lacto-ovo-vegetarian diet containing legumes and whole grains for 8 weeks maintained zinc status within normal limits, even though the diet was lower in total zinc and higher in phytate and fiber than a control omnivorous diet (65). The authors advised that legumes and whole grains be consumed regularly, which is a wise suggestion for active vegetarians and athletes in heavy training. In addition to legumes and whole-grain products, other sources of zinc in a vegetarian diet include hard cheeses, fortified cereals, nuts, and soy and commercial vegetarian products (25). The zinc content of selected protein-containing plant foods is shown in Table 16.1.

Iodine

Iodine status is not generally a concern for athletes living in industrial countries. Recent evidence is mounting, however, that vegetarians and particularly vegans may be at increased risk for iodine deficiency (66–68). A recent study assessing the iodine status of 81 nonathletic adults found that 25% of the vegetarians and 80% of the vegans suffered from iodine deficiency (urinary iodine excretion value below 100 µg/L) compared with 9% in those on a mixed diet (66). Researchers have suggested that the higher prevalence of iodine deficiency among vegetarians might be a consequence of prevailing (or exclusive) consumption of plant foods (66) grown in soil with low iodine levels (67), limited consumption of cow's milk (68), no intake of fish or sea products (66), and reduced iodine intake from iodized salt (66,67). These studies have exposed a need for more research in this area and its possible effect on the health and performance of athletic individuals. Vegetarian athletes can ensure adequate iodine status by consuming one-half teaspoon of iodized salt daily (25). On the other hand, vegetarians who consume sea vegetables on a regular basis (ie, at least once a week) may have high iodine status (25).

B Vitamins

Vegetarian diets can easily meet the requirements for most B vitamins. Depending on the type of vegetarian diet, however, riboflavin and vitamin B-12 are potential exceptions. Several studies have suggested that riboflavin needs are increased in individuals who begin an exercise program, particularly if riboflavin status is marginal (69,70). This could also be applicable to athletes who suddenly increase their training. Because riboflavin intakes are reportedly low in some vegans (4), active vegetarians who avoid dairy products should be educated about the plant sources of riboflavin to ensure adequate intake. Good plant sources of riboflavin include whole-grain and fortified breads and cereals, beans, peas, lentils, tofu, nuts, seeds, tahini, bananas, asparagus, figs, dark-green leafy vegetables, avocado, and most sea vegetables (seaweed, kombu, arame, sulse).

Vitamin B-12 has been of interest in athletic populations possibly due to its role in maintaining the cells of the hematopoietic and nervous systems. Injections of vitamin B-12 are popular with some athletes, trainers, and coaches because of the belief that the vitamin will increase oxygen uptake and thereby enhance endurance performance. In the absence of actual deficiency, however, studies have not supported any benefit of vitamin B-12 injections (71) or of high-dose supplementation with a multivitamin (63).

Because cobalamin, the active form of vitamin B-12, is found exclusively in animal products (72), vegan athletes need to regularly consume vitamin B-12–fortified foods or a vitamin B-12–containing multivitamin. Food sources of vitamin B-12 include Redstar brand nutritional yeast T6635 (Universal Foods, Milwaukee, WI), soymilk, breakfast cereals, and meat analogs that are vitamin B-12–fortified. Because vitamin B-12 fortification is brand-specific, the vegan athlete should be encouraged to check food labels. Although there is some thought that large quantities of nori and chorella seaweeds can supply bioavailable vitamin B-12, sea vegetables should not be considered a reliable source of this vitamin because the standard assay for determining vitamin B-12 content does not distinguish between biologically active forms and analogues (73).

Vegetarians who consume dairy products or eggs are likely to have adequate intakes of vitamin B-12 (25,72). However, because of the irreversible neurological damage that can occur with vitamin B-12 deficiency, markers of vitamin B-12 status (homocysteine, methylmalonic acid, and holotranscobalamin II) should be measured if there is concern (72). The typical hematological symptoms of vitamin B-12 deficiency can be masked by high folate intake, a probable finding in the vegan or vegetarian athlete.

Sports Nutrition Considerations: Supplements

Vegetarian athletes, like other athletes, may inquire about nutritional supplements or ergogenic aids to assist their athletic training and performance. An extensive discussion of supplements can be found in Chapter 7, but those of particular interest to vegetarian athletes—protein, creatine, and carnitine—are included here.

Protein

As discussed earlier, the protein needs of vegetarian and vegan athletes can be met by diet alone. For convenience, protein-containing nutrition beverages (eg, Go Energy-Recovery shake, Silsco Marketing, Brantford, Canada; Boost, Novartis Pharmaceuticals, East Hanover, NJ; Carnation Instant Breakfast, Nestle USA, Glendale, CA) or protein bars (eg, Genisoy, MLO/Genisoy Products, Fairfield, CA) can be used occasionally to supplement the diet. The athlete, nevertheless, should understand that these products are not necessary and are not a replacement for food.

Research has confirmed that protein or amino acid supplements consumed in excess of daily needs do not improve performance or stimulate more lean muscle gain (74). Provocative findings from several recent studies, however, have suggested that consumption of certain isolated proteins (mainly casein isolated from cow's milk) in a single feeding after exercise may promote greater gains in protein accretion than other proteins (ie, whey, also isolated from cow's milk) (75,76). Although intriguing, professionals and athletes are cautioned that this research is in its infancy and currently does not address protein consumption as it naturally occurs, in multiple mixed meals containing whole foods.

Nitrogen balance studies in humans have also found that isolated soy protein is comparable to that of animal proteins (77). A small study in two groups of six young nonathletic males found no difference in daily protein turnover in men fed a soy-based compared with an animal-based protein diet (78). Although studies specifically addressing the merit of consuming protein that is primarily plant- or animal-based during training would be of interest, there is currently little evidence to suggest that active vegetarians should consume a particular type of dietary and/or supplemental protein.

Creatine

Since the early 1990s, a considerable body of evidence has supported the efficacy of oral creatine supplementation to increase body mass and performance in high-intensity, short-duration exercise tasks including strength-training and repetitive sprint cycling or running (79–82). Supplementation, however, does not seem to be effective for performance during swimming or endurance running and cycling (79–82).

Most of the creatine found in the body is in skeletal muscle, where it exists primarily as creatine phosphate (83), an important storage form of energy that buffers adenosine triphosphate (ATP) and thus serves to maintain the bioenergetic state of exercising muscle. The average dietary intake is approximately 2 g per day in omnivores (83) and negligible in vegetarians because it is found primarily in muscle tissue (ie, meats). Even though creatine can be synthesized extramuscularly from amino acid precursors (83), serum (84,85) and skeletal muscle (86–88) creatine concentrations have been found to be lower in both vegetarians and nonvegetarians consuming a vegetarian diet compared with those consuming a meat-containing diet.

Interestingly, several (85,88) but not all studies (89) have noted that vegetarians who take creatine supplements have a greater response to supplementation than nonvegetarians. Vegetarians have been found to experience greater increases in skeletal muscle total creatine, phosphocreatine, lean tissue mass, and work performance during weight-training (88) and anaerobic bicycle performance (85) than their nonvegetarian teammates. Thus, there is some thought that vegetarian athletes in particular may benefit from creatine supplementation. According to most manufacturers, creatine is not synthesized using animal derivatives (personal communication), but interested vegans should assure this before initiating its use.

Carnitine

Carnitine plays a central role in the metabolism of fatty acids by transporting them from the cytosol to the mitochondrial matrix for beta oxidation, and also has many other important metabolic roles (90). Carnitine is supplied by the diet from meats and dairy products but is not found in plant foods. Like creatine, serum concentrations of carnitine have been found to be lower in vegetarians (84) despite endogenous synthesis from lysine and methionine in the liver (91). Not surprisingly, carnitine has been targeted as a potential promoter of fat loss and endurance performance. Available clinical experimental studies, however, did not support the claims that carnitine supplementation alters fuel utilization at rest or during exercise, improves maximum oxygen uptake or performance, or promotes body fat loss (90,92). Nevertheless, vegetarian athletes may be a target of aggressive marketing and may express interest in this supplement.

Nutrition Before, During, and After Exercise

Pre-exercise Nutrition

The meal before a competition or exercise session should increase fuel stores, provide adequate hydration, and prevent both hunger and gastrointestinal distress. Studies have shown that consumption of between 1 and 5 g of carbohydrate per kilogram body weight 1 to 4 hours before endurance exercise has the potential to improve endurance performance by as much as 14% (93) and is also thought to benefit high-intensity activity lasting several hours. Vegetarian athletes should be encouraged to consume familiar, well-tolerated, high-carbohydrate meals that are low in sodium, simple sugars, and fiber (21). Vegetarian athletes who are accustomed to eating gas-producing foods such as legumes, which are not typically recommended in the pre-event meal, may tolerate these foods without complications.

Several studies have suggested that before exercise consumption of carbohydrate with a low glycemic index (GI) compared with carbohydrate with a high GI (eg, lentils vs mashed potatoes) may prolong endurance during strenuous exercise by maintaining higher blood glucose concentrations toward the end of exercise (94–96). These foods may offer an advantage by providing a slow-release source of glucose without an accompanying insulin surge (94). An improvement in endurance performance with the intake of a low-GI pre-event meal, however, has not been consistently reported, despite a rather consistent shift toward greater fat oxidation (97). (For a discussion of the GI, see Chapter 2.)

As with all athletes, vegetarian athletes should follow guidelines for fluid consumption. These include consuming 400 to 600 mL (approximately 1.5 to 2.5 cups) 2 to 3 hours before exercise (21,98).

Supplementation During Exercise

Carbohydrate ingestion at levels between 40 and 75 g/hour have been shown to benefit prolonged, moderate-intensity exercise (more than 2 hours) (16) and variable-intensity exercise of shorter duration (99–101), presumably by maintaining blood glucose levels and preserving carbohydrate oxidation as endogenous glycogen stores become depleted. Ingestion of fluid-replacement beverages, at the recommended carbohydrate concentration of 4% to 8% (21,102), easily provides carbohydrate requirements while simultaneously meeting fluid needs. Both fluid and carbohydrate are shown to have a cumulative effect on performance (99).

Although commercial sport drinks work well for delivering easily absorbed carbohydrate, some vegetarian athletes may prefer natural or noncommercial sources of carbohydrate. In this case, diluted fruit juices (4 oz juice in 4 oz water = 6% solution), low-sodium vegetable juices such as carrot juice (7% solution), and honey or solid foods ingested with water may be appropriate. Research has shown that solid food (103–107) and honey (108) are as effective as liquids in increasing blood glucose and enhancing performance, provided that they are ingested with water and are easily digestible. The guideline is to drink approximately 240 mL (8 oz) of water with every 15 g carbohydrate ingested to create a 6% solution. A pinch of table salt can also be added to juices or low-sodium solids as necessary for events lasting longer than 3 to 4 hours (109). As a final point, it should be noted that although many vegetarians may be interested in honey because it is perceived as "natural" sugar, vegans may be opposed to it because it is an animal product (110).

Post-exercise Nutrition

The most recent recommendation by the American College of Sports Medicine, the American Dietetic Association, and the Dietitians of Canada is that athletes should consume a mixed meal providing carbohydrates, protein, and fat soon after a strenuous competition or training session (21). Vegetarian athletes who have performed prolonged or strenuous exercise should make an effort to consume carbohydrate and possibly protein immediately after exercise to promote recovery, particularly if exercise training is to be resumed the following day.

Carbohydrate intake of 1.5 g/kg within 30 minutes of exercise and again every 2 hours for the next 4 to 6 hours is recommended to replace muscle glycogen and ensure rapid recovery (21). Foods with a high GI (111,112) or those containing both carbohydrate and protein (approximately 1 g protein to 3 g carbohydrate) (113) may increase the rate of muscle glycogen storage after exercise by stimulating greater insulin secretion. Evidence suggests that consuming protein along with carbohydrate after endurance or resistance training may provide needed amino acids to maximize nitrogen retention and stimulate muscle protein synthesis (114–118). Including fat during the recovery period may also be important to replace intramyocellular lipid stores during periods of high-volume endurance training (37).

Current recommendations for post-exercise fluid requirements are to consume up to 150% of the weight lost during the exercise session (98,119). Athletes participating in heavy, prolonged workouts should also include sodium and potassium in the recovery meal(s) (120). Vegetarians are likely to choose foods containing ample potassium (eg, fruits, vegetables), but they may intentionally or unintentionally avoid sodium-containing foods. Sodium intake can be of concern during periods of heavy training in athletes who avoid salt or processed foods (ie, the typical sweat loss is about 30 mEq/L or 690 mg sodium per hour) (108). Thus, more liberal intakes of sodium are often appropriate in the athletic population.

Special Concerns for the Female Athlete

The prevalence of amenorrhea among exercising women is reported to be between 1% and 44% (121) with higher prevalence in sports that emphasize thin physique (eg, distance runners, gymnasts). The mechanism mediating the disruption of normal hypothalamic reproductive function is unknown, but evidence points to a favoring of energy availability (ie, the energy drain hypothesis), rather than stress or an overly lean body composition (122). Although there is some indication that menstrual cycle disturbances may be higher in vegetarians (123) and vegetarian athletes (124,125), these findings are not consistent (123,126) and can most likely be explained by study designs (123). For example, studies commonly define vegetarians as those having "a low-meat" diet and not necessarily vegetarian diet (124,125) and may tend to recruit a biased sample of vegetarians (ie, those with menstrual cycle disturbances may be more likely to volunteer for a study on menstrual cycle disturbances) (123).

In nonathletic females, Goldin et al (127) found that vegetarians, compared with nonvegetarians, had lower circulating estrogen levels, which were associated with higher fiber and lower fat intakes, higher fecal outputs, and two to three times more estrogen in feces. Among athletes, recall studies have generally documented lower intakes of energy (125, 128), protein (125,128), fat (125,129), and zinc (129), and higher intakes of fiber (129,130) and vitamin A (129) in amenorrheic compared with eumenorrheic athletes. Collectively, these findings suggest that the energy and/or nutrient composition of some vegetarian diets could predispose vegetarian athletes to amenorrhea.

Given the high prevalence of amenorrhea among athletic women and possible higher prevalence among some vegetarians, nutrition professionals should obtain menstrual cycle history as part of the screening procedure and, if appropriate, refer the athlete for medical evaluation and treatment. Nutrition evaluation and education of vegetarian athletes should focus on adequacy of energy, protein, fat, zinc, and fiber intakes. Available research suggests that reproductive disruption seems to occur when energy availability (dietary energy intake minus exercise energy expenditure) is less than a threshold between 20 and 30 kcal per kilogram of lean body mass, and that some athletes are more sensitive to this threshold than others (122).

If excess fiber intake is a concern, amenorrheic athletes can decrease fiber and possibly increase energy intake by consuming one third to one half of their cereal/grain servings from refined rather than whole-grain sources and by replacing some high-fiber fruit or vegetable servings with juice servings. A high-fiber intake may be detrimental to athletes in heavy training by causing lower energy intake (4) and potentially reducing enterohepatic circulation of sex steroid hormones (127,131). Energy intake may also be increased by encouraging consumption of regular meals and snacks and energy-dense foods as appropriate.

Assessing, Counseling, and Working with Vegetarian Athletes

The body sizes and shapes of vegetarian athletes vary, and these athletes have different reasons for being vegetarian. In the counseling session, a dietary assessment is necessary to determine which foods the athlete eliminates from the diet and which foods are acceptable. This will help evaluate nutrient adequacy to ensure that the nutrients in avoided foods can be met with acceptable foods. Although terms such as *lacto-ovo-vegetarian*, *lacto-vegetarian*, *vegan*, or *strict vegetarian* are commonly used to describe vegetarians, they are not always realistic. Vegetarians do not necessarily fall into distinct categories based on food selection or philosophies on vegetarianism. For example, two lacto-ovo-vegetarian athletes may have different philosophies about dairy products that would require different types of nutrition education. One may consume several servings of dairy products per day, while the other may eat only cheese and small amounts of dairy found in processed foods. Similarly, some vegans may be extremely strict, eliminating all commercially available foods that contain any ingredient that is animal derived or processed with an animal derivative (eg, commercial bread), while another will simply avoid foods of obvious animal origin. Also, some individuals claim to follow vegetarian diets when they mean that they avoid red meat but eat fish or poultry.

A thorough diet history followed by an analysis of energy and key nutrients such as carbohydrate, protein, fat, fiber, calcium, vitamin D, iron, zinc, iodine, riboflavin, and vitamin B-12 is the best way to reliably assess the vegetarian athlete's diet. Computer nutrient databases may be helpful, but many do not contain an adequate selection of vegetarian foods. In many cases it is useful to have the athlete keep food records and bring in food labels from vegetarian products that he or she consumes.

In addition to the diet assessment, it is often valuable to discuss why the active vegetarian has chosen to follow a vegetarian diet. Health, ecology, animal welfare, and religion are admirable reasons, but desire to lose weight or lack of time are not. Individuals who "don't eat meat" because it is the socially acceptable way to lose weight or because of limited time or food budgets have been labeled "new wave" vegetarians (132). These individuals may be at health and nutritional risk due to their haphazard eating patterns and lack of a solid philosophy that drives many vegetarians in their desire to eat well. The focus in "new wave" vegetarians should be on improving the diet with more healthful plant-based but not necessarily vegetarian foods.

A final concern is that vegetarianism may be used as a convenient and socially acceptable way for individuals with eating disorders to reduce energy and fat intake and thus mask their disordered eating behaviors. Clinical studies have found that a large number of anorexia nervosa patients profess to be vegetarian (133,134). Several recent studies have also noted that adolescents who report being vegetarian were more likely to engage in disordered eating behaviors (frequent dieting, binge eating, and self-induced vomiting) (135) and food restriction, and were more concerned with being slim (136) than those who did not report being vegetarian. Similar findings were noted in college women with those who reported being vegetarian displaying higher dietary restraint and having Eating Attitude Test (EAT) scores that were indicative of eating disorders (EAT > 30) (137). Again, the motivation for following a vegetarian diet and the adequacy of energy intake may be valuable when screening for potential eating disorders or weight preoccupation.

The role of the nutrition professional during counseling and education is to work with the athlete to ensure adequate nutritional status given his or her vegetarian beliefs, income, and lifestyle. Guidelines have been developed for counseling pregnant vegetarians (138). These guidelines are useful when working with the vegetarian population in general (139) and include establishing rapport, reinforcing positive nutrition practices, prioritizing nutrition concerns, and individualizing counseling (138). It is also important to remember that nutritional requirements are for individual essential nutrients (eg, protein, calcium, iron,) rather than for specific foods (eg, meat or dairy) or food groups (eg, meat group or dairy group).

Resources for Improving the Diet

Some athletes or active individuals, vegetarian or omnivorous, find it difficult to select a varied diet (139). Factors such as lack of knowledge about food preparation, lack of time, and economic constraints may lead to a monotonous diet. This pattern is common in college athletes. Vegetarian cookbooks (particularly with pictures) and videos can be used to provide ideas for increased dietary variety. A tour of a supermarket or natural food store may help identify products that are suitable for use by vegetarians. Vegetarian cooking classes for teams or individual athletes are also a great way to provide hands-on education and introduce new vegetarian foods and recipes. (See Box 16.2 for recommended resources).

Summary

Athletes at all levels of performance can meet their energy and nutrient needs on a vegetarian diet that contains a variety of plant foods. Depending on their food preferences, however, some athletes may have trouble meeting needs of certain key nutrients, which include total energy, carbohydrate, protein, fat, calcium, vitamin D, iron, zinc, iodine, riboflavin, and vitamin B-12. Thus, vegetarian athletes, like most athletes, may benefit from education about food choices that provide adequate nutrients for promoting optimal training, optimal performance, and good health. Nutrition professionals can play an essential role in optimizing the health and performance of athletes and active individuals who consume vegetarian diets.

However, nutrition professionals who work with vegetarian athletes and their coaches and trainers need to be sensitive to and knowledgeable about vegetarianism and exercise training. Athletes should be encouraged to eat a wide variety of plant foods; they should not be told that they need poultry, fish, or dairy products to obtain adequate nutrition. It is the

Box 16.2   Vegetarian Resources

General Publications
- *Vegetarian Journal.* Bimonthly publication by the Vegetarian Resource Group, PO Box 1463, Baltimore, MD 21203. ISSN 0885-7636. http://www.vrg.org.
- *Vegetarian Nutrition DPG Fact Sheet*s. Topics include: Making the Change to a Vegetarian Diet, Vegetarian Nutrition Resources on the Internet, Dining out for Vegetarians, Quick Vegetarian Meals. Available from Vegetarian Nutrition, a Dietetic Practice Group of the American Dietetic Association. http://www.vegetariannutrition.net.
- *The Vegetarian Way: Total Health for You and Your Family*, by Virginia Messina, MPH, RD, and Mark Messina. Crown Trade Paperbacks; 1997. ISBN 0-15788-275-2.

Cookbooks
- *Low-Fat Ways to Cook Vegetarian*, edited by Susan M. McIntosh, MS, RD. Oxmoor House; 1996. ISBN 0-8487-2206-x.
- *The Essential Vegetarian Cookbook*, by Diana Shaw. Clarkson Potter/Publishers; 1997. ISBN 0-517-88268-x.
- *Vegan Meals for One or Two,* by Nancy Berkoff, EdD, RD. The Vegetarian Resource Group. ISBN 0-93141-123-8. http://www.vrg.org.

Professional Publications
- *Vegetarian Nutrition*, edited by Joan Sabate, MD, DrPH. CRC Press; 2001. ISBN 0-8493-8508-3.
- *A Dietitian's Guide to Vegetarian Diets. Issues and Applications, Second Edition,* by Virginia Messina, MPH, RD, Reed Mangels, PhD, RD, and Mark Messina, PhD, MS. Jones and Bartlett Publishers; 2004. ISBN 0-76373-241-9.

Quantity Recipes
- *Vegetarian Journal's Foodservice Update.* Quarterly publication by the Vegetarian Resource Group, PO Box 1463, Baltimore, MD 21203. ISSN 1072-0820. http://www.vrg.org.
- *Vegan Quantity Recipes for Every Occasion*, by Nancy Berkoff, EdD, RD. The Vegetarian Resource Group. ISBN 0-93141-121-1.

Resource Groups
- Vegetarian Nutrition. A Dietetic Practice Group of the American Dietetic Association. http://www.vegetariannutrition.net.
- The Vegetarian Resource Group, PO Box 1463, Baltimore, MD 21203. http://www.vrg.org.

Travel Book
- *Vegetarian Journal's Guide to Natural Food Restaurants in the US & Canada*, 3rd edition. Avery Publishing Group; 1998. ISBN 0-89529-837-6.

position of the American Dietetic Association and Dietitians of Canada that "appropriately planned vegetarian diets are healthful, nutritionally adequate, and provide health benefits in the prevention and treatment of certain diseases" and "can meet the needs of competitive athletes" (25).

References

1. Goran M. Variation in total energy expenditure in humans. *Obes Res.* 1995;3:59–66.
2. Borsheim E, Bahr R. Effect of exercise intensity, duration and mode on post-exercise oxygen consumption. *Sports Med.* 2003;33:1037–1060.
3. Bahr R, Sejersted O. Effect of intensity of exercise on excess postexercise O_2 consumption. *Metabolism.* 1991;40:836–841.
4. Grandjean A. The vegetarian athlete. *Phys Sportsmed.* 1987;15:191–194.
5. Messina V, Melina V, Mangels AR. A new food guide for North American vegetarians. *J Am Diet Assoc.* 2003;103:771–775.
6. Messina M, Messina V. *The Dietitian's Guide to Vegetarian Diets: Issues and Applications.* Gaithersburg, Md: Aspen Publishers; 1996.
7. Messina V, Mangels AR, Messina M. *A Dietitian's Guide to Vegetarian Diets: Issues and Applications.* 2nd ed. Boston, Mass: Jones and Bartlett Publishers; 2004.
8. Houtkooper L. Food selection for endurance sports. *Med Sci Sports Exerc.* 1992;24(9 Suppl):S349-S359.
9. Casey A, Mann R, Banister K, Fox J, Morris PG, Macdonald IA, Greenhaff PL. Effect of carbohydrate ingestion on glycogen resynthesis in human liver and skeletal muscle, measured by (13)C MRS. *Am J Physiol.* 2000;278:E65–E75.
10. Bergstrom J, Hermansen L, Hultman E, Saltin B. Diet, muscle glycogen and physical performance. *Acta Physiol Scand.* 1967;71:140–150.
11. Nilsson L, Hultman E. Liver glycogen in man-the effect of total starvation or a carbohydrate-poor diet followed by carbohydrate refeeding. *Scand J Clin Lab Invest.* 1973;32:325–330.
12. Goforth HW Jr, Laurent D, Prusaczyk WK, Schneider KE, Petersen KF, Shulman GI. Effects of depletion exercise and light training on muscle glycogen supercompensation in men. *Am J Physiol Endocrinol Metab.* 2003;285:E1304–E1311.
13. Spencer M, Yan Z, Katz A. Carbohydrate supplementation attenuates IMP accumulation in human muscle during prolonged exercise. *Am J Physiol.* 1991;261:C71–C76.
14. O'Keeffe K, Keith R, Wilson G, Blessing D. Dietary carbohydrate intake and endurance exercise performance of trained female cyclists. *Nutr Res.* 1989;9:819–830.
15. Brewer J, Williams C, Patton A. The influence of high carbohydrate diets on endurance running performance. *Eur J Appl Physiol Occup Physiol.* 1988;57:698–706.
16. Coggan AR, Swanson SC. Nutritional manipulations before and during endurance exercise: effects on performance. *Med Sci Sports Exerc.* 1992;24:S331–S335.
17. Pizza FX, Flynn MG, Duscha BD, Holden J, Kubitz ER. A carbohydrate loading regimen improves high intensity, short duration exercise performance. *Int J Sport Nutr.* 1995;5:110–116.
18. Larson DE, Hesslink RL, Hrovat MI, Fishman RS, Systrom DM. Dietary effects on exercising muscle metabolism and performance by ^{31}P-MRS. *J Appl Physiol.* 1994;77:1108–1115.
19. Hargreaves M, Costill DL, Coggan A, Fink WJ, Nishibata I. Effect of carbohydrate feedings on muscle glycogen utilization and exercise performance. *Med Sci Sports Exerc.* 1984;16:219–222.
20. Sugiura K, Kobayashi K. Effect of carbohydrate ingestion on sprint performance following continuous and intermittent exercise. *Med Sci Sports Exerc.* 1998;30:1624–1630.

21. American College of Sports Medicine, American Dietetic Association, Dietitians of Canada. Nutrition and athletic performance. Joint position statement. *Med Sci Sports Exerc.* 2000;32: 2130–2145.

22. Lemon PW, Mullin JP. Effect of initial muscle glycogen levels on protein catabolism during exercise. *J Appl Physiol.* 1980;48:624–629.

23. Institute of Medicine. *Recommended Dietary Allowances.* 10th ed. Washington, DC: National Academy Press; 1989.

24. Young VR, Pellett PL. Plant proteins in relation to human protein and amino acid nutrition. *Am J Clin Nutr.* 1994;59(5 Suppl):1203S–1212S.

25. Position of the American Dietetic Association and Dietitians of Canada: vegetarian diets. *J Am Diet Assoc.* 2003;103:748–765.

26. Bergstrom J, Furst P, Vinnars E. Effect of a test meal, without and with protein, on muscle and plasma free amino acids. *Clin Sci (Lond).* 1990;79:331–337.

27. Decombaz J, Schmitt B, Ith M, Decarli B, Diem P, Kreis R, Hoppeler H, Boesch C. Postexercise fat intake repletes intramyocellular lipids but no faster in trained than in sedentary subjects. *Am J Physiol Regul Integr Comp Physiol.* 2001;281:R760–R769.

28. Larson-Meyer DE, Newcomer BR, Hunter GR, Joanisse DR, Weinsier RL, Bamman MM. Relation between in vivo and in vitro measurements of skeletal muscle oxidative metabolism. *Muscle Nerve.* 2001;24:1665–1676.

29. Romijn J, Coyle EF, Sidossis LS, Gastaldelli A, Horowitz JF, Endert E, Wolfe RR. Regulation of endogenous fat and carbohydrate metabolism in relation to exercise intensity and duration. *Am J Physiol.* 1993;265:E380–E391.

30. Romijn JA, Coyle EF, Sidossis LS, Rosenblatt J, Wolfe RR. Substrate metabolism during different exercise intensities in endurance- trained women. *J Appl Physiol.* 2000;88:1707–1714.

31. Muoio DM, Leddy JJ, Horvath PJ, Awad AB, Pendergast DR. Effect of dietary fat on metabolic adjustments to maximal VO_2 and endurance in runners. *Med Sci Sports Exerc.* 1994;26:81–88.

32. Hoppeler H, Billeter R, Horvath PJ, Leddy JJ, Pendergast DR. Muscle structure with low- and high-fat diets in well trained male runners. *Int J Sports Med.* 1999;20:522–526.

33. Ornish D, Brown SE, Scherwitz LW, Billings JH, Armstrong WT, Ports TA, McLanahan SM, Kirkeeide RL, Brand RJ, Gould KL. Can lifestyle changes reverse coronary heart disease? The Lifestyle Heart Trial. *Lancet.* 1990;336:129–133.

34. Gould KL, Ornish D, Scherwitz L, Brown S, Edens RP, Hess MJ, Mullani N, Bolomey L, Dobbs F, Armstrong WT, Merritt T, Ports T, Sparler S, Billings J. Changes in myocardial perfusion abnormalities by positron emission tomography after long-term, intense risk factor modification. *JAMA.* 1995;274:894–901.

35. Gould KL, Ornish D, Kirkeeide R, Brown S, Stuart Y, Buchi M, Billings J, Armstrong W, Ports T, Scherwitz L. Improved stenosis geometry by quantitative coronary arteriography after vigorous risk factor modification. *Am J Cardiol.* 1992;69:845–853.

36. Horvath PJ, Eagen CK, Ryer-Calvin SD, Pendergast DR. The effects of varying dietary fat on the nutrient intake in male and female runners. *J Am Coll Nutr.* 2000;19:42–51.

37. Larson-Meyer DE, Hunter GR, Newcomer BR. Influence of endurance running and recovery diet on intramyocellular lipid content in women: A ^{1}H-NMR study. *Am J Physiol.* 2002;282: E95–E106.

38. Institute of Medicine. *Dietary Reference Intakes for Calcium, Phosphorus, Magnesium, Vitamin D, and Fluoride.* Washington, DC: National Academy Press; 1997.

39. Heaney RP, Recker RR, Saville PD. Menopausal changes in calcium balance performance. *J Lab Clin Med.* 1978;92:953–962.

40. Myburgh KH, Hutchins J, Fataar AB, Hough SF, Noakes TD. Low bone density is an etiologic factor for stress fractures in athletes. *Ann Intern Med.* 1990;113:754–759.

41. Wolman RL, Clark P, McNally E, Harries MG, Reeve J. Dietary calcium as a statistical determinant of trabecular bone density in amenorrhoeic and oestrogen-replete athletes. *Bone Miner.* 1992;17:415–423.

42. Weaver CM, Plawecki KL. Dietary calcium: adequacy of a vegetarian diet. *Am J Clin Nutr.* 1994;59(5 Suppl):1238S–1241S.

43. Weaver CM, Proulx WR, Heaney R. Choices for achieving adequate dietary calcium with a vegetarian diet. *Am J Clin Nutr.* 1999;70(3 Suppl):543S–548S.

44. Heaney RP, Dowell MS, Rafferty K, Bierman J. Bioavailability of the calcium in fortified soy imitation milk, with some observations on method. *Am J Clin Nutr.* 2000;71:1166–1169.

45. Kohlenberg-Mueller K, Raschka L. Calcium balance in young adults on a vegan and lactovegetarian diet. *J Bone Miner Metab.* 2003;21:28–33.

46. Minihane AM, Fairweather-Tait SJ. Effect of calcium supplementation on daily nonheme-iron absorption and long-term iron status. *Am J Clin Nutr.* 1998;68:96–102.

47. Hallberg L. Does calcium interfere with iron absorption? (Editorial). *Am J Clin Nutr.* 1998;68: 3–4.

48. Holick MF. Evolution and function of vitamin D. *Recent Results Cancer Res.* 2003;164:3–28.

49. Fogelholm M. Indicators of vitamin and mineral status in athletes' blood: a review. *Int J Sport Nutr.* 1995;5:267–284.

50. Robertson JD, Maughan RJ, Davidson RJ. Faecal blood loss in response to exercise. *BMJ.* 1987;295:303–305.

51. Waller MF, Haymes EM. The effects of heat and exercise on sweat iron loss. *Med Sci Sports Exerc.* 1996;28:197–203.

52. Eichner E. Runner's macrocytosis: a clue to footstrike hemolysis. *Am J Med.* 1985;78:321–325.

53. Malczewska J, Raczynski G, Stupnicki R. Iron status in female endurance athletes and in nonathletes. *Int J Sport Nutr Exerc Metab.* 2000;10:260–276.

54. Snyder AC, Dvorak LL, Roepke JB. Influence of dietary iron source on measures of iron status among female runners. *Med Sci Sports Exerc.* 1989;21:7–10.

55. Craig W. Iron status of vegetarians. *Am J Clin Nutr.* 1994;59(5 Suppl):1233S–1237S.

56. Lamanca JJ, Haymes EM. Effects of low ferritin concentrations on endurance performance. *Int J Sports Med.* 1992;2:376–385.

57. Zhu Y, Haas J. Iron depletion without anemia and physical performance. *Am J Clin Nutr.* 1997; 66:334–341.

58. Hurrell RF, Reddy M, Cook JD. Inhibition of non-haem iron absorption in man by polyphenolic-containing beverages. *Br J Nutr.* 1999;81:289–295.

59. Schumacher YO, Schmid A, Grathwohl D, Bultermann D, Berg A. Hematological indices and iron status in athletes of various sports and performances. *Med Sci Sports Exerc.* 2002;34:869–875.

60. Herbert V. Everyone should be tested for iron disorders. *J Am Diet Assoc.* 1992;92:1502–1509.

61. Lukaski HC. Micronutrients (magnesium, zinc, and copper): are mineral supplements needed for athletes? *Int J Sport Nutr.* 1995;5(suppl):S74–S83.

62. Manore MM, Helleksen JM, Merkel J, Skinner JS. Longitudinal changes in zinc status in untrained men: effects of two different 12-week exercise training programs and zinc supplementation. *J Am Diet Assoc.* 1993;93:1165–1168.

63. Singh A, Moses FM, Deuster PA. Chronic multivitamin-mineral supplementation does not enhance physical performance. *Med Sci Sports Exerc.* 1992;24:726–732.

64. Hunt JR. Bioavailability of iron, zinc, and other trace minerals from vegetarian diets. *Am J Clin Nutr.* 2003;78(3 Suppl):633S–639S.

65. Hunt JR, Matthys LA, Johnson LK. Zinc absorption, mineral balance, and blood lipids in women consuming controlled lacto-ovo-vegetarian and omnivorous diets for 8 wk. *Am J Clin Nutr.* 1998;67:421–430.

66. Krajcovicova-Kudlackova M, Buckova K, Klimes I, Sebokova E. Iodine deficiency in vegetarians and vegans. *Ann Nutr Metab.* 2003;47:183–185.

67. Remer T, Neubert A, Manz F. Increased risk of iodine deficiency with vegetarian nutrition. *Br J Nutr.* 1999;81:45–49.

68. Lightowler HJ, Davies GJ. Iodine intake and iodine deficiency in vegans as assessed by the duplicate-portion technique and urinary iodine excretion. *Br J Nutr.* 1998;80:529–535.

69. Belko A. Vitamins and exercise—an update. *Med Sci Sports Exerc.* 1987;19(5 Suppl): S191–S196.

70. Soares M, Satyanarayana K, Bamji M, Jacob C, Ramana Y, Rao S. The effect of exercise on the riboflavin status of adult men. *Br J Nutr.* 1993;69:541–551.

71. Than T-M, May M-W, Aug K-S, Mya-Tu M. The effect of vitamin B12 on physical performance capacity. *Br J Nutr.* 1978;40:269–273.

72. Herrmann W, Geisel J. Vegetarian lifestyle and monitoring of vitamin B-12 status. *Clin Chim Acta.* 2002;326:47–59.

73. Rauma AL, Torronen R, Hanninen O, Mykkanen H. Vitamin B-12 status of long-term adherents of a strict uncooked vegan diet ("living food diet") is compromised. *J Nutr.* 1995;125:2511–2515.

74. Kreider RB, Miriel V, Bertun E. Amino acid supplementation and exercise performance. Analysis of the proposed ergogenic value. *Sports Med.* 1993;16:190–209.

75. Boirie Y, Dangin M, Gachon P, Vasson MP, Maubois JL, Beaufrere B. Slow and fast dietary proteins differently modulate postprandial protein accretion. *Proc Natl Acad Sci U S A.* 1997;94: 14930–14935.

76. Dangin M, Boirie Y, Garcia-Rodenas C, Gachon P, Fauquant J, Callier P, Ballevre O, Beaufrere B. The digestion rate of protein is an independent regulating factor of postprandial protein retention. *Am J Physiol Endocrinol Metab.* 2001;280:E340–E348.

77. Young V. Soy protein in relation to human protein and amino acid nutrition. *J Am Diet Assoc.* 1991;91:828–835.

78. Gausseres N, Catala I, Mahe S, Luengo C, Bornet F, Guy-Grand B, Tome D. Whole-body protein turnover in humans fed a soy protein-rich vegetable diet. *Eur J Clin Nutr.* 1997;51:308–311.

79. Juhn MS, Tarnopolsky M. Oral creatine supplementation and athletic performance: a critical review. *Clin J Sport Med.* 1998;8:286–297.

80. Juhn M. Popular sports supplements and ergogenic aids. *Sports Med.* 2003;33:921–939.

81. Branch JD. Effect of creatine supplementation on body composition and performance: a meta-analysis. *Int J Sport Nutr Exerc Metab.* 2003;13:198–226.

82. Terjung RL, Clarkson P, Eichner ER, Greenhaff PL, Hespel PJ, Israel RG, Kraemer WJ, Meyer RA, Spriet LL, Tarnopolsky MA, Wagenmakers AJ, Williams MH. American College of Sports Medicine roundtable. The physiological and health effects of oral creatine supplementation. *Med Sci Sports Exerc.* 2000;32:706–717.

83. Balsom PD, Soderlund K, Ekblom B. Creatine in humans with special reference to creatine supplementation. *Sports Med.* 1994;18:268–280.

84. Delanghe J, De Slypere J-P, De Buyzere M, Robbrecht J, Wieme R, Vermeulen A. Normal reference values for creatine, creatinine, and carnitine are lower in vegetarians. *Clin Chem.* 1989;35:1802–1803.

85. Shomrat A, Weinstein Y, Katz A. Effect of creatine feeding on maximal exercise performance in vegetarians. *Eur J Appl Physiol.* 2000;82:321–325.

86. Harris RC, Soderlund K, Hultman E. Elevation of creatine in resting and exercised muscle of normal subjects by creatine supplementation. *Clin Sci.* 1992;83:367–374.

87. Lukaszuk JM, Robertson RJ, Arch JE, Moore GE, Yaw KM, Kelley DE, Rubin JT, Moyna NM. Effect of creatine supplementation and a lacto-ovo-vegetarian diet on muscle creatine concentration. *Int J Sport Nutr Exerc Metab.* 2002;12:336–348.

88. Burke DG, Chilibeck PD, Parise G, Candow DG, Mahoney D, Tarnopolsky M. Effect of creatine and weight training on muscle creatine and performance in vegetarians. *Med Sci Sports Exerc.* 2003;35:1946–1955.

89. Clarys P, Zinzen E, Hebbelinck M. The effect of oral creatine supplementation on torque production in a vegetarian and non-vegetarian population: a double blind study. *Vegetarian Nutrition.* 1997;1:100–105.

90. Brass EP. Supplemental carnitine and exercise. *Am J Clin Nutr.* 2000;72(2 Suppl):618S–623S.

91. Rebouche C, Chenard C. Metabolic fate of dietary carnitine in human adults: identification and quantification of urinary and fecal metabolites. *J Nutr.* 1991;121:539–546.

92. Dyck DJ. Dietary fat intake, supplements, and weight loss. *Can J Appl Physiol.* 2000;25:495–523.

93. Coyle E, Coggan A, Davis J, Sherman W. Current thoughts and practical considerations concerning substrate utilization during exercise. *Sports Sci Exch.* 1992;Spring:1–4.

94. Thomas DE, Brotherhood JR, Brand JC. Carbohydrate feeding before exercise: effect of glycemic index. *Int J Sports Med.* 1991;12:180–186.

95. Thomas D, Brotherhood J, Miller J. Plasma glucose levels after prolonged strenuous exercise correlate inversely with glycemic response to food consumed before exercise. *Int J Sport Nutr.* 1994;4:361–373.

96. DeMarco HM, Sucher KP, Cisar CJ, Butterfield GE. Pre-exercise carbohydrate meals: application of glycemic index. *Med Sci Sports Exerc.* 1999;31:164–170.

97. Siu PM, Wong SH. Use of the glycemic index: effects on feeding patterns and exercise performance. *J Physiol Anthropol Appl Human Sci.* 2004;23:1–6.

98. Convertino VA, Armstrong LE, Coyle EF, Mack GW, Sawka MN, Senay LC Jr, Sherman WM. American College of Sports Medicine. Position Stand. Exercise and Fluid Replacement. *Med Sci Sports Exerc.* 1996;28:i–vii.

99. Below P, Mora-Rodriguez R, Gonzalez-Alonso J, Coyle E. Fluid and carbohydrate ingestion independently improve performance during 1 h of intense exercise. *Med Sci Sports Exerc.* 1995;27:200–210.

100. Ball TC, Headley SA, Vanderburgh PM, Smith JC. Periodic carbohydrate replacement during 50 min of high-intensity cycling improves subsequent sprint performance. *Int J Sport Nutr.* 1995;5:151–158.

101. Nicholas CW, Williams C, Lakomy HK, Phillips G, Nowitz A. Influence of ingesting a carbohydrate-electrolyte solution on endurance capacity during intermittent, high intensity shuttle running. *J Sports Sci.* 1995;13:283–290.

102. Gisolfi CV, Summers RW, Schedl HP, Bleiler TL. Intestinal water absorption from selected carbohydrate solutions in humans. *J Appl Physiol.* 1992;73:2142–2150.

103. Neufer PD, Costill DL, Flynn MG, Kirwan JP, Mitchell JB, Houmard J. Improvements in exercise performance: effects of carbohydrate feedings and diet. *J Appl Physiol.* 1987;62:983–988.

104. van der Brug GE, Peters HP, Hardeman MR, Schep G, Mosterd WL. Hemorheological response to prolonged exercise—no effects of different kinds of feedings. *Int J Sports Med.* 1995;16:231–237.

105. Coleman E. Update on carbohydrate: solid versus liquid. *Int J Sport Nutr.* 1994;4:80–88.

106. Lugo M, Sherman WM, Wimer GS, Garleb K. Metabolic responses when different forms of carbohydrate energy are consumed during cycling. *Int J Sport Nutr.* 1993;3:398–407.

107. Roberts RA, McMinn SB, Mermier C, Leadbetter Gr, Ruby B, Quinn C. Blood glucose and glucoregulatory hormone responses to solid and liquid carbohydrate ingestion during exercise. *Int J Sport Nutr.* 1998;8:70–83.

108. Lancaster S, Kreider RB, Rasmussen C, Kerksick C, Greenwood M, Milnor P, Almada AL, Earnest CP. Effects of honey supplementation on glucose, insulin, and endurance cycling performance. *FASEB J.* 2001;15:LB315.

109. Gisolfi CV, Duchman SM. Guidelines for optimal replacement beverages for different athletic events. *Med Sci Sports Exerc.* 1992;24:679–687.

110. Why honey is not vegan. Available at: http://www.vegetus.org/honey/honey.htm. Accessed November 11, 2004.

111. Burke LM, Collier GR, Hargreaves M. Muscle glycogen storage after prolonged exercise: effect of the glycemic index of carbohydrate feedings. *J Appl Physiol.* 1993;75:1019–1023.

112. Jozsi AC, Trappe TA, Starling RD, Goodpaster B, Trappe SW, Fink WJ, Costill DL. The influence of starch structure on glycogen resynthesis and subsequent cycling performance. *Int J Sports Med.* 1996;17:373–378.

113. Ivy JL, Goforth HW Jr, Damon BM, McCauley TR, Parsons EC, Price TB. Early postexercise muscle glycogen recovery is enhanced with a carbohydrate-protein supplement. *J Appl Physiol.* 2002;93:1337–1344.

114. Tipton KD, Rasmussen BB, Miller SL, Wolf SE, Owens-Stovall SK, Petrini BE, Wolfe RR. Timing of amino acid-carbohydrate ingestion alters anabolic response of muscle to resistance exercise. *Am J Physiol Endocrinol Metab.* 2001;281:E197–206.

115. Levenhagen DK, Gresham JD, Carlson MG, Maron DJ, Borel MJ, Flakoll PJ. Postexercise nutrient intake timing in humans is critical to recovery of leg glucose and protein homeostasis. *Am J Physiol Endocrinol Metab.* 2001;280:E982–E993.

116. Miller SL, Tipton KD, Chinkes DL, Wolf SE, Wolfe RR. Independent and combined effects of amino acids and glucose after resistance exercise. *Med Sci Sports Exerc.* 2003;35:449–455.

117. Roy BD, Tarnopolsky MA, MacDougall JD, Fowles J, Yarasheski KE. Effect of glucose supplement on protein metabolism after resistance training. *Clin J Sport Med.* 1997;82:1882–1888.

118. Roy BD, Luttmer K, Bosman MJ, Tarnopolsky MA. The influence of post-exercise macronutrient intake on energy balance and protein metabolism in active females participating in endurance training. *Int J Sport Nutr Exerc Metab.* 2002;12:172–188.

119. Shirreffs SM, Taylor AJ, Leiper JB, Maughan RJ. Post-exercise rehydration in man: effects of volume consumed and drink sodium content. *Med Sci Sports Exerc.* 1996;28:1260–1271.

120. Maughan R, Leiper J, Shirreffs S. Restoration of fluid balance after exercise-induced dehydration: effects of food and fluid intake. *Eur J Appl Physiol Occup Physiol.* 1996;73:317–325.

121. Loucks AB. Physical health of the female athlete: observations, effects, and causes of reproductive disorders. *Can J Appl Physiol.* 2001;26(Suppl):S176–S185.

122. Loucks AB. Energy availability, not body fatness, regulates reproductive function in women. *Exerc Sport Sci Rev.* 2003;31:144–148.

123. Barr SI. Vegetarianism and menstrual cycle disturbances: is there an association? *Am J Clin Nutr.* 1999;70(3 Suppl):549S–554S.

124. Brooks SM, Sanborn CF, Albrecht BH, Wagner WW Jr. Diet in athletic amenorrhoea [letter]. *Lancet.* 1984;2:559–560.

125. Kaiserauer S, Snyder AC, Sleeper M, Zierath J. Nutritional, physiological, and menstrual status of distance runners. *Med Sci Sports Exerc.* 1989;21:120–125.

126. Slavin J, Lutter J, Cushman S. Amenorrhea in vegetarian athletes [letter]. *Lancet.* 1984;1984:1474–1475.

127. Goldin B, Adlercreutz H, Gorbach S, Warram J, Dwyer J, Swenson L, Woods M. Estrogen excretion patterns and plasma levels in vegetarian and omnivorous women. *N Engl J Med.* 1982;307:1542–1547.

128. Nelson ME, Fisher EC, Catsos PD, Meredith CN, Turksoy RN, Evans WJ. Diet and bone status in amenorrheic runners. *Am J Clin Nutr.* 1986;43:910–916.

129. Deuster PA, Kyle SB, Moser PB, Vigersky RA, Singh A, Schoomaker EB. Nutritional intakes and status of highly trained amenorrheic and eumenorrheic women runners. *Fertil Steril.* 1986;46:636–643.

130. Lloyd T, Buchanan J, Bitzer S, Waldman CJ, Myers C, Ford BG. Interrelationship of diet, athletic activity, menstrual status, and bone density in collegiate women. *Am J Clin Nutr.* 1987;46: 681–684.

131. Raben A, Kiens B, Richter EA, Rasmussen LB, Svenstrup B, Micic S, Bennett P. Serum sex hormones and endurance performance after a lacto-ovo vegetarian and a mixed diet. *Med Sci Sports Exerc.* 1992;24:1290–1297.

132. Szabo L. The health risks of new-wave vegetarianism. *Can Med Assoc J.* 1997;156:1454–1455.

133. O'Connor MA, Touyz SW, Dunn SM, Beumont JV. Vegetarianism in anorexia nervosa? A review of 116 consecutive cases. *Med J Aust.* 1987;147:540–542.

134. Huse DM, Lucas AR. Dietary patterns in anorexia nervosa. *Am J Clin Nutr.* 1984;40:251–254.

135. Neumark-Sztainer D, Story M, Resnick MD, Blum RW. Adolescent vegetarians. A behavioral profile of a school-based population in Minnesota. *Arch Pediatr Adolesc Med.* 1997;151:833–838.

136. Worsley A, Skrzypiec G. Teenage vegetarianism: prevalence, social and cognitive contexts. *Appetite.* 1998;30:151–170.

137. Klopp SA, Heiss CJ, Smith HS. Self-reported vegetarianism may be a marker for college women at risk for disordered eating. *J Am Diet Assoc.* 2003;103:745–747.

138. Johnston P. Counseling the pregnant vegetarian. *Am J Clin Nutr.* 1988;48(3 Suppl):901–905.

139. Mangels A. Working with vegetarian clients. *Issues in Vegetarian Dietetics.* 1995;5:1,4,5.

Chapter 17

PREGNANCY AND EXERCISE

Ann F. Cowlin, MA, CSM, CCE

Introduction

Regular exercise can provide health benefits for pregnant women and their offspring. Consequently, prenatal health care providers now advocate a level of exercise during pregnancy appropriate to each woman's circumstances (1,2). Underlying this advocacy is the assumption of adequate nutrition.

On one hand, exercise is a source of stress in pregnancy. Both exercise and pregnancy require energy beyond what is needed for activities of daily living, and they compete for nutrients and produce physiological stresses. In addition, childbearing changes a woman's identity, and the alterations in lifestyle can be stressful—waking frequently in the middle of the night to urinate while pregnant, and later to feed the baby, for example. A woman accustomed to high levels of activity may experience conflict about the need to alter her level of activity, about her changing body shape, or about shifting her focus to the well-being of her infant. Of all the roles in a woman's life, motherhood produces the greatest barriers to participation in exercise (3).

On the other hand, in a healthy pregnancy aerobic exercise provides a woman with confidence in her body and the prowess of physical fitness (4), which constitute excellent preparation for the rigors of childbirth and parenting. Clapp (5) has found that aerobic activity is associated with a slight protection from congenital anomalies, spontaneous abortion, placental abruption, and other negative outcomes in early pregnancy. Birth outcomes for athletic mothers and their babies are good (6,7) as are long-term outcomes for infants (8), and a fit woman's physiological tolerance for the long duration of labor and her ability to recover seem enhanced (9–11). Strength and flexibility help mothers-to-be deal with common discomforts and prepare for birth and moving with an infant, while mind/body strategies help women learn mental focus, stress management, and calming techniques.

Adequate nutrition is necessary to prevent low birth weight (LBW) and prematurity and their sequellae of mental and physical disabilities. Babies born weighing less than 5.5 pounds (2,500 g) are considered LBW. Most LBW births—even small reductions in birth weight due to reduced access to prenatal health care because of race or economic status—can be virtually eradicated through improved prenatal nutrition (12). Moderate aerobic exercise has also been shown to reduce the risk for LBW (13), as well as for maternal preeclampsia (pregnancy-induced hypertension with proteinurea) (14,15), a gene-linked disorder that is aggravated by low protein intake, lack of recreational exercise, and stress. These are two major health risks related to pregnancy in the United States, and although technology is improving survival rates, prenatal care, nutrition, and moderate exercise are keys to their prevention.

Principles of adequate nutrition during pregnancy are well-established and are reviewed in several publications (2,16,17). The following sections highlight nutrition issues known to be affected by exercise during pregnancy—energy balance, and carbohydrate, fat, protein, and fluid needs.

Nutritional Needs During Pregnancy

Energy Balance: Maternal Weight Gain and Energy Needs

Maternal weight gain is a measurable factor that has traditionally been used to evaluate the state of a pregnancy. The National Academy of Science (12) recommends that pregnancy weight gain be predicated on a woman's pre-pregnancy body mass index (BMI). A woman whose pre-pregnancy BMI is less than 19.8 (low) should have a total weight gain of 28 to 40 pounds; whose BMI is 19.8 to 26.0 (normal) should gain 25 to 35 pounds; and whose BMI is 26.0 to 29.0 (high) should gain 15 to 25 pounds. Weight gain in obese women (BMI > 29.0) should be at least 15 pounds, but must be closely managed in consultation with the physician or midwife and dietitian.

First-trimester weight gain occurs at a slower pace than second- or third-trimester weight gain and may be negatively influenced by nausea and vomiting. If dietary intake is based on adequate energy and protein, weight gain should be in the correct range for an individual woman, unless there is an underlying medical condition. With recent advancements in ultrasound imaging, health care providers now rely as much on this technology as on weight gain or fundal height (the measurement from pubic bone to top of the uterus) to determine if fetal growth is progressing at a satisfactory rate.

Energy requirements are based on height, weight, activity level, and nutritional stress factors, plus approximately 300 kcal/day. Nutritional stresses include nausea, vomiting, and weight loss for a prolonged period; pregnancy spacing of less than 1 year apart; prior poor obstetrical outcomes (stillbirth, spontaneous abortion, preterm delivery); failure to gain adequate weight; age younger than 20 years; and emotional stress. For each stress factor, an additional 200 kcal/day (400 extra kcal/day maximum) should be added (2).

Energy requirements must be calculated regularly during pregnancy to account for changes. Very athletic women may become less active, there may be too great a weight gain or loss, and stress factors may change. A 2004 study by Butte et al (18) examined energy requirements during pregnancy and confirmed a gradual increase in basal metabolic rate throughout pregnancy. They concluded that energy needs in healthy women who start pregnancy with a normal BMI are approximately 500 kcal/day more than their pre-pregnancy requirements during their third trimester.

The metabolic stress of pregnancy implies the need for careful attention to energy balance. Because of fetal needs, the decreased availability of glucose for maternal energy, and the potential for hyperinsulinemia, small frequent meals including all three macronutrients can help reduce the risk of fatigue. In addition, developing a pattern of recurring cycles of activity, food intake, and rest during the day can help maintain energy balance. The inclusion of prenatal aerobic exercise is considered state of the art treatment for gestational diabetes, and resumption of vigorous exercise prior to 6 weeks' postpartum reduces the amount of weight gain that remains following birth.

Carbohydrate Needs

As it was prior to pregnancy, carbohydrate intake is a major nutrient in the pregnant athlete's diet. The Dietary Reference Intake (DRI) report suggests that pregnant women consume a daily minimum intake of 175 g carbohydrate (19). Although no specific recommendations have been made for pregnant athletes, it seems prudent to recommend 6 to 8 g carbohydrate per kilogram of pre-pregnancy body weight based on the American College of Sports Medicine, American Dietetic Association, and Dietitians of Canada joint position statement on nutrition and athletic performance (20).

Birth size is modified in part by the effects of maternal carbohydrate intake and physical activity on the availability of feto-placental glucose (21–23), with a diet containing low–glycemic index (GI) carbohydrate foods associated with better maternal and fetal outcomes. The interactions among low- and high-GI carbohydrate intakes, and pre-pregnancy, early pregnancy, and late pregnancy activity levels are complex, but there are indications that insulin-like growth factor-1 (IGF-1) may be a marker for potential low or high birth weight partly due to this interaction (24). Low levels of IGF-1 after 16 weeks' gestation could indicate a need for reduced physical activity and/or increased carbohydrate intake, whereas high IGF-1 may indicate a need for a more emphasis on low-GI carbohydrates and/or the possibility that activity tapering may have occurred in a pregnant athlete. Low-GI carbohydrates before exercise help to stabilize the pregnant athlete's blood glucose during exercise (25). Low-carbohydrate diets are not recommended for pregnant athletes because data in laboratory animals suggest that exercise done in conjunction with a low-carbohydrate diet hampers fetal development (26).

Fat Needs

Health-inducing fats continue to be essential in pregnancy. Fetal fatty acids are provided solely by maternal supplies. There is some evidence that during pregnancy maternal DHA levels decrease and the potential for developing a deficiency increases (27). Increasing maternal intake of n-3 fatty acids has been shown to increase fetal DHA levels (28) and may reduce the risk of preeclampsia. One researcher found that women with the lowest levels of n-3 fatty acids were 7.6 times more likely to have preeclampsia compared with those with the highest level (29). n-6 fats aid the absorption of vitamins A, D, E, and K as well as calcium, all of which are critical in fetal development.

Protein Needs

In pregnancy, protein is needed for growth of the uterus, placenta, and breast tissue, for production of amniotic fluid and a 40% increase in maternal blood volume, for storage reserves for labor, birth, and breastfeeding, and to facilitate rapid fetal tissue growth, in addition to the nonpregnant needs of an athlete. Adequate protein assists in magnesium retention, which reduces the risk for and/or severity of pregnancy-induced hypertension (PIH).

Professional viewpoints vary about protein needs in pregnancy. The American College of Obstetricians and Gynecologists (16) recommends an extra 10 g protein per day, and notes that women who are very active or younger than 14 years may require 1.0 g protein per kilogram of body weight. In this case, a 135-pound pregnant woman would require 60 to 70 g protein per day. However, there are other points of view (2,30), based on the fact that as much as 30% of protein intake may be stored during pregnancy and some used for maternal fuel if total energy intake is inadequate. This equates to 70 to 90 g protein per day for an average American woman with a singleton pregnancy. By adding 25 to 30 g protein per day to her needs based on weight and activity level, and consuming sufficient total energy, an athletic pregnant woman can be assured that she will provide the building blocks required.

Fluid Needs

During pregnancy, water does extra duty, helping to maintain an increased maternal blood volume, cooling both mother and fetus, and carrying waste from increased metabolic functions. While pregnancy tends to reduce the threshold for thirst and attenuate the body's ability to maintain central blood volume (31), eight 8-oz glasses of fluids per day continues to be the commonly accepted amount recommended to maintain an adequate central blood volume. Athletic women may need more and pregnant women living at high altitudes may need to consume twice this amount. Although sport drinks may be useful for those with an intense or long duration work load, a low-GI carbohydrate snack consumed approximately 1 hour before exercise with water or diluted fruit juice consumed during the workout may be sufficient for the recreational exerciser. A few ounces of water consumed every 10 or 15 minutes during intense work is advisable. Athletes should drink water until their urine is clear.

Postpartum Energy Needs

Following birth, a woman's nutritional needs change. If a new mother is not breastfeeding, her metabolic needs can be calculated based on those of a nonpregnant woman. Most experts agree that if breastfeeding is the only source of nourishment for the newborn, the new mother will require approximately 500 extra kcal/day to produce an adequate milk supply. It is essential to continue with the additional protein and even more fluids. Counseling—especially with elite athletes—must include information about increased fluid intake (32). Before exercising, a nursing athlete should drink an extra 6 or 8 oz of water and drink enough throughout the workout to prevent thirst. The volume of milk production will not be compromised if the mother is drinking adequately (33,34). If the infant of an elite athlete is not gaining weight at an acceptable pace, the health care provider should inquire about the extent of exercise by the nursing mother.

Research has found that although lactic acid in breastmilk was significantly increased through 90 minutes postexercise after a maximal intensity treadmill session, there was no significant increase after sessions at 50% or 75% maximum oxygen consumption (VO_{2max}) (35). Women whose infants have an aversion to postexercise breastmilk often express their milk before exercising and give this to their infants in a bottle after exercise, then express and discard postexercise breastmilk. Effects of exercise on mineral and immunoglobin content of breastmilk are minimal and transient (36,37).

In a review of research findings on the effects of energy restriction (as opposed to malnutrition) and maternal weight loss, Dewey (38) concluded that short-term energy deficit in conjunction with exercise and resulting weight loss does not adversely affect lactation, perhaps because of the increase in maternal plasma prolactin concentration associated with a negative energy balance. Little and Clapp (39) compared lactation-induced bone changes in women who participated in self-selected recreational exercise in the early postpartum period with those who did not, and found that exercise had no impact on the bone mineral density loss associated with early postpartum lactation.

Conditions and Situations That May Affect Energy Balance

The value of adequate nutrition and an active pregnancy is evident in the outcome: a healthy, well-developed infant and a healthy mother. Eating disorders, pregnancy-induced hypertension, anemia, or age-related factors can have adverse effects. Postnatal distress is associated with body weight and shape concerns, disordered eating before and during pregnancy, and vomiting during pregnancy (40). Low-intensity exercise during early pregnancy plays a protective role. The most distressed mothers suffer from an eating disorder at the time of pregnancy. The binge and purge type of eating disorder is associated with more psychological distress than a food-restriction type of disorder.

Nausea and vomiting are fairly common in early pregnancy and usually abate around the 12th week. In practice, helping women through early pregnancy nausea and vomiting consists of encouraging them to find out which proteins they can eat and retain, drink plenty of fluids, and maintain electrolyte balance. Sport drinks with 6% to 8% carbohydrate can be useful. Some women find moderate exercise helpful. Eating plenty of protein and eating often in small quantities often alleviates nausea caused by fluctuating plasma glucose levels.

How Much of What Type of Exercise Is Safe and Beneficial?

Most of the seminal research on prenatal and postnatal exercise outcomes involves women who were active before pregnancy, have no underlying pathology contraindicating exercise, and continue to be active during their pregnancies and the immediate postpartum period. Outcomes associated with this group have been cited to illustrate the safety and benefits of regular prenatal and postnatal exercise. There has also been sufficient research involving women with healthy pregnancies who become active in the first half of pregnancy to indicate that the benefits of regular, moderate aerobic activity begun in early pregnancy may extend to all women with a healthy pregnancy. Readers are referred to the extensive discussion of pregnancy and exercise found in the major texts on the subject (1,11,41–43) as references for information in the remainder of this chapter.

Safety and Potential Benefits

Research and evidence-based practice indicate that the traditional threshold for cardiovascular conditioning—20 to 30 minutes of moderate aerobic exercise, 3 to 5 days per week—is also an effective threshold for positive health and birth outcomes in a healthy pregnancy. Forty-five minutes of continuous aerobic activity 4 to 5 days per week may be an upper limit at which fetal fat stores—and consequently birth weight—are negatively affected. In developing exercise prescriptions, prenatal and postnatal fitness professionals use an exercise classification system of five categories to identify the starting point for a given individual (see Box 17.1) (11).

Before determining if, and which, alterations in activity are indicated, it is important to determine the goals of the exercising woman. The main goal is to have a healthy baby. For a woman in either category 1 or 2 (see Box 17.1), if her secondary goals include preparation for birth, controlling weight gain, and a quick postpartum recovery, she must move into category 3. If her secondary goals are to prevent discomfort and meet other pregnant women for social support, it is less critical that she move into the third category, or she can participate in a low-intensity activity such as yoga. Women in categories 3, 4, or 5 also need to identify their secondary goals. Modifications of activities based on pregnancy-related factors (described later in this chapter) may be all that is required. However, women with extensive workout programs may need to reduce the duration of high-intensity aerobic sessions to prevent a negative impact on the baby's health.

Some exercise components have been studied less than aerobic activities. However, these exercises—such as strength training, flexibility, special pregnancy exercises, and mind-body techniques—practiced twice per week can all be helpful in dealing with discomfort and stress, and in preparing for labor. Examples include strengthening the upper

---

Box 17.1   Exercise Classification

1. Inactive or sedentary—does no exercise; performs most activities of daily living, but not more strenuous tasks, such as moving furniture or mowing the lawn.
2. A little activity—accumulates one to three 30-minute activity sessions over the course of a week; these may involve walking, gardening, bicycling, badminton, or other recreational activity.
3. Active—accumulates at least 30 minutes of activity or exercise almost daily, with at least three days involving 15 to 30 minutes of sustained moderate-intensity cardiovascular work; two days involving strength and stretch work; and some centering, relaxation/imagery, or other stress management.
4. Very active—has five or more regular exercise days per week, involving moderate- to high-intensity aerobics, strength, stretch, relaxation, centering/imagery, or other stress management.
5. Professional or competitive—does exercise as a job or lifestyle, involving strenuous exercise daily and appropriate recovery work.

Source: Reprinted with permission from Cowlin AF. *Women's Fitness Program Development.* Champaign, Ill: Human Kinetics; 2002:140.

back and stretching the lower back to help relieve some back discomforts; strengthening the transverse abdominal muscle with the hiss/compress exercise to prepare for pushing during birth; kegel exercises to strengthen the pelvic floor muscles; and centering activities such as yoga, relaxation, and guided imagery (mind-body strategies), which help women learn to work with their bodies rather than fear the intense and painful sensations that can accompany labor.

Perhaps the most important finding of research on physical activity in pregnancy is the effect on placental development from aerobic conditioning in the first and second trimesters. Regular, moderate exercise during this time helps increase placental volume and area for nutrient transport. This enhances nutrient delivery in general and protects the fetus during periods of maternal physical activity when uterine blood flow is reduced. The fetal heart rate increases during maternal exercise, the magnitude of which is dependent on intensity and duration of activity. In a healthy pregnancy, variability is maintained, and the rate returns to baseline within 30 to 90 minutes after exercise. Readers are referred to the extensive discussion of pregnancy and exercise found in the major texts on the subject (1,11,41–43) for more information on the topics covered in the remainder of this chapter.

Women who participate in regular vigorous exercise throughout their pregnancies report lower levels of perceived exertion during pregnancy and labor, less discomfort, and more rapid recovery than those who do not exercise or who stop exercising during pregnancy. Findings concerning length of labor, Cesarean rates, birth weight and Apgar scores are mixed, in part due to the differences in birthing practices, although some studies demonstrate significant decreases in the need for Cesarean delivery among recreational exercisers.

Classic signs of hypoxia or fetal distress in labor—fetal heart rate abnormalities, cord entanglement, the presence of meconium and erythropoietin levels—can be significantly reduced for babies of exercising women. Although there is no increase in gestations of less than 260 days, there may be less postdate gestation and less incidence of low Apgar scores among newborns of exercising mothers. There is no indication of neurological or physical deficits in these infants (44).

Clapp et al (45) have published data demonstrating that morphometric parameters were similar, and no significant differences were observed in psychomotor or mental scales between two groups (exercising mothers and control subjects) of 1-year-olds. Additionally, published data on morphometrics and psychomotor and mental function of 5-year-olds with the same birth history found that motor, integrative, and academic readiness skills were similar to control subjects (8). However, the offspring of exercising mothers performed significantly better on the Wechsler revised intelligence scale and tests of oral language skills. The interpretation of this information is difficult because the results could be influenced by the lifestyle of mothers who choose regular vigorous exercise.

Dangers

Any condition in which physical exertion poses a threat to the life or quality of life of the infant and/or mother is contraindication for exercise. The prenatal health care provider is the appropriate professional to screen pregnant women for exercise. The care provider can rule out clients with contraindications to exercise, note conditions that may benefit from exercise, and review conditions that may require ongoing assessment. Fitness and nutrition professionals must monitor warning signs and symptoms. In this way, problems are most easily avoided and the chance of a positive outcome is maximized. Box 17.2 (11) lists conditions, signs, and symptoms for medical screening that fall into each of these categories.

Box 17.2   Medical Screening for Prenatal Exercise Participation

Contraindications for Exercise
- Placenta previa
- Premature rupture of membranes (PROM)
- Incompetent cervix
- Chronic heart disease
- Premature labor
- Preeclampsia, eclampsia, or pregnancy-induced hypertension
- Tearing or separation of placenta (abruption)
- Fever (or presence of infection)
- Acute and/or chronic life-threatening condition

Conditions That May Benefit from Exercise
- Diabetes
- Gestational diabetes
- Hyperinsulinemia
- Overweight
- Discomforts
- Depression
- Weakness
- Lack of stamina
- Elevated blood pressure

Conditions for Assessment
- Marginal or low-lying placenta
- History of intrauterine growth restriction
- Diabetes or hyperinsulinemia
- Irregular heart beat or mitral valve prolapse
- Anemia
- Multiple gestations
- Thyroid disease
- 3 or more spontaneous abortions
- Excessive over- or underweight
- Extremely sedentary lifestyle
- Asthma

Warning Signs or Symptoms
- Edema of face and hands
- Severe headaches
- Hypertension
- Dizziness or disorientation
- Palpitations or chest pain
- Difficulty walking
- Nausea
- Bleeding or fluid discharge
- Regular strong contractions
- Cramps
- Fever

Source: From Cowlin AF. *Women's Fitness Program Development.* Champaign, Ill: Human Kinetics; 2002:144. Copyright (c) 2002 by Ann F. Cowlin. Modified with permission from Human Kinetics.

Exercise Performance and Indications for Modification in Pregnancy

Due to the physiological and psychosocial changes that occur in pregnancy, exercise regimens are subject to several modifications. Issues that need to be monitored include the potential for orthostatic hypotensive syndromes (low blood pressure due to position); hypertensive disorders of pregnancy; shifts in measurement of exercise intensity, thermoregulation, maintenance of energy balance, respiration, and acid-base balance; biomechanics; and psychophysiology.

Standing still and lying still in the supine (on the back) position for long periods of time are both contraindicated after the first trimester because they lead to reduced venous return and the possibility of reduced blood pressure and reduced uterine perfusion. Resting for 10 to 20 minutes in the side-lying position maximizes blood flow and provides an antidote to the problem of standing for long periods and even for sitting for many hours at a computer. Exercises normally performed on the back can be altered by doing variations on the side, seated, or on hands and knees. After the first trimester, modified curl downs should be substituted for abdominal crunches.

When pregnancy-induced hypertension, preeclampsia, or eclampsia are diagnosed, exercise is generally contraindicated. However, recent evidence indicates that increased blood pressure may respond positively to moderate intensity activity. Regular aerobic activity started before or during early pregnancy probably prevents, or reduces the severity of, hypertensive disorders of pregnancy.

Pregnancy affects the measurement of submaximal exertion intensity. Most frequently, the use of perceived exertion is recommended as a means of delineating an appropriate intensity. Moderate intensity, defined as somewhat hard to hard exertion, will produce adequate intensity for cardiovascular conditioning in pregnancy. An upper limit has been difficult to assess due to genetic variations, the influence of environmental factors on each pregnancy, and the effect of individual pre-pregnancy training regimens. Table 17.1 (11) demonstrates the range of heart rates that may indicate a safe and effective moderate aerobic intensity for healthy pregnant women.

Pregnant women are subject to additional concerns about body temperature. Due to the potential for detrimental teratogenic effects from increased core body temperature, hot tubs, and saunas are contraindicated for pregnant women. Moderate- to high-intensity aerobic exercise for periods of 30 to 45 minutes in well-conditioned women do not seem to increase core temperature enough for potential danger in the presence of adequate hydration. However, the potential exists for overheating in the absence of hydration, in a hot humid environment, or during prolonged high-intensity activity. Professional and highly competitive amateur athletes should be regularly monitored for elevations in core temperature.

There are two periods in a pregnancy during which women often experience dyspnea, or difficulty breathing, regardless of level of physical fitness. When the placenta takes over production of progesterone at the end of the first trimester, the area of the brain that responds to carbon dioxide becomes more sensitive, which causes hyperventilation. In the final months of pregnancy, as the uterus takes up more and more space in the abdomen, the diaphragm can be crowded, which limits its motion. In both cases, dyspnea can occur upon exertion. Slowing movement and breathing slowly using intercostal expansion (expanding the sides and back when inhaling) will generally improve the sensation. If a woman experiences dyspnea while sedentary for a period of time, this can be an indication of deep vein thrombosis and she must be referred to a health care provider.

Women who are physically fit during pregnancy are capable of greater maximal aerobic power and have a greater capacity for sustained aerobic endurance than those who are not. Maintaining fitness through the third trimester also tends to preserve an increased anaerobic threshold in later pregnancy and reduce the metabolic consequences of labor by preventing extensive production of free radicals resulting from the body's exertion during labor and birth.

The changing center of gravity due to the forward and slightly upward growth of the abdomen dictates that each woman reduce the impact of ground forces in aerobic activities and control ballistic impact on joints in open-chain movements (example: free weights) to the degree necessary for her to prevent damage to nerves, blood vessels, and joint facets.

TABLE 17.1   Range of Aerobic Intensities for Healthy Pregnant Women

Intensity	RPE*	Functional Capacity, % VO_{2max}	Heart Rate†, beats/min
	Very light		
		50	
			100–120
			103–123
Low (safe)			106–126
	Fairly light		109–129
			112–132
		60	115–135
			118–138
			121–141
	Somewhat hard		124–144
			127–147
		70	130–150
Moderate (safe and effective)			133–153
			136–156
	Hard		139–159
			142–162
		80	145–165
			148–168
			151–171
	Very hard		154–174
			157–177
High (safety in question)		90	160–180
			163–183
			167–187
	Very, very hard	95	170–190

Abbreviation: RPE, rate of perceived exertion.

*In this setting, only subjective description of RPE has been used.

†Heart rates shown are for women aged 20 to 40 years. Lower values in ranges are likely values for women who are close to age 40 or less fit. Higher values in ranges are likely values for women who are close to age 20 or extremely fit. The correspondence of exercising heart rates and the percentage of functional capacity is a complex relationship, which is dependent on genetic potential, training, and age, and further complicated by the responses of pregnancy. *Source:* From Cowlin AF. *Women's Fitness Program Development.* Champaign, Ill: Human Kinetics; 2002:106 (Figure 6.2). Copyright © 2002 by Ann F. Cowlin. Modified with permission from Human Kinetics.

For some women, particularly in later pregnancy, increases in hormones that soften connective tissue also require adjustments in size and speed of motion. For example, some women find they need to stop running in the second trimester because the impact is too painful, while others continue running, but at a slower pace and with less arm swing, through the end of their pregnancies. To help prevent or reduce the degree of diastasis recti (abdominal muscles pulling away from the linea alba) after 20 weeks, abdominal exercises should be done with a splinting action of the hands pressing the sides of the abdomen toward the center line. This condition will need to be evaluated postpartum and remedial exercises are often helpful.

Active women who are placed on bed rest during pregnancy will experience deconditioning. Some will be able to resume activities of daily living after an episode of premature labor, but others may not. In any case, exercise will likely be contraindicated or the level reduced, and energy requirements will need to be refigured.

Athletic women who are accustomed to exercising alone may find group exercise to be a good way to gain social support. The changing identity that occurs during the childbearing process often provokes the need to be with other mothers-to-be. In addition, the effects of hormonal shifts on the mind and emotions are profound. A woman's sense of well-being and feelings of competency may be affected, and social support during this major life transition can be very helpful. Pre/postnatal group exercise is an ideal way to gain support and prepare for birth at the same time. Even elite athletes benefit from spending 1 or 2 hours per week with a special exercise group.

Sport-Specific Recommendations

Factors that constitute risks in physical activities during pregnancy include danger from equipment, other participants, or the activity environment. Skydiving and scuba diving are examples of sports that are unsafe at any stage of pregnancy. Another factor is the Effort/Shape (46), or combination of energy, timing, and direction used in movements normally done in the execution of an event or activity. Slashing motions pose risks, for example, because they involve forceful, quick movements that are not precisely directed in space at the distal end, and can, therefore, be highly ballistic to proximal joints. An example would be trying to strip a basketball from another player, or defending against such a move. For this reason, only friendly games of basketball are recommended. Another example would be a high leg kick that is not controlled on the way down. Thus, the more percussive martial arts are only recommended early in pregnancy before balance changes affect proprioception and limit the ability to maintain controlled direction of a large movement of the leg. Table 17.2 outlines recommendations for several sports and fitness activities based on these factors.

Management Procedures in Pregnancy

Box 17.3 outlines nutrition management procedures during pregnancy. This outline can be used to augment procedures normally followed when working with nonpregnant women of childbearing age. It is important to keep in mind that modification of activities may have an effect on nutritional needs at several points in the pregnancy.

Summary

Pregnancy presents unique challenges for active women. Although exercise has many benefits for both mother and baby, it needs to be appropriate to each woman's situation to be safe and effective. A mother-to-be must consume the required nutrients to support both her physical activities and her growing baby. She also needs to be willing to modify her routine to accommodate physical changes and safety requirements. By requiring medical screening, identifying goals and an appropriate activity level for a pregnant client, deter-

TABLE 17.2   Prenatal Cardiovascular Activity Chart

> **KEY:** 1 = first trimester; 2 = second trimester; 3 = third trimester. Assessment of activity level is during the trimester under consideration.
>
> Activities marked with * require special skills and/or familiarity with equipment that should already be present and pose dangers because of demands of those skills or equipment.
>
> Activities marked with † are risky even with previous experience because of contraindicated effort/shape or lack of control in the environment, and become increasingly dangerous as pregnancy progresses.
>
> **REMINDER:** The appropriateness of any activity is ultimately a matter only the pregnant woman can assess. If no number is listed, the activity is not recommended at that point in pregnancy.

Activity	Inactive	A Little Inactive	Active	Very Active	Competitive or Professional
Walking, running, and track					
Walking	1 2 3	1 2 3	1 2 3	1 2 3	1 2 3
Speed walking		2 3	1 2 3	1 2 3	1 2 3
Jogging*			1 2	1 2 3	1 2 3
Running*			1 2	1 2	1 2 3
Track events*			1	1 2	1 2
Use of Exercise Machines					
Treadmill*		1 2	1 2 3	1 2 3	1 2 3
Stair machine*			1 2	1 2 3	1 2 3
Slide*†					
Glidewalker*†				1 2	1 2
Cycling					
Stationary cycling	1 2	1 2	1 2 3	1 2 3	1 2 3
Recreational cycling*†		1 2	1 2	1 2	1 2
Competitive cycling*†					1
Swimming and other water activities					
Recreational swimming*†	1 2 3	1 2 3	1 2 3	1 2 3	1 2 3
Water aerobics	2	1 2 3	1 2 3	1 2 3	1 2 3
Lap swimming*			1 2 3	1 2 3	1 2 3
Competitive swimming*†				1 2	1 2
Snorkeling*†		1 2	1 2 3	1 2 3	1 2 3
Water skiing*†					
Scuba diving*†					
Surfing*†					
Day sailing*†			1 2	1 2	1 2 3
Sail boarding*†				1	1
Rowing or sculling, carefully*†				1 2	1 2 3
Ergometer rowing*			1 2	1 2 3	1 2 3
Whitewater canoeing, kayaking*†					

continues

TABLE 17.2   Prenatal Cardiovascular Activity Chart (continued)

Activity	Inactive	A Little Inactive	Active	Very Active	Competitive or Professional
Aerobic classes					
Prenatal aerobic/exercise class	1 2 3	1 2 3	1 2 3	1 2 3	1 2 3
Low-impact/low-intensity aerobics	1 2	1 2 3	1 2 3	1 2 3	1 2 3
Low-impact/high-intensity aerobics*			1 2	1 2 3	1 2 3
High-impact/high-intensity aerobics*†					
Low-step aerobics, beginning*		1 2	1 2 3	1 2 3	1 2 3
Low-step aerobics, advanced*†			1 2	1 2 3	1 2 3
High-step aerobics, advanced*†				1	1
Dance and gymnastics					
Modern dance, beginning	1 2	1 2 3	1 2 3	1 2 3	1 2 3
Modern dance, advanced*			1 2	1 2 3	1 2 3
African/Caribbean dance, beginning		1 2	1 2 3	1 2 3	1 2 3
African/Caribbean dance, advanced			1	1 2	1 2
Mideastern (belly) dance	1 2	1 2 3	1 2 3	1 2 3	1 2 3
Ballet, beginning*		1 2	1 2 3	1 2 3	1 2 3
Ballet, advanced*			1 2	1 2	1 2 3
Jazz dance, beginning*		1 2	1 2	1 2	
Jazz dance, advanced*†		1	1 2	1 2	
Ballroom dance, beginning	1 2	1 2 3	1 2 3	1 2 3	1 2 3
Ballroom dance, advanced*†			1 2	1 2	1 2 3
Contra dance		1 2	1 2 3	1 2 3	1 2 3
Gymnastics*†				1	1
Yoga					
Prenatal yoga	1 2 3	1 2 3	1 2 3	1 2 3	1 2 3
Yoga, beginning*			1	1 2	1 2
Yoga, advanced*			1	1	1
Martial arts					
Tai chi	1 2	1 2 3	1 2 3	1 2 3	1 2 3
Karate, beginning*			1	1	1 2
Karate, advanced*					
Judo, beginning*			1	1	1 2
Judo, advanced*					
Friendly games of . . .					
Badminton*	1 2	1 2 3	1 2 3	1 2 3	1 2 3
Basketball*†			1	1 2	1 2
Frisbee*†	1	1 2	1 2	1 2	1 2
Golf*		1	1 2	1 2	1 2

continues

TABLE 17.2   Prenatal Cardiovascular Activity Chart (continued)

Activity	Inactive	A Little Inactive	Active	Very Active	Competitive or Professional
Handball*†					
Ping-pong*		1	1 2	1 2	1 2
Racquetball*†			1	1	1
Soccer*†			1	1	1
Softball*†			1	1	1
Squash*†					
Tennis*†			1 2	1 2	1 2 3
Volleyball*†			1	1 2	1 2
Skiing, snow boarding, and skating					
Cross-country skiing*†			1 2	1 2	1 2
Ski machine*†			1	1	1
Downhill skiing*†					
Snowboarding or skateboarding*†					
Roller skating or in-line skating*†			1	1 2	1 2
Ice skating*†			1 2	1 2	1 2 3
Other					
Rock climbing*†				1	1
Skydiving*†					

Source: Adapted with permission from *Dancing Thru Pregnancy® Instructor's Manual.* Stony Creek, Conn: DTP, Inc; 1996. Copyright © 1996, 2002 Ann Cowlin.

Box 17.3   Nutrition and Exercise Management Procedures in Pregnancy

1. Have client obtain medical screening (see Box 17.2).
2. Determine prenatal exercise goals.
3. Determine initial exercise category (see Box 17.1).
4. Determine target exercise category and appropriate aerobic intensity to meet goals (see Table 17.1).
5. Determine target weight gain.
6. Compute energy, protein, and water needs.
7. Assess food and water intake, energy expenditure, and weight gain.
8. Get feedback from client and obstetrician or midwife.
9. Modify strategy for comfort, safety, and appropriateness (ongoing).

Source: Copyright © 2004 Ann Cowlin. Used by permission.

mining target weight gain and nutritional requirements, and being supportive about necessary modifications as the pregnancy progresses, the nutrition professional can contribute to a healthy pregnancy outcome. Sports nutrition guidelines for the pregnant athlete are found in Box 17.4 (12,17–22, 25,26,42).

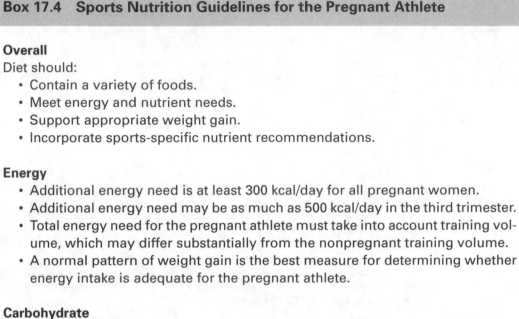

Box 17.4   Sports Nutrition Guidelines for the Pregnant Athlete

Overall
Diet should:
- Contain a variety of foods.
- Meet energy and nutrient needs.
- Support appropriate weight gain.
- Incorporate sports-specific nutrient recommendations.

Energy
- Additional energy need is at least 300 kcal/day for all pregnant women.
- Additional energy need may be as much as 500 kcal/day in the third trimester.
- Total energy need for the pregnant athlete must take into account training volume, which may differ substantially from the nonpregnant training volume.
- A normal pattern of weight gain is the best measure for determining whether energy intake is adequate for the pregnant athlete.

Carbohydrate
- 6–8 g/kg of pre-pregnancy body weight daily.
- Low-glycemic index (GI) carbohydrates should be emphasized.

Protein
- Dietary Reference Intake (DRI) of 71 g/day for pregnant women may not meet the needs of the pregnant athlete.
- Strive for 1.2 to 1.7 g/kg pre-pregnancy body weight daily and adjust appropriately.

Fat
- Emphasize the need for fat for proper maternal and fetal development.
- Emphasize the intake of n-3 fatty acids and other heart healthy fats.

Fiber
- 28 g/day (DRI) to maintain fecal volume and help prevent constipation and hemorrhoids.

Vitamins and Minerals
- Incorporate iron- and folate-rich foods in the diet.
- Include nutrient-dense foods such as fruits, vegetables, and whole grains.
- Prenatal vitamins are routinely prescribed and their consumption is encouraged.

continues

Box 17.4   Sports Nutrition Guidelines for the Pregnant Athlete (continued)

Fluid
- At least 8 to 10 cups of fluid per day. Fruits, vegetables, and other foods with a high water content can help to meet this guideline.
- Moderate to strenuous exercise induces significant water loss through sweat. Fluid loss must be balanced with fluid intake.
- Beverages with 4% to 8% carbohydrate may help prevent hypoglycemia when exercise lasts longer than 45 to 60 minutes and can be used to conveniently replete carbohydrate, fluid, and electrolyte losses.

Nutrition Before, During, and After Exercise
- Eat a small carbohydrate-containing snack approximately 1 hour before exercise and/or consume a fluid-replacement beverage during exercise to prevent hypoglycemia.
- Low-GI carbohydrate-containing foods before exercise can help stabilize blood glucose during exercise.
- During prolonged exercise, use high-GI foods or beverages to prevent hypoglycemia.
- Postexercise snacks that contain both carbohydrate and protein (such as fruit, milk, yogurt, or crackers and peanut butter or juice) are recommended.

Morning Sickness
To reduce the nausea and vomiting associated with morning sickness:
- Drink plenty of fluid in the evening (and middle of the night if awake).
- Avoid becoming hypoglycemic.
- Consume a beverage with 6% to 8% carbohydrate, fruit, whole grain dry toast, granola, and/or dry salty foods (including crackers, potato chips). This may help ameliorate symptoms.
- Perform warm-up exercises to increase circulation.

Source: Box created by D. Enette Larson-Meyer, PhD, RD, FACSM. Data are from references 12, 17–22, 25, 26, and 42.

References

1. American College of Obstetricians and Gynecologists. *ACOG Committee Opinion: Exercise During Pregnancy and the Postpartum Period.* Washington, DC: American College of Obstetricians and Gynecologists; 2002.
2. Varney H, Kriebs JM, Gegor, CL, eds. *Varney's Midwifery.* 4th ed. Boston, Mass: Jones & Bartlett; 2003.
3. Verhoef MJ, Love EJ. Women and exercise participation: the mixed blessings of motherhood. *Health Care Women Int.* 1994;15:297–306.
4. Kramer MS. Aerobic exercise for women during pregnancy (Cochrane Review). In: *The Cochrane Library.* Chichester, England: John Wiley & Sons, Ltd; 2004.

5. Clapp JF 3rd. The athletic woman: a clinical approach to exercise in pregnancy. *Clin Sports Med.* 1994;13:443–458.

6. Bungum TJ, Peaslee DL, Jackson AW, Perez MA. Exercise during pregnancy and type of delivery in nulliparae. *J Obstet Gynecol Neonatal Nurs.* 2000;29:258–264.

7. Lokey EA, Tran ZV, Wells CL, Myers BC, Tran AC. Effects of physical exercise on pregnancy outcomes: a meta-analytic review. *Med Sci Sports Exerc.* 1991;23:1234–1239.

8. Clapp JF 3rd. Morphometric and neurodevelopmental outcome at age five years of the offspring of women who continued to exercise regularly throughout pregnancy. *J Pediatr.* 1996;129: 856–862.

9. Ohtake PJ, Wolfe LA. Physical conditioning attenuates respiratory responses to steady-state in late gestation. *Med Sci Sports Exerc.* 1998;30:17–27.

10. Kobe H, Nakai A, Koshino T, Araki T. Effect of regular maternal exercise on lipid peroxidation levels and antioxidant enzymatic activities before and after delivery. *J Nippon Med Sch.* 2002;69:542–548.

11. Cowlin AF. *Women's Fitness Program Development.* Champaign, Ill: Human Kinetics; 2002.

12. Institute of Medicine Committee on Nutritional Status During Pregnancy and Lactation. *Nutrition During Pregnancy.* Washington, DC: National Academy Press; 1990.

13. Leiferman JA, Evenson KR. The effect of regular leisure physical activity on birth outcomes. *Matern Child Health J.* 2003;7:59–64.

14. Sorensen TK, Williams MA, Lee IM, Dashow EE, Thompson ML, Luthy DA. Recreational physical activity during pregnancy and risk of preeclampsia. *Hypertension.* 2003;41:1273–1280.

15. Yeo S, Davidge ST. Possible beneficial effect of exercise by reducing oxidative stress, on the incidence of preeclampsia [review]. *J Womens Health Gend Based Med.* 2001;10:983–989.

16. American College of Obstetricians and Gynecologists. *Nutrition During Pregnancy.* Washington, DC: American College of Obstetricians and Gynecologists; 2002. ACOG patient education pamphlet AP001.

17. Kaiser LL, Allen L. Position of the American Dietetic Association: nutrition and lifestyle for a healthy pregnancy outcome. *J Am Diet Assoc.* 2002;102:1479–1490.

18. Butte NF, Wong WW, Treuth MS, Ellis KJ, O'Brian Smith E. Energy requirements during pregnancy based on total energy expenditure and energy deposition. *Am J Clin Nutr.* 2004;79: 1078–1087.

19. Institute of Medicine. *Dietary Reference Intakes for Energy, Carbohydrate, Fiber, Fat, Fatty Acids, Cholesterol, Protein, and Amino Acids (Macronutrients).* Washington, DC: National Academy Press; 2002. Available at: http://www.nap.edu/books. Accessed November 16, 2004.

20. American College of Sports Medicine, American Dietetic Association, and Dietitians of Canada. Nutrition and athletic performance. Joint position statement. *Med Sci Sports Exerc.* 2000;32:2130–2145.

21. Clapp JF 3rd. Maternal carbohydrate intake and pregnancy outcome. *Proc Nutr Soc.* 2002;61:45–50.

22. Clapp JF 3rd. The effect of dietary carbohydrate on the glucose and insulin response to mixed caloric intake and exercise in both nonpregnant and pregnant women. *Diabetes Care.* 1998; 21(Suppl 2):B107–B112.

23. Clapp JF 3rd. The effects of maternal exercise on fetal oxygenation and feto-placental growth. *Eur J Obstet Gynecol Reprod Biol.* 2003;110(Suppl 1):S80–S85.

24. Clapp JF 3rd, Schmidt S, Paranjape A, Lopez B. Maternal insulin-like growth factor-I levels (IGF-I) reflect placental mass and neonatal fat mass. *Am J Obstet Gynecol.* 2004;190:730–736.

25. Siu PM, Wong SH. Use of the glycemic index: effects on feeding patterns and exercise performance. *J Physiol Anthropol Appl Hum Sci.* 2004;23:1–6.

26. Cobrin M, Koski KG. Maternal dietary carbohydrate restriction and mild-to-moderate exercise during pregnancy modify aspects of fetal development in rats. *J Nutr.* 1995;125:1617–1627.

27. Holman RT, Johnson SB, Ogburn, PL. Deficiency of essential fatty acids and membrane fluidity during pregnancy and lactation. *Proc Nat Acad Sci.* 1991;88:4835–4839.

28. Connor WE, Lowensohn R, Hatcher L. Increased doosahexaenoic acid levels in human newborn infants by administration of sardines and fish oil during pregnancy. *Lipids.* 1996; 31(suppl): 183S–187S.

29. Williams MA, Zingheim RW, King IB. Omega-3 fatty acids in maternal erythrocytes and risk of preeclampsia. *Epidemiology.* 1995;6:232–237.

30. Brewer TH, Brewer GS. *The Brewer Medical Diet for Normal and High-Risk Pregnancy.* New York, NY: Simon and Schuster; 1983.

31. Heenan AF, Wolfe LA, Davies GA, McGrath MJ. Effects of human pregnancy on fluid regulation responses to short-term exercise. *J Appl Physiol.* 2003;95:2321–2327.

32. Hale RW, Milne L. The elite athlete and exercise in pregnancy. *Semin Perinatol.* 1996;20: 277–284.

33. Dewey KG, Lovelady CA, Nommsen-Rivers LA, McCrory MA, Lonnerdal B. A randomized study of the effects of aerobic exercise by lactating women on breast milk volume and composition. *N Engl J Med.* 1994;330:449–453.

34. Lovelady CA, Lonnerdal B, Dewey KB. Lactation performance of exercising women. *Am J Clin Nutr.* 1990;52:103–109.

35. Carey GB, Quinn TJ, Goodwin SE. Breast milk composition after exercise of different intensities. *J Hum Lact.* 1997;13:115–120.

36. Fly AD, Uhlin KL, Wallace JP. Major mineral concentrations in human milk do not change after maximal exercise testing. *Am J Clin Nutr.* 1998;68:345–349.

37. Gregory RL, Wallace JP, Gfell LE, Marks J, King BA. Effect of exercise on milk immunoglobin A. *Med Sci Sports Exerc.* 1997;29:1596–1601.

38. Dewey KG. Effects of maternal caloric restriction and exercise during lactation. *J Nutr.* 1998;128(2 Suppl):386S–389S.

39. Little KD, Clapp JF 3rd. Self-selected recreational exercise has no impact on early postpartum lactation-induced bone loss. *Med Sci Sports Exerc.* 1998;30:831–836.

40. Abraham S, Taylor A, Conti J. Postnatal depression, eating, exercise, and vomiting before and during pregnancy. *Int J Eat Disord.* 2001;29:482–487.

41. American College of Obstetricians and Gynecologists. *Exercise During Pregnancy and the Postpartum Period.* Washington, DC: American College of Obstetricians and Gynecologists; 1994. Technical Bulletin No. 179.

42. Clapp JF 3rd. *Exercising Through Your Pregnancy.* Champaign, Ill: Human Kinetics; 1998.

43. Clapp JF 3rd. The athletic woman: exercise during pregnancy. A clinical update. *Clin Sports Med.* 2000;19:273–286.

44. Clapp JF 3rd. The effects of maternal exercise on early pregnancy outcome. *Am J Obstet Gynecol.* 1989;161:1453.

45. Clapp JF 3rd, Simonian S, Lopez B, Appley-Wineberg S, Harcar-Sevik R. The one-year morphometric and neurodevelopmental outcome of the offspring of women who continued to exercise regularly throughout pregnancy. *Am J Obstet Gynecol.* 1998;178:594–599.

46. Bartenieff I. *A Primer for Movement Description: Using Effort/Shape and Supplementary Concepts.* New York, NY: Dance Notation Bureau; 1970.

47. *Dancing Thru Pregnancy® Instructor's Manual.* Stony Creek, Conn: DTP, Inc; 1996.

Chapter 18

DISORDERED EATING IN ATHLETES

Katherine A. Beals, PhD, RD, FACSM

Introduction

Since the early 1980s, a growing body of literature has documented eating disturbances and body weight issues in athletes. Despite the interest of the scientific community, disordered eating in athletes did not garner mainstream attention until Christy Henrich's much-publicized battle with, and eventual death from, anorexia nervosa. The death of this 22-year-old gymnast seemed to open the door to the eating disorder closet, as several other well-recognized athletes (eg, Nadia Comaneci, Dara Torres, and Zina Garrison) as well as collegiate and even recreational athletes began to reveal their own personal struggles with disordered eating.

With the increasing visibility of eating disorders in athletes has come the need to create programs and recruit personnel to identify, prevent, and treat them. The sports dietitian is often the first person to come into contact with an eating-disordered athlete and is almost always an integral member of the treatment team. Thus, it is essential that he or she have a firm understanding of eating disorders and is prepared to provide appropriate nutritional care. This chapter provides sports nutrition professionals with background information as well as the tools needed to successfully manage disordered eating in athletes.

Eating Disorder Categories and Classification

The terms *eating disorder* and *disordered eating* are frequently, yet erroneously, used interchangeably, both in the literature and in general practice. Strictly speaking, the term *eating disorder* refers to one of the three clinically diagnosable conditions—anorexia nervosa, bulimia nervosa, or eating disorders not otherwise specified (EDNOS)—recognized in the 4th edition of the American Psychiatric Association's *Diagnostic and Statistical Manual of Mental Disorders* (DSM-IV) (1). To be diagnosed with a clinical eating disorder, an individual must meet a standard set of criteria as outlined in the DSM-IV (1). The criteria can be found in Appendix D. Disordered eating, on the other hand, is a general term used to describe the spectrum of abnormal and harmful eating behaviors that are used in a misguided attempt to lose weight or maintain a lower than normal body weight (2).

The Clinical Conditions

According to the most recent edition of the DSM, the clinical eating disorders—anorexia nervosa, bulimia nervosa, and EDNOS—are characterized by severe disturbances in eating behavior and body image (1). It must be emphasized that the clinical eating disorders are psychiatric conditions and, as such, they go beyond simple body weight/shape dissatisfaction and involve more than just abnormal eating patterns and pathogenic weight-control behaviors. Individuals with clinical eating disorders often experience comorbid psychological conditions, such as obsessive-compulsive disorder, depression, and anxiety disorder (3). They often come from dysfunctional families and have a history of physical and emotional abuse. In addition, they often display severe feelings of insecurity and worthlessness, have trouble identifying and displaying emotions, and experience difficulty in forming close relationships with others.

Athletes with clinical eating disorders resemble their nonathletic counterparts in many ways; however, there are subtle but important differences that sports dietitians should be aware of. Athletes with anorexia nervosa, like their nonathletic counterparts, are obsessed with the desire to be thin. However, unlike nonathletes with anorexia, who generally view thinness as the only goal, athletes with anorexia strive for thinness *and* the improvement in performance that they believe will accompany it. This is particularly (although not exclusively) true for female athletes, especially those participating in sports that emphasize leanness. Although starving in the name of improved performance may seem counterproductive to the objective eye, the athlete with anorexia is not logical when it comes to body weight and often has come to embrace (and embody) the notion that thinner is better (ie, faster, stronger, more pleasing to the judges, etc).

Athletes with anorexia are generally more resistant to intervention and often more difficult to identify. To be competitive, athletes often follow rigid dietary practices and engage in intense, and what might be considered excessive, physical training, thus making it difficult to distinguish the committed athlete from the diet- and exercise-obsessed individual with anorexia (4).

Athletes with bulimia nervosa, like nonathletes with the same condition, engage in regular binge–purge cycles; however, both the binge and purge may be somewhat less clear when it comes to athletes. According to the DSM-IV (1), a binge is defined as eating "a large amount of food in a discrete period of time." As might be expected, problems arise in interpreting the phrases "large amount of food" (larger than most individuals under similar circumstances) and "discrete period of time," particularly as they apply to athletes. It could be argued that, because of increased energy expenditure and therefore increased energy requirements, athletes generally consume more food than most individuals. Moreover, the varied energy needs of athletes make it difficult to characterize or compare "similar circumstances." The context of eating must also be considered. For example, what may be thought of as excessive consumption at a typical meal might be considered normal under certain circumstances, such as carbohydrate loading for a competitive event or refueling after a particularly prolonged or intense training session or competition.

The factors precipitating binge–purge cycles and the rationalizations accompanying them also serve to differentiate athletes with bulimia nervosa from their nonathletic counterparts (4). For example, the nonathlete with bulimia generally restricts food intake for weight loss alone, whereas food restriction for the athlete with the same condition often serves a dual purpose: weight loss and performance enhancement (or at least the athlete uses the guise of performance to justify food restriction). Although typically triggered by periods of food restriction or dieting, the bingeing and purging cycles of the athlete with bulimia nervosa may be caused by other factors unique to the sport setting, including athletic identity crises and performance dynamics. As is true for athletes with anorexia, athletes with bulimia tend to connect self-esteem and self-worth to athletic performance. Anything that threatens these athletes' fragile sense of self-esteem (eg, a poor performance, negative comment from a coach or teammates) can serve to elicit a binge-and-purge cycle.

Finally, the athletic environment provides unique situations for bingeing as well as purging that are generally not available to the nonathlete with bulimia. The common practice of carbohydrate loading before an endurance event is a key example of a situation in which the athlete with bulimia is actually encouraged to engage in the very behavior that epitomizes the disease. Team meals may serve to further complicate matters because the social situation and peer pressure may serve to increase food consumption. These environmental cues, individually or collectively, can increase the likelihood of a binge and a subsequent purge.

It has also been suggested that athletes with bulimia nervosa are more likely to engage in excessive exercise after a binge than their nonathletic counterparts, who are more apt to purge using vomiting or laxatives (5). This difference in purging behaviors is again largely explained by the nature of the sport setting. That is, because exercise is a behavior that athletes already engage in, it is easier for athletes with bulimia, like those with anorexia, to disguise their condition with excessive physical activity or at least to rationalize increased exercise in the name of improved performance. Conversely, concealing vomiting or the use of laxatives and diuretics is much more difficult for the athlete, particularly during road trips or other team functions (5).

Subclinical Variants

In some cases, athletes may exhibit all of the overt behaviors of a clinical eating disorder but do not harbor the severe psychological disturbances that underlie the clinical disorders (5–9). These partial or eating disorder syndromes have been classified and characterized in a variety of ways by several researchers and practitioners. Some of the more common of these classifications include the following.

Anorexia Athletica/Fear of Obesity

A prominent researcher in the area of eating disorders in athletes, Jorunn Sundgot-Borgen (10) has developed a set of criteria to describe a variant of anorexia nervosa in athletes, which she refers to as *anorexia athletica*. The following is a list of essential features of anorexia athletica. Features marked with + are absolute criteria; (+) are relative criteria.

- Weight loss of more than 5% of expected body weight   +
- Delayed menarche (ie, no menstrual bleeding by age 16 years)   (+)
- Menstrual dysfunction (amenorrhea or oligomenorrhea)   (+)
- Gastrointestinal complaints   (+)
- Absence of medical illness or affective disorder to explain the weight loss +
- Body image distortion   (+)
- Excessive fear of weight gain or becoming obese   +

- Restriction of energy intake (less than 1,200 kcal/day)   +
- Use of purging methods (eg, self-induced vomiting, laxatives, diuretics)   (+)
- Binge eating   (+)
- Compulsive exercise   (+)

It should be noted that the criteria for anorexia athletica were derived largely from a set criteria used to describe a disorder referred to as "fear-of-obesity" observed in a small sample of nonathletic adolescents (11).

Subclinical Eating Disorders

The term *subclinical eating disorder* has frequently been used by researchers to describe individuals, both athletes and nonathletes, who present with considerable eating pathology and body weight concerns but do not demonstrate significant psychopathology and/or fail to meet all of the DSM-IV (1) criteria for anorexia nervosa, bulimia nervosa, or EDNOS (6–8,12,13). Indeed, many athletes who report using pathogenic weight control methods (eg, laxatives, diet pills, and excessive exercise) do not technically meet the criteria for a clinical eating disorder. Conversely, athletes may use none of these methods but still have an obvious eating disorder.

For example, one female collegiate distance runner reported routinely eating approximately 1,000 kcal/day while averaging 60 miles/week (and "working out" at the gym in addition to her regular training regimen). She ate similar foods every day and severely limited her fat intake (no more than 20 g/day). Occasionally she would "binge" by eating a forbidden food (eg, a piece of cake or an order of french fries) and she would have to exercise afterward to "burn off" what she had eaten. Although she was openly dissatisfied with her body weight and shape (despite the fact her body weight was on the low end of normal for her height), she did not display any significant emotional distress or psychological disturbance.

This athlete definitely displays disordered eating behaviors; however, she does not meet the diagnostic criteria for either anorexia nervosa or bulimia nervosa. In fact, depending on the context of the evaluation, she might not even meet the criteria necessary for a diagnosis of EDNOS. This example serves to emphasize that it should not be the precise eating disorder diagnosis that is of primary concern, but rather the extent to which the disordered eating compromises the athlete's physical and mental health. In this case, it is only a matter of time before the athlete's disordered eating behaviors negatively affect her performance as well as her health.

Prevalence

Current estimates of the prevalence of disordered eating among athletes are highly variable, ranging from less than 1% to as high as 62% in female athletes (2,14,15), and between 0% and 57% in male athletes (15,16). This wide-range of estimates is due to differences in screening instruments/assessment tools used (eg, self-report questionnaires vs in-depth interviews), definitions of eating disorders applied (few have used the DSM-IV criteria), and the athletic populations studied (eg, collegiate vs high school athletes, elite athletes vs recreational athletes vs those who are physically active but noncompetitive). Only four studies (10,13,17,18) have used large (N > 400) heterogeneous samples of athletes and validated measures of disordered eating (10,17,19) (see Table 18.1). The remainder had inadequate

TABLE 18.1   Summary of Prevalence Studies Including Large, Heterogeneous Samples of Athletes and Validated Assessments of Disordered Eating

Study	Subjects	Instruments	Findings
Beals and Manore (17)	425 female collegiate athletes	EAT-26 and EDI-BD	3.3% and 2.4% of the athletes self-reported a diagnosis of clinical anorexia and bulimia nervosa, respectively; 15% and 31.5% of the athletes scored more than the designated cutoff scores on the EAT-26 and EDI-BD, respectively.
Johnson, Powers, and Dick (19)	1,445 collegiate athletes (883 men and 562 women) from 11 NCAA Division I Schools	EDI-2 and questionnaire developed by the authors using DSM-IV criteria	None of the men met the criteria for anorexia or bulimia nervosa; 1.1% of the women met the criteria for bulimia nervosa. 9.2% of the women and 0.01% of the men met the criteria for subclinical bulimia; 2.8% met the criteria for subclinical anorexia. 5.5% of the women and 2% of the men reported purging (vomiting, using laxatives or diuretics) on a weekly basis.
Sundgot-Borgen (10)	522 Norwegian elite female athletes	EDI and in-depth interview developed by the author based on DSM-III criteria	1.3%, 8.0%, and 8.2% were diagnosed with anorexia nervosa, bulimia nervosa, and anorexia athletica, respectively.
Sundgot-Borgen et al (18)	The total population of Norwegian elite athletes (960 men and 660 women) representing 60 different sporting events	A questionnaire developed by the authors, including subscales of the EDI, weight history, and self-reported history of eating disorders	20% (n = 156) of the female athletes and 8% (n = 27) of the male athletes met the DSM-IV criteria for a clinical eating disorders (ie, anorexia nervosa, bulimia nervosa, or EDNOS).

Abbreviations: DSM, *Diagnostic and Statistical Manual of Mental Disorders;* EAT-26, Eating Attitudes Test; EDI, Eating Disorder Inventory; EDI-2, Eating Disorder Inventory 2; EDI-BD, Eating Disorder Inventory Body Dissatisfaction Subscale; EDNOS, eating disorders not otherwise specified; NCAA, National Collegiate Athletic Association.

sample sizes, examined single sports, or used incorrect measures of disordered eating, all of which can bias prevalence estimates.

Despite the conflicting prevalence estimates derived from the available research, the current data are consistent in indicating the following three points: (*a*) female athletes are at more risk for disordered eating behaviors than their male counterparts; (*b*) there is a higher incidence of disordered eating (including both clinical and subclinical eating disorders) in athletes participating in sports or activities in which a lean physique is considered advantageous or the norm; and (*c*) the prevalence of subclinical eating disorders exceeds that of the clinical eating disorders (6,14,20,21).

Etiology

Most eating disorders experts maintain that the etiology of disordered eating is multifactorial and encompasses a complex interaction between sociocultural, demographic, environmental, biological, psychological, and behavioral factors (22). Many of these same factors have been shown to place the athlete at risk for disordered eating. In addition, research has identified some sport-specific risk factors for the development of disordered eating among athletes (23). The etiological factors for disordered eating are described in the following sections.

Sociocultural Factors

Eating disorders are more prevalent in industrialized/developed countries (eg, Australia, Canada, England, France, and the United States) compared with less industrialized/developed countries. The reasons for this cultural difference is not completely understood, but it is thought to be largely due to the sociocultural influences unique to developed countries, one of the most pervasive being attitudes about body weight. In most modern societies, being thin is equated with beauty, as well as a several other positive attributes, including goodness, success, and power (24).

Although women experience the brunt of societal pressure to be thin, men are beginning to react to body weight and shape pressures with increasing frequency. Little formal research has been done, but indirect evidence and anecdotal reports suggest that men, particularly those engaged in athletics or who are regularly physically active, are becoming increasingly concerned and subsequently dissatisfied with their bodies (25).

Athletes may face even more pressure than nonathletes to achieve or maintain a particular body weight or shape (23). Indeed, athletes must not only meet the current body weight ideals held by society in general but also conform to the specific aesthetic and performance demands of their sport. This pressure may be particularly high for athletes in thin-build sports or activities that require a low body weight or lean physique, such as dance (especially ballet), gymnastics, distance running, triathlon, swimming, diving, figure skating, cheerleading, wrestling, and lightweight rowing. This pressure can be particularly strong (rendering the development of an eating disorder much more likely) when there is a discrepancy between the athlete's actual body weight and the perceived ideal body weight for the athlete's particular sport (14). For example, a naturally larger athlete who wishes to compete in gymnastics or a naturally heavier wrestler who is trying to compete in a lower weight class may feel especially strong pressure to alter his or her body weight.

Psychosocial Factors

Individuals with eating disorders often come from dysfunctional families, particularly those with overbearing or controlling parents, victims of physical or sexual abuse, or those whose parents have a history of alcoholism or substance abuse (22,26). Such family environments can cause severe psychological and emotional distress, undermine the development of self-esteem, and lead to inadequate coping skills, all of which may increase the risk that an eating disorder might develop. Although family dysfunction may not be a common causative factor in athletes, it should always be considered a possibility. For example, an athlete may feel overwhelmed or out of control as a result of an injury, a particularly poor performance, or the excessive demands of a coach. Because of a dysfunctional family environment, the athlete may have never developed the coping skills necessary to handle these problems, and thus the athlete concentrates on something that can be managed, such as body weight.

Biological Factors

A biological-behavioral model of activity-based anorexia nervosa was proposed in a series of studies by Epling and Pierce (27) and Epling et al (28). These researchers theorized that dieting and exercising initiate the anorexic cycle and claimed that as many as 75% of the cases of anorexia nervosa are exercise-induced. The theory holds that strenuous exercise suppresses appetite, which leads to a decrease in food intake and subsequent reduction in body weight. It should be noted that this research was conducted with rats and has not been replicated in humans (29). Additional biological factors that have been implicated in the development of disordered eating include gender (it is estimated that females outnumber males 10 to 1), early onset of menarche (younger than age 12 years), and propensity toward obesity (1,25).

Psychological and Behavioral Factors

Personality traits contribute largely to the psychological predisposition for disordered eating. Some of the general personality traits characteristic of athletes are similar to those manifested by patients with eating disorders (30). For example, both groups tend to be goal-oriented, achievement-driven, independent, persistent, and tolerant of pain and discomfort. In addition, it has been hypothesized that athletes, particularly female athletes, may be more vulnerable to eating disorders than the general female population because of additional stressors associated with the fitness or athletic environment (5,23).

Sport-Specific Factors

Recent research findings indicate that certain inherent pressures and/or demands of the sport setting may serve to "trigger" the development of an eating disorder in psychologically susceptible athletes (5,13,23). In a study investigating risk and trigger factors for the development of eating disorders, Sundgot-Borgen (23) found that female athletes suffering from eating disorders often started sport-specific training and dieting at significantly earlier ages than athletes without eating disorders . In addition, prolonged periods of dieting, frequent weight fluctuations, sudden increases in training volume, or traumatic life events such as an injury or a change of coach tended to trigger the development of eating disorders (23).

Some researchers have proposed that specific sports or physical activities (ie, those that emphasize leanness or require large training volumes) may "attract" individuals with eating disorders, particularly anorexia nervosa, because these activities provide a setting in which individuals can use or abuse exercise to expend extra energy and hide or justify their abnormal eating and dieting behaviors (20,31). Moreover, the stereotypical standards of body shape in women's sports and physical activities that emphasize leanness make it difficult for observers to notice when an individual has lost too much weight. These common and accepted low weight standards may help active women with disordered eating hide and/or justify their problem and delay intervention (23,31).

Effects on Health and Performance

The effects of disordered eating on health and performance of the athlete can be surprisingly variable, but they are generally dependent on the severity and chronicity of the disorder. Some athletes may be able to engage in disordered eating behaviors for extended periods of time with few long-term negative effects (5). For most, however, it is simply a matter of time before the pathogenic weight control behaviors and chronic energy restriction negatively affect their physical performance and, more importantly, their physical and emotional health.

Health

The morbidity associated with disordered eating can be explained by (*a*) the restriction of calories and the resulting state of starvation or semistarvation, and (*b*) the purging techniques used to rid the body of ingested energy. Athletes who chronically or severely restrict energy intake will likely have macro- and micronutrient deficiencies, anemia, chronic fatigue, and an increased risk of infections, injury, and illnesses (32,33). Additional health effects associated with chronic or severe energy restriction and the resulting weight loss (or maintenance of a dangerously low body weight) include decreased basal metabolic rate, cardiovascular and gastrointestinal disorders, depression, menstrual dysfunction, and the resulting decrease in bone mineral density (34) (Table 18.2 [4] and Box 18.1 [2]).

Athletes who engage in bingeing and purging have many of the same health complications as those with anorexia nervosa (eg, nutrient deficiencies, chronic fatigue, endocrine abnormalities, and bone mineral density reductions); however, the gastrointestinal and cardiovascular complications are somewhat distinct. Bingeing frequently causes gastric distention that, in rare cases, can result in gastric necrosis and even rupture (35). Esophageal reflux and subsequent chronic throat irritation are also common and may increase the risk for esophageal cancer (36). The gastrointestinal complications associated with purging depend on the purging methods used and can include throat and mouth ulcers, dental caries, abdominal cramping, diarrhea, and hemorrhoids (35,37) (refer to Table 18.2).

Electrolyte imbalances, particularly hypokalemia (ie, low blood potassium levels), are also common in individuals who engage in purging behaviors and can have debilitating effects on health. The cardiovascular complications associated with bingeing and purging are usually secondary to the electrolyte imbalances induced by purging. As described earlier, hypokalemia can result in potentially life-threatening cardiac arrhythmia. In addition, individuals who abuse ipecac may have myocarditis (inflammation of the middle layer of the heart muscle) and various cardiomyopathies (36). Alterations in electrolyte levels as a result of purging can lead to dangerous disruptions in the body's acid-base balance and life-threatening alterations in the body's pH. Self-induced vomiting typically results in an increase in serum bicarbonate levels and thus leads to metabolic alkalosis (increase in blood pH). On the other hand, individuals who abuse laxatives are most likely to develop metabolic acidosis (decrease in blood pH) secondary to loss of bicarbonate in the stool (36).

Performance

Surprisingly, anecdotal evidence (ie, reports from coaches and personal accounts by athletes with disordered eating) suggests that athletes practicing disordered eating behaviors often experience an initial, albeit transient, increase in performance. The reasons for this temporary increase in performance are not completely understood but are thought to be related to the initial physiological and psychological effects of starvation and purging (38). Starvation and purging are physiological stressors and, as such, produce an up-regulation of

TABLE 18.2 Health Consequences of Disordered Eating Behaviors

Weight Control Behavior	Physiological Effects and Health Consequences
Fasting or starvation	Promotes loss of lean body mass, a decrease in metabolic rate, and a reduction in bone mineral density. Increases the risk of nutrient deficiencies. Promotes glycogen depletion, resulting in poor exercise performance.
Diet pills	Typically function by suppressing appetite and may cause a slight increase in metabolic rate (if they contain ephedrine or caffeine). May induce rapid heart rate, anxiety, inability to concentrate, nervousness, inability to sleep, and dehydration. Any weight lost is quickly regained once use is discontinued.
Diuretics	Weight loss is primarily water, and any weight lost is quickly regained once use is discontinued. Dehydration and electrolyte imbalances are common and may disrupt thermoregulatory function and induce cardiac arrhythmia.
Laxatives or enemas	Weight loss is primarily water, and any weight lost is quickly regained once use is discontinued. Dehydration and electrolyte imbalances, constipation, cathartic colon (a condition in which the colon becomes unable to function properly on its own), and steatorrhea (excessive fat in the feces) are common. May be addictive, and athlete can develop resistance, thus requiring larger and larger doses to produce the same effect (or even to induce a normal bowel movement).
Self-induced vomiting	Largely ineffective in promoting weight (body fat) loss. Large body water losses can lead to dehydration and electrolyte imbalances. Gastrointestinal problems, including esophagitis, esophageal perforation, and esophageal and stomach ulcers, are common. May promote erosion of tooth enamel and increase the risk for dental caries. Finger calluses and abrasions are often present.
Fat-free diets	May be lacking in essential nutrients, especially fat-soluble vitamins and essential fatty acids. Total energy intake must still be reduced to produce weight loss. Many fat-free convenience foods are highly processed, with high sugar contents and few micronutrients unless the foods are fortified. The diet is often difficult to follow and may promote binge eating.
Saunas	Weight loss is primarily water, and any weight lost is quickly regained once fluids are replaced. Dehydration and electrolyte imbalances are common and may disrupt thermoregulatory function and induce cardiac arrhythmia.
Excessive exercise	Increases risk of staleness, chronic fatigue, illness, overuse injuries, and menstrual dysfunction.

Source: Reprinted with permission from Beals KA. *Disordered Eating Among Athletes: A Comprehensive Guide for Health Professionals.* Champaign, Ill: Human Kinetics; 2004:84–85. Originally adapted with permission from *ACSM's Health and Fitness Journal.* Lippincott, Williams, and Wilkins.

the hypothalamic-pituitary-adrenal axis, (ie, "the fight-or-flight response") and an increase in the adrenal hormones: cortisol, epinephrine, and norepinephrine. These hormones have a stimulatory effect on the central nervous system that can mask fatigue and evoke feelings of euphoria in the eating disordered athlete. In addition, the initial decrease in body weight (particularly before there is a significant decrease in muscle mass) may induce a transient increase in relative maximal oxygen uptake (VO_{2max}) per kilogram of body weight (39).

Box 18.1   The Female Athlete Triad

The *female athlete triad* (Triad) refers to three distinct yet interrelated disorders: (*a*) disordered eating, (*b*) menstrual dysfunction, and (*c*) osteoporosis. Although any of these disorders can, and do, occur in isolation, they often follow a typical developmental pattern. In an attempt to improve performance or meet the aesthetic demands of her sport, the female athlete engages in disordered eating behaviors. The energy imbalance and hormonal alterations resulting from the disordered eating leads to menstrual dysfunction, which eventually causes decreases in bone mineral density and possibly premature osteoporosis. Because of the difficulty of measuring all three disorders of the triad simultaneously, there is currently no data describing the prevalence of the Triad among female athletes.

Source: Data are from reference 2.

Moreover, with weight loss, athletes may feel lighter, which may afford them a psychological boost, particularly if they believe that lighter is always better in terms of performance.

It should be emphasized that the increase in performance sometimes seen with disordered eating is only temporary. Eventually, the body will break down and performance will suffer. The decrement in performance seen with chronic or severe energy restriction is likely due to one or more of the following factors: nutrient deficiencies, anemia, fatigue, reduced cardiovascular function, frequent infection, illness, and/or injuries (4). As previously described, individuals with bulimia nervosa may purge or attempt to compensate for their bingeing episodes by using diuretics, laxatives, or enemas; self-induced vomiting; or exercising excessively. If the purging or compensatory behaviors place the athlete in a state of negative energy balance, then the potential effects on performance are similar to those seen with chronic or severe energy restriction. Also, the gastrointestinal blood losses that often result from chronic vomiting can contribute to iron losses and increase the risk of iron deficiency anemia. Excessive exercise, especially given inadequate energy and nutrient intakes, invariably leads to overuse injuries. In addition to the resulting energy and nutrient deficiencies, purging poses some unique problems regarding athletic performance, most notably dehydration and electrolyte abnormalities (40).

The effects of disordered eating on athletic performance are a function of the severity and duration of the disordered eating behaviors as well as the physiological demands of the sport (4). Thus, an individual who engages in severe energy restriction or who has been bingeing and purging for a long time will likely experience a greater decrement in performance than one who has engaged in milder weight-control behaviors for a shorter period of time. Likewise, endurance sports and other physical activities with high energy demands (eg, distance running, swimming, cycling, basketball, and field and ice hockey) are likely to be more negatively affected than sports with lower energy demands (eg, diving, gymnastics, weightlifting). Finally, athletes who train at a high intensity (eg, elite athletes) are apt to have greater performance decrements than those who engage in lower-intensity exercise (eg, recreational athletes).

Prevention

According to Thompson and Sherman (5), the goal of eating disorder prevention is to "inoculate" athletes against the factors that predispose them to disordered eating. Unfortunately, as was previously described, many of the factors that predispose an athlete to disordered eating (eg, biological or psychological predisposition; dysfunctional family life; being female, white, or of adolescent age) are considered unalterable and as such are largely outside the control of coaches, athletic staff, or health professionals. Prevention efforts must therefore focus on those predisposing factors that can be controlled, including the sociocultural emphasis on thinness, unrealistic body weight ideals, and unhealthful eating and weight-control practices that permeate the athletic environment. A combination of education and preventive strategies are recommended for preventing disordered eating in athletes.

Educational programming for the prevention of disordered eating in athletes should be provided by the appropriate health professional, such as an exercise physiologist, psychiatrist/psychologist, registered dietitian (RD), or physician, and should target coaches, trainers, athletic support staff and administration, and the athletes themselves. For the younger athlete with disordered eating, education should also be directed toward the athlete's parents as they maintain a significant influence over the athlete and may facilitate, albeit unknowingly, the athlete's disordered eating behaviors. The focus of education should be on dispelling the myths and misconceptions about nutrition, body weight and composition, weight loss, and the impact of these factors on athletic performance. Equally important is providing accurate and appropriate nutritional information and dietary guidelines to promote optimal health and athletic performance. An RD with expertise in sports nutrition as well as eating disorders is the most qualified and best suited individual to provide such nutritional education (4).

Nonetheless, education is unlikely to be effective unless it is accompanied by preventive efforts designed to change the beliefs and behaviors of athletes and athletic staff. Prevention strategies should build on the educational information supplied and thus should de-emphasize body weight and body composition, promote healthful eating behaviors, destigmatize disordered eating, and recognize and encourage the athlete's individuality while fostering a team environment (4). Examples of these strategies follow.

De-emphasizing Weight and Body Composition

There are several ways that coaches, trainers, and athletic staff can help de-emphasize body weight and composition among their athletes. As mentioned in the previous section, simply educating the athletes and athletic staff about the limitations of anthropometric measures can help to reduce the emphasis on body weight and composition (or at least put it into proper perspective). Of course, the most obvious way to de-emphasize body weight or composition is to simply eliminate anthropometric assessments altogether (41).

Promoting Healthful Eating Behaviors

To successfully promote healthful eating behaviors among athletes, nutrition education and information must be reinforced by practice. All those involved in the management of athletes must therefore practice what they preach. Coaches are probably in the best position to reinforce nutrition education messages by bringing healthful foods to practice, choosing healthful restaurants before and after competitions, and, of course, eating healthfully themselves.

Destigmatizing Eating Disorders

Coaches, trainers, and other athletic personnel can help reduce the stigma of disordered eating by creating an atmosphere in which athletes feel comfortable discussing their concerns about body image, eating, and weight control. Athletic personnel should strive to promote understanding and foster trust between themselves and their athletes. The goal is to create an atmosphere in which athletes feel comfortable confiding an eating problem. In short, coaches, trainers, and athletic administrators must make it clear that they place the athletes' health and well-being ahead of athletic performance.

Fostering Individuality Within a Team Environment

Most coaches, trainers, and athletes have come to realize the importance of individualizing physical training regimens. Thus, it is surprising that they still have difficulty accepting that each athlete has a unique body size, shape, and composition with distinct nutritional requirements. Individualization of each athlete's body weight or composition goals and dietary practices, taking into account weight and nutritional history, current training and dietary practices, and weight, diet, and performance goals, is not only key to optimal performance but also to the prevention of disordered eating.

Although it is important to recognize and respect the athlete's individuality, it is also important to foster a team environment, one in which all athletes work together toward the common goal of optimal health and performance. This may be somewhat challenging because athletes, by their very nature, are competitive. The environment dictates that athletes be competitive not only with their opponents, but often within their own team to secure playing time or their position on the team. Unfortunately, this competitive drive sometimes goes beyond the playing field and affects other aspects of the athlete's existence, such as eating behaviors, body weight, and/or body composition.

Comparing oneself physically to another individual is certainly not a practice confined to athletes, but it may be more prevalent in the athletic setting simply because athletes have more opportunities for comparison (eg, athletes frequently change clothes and shower in the same locker room; athletic apparel or uniforms are becoming increasingly revealing; group weigh-ins and body composition assessments remain prevalent in many sports) (5). Coaches, trainers, and athletic administrators can help reduce this "competitive thinness" by not comparing athletes' body weights or body compositions and by not using the bodies of certain athletes on the team as the gold standard by which all others are measured. Instead, coaches and trainers should try to downplay body weight and encourage healthful eating behaviors among all of their athletes.

Identification, Approach, and Referral

Athletes with disordered eating often either deny that the problem exists or do not realize that they have a problem. In either case, they are unlikely to come forward and admit to disordered eating of their own accord. Thus, it is up to others to recognize the signs and symptoms of disordered eating and initiate intervention. Table 18.3 (4,42–47) presents a variety of eating disorder questionnaires, and screening instruments are available. However, many researchers and practitioners contend that the best method for identifying athletes with disordered eating is probably direct observation (4,48). A list of common signs and symptoms of disordered eating are listed in Table 18.4 (4). For direct observation to be effective, every individual who works closely with athletes needs to be familiar with the warning signs and symptoms of disordered eating.

TABLE 18.3 Self-Report Surveys and Questionnaires for Identifying Disordered Eating in Athletes

Instrument	Description
Bulimia Test-Revised (BULIT-R) (42)	A 28-item multiple-choice questionnaire designed to assess the severity of symptoms and behaviors associated with bulimia nervosa (eg, weight preoccupation and bingeing and purging frequency). Respondents rate each item on a 5-point Likert scale in which higher scores are more indicative of bulimia nervosa.
Eating Attitudes Test, 40 items (EAT-40) (43)	A 40-item inventory designed to assess thoughts, feelings, and behaviors associated with anorexia nervosa. Items are scored on a 6-point Likert scale ranging from *never* to *always*. A score of ≥ 30 indicates risk of anorexia nervosa.
Eating Attitudes Test, 26 items (EAT-26) (44)	A shortened (26-item) version of the EAT-40 that also identifies thoughts, feelings, and behaviors associated with anorexia nervosa. Uses a 6-point Likert scale ranging from *rarely* to *always*. A score of ≥ 20 indicates risk of anorexia nervosa.
Eating Disorder Inventory (EDI) (45)	A 64-item questionnaire with 8 subscales. The first 3 subscales (Drive for Thinness, Bulimia, and Body Dissatisfaction) assess behaviors regarding body image, eating, and weight control practices. The remaining 5 subscales (Interpersonal Distrust, Perfectionism, Interoceptive Awareness, Maturity Fears, and Ineffectiveness) assess the various psychological disturbances characteristic of those with clinical eating disorders. Items are answered using a 6-point Likert scale ranging from *always* to *never*.
Eating Disorder Inventory-2 (EDI-2) (46)	A 91-item multidimensional inventory designed to assess the symptoms of anorexia nervosa and bulimia nervosa. The EDI-2 contains the same 8 subscales as the EDI and adds 3 additional subscales (27 more items), including Asceticism, Impulse Regulation, and Social Insecurity. Items are answered using a 6-point Likert scale ranging from *always* to *never*.
Three-Factor Eating Questionnaire (TFEQ) (47)	A 58-item true/false and multiple-choice questionnaire that measures the tendency toward voluntary and excessive restriction of food intake as a means of controlling body weight. The questionnaire contains 3 subscales: Restrained Eating (eg, "I often stop eating when I am not full as a conscious means of controlling my weight"), Tendency Toward Disinhibition (eg, "When I feel lonely, I console myself by eating"), and Perceived Hunger (eg, "I am always hungry enough to eat at any time").

Source: Reprinted with permission from Beals KA. *Disordered Eating Among Athletes: A Comprehensive Guide for Health Professionals.* Champaign, Ill: Human Kinetics; 2004:120–122.

TABLE 18.4   Signs and Symptoms of Disordered Eating

Behavioral	*Physical*
• Excessive criticism of one's body weight or shape	• Chronic fatigue
• Preoccupation with food, calories, or weight	• Noticeable weight loss or gain
• Compulsive, excessive exercise	• Anemia
• Mood swings, irritability	• Frequent gastrointestinal problems or complaints (eg, excessive gas, abdominal bloating, constipation, ulcers)
• Depression	• Cold intolerance
• Social withdrawal	• Lanugo (fine hair on the face and body)
• Secretly eating or stealing food	• Tooth erosion, excessive dental caries
• Bathroom visits after eating	• Callused fingers
• Avoiding food-related social activities	• Frequent musculoskeletal injuries (particularly stress fractures)
• Excessive use of laxatives, diuretics, or diet pills	• Delayed or prolonged healing of wounds or injuries
• Consumption of large amounts of food inconsistent with the athlete's weight	• Frequent or prolonged illnesses
• Excessive fear of being overweight or becoming fat that does not diminish as weight loss continues	• Dry skin and hair
• Preoccupation with the dietary patterns and eating behaviors of other people	• Brittle nails
• Lack of concern for excessive weight loss or extremely low body weight	• Alopecia (hair loss)
	• In women, irregular or absent menstrual cycles

Source: Adapted with permission from Beals KA. *Disordered Eating Among Athletes: A Comprehensive Guide for Health Professionals.* Champaign, Ill: Human Kinetics; 2004:129.

Once disordered eating has been identified, the next steps are approaching and referring the athlete to a treatment program. Approaching an athlete with disordered eating and convincing him or her to seek treatment can be extremely difficult. Although the athlete with disordered eating may seem to be the most compliant individual on the team, when threatened with exposure and the potential consequences (eg, embarrassment, disapproval by coaches and teammates, being withheld from competition or removed from the team, having to relinquish the pathogenic weight-control behaviors and possibly gain weight), denial and defiance often take over (5). Thus, it is crucial to be sensitive yet firm when approaching an athlete who is suspected of having an eating disorder and attempting to convince him or her to seek treatment.

The potential for a successful intervention increases if the following three conditions are met: (*a*) the athlete is approached in a timely fashion; (*b*) there is an established rapport between the athlete and the individual attempting the intervention; and (*c*) the athlete is approached with caring and concern. Ohio State University's athletic department recently issued an eating disorders policy, which is presented in Box 18.2, for approaching and referring athletes identified with disordered eating (49).

Treatment

Treatment of disordered eating involves the application of specific therapeutic modalities—psychological, nutritional, and medical—by qualified health professionals, such as

---

Box 18.2   Strategies for Approaching an Athlete Suspected of Having an Eating Disorder

- The individual (eg, coach, staff member) who has the best rapport with the student athlete should be the one to approach the athlete, and it should be done in a private setting (eg, a private meeting).
- In a respectful tone, indicate specific observations that led to the concern, being sure to give the athlete time to respond.
- Choose "I" statements over "you" statements to avoid placing the athlete on the defensive. For example, "I've noticed that you've been fatigued lately, and I'm concerned about you" is preferable to "You need to eat and everything will be fine."
- Avoid giving simple solutions (eg, "Just eat something") to a complex problem. This will only encourage the student athlete to hide the behavior from you in the future.
- Avoid discussing implications for team participation and instead affirm that the student athlete's role on the team will not be jeopardized by an admission to a problem. The team may be the athlete's only diversion from his or her disordered eating. By eliminating this opportunity for social support and the supervision of a coach or trainer, the athlete may dive into further pathology.
- Regardless of whether the student athlete responds with denial or hostility, it is important to encourage him or her to meet with a professional for an assessment. Acknowledge that seeking outside help is often beneficial and is not a sign of weakness.

Source: Data are from reference 49.

---

psychiatrists, psychologists, RDs, and physicians. Because eating disorders are psychological disorders, psychological counseling is considered the cornerstone of treatment. Because of the medical complications that often accompany disordered eating, a physician should also be included in the overall treatment plan. Finally, nutrition counseling, provided by an RD specializing in eating disorders, is a vital component of the total treatment regimen for disordered eating.

Psychological Treatment

A variety of psychological approaches have been used successfully to treat eating disorders, including psychodynamic, cognitive-behavioral, and behavioral methods. Additional variables to consider when selecting a treatment approach include the treatment setting (eg, inpatient vs outpatient) and format (eg, individual vs group, with or without family). For additional information of psychological treatment, refer to the *Handbook of Treatment for Eating Disorders* (50).

Nutrition Treatment

Psychological counseling aims to uncover and correct the underlying mental and emotional issues fueling the eating disorder, and nutrition counseling focuses on changing the disordered eating behaviors (ie, the energy restriction, bingeing, and/or purging), treating any nutritional deficiencies, addressing nutrition beliefs and thoughts about food and body, and reeducating the athlete about sound nutritional practices.

Athletes with disordered eating often have nutritional deficiencies that can range from mild to severe. In fact, abnormal nutritional status measures are often used to verify the presence of disordered eating (Table 18.5) (40). Thus, one of the first steps in treatment should be to identify and rectify existing nutritional deficiencies. Micronutrient status, particularly vitamin B-12, iron, calcium (via bone density assessment), and electrolytes, should be measured. Because the disordered eating athlete will likely be resistant to immediate and significant increases in food intake, supplementation is frequently necessary during the early stages of treatment.

Individuals with disordered eating are obsessed with nutrition and often seem to be experts on the topic; however, the knowledge that they possess is generally wrought with myths and misconceptions (4). Moreover, they have often been engaged in abnormal eating patterns for so long that they have no concept of what constitutes normal or healthful eating. Thus, the primary goals of nutritional management for eating disorders are to dispel the myths and misconceptions regarding food and diet and to reestablish healthful eating patterns. Providing accurate information about such topics as energy balance, vitamin and mineral functions and requirements, and fluid needs is key to extinguishing disordered eating beliefs and behaviors.

Individuals with disordered eating have often lost touch with internal (physiological) feelings of hunger and satiety, instead relying on external cues and rigid rules for eating. Thus, nutrition counseling must focus on helping them recognize and respond appropriately to bodily signals of hunger and satiety (51). Meal management (ie, creating meal plans and strategies to deal with irrational food thoughts and behaviors) can aid in the reestablishment of "normal eating" and may also help empower the individual with an eating disorder to take control of mealtimes and food intake.

TABLE 18.5 Laboratory and Biochemical Findings Associated With Eating Disorders

Anorexia Nervosa	Bulimia Nervosa
• Decreased iron status measures (anemia is common)	• Decreased iron status measures (anemia is common)
• Elevation of liver enzymes	• Hyponatremia
• Hypoglycemia	• Hypokalemia
• Decreased serum creatinine	• Metabolic alkalosis (associated with self-induced vomiting)
• Decreased BUN	• Metabolic acidosis (associated with laxative abuse; may mask a potassium deficiency)
• Low thyroid function (decreased T4)	
• Hypophosphatemia	• Hypomagnesemia
• Hypocholesterolemia (low HDL and LDL cholesterol levels)	• Hypoglycemia (due to purging)
	• Hyperglycemia (due to bingeing)
	• Dehydration

Abbreviations: BUN, blood urea nitrogen; HDL, high-density lipoprotein; LDL, low-density lipoprotein.
Source: Adapted with permission from Beals KA. *Disordered Eating Among Athletes: A Comprehensive Guide for Health Professionals.* Champaign, Ill: Human Kinetics; 2004:185–188.

Summary

In the world of athletics, a fraction of a second or one tenth of a point can mean the difference between winning and losing. These high stakes can place enormous pressure on athletes. Under such pressure, many athletes develop a "win at all cost" attitude and some may resort to disordered eating behaviors in an attempt to lose weight so as to improve performance. Unfortunately, these weight-loss behaviors are often self-defeating. Any initial improvement in performance (as a result of weight loss) is transient. The pathogenic weight-control practices will eventually take their toll on the athlete's health and performance.

Prevention of disordered eating in athletes involves the development of educational programs and strategies designed to dispel the myths and misconceptions surrounding nutrition, dieting, body weight, and body composition, and their impact on performance, as well as stressing the role of nutrition in promoting health and optimal physical performance. Early identification is paramount to limiting the progression and shortening the duration of the disordered eating. Thus, all those individuals working with athletes must be familiar with the warning signs and symptoms of disordered eating in athletes.

The primary treatment goals for eating disorders in athletes are to normalize eating behaviors and body weight and identify and correct the underlying psychological issues that initiated and perpetuate the eating disorder. As the individual who is most knowledgeable in the area of nutrition as it relates to athletes, the sports dietitian plays an integral role in the treatment of disordered eating in athletes.

References

1. *Diagnostic and Statistical Manual of Mental Disorders.* 4th ed. Washington, DC: American Psychiatric Association; 1994.
2. Otis CL, Drinkwater B, Johnson M, Louks A, Wilmore JH. American College of Sports Medicine position stand. The female athlete triad: disordered eating, amenorrhea, and osteoporosis. *Med Sci Sports Exerc.* 1997;29:i–ix.
3. Fairburn CG, Brownell KD, eds. *Eating Disorders and Obesity: A Comprehensive Handbook.* 2nd ed. New York, NY: Guilford Press; 2001.
4. Beals KA. *Disordered Eating Among Athletes: A Comprehensive Guide for Health Professionals.* Champaign, Ill: Human Kinetics; 2004.
5. Thompson RA, Sherman RT. *Helping Athletes with Eating Disorders.* Champaign, Ill: Human Kinetics; 1993.
6. Beals KA, Manore MM. The prevalence and consequences of subclinical eating disorders in female athletes. *Int J Sport Nutr.* 1994;4:175–195.
7. Beals KA, Manore MM. Subclinical eating disorders in active women. *Topics Clin Nutr.* 1999;14:14–24.
8. Beals KA, Manore MM. Behavioral, psychological and physical characteristics of female athletes with subclinical eating disorders. *Int J Sport Nutr Exerc Metab.* 2000;10:128–143.
9. Smith NJ. Excessive weight loss and food aversion in athletes simulating anorexia nervosa. *Pediatrics.* 1980;66:139–142.
10. Sundgot-Borgen J. Prevalence of eating disorders in elite female athletes. *Int J Sport Nutr.* 1993;3:29–40.
11. Pugliese MT, Liftshitz F, Grad G, Fort P, Marks-Katz M. Fear of obesity: a cause for short stature and delayed puberty. *N Engl J Med.* 1983;309:513–518.

12. Bunnell DW, Shenker IR, Nussbaum MP, Jacobson MS, Cooper P. Subclinical versus formal eating disorders: differentiating psychological features. *Int J Eat Disord.* 1990;9:357–362.

13. Williamson DA, Netemeyer RG, Jackman LP, Anderson DA, Funsch CL, Rabalais JY. Structural equation modeling for risks for the development of eating disorder symptoms in female athletes. *Int J Eat Disord.* 1995;4:387–393.

14. Brownell KD, Rodin J. Prevalence of eating disorders in athletes. In: Brownell KD, Rodin J, Wilmore JH, eds. *Eating, Body Weight and Performance in Athletes: Disorders of Modern Society.* Philadelphia, Pa: Lea and Febiger; 1992:128–145.

15. Byrne S, McLean N. Eating disorders in athletes: a review of the literature. *J Sci Med Sport.* 2001;4:145–159.

16. Andersen AE. Eating disorders in male athletes: a special case? In: Brownell KD, Rodin J, Wilmore JH, eds. *Eating, Body Weight and Performance in Athletes: Disorders of Modern Society.* Philadelphia, Pa: Lea and Febiger; 1992:172–188.

17. Beals KA, Manore MM. Disorders of the female athlete triad among collegiate athletes. *Int J Sport Nutr Exerc Metab.* 2002;12:281–293.

18. Sundgot-Borgen J, Dlungland M, Torstveit G, Rolland C. Prevalence of eating disorders in male and female elite athletes. *Med Sci Sports Exerc.* 1999;31(suppl):S297.

19. Johnson C, Powers PS, Dick R. Athletes and eating disorders: the National Collegiate Athletic Association study. *Int J Eat Disord.* 1999;26:179–188.

20. Sundgot-Borgen J. Eating disorders. In: Berning JR, Steen SN, eds. *Nutrition for Exercise and Sport.* Gaithsburg, Md: Aspen Publishers; 1998:187–204.

21. Wilmore JH. Eating and weight disorders in the female athlete. *Int J Sport Nutr.* 1991;1:104–107.

22. Brownell KD, Foryet JP, eds. *Handbook of Eating Disorders: Physiology, Psychology, and Treatment of Obesity, Anorexia Nervosa, and Bulimia Nervosa.* New York, NY: Basic Books; 1986.

23. Sundgot-Borgen J. Risk and trigger factors for the development of eating disorders in female athletes. *Med Sci Sports Exerc.* 1994;26:414–419.

24. Rodin J. Cultural and psychosocial determinants of weight concerns. *Ann Intern Med.* 1993; 119:643–645.

25. Pope HG Jr, Phillips KA, Olivardia R. *The Adonis Complex: The Secret Crisis of Male Body Obsession.* New York, NY: Free Press; 2000.

26. Fairburn CG, Welch SL, Doll HA, Davies BA, O'Connor ME. Risk factors for bulimia nervosa: a community-based, case-control study. *Arch Gen Psychiatry.* 1997;54:509–517.

27. Epling WF, Pierce WD. Activity-based anorexia nervosa. *Int J Eat Disord.* 1988;7:475–485.

28. Epling WF, Pierce WD, Stefan L. A theory of activity-based anorexia nervosa. *Int J Eat Disord.* 1983;3:27–46.

29. O'Connor PJ, Smith JC. Physical activity and eating disorders. In: Rippe JM, ed. *Lifestyle Medicine.* Oxford, England: Blackwell Science; 1999:1005–1015.

30. Garfinkel PE, Garner DM, Goldbloom DS. Eating disorders: implications for the 1990's. *Can J Psychiatry.* 1987;32:624–631.

31. Sacks MH. Psychiatry and sports. *Ann Sports Med.* 1990;5:47–52.

32. Beals KA, Manore MM. Nutritional status of female athletes with subclinical eating disorders. *J Am Diet Assoc.* 1998;98:419–425.

33. Manore MM. Running on empty: chronic dieting in active women. *ACSM's Health Fit J.* 1998;2:24–31.

34. Eichner ER. General health issues of low body weight and undereating in athletes. In: Brownell KD, Rodin J, Wilmore JH, eds. *Eating, Body Weight and Performance in Athletes: Disorders of Modern Society.* Philadelphia, Pa: Lea and Febiger; 1992:191–201.

35. Pomeroy C, Mitchell JE. Medical issues in the eating disorders. In: Brownell KD, Rodin J, Wilmore JH, eds. *Eating, Body Weight and Performance in Athletes: Disorders of Modern Society.* Philadelphia, Pa: Lea and Febiger; 1992:202–221.

36. Carney CP, Andersen AE. Eating disorders: guide to medical evaluation and complications. *Psychiatr Clin North Am.* 1996;19:657–679.

37. Bo-Linn GW. Understanding medical complications in eating disorders. In: Larocca F. *Eating Disorders.* San Francisco, Calif: Jossey-Bass; 1986:5–12.

38. Johnson MD. Disordered eating in active and athletic women. *Clin Sports Med.* 1994;13: 355–369.

39. Ingjer F, Sundgot-Borgen J. Influence of body weight reduction on maximal oxygen uptake in female elite athletes. *Scand J Med Sci Sport.* 1991;1:141–146.

40. Otis CL, Goldingay R. *The Athletic Woman's Survival Guide: How to Win the Battle against Eating Disorders, Amenorrhea, and Osteoporosis.* Champaign, Ill: Human Kinetics; 2000.

41. Carson JD, Bridges E. Abandoning routine body composition assessment: a strategy to reduce disordered eating among female athletes and dancers. Canadian Academy of Sport Medicine position statement. *Clin J Sports Med.* 2001;11:280.

42. Thelen MH, Farmer J, Wonderlich S, Smith M. A revision of the bulimia test: the BULIT-R. *J Consult Clin Psychol.* 1991;3:119–124.

43. Garner DM, Garfinkel PE. The Eating Attitudes Test: an index of the symptoms of anorexia nervosa. *Psychol Med.* 1979;9:273–279.

44. Garner DM, Olmstead MP, Bohr Y, Garfinkel PE. The Eating Attitudes Test: psychometric features and clinical correlates. *Psychol Med.* 1982;12:871–878.

45. Garner DM, Olmsted MP, Polivy J. Development and validation of a multidimensional eating disorder inventory for anorexia nervosa and bulimia. *Int J Eat Disord.* 1983;2:15–34.

46. Garner DM. *Eating Disorder Inventory-2 Manual.* Odessa, Fla: Psychological Assessment Resources; 1991.

47. Stunkard AJ. "Restrained eating": what it is and a new scale to measure it. In: Cioffi LA, ed. *The Body Weight Regulatory System: Normal and Disturbed Mechanisms.* New York: Raven Press; 1981:243–251.

48. Ryan R. Management of eating problems in the athletic setting. In: Brownell KD, Rodin J, Wilmore JH, eds. *Eating, Body Weight and Performance in Athletes: Disorders of Modern Society.* Philadelphia, Pa: Lea and Febiger; 1992:344–362.

49. Hill L. The Ohio State University Department of Athletics Eating Disorder Policy 2001. Available at: http://ohiostatebuckeyes.collegesports.com/genrel/sa-handbook/conduct.pdf. Accessed November 18, 2004.

50. Garner DM, Garfinkel PE. *Handbook of Treatment for Eating Disorders.* New York, NY: Guilford Press; 1997.

51. Kahm A. Recovery through nutritional counseling. In: Kinovy BP. *Eating Disorders: New Directions in Treatment and Recovery.* 2nd ed. New York, NY: Columbia University Press; 2001:15–47.

Chapter 19

MANAGEMENT OF DIABETES AND EXERCISE

Charlotte Hayes, MMSc, MS, RD, CDE

Introduction

Physical activity is a cornerstone in diabetes management (1). The important health benefits of activity for people with diabetes and for those at risk for developing diabetes include a reduction in cardiovascular risk factors, achievement and maintenance of a healthy body weight, reduced body fat, and a heightened sense of well-being (1–4). Exercise also significantly affects blood glucose control (3,5). It increases peripheral insulin sensitivity, reduces insulin requirements, and improves glucose tolerance (3,5). Metabolic adaptations to exercise can improve glycemic control for individuals with type 2 diabetes and can normalize glucose homeostasis in those with prediabetes (4–6), or blood glucose levels that are higher than normal but less than the diagnostic threshold for diabetes (6). (Pre-diabetes is identified by impaired fasting glucose [fasting plasma glucose level more than 100 mg/dL but less than 126 mg/dL] or by impaired glucose tolerance [2-hour blood glucose value in an oral glucose tolerance test equal to or more than 140 mg/dL but less than 200 mg/dL [7]). However, these same adaptations to exercise can lead to significant blood glucose fluctuations and result in management challenges for individuals with type 1 diabetes (5,8).

The casual exerciser as well as the elite athlete with diabetes often face the need to adjust diabetes management to achieve and maintain euglycemia with activity. Adjustments may be necessary in medications, meal planning, and in the exercise regimen itself. The need for multiple, complex adjustments may require input from a specialized diabetes team. The registered dietitian (RD) plays a central role in integrating diabetes nutrition management and activity. The desired outcome of nutrition intervention is the achievement of optimal glycemic control with exercise so that the individual with diabetes can realize the many health benefits of an active lifestyle.

The Role of Exercise in Diabetes Prevention

Type 2 diabetes is a progressive disorder that is closely linked to obesity. The prevalence of both disease states has dramatically increased during the past decade (9). Furthermore, the prevalence of type 2 diabetes in youth has increased at an alarming rate (10). In part, the epidemics of both obesity and diabetes are attributed to the environment we live in, which supports physical inactivity and enables effortless access to high-calorie foods (9).

Prior to the onset of type 2 diabetes, metabolic syndrome (syndrome X) and associated cardiovascular risk factors often become apparent. Unless lifestyle changes are made, the metabolic syndrome typically progresses to pre-diabetes, and within 10 years of onset, pre-diabetes progresses to overt type 2 diabetes (11). Recognition of the link between the metabolic disorders associated with pre-diabetes/type 2 diabetes and cardiovascular diseases is essential. Approximately 65% of people with diabetes die from heart disease or stroke (12). Thus, the dramatic increases in obesity and type 2 diabetes are significant public health concerns.

The role of exercise in diabetes prevention should not be overlooked. Exercise reduces insulin resistance, improves insulin action, and increases glucose tolerance. Furthermore, exercise improves cardiovascular risk factors and aids with weight loss and maintenance (2). Because exercise improves the constellation of metabolic abnormalities that lead to type 2 diabetes (see Box 19.1 [13–15]), and its complications, it is considered an essential modality for its prevention (7).

Landmark clinical trials investigating the feasibility and effectiveness of preventing type 2 diabetes with lifestyle interventions have provided strong evidence that early lifestyle intervention can lead to prevention (16–19). In these trials, modest lifestyle modifications aimed at increasing physical activity to an average of 150 minutes per week, reducing dietary fat and energy intake, and moderately reducing weight by 5% to 7% of starting weight were shown to prevent progression of pre-diabetes to overt diabetes. Intensive lifestyle interventions resulted in a 58% reduction in risk of developing type 2 diabetes in both the Diabetes Prevention Program (16) and Finnish Diabetes Prevention Program (17), two large-scale randomized clinical trials.

Type 2 Diabetes

Type 2 diabetes is the predominant form of diabetes. It is characterized by reduced insulin-mediated glucose uptake due to insulin resistance, defects in insulin secretion, and, over

---

Box 19.1   Risk Factors for Development of Type 2 Diabetes

Lack of physical activity
Age
Obesity
Abdominal fat distribution (ie, waist circumference > 40 inches for men or
    > 35 inches for women)
Hypertension
Dyslipidemia
Family history
History of gestational diabetes
Racial/ethnic group (eg, Native Americans, Pacific Islanders, African
    Americans, Hispanics/Latinos)

Source: Data are from references 13 to 15.

time, insulin deficiency (7). Risk factors for developing type 2 diabetes are multiple (7) (see Box 19.1 [13]). Lack of physical activity is a considerable risk factor, and potential benefits of exercise to the individual with type 2 diabetes are numerous (1,2) (see Box 19.2 [1]). The benefit of exercise in improving the metabolic abnormalities associated with type 2 diabetes seems to be greatest early in the progression of the disease (1).

Medical nutrition therapy (MNT) is an integral part of type 2 diabetes management. Desired outcomes of MNT include achievement and maintenance of glucose, lipid, and blood pressure goals (20). Weight loss is often an important aspect of management as well. A moderate loss of 5% to 7% of initial body weight (approximately 10 to 20 lb) is sufficient to considerably improve glycemic control, blood lipids, and blood pressure (20). The combination of diet plus exercise has been shown to optimize weight loss (21), decrease the reductions in lean body mass and resting metabolic rate that often accompany weight loss (22), and improve cardiovascular risk factors more than either diet or exercise therapy alone (23). Thus, diet and exercise should be considered adjunctive therapies in type 2 diabetes management.

Diabetes MNT and Exercise for Optimal Glycemic Control

When advising individuals with type 2 diabetes, it is important to emphasize that the combined therapies of meal planning plus exercise can lead to optimal blood glucose control and provide other health benefits. In contrast, the consumption of unnecessary extra calories when exercising can easily counter the energy deficit and blood glucose–lowering effect created by activity, especially if an individual's physical capacity is limited and the energy deficit created is small.

Individuals who control their diabetes by diet and exercise only are not at increased risk of hypoglycemia when active (4). Extra food for exercise is often unnecessary and should certainly be avoided if weight management is a goal. An exception is during periods of prolonged, vigorous exercise, when intake of extra calories is typically necessary to support sustained, increased energy expenditure.

For those on oral antidiabetes medication(s), moderate exercise typically leads to a gradual reduction in blood glucose that is unlikely to result in hypoglycemia. However, with certain medications, hypoglycemia is still possible (24) (see Table 19.1 [24,25]), and prolonged activity increases the possibility of blood glucose levels falling too low (4). If the blood glucose falls below a desirable range, a reduction in the dosage of medication(s)

Box 19.2   Potential Health Benefits of Exercise in Type 2 Diabetes

Improved glycemic control
Improved insulin sensitivity; decreased plasma insulin levels
Reduced cardiovascular risk factors
Improved lipid profile; decrease in triglyceride-rich very-low-density lipoproteins
Lower blood pressure
Increased fibrinolytic activity
Greater success with weight loss and maintenance
Can delay or prevent onset of type 2 diabetes

Source: Data are from reference 1.

TABLE 19.1   Oral Antidiabetes Agents and Associated Hypoglycemia Risk

Medication	*Potential for Hypoglycemia*
First generation sulfonylureas	Moderate
Second-generation sulfonylureas (glyburide, glipizide, glimepiride)	Moderate
Alpha-glucosidase inhibitors (acarbose, miglitol)*†	Low
Biguanides (metformin)	Low
Thiazolidinediones (rosiglitazone, pioglitazone)*	Low
Meglitinides (repaglinide, nateglinide)	Low-moderate
Combination drugs	Varies

*Can contribute to hypoglycemia if used as combination therapy with insulin or sulfonylureas.
†Glucose must be used as treatment for hypoglycemia; alpha-glucosidase inhibitors prevent the conversion of sucrose to metabolically available sugars.
Source: Data are from references 24 and 25.

should be discussed with the diabetes team. Extra food to maintain adequate blood glucose values should be used conservatively.

Individuals treated with insulin are at risk of experiencing exercise-related blood glucose fluctuations and hypoglycemia. To maintain euglycemia with activity, the principles of adjusting insulin, carbohydrates, and exercise that guide individuals with type 1 diabetes should be applied to type 2 diabetes management (4).

Post-meal exercise may reduce blood glucose response to food consumed (26). Individuals who experience postprandial hyperglycemia may benefit from exercising 1 to 2 hours after eating. Exercise at this time may reduce post-meal blood glucose increases and certainly will reduce risk of exercise-related hypoglycemia.

Exercise Recommendations for Type 2 Diabetes

The 2005 *Dietary Guidelines for Americans* (27) recommends that all people older than 2 years accumulate at least 30 minutes of moderate activity on most days of the week. Individuals are encouraged to begin by taking small steps each day to informally increase activity levels. These general recommendations are safe and effective for most people with type 2 diabetes and are consistent with recommendations that successfully guided increases in physical activity in the diabetes prevention trials (4). The emphasis on routine activity is important. Because the beneficial metabolic effects of exercise on glycemic control last only a few days (3,28,29), exercise must be performed regularly and consistently to achieve an optimal reduction in blood glucose. Planned exercise 5 to 7 days per week for 20 to 45 minutes per session may offer additional health benefits and more improvement in glycemic control (3).

The optimal level of exercise to support weight loss and maintenance is currently under debate. The Institute of Medicine has suggested that 60 minutes per day of exercise may be necessary to control weight (30). However, when advising individuals with type 2 diabetes, the majority of whom are overweight, it is important to apply strategies that will encourage adoption and maintenance of lifelong activity (31). Activity goals that seem beyond reach will only dissuade the most sedentary, who have the most to gain from moderate increases in physical activity.

Prior to beginning exercise, a thorough medical evaluation to screen for macrovascular and microvascular complications of diabetes is indicated (1) (see Box 19.3 [7]). This will minimize exercise risk and assure appropriateness of an exercise prescription.

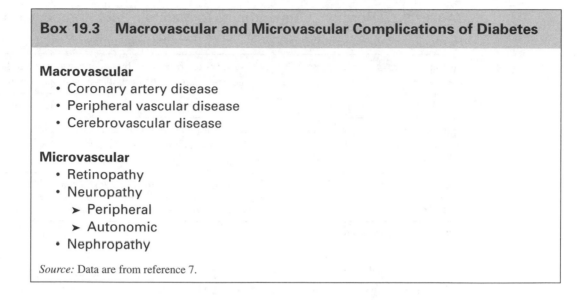

Box 19.3   Macrovascular and Microvascular Complications of Diabetes

Macrovascular
- Coronary artery disease
- Peripheral vascular disease
- Cerebrovascular disease

Microvascular
- Retinopathy
- Neuropathy
  - Peripheral
  - Autonomic
- Nephropathy

Source: Data are from reference 7.

Type 1 Diabetes

Type 1 diabetes accounts for 5% to 10% of all cases of diabetes and is characterized by the loss of insulin production by the pancreatic islet cells (7,32). Individuals with this type of diabetes must overcome considerable obstacles during exercise because for them metabolic adjustments to maintain fuel homeostasis (see Table 19.2 [5,26]) are lacking (5,8). The result can be a mismatch between hepatic glucose production and muscle glucose utilization, and substantial deviation from euglycemia (33). Exercise must be carefully integrated into the diabetes management regimen so that optimal blood glucose levels can be maintained with activity.

Many variables influence blood glucose response to exercise (1,8,33,34) (see Box 19.4 [1,3,5,34]). Those that can most readily be modified are circulating insulin levels and nutritional status. Insulin adjustments and carbohydrate supplementation can be used independently or together to maintain optimal blood glucose levels during activity. The individual with type 1 diabetes must monitor blood glucose regularly with exercise to understand glycemic response to activity, learn to make appropriate exercise-related management decisions, and evaluate the effectiveness of these decisions.

Self-monitoring of Blood Glucose and Pattern Management

Self-monitoring of blood glucose (SMBG), careful record keeping, and recognition of blood-glucose patterns with activity are important skills for the individual with type 1 diabetes. These skills enhance the ability to make sound self-adjustment decisions that improve exercise safety and optimize competitive performance (1). SMBG should be conducted regularly before exercise, after exercise, during prolonged activity, or when doing activities that are not routine. Frequent monitoring helps predict potential for hypoglycemia or hyperglycemia occurring during or after exercise and thus reduces risk for these acute complications. Data from monitoring, when carefully recorded and analyzed, become the basis for decision-making about adjustments in management for subsequent exercise (5) (see Figure 19.1). Pattern management, the methodical process of data collection, analysis, and decision-making (see Box 19.5 [34,35]), is the foundation of successful blood-glucose control with activity.

TABLE 19.2   Hormonal Adjustments to Maintain Fuel Homeostasis

Hormone	Response to Exercise	Metabolic Effect
Insulin	Decreases	Restricts use of glucose by nonexercising skeletal muscle; increases hepatic glycogenolysis; facilitates lipolysis
Glucagon	Increases	Stimulates hepatic glycogenolysis and gluconeogenesis
Epinephrine	Increases	Stimulates glucose production during prolonged exercise Increases muscle glycogenolysis Increases adipose tissue lipolysis
Norepinephrine	Increases	Modulates initial hepatic glucose release
Cortisol	Increases	Increases hepatic glucose production

Source: Data are from references 5 and 26.

Box 19.4   Variables That Influence the Effect of Exercise on Blood Glucose Levels in Type 1 Diabetes

Level of training and fitness
Intensity of exercise
Duration of exercise
Time of exercise
Type of exercise
Metabolic control
Nutritional status and glycogen stores
Circulating insulin levels

Source: Data are from references 1, 3, 5, and 34.

Carbohydrate Supplements

Carbohydrate supplements, though useful in some exercise situations, should be used conservatively. When deciding about the need for additional carbohydrate during exercise, several factors should be considered (1) (see Box 19.6 [1,5]). Unnecessary or immoderate carbohydrate intake can quickly neutralize the beneficial blood glucose–lowering effects of exercise and can supply excessive energy.

Carbohydrate supplements are useful when activity is spontaneous or unplanned and is typically necessary during long-duration exercise or competitive events when energy expenditure is high. Carbohydrate can be consumed before, during, or after such exercise. As a general rule, intake of supplemental carbohydrate is indicated pre-exercise when the blood glucose is less than 100 mg/dL prior to the start of activity (1). Individuals who participate in long-duration activities or competitive events that last longer than 30 to 60 minutes may need to consume carbohydrate during exercise to maintain optimal blood glucose control and delay fatigue. Muscle efficiency and performance are best when blood glucose values are maintained between 70 and 150 mg/dL, or as near normal as possible, during exercise (34).

Enough carbohydrate should be consumed during exercise to keep the blood glucose in this optimal range. Intake of 15 to 30 g of carbohydrate every 30 to 60 minutes of exercise

Name: _____   For: Month _____   Year _____

Address: _____   Home Phone: _____   Work: _____

City: _____   State: _____   Zip: _____

Blood Glucose Target Range: 70–140 mg/dL

Blood Glucose Target Range at Bedtime: 90–150 mg/dL

TIME	2–4 AM		PRE-BREAKFAST			PC	NOON			PC	PRE-SUPPER			PC	BEDTIME			REMARKS
DATE	BG		BG	RA	Sup		BG	RA	Sup		BG	RA	Sup		BG	L	Sup	*Reaction # Exercise
6/14	98		126	7	0	(57)	(61)	7	−1 / 0		77	7	−1 / 0		106	17	0	*#Work in yard 2 hrs. 9:30–11:30a
6/15	—		121	5	0		[178]	7	2	2:30 (59)	[157]	7	1		120	17	0	*#Aerobics class 1:00–2:00p ↑ 30 g CHO
6/16	133		132	5	0		136	5	0		125	7	0		97	17	0	
6/17	97		104	5	0		[141]	5	1	3:00 (63)	97	7	0		112	17	0	*#Brisk walk 1:30–12:25p ↑ 20 g CHO
6/18	—		110	5	0		137	4	0		129	7	0		141	17	0	
6/19	141		97	5	0		115	4	0	2:30 108	134	7	0		138	17	0	#Aerobics class 1:00–2:00p 0 ↑ CHO
6/20	104		[152]	5	1		75	4	−1 / 0	3:00 92	86	7	0		126	17	0	*#Brisk walk 2:00–3:00p 0 ↑ CHO
6/21	—		128	5	0		[148]	4	1		112	7	0		1	17	0	

○ = BG < target range
☐ = BG > target range

FIGURE 19.1 Sample blood glucose flow sheet. Abbreviations: BG, blood glucose; L, long-acting insulin; RA, rapid-acting insulin; Sup, supplement/compensatory insulin. Copyright © Atlanta Diabetes Associates.

Box 19.5   Pattern Management: A 6-Step Process

Step 1: Record blood glucose readings.
Step 2: Study the recorded information.
Step 3: Find and interpret blood glucose patterns.
Step 4: Make adjustment decisions based on identified patterns.
Step 5: Implement adjustments (modified management strategies).
Step 6: Evaluate blood glucose response.

Source: Data are from references 34 and 35.

---

is a general, safe starting guideline for supplementing carbohydrate (36). Sport drinks and diluted juices (< 8% carbohydrate) serve to replace fluid, as well as to provide carbohydrate, and are certainly appropriate for individuals with diabetes. Sports bars are easy to carry, portion-controlled, carbohydrate-controlled supplement options and are convenient to use during periods of activity. Additional insulin should not be taken to cover carbohydrate consumed for the purpose of maintaining target range blood glucose levels with activity (37). Because numerous variables can influence blood glucose response to exercise, strategies for

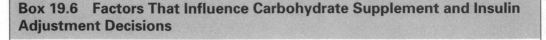

Box 19.6   Factors That Influence Carbohydrate Supplement and Insulin Adjustment Decisions

Blood glucose level before exercise
Planned exercise intensity
Planned exercise duration
Level of training
Time of day for planned exercise
Time of last meal
Insulin therapy
Previously measured metabolic response to exercise

Source: Data are from references 1 and 5.

supplementing carbohydrate must be highly individualized (1,5). SMBG and pattern management allow the individual to draw on prior exercise experience, fine-tune carbohydrate supplementation strategies, and achieve optimal blood glucose levels for peak performance.

Endurance athletes with diabetes may use strategies of manipulating carbohydrate intake to optimize muscle and liver glycogen stores prior to long events. Frequent SMBG and insulin adjustment is necessary to maintain glycemic control when carbohydrate intake and training are altered before an event. Carbohydrate loading can be used with caution and meticulous care by athletes with diabetes (38). Extra carbohydrate may be needed after exercise when insulin sensitivity is increased and glycogen synthesis is enhanced (3,5,34,38). Intake of additional carbohydrate at this time can promote glycogen storage and reduce the likelihood of hypoglycemia. SMBG should be done every 1 to 2 hours after exercise to assess the blood glucose response to activity and make necessary adjustments in food intake and insulin dosages (36).

Insulin Adjustment

Because insulin sensitivity and responsiveness change with exercise, significant blood glucose fluctuations can occur if circulating insulin levels are too high or too low (3,5,34) (see Table 19.3 [3,5]). Pre-exercise insulin adjustment to reduce the usual dosage and thus reduce circulating insulin levels is often necessary, especially before long-duration or competitive activity. Insulin adjustment to reduce insulin can also be used by those who exercise for weight management and therefore wish to minimize the need to supplement carbohydrate (37). Elevated pre-exercise blood glucose can indicate insulin deficiency. Supplemental insulin may be necessary to correct low insulin levels and improve metabolic control before beginning exercise. Adjustment decisions should always be made with consideration of several significant variables (refer to Box 19.6). SMBG, careful record-keeping, and evaluation of blood glucose patterns are crucial for determining successful adjustment strategies.

A number of guidelines for reducing insulin dosages prior to planned exercise have been suggested (5,34,36,37,39). A 30% to 50% reduction in the dose of insulin acting during the time of exercise is generally accepted as a safe starting guideline. Greater reductions may be needed for prolonged or extreme exercise (36,39). Because adjustment decisions require recognition of the insulin acting during the time of exercise, familiarity with the time course of insulin action (see Figure 19.2 [40,41]) is important.

TABLE 19.3   Metabolic Response to Exercise Based on Insulin Status

Insulin Level	Liver Glucose Output	Muscle Glucose Uptake	Metabolic Effect
High	↑	↑↑	↓ BG ↑ Hypoglycemia risk ↓ FFA mobilization
Desirable	↑↑	↑↑	Stable BG Efficient fuel flux
Low	↑↑	↑	↑BG ↑ Potential for hyperglycemia ↑ Lipolysis ↑ Ketones

Key: ↑ = moderate increase; ↑↑ = large increase; ↓ = decrease.
Abbreviations: BG, blood glucose level; FFA, free fatty acid.
Source: Data are from references 3 and 5.

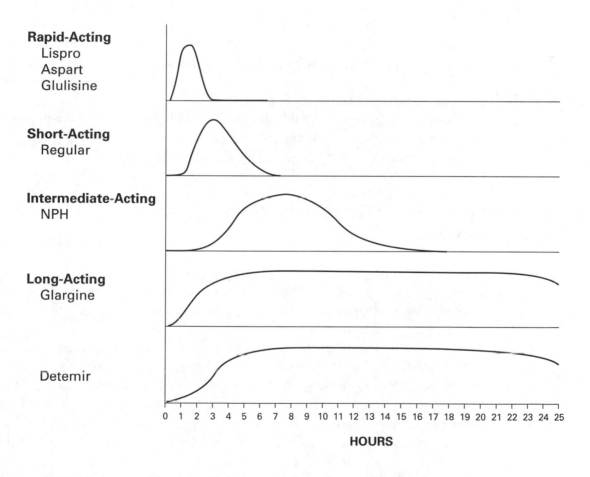

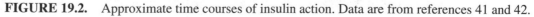

HOURS

FIGURE 19.2.   Approximate time courses of insulin action. Data are from references 41 and 42.

Intensive insulin therapy, either multiple daily injections (MDI) or continuous subcutaneous insulin infusion (CSII), is considered standard treatment for type 1 diabetes (39). The advantage of intensive therapy is that it offers multiple opportunities to adjust insulin doses throughout the day. Adjustments for exercise can then be made with great precision. Conventional (or twice-daily insulin therapy) offers fewer opportunities to manipulate doses to reflect changes in insulin requirements. Therefore, adjustments for exercise tend to be less precise. Dosages of intermediate or long-acting insulin are substantially higher in conventional therapy than in intensive therapy, which predominately uses rapid- or short-acting insulin. Longer-acting insulin(s), with the exception of the "peakless" insulin analog glargine, can cause sustained hyperinsulinemia and impede glycemic control during and after intense or prolonged activity (39,42). For these reasons, intensive therapy is more likely to allow safe and optimal exercise performance and is certainly the therapy of choice for athletes with type 1 diabetes.

Doses of insulin may need to be modified for an extended time after extreme or prolonged activity, when insulin sensitivity and muscle glycogen repletion are increased. The period of heightened sensitivity to insulin can last for up to 36 hours after extreme or unusual exercise. Reduction in insulin doses during this period may be necessary to prevent postexercise hypoglycemia, which can be quite severe. Frequent SMBG, including monitoring during the night (eg, at 3:00 am), is an advisable precautionary measure. In contrast, high-intensity, short-duration activity can result in postexercise hyperglycemia due to release of the counterregulatory hormones norepinephrine and epinephrine and excessive hepatic glucose production (33,39).

Blood glucose elevation in this situation is usually transient, and use of supplemental insulin as a corrective measure is not indicated. Extra insulin could cause hypoglycemia if its action coincides with an increase in insulin sensitivity postexercise (39).

Interpretation of Blood Glucose Patterns and Appropriate Corrective Actions

Pre-exercise blood glucose levels and changes that occur during and after exercise reflect circulating insulin levels (34). When diabetes medications are properly adjusted and carbohydrate intake appropriate, blood glucose levels should remain within a desired target range during and after exercise.

If circulating insulin levels are elevated, glucose will enter the exercising muscle cell rapidly, resulting in a significant decrease in blood glucose (33). Too much circulating insulin also restricts glucose production by the liver and reduces free fatty acid mobilization from fat cells, thus making other important fuels for exercise unavailable (34). The result can be hypoglycemia. The appropriate corrective action is to reduce the dose of insulin or oral antidiabetes medication and supplement carbohydrate in controlled amounts at the next exercise session. Whenever hypoglycemia is suspected, exercise must be delayed until the blood glucose level is verified by SMBG. A blood glucose value less than 70 mg/dL indicates hypoglycemia (40). This must be treated appropriately before exercise is resumed (see Figure 19.3 [35]).

If circulating insulin levels are too low, glucose has difficulty entering exercising muscle cells. Glucose production and release from the liver and fatty acid mobilization are

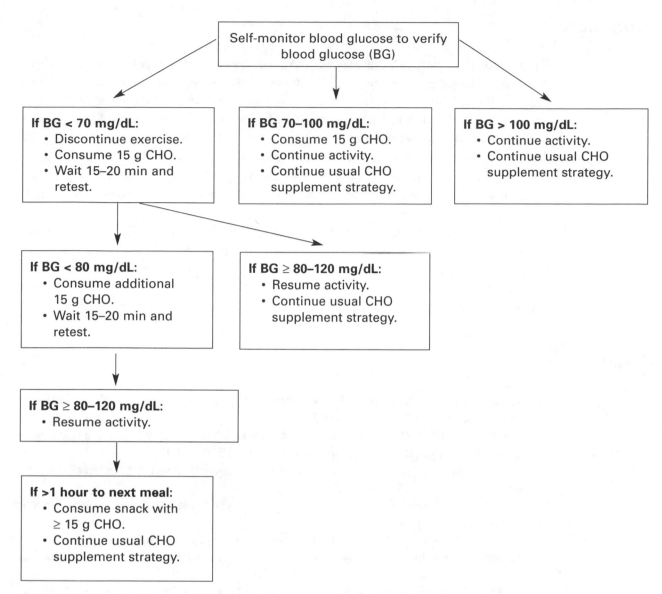

FIGURE 19.3.   Carbohydrate (CHO) supplement use during exercise. Data are from reference 33.

increased. The result can be severe hyperglycemia and ketosis (5,33,34). If the fasting blood glucose prior to anticipated exercise is more than 250 mg/dL, urine ketones should always be tested. The combination of a fasting blood glucose value more than 250 mg/dL and positive ketones or blood glucose more than 300 mg/dL with or without ketones indicates insulinopenia and poor metabolic control (1). Supplemental insulin should be administered and exercise should be delayed until improved metabolic control is achieved (5). Intake of noncaloric fluids should be encouraged to prevent dehydration associated with hyperglycemia and to help clear ketones. Moderate hyperglycemia in the absence of ketones is often due to factors such as prior dietary indiscretion or psychological stress. If such is the case, exercise will usually result in a reduction in blood glucose and improved control.

Summary

For individuals with type 2 diabetes and those with pre-diabetes, regular physical activity can improve blood glucose control and may even alleviate symptoms of the disease. However, for individuals with type 1 diabetes, exercise does not have the same tendency to improve glycemic control. Rather, it has the potential to cause significant blood glucose fluctuations and considerable management challenges (5). Even so, all individuals with diabetes should be encouraged to follow active lifestyles to achieve the many health benefits of physical activity. The athlete with diabetes, who is striving for competitive performance, should be offered the support and self-management training needed to achieve optimal performance.

This chapter presents general guidelines and strategies for adapting diabetes medications and MNT to accommodate exercise. The information presented should be considered a starting point. Strategies must be modified and individualized based on the uniqueness of each client and each exercise situation. SMBG and pattern management allow successful strategies to be developed and fine-tuned to minimize exercise risk while maximizing performance.

References

1. American Diabetes Association. Position Statement: physical activity/exercise and diabetes. *Diabetes Care*. 2004;27(Suppl 1):S58–S62.
2. Albright A, Franz M, Hornsby G, Kriska A, Marrero D, Ullrich I, Verity L. Position stand: exercise and type 2 diabetes. *Med Sci Sports Exerc*. 2000;32:1345–1360.
3. Young JC. Exercise prescription for individuals with metabolic disorders: practical considerations. *Sports Med*. 1995;19:43–45.
4. Kriska A. Can a physically active lifestyle prevent type 2 diabetes? *Exerc Sports Sci Rev*. 2003;31:132–137.
5. Wasserman D, Davis S, Zinman B. Fuel metabolism during exercise in health and diabetes. In: Ruderman N, Devlin J, Schneider S, eds. *Handbook of Exercise in Diabetes*. Alexandria, Va: American Diabetes Association; 2002:63–99.
6. American Diabetes Association, National Institute of Diabetes, Digestive and Kidney Diseases. Position statement: the prevention or delay of type 2 diabetes. *Diabetes Care*. 2004;27(Suppl 1):S47–S54.
7. American Diabetes Association. Diagnosis and classification of diabetes mellitus. *Diabetes Care*. 2004;27(Suppl 1):S5–S10.
8. Raguso CA, Coggan AR, Gastadelli A, Sidossis LS, Bastyr EJ III, Wolfe RR. Lipid and carbohydrate metabolism in IDDM during moderate and intense exercise. *Diabetes*. 1995;44:1066–1074.
9. Mokdad A, Bowman B, Ford E, Vinicor F, Marks J, Koplan J. The continuing epidemics of obesity and diabetes in the United States. *JAMA*. 2001;286:1195–1200.
10. Fagot-Campagna A, Pettit D, Engelgau M. Type 2 diabetes among North American children and adolescents: an epidemiological review and public health perspective. *J Pediatr*. 2000;136:664–672.
11. *Insulin Resistance and Pre-diabetes*. Bethesda, Md: National Institute of Diabetes and Digestive and Kidney Diseases; 2003. NIH Publication 03-4893.
12. Grundy S, Benjamin I, Burke G, Chait A, Eckel R, Howard B, Mitch W, Smith S, Sowers J. Diabetes and cardiovascular disease: a statement for healthcare professionals from the American Heart Association. *Circulation*. 1999;100:1134–1146.

13. American Diabetes Association. Screening for type 2 diabetes. *Diabetes Care.* 2004;27(Suppl 1):S11–S14.

14. *Third Report of the National Cholesterol Education Program (NCEP) Expert Panel on Detection, Evaluation and Treatment of High Blood Cholesterol in Adults (Adult Treatment Panel III) Executive Summary.* Bethesda, Md: National Heart, Lung and Blood Institute; 2001. NIH publication no. 01–3670.

15. National Diabetes Fact Sheet. Available at: http://www.diabetes.org/diabetes statistics/ nationaldiabetes-fact-sheet.jsp. Accessed April 6, 2005.

16. Diabetes Prevention Research Group. Reduction in the incidence of type 2 diabetes with lifestyle intervention or metformin. *N Engl J Med.* 2002;346:393–403.

17. Tuomilehto J, Lindstrom J, Eriksson T, Valle T, Hamalainen H, Ilanne-Paprikka P, Keinanen-Kiukaanniemi S, Laasko M, Louheranta A, Rastas M, Salminen V, Uusitupa M. Prevention of type 2 diabetes mellitus by changes in lifestyle among subjects with impaired glucose tolerance. *N Engl J Med.* 2001;344:1343–1350.

18. Eriksson K, Lindgarde F. Prevention of type 2 (non-insulin dependent) diabetes by diet and physical exercise. *Diabetologia.* 1991;34:891–898.

19. Pan X, Li G, Hu Y, Wang J, Yang W, An Z, Hu Z, Lin J, Xiao J, Cao H, Liu P, Jiang X, Jiang Y, Wang J, Zheng H, Zhang H, Bennett P, Howard B. Effects of diet and exercise in preventing NIDDM in people with impaired glucose tolerance: the Da Quin IGT and Diabetes Study. *Diabetes Care.* 1997;20:537–544.

20. American Diabetes Association. Nutrition principles and recommendations in diabetes. *Diabetes Care.* 2004;27(Suppl 1):S36–S46.

21. King AC, Tribble DL. The role of exercise in weight regulation in nonathletes. *Sports Med.* 1991;11:331–349.

22. Bouchard C, Depres JP, Tremblay A. Exercise and obesity. *Obes Res.* 1993;1:133–147.

23. Wood PD, Stefanick ML, Williams PT, Haskell WL. The effects on plasma lipoproteins of a prudent weight-reducing diet, with or without exercise, in overweight men and women. *N Engl J Med.* 1991;325:461–466.

24. Meece J. Oral agent use in type 2 diabetes. *On The Cutting Edge.* 2004;25:23–27.

25. White JR, Campbell RK, Yarborough PC. Pharmacologic therapies. In: Franz MJ, ed. *A Core Curriculum for Diabetes Education.* 4th ed. Chicago, Ill: American Association of Diabetes Educators; 2001:89–147.

26. Rassmussen OW, Lauszus FF, Hermansen K. Effects of postprandial exercise on glycemic response in IDDM subjects. *Diabetes Care.* 1994;17:1203–1205.

27. US Department of Agriculture and US Department of Health and Human Services. Dietary Guidelines for Americans 2005. Available at: http://www.healthierus.gov/dietaryguidelines. Accessed May 17, 2005.

28. Dela F, Larsen JJ, Mikines KJ, Plough T, Petersen LN, Galbo H. Insulin-stimulated muscle glucose clearance in patients with NIDDM: effects of one-legged physical training. *Diabetes.* 1995;44:1010–1020.

29. Yamanouchi K, Shinozaki T, Chikada K, Nishikawa T, Ito K, Shimizu S, Ozawa N, Suzuki Y, Maeno H, Kato K. Daily walking combined with diet therapy is a useful means for obese NIDDM patients not only to reduce body weight but also to improve insulin sensitivity. *Diabetes Care.* 1995;18:775–778.

30. Institute of Medicine. *Dietary Reference Intakes for Energy, Carbohydrates, Fiber, Fat, Protein and Amino Acids (Macronutrients).* Washington, DC: National Academy Press; 2002.

31. Jakicic M, Gallagher K. Exercise considerations for the sedentary overweight adult. *Exerc Sport Sci Rev.* 2003;31:91–95.

32. Koplan J. Diabetes: Disabling, Deadly, and on the Rise. At a Glance 2003. Available at: http://www.CDC.gov/nccdphp/aag_ddt.htm. Accessed Jan. 21, 2004.

33. Richter EA, Turcotte L, Hespel P, Kiens B. Metabolic responses to exercise: effects of endurance training and implications for diabetes. *Diabetes Care*. 1992;15:1767–1776.

34. Exercise. In: Walsh J, Roberts R, eds. *Pumping Insulin*. 2nd ed. San Diego, Calif: Torrey Pines Press; 1995:83–95.

35. Hinnen DA, Guthrie DW, Childs BP, Guthrie RA. Pattern management of blood glucose. In: Franz MJ, ed. *A Core Curriculum for Diabetes Education*. 4th ed. Chicago, Ill: American Association of Diabetes Educators; 2001:173–197.

36. Franz M. Nutrition, physical activity, and diabetes. In: Ruderman N, Devlin J, Schneider S, eds. *Handbook of Exercise in Diabetes*. Alexandria, Va: American Diabetes Association; 2002:321–337.

37. Zinman B. Exercise and the pump. In: Fredrickson L, ed. *The Insulin Pump Therapy Book*. Los Angeles, Calif: Minimed; 1995:106–115.

38. Sherman W, Jacobs K, Ferrara C. Nutritional strategies to optimize athletic performance. In: Ruderman N, Devlin J, Schneider S, eds. *Handbook of Exercise in Diabetes*. Alexandria, Va: American Diabetes Association; 2002:339–354.

39. Berger M. Adjustment of insulin and oral agent therapy. In: Ruderman N, Devlin J, Schneider S, eds. *Handbook of Exercise in Diabetes*. Alexandria, Va: American Diabetes Association; 2002:365–376.

40. Gonder-Frederick L. Hypoglycemia. In: Franz MJ, ed. *A Core Curriculum for Diabetes Educators*. 4th ed. Chicago, Ill: American Association of Diabetes Educators; 2001:231–260.

41. Management of diabetes: self-monitoring of blood glucose. In: Holler HJ, Pastors JG, eds. *Diabetes Medical Nutrition Therapy*. Chicago, Ill: American Dietetic Association; 1997:43–49.

42. Bennett J. An overview of management of insulin therapy. *On the Cutting Edge*. 2004;25(2).

Resources

Diabetes Exercise and Sports Association (DESA). 8001 Montcastle Dr., Nashville, TN 37221. 800/898-4322. (This nonprofit service association is dedicated to encouraging an active lifestyle for people with diabetes. Members include individuals with diabetes who participate in fitness activities at all levels, health care professionals, and everyone interested in the relationship between diabetes and exercise.)

National Diabetes Education Program. Available at: http://ndep.nih.gov. Accessed November 18, 2004. (This is a valuable resource. Its *Small Steps, Big Rewards* materials focus on the prevention of type 2 diabetes.)

Chapter 20

CARDIOVASCULAR DISEASE PREVENTION AND MANAGEMENT

Satya S. Jonnalagadda, PhD, RD

Introduction

Cardiovascular disease (CVD) is a general term that encompasses many different diseases of the heart and circulatory system. CVD accounts for 38.5% of all deaths in the United States (1). Coronary artery disease (also referred to as coronary heart disease [CHD]) is associated with a narrowing or total blocking of coronary arteries due to build up of fatty plaque, thus reducing the blood flow to the heart. In the United States CHD, or ischemic heart disease (IHD), is the most prevalent form of CVD and accounts for 54% of all CVD deaths (1). Additionally, peripheral vascular disease can affect the arteries, the veins, or the lymph vessels, with the most common form being peripheral arterial diseases, which affect 8 million to 12 million Americans, and is more common among individuals older than 70 years. Other major CVDs include hypertensive heart disease, or elevated blood pressure (5% of CVD deaths), and cerebrovascular disease, or the disruption of blood flow to brain resulting in a stroke (18% of CVD deaths) (1).

In this chapter, the first section reviews the lifestyle and behavioral factors involved in the management of CHD and the second section reviews the lifestyle and behavioral factors involved in the management of hypertension.

Atherosclerosis and CHD Risk

CHD occurs as a result of atherosclerosis of the coronary arteries. Atherosclerosis is the result of a complex biological process initiated by chronic endothelial injury or damage. The earliest lesion is referred to as a fatty streak. By puberty, flat or slightly raised fatty streaks are present in most children, although in some the lesion is more advanced (atheroma), which can progress and evolve into a fibrous plaque (2). Fibrous plaques, which appear during early adulthood and progress with age, are formed particularly in coronary arteries and the abdominal aorta as a result of continuous lipid deposition, chronic

369

inflammation, and repair (Figure 20.1) (2). The progression of lesions to enlarged atherosclerosis plaques is especially rapid in individuals with coronary risk factors (3).

As atherosclerosis progresses, fibrous plaques increase in size, protrude into the arterial lumen, and thereby impede blood flow (2). Usually by this time the plaques are covered with a dense cap of connective tissue that contains embedded smooth muscle cells, which typically overlay a core of lipid and necrotic debris. This sequence of events can result in the ulceration of the connective tissue and smooth muscle cap, thereby exposing blood to the lipid layer and necrotic debris and precipitating thrombosis. Hemorrhage into the plaque and subsequent swelling are another serious complication, which may also induce ulceration and thrombosis. If atherosclerosis affects the cerebral arteries, the clinical outcome is a stroke that results from a cerebral infarct or a cerebral hemorrhage. CHD occurs as a result of atherosclerosis of the coronary arteries and affects the cardiac muscle. Blood flow to the heart is interrupted, which can eventually result in death.

Lipoproteins and CHD Risk

Lipoproteins are macromolecular complexes composed of different lipids and proteins. The major lipids are triacylglycerols (TAG), cholesterol, and phospholipids; the proteins in these lipids are referred to as apolipoproteins. The lipoprotein classes are chylomicrons, very-low-density lipoproteins (VLDL), intermediate-density lipoproteins (IDL), low-density lipoproteins (LDL), and high-density lipoproteins (HDL). Chylomicrons and VLDL are TAG-rich particles, IDL and LDL are rich in cholesterol, and HDL is a smaller, denser particle containing proportionally more protein than lipid. The physical and chemical characteristics of major lipoprotein classes are shown in Table 20.1. Nine major apolipoproteins, commonly referred to as *apo* and associated with the various lipoprotein classes, provide structural stability to the particles and play a key role in regulating the metabolic fate of these lipoproteins (Table 20.2). Apo AI and AII are affected by diet-induced changes in HDL cholesterol, whereas apo B usually changes in parallel with LDL

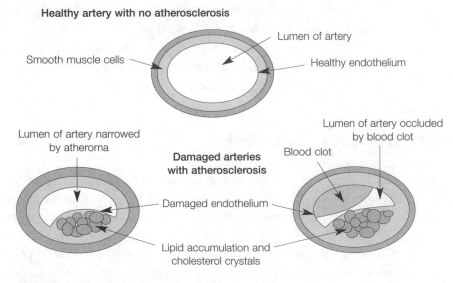

FIGURE 20.1. Development of atherosclerosis.

TABLE 20.1   Characteristics of Major Lipoproteins

Lipoprotein	Density, g/dL	Percent Lipid*		
		Triacylglycerol	*Cholesterol*	*Phospholipids*
Chylomicron	0.95	80–95	2–7	3–9
VLDL	0.95–1.006	55–80	5–15	10–20
IDL	1.006–1.019	20–50	20–40	15–25
LDL	1.019–1.063	5–15	40–50	20–25
HDL	1.063–1.21	5–10	15–25	20–30

Abbreviations: HDL, high-density lipoprotein; IDL, intermediate-density lipoprotein; LDL, low-density lipoprotein; VLDL, very-low-density lipoprotein.
*Percent composition of lipids; apolipoproteins make up the rest.

TABLE 20.2   Characteristics of Major Apolipoproteins

Apolipoprotein	Lipoprotein	Metabolic Functions
Apo AI	HDL Chylomicrons	Component of HDL LCAT activator
Apo AII	HDL Chylomicrons	Unknown
Apo AIV	HDL Chylomicrons	Unknown
Apo B48	Chylomicrons	Needed for assembly and secretion of chylomicrons from small intestine
Apo B100	VLDL IDL LDL	Needed for assembly and secretion of VLDL from liver Structural protein of VLDL, IDL, and LDL Ligand for LDL receptor
Apo CI	All major lipoproteins	Unknown
Apo CII	All major lipoproteins	Activator of lipoprotein lipase
Apo CIII	All major lipoproteins	Inhibitor of lipoprotein lipase May inhibit hepatic uptake of chylomicrons and VLDL remnants
APO E	All major lipoproteins	Ligand for binding of several lipoproteins to the LDL receptor and possibly to separate hepatic apo E receptor

Abbreviations: HDL, high-density lipoprotein; IDL, intermediate-density lipoprotein; LCAT, lecithin cholesterol acyl transferase; LDL, low-density lipoprotein; VLDL, very-low-density lipoprotein.

cholesterol. In addition to the major lipoprotein classes, a genetic variant of LDL, namely Lipoprotein (a) [Lp(a)], is produced from LDL and apoprotein (a). This apoprotein (a) portion of the Lp(a) molecule has a structural resemblance to plasminogen and can prevent the plasminogen from dissolving blood clots. Current evidence suggests that Lp(a) may bind to the fibrin clots, thereby delivering cholesterol to the site of injury, resulting in the blockage of blood vessels and eventually causing a myocardial infarction (MI).

The National Cholesterol Education Program (NCEP) Adult Treatment Panel III (ATP III) guidelines (4) focus on primary prevention in individuals with multiple risk factors and emphasize intensive LDL cholesterol–lowering treatment. In adults older than age 20 years, a fasting lipoprotein profile (total cholesterol, LDL cholesterol, HDL cholesterol, and TAG) should be obtained once every 5 years. Table 20.3 (4) shows the risk classification based on plasma lipoprotein levels.

Risk Factors of CVD

CVD is progressive, develops silently over decades, and is the result of chronic exposure to both modifiable and nonmodifiable risk factors. Risk factors, in addition to LDL cholesterol, include presence or absence of CHD and other atherosclerotic diseases (4). Other major CVD risk factors include cigarette-smoking, hypertension, low HDL cholesterol, family history of premature CHD (CHD in male first-degree relative younger than 55 years; CHD in female first-degree relative younger than 65 years), and age (men 45 years of age or older and women 55 years of age and older) (see Box 20.1 for a complete list of

TABLE 20.3   ATP III Classifications of Plasma Lipoprotein Levels

Lipoprotein Level, mg/dL	Classification
Total cholesterol	
< 200	Desirable
200–239	Borderline high
≥ 240	High
LDL cholesterol	
< 100	Optimal
100–129	Near optimal/above optimal
130–159	Borderline high
160–189	High
≥ 190	Very high
HDL cholesterol	
< 40	Low
> 60	High
Triacylglycerol	
< 150	Normal
150–199	Borderline high
200–499	High
≥ 500	Very high

Abbreviations: ATP III, Adult Treatment Panel III; HDL, high-density lipoprotein; LDL, low-density lipoprotein.
Source: Adapted from National Cholesterol Education Program. *Third Report of the Expert Panel on Detection, Evaluation, and Treatment of High Blood Cholesterol in Adults (Adult Treatment Panel III).* Bethesda, Md: National Heart, Lung, and Blood Institute; 2001. NIH publication no. 01-3305. Available at: http://www.nhlbi.nih.gov/guidelines/cholesterol. Accessed March 28, 2005.

Box 20.1   Nonlipid Coronary Heart Disease Risk Factors

Modifiable Risk Factors
  Hypertension
  Cigarette smoking
  Thrombogenic/hemostatic state
  Diabetes
  Obesity
  Physical inactivity
  Atherogenic diet

Nonmodifiable Risk Factors
  Age
  Male gender
  Family history of premature coronary heart disease

Emerging Risk Factors
  Elevated total homocysteine levels
  C-Reactive protein
  Impaired fasting glucose

Source: Adapted from National Cholesterol Education Program. *Third Report of the Expert Panel on Detection, Evaluation, and Treatment of High Blood Cholesterol in Adults (Adult Treatment Panel III)*. Bethesda, Md: National Heart, Lung, and Blood Institute; 2001. NIH publication no. 01-3305. Available at: http://www.nhlbi.nih.gov/guidelines/cholesterol. Accessed March 28, 2005.

CVD risk factors) (4). These categories of risk factors encompass life habit risk factors and emerging risk factors. Life habit risk factors include physical inactivity and atherogenic diet, which may lead to obesity. All are direct targets for therapeutic intervention.

The emerging risk factors include Lp(a), homocysteine, prothrombotic and proinflammatory factors, impaired fasting glucose, and evidence of subclinical atherosclerotic disease. These emerging risk factors do not specifically modify LDL cholesterol treatment goals, but contribute to CHD risk and may be useful to assess when determining an individual's therapeutic regimen.

ATP III identifies three risk categories that define the goals for LDL cholesterol–lowering therapy (see Table 20.4) (4). Based on results of several recent drug trials, modifications have been recommended for the ATP III treatment guidelines (5). A therapeutic LDL cholesterol goal of less than 70 mg/dL has been recommended for individuals considered very high risk (ie, those with established CVD, plus other multiple major risk factors like diabetes, severe and poorly controlled risk factors, multiple risk factors of metabolic syndrome, and those with acute coronary syndromes) (5). This reduction in LDL cholesterol can be achieved with the initiation of LDL-lowering drug therapies, primarily statins, along with Therapeutic Lifestyle Changes (TLC) (5). Additionally, for individuals considered moderately high-risk (2 or more risk factors and 10-year risk of 10% to 20%) and with baseline LDL cholesterol of 100 to 129 mg/dL, a LDL cholesterol goal of less than

TABLE 20.4   LDL Cholesterol Goals Based on Risk Category

Risk Category	Goal, mg/dL
CHD and CHD risk equivalents*	< 100
Multiple (≥ 2) risk factors	< 130
0–1 risk factor	< 160

Abbreviations: CHD, coronary heart disease; LDL, low-density lipoprotein.

*Risk equivalents = other clinical forms of atherosclerosis; diabetes; and multiple risk factors that confer a 10 y risk of CHD > 20%.

Source: Adapted from National Cholesterol Education Program. *Third Report of the Expert Panel on Detection, Evaluation, and Treatment of High Blood Cholesterol in Adults (Adult Treatment Panel III).* Bethesda, Md: National Heart, Lung, and Blood Institute; 2001. NIH publication no. 01–3305. Available at: http://www.nhlbi.nih.gov/guidelines/cholesterol. Accessed March 28, 2005.

130 mg/dL is recommended, with a therapeutic goal of less than 100 mg/dL (5). The overall goal for high- to moderately high–risk individuals is to achieve a 30% to 40% reduction in LDL cholesterol levels (5).

Metabolic Syndrome

Metabolic syndrome constitutes a constellation of major risk factors, including life habits, and is increasingly becoming common among both young and older individuals, predisposing them to CVD and other chronic disease states (4). Metabolic syndrome is characterized by abdominal obesity, atherogenic dyslipidemia (elevated TAG, small LDL cholesterol particles, low HDL cholesterol levels), elevated blood pressure, insulin resistance (with or without glucose intolerance), and prothrombotic and proinflammatory states. The presence of metabolic syndrome is identified by the presence of at least three of the following:

- Abdominal obesity: waist circumference for men more than 102 cm (40 inches); waist circumference for women more than 88 cm (35 inches)
- TAG of 150mg/dL or more
- HDL cholesterol less than 40 mg/dL for men and less than 50 mg/dL for women
- Blood pressure 130/85 mm Hg or more
- Fasting glucose 110 to 125 mg/dL

The primary management goals of metabolic syndrome include weight reduction, increased physical activity, and TLC (4). To reduce risk, ATP III calls for primary prevention, which encompasses TLC, including physical activity to reduce the short-term (less than 10 years) and long-term (more than 10 years) risk of CHD. Secondary prevention, which targets LDL cholesterol reduction to less than 100 mg/dL through TLC, increased physical activity, and drug therapy, focuses on reducing total and coronary mortality, major coronary events, coronary artery procedures, and stroke in individuals with established CHD (4).

In addition, the Framingham Heart Study (6) has helped develop a simple coronary disease prediction algorithm based on current guidelines for blood pressure, total cholesterol, and LDL cholesterol. This algorithm allows physicians to predict multivariate CHD risk in clients without overt CHD and can be found in ATP III documentation (4) and a study by Wilson et al (6).

Therapeutic Lifestyle Changes

Based on the existing evidence, TLC is a multifaceted approach to reducing risk of CHD in the general population (4,7,8). It includes the following:

- Reducing saturated fat intake (< 7% of total energy intake) and minimizing *trans* fatty acid intake
- Reducing dietary cholesterol intake (< 200 mg/day)
- Polyunsaturated fat intake of up to 10% of total energy intake
- Monounsaturated fat intake of up to 20% of total energy intake
- Total fat intake of 25% to 35% of total energy (predominantly unsaturated fat)
- Carbohydrate intake of 50% to 60% of total energy (predominantly from whole grains, fruits, and vegetables)
- Dietary fiber intake of 20 to 30 g/day, predominantly viscous (soluble) fiber (10–25 g/day)
- Plant stanols/sterols (2 g/day)
- Increased physical activity (a daily minimum of 30 minutes)
- Weight reduction by balancing energy intake and expenditure to maintain desirable body weight and/or prevent weight gain

Drug Therapy

Individuals with elevated short- and long-term risk in addition to TLC will require LDL-lowering drugs, which include statins, bile acid sequestrants, nicotinic acid, and fibric acids (4,5). Table 20.5 summarizes the cholesterol-lowering effects of these various drug categories. The choice and dose of the drug therapy are dependent on the individual's LDL cholesterol level and lipoprotein profile, and combined drug therapy may be indicated for some individuals. However, even with the use of cholesterol-lowering drugs, TLC should be continued because it can enhance the drugs' actions and reduce the risk of recurrent events (4,5,7,8).

Nonmodifiable Risk Factors

Age

Advancing age is a major independent risk factor of CHD and should be counted as a risk factor to modify LDL cholesterol goals in primary prevention (4). Because of the progressive

TABLE 20.5   Cholesterol-Lowering Effects of Common Prescription Drugs

Drug Category	Lipid Effects		
	LDL Cholesterol	HDL Cholesterol	Triacylglycerols
HMG-CoA reductase inhibitors (statins)*	↓ 18%–55%	↑ 5%–15%	↓ 7%–30%
Bile acid sequesterants†	↓ 15%–30%	↑ 3%–5%	No change
Nicotinic acid	↓ 5%–25%	↑ 15%–35%	↓ 20%–50%
Fibric acids‡	↓ 5%–20%	↑ 10%–20%	↓ 20%–50%

Abbreviations: HDL, high-density lipoprotein; LDL, low-density lipoprotein.
*For example, lovastatin, pravastatin, simvastatin.
†For example, cholestyramine, colestipol.
‡For example, gemfibrozil, fenofibrate.
Source: Adapted from National Cholesterol Education Program. *Third Report of the Expert Panel on Detection, Evaluation, and Treatment of High Blood Cholesterol in Adults (Adult Treatment Panel III).* Bethesda, Md: National Heart, Lung, and Blood Institute; 2001. NIH publication no. 01–3305. Available at: http://www.nhlbi.nih.gov/guidelines/cholesterol. Accessed March 28, 2005.

nature of coronary atherosclerosis, age reflects the progressive nature of the disease and exposure to atherogenic risk factors. Both young (younger than 45 years) and older (older than 65 years) individuals benefit from LDL cholesterol-lowering therapy.

Gender

Men have a higher baseline risk of CHD than women (4). Risk in women lags 10 to 15 years behind that of men, which may be due to lower LDL cholesterol, lower blood pressure, and higher HDL cholesterol levels among women. Estrogen may contribute to the protective effect among women with respect to the blood lipids. However, oral estrogen has been observed to increase the risk of coagulation and inflammation among postmenopausal women, and the evidence is limited regarding its independent protective role (4).

Family History of Premature CHD

A positive family history of CHD among first-degree relatives (parents, siblings, children) is a major risk factor of CHD, which is typically also associated with a high prevalence of modifiable risk factors (4). Higher risk for CHD is present with younger age of onset in affected family members and greater number of affected first-degree relatives. Existing evidence also suggests that a family history of premature CHD is an independent risk factor of CHD.

Modifiable Risk Factors

Serum LDL Cholesterol

There is strong causal relationship between elevated LDL cholesterol and CHD risk—even LDL cholesterol levels between 100 and 129 mg/dL can initiate the atherogenesis process

(4). Fatty streaks, which consist of cholesterol-filled macrophages and are the first step in atherogenesis, derive cholesterol from LDL cholesterol. Elevated LDL cholesterol levels can thus not only contribute to the development of plaque but can also result in plaque instability. Therefore, the primary target of the ATP III guidelines is LDL cholesterol reduction (4).

Serum Triacylglycerols

Elevated TAG levels are associated with increased risk of CHD and are commonly associated with other lipid and nonlipid risk factors (4). Additionally, triglyceride-rich lipoproteins, which are remnant lipoproteins, namely small VLDL and IDL particles, are also considered atherogenic in nature. An elevation in serum TAG could be attributed to overweight and obesity, physical inactivity, cigarette smoking, excessive alcohol consumption, very high-carbohydrate diets (more than 60% of total energy), other diseases (such as type 2 diabetes and chronic renal failure), certain medications (such as cortiocosteroids and protease inhibitors), and genetic factors (4).

Non-HDL Cholesterol

In individuals with elevated TAG levels (> 200 mg/dL), VLDL cholesterol levels are increased. Therefore, levels of non-HDL cholesterol, which includes all lipoproteins that contain apoB, should be determined and targeted for therapy (4). The sum of VLDL plus LDL cholesterol is called non-HDL cholesterol. It is calculated as total cholesterol minus HDL cholesterol, and includes all lipoproteins that contain apo B.

Low HDL cholesterol

A strong, independent, inverse association between HDL cholesterol level and CHD risk has been established. High HDL cholesterol levels are associated with reduced risk of CHD. High HDL cholesterol levels may protect against atherogenesis, partly due to its antioxidant and anti-inflammatory properties and its role in the reverse cholesterol transport (4). A 1% decrease in HDL cholesterol is associated with a 2% to 3% increase in CHD risk (4). Low HDL cholesterol may also be associated with elevated levels of VLDL remnants, small LDL particles, and insulin resistance, thereby increasing risk of disease. Low HDL cholesterol levels could be attributable to elevated serum TAG, overweight and obesity, physical inactivity, cigarette smoking, very high-carbohydrate diets (> 60% of total energy), type 2 diabetes, certain drugs such as beta-blockers and anabolic steroids, and genetic factors (4). Smoking cessation, weight control, and regular exercise have been shown to increase HDL cholesterol levels. Hormone replacement therapy in postmenopausal women tends to increase HDL cholesterol levels.

Atherogenic Dyslipidemia

The lipid triad, which includes elevated TAG, small LDL particles, and reduced HDL cholesterol, commonly occurs in individuals with premature CHD (4). These individuals are characterized by obesity, abdominal obesity, insulin resistance, and physical inactivity.

Weight reduction and increased physical activity can alleviate the negative effects of atherogenic dyslipidemia.

Cigarette Smoking

Cigarette smoking is a strong independent risk factor for CHD, and other forms of CVD. Smoking cessation should be emphasized in the clinical management of CHD (4).

Hypertension

Elevated blood pressure is an independent risk factor for CHD in both men and women, and in both young and older individuals (4). Reduction in blood pressure among hypertensive individuals can reduce the risk of CHD, but it does not completely remove all of the associated risk.

Diabetes Mellitus

Individuals with type 1 and 2 diabetes are at increased risk for CHD and other forms of CVD, and diabetes is considered an independent risk factor (4). Improved glycemic control can reduce microvascular complications commonly observed in these individuals. Typically, these individuals also have other CHD risk factors such as hypertension, low HDL cholesterol, and increased TAG levels.

Overweight and Obesity

It is estimated that approximately 64% of adults in the United States are overweight or obese, which can increase risk of CHD, stroke, other chronic conditions, and all-cause mortality. A BMI of 25 to 29.9 is considered overweight and a BMI of 30 or more is considered obese (9). Obesity is a major modifiable risk factor of CHD, and this risk increases with increased abdominal obesity (4,10). Individuals who are overweight or obese may also have other CHD risk factors such as dyslipidemia, type 2 diabetes, and hypertension. A modest weight reduction of 5% to 10% has been show to reduce blood pressure and total cholesterol and improve glucose tolerance in individuals with diabetes. Evidence-based obesity clinical guidelines (9) consider everyone with a BMI of more than 25 at risk for disease (Table 20.6). Although weight-reduction treatment is recommended for overweight individuals only when two or more risk factors are present, it is generally recommended that treatment of obese individuals focus on weight loss over a prolonged period, which can result in improvement of CVD risk factors (ie, weight loss lowers blood pressure, TAG, total cholesterol, and LDL cholesterol, and raises HDL cholesterol).

Atherogenic Diet

An atherogenic diet (high saturated fat and cholesterol) is a major modifiable risk factor for CHD because it can increase LDL cholesterol levels (4,7,8). Dietary patterns that include plenty of fruit, vegetables, whole grains, and unsaturated fatty acids seem to reduce the baseline CHD risk of populations, which may be attributable to the antioxidant nutrients, folic acid, other B-vitamins, n-3 fatty acids, and other micronutrients and nonnutritive substances present in these diets (4,11).

TABLE 20.6   Classification of Overweight and Obesity by BMI, Waist Circumference, and Associated Disease Risks

| Classification | BMI | Obesity Class | Disease Risk* Relative to Normal Weight and Waist Circumference | |
			Men ≤ 102 cm (≤ 40 in) Women ≤ 88 cm (≤ 35 in)	Men > 102 cm (> 40 in) Women > 88 cm (> 35 in)
Underweight	< 18.5		—	—
Normal†	18.5–24.9		—	—
Overweight	25.0–29.9		Increased	High
Obesity	30.0–34.9	I	High	Very high
	35.0–39.9	II	Very high	Very high
Extreme obesity	≥ 40	III	Extremely high	Extremely high

*Disease risk for type 2 diabetes, hypertension, and cardiovascular disease.

†Increased waist circumference can also be a marker for increased risk even in persons of normal weight.

Source: Adapted from Obesity Education Initiative. *Clinical Guidelines on the Identification, Evaluation and Treatment of Overweight and Obesity in Adults: The Evidence Report.* Bethesda, Md: National Heart, Lung, and Blood Institute; 1998. Available at: http://www.nhlbi.nih.gov/guidelines/obesity/ob_gdlns.htm. Accessed March 28, 2005.

Physical Inactivity

Physical inactivity is another major modifiable risk factor for CHD (12). Physical inactivity not only has a direct impact on CHD risk, but also an indirect impact by influencing other risk factors, such as blood pressure, overweight, and obesity. A strong inverse, dose-response relationship has been observed between vigorous physical activity, physical fitness, and CHD mortality. Regular exercise and lifelong physical activity has been shown to slow the age-related decrease in functional ability, to prevent or delay the onset of degenerative diseases, and to add 2 to 7 years to the average lifespan. Vigorous physical activity has been observed to directly influence the functioning of the vascular system by maintaining and improving vessel function. Additionally, regular vigorous physical activity has been shown to increase HDL cholesterol levels; improve insulin sensitivity; enhance fibrinolysis; and decrease TAG, small dense LDL cholesterol, blood pressure, platelet adherence, and risk of cardiac arrhythmias. Physical activity has also been observed to prevent the increase in TAG levels among individuals who consume a high-(simple) carbohydrate diet (4).

Regular aerobic endurance physical activity increases cardiovascular functional capacity and decreases myocardial oxygen demand. The energy demands of these prolonged endurance activities, such as jogging, bicycling, hiking, and swimming, are not only beneficial to the cardiovascular system but can also reduce the body fat mass, further reducing the risk of CHD. Thus, exercise helps control elevated blood lipids, glucose, blood pressure, and obesity (Box 20.2) (12). Exercise capacity is defined as the point of maximum ventilatory oxygen uptake or the highest work intensity that can be achieved. Low-intensity activities at a range of 40% to 60% of maximum capacity include walking for pleasure, gardening, yard work, housework, dancing, and prescribed home exercises (Table 20.7) (12). To promote good health and modify risk of CHD, 60 minutes of daily moderate physical activity (60% to 75% of maximal capacity) is recommended (13) (Box 20.3).

Box 20.2   Benefits of Physical Activity

- Increases maximum ventilatory oxygen
- Increases cardiac output
- Increases ability of muscle to extract and use oxygen from blood
- Reduces myocardial oxygen demand
- Encourages beneficial changes in hemodynamic, hormonal, metabolic, neurological, and respiratory functions
- Reduces blood lipids and blood glucose
- Increases blood high-density lipoprotein cholesterol
- Reduces body weight
- Alters adipose tissue distribution
- Improves flexibility and quality of life

Source: Data are from reference 12.

TABLE 20.7   Examples of Activities at Various Intensities

Less vigorous, more time	Washing and waxing car for 45 to 60 min
	Washing windows or floors for 45 to 60 min
	Gardening for 30 to 45 min
	Wheeling self in wheelchair for 30 to 40 min
	Bicycling 5 miles in 30 min
	Raking leaves for 30 min
	Walking 2 miles in 30 min (15 min/mile)
	Water aerobics for 30 min
	Swimming laps for 20 min
	Bicycling 4 miles in 15 min
	Running 1½ miles in 15 min (10 min/mile)
	Shoveling snow for 15 min
More vigorous, less time	Stair walking for 15 min

Note: With the increasing intensity of the activities, from top to bottom, the time spent is decreased.
Source: Adapted from *Physical Activity and Health: A Report of the Surgeon General.* Atlanta, Ga: National Center for Chronic Disease Prevention and Health Promotion; 1996.

Strength training exercise alone has only a modest effect on risk factors compared with aerobic exercise; however, resistance training using 8 to 10 different sets with 10 to 15 repetitions each at moderate to high intensity for a minimum of 3 days per week is recommended for the reduction of body fat and the maintenance of muscle mass, strength, flexibility, functional capacity, bone-mineral density, as well as the prevention and/or rehabilitation of musculoskeletal problems.

Multiple mechanisms may contribute to the protective effects of physical activity to combat CVD. Endurance exercise training, along with other CVD risk factor interventions,

Box 20.3   Exercise Recommendations for Primary and Secondary Prevention of Cardiovascular Disease

Primary Prevention
- 30 to 60 minutes, four to six times per week *or* 30 minutes on most days of the week
- End point of exercise is subjective:
  1. Breathlessness
  2. Fatigue levels such as "Somewhat hard" or "Hard" in Borg Perceived Exertion Scale

Aerobic activity such as
  1. Bicycling—stationary or routine
  2. Walking, jogging
  3. Swimming

Resistive exercise:
  1. Two to three times per week
  2. 8 to 10 exercise sets
  3. 10 to 15 repetitions per set
  4. Moderate intensity
  5. Use of free weights (15 to 30 lb)

Secondary Prevention
Initial activity: Walking
  1. Gradual increase in duration
  2. Active, nonresistive range of motion of upper extremities
  3. Should be supervised

Long-term activity:
  1. Symptom-limited exercise test after stabilization
  2. Regular conditioning program
     - Large muscle group activities for 20 minutes
     - Warm-up and cool down

has been shown to prevent progression and reduce the severity of atherosclerosis (12–14). Exercise training increases HDL cholesterol, which acts as a lipid scavenger and removes the extra hepatic cholesterol. Exercise training can also increase lipoprotein lipase activity, which helps remove cholesterol and fatty acids from circulation and can reduce TAG levels. Additionally, the weight loss that can be achieved with increased physical activity also contributes to these beneficial effects of physical activity. Exercise increases coronary blood flow and improves the efficiency of oxygen exchange. Endurance training reduces thrombosis by increasing the breakdown of blood clots and decreasing platelet adhesiveness and aggregation. A dose-response association has been observed between amount of exercise performed and all-cause mortality, as well as CVD mortality in middle-aged and elderly populations (15,16).

Emerging Non-Lipid Risk Factors

Homocysteine

Elevated serum homocysteine levels have been positively correlated with risk for CHD (4). However, ATP III does not recommend routine measurement of homocysteine as part of the risk assessment to modify LDL cholesterol goals because the relationship between homocysteine and CHD is not well understood among different subgroups of the population, and the strength of the relationship between homocysteine and CHD risk is not as strong as that of the major established risk factors (4). Elevated homocysteine is treated with dietary folic acid and, if necessary, combined with vitamins B-6 and B-12 (4).

Thrombogenic/Hemostatic Factors

The process of thrombosis, which includes platelets and coagulation factors, is a key player in acute coronary syndrome (4). Platelet hyperaggregability, high fibrinogen levels, activated factor VII, plasminogen activator inhibitor-1 (PAI-1), tissue plasminogen activator (tPA), von Willebrand factor, factor V Leiden, protein C, and antithrombin III have been suggested to be associated with CHD risk (4). However, at the present time, evidence is insufficient to warrant routine screening to assess CHD risk.

Inflammatory Markers

Considering that atherosclerosis involves chronic inflammatory processes, levels of serum inflammatory markers, such as C-reactive protein, may be indicative of coronary events and unstable plaques (4,17). However, at the present time, routine testing of inflammatory markers to determine LDL cholesterol goals is not recommended because the measurement of C-reactive protein adds little to the risk assessment profile provided by the established risk factors (4,17). Additionally, evidence is limited regarding appropriate treatment intervention for elevated C-reactive protein levels because the levels can be influenced by both acute and chronic inflammatory conditions.

Cholesterol-Reduction Therapy

Dietary Interventions

Diet is the primary therapeutic approach for individuals at risk for CHD (4,7,8,18). Based on the scientific evidence, ATP III recommends dietary modifications as part of the TLC program (4). The roles of some of the individual dietary components in the management of CHD are briefly discussed in the following sections.

Total Fat

Diets providing approximately 25% of energy from total fat have been shown to reduce plasma total cholesterol and LDL cholesterol by approximately 9% to 11%, which is primarily attributed to a reduction in dietary saturated fatty acid (SFA) content (18).

Saturated Fatty Acids

Clinical trials have consistently shown SFA to increase blood LDL cholesterol. A dose-response relationship has been observed between SFA and LDL-cholesterol levels, with high SFA diets increasing LDL cholesterol and low SFA diets reducing LDL cholesterol levels. Meta-analysis of existing studies show that for every 1% increase in energy from saturated fatty acids, as a percent of total energy, LDL cholesterol increased by 2% (4,18). Furthermore, high SFA intakes have been associated with increased risk of CHD. SFA are commonly found in animal fats, coconut oil, palm kernel oil, and palm oil. The main contributors to the dietary intake of SFA are meat, poultry, eggs, and dairy products.

Monounsaturated Fatty Acids

Studies have demonstrated a negative association between *cis*-monounsaturated fatty acid (MUFA) intake and CHD incidence, when SFA and cholesterol intake are controlled (18). MUFAs reduce LDL cholesterol levels relative to SFA and do not reduce HDL cholesterol or increase TAG levels. Contributors to the dietary intake of MUFA include olive oil, canola oil, nuts such as walnuts, and avocados.

Polyunsaturated fatty acids

Polyunsaturated fatty acid (PUFA) intake has been shown to be negatively correlated with CHD mortality and to reduce LDL cholesterol levels (18). However, compared with MUFAs, PUFAs can cause reductions in HDL cholesterol. n-6 linoleic acid has been shown to reduce total cholesterol and LDL cholesterol levels, when substituted for SFA. Salad dressings, corn oil, soybean oil, safflower oil, sunflower seed oil, canola oil, and cottonseed oils are all rich in linoleic acid. n-3 fatty acids include alpha-linolenic acid (LNA), eicosapentaenoic acid (EPA), and docosahexaenoic acid (DHA). LNA, found in soybean and canola oil, tofu, and nuts, is an important plant-based n-3 fatty acid for vegetarians. EPA and DHA are long-chain PUFAs mainly from marine sources, namely fish and shellfish. These n-3 fatty acids reduce TAG especially in individuals with hypertriglyceridemia and influence cellular responses in platelets, monocytes, and endothelial cells by decreasing platelet aggregation and prolonging bleeding time (19–21). Fish oil supplements are generally not recommended except for individuals with severe, treatment-resistant hypertriglyceredemia, because of their potential adverse effects such as fishy odor, gastrointestinal upset, increased bleeding time, frequent nosebleed, easy bruising, increased total cholesterol in individuals with hyperlipidemia, and increased oxidation potential (19–21). Typically, high-PUFA diets (> 10% energy) are not recommended due to the increase in LDL cholesterol susceptibility to oxidation and the lack of long-term studies examining the safety of high PUFA intakes (4,18–23).

Trans Fatty Acids

Trans fatty acids have been observed to increase LDL-cholesterol levels and risk of CHD (4,8). *Trans* MUFA increase LDL cholesterol approximately two thirds as much as palmitic acid, may have a HDL cholesterol-reducing effect, and may potentially increase Lp(a). Major sources of *trans* fatty acids are margarine and hydrogenated fats. Liquid vegetable oil, soft margarine, and *trans* fatty acid-free margarine should replace the use of butter, stick margarine, and shortening.

Dietary Cholesterol

Dietary cholesterol increases total cholesterol, primarily LDL cholesterol, although this has less of a hypercholesterolemic effect than SFA (19,22). An increase of approximately 4 mg/dL in plasma total cholesterol has been observed for every 100 mg increase in dietary cholesterol in a 2,500-kcal diet. Individual variation in response to dietary cholesterol is substantial. A diet high in SFA has been shown to elicit a greater hypercholesterolemic response to dietary cholesterol, whereas a diet high in PUFA attenuates the response.

Fat Substitutes

Because of inadequate information on long-term health effects and overall health benefits of fat substitutes, the American Heart Association discourages use of these products (18). Additionally, it believes that an emphasis on low-fat or reduced-fat foods may make individuals overlook total energy intake. Therefore, adequate nutrition education is required when recommending these products to individuals attempting to reduce total fat intake.

High-Carbohydrate Diets

Typically low-fat diets are high in carbohydrates (> 60% total energy), which have been shown to increase VLDL and TAG (4,8). However, if these high-carbohydrate diets are rich in fiber and complex carbohydrates, low in simple sugars, and are accompanied with weight loss, then the elevation in TAG can be minimized and can result in the reduction of LDL cholesterol levels (4,8).

Dietary Protein

The amount and type of dietary protein has little effect on LDL cholesterol levels (4). Substituting animal protein with soy protein (25 g/day) in a low-SFA, low-cholesterol diet has been shown to reduce LDL cholesterol by 5% (4,23).

Dietary Fiber

Dietary fiber that includes components of vegetables and fruits that are resistant to human digestive enzymes encompasses polysaccharides (eg, cellulose, hemicellulose, pectin, gums) and nonpolysaccharides (eg, lignin and other indigestible plant components). Properties such as fermentability, viscosity, and bile acid-binding capacity have been attributed to the physiological functions of dietary fiber. A 5 to 10 g increase in viscous fiber per day has been observed to reduce LDL cholesterol by approximately 5% (4,24–27). Table 20.8 and Box 20.4 provide examples of the sources of major types of dietary fiber and some of their proposed physiological functions.

High-Protein, High-Total Fat, and High-Saturated Fat Weight-Loss Regimens

Based on a limited number of studies, it seems that the low-carbohydrate, high-protein, high-fat diet approach may be more efficacious than the conventional approach for short-term weight loss (6 to 12 months) (28–33). Moreover, during weight loss, these diets seem to be less harmful than anticipated in terms of traditional measures of CVD risk. However, given the small sample sizes, limited study population, and the short duration of treatment, these preliminary data do not suggest any modification of the current recommendations (28,29). Because long-term improvement in health is the overall goal, and high-protein and high-fat diets have a strong association with atherogenesis in the long-term, an effective diet is one that can be sustained.

TABLE 20.8 Sources of Dietary Fiber

Insoluble Fiber	Soluble Fiber	Lignin
Wheat	Oats	Carrots
Rye	Legumes	Wheat
Rice	Beans	Fruit with edible seeds
Most whole grains	Peas	
Bran	Fruits and vegetables	
	Guar gum	
	Carrots	

Box 20.4   Physiological Functions of Dietary Fiber

- Increases fecal bulk
- Increases frequency of defecation
- Increases postprandial satiety
- Decreases intralumninal pressure
- Increases bile acid excretion
- Reduces intestinal transit time
- Delays gastric emptying
- Reduces glucose and cholesterol absorption
- Binds with minerals, altering mineral balance
- Is a substrate for colon bacteria

Antioxidants and CVD

Antioxidants

Oxidation of LDL cholesterol in vitro promotes the deposition of cholesterol esters in macrophages and arterial smooth muscle cells (34,35). Oxidized LDL is thought to promote adhesion of blood monocytes to the endothelium, which could lead to a narrowing of the artery. Additionally, oxidized LDL may also induce endothelial damage, promoting atherosclerosis by increasing the entry of blood components and platelet aggregation at the site of injury, and may interfere with the response of arteries to endothelial-derived relaxation factors (nitric oxide). Therefore, antioxidants, especially those derived from the diet, may aid in inhibiting or reducing LDL oxidation and in preventing the atherogenesis process (Table 20.9) (34). Generally, fruits and vegetables are good sources of these antioxidants and also contain additional compounds that together may inhibit the development of atherosclerosis.

In addition to dietary factors, moderate-intensity physical activity has also been shown to enhance the body's antioxidant system in proportion to the exercise-induced oxidative stress, due to the energy demands of the activity (36,37). Thus, regular physical activity is critical to promote the endogenous antioxidant defense mechanisms to reduce or delay the risk of chronic diseases such as CHD. A few of the well-known, naturally occurring antioxidants are briefly discussed in the following paragraphs.

TABLE 20.9 Sources of Dietary Antioxidants

Antioxidants	*Dietary Sources*
Vitamin E	Vegetable oils, nuts, whole grains (germ), butter, liver, egg yolk, some fruits and vegetables
Carotene	Orange fruits and vegetables, spinach, broccoli, green beans, peas, peppers
Beta carotene	Carrots, cantaloupe, broccoli, spinach
Lycopene	Tomatoes, tomato products
Lutein	Spinach, greens, broccoli, corn, green beans, peas
Ascorbic acid	Fresh fruits, cruciferous vegetables, potatoes, other vegetables
Flavonoids	Colored fruits and vegetable skins, apples, citrus fruits, onions, potatoes, tea
Ubiquinone-10	Soybean oil, meats, sardines, nuts, wheat germ, beans, garlic, spinach
Selenium	Grains, meat, fish, garlic

Source: Data are from reference 34.

Vitamin E (Tocopherols and Tocotrienols)

Tissue, plasma, and LDL-cholesterol contain alpha tocopherol, a lipid-soluble antioxidant. Vitamin E traps the free radicals, a chain-breaking reaction, thereby providing protection against lipid peroxidation. Despite this protective effect, human intervention studies with vitamin E supplements have not provided any conclusive evidence about the role of vitamin E in protecting against CVD (38,39).

Carotenoids

Approximately 600 carotenoid compounds have been identified in plants, some of which are beta carotene, alpha carotene, lycopene, beta cryptoxanthin, and crocetin (40). Beta carotene is an antioxidant that traps free radicals and quenches singlet oxygen, suggesting a potential protective role against the development of atherosclerosis by inhibiting oxidative modification of LDL. Although prospective cohort studies have demonstrated an inverse association between plasma beta carotene, myocardial infarction, and CVD, no protective effects have been demonstrated for beta carotene supplementations (40).

Ascorbic Acid

Ascorbic acid is a water-soluble antioxidant, which reacts directly with superoxide, hydroxyl radicals, and singlet oxygen in a chain-breaking reaction (35). Ascorbic acid also plays a role in regenerating reduced tocopherol, and may prevent LDL oxidation. Its exact role and the amount required to provide a protective role against CVD are unclear.

Although it is not possible to make recommendations about consumption of antioxidant supplements, a balanced, moderate-fat diet rich in fruits, vegetables, legumes, and fiber may have an overall protective role (11,34).

Phytochemicals and CVD

A strong protective association has been observed between fruit and vegetable consumption and CHD (41,42). Current evidence suggests that certain components of fruits and vegetables (ie, plant sterols, flavonoids, and sulfur-containing compounds) may play a significant role in their protective effect (41,42). Some of these compounds are briefly discussed here.

Plant Sterols and Stanols

Plant sterols include compounds that are structurally related to cholesterol. The main plant sterols in the US diet are sitosterol, stigmasterols, and campesterol; the most predominant one is beta sitosterol. Sources of plant sterols and stanols are vegetable oils, nuts, seeds, legumes (dried peas, dried beans, and lentils), breads and cereals, fruits, vegetables, and other plant-based foods. Clinical trials have shown that 2 to 3 g/day of plant sterols have a significant cholesterol-lowering effect of approximately 6% to 15% or more by reducing dietary cholesterol absorption (8,43).

Flavonoids

Flavonoids are found in fruits, vegetables, nuts, and seeds. This group includes flavanols, flavones, catechins, flavanones, and anthocyanins, which in the US diet are commonly provided by tea, onions, soy, and wine. Epidemiological studies have shown an inverse association between flavonoid intake and CHD; however, the exact nature of this relationship is unclear (42). It has been suggested that some flavonoids may possess antioxidant properties preventing LDL oxidation, which is one of the mechanisms proposed for the cholesterol-lowering effects of the phenolic compounds found in red wine (44). Compounds such as quercetin inhibit macrophage-mediated LDL oxidation and potentially block the cytotoxic effects of oxidized LDL. Phenolic compounds found in red wine and olives may also protect against LDL oxidation, which may explain the reduction in CVD among individuals who consume wine (43,44). Polyphenols in red wine inhibit both cyclo-oxygenation and lipo-oxygenation of platelets and therefore may potentially decrease thrombosis tendencies (45). Similar findings have been found with tea and grape juice. Additionally, isoflavones, found in high concentration in soy foods, have also been observed to reduce cholesterol (46).

Sulfur Compounds

Plants containing sulfur compounds, namely the allium family, have been shown to reduce plasma total cholesterol. Garlic in various forms in conjunction with a low-fat, low-cholesterol diet has been shown to have a hypocholesterolemic effect (approximately 9%), potentially by inhibiting cholesterol synthesis (47). In spite of these potential effects, it should be recognized that all these compounds are effective in their natural forms and excess intake of individual supplements of these compounds may have adverse effects such as gastrointestinal disturbances and allergic reactions in some individuals. Therefore, it is more prudent and cost effective to consume a balanced diet containing a variety of fruits, vegetables, and whole-grain products than to consume individual supplements.

Alcohol and CVD

Extensive observational studies suggest that total mortality may be reduced in individuals consuming one to two alcoholic drinks per day. This protective effect could be attributed to the increase in HDL cholesterol levels observed in these individuals or by alcohol's influence on tissue plasminogen activator, a major component of the fibrinolytic system, thereby activating the antithrombotic mechanism (48). However, this association between alcohol intake and mortality has a J-shaped curve, suggesting that with high-alcohol intake (more than 3 drinks per day), mortality increases (48,49).

Caffeine and CVD

Caffeine in coffee, tea, and cola soft drinks is the most widely consumed stimulant in the United States. More than 50% of the adult population consumes an average of 3.4 cups of coffee per day. A J-shaped association was observed between risk of acute coronary syndromes and quantity of coffee consumed (50). It has been suggested that coffee consumption alters blood lipids, which may be associated with factors such as the method of coffee brewing, diet, body fat, or smoking. Boiled coffee has been observed to increase serum cholesterol, probably due to cafestol, a lipid compound in coffee that is typically removed when coffee is brewed using paper filters (51,52).

Herbal or Botanical Dietary Supplements

Although the use of herbal or botanical supplements, such as grape seed extract and ginseng, is popular and has been touted to reduce CHD risk, the scientific evidence regarding the efficacy of these supplements is limited. ATP III does not recommend the use of herbal or botanical dietary supplements to reduce risk for CHD (4).

Athletes and CVD

Athletes' aerobic training provides an advantage with respect to cardiovascular fitness by widening the arterial lumen and improving the tone of the smooth muscles of the arteries. Additionally, aerobic training enhances the arteries' response to the vasodilating factors and inhibits their response to vasoconstrictive factors. Among athletes, age, sexual maturity, training status, peak oxygen consumption, and body fatness are determinants of blood lipid concentrations. Peak oxygen consumption is a significant, independent, positive predictor of HDL cholesterol levels among athletes. Given the impact of physical activity on CHD risk factors, athletes in general gain a protective advantage from participation in regular daily exercise activities.

Although an inverse relationship exists between the level of activity and the incidence of CHD, it should be recognized that even among athletes exercise does not provide immunity from the disease and they should be monitored on a regular basis. Sudden and unexpected deaths of young, trained athletes have occurred (53–55). However, these occur only in about 1 in 200,000 individual athletes per year and should not deter young individuals from participating in sports. Cardiovascular lesions, such as a ruptured aortic aneurysm, aortic valve stenosis, and myocarditis, account for less than 5% of the total causes of death in the trained athlete (53–55).

Approximately one third of the deaths in young athletes are attributed to hypertrophic cardiomyopathy associated with sudden and unexpected cardiac death, usually occurring after moderate to severe exertion (56). This risk of sudden death may be compounded by alterations in blood volume, dehydration, and electrolyte imbalance commonly encountered in the competitive athlete. Another common cause of sudden death in athletes is congenital abnormalities of the coronary arteries. Additionally, African-American male athletes seem to be more susceptible to sudden death on the athletic field. Therefore, in the presence of risk factors, intense physical activity along with the tremendous stress that athletes are under during training and competition may act as a trigger to and precipitating factor of the sudden death of an athlete, especially in sports such as football and basketball. It may be prudent for athletes and individuals with hypertrophic cardiomyopathy to withdraw from competitive sports. The American Heart Association recommends obtaining a personal and family medical history and physical exam to detect cardiovascular lesions in athletes (55).

In individuals older than age 30, the major cause of death during or soon after exercise is attributed to CHD, which is mainly associated with rupturing of the plaque or thrombosis (53–55). Therefore, active individuals should be aware of the symptoms of exercise intolerance, such as chest discomfort, unusual dyspnea, and physical or verbal manifestation of severe fatigue, and seek medical attention promptly (53–55).

TLC Principles

The principles of TLC (total fat intake of 25% to 35% of total energy, reducing intake of saturated fat to less than 7% of total energy, reducing dietary cholesterol intake to less than 200 mg/day, PUFA intake of up to 10% of total energy, MUFA intake of up to 20% of total energy, carbohydrate intake of 50% to 60% of total energy, dietary fiber intake of 20–30 g/day, plant stanols and sterols of 2 g/day, balancing energy intake and energy expenditure, and daily moderate physical activity) can result in significant reductions in known CHD risk factors. Therefore, a prudent dietary intake, in combination with 60 minutes of daily moderate physical activity and other life habit changes will play a major role in the prevention and treatment of CVD regardless of the individual's age, gender, or physical fitness.

Hypertension Overview

Approximately 50 million adult Americans have hypertension, one of the major modifiable risk factors associated with the development of CVD (57,58). The risk of CVD is directly related to blood pressure level, sometimes even at relatively normal blood pressure levels (ie, 120 mm Hg of systolic blood pressure and 80 mm Hg of diastolic blood pressure) (57,58). Morbidity and mortality risk increases curvilinearly with rising levels of systolic and diastolic blood pressure. Risk increases progressively and incrementally when of systolic and diastolic blood pressure are more than 120 mm Hg and more than 80 mm Hg, respectively.

The most recent hypertension guidelines classify a systolic blood pressure of 120 to 129 mm Hg or diastolic blood pressure of 80 to 89 mm Hg as prehypertension, with hypertension being defined as a systolic blood pressure of more than 140 mm Hg and a diastolic blood pressure of more than 90 mm Hg (see Table 20.10) (57,58). Individuals in the prehypertension stage are at increased risk for progression to hypertension, and those with blood pressure in the 130/80 mm Hg to 139/89 mm Hg range are at twice the risk of developing hypertension.

TABLE 20.10   Classification and Management of Blood Pressure for Adults Aged 18 Years or Older

Blood Pressure Classification	Systolic Blood Pressure, mm Hg		Diastolic Blood Pressure, mm Hg	Management		
					Initial Drug Therapy	
				Lifestyle Modification	Without Compelling Indication	With Compelling Indication
Normal	< 120	And	< 80	Encourage		
Prehypertension	120–139	Or	80–89	Yes	No antihypertensive drug indicated	Drug(s) for the compelling indications
Stage 1 hypertension	140–159	Or	90–99	Yes	Thiazide-type diuretics for most	Drug(s) for the compelling indications Other antihypertensive drugs
Stage 2 hypertension	≥ 160	Or	≥ 100	Yes	2-drug combination for most	Drug(s) for the compelling indications Other antihypertensive drugs

Source: Adapted from National High Blood Pressure Education Program. *The Seventh Report of the Joint National Committee on Prevention, Detection, Evaluation, and Treatment of High Blood Pressure (JNC 7).* Bethesda, Md: National Heart, Lung, and Blood Institute; 2003. Available at: http://www.nhlbi.nih.gov/guidelines/hypertension. Accessed March 28, 2005.

To reduce the morbidity and disability associated with hypertension, it is necessary to shift the entire blood pressure distribution to lower levels. A change of even a few millimeters of Hg would reduce both the extent and severity of disease in the population. It has been established that a 2 mm shift downward in the entire distribution of systolic blood pressure may reduce the annual mortality from stroke, CHD, and all-cause mortality by 6%, 4%, and 3% respectively (57,58). An intervention that would lower diastolic blood pressure by 1 to 3 mm Hg could reduce the incidence of hypertension by as much as 20% to 50%. Antihypertension treatment has been observed to reduce the incidence of myocardial infarction by 20% to 25% and stroke by 35% to 40% (57,58). The overall goal of antihypertensive therapy is to reduce cardiovascular and renal morbidity and mortality. The primary focus is to achieve blood pressure goals of less than 140/90 mm Hg; this goal is reduced to less than 130/80 mm Hg for individuals with diabetes or renal disease.

Factors Affecting Hypertension

Hypertension is an inherited, multifactorial trait (57–59). Blood pressure is influenced by pathological conditions, genetics, age, overweight and obesity, and dietary factors (see Box 20.5) (58). Blood pressure tends to increase with age and levels seem to be correlated among family members, probably due to common genetic, lifestyle, and environmental backgrounds. A decrease in renal function common with increasing age has been suggested

Box 20.5   Identifiable Causes of Hypertension

- Sleep apnea
- Drug-induced or drug-related
- Chronic kidney disease
- Primary aldosteronism
- Renovascular disease
- Chronic steroid therapy and Cushing syndrome
- Pheochromocytoma
- Coarctation of the aorta
- Thyroid or parathyroid disease

Source: Adapted from National High Blood Pressure Education Program. *The Seventh Report of the Joint National Committee on Prevention, Detection, Evaluation, and Treatment of High Blood Pressure (JNC 7).* Bethesda, Md: National Heart, Lung, and Blood Institute; 2003. Available at: http://www.nhlbi.nih.gov/guidelines/hypertension. Accessed March 28, 2005.

as a primary cause of this age-associated increase in blood pressure (59). Lifestyle modification (see Table 20.11) (58) has been shown to prevent or delay the expected increase in blood pressure in susceptible individuals. Lifestyle modifications can not only reduce blood pressure and prevent increases in blood pressure, but can also prevent other CVD risk factors. These lifestyle modifications can also assist with a reduction in the number and dosage of antihypertensive medications (57,58).

TABLE 20.11   Lifestyle Modifications to Manage Hypertension

Modification	Recommendation	Approximate Systolic Blood Pressure Reduction, mm Hg
Weight reduction	Maintain normal body weight (BMI 18.5–24.9)	5–20 per 10-kg weight loss
Adopt DASH eating plan	Consume a diet rich in fruits, vegetables, and low-fat dairy products with a reduced content of saturated and total fat	8–14
Dietary sodium reduction	Reduce dietary sodium intake to no more than 100 mEq/L (2.4 g sodium or 6 g sodium chloride)	2–8
Physical activity	Engage in regular aerobic physical activity such as brisk walking (at least 30 min per day, most days of the week)	4–9
Moderation of alcohol consumption	Limit consumption to no more than 2 drinks/day for men and no more than 1 drink/day for women*	2–4

Abbreviations: BMI, body mass index; DASH, Dietary Approaches to Stop Hypertension.
*1 drink = 1 oz or 30 mL ethanol—eg, 24 oz beer, 10 oz wine or 2 oz 100-proof whiskey.
Source: Adapted from National High Blood Pressure Education Program. *The Seventh Report of the Joint National Committee on Prevention, Detection, Evaluation, and Treatment of High Blood Pressure (JNC 7).* Bethesda, Md: National Heart, Lung, and Blood Institute; 2003. Available at: http://www.nhlbi.nih.gov/guidelines/hypertension. Accessed March 28, 2005.

Weight Reduction

In the United States, obesity and weight gain are the most important determinants of the increase in blood pressure. Weight loss is one of the most successful methods for reducing blood pressure levels among both normotensive and hypertensive individuals (57,58). Additionally, the distribution of body fat also seems to affect blood pressure. For example, visceral obesity (waist circumference of more than 34 inches for women and more than 39 inches for men) is a strong risk factor for hypertension and consequently increased risk of CVD. Weight loss, as little as 10 lb in overweight individuals, can enhance the blood pressure-lowering effect of antihypertensive agents and also reduce other CVD risk factors (60,61).

Alcohol Consumption

Increased alcohol consumption is an important risk factor for high blood pressure, causing resistance to antihypertensive therapy (57,58,62). Epidemiological studies suggest that increased blood pressure in heavy drinkers can be normalized within a week upon abstinence from alcohol (63). Alcohol consumption should be limited to 1 oz of ethanol per day (64), which is equivalent to 24 oz of beer, 10 oz of wine, or 2 oz of 100-proof whiskey.

Women and lower-weight/lean individuals are more susceptible to the effects of alcohol because the absorption rate is increased; therefore, these individuals should limit their ethanol intake to 0.5 oz per day (57,58). Changes in intracellular sodium metabolism, effect on smooth muscle, insulin resistance, and an overactive sympathetic nervous system have all been suggested as potential mechanisms for the role of alcohol in hypertension (62,63).

Physical Activity

Moderate physical activity via aerobic exercise can increase weight loss, improve functional health status, and reduce the risk of CVD and all-cause mortality. Risk of hypertension is increased 20% to 50% in sedentary individuals, compared with their active counterparts (12). Moderate physical activity can be achieved with brisk walking for 30 to 45 minutes each day, which can also help reduce elevated blood pressure (12). However, individuals with CVD and other related health problems require a thorough evaluation, such as a cardiac stress test, before embarking on an exercise program.

Physical activity is an effective nonpharmacologic way to reduce blood pressure. Walking, running, and exercising on a cycle ergometer have all been shown to be associated with reducing blood pressure. The overall goal of physical activity is to increase total energy expenditure. The benefits of physical activity for reducing blood pressure disappear within 2 weeks after exercise cessation and, therefore, physical activity must be maintained over time (12).

The mechanism of exercise-induced reduction in blood pressure is unclear, but it may be associated with a reduction in peripheral vascular resistance and an increase in cardiac output. A recent meta-analysis on the effects of regular exercise on blood pressure revealed that aerobic exercise training could reduce resting systolic and diastolic blood pressure by approximately 4 to 5 mm Hg and 3 to 4 mm Hg, respectively (65). Long-term prospective studies on the impact of blood pressure-reducing effects of physical activity on CVD morbidity and mortality have not been conducted. However, pharmacological interventions have shown that a reduction in diastolic blood pressure of 5 to 6 mm Hg is associated with a 42% reduction in the incidence of stroke and a 14% reduction in CHD (57,58,66,67), thereby suggesting that physical activity could also have a potentially similar impact on overall morbidity and mortality.

Lower intensity physical activities have been found to be as effective or more effective than higher intensity activities. Typically, lower intensity exercises, such as walking, cycling, and swimming, are associated with greater compliance, adherence, and lower risk of CVD and are easier to implement. In addition to reducing blood pressure, regular physical activity can also favorably influence dyslipidemia, insulin resistance, body weight, left ventricular hypertrophy, risk of stroke, and other CVD events.

Dietary Sodium

Studies have demonstrated a positive association between sodium intake and blood pressure (57,58). A meta-analysis of clinical trials observed that reducing dietary sodium to 75 to 100 mmol (1 mmol sodium = 23 mg sodium; to convert milligrams of sodium to milligrams of sodium chloride multiply by 2.54) reduced blood pressure over several weeks to several years (68). However, individual response to sodium restriction varies considerably (69). Typically, a reduction in dietary sodium is also associated with reduction in antihypertensive medication, reduction in diuretic-induced potassium wasting, regression in left ventricular hypertrophy, protection from osteoporosis, and reduction in renal stones (6,70).

The average consumption of sodium in North America is more than 150 mmol/day. However, the latest dietary recommendations indicate that the Adequate Intake (AI) of sodium for young adults is 1.5 g/day (65 mmol/day; 3.8 g sodium chloride/day) (71). Similarly, the AI for individuals 50 to 70 years of age is 1.3 g/day (55 mmol/day; 3.2 g sodium chloride/day) and for those older than 70 years it is 1.2 g/day (50 mmol/day; 2.9 g sodium chloride/day). Approximately 75% of dietary sodium intake is derived from processed foods; therefore, individuals should be educated on reading food labels and selecting low-sodium foods.

The Third National Health and Nutrition Examination Survey observed higher intakes of sodium by males than by females (72). Although in adults the mean sodium intake was similar among racial and ethnic groups, African-American children were observed to have higher intakes than white children (3.2 g vs 2.9 g in ages 6 to 11 years, 3.6 g vs 3.4 g in ages 12 to 15 years, respectively). Although the sodium intakes paralleled reductions in total energy intakes, the nutrient density of sodium in the diet increased with age. This may be due to the increased use of discretionary salt by the elderly to compensate for diminished taste sensitivity.

In hypertensive individuals, severe (1 g sodium chloride per day) and moderate (4 to 6 g sodium chloride per day) salt restriction can reduce blood pressure. However, modest salt restriction combined with anti-hypertensive therapy can increase blood pressure in some individuals because of an active rennin-angiotensin system.

Adherence with low-salt diets is variable, and sodium restriction can have both a positive and a negative impact on intake of certain nutrients. Typically with salt restriction, intake of energy, fat, and sugar is reduced. Salt restriction also reduces the intake of some other micronutrients. Three food groups are the main sources of dietary sodium: meats, poultry, and fish; grain products; and milk and dairy products. These food groups are also good sources of dietary calcium, iron, magnesium, and vitamin B-6. Therefore, a decrease in the intake of these foods will also decrease the intake of these micronutrients. Proper measures need to be taken to prevent any detrimental effects that can result due to alterations in other micronutrients.

Athletes on medications that increase fluid losses (and thereby sodium losses) and those on a low-sodium diet need to be pay attention to their dietary sodium intake because reductions in blood sodium levels can occur during athletic events due to sweat losses, which can have detrimental effects on blood volume, muscle contractility, and performance. This is especially true for athletes engaged in long duration endurance activities such as triathlons and marathons. These individuals may need to increase their dietary sodium intake prior to the event by consuming higher sodium foods such as cereals, beans, vegetable juices, and during the event they should consume sport drinks that contain sodium.

Chloride Intake

An increase in dietary chloride alone, similar to an increase in dietary sodium alone, fails to produce hypertension, whereas high amounts of chloride in the form of sodium chloride can produce hypertension (73). Expansion of extracellular fluid volume may be responsible for the development of hypertension in this case.

Potassium Intake

The amount of potassium in the diet contributes to blood pressure levels (ie, high potassium intake can reduce blood pressure as well as the risk of CVD). The AI for potassium is set at 4.7 g/day (120 mmol/day) for adults (71). Inadequate dietary potassium intake can increase blood pressure, and therefore adequate potassium intake from fresh fruits and vegetables should be achieved. Meta-analysis of randomized controlled trials found a significant reduction in systolic and diastolic blood pressure with potassium supplements (3.11 mm Hg and 1.97 mm Hg, respectively), and this effect was enhanced in individuals with high sodium intakes (74). However, potassium-containing salt substitutes, potassium supplements, and potassium-sparing diuretics should be used with caution, especially in individuals susceptible to hyperkalemia and those with renal insufficiency.

Calcium Intake

Low calcium intake (< 800 mg/day) has been associated with an increased prevalence of hypertension (75). However, only a minimal reduction in hypertension has been observed with an increased (> 800 mg/day) calcium intake. It has been postulated that the blood pressure-lowering effects of both potassium and calcium may be related to their ability to increase the excretion of sodium salts, thereby reducing the negative impact of sodium on blood pressure, especially in salt-sensitive individuals. Additionally, deficiencies of potassium and calcium have been observed to increase individuals' sensitivities to salt, which can adversely impact blood pressure (73). Although currently no rationale exists for recommending calcium supplements to reduce blood pressure, it is the general recommendation that all individuals meet the daily recommended intakes for dietary calcium to reduce their risk of sodium chloride-induced hypertension.

Magnesium Intake

Although cohort studies suggest an association between low dietary magnesium intake and hypertension, the mechanism of action is unclear and therefore does not justify an increase in magnesium intake to more than the current dietary recommended intakes of 420 mg for adult men and 320 mg for adult women (62).

Dietary Fat

There is little substantive evidence that dietary fat plays a role in blood pressure regulation (8,62). Of the many ways that dietary fat and fatty acids can affect risk factors for CHD, it is clear from epidemiological and clinical studies that this is not due to any appreciable change in blood pressure. There is little consistent evidence from experimental studies that the type and amount of fat significantly affect blood pressure. High doses of long-chain n-3 fatty acids (EPA and DHA) (3 to 15 g per day) have been shown to have a modest reduction effect on systolic blood pressure (2.1 mm Hg) and diastolic blood pressure (1.6 mm Hg), especially in individuals with elevated blood pressure, but the long-term treatment effect of n-3 fatty acids remains to be elucidated (8).

Caffeine

Caffeine may increase blood pressure, but tolerance to this effect develops rapidly (62). With chronic caffeine consumption, a blunted response to individual challenge doses has been observed. A small but significant decrease in blood pressure (1.5 mm Hg systolic blood pressure and 1.0 mm Hg diastolic blood pressure) was observed in normotensive individuals when caffeinated coffee was substituted with decaffeinated coffee. Additionally, a reduction in heart rate response to mental stress was observed with abstinence from caffeinated coffee. However, no direct relationship has been reported between caffeine consumption and blood pressure and the mechanism of action is unclear at the present time.

Cigarette Smoking

Cigarette smoking is a major modifiable risk factor of CVD, which is associated with a significant increase in blood pressure (57). Smoking cessation has been associated with reduction in blood pressure and CVD risk. Additionally, appropriate counseling is required with smoking cessation to prevent or minimize weight gain.

The Dietary Approaches to Stop Hypertension Diet Plan

Dietary Approaches to Stop Hypertension (DASH) was a multicenter clinical trial funded by the National Institutes of Health (NIH) to examine the influence of dietary modification on hypertension. The results of this study demonstrated that a reduction in blood pressure (5.5 mm Hg systolic and 3.0 mm Hg diastolic) can be achieved with a combination diet within 2 weeks of initiation of the diet, similar in magnitude to that observed in monotherapy antihypertensive drug trials, suggesting that this diet combination could be an effective alternate for individuals with stage 1 hypertension and could potentially prevent or delay the initiation of drug therapy (76). This combination diet is rich in fruits, vegetables, and low-fat dairy foods; low in total fat, saturated fat, and cholesterol; high in dietary fiber, potassium, calcium, and magnesium; and moderately high in protein (see Table 20.12) (77). In the DASH-Sodium study, a reduction in dietary sodium resulted in further reductions in blood pressure, with the greatest reduction observed in the low-sodium diet plan (DASH plus < 1,500 mg sodium) (78).

Exercise Prescription

Physical activity has both a direct and indirect effect on blood pressure. In addition to reducing systolic and diastolic blood pressure, weight loss and reduction in blood lipids due to physical activity also have an impact on blood pressure reductions (13,79,80). Therefore, in addition to the nonpharmacologic treatments for hypertension, such as

TABLE 20.12   The Dietary Approaches to Stop Hypertension (DASH) Diet Plan

Food Groups	Daily Servings	Serving Sizes	Examples	Nutritional Significance
Grains and grain products	7–8	1 slice bread, ½ cup dry cereal	Whole-wheat bread, bagels	Major source of energy and fiber
Vegetables	4–5	1 cup raw leafy vegetables, 6 oz vegetable juice	Tomatoes, spinach, beans	Rich sources of potassium, magnesium, and fiber
Fruits	4–5	1 medium fruit, 6 oz fruit juice	Bananas, melons, raisins	Important sources of potassium, magnesium, and fiber
Low-fat or nonfat dairy products	2–3	8 oz milk, 1 cup yogurt	Fat-free or low-fat milk, nonfat or low-fat yogurt	Major sources of calcium and protein
Meats, poultry, and fish	2 or less	3 oz cooked meat, poultry, or fish	Select only lean cuts; trim visible fat; broil, roast, or boil; remove skin from poultry	Rich sources of protein and magnesium
Nuts, seeds, and legumes	4–5 per week	⅓ cup nuts, ½ cooked legumes	Almonds, peanuts, kidney beans, lentils	Rich sources of energy, potassium, magnesium, protein, and fiber
Fats and oils	2–3	1 tsp soft margarine, 1 Tbsp low-fat mayonnaise, 1 tsp vegetable oil	Soft margarine, low-fat mayonnaise, light salad dressing, vegetable oil (olive, canola, corn)	DASH has 27% of calories as fat, including fat in or added to foods
Sweets	5 per week	1 Tbsp sugar, 1 Tbsp jelly/jam, 8 oz lemonade	Maple syrup, sugar, jelly, jam, hard candy, fruit punch, sorbet, ices	Sweets should be low fat

Source: Adapted from National Heart, Lung, and Blood Institute. Facts about the DASH Eating Plan. 2003. National Institutes of Health publication no. 03-4082. Available at: http://www.nhlbi.nih.gov/health/public/heart/hbp/dash/new_dash.pdf. Accessed November 23, 2004.

weight loss, alcohol restriction, and sodium restriction, daily aerobic activity should be prescribed for individuals with hypertension. The recommended exercise program for individuals with moderate hypertension includes large-muscle activities at moderate intensity (50% to 85% of maximum oxygen intake [VO_{2max}]), low-resistance and dynamic aerobic activities, such as cycling, walking on a treadmill, dancing, or gardening, three to five times per week for 20 to 60 minutes (57,58,81). Lower intensity exercise (40% to 70% VO_{2max}) may also be effective in reducing blood pressure, especially in the elderly (79–81). The exercise program for individuals with hypertension should be initiated at a comfortable pace and increased gradually by 5 minutes every week until individuals can perform the activity comfortably for at least 45 minutes.

This endurance exercise training has been observed to reduce systolic and diastolic blood pressure by 10 mm Hg in individuals with mildly elevated blood pressure, but these benefits remain only as long as the endurance training is maintained (79–81). Hypertensive individuals who are active in athletics should include moderate, dynamic activities and should increase their level of activity gradually. All hypertensive individuals participating in some kind of a regular activity program should have their blood pressure measured every 2 to 4 months to monitor the impact of exercise training. It should also be recognized that certain individuals with essential hypertension may not respond to endurance exercise training and may require pharmacologic intervention.

Unlike endurance exercise, resistive or strength training exercises have not been shown to reduce blood pressure. Although resistive or strength training exercises are not contraindicated for those with hypertension, these individuals should monitor their blood pressure while undertaking these activities because of the potential blood pressure-increasing effects (79–81).

Overall, endurance exercise not only reduces blood pressure, but also favorably modifies the risk factors of CVD. Therefore, all individuals should participate in daily moderate physical activity to reduce their risk of CVD.

Pharmacologic Treatment

Reducing blood pressure with several classes of drugs can reduce complications of hypertension (57,58). Thiazide-type diuretics are common antihypertension medications, which have been observed to prevent cardiovascular complications of hypertension (57,58). Diuretics could potentially enhance the efficacy of multidrug therapies and should be used as the first line of therapy for patients with hypertension, either alone or in combination with other drug classes, such as angiotensin-converting enzyme inhibitors, beta-blockers, and calcium channel blockers (see Table 20.13).

TABLE 20.13 Examples of Oral Antihypertensive Drugs

Class	Drugs
Thiazide diuretics	Chlorothiazide; hydrocholorathiazide
Loop diuretics	Furosemide; torsemide
Potassium-sparing diuretics	Amiloride; triamterene
Aldosterone-receptor blockers	Eplerenone; spironolactone
Beta-blockers	Atenolol; metoprolol
Combined alpha and beta blockers	Carvedilol; labetalol
Angiotensin-converting enzyme inhibitors	Captopril; lisinopril
Angiotensin II antagonists	Candesartan
Calcium channel blockers—non-dihydropyridines	Diltiazem extended release
Calcium channel blockers—dihydropyridines	Amlodipine
Alpha 1–blockers	Doxazosin
Central alpha 2–agonists and other centrally acting drugs	Clonidine

References

1. American Heart Association. 2004 Heart Disease and Stroke Statistics. Dallas, Texas: American Heart Association; 2004. Available at: http://www.americanheart.org/downloadable/heart/1072969766940HSStats2004Update.pdf. Accessed January 2, 2004.

2. Ross R. The pathogenesis of atherosclerosis: a perspective for the 1990s. *Nature.* 1993;362: 801–809.

3. Fuster V, Badimon L, Badimon JJ, Chesebro JH. The pathogenesis of coronary artery disease and the acute coronary syndrome. *N Engl J Med.* 1992;326:242–250.

4. National Cholesterol Education Program. *Third Report of the Expert Panel on Detection, Evaluation, and Treatment of High Blood Cholesterol in Adults (Adult Treatment Panel III).* Bethesda, Md: National Heart, Lung, and Blood Institute; 2001. NIH publication no. 01-3305. Available at: http://www.nhlbi.nih.gov/guidelines/cholesterol/. Accessed March 28, 2005.

5. Grundy SM, Cleeman JI, Merz CN, Brewer HB Jr, Clark LT, Hunninghake DB, Pasternak RC, Smith SC Jr, Stone NJ for the Coordinating Committee of the National Cholesterol Education Program. Implications of recent clinical trials for the National Cholesterol Education Program Adult Treatment Panel III Guidelines. *Circulation.* 2004;110:227–239.

6. Wilson PWF, D'Agostino RB, Levy D, Belanger AM, Silbershatz H, Kannel WB. Prediction of coronary heart disease using risk factor categories. *Circulation.* 1998;97:1837–1847.

7. Van Horn L, Ernst N. A summary of the science supporting the new National Cholesterol Education Program dietary recommendation: what dietitians should know. *J Am Diet Assoc.* 2001;10:1148–1154.

8. Van Horn L, McDonald A, Peters E, Gernhofer N. Dietary management of cardiovascular disease: a year 2002 perspective. *Nutr Clin Care.* 2001;4:314–331.

9. Obesity Education Initiative. *Clinical Guidelines on the Identification, Evaluation and Treatment of Overweight and Obesity in Adults: The Evidence Report.* Bethesda, Md: National Heart, Lung, and Blood Institute; 1998. Available at: http://www.nhlbi.nih.gov/guidelines/obesity/ob_gdlns.htm. Accessed March 28, 2005.

10. Eckel RH, Krauss RM for the AHA Nutrition Committee, American Heart Association. Call to action: obesity as a major risk factor for coronary heart disease. *Circulation.* 1998;97:2099–2100.

11. Jenkins DJ, Kendall CW, Marchie A, Faulkner DA, Wong JM, de Souza R, Emam A, Parker TL, Vidgen E, Lapsley KG, Trautwein EA, Josse RG, Leiter LA, Connelly PW. Effects of a dietary

portfolio of cholesterol-lowering foods vs Lovastatin on serum lipids and C-reactive protein. *JAMA*. 2003;290:502–510.

12. *Physical Activity and Health: A Report of the Surgeon General*. Atlanta, Ga: National Center for Chronic Disease Prevention and Health Promotion; 1996.

13. Institute of Medicine. *Dietary Reference Intakes for Energy, Carbohydrate, Fiber, Fat, Fatty Acids, Cholesterol, Protein and Amino Acids (Macronutrients)*. Washington, DC: National Academy Press; 2002. Available at: http://www.nap.edu. Accessed December 30, 2003.

14. Stefanick ML, Mackey S, Sheehan M, Ellsworth N, Haskell WL, Wood PD. Effects of diet and exercise in men and post-menopausal women with low levels of HDL cholesterol and high levels of LDL cholesterol. *N Engl J Med*. 1998;339:12–20.

15. Lee IM, Hsieh CC, Paffenbarger RS. Exercise intensity and longevity in men: the Harvard Alumni Health Study. *JAMA*. 1995;273:1179–1184.

16. Blair SN, Kohl HW, Barlow CE, Paffenbarger RS, Gibbons LW, Macera CA. Changes in physical fitness and all-cause mortality: a prospective study of healthy and unhealthy men. *JAMA*. 1995;273:1093–1098.

17. Danesh J, Wheeler JG, Hirschfield GM, Eda S, Eiriksdottir G, Rumley A, Lowe GDO, Pepys MB, Gudnason V. C-reactive protein and other circulating markers of inflammation in the prediction of coronary heart disease. *N Engl J Med*. 2004;350:1387–1397.

18. Stone NJ, Nicolosi RJ, Kris-Etherton P, Ernst ND, Krauss RM, Winston M. Summary of the scientific conference on the efficacy of hypocholesterolemic dietary interventions. *Circulation*. 1996;94:3388–3391.

19. Stone NJ. Fish consumption, fish oil, lipids and coronary heart disease. *Circulation*. 1996;94:2337–2340.

20. Din JN, Newby DE, Flapan AD. Omega 3 fatty acids and cardiovascular disease-fishing for a natural treatment. *BMJ*. 2004;328:30–35.

21. Djousse L, Hunt SC, Arnett DK, Province MA, Eckfeldt JH, Ellison RC. Dietary linolenic acid is inversely associated with plasma triacylglycerol: the National Heart, Lunch, and Blood Institute Family Heart Study. *Am J Clin Nutr*. 2003;78:1098–1102.

22. Krauss RM, Deckelbaum RJ, Ernst N, Fisher E, Howard BV, Knopp RH, Kotchen T, Lichtenstein AH, McGill HC, Pearson TA, Prewitt TE, Stone NJ, Horn LV, Weinberg R. Dietary guidelines for healthy American adults. A statement for health professionals from the Nutrition Committee, American Heart Association. *Circulation*. 1996;94:1795–1800.

23. Anderson JW, Johnstone BM, Cook-Newell ME. Meta-analysis of the effects of soy protein intake on serum lipids. *N Engl J Med*. 1995;333:276–282.

24. Ripsin CM, Keenan JM, Jacobs DR Jr, Elmer PJ, Welch RR, Van Horn L, Liu K, Turnbull WH, Thye FW, Kestin M, et al. Oat products and lipid lowering: a meta-analysis. *JAMA*. 1992;267:3317–3325.

25. Anderson JW, Smith BM, Gustafson NJ. Health benefits and practical aspects of high-fiber diets. *Am J Clin Nutr*. 1994;59(5 Suppl):1242S-1247S.

26. Rimm EB, Ascherio A, Giovannucci E, Spiegelman D, Stampher MJ, Willett WC. Vegetables, fruit and cereal fiber intake and risk of coronary heart disease among men. *J Am Diet Assoc*. 1996;275:447–451.

27. Van Horn L. Fiber, lipids and coronary heart disease. A statement for healthcare professionals from the Nutrition Committee, American Heart Association. *Circulation*. 1997;95:2701–2704.

28. St. Jeor ST, Howard BV, Prewitt E, Bovee V, Bazzarre T, Eckel RH for the AHA Nutrition Committee. Dietary protein and weight reduction. A statement for healthcare professionals from the nutrition committee of the council on nutrition, physical activity, and metabolism of the American Heart Association. *Circulation*. 2001;104:1869–1874.

29. Bravata DM, Sanders L, Huang J, Krumholz HM, Olkin I, Gardner CD, Bravata DM. Efficacy and safety of low carbohydrate diets: a systematic review. *JAMA*. 2003;298:1837–1850.

30. Farnsworth E, Luscombe ND, Noakes M, Wittert G, Argyiou W, Clifton PM. Effects of a high-protein, energy-restricted diet on body composition, glycemic control, and lipid concentrations in overweight and obese hyperinsulinemic men and women. *Am J Clin Nutr.* 2003;78:31–39.

31. Foster GD, Wyatt HR, Hill JO, McGuckin BG, Brill C, Mohammed BS, Szapary PO, Rader DJ, Edman JS, Klein S. A randomized trial of a low-carbohydrate diet for obesity. *N Engl J Med.* 2003;348:2082–2090.

32. Samaha FF, Iqbal N, Seshadri P, Chicano KL, Daily DA, McGrory J, Williams T, Williams M, Gracely EJ, Stern L. A low-carbohydrate as compared with a low-fat diet in severe obesity. *N Engl J Med.* 2003;348:2074–2081.

33. Brehm BJ, Seeley RJ, Daniels SR, D'Alessio DA. A randomized trial comparing a very low carbohydrate diet and a calorie-restricted low fat diet on body weight and cardiovascular risk factors in healthy women. *J Clin Endocrinol Metab.* 2003;88:1617–1623.

34. Duell PB. Prevention of atherosclerosis with dietary antioxidants: fact or fiction? *J Nutr.* 1996;126(suppl):1067S–1071S.

35. Kwiterovich PO. The effect of dietary fat, antioxidants and pro-oxidants on blood lipids, lipoproteins and atherosclerosis. *J Am Diet Assoc.* 1997;97(7 Suppl):S31–S41.

36. Alessio HM, Blasi ER. Physical activity as a natural antioxidant booster and its effect on a healthy life span. *Res Q Exerc Sport.* 1997;68:292–302.

37. Powers SK, DeRuisseau KC, Quindry J, Hamilton KL. Dietary antioxidants and exercise. *J Sports Sci.* 2004;22:81–94.

38. Stampfer MJ, Hennekens CH, Manson JE, Colditz GA, Rosner B, Willett WC. Vitamin E consumption and the risk of coronary heart disease in women. *N Engl J Med.* 1993;328:1444–1449.

39. The Alpha-Tocopherol, Beta Carotene Prevention Cancer Prevention Study Group. The alpha-tocopherol beta-carotene lung cancer prevention study: initial results from a controlled trial. *N Engl J Med.* 1994;330:1029–1035.

40. Osganian SK, Stampfer MJ, Rimm E, Spiegelman D, Manson JE, Willett WC. Dietary carotenoids and risk of coronary artery disease in women. *Am J Clin Nutr.* 2003;77:1390–1399.

41. Howard BV, Kritchevsky D. Phytochemicals and cardiovascular disease. A statement for health professionals from the American Heart Association. *Circulation.* 1997;95:2591–2593.

42. Sesso HD, Gaziano JM, Liu S, Buring JE. Flavonoid intake and the risk of cardiovascular disease in women. *Am J Clin Nutr.* 2003;77:1400–1408.

43. Law M. Plant sterol and stanol margarine and health. *BMJ.* 2000;320:861–864.

44. Waterhouse AL, German JB, Walzem RL, Hansen RJ, Kasim-Karakas SE. Is it time for a wine trial? *Am J Clin Nutr.* 1998;68:220–221.

45. Nigdikar SV, Williams NR, Griffin BA, Howard AN. Consumption of red wine polyphenols reduces the susceptibility of low-density lipoproteins to oxidation in vivo. *Am J Clin Nutr.* 1998;68:258–265.

46. Lichtenstein AH. Soy protein, isoflavones and cardiovascular risk. *J Nutr.* 1998;128:1589–1592.

47. Spigelski D, Jones PJH. Efficacy of garlic supplementation in lowering serum cholesterol levels. *Nutr Rev.* 2001;59:236–244.

48. Ridker PM, Vaughan DE, Stampfer MJ, Glynn RJ, Hennekens CH. Association of moderate alcohol consumption and plasma concentration of endogenous tissue-type plasminogen activator. *JAMA.* 1994;272:929–933.

49. Gronbaek M, Deis A, Sorensen TI, Becker U, Schnohr P, Jensen G. Mortality associated with moderate intakes of wine, beer or spirits. *BMJ.* 1995;310:1165–1169.

50. Panagiotakos DB, Pitsavos C, Chrysohoou C, Kokkinos P, Toutouzas P, Stefanadis C. The J-shaped effect of coffee consumption on the risk of developing acute coronary syndromes: the CARDIO2000 case-control study. *J Nutr.* 2003;133:3228–3232.

51. Bak AA, Grobbee DE. The effect of serum cholesterol levels of coffee brewed by filtering or boiling. *N Engl J Med.* 1989;321:1432–1437.

52. Urgert R, Meyboom S, Kuilman M, Rexwinkel H, Vissers MN, Klerk M, Katan M. Comparison of effect of cafetiere and filtered coffee on serum concentrations of liver aminotransferases and lipids: six month randomised controlled trial. *BMJ*. 1996;313:1362–1366.

53. Maron BJ. Cardiovascular risks of young persons on the athletic field. *Ann Intern Med*. 1998;129:379–386.

54. Sharma S, Whyte G, McKenna WJ. Sudden death from cardiovascular disease in young athletes: fact or fiction? *Br J Sports Med*. 1997;31:269–276.

55. Maron BJ, Thompson PD, Puffer JC, McGrew CA, Strong WB, Douglas PS, Clark LT, Mitten MJ, Crawford MH, Atkins DL, Driscoll DJ, Epstein AE. Cardiovascular preparticipation screening of competitive athletes. A statement for health professionals from the Sudden Death Committee (clinical cardiology) and Congenital Cardiac Defects Committee (cardiovascular disease in the young), American Heart Association [published addendum in *Circulation*. 1998;97:2294]. *Circulation*. 1996;94:850–856.

56. Maron BJ. Hypertrophic cardiomyopathy: a systematic review. *JAMA*. 2002;287:1308–1320.

57. Chobania AV, Bakris GL, Black HR, Cushman WC, Green LA, Izzo JL, Jones DW, Materson BJ, Oparil S, Wright JT, Rocella EJ and the National High Blood Pressure Education Program Coordinating Committee. The seventh report of the Joint National Committee on Prevention, Detection, Evaluation, and Treatment of High Blood Pressure. The JNC 7 report. *JAMA*. 2003;289;2560–2572.

58. National High Blood Pressure Education Program. *The Seventh Report of the Joint National Committee on Prevention, Detection, Evaluation, and Treatment of High Blood Pressure (JNC 7)*. Bethesda, Md: National Heart, Lung, and Blood Institute; 2003. Available at: http://www.nhlbi.nih.gov/guidelines/hypertension. Accessed March 28, 2005.

59. Preuss HG. Diet, genetics and hypertension. *J Am Coll Nutr*. 1997;16:296–305.

60. Neaton JD, Grimm RH Jr, Prineas RJ, Stamler J, Grandits GA, Elmer PJ, Cutler JA, Flack JM, Schoenberger JA, McDonald R; Treatment of Mild Hypertension Study Group. Treatment of Mild Hypertension Study: final results. *JAMA*. 1993;270:713–724.

61. Trials for Hypertension Prevention Collaborative Research Group. Effects of weight loss and sodium reduction intervention on blood pressure and hypertension incidence in overweight people with high-normal blood pressure: the Trials of Hypertension Prevention, Phase II. *Arch Intern Med*. 1997;157:657–667.

62. Stamler J, Caggiula AW, Grandits GA. Relation of body mass and alcohol, nutrient, fiber, and caffeine intakes to blood pressure in the special intervention and usual care groups in the Multiple Risk Factor Intervention Trial. *Am J Clin Nutr*. 1997;65(1 Suppl):338S-365S.

63. Klatsky AL. Alcohol, coronary heart disease and hypertension. *Ann Rev Med*. 1996;47:149–160.

64. US Dept of Agriculture and US Dept of Health and Human Services. *Nutrition and Your Health: Dietary Guidelines for Americans*. Available at: http://www.usda.gov/cnpp/DietGd.pdf. Accessed August 15, 2003.

65. Halbert JA, Silagy CA, Finucane P, Withers RT, Hamdorf PA, Andrews GR. The effectiveness of exercise training in lowering blood pressure: a meta-analysis of randomized trials of four weeks or longer. *J Hum Hypertens*. 1997;11:641–649.

66. Psaty BM, Lumley T, Furberg CD, Schellenbaum G, Pahor M, Alderman MH, Weiss NS. Health outcomes associated with antihypertensive therapies used as first-line agents: a network meta-analysis. *JAMA*. 1997;277:739–745.

67. Collins R, Peto R, MacMahon S, Hebert P, Fiebach NH, Eberlein KA, Godwin J, Qizilbash N, Taylor JO, Hennekens CH. Blood pressure, stroke and coronary heart disease. Part 2: Short-term reductions in blood pressure: overview of randomized drug trials in their epidemiological context. *Lancet*. 1990;335:827–838.

68. Cutler JA, Follmann D, Allender PS. Randomized trials of sodium restriction: an overview. *Am J Clin Nutr*. 1997;65(2 Suppl):643S-651S.

69. Luft FC, Weinberger MH. Heterogeneous responses to changes in dietary salt intake: the salt-sensitivity paradigm. *Am J Clin Nutr*. 1997;65(2 Suppl):612S–617S.

70. Devine A, Criddle RA, Dick IM, Kerr DA, Prince RL. A longitudinal study of the effect of sodium and calcium intakes on regional bone density in post-menopausal women. *Am J Clin Nutr*. 1995;62:740–745.

71. Institute of Medicine. Dietary Reference Intakes for Water, Potassium, Sodium, Chloride, and Sulfate. Washington, DC: National Academy Press; 2004. Available at: http://www.nap.edu. Accessed April 1, 2004.

72. McDowell MA, Briefel RR, Alaimo K, Biscof AM, Caughman CR, Carroll MD, Loria CM, Johnson CL. Energy and macronutrient intake of persons ages 2 months and over in the United States: Third National Health and Nutrition Examination Survey, Phase I, 1988–1991. *Advance Data from Vital and Health Statistics No. 255*. Hyattsville, Md: National Center for Health Statistics; 1994.

73. Kotchen TA, Kotchen JM. Dietary sodium and blood pressure: interactions with other nutrients. *Am J Clin Nutr*. 1997;65(2 Suppl):708S–711S.

74. Whelton PK, He J, Cutler JA, Brancati FL, Appel LJ, Follmann D, Klag MJ. Effects of oral potassium on blood pressure: meta-analysis of randomized controlled clinical trials. *JAMA*. 1997;277:1624–1632.

75. McCarron DA. Role of adequate dietary calcium intake in the prevention and management of salt-sensitive hypertension. *Am J Clin Nutr*. 1997;65(2 Suppl):712S–716S.

76. Appel LJ, Moore TJ, Obarzanek E, Vollmer WM, Svetkey LP, Sacks FM, Bray GA, Vogt TM, Cutler JA, Windhauser MM, Lin PH, Karanja N. A clinical trial of the effects of dietary patterns on blood pressure. DASH Collaborative Research Group. *N Engl J Med*. 1997;336:1117–1124.

77. National Heart, Lung, and Blood Institute. Facts about the DASH Eating Plan. 2003. National Institutes of Health publication No. 03-4082. Available at: http://www.nhlbi.nih.gov/health/public/heart/hbp/dash/new_dash.pdf. Accessed November 23, 2004.

78. Sacks FM, Svetkey LP, Vollmer WM, Appel LJ, Bray GA, Harsha D, Obarzanek E, Conlin PR, Miller ER 3rd, Simons-Morton DG, Karanja N, Lin PH; DASH-Sodium Collaborative Research Group. Effects on blood pressure of reduced dietary sodium and the Dietary Approaches to Stop Hypertension (DASH) diet. *N Engl J Med*. 2001;344:3–10.

79. Kelley GA, Kelley KS. Aerobic exercise and resting blood pressure in older adults: a meta-analytic review of randomized controlled trials. *J Gerontol A Biol Sci Med Sci*. 2001;56:M298–M303.

80. Stewart KJ. Exercise training and the cardiovascular consequences of type 2 diabetes and hypertension. Plausible mechanisms for improving cardiovascular health. *JAMA*. 2002;288:1622–1631.

81. American College of Sports Medicine Position Stand. Physical activity, physical fitness, and hypertension. *Med Sci Sports Exerc*. 1993;25:i–x.

Additional Resources

ATP III Guidelines At-A-Glance Quick Desk Reference. Bethesda, Md: National Heart, Lung, and Blood Institute; 2001. NIH publication No. 01–3305. Available at: http://www.nhlbi.nih.gov/guidelines/cholesterol/atglance.htm. Accessed November 23, 2004.

National High Blood Pressure Education Program. The DASH Eating Plan. Available at: http://www.nhlbi.nih.gov/health/public/heart/hbp/dash/index.htm. Accessed November 23, 2004.

National High Blood Pressure Education Program. Your Guide to Lowering Blood Pressure. Available at: http://www.nhlbi.nih.gov/health/public/heart/hbp/hbp_low/index.htm. Accessed November 23, 2004.

Section 4

Sports-Specific Nutrition Guidelines

Much of the sports nutrition information available to both athletes and practitioners is general in nature. Athletes often ask for specific information about their particular sport. Some sports, such as soccer and distance running, have been studied extensively and there is a large of body of scientific literature published. Athletes in other sports have been studied to a small degree, if at all, and practitioners must answer specific questions as best they can.

This section has grouped sports together based primarily on their physiological demands. Very high–intensity sports include sprints (ie, running 50 to 200 meters, swimming 50 meters, or cycling 200 meters), jumping or hurdling, and weight or power lifting. High-intensity, short-duration sports last from 1½ to 30 minutes and include running or swimming 1,500 meters, rowing, and short-distance cycling. Intermittent, high-intensity sports have been well-studied in some cases and include soccer, football, basketball, hockey, and tennis. Endurance and ultraendurance sports, such as distance running, cycling, swimming, or combinations of these events, are included in one chapter. Sports in which weight is restricted and/or the body is judged aesthetically, such as wrestling, gymnastics, or bodybuilding are grouped together because weight or body composition is such an important factor. The final chapter is devoted to sports that depend on precision and reaction time but are low endurance, such as baseball and golf.

Chapter 21

NUTRITION FOR VERY HIGH–INTENSITY SPORTS

JANET WALBERG RANKIN, PhD

Introduction

This chapter reviews the evidence that the diet of athletes performing very high–intensity efforts for a brief period (as defined as maximal effort of less than 30 seconds) affects athletic success. Numerous sports and events involve very high–intensity efforts (see Table 21.1). Running sprints, jumps, throws, or hurdles from track and field events as well as some cycle and swim events are brief and intense. In addition to these single-effort events, some team sports depend on episodic, maximal but brief physical effort (eg, football, volleyball, baseball).

These athletes are involved in intensive workouts, often daily or sometimes several workouts per day, which influence their dietary needs. Although a high school level athlete may work out approximately 3 or 4 days per week for 1 to 2 hours per session, a college or elite athlete may be involved in as many as 14 sessions per week or more. On the day of competition, although the actual event is brief, the athlete may compete in multiple events in one day (eg, relay, sprint, and jump). This chapter reviews the energy systems used to fuel very high–intensity activity, diets typically consumed, and dietary recommendations for athletes doing very high–intensity exercise.

Energy System and Fuel Use

The performance of very high–intensity efforts depends on many factors, including reaction time, muscle power, skill, muscle fiber type, and psychological issues. From a metabolic standpoint, adenosine triphosphate (ATP) availability, rate of breakdown, and rate of ATP resynthesis are critical. The rate of ATP needed to perform these events is high. For example, the power output during a 30-second sprint is approximately twice that achieved at maximum oxygen consumption (VO_{2max}). These events are fueled primarily through anaerobic metabolic pathways. The shorter the maximal effort, the higher the percentage of

TABLE 21.1   Events and Sports That Involve Very High–Intensity Exercise (< 30 sec)

Mode	Event (Approximate Duration)
Run sprint	50-m dash (6 sec), 100 m (10 sec), 200 m (20 sec)
Jumping or hurdles	100/110 m hurdle, high jump, long jump, triple jump, pole vault
Cycle sprint	200 m (10 sec)
Swim sprint	50 m (22 sec)
Throwing	Shot, javelin, discus, hammer (several seconds)
Olympic weight lifting	Snatch, clean and jerk (≤ 1 sec)
Power lifting	Bench press, squat, dead lift (seconds)
Gymnastics	Multiple events
Team sports with sprints	Multiple, including football, baseball

ATP from anaerobic (as compared with aerobic) sources. For example, the ATP used in a 30-second maximal sprint is approximately 80% anaerobically generated, whereas a 10-second sprint is approximately 97% anaerobically fueled (1).

Most of the anaerobic ATP production during very high–intensity exercise occurs by the breakdown of creatine phosphate (PCr) within the muscle. This is the most rapid source of energy for ATP regeneration. Estimates are that the maximal rate of ATP production (μmol/second/kg) is 6.0 for PCr but only 1.5 for anaerobic glycolysis and 0.24 and 0.5 for aerobic generation via fat and carbohydrate, respectively (2). This means that efforts that require very rapid ATP use will rely heavily on PCr breakdown. Because creatine phosphate stores are limited and use is rapid with high-intensity work, it is possible to significantly reduce these stores during a brief exercise bout. For example, research shows that a 30-second maximal effort sprint decreased PCr by 75%, a 20-second sprint (eg, 200-meter run, 50-meter swim) by about half, while even a 10-second maximal effort (eg, 100-meter run, 200-meter cycle) can decrease PCr by 40%. (1,2). So, a limiting factor for performance of these very high–intensity efforts could be initial muscle PCr stores. It is logical to begin the event, game, or match with high muscle PCr. Sprint training can increase PCr stores. Another way to boost muscle creatine stores is through a supplementation strategy with oral creatine (discussed later in this chapter).

In addition to PCr, the other fuel that provides ATP during high-intensity efforts of up to 30 seconds is carbohydrate through glycolysis. The use of glycolysis for ATP generation becomes more and more of a critical factor as the duration of a sprint increases. A 10-second sprint depends on glycolysis for approximately 44% of the ATP used, whereas a 30-second sprint will likely get more than 50% of the ATP from this system (1). Even so, because muscles have much more glycogen than PCr, these brief, very high–intensity efforts do not substantially reduce muscle glycogen. The magnitude of reduction in muscle glycogen depends on the intensity and duration of an exercise bout as well as the type of activity (see Figure 21.1) (3–5) The magnitude of glycogen depletion during resistance exercise will be related to the intensity of the lift and to the amount of work performed. Most of these studies used a high-volume resistance exercise workout; little research has been done on glycogen use with low-volume, high-intensity workouts.

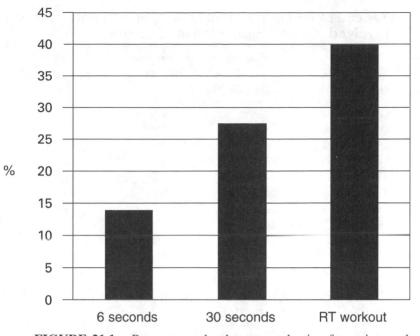

FIGURE 21.1.   Percent muscle glycogen reduction for sprints and resistance exercise workout. RT = multiple-set resistance training. Data are from references 3, 4, and 5.

Although the reductions described earlier are meaningful, glycogen is not being reduced to the level shown to be detrimental to performance of aerobic events (6). Thus, it is not clear if modestly reduced glycogen stores are likely to influence performance of a single very high–intensity effort. However, if the very high–intensity effort is interspersed within a game that involves substantial aerobic exercise (eg, basketball) or is concurrent with a low-carbohydrate diet (eg, < 4 g/kg body weight), muscle glycogen may be reduced enough to impair performance of very high–intensity efforts. In addition, quality of workouts may be compromised if they begin with low muscle glycogen.

In summary, brief, very high–intensity efforts rely primarily on PCr stores and partially on glycogen stores with the longer sprints. This can result in substantial use of the PCr stores but typically less than one third of the muscle glycogen stores.

Typical Diets

Much less information has been published describing the diet of very high–intensity athletes compared with endurance athletes. Also, the manner in which athletes are often grouped in these reports (eg, using the category "swimmers") can make it difficult to differentiate those who are involved with short-duration events from those who participate in long-duration events (7). In addition, some of this data are collected on athletes from different countries, which introduces the difficulty of comparing athletes' diets from different cultures and different levels of competition (7–11). Some of the studies that evaluated the diet of sprint or very high–intensity athletes using dietary records are shown in Tables 21.2 (6–10) and 21.3 (6–8).

TABLE 21.2   Reported Diet Quality and Quantity for Female Athletes Involved in Brief, High-Intensity Exercise

Type (Reference)	Energy, kcal/d (kcal/kg)	Energy from Carbohydrate, %	Carbohydrate (g/kg)	Energy from Protein, %	Energy from Fat, %
Gymnasts (6)	2298 (51.0)	42	5.4	16	42
Gymnasts (10)	1838 (42.5)	49	5.1	15	36
Gymnasts (9)	1678 (34.4)	66	5.8	17	18
Field Athletes (8)	2215 (26.2)	46	3.0	17	38
Throwing (6)	4446 (53.0)	35	4.6	19	47
Throwers (7)	2617 (40.0)	54	5.1	14	32
Sprinters (7)	2393 (45.7)	53	5.8	15	33
Jumpers (7)	1982 (36.5)	51	4.5	16	33
Swimmers (6)	4595 (71)	35	6.2	26	49

TABLE 21.3   Reported Diet Quality and Quantity for Male Athletes Involved in Brief, High-Intensity Exercise

Type (Reference)	Energy, kcal/d (kcal/kg)	Energy from Carbohydrate, %	Carbohydrate (g/kg)	Energy from Protein, %	Energy from Fat, %
Gymnasts (6)	3310 (56.0)	43	6.1	18	38
Throwing (6)	5353 (49.0)	34	4.1	20	47
Throwers (7)	3591 (34.6)	55	4.1	15	30
Field athletes (8)	3485 (36.0)	41	3.7	19	40
Sprinters (7)	2653 (40.0)	54	5.1	15	30
Jumpers (7)	2863 (41.6)	54	5.2	15	31
Swimming (6)	5938 (80)	33	6.5	22	48
Weightlifting (6)	4597 (57)	38	5.4	22	40

The study of Japanese track-and-field athletes separated the athletes by event (8). The diets of male sprinters and jumpers were similar in energy content, whereas throwers and long-distance runners were similar to each other but they consumed approximately 30% more energy than the sprinters or jumpers. The proportion of macronutrients in the diet was remarkably consistent among types of athletes, although the absolute amount of all macronutrients was higher for athletes with the greatest energy consumption. All of the athletic groups consumed at least 1.3 g of protein per kilogram of body weight. The protein intake per kilogram of body weight was least for both male and female throwers and highest for the long-distance runners. The female throwers consumed more than the female sprinters or jumpers, but the difference was much less than for males. The elite South African field athletes studied at a national championship (9) and Chinese field athletes (7) consumed a diet of similar high energy value but much higher in fat and protein than that of the Japanese athletes. Although it is difficult to find consistent patterns, the sprinters and jumpers tend to consume lower energy diets than throwers and weight lifters. The absolute daily energy intake of the latter was similar to that of endurance runners.

Nutritional Issues

There has been little attention focused on the effect of nutritional quality or quantity on performance of very high–intensity efforts. There are several dietary factors that theoretically could affect performance; research concerning these factors is reviewed here.

Energy, Body Weight and Composition

Track-and-field coaches encourage athletes to minimize body fat for most events (except throwers). More energy is required to perform these events at a heavier body weight. The value of muscle mass is balanced by the increased force generation, but there is no performance advantage and actually a disadvantage to weight from body fat. Measurement of body composition and aerobic capacity in 100 youths showed that although fat-free mass was positively correlated with maximal power output and total work completed on the treadmill test, percentage body fat was negatively correlated with endurance time on the test of aerobic capacity (12). However, this should not be interpreted as proving that if a specific sprinter who is already lean reduces his or her body fat even further that performance will directly improve. There are too many other important factors that determine performance and, as discussed later in this chapter, potential unintended consequences of weight loss to encourage rigid minimum body-fat standards.

Sprinters tend to have much higher muscularity and somewhat higher body fat than distance runners. The higher muscularity obviously helps produce more power for rapid acceleration and maximal speed. Most elite sprinters are lean but not as lean as athletes from endurance sports. Wilmore (13) evaluated the body fat for a cross section of athletes and reported that male sprinters and discus throwers had approximately 16% body fat whereas those performing the shot-put ranged from 16% to 20% body fat. The female athletes in these events had more body fat than men, with sprinters and jumpers approximately 19% to 20% fat and the throwers from 25% to 28% body fat.

There is evidence that weight loss is common in high-power athletes. Folgelholm and Hiilloskorpi (14) reported that approximately 50% of men and women in speed sports were trying to lose weight. Almost half of the elite gymnasts studied by Jannalagadda et al (10) were on a "self-prescribed diet."

Weight loss and negative energy balance may impair physical performance. Some studies report no effect of short-term weight loss on performance of high-intensity exercise, whereas others report decrements. McMurray et al (15) observed decreased total and average power in collegiate wrestlers in a 30-second maximal effort cycling test after 7 days of weight loss (2.4 kg) on a reduced-energy diet. Subjects in another study lost less weight and more slowly (1.3 kg over 2 weeks) and actually had a slight increase in performance of the same 30-second test (16). A series of studies at Virginia Tech has looked at the effect of short-term weight loss through energy restriction on anaerobic performance (17). Dynamic muscle strength of the quadriceps and biceps brachii was reduced by approximately 8% in athletes who lost 3.3 kg during a 10-day period of dieting (17). So, substantial weight loss that is done quickly (eg, 5% within several days) is more likely to detrimentally affect high–intensity performance than more gradual weight loss.

The macronutrient mix, especially the amount of carbohydrate in a weight-loss diet, may influence performance. For example, resistance trainers who consumed a low-energy diet with 50% (2.3g/kg) of energy from carbohydrate had decreased muscle endurance after 7 days of the diet, whereas those who consumed the same amount of energy, but with 70% (3.2 g/kg) of the energy derived from carbohydrate, maintained their rates of isometric fatigue at baseline levels (18). In summary, there is evidence for a reduction in sprint performance and muscle strength or endurance in some but not all studies examining acute weight loss in athletes. Very high–intensity efforts are likely less affected by negative energy balance than more prolonged exercise bouts.

Because there could be a negative impact of energy restriction on performance, body composition recommendations should be flexible and individualized for athletes with different body types and weight histories. There is no guarantee that any individual athlete will improve performance as a result of weight loss. In fact, as discussed previously in this chapter, performance may be impaired during the weight loss. Other potential consequences of rapid weight loss include decreases in muscle mass and possible effects on linear growth, hormonal changes, and nutrient deficiencies (19). Female athletes dieting for weight loss are particularly susceptible to the female athlete triad: disruption of reproductive hormones, reduced bone strength concurrent with disordered eating, and poor diet. Athletes who need to lose weight should be encouraged to lose weight gradually, at a modest rate, and during the off-season to minimize any detrimental effect on performance.

Hydration

The detrimental effect of dehydration on aerobic performance is well-documented, but the effect on muscle strength or performance of power events is less clear. One study (20) found a 7.8% reduction in isometric muscle strength in athletes who lost 3.4% of their body weight via dehydration in a sauna. Another study showed that a 3.8% loss of body weight using sauna exposure had no effect on muscle isometric strength and endurance (21). Recently, a study with more modest dehydration evaluated the effect on performance in both men and women. Neither strength nor jump capacity in men was affected by loss of 1.8% of body weight through sauna, but a similar amount of dehydration reduced jump capacity linearly with percentage reduction in body weight in women (22).

The value of hydration on maximal power output following an endurance bout was illustrated in a study by Fritzsche et al (23). Eight endurance-trained cyclists exercised 122 minutes at 62% VO_{2max} in a hot and humid environment at four separate times. They were provided with either 3.3 liters of water, 3.4 liters of water with approximately 200 g of carbohydrate, the same amount of carbohydrate in a small fluid volume (about one-half liter), or this small amount of water alone. Maximal power production over 4 seconds was measured at four times during the 2-hour cycling bout (every 26 minutes). Although there was no difference in maximum power production sprints among the treatments at the first power test, the decrease in power between 26 minutes and near the end of the bout was the least for the treatment with the highest fluid and carbohydrate content (Figure 21.2). The subjects could produce more power with this treatment than when they had the same volume of water alone. Both of these treatments were superior to both trials with the small amount of water (whether containing carbohydrate or not). The researchers concluded that maximal power is best maintained by consuming high amounts of fluid, especially if it contains carbohydrate. This illustrates the importance of hydration to athletes involved in games that include significant aerobic activity with sporadic sprints or high muscle-power generation.

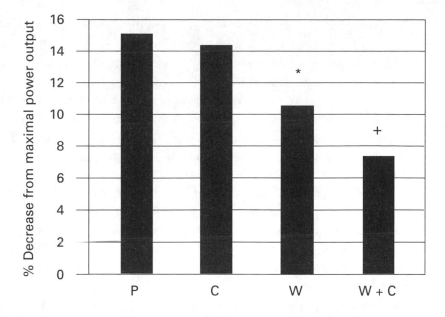

FIGURE 21.2.   Decrease in power output for 4-sec maximal power test during 2-h endurance exercise bout for treatments varying in hydration and carbohydrate. **Key:** P, placebo consumed (0.4 L water); C, carbohydrate consumed (204 g carbohydrate in 0.5 L water); W, water consumed (3.3 L water); W + C, water with carbohydrate consumed (3.4 L water with 204 g carbohydrate). * indicates significantly different from P or C; + indicates significantly different from all other groups. Data are from reference 23.

As with weight loss through energy restriction, the magnitude of dehydration will likely influence performance. Because there is some evidence suggests that even modest amounts of dehydration can impair performance in some athletes (22), weight loss through dehydration should not exceed 2% of body weight.

Carbohydrate

Dietary carbohydrate can ensure that glycogen stores are adequate and that blood glucose is maintained. An important question is: how much glycogen is adequate for performance of very high–intensity exercise? As discussed previously in this chapter, very high–intensity exercise drains some muscle glycogen, but not to the extent that it causes impaired performance as may occur in longer or events involving repeated sprints. Therefore, the value of high initial muscle glycogen on short, maximal efforts is debatable and has been studied in a small number of studies reviewed here.

Muscle Strength and Power

Some studies suggest that a low initial muscle glycogen concentration will adversely affect muscle strength and power (24), but a careful subsequent study suggested that some of this impairment was due to the exhaustive exercise performed, which resulted in reduced glycogen, rather than the glycogen reduction itself (25). A reduction of more than half of the muscle glycogen through diet and exercise resulted in a decrease in muscle strength and endurance, but repletion of muscle glycogen through diet did not allow recovery of muscle force. This showed that it was the strenuous exercise rather than the muscle glycogen reduction, per se, that impaired performance. Thus, there is not good evidence that muscle glycogen has any effect on maximal muscle strength or power.

The effect of muscle glycogen on muscle endurance is not supported in a study of resistance-trained athletes who completed a resistance training workout in a carbohydrate-loaded or carbohydrate-depleted condition (26). There was no difference in total volume lifted between the two dietary conditions, suggesting that muscle glycogen was not a limiting factor for the resistance exercises.

The effect of acute consumption of carbohydrate on muscle endurance is controversial. Several studies support the value of consuming carbohydrate just before and during a resistance exercise bout on total work performed during a workout. Resistance-trained males who consumed a glucose polymer solution (1 g/kg) before and during (0.17 g/kg) a repeated-set leg-extension bout tended to have better muscle endurance, as reflected by number of repetitions (149 vs 129 for carbohydrate vs placebo) and sets (17.1 vs 14.4 for carbohydrate vs placebo), but statistical significance was not quite achieved (27). Haff et al (28) reported that resistance-trained males could do approximately 8% more total and average work during an exercise test of 16 sets of 10 reps at 120 degrees/second. However, another study from that laboratory (29) using a similar design found no effect of acute carbohydrate ingestion (0.5 g/kg) before and every 10 minutes during a 39-minute isotonic exercise bout on isokinetic exercise test performance (3 sets of 10 reps at 2.09 rad/second). This was in spite of the fact that the carbohydrate ingestion reduced the total muscle glycogen reduction during the exercise workout.

A study from the author's laboratory at Virginia Tech did not support the value of a single high-carbohydrate feeding (1 g/kg) on performance of multiple-set resistance exercise when subjects were losing weight on a low-energy diet for 3 days (30). Resistance exercise performance was tested before and after the body weight loss by having the subjects perform repetitions to exhaustion in the last set of leg extension and bench press exercises within a four-exercise resistance workout. The performance was not different if the subjects consumed a high-carbohydrate beverage compared to a placebo beverage.

In summary, most studies do not support the value of high muscle glycogen or acute carbohydrate ingestion on muscle strength or endurance. Most of the studies performed in a weight-room setting with multiple sets and exercise workouts have not demonstrated a benefit of a chronically high-carbohydrate diet or acute carbohydrate ingestion on performance. Some of the variation among studies may relate to the performance tests used (eg, large-muscle vs small-muscle exercises, number of repetitions, and intensity) as well as the subjects (athletes trained in that event compared with those less familiar and thus less reliable in their performance of the test).

Sprint Performance

Few studies have examined the effect of muscle glycogen on single sprint performance. However, one study (31) reported a detrimental effect of a low-carbohydrate diet for 3 days on high-intensity exercise. Subjects produced a higher mean power output (but the same peak power) in a 30-second maximal cycling test when they consumed a 50% carbohydrate diet with 130 kJ/kg (~ 3.9 g carbohydrate per kg) compared with an isocaloric diet of only 5% carbohydrate (~ 0.4 g/kg) for 3 days (Figure 21.3).

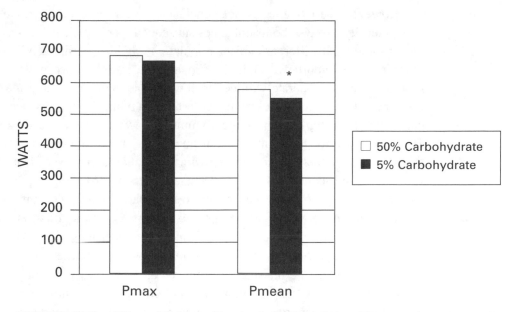

FIGURE 21.3. Effect of 3 days of low-carbohydrate diet on 30-sec cycle sprint maximum and mean power. Pmax = maximum power; Pmean = mean power. * indicates significant difference between dietary treatment groups. Data are from reference 31.

Even if sprint performance is impaired by a very low–carbohydrate diet, most studies do not observe a benefit of moving from a moderate-carbohydrate diet to a high-carbohydrate diet for sprint performance. Lamb et al (32) found no benefit of a high-carbohydrate (80% of energy, 12.1 g/kg) diet compared with a moderate-carbohydrate (43% of energy, 6.5 g/kg) diet consumed for 9 days on 50-meter swim sprint performance in collegiate male swimmers. Vandenberghe et al (33) found no difference in cycling time to exhaustion (~ 125% of VO_{2max}) for a moderate- compared with a high-carbohydrate diet (70% of energy and ~ 7.7 g/kg vs 50% of energy and ~ 4.6 g/kg).

In summary, limited research suggests that sprint performance may be reduced with very low–carbohydrate diets but, in reality, few athletes are likely to actually consume diets too low in carbohydrate. The exception could be athletes attempting to lose weight on the low-carbohydrate diets that recommend severe limits on carbohydrate intake, a practice that should be discouraged. There is little evidence for the value of increasing dietary carbohydrate to higher than moderate levels (~ 60% of energy).

Recovery

Some athletes perform repeated events or games during a single day, so they need to recover as quickly as possible. Consumption of carbohydrate after exercise will accelerate glycogen replenishment. For example, Pascoe et al (34) showed that muscle glycogen decreased to approximately 70% of resting values after a resistance exercise bout, but consumption of a carbohydrate beverage (1.5 g/kg) after exercise increased muscle glycogen to 75% of baseline after 2 hours and to 91% of baseline after 6 hours. On the other hand, there was no restoration of muscle glycogen after 6 hours when a water placebo was ingested after exercise.

However, the evidence is not conclusive that a high-carbohydrate diet between two high-intensity exercise bouts enhances subsequent performance. Two studies using similar methodology but different subject populations yielded completely different conclusions regarding the importance of high carbohydrate intake between bouts. Haub et al (35) reported that six moderately trained men were able to maintain their maximal exercise performance of a 100-KJ cycle ergometer test to that of an initial test when they had consumed carbohydrate (0.7 g/kg) during the 60 minutes between the two tests; time to complete the 100-KJ test was longer if subjects consumed a placebo during the recovery period. Although this suggests a benefit of high carbohydrate ingestion on recovery from high-intensity performance, a subsequent study with the same protocol (36) using seven competitive cyclists found no benefit on performance due to high carbohydrate consumption between bouts. Because training, especially sport-specific training, is such an important variable, it is difficult to compare the two studies. The differences between these studies emphasize the importance of using athletes specific to the event in these dietary intervention studies.

To summarize, the information from research on dietary carbohydrate for sprinting or muscle strength translates into more flexibility for the diet of athletes involved in very high–intensity events than for those participating in prolonged, endurance exercise. Several studies show superior performance of single sprints when athletes have consumed high-carbohydrate diets (> 65% of energy from carbohydrate, > 7 g/kg) compared with low-carbohydrate diets (< 10% of energy, < 1.5 g/kg), but this is not consistent among studies. There is no consensus that a high-carbohydrate diet is superior to a moderate-carbohydrate diet for performance of single sprints or maximum muscle power. Therefore, although glycogen stores can be supercompensated using glycogen loading, there is no evidence that this could help performance, and, in fact, it may be counterproductive, owing to weight gain that coincides with the additional carbohydrate stores. The carbohydrate content of the diet may come into play for athletes performing multiple events over a day or for those doing significant amounts of aerobic activity in addition to the sprints. It is recommended that athletes involved in very high–intensity sports or events consume approximately 6 to 8 g/kg, with the lower end of the range recommended for athletes with lower energy needs. Consumption of carbohydrate foods after an event will enhance the rate of glycogen replacement.

Protein

Because most athletes performing brief, maximal efforts depend on high muscularity and function, they want nutritional strategies that enhance lean body mass. Although most research does not support consuming a chronically high protein intake (> 1.8 g/kg) in the daily diet (37), research is accumulating that timing of food consumption just before or after a resistance exercise bout can modify muscle protein balance. Several studies show that acute resistance exercise stimulates an anabolic state for up to 24 hours. However, if resistance exercise is done in the fasted state, the protein balance remains negative. If food is consumed, protein balance will become positive, suggesting muscle growth. Specific studies from one laboratory have shown that consumption of as little as 6 g of amino acids or amino acids with about 35 g of carbohydrate just after or before a resistance exercise bout improves the protein balance across the exercised muscle (38). Most of this research used purified solutions rather than whole foods, tested a single exercise bout, and used untrained subjects. These issues limit its practical application for a training athlete and demonstrate that more research using whole foods for prolonged training periods must be done to validate that consuming certain foods or supplements at specific times will result in greater muscle gains.

Because there is no disadvantage and some evidence of benefit to consuming foods with protein just after a workout, this could be recommended as a potential advantage to athletes desiring lean mass gain. This could be accomplished, for example, by consuming a dairy product, a lean meat sandwich, or nuts after a resistance workout. However, overemphasis on protein could reduce carbohydrate intake or increase ingestion of fats associated with heart disease (eg, saturated and *trans* fat). It should be emphasized that the most important dietary factor for weight gain is energy. An athlete will not gain lean tissue without a positive energy balance.

Supplements and Ergogenic Aids

Dietary supplements that are attractive to athletes involved in very high–intensity events or sports are those that may increase the availability of PCr, increase lean body mass, or improve reaction time. The most common dietary supplement is likely creatine, with reports that as many as 28% of collegiate athletes use this supplement. One survey of more than 1,000 middle and high school students showed that 5.6% of all the students reported using creatine, whereas 44% of 12th-grade students reported using this supplement (39).

Research shows that daily consumption of creatine monohydrate increases muscle stores of PCr up to 20%. Apparently, some individuals are responders while others are non-responders, and athletes cannot predict to which group they belong (40). A meta-analysis showed that supplemental creatine was effective in improving performance for the major-ity of the studies and was most likely to improve performance of repeated bouts of less than 30 seconds (eg, resistance exercise, cycle sprints) and upper-body exercise (41). However, there was no clear evidence for a benefit on run or swim sprints. Predictably, the benefits diminished as the bouts lengthened in duration because the use of PCr is highest for brief efforts. There have been claims that creatine supplementation will enhance muscle hyper-trophy, but this has not been clearly validated. Fortunately, there is not much evidence of harm of creatine supplementation for healthy adult athletes. However, it should not be rec-ommended for children (because not enough research can support its safety in this popula-tion) and is potentially dangerous for those with abnormal kidney function (42).

A variety of supplements have been sold with claims that they promote muscle gain. There is inadequate research on most of these supplements to make an unequivocal state-ment of efficacy, but the majority of studies do not support a benefit of chromium, boron, vanadyl sulfate, androstenedione, or dehydroepiandrosterone (DHEA) (43–46). The Food and Drug Administration (FDA) has banned androstenedione.

The two supplements that have more positive reports of an anabolic effect are creatine and beta-hydroxy beta-methylbuterate (HMB). A meta-analysis suggested that both of these supplements increased lean body mass and strength compared with placebo in the set of studies included (45).

An important factor that is not included in most of those studies is the composition of the lean tissue gain. Creatine, for example, is known to increase water retention, which could contribute to the lean gain. Careful studies of protein synthesis and degradation are needed to clarify the effect of these supplements on muscle protein accretion and mass.

Stimulants can improve reaction time and are tempting for those who must react with quick acceleration from a start signal. These chemicals can also reduce perception of effort and influence fuel utilization. Caffeine and ephedra are two examples of stimulants that have been used by athletes. Research supports the benefit of caffeine for moderately intense exercise (~ 85% VO_{2max}), but most evidence does not support its benefit for maximal exercise bouts of less than 90 seconds (46). Caffeine (5 mg/kg) did not improve power output during a 30-second Wingate test but increased time to exhaustion during a longer test at 125% of VO_{2max} lasting less than 2 minutes (47). The authors interpret this as evidence that caffeine enhances anaerobic ATP production. Ephedrine, on the other hand, increased peak power output during the Wingate test in this study. Although this shows there is some evidence that these two chemicals can improve performance, both can have adverse effects. Nervousness, sleeplessness, and cardiac arrhythmia are possible side effects of caffeine ingestion (48). Several recent medical reviews (49,50) identify significant health risks of ephedra use. The Food and Drug Administration has banned the sale of dietary supplements with ephedra. A federal judge struck down the ban for doses of 10 mg or less.

Summary of Research

Most benefits of nutrition observed for studies of high-intensity athletes are tests that include substantial amounts of other aerobic exercise (eg, sprints interspersed within endurance exercise, muscle strength tests after full multi-set workouts). Only very low–carbohydrate diets or moderately low-carbohydrate diets paired with low energy had a detrimental effect on performance of single, maximal efforts. For most very high–intensity, brief exercise events, the diet will have less of an impact than other genetic, training, and motivational factors. Some supplements may enhance performance but ethical, health, and legal issues may discourage their use.

Translation to Diets

The overall goals of nutrition planning for athletes in a maintenance state in very high–intensity sports/events should be to maintain:

- Energy balance (or positive if muscle growth is a goal)
- Hydration
- Blood glucose
- Adequate muscle glycogen
- Muscle mass
- Comfort before competition
- A healthful diet (eg, micronutrients)

This can be accomplished by recommending a balanced, varied diet that maintains body weight, with 6 to 8 g/kg or at least 60% of energy from carbohydrate and 1.2 g/kg protein. Fluids should be consumed at each meal, between meals, and during workouts to maintain hydration. Measurement of body weight before and after a workout can be used as an index of dehydration and effort should be made to rehydrate before the next workout or competition. To avoid gastrointestinal distress during the event, a pre-event meal should be consumed at least 1½ hours prior, with only fluids closer to the event. A low-fiber, low-fat meal is recommended because it will leave the stomach and intestine more quickly. Inclusion of protein with carbohydrate in the meal or low–glycemic index foods will make it more likely that blood glucose will be at a normal concentration before the event.

During a high volume of training or initiation of training, athletes may require a higher energy intake (~ 500 additional kcal/day), with special efforts to consume food with protein and carbohydrate just before or after (as tolerated) each resistance training workout to maximize muscle glycogen replacement and protein synthesis.

Many athletes are tempted by various claims from supplement companies, so care should be taken by the sports nutritionist to find out what supplements the athletes may be taking (see Chapter 7). Supplements that have no evidence of benefit, have evidence that they could be harmful, or are banned by sports governing bodies should be strongly discouraged. Ongoing education should be provided as new supplements become popular.

Athletes competing in several events or matches during one day have a special challenge in deciding what they can tolerate that will also help their performance. A light snack such as yogurt with fruit, small sandwich (without high-fat sauces or cheeses), cereal with milk, regular or dried fruit, a commercial liquid meal, fruit cookies, or muffins along with sport drinks or water are appropriate for between events. Because the food provided at the concession stands at most sporting events do not fit this profile, it is best if athletes or the trainers packs their own snacks for the day.

Although there is less emphasis on a high-carbohydrate diet in very high–intensity sports compared with athletes competing in endurance events, all athletes should be discouraged from consuming a very low–carbohydrate diet. This diet may impair their performance and is often less healthful due to low vitamin, mineral, and fiber content.

Some athletes may consider the fact that there is less evidence for an effect of diet on performance in very high–intensity events, so they can eat whatever they want. Any dietary recommendations for these athletes must consider the same health issues as for any other individual. Therefore, it is important that the nutrition counselor look at the overall diet and provide education about making changes to improve the quality and healthfulness of the diet as well to improve performance.

References

1. Spriet LL. Anaerobic metabolism during high-intensity exercise. In: Hargreaves EM. *Exercise Metabolism*. Champaign, Ill: Human Kinetics; 1995:10–20.
2. Lamb DR. *Physiology of Exercise*. 2nd ed. New York, NY: Macmillan; 1984:71.
3. Gaitanos GC, Williams C, Boobis LH, Brooks S. Human muscle metabolism during intermittent maximal exercise. *J Appl Physiol*. 1993;75:712–719.
4. Esbjornsson-Liljedahl M, Sundberg CJ, Norman B, Jansson E. Metabolic response in type I and type II muscle fibers during a 30-s cycle sprint in men and women. *J Appl Physiol*. 1999;87: 1326–1332.
5. Haff GG, Lehmkuhl MJ, McCoy LB, Stone MH. Carbohydrate supplementation and resistance training. *J Stength Cond Res*. 2003;17:187–196.
6. Bergstrom, J, Hermansen L, Saltin B. Diet, muscle glycogen and physical performance. *Acta Physiol Scand*. 1967;71:140–150.
7. Chen, JD, Wang JF, Li KJ,. Zhao YW, Wang SW, Jiao Y, Hou XY. Nutritional problems and measures in elite and amateur athletes. *Am J Clin Nutr*. 1989;49:1084–1089.

8. Sugiura K, Suzuki I, Kobayashi K. Nutritional intake of elite Japanese track-and-field athletes. *Int J Sport Nutr.* 1999;9:202–212.

9. Faber M, Benade AJ. Mineral and vitamin intake in field athletes (discus-, hammer-, and javelin-throwers and shotputters). *Int J Sports Med.* 1991;12:324–327.

10. Jannalagadda SS, Bernadot D, Nelson M. Energy and nutrient intakes of the United States National Women's Artistic Gymnastics Team. *Int J Sport Nutr.* 1998;8:331–344.

11. Loosli, AR, Benson J, Gillien DM, Bourdet K. Nutrition habits and knowledge in competitive adolescent female gymnasts. *Phys Sportsmed.* 1986;14:118–130.

12. Rump P, Verstappen F, Gerver WJ, Hornstra G. Body composition and cardiorespiratory fitness indicators in prepubescent boys and girls. *Int J Sports Med.* 2002;23:50–54.

13. Wilmore JH. Body composition in sports medicine: directions for future research. *Med Sci Sports Exerc.* 1983;15:21–31.

14. Fogelholm M, Hiilloskorpi H. Weight and diet concerns in Finnish female and male athletes. *Med Sci Sports Exerc.* 1999;31:229–235.

15. McMurray RG, Proctor CR, Wilson WL. Effect of caloric deficit and dietary manipulation on aerobic and anaerobic exercise. *Int J Sports Med.* 1991;12:167–172.

16. Zachwiega JJ, Ezell DM, Cline AD, Ricketts JC, Vicknair PC, Schorle SM, Ryan DH. Short-term dietary energy restriction reduces lean body mass but not performance in physically active men and women. *Int J Sports Med.* 2001;22:310–316.

17. Walberg-Rankin J, Hawkins CE, Fild DS, Sebolt DR. The effect of oral arginine during energy restriction in male weight trainers. *J Strength Cond Res.* 1994;8:170–177.

18. Walberg J, Leidy M, Sturgill D, Hinkle D, Ritchey S, Sebolt D. Macronutrient content of a hypoenergy diet affects nitrogen retention and muscle function in weight lifters. *Int J Sports Med.* 1988;4:261–266.

19. Walberg Rankin J. Changing body weight and composition in athletes. In: Lamb D, Murray R, eds. *Exercise, Nutrition, and Control of Body Weight.* Carmel, Ind: Cooper Publishing; 1998:199–242. Perspectives in Exercise and Sports Medicine vol 11.

20. Viitasalo JR, Kyrolainen H, Bosco C, Alen M. Effects of rapid weight reduction on force production and vertical jumping height. *Int J Sports Med.* 1987;8:281–185.

21. Greiwe JS, Staffey KS, Melrose DR, Narve MD, Knowlton RG. Effects of dehydration on isometric muscular strength and endurance. *Med Sci Sports Exerc.* 1998;30:284–288.

22. Gutierrez A, Mesa JLM, Ruiz JR, Chirosa LJ, Castillo MJ. Sauna-induced rapid weight loss decreases explosive power in women but not men. *Int J Sports Med.* 2003;24:518–522.

23. Fritzsche RG, Switzer TW, Hodgkinson BJ, Lee SH, Martin JC, Coyle EF. Water and carbohydrate ingestion during prolonged exercise increase maximal neuromuscular power. *J Appl Physiol.* 2000;88:730–737.

24. Jacobs I, Kaiser P, Tesch P. Muscle strength and fatigue after selective glycogen depletion in human skeletal muscle fibers. *Eur J Appl Physiol.* 1981;46:47–53.

25. Grisdale RK, Jabobs I, Cafarelli E. Relative effects of glycogen depletion and previous exercise on muscle force and endurance capacity. *J Appl Physiol.* 1990;69:1276–1282.

26. Mitchell JB, DiLauro PC, Pizza FX, Cavender DL. The effect of preexercise carbohydrate status on resistance exercise performance. *Int J Sport Nutr.* 1997;7:185–196.

27. Lambert CP, Flynn MG, Boone JB, Michaud T, Rodriguez-Zayas J. Effects of carbohydrate feeding on multiple-bout resistance exercise. *J Appl Sport Sci Res.* 1991;5:192–197.

28. Haff GG, Schroeder CA, Koch AJ, Kuphal KE, Comeau MJ, Potteiger JA. The effects of supplemental carbohydrate ingestion on intermittent isokinetic leg exercise. *J Sports Med Phys Fitness.* 2001;41:216–222.

29. Haff GG, Koch AJ, Potteiger JA, Kuphal KE, Magee LM, Green SB, Jakicic JJ. Carbohydrate supplementation attenuates muscle glycogen loss during acute bouts of resistance exercise. *Int J Sport Nutr Exerc Metab.* 2000;10:326–339.

30. Dalton RA, Walberg Rankin J, Sebolt D, Gwazdauskas F. Acute carbohydrate consumption does not influence resistance exercise performance during energy restriction. *Int J Sport Nutr.* 1999;9:319–332.

31. Langfort J, Zarzeczny R, Pilis W, Nazar K. The effect of a low-carbohydrate diet on performance, hormonal and metabolic responses to a 30-s bout of supramaximal exercise. *Eur J Appl Physiol.* 1997;76:128–133.

32. Lamb DR, Rinehardt K, Bartels RL, Sherman WM, Snook JT. Dietary carbohydrate and intensity of interval swim training. *Am J Clin Nutr.* 1990;52:1058–1063.

33. Vandenberghe K, Hespel P, Vanden Eynde B, Lysens R, Richter EA. No effect of glycogen level on glycogen metabolism during high intensity exercise. *Med Sci Sports Exerc.* 1995;27: 1278–1283.

34. Pascoe DD, Costill DL, Fink WJ, Roberts RA, Zachwieja JJ. Glycogen resynthesis in skeletal muscle following resistance exercise. *Med Sci Sports Exerc.* 1993;25:349–354.

35. Haub MD, Potteiger JA, Jacobsen DJ, Nau KL, Magee LA, Comeau MJ. Glycogen replenishment and repeated maximal effort exercise: effect of liquid carbohydrate. *Int J Sport Nutr.* 1999;9:406–415.

36. Haub MD, Haff GG, Potteiger JA. The effect of liquid carbohydrate ingestion on repeated maximal effort exercise in competitive cyclists. *J Strength Cond Res.* 2003;17:20–25.

37. Walberg Rankin J. Role of protein in exercise. *Clinics Sports Med.* 1999;18:499–512.

38. Tipton KD, Wolfe RR. Exercise, protein metabolism, and muscle growth. *Int J Sport Nutr Exerc Metab.* 2001;11:109–132.

39. Metzl JD, Small E, Levine SR, Gerhsel JC. Creatine use among young athletes. *Pediatrics.* 2001;108:421–425.

40. Rawson ES, Volek JS. Effects of creatine supplementation and resistance training on muscle strength and weightlifting performance. *J Strength Cond Res.* 2003;17:822–831.

41. Branch JD. Effect of creatine supplementation on body composition and performance: a meta-analysis. *Int J Sport Nutr Exerc Metab.* 2003;13:198–226.

42. Pritchard NR, Kalra PA. Renal dysfunction accompanying oral creatine supplements. *Lancet.* 1998; 351:1252–1253.

43. Clarkson PM, Rawson ES. Nutritional supplements to increase muscle mass. *Crit Rev Food Sci Nutr.* 1999;39:317–328.

44. Kreider RB. Dietary supplements and the promotion of muscle growth with resistance exercise. *Sports Med.* 1999;27:97–110.

45. Nissen SL, Sharp RL. Effect of dietary supplements on lean mass and strength gains with resistance exercise: a meta-analysis. *J Appl Physiol.* 2003;94:651–650.

46. Graham TE. Caffeine, coffee, and ephedrine: impact on exercise performance and metabolism. *Can J Appl Physiol.* 2001;26(suppl):S103–S119.

47. Bell DG, Jacobs I, Ellerington K. Effect of caffeine and ephedrine ingestion on anaerobic exercise performance. *Med Sci Sports Exerc.* 2001;33:1399–1403.

48. Clarkson PM. Nutritional ergogenic aids: caffeine. *Int J Sport Nutr.* 1993;3:103–111.

49. Bent S, Tiedt TN, Odden MC, Shlipac MG. The relative safety of ephedra compared with other herbal products. *Ann Intern Med.* 2003;138:468–471.

50. Haller CA, Benowitz NL. Adverse cardiovascular and central nervous system events associated with dietary supplements containing ephedra alkaloids. *New Engl J Med.* 2000;343:1833–1838.

Chapter 22

NUTRITION FOR HIGH-INTENSITY, SHORT-DURATION SPORTS

Marie Dunford, PhD, RD

Introduction

High-intensity, short-duration sports include swimming (200 to 1,500 meters), running (200 to 1,500 meters and elite 10,000-meter runners), rowing (crew), short-distance cycling, downhill mountain biking, and many speed skating events. Athletes in these sports typically perform between 1½ and 30 minutes. During training, exercise intensity may increase to 75% of maximum oxygen consumption (VO_{2max}), and in the case of interval training, 85% to 100% VO_{2max} (1–3). Successful performance will require both anaerobic and aerobic conditioning. Genetic predisposition, training, and nutrition are all important influences.

Athletes in high-intensity, short-duration sports train for hours at a time, even though the actual event is over in minutes. All engage in resistance training to build and then maintain muscle mass, as well as plyometric training, which is needed to provide power. In addition, they focus on cardiovascular training. Although there is some degree of cross-training, training specificity is essential. Mental discipline is important, as is race-day strategy.

Compared with athletes who perform longer distances or who engage in very high–intensity sports, there is not as much research about high-intensity, short-duration athletes (1,2,4–7). Most of the research has been conducted on rowers and swimmers. This chapter contains general nutrition recommendations that should be adjusted on an individual basis. Other nutrition-related issues, such as body composition, disordered eating patterns, and supplements, are discussed.

Energy Systems Used

Use of the body's energy systems is determined by the intensity of exercise. The predominant energy system used for exercise lasting 30 seconds to 2 minutes (eg, 200- to 800-meter runs) is glycolysis, although the adenosine triphosphate–phosphocreatine (ATP-PCr) system also contributes. Such sports are referred to as anaerobic. The anaerobic contribution for male and female 400-meter runners is approximately 60% to 63% of the total energy expenditure (2,4). Although not the predominant system, the aerobic system (using pyruvate as the energy source) does make an important contribution even in exercise lasting less than 2 minutes (3).

As intense exercise extends beyond 2 minutes, the aerobic energy system becomes the predominant system. The sub-4-minute 1,500-meter runner depends predominantly (approximately 80% to 84%) on aerobic (carbohydrate) sources. The remaining 16% to 20% of energy is provided by the anaerobic systems, ATP-PCr, and lactic acid (2,4). Similarly, 20% to 25% of the energy used in a 2,000-meter crew race is anaerobic (5). Athletes in events approaching the 30-minute mark, such as 10,000-meter runners, do use some fat to fuel the exercise, but carbohydrate provides the majority of the energy used.

Dietary Needs

Energy

Highly trained athletes in these sports will likely spend 4 hours per day specifically training for their sport. In addition, they will lift weights at least three times per week, sometimes more. Although there are rest and travel days, in general daily energy expenditure is high. Reported daily intakes are often less than estimated needs (6,8). For example, female middle-distance runners report a mean daily energy intake of 2,431 kcal, but the estimated daily need is calculated at 2,635 kcal (8). It is unclear if the less-than-expected energy intake is due to underreporting or overcalculating energy needs, or if it is a result of chronic undereating, which may suppress metabolism and reduce energy needs (8,9). Assessing each athlete's usual energy intake and comparing it to long-term body composition is important.

At the elite and highly competitive collegiate levels, training and competing is like a job. Elite athletes often have demanding worldwide travel schedules. For collegiate athletes, the demands of classes, in addition to training, leave little free time. These athletes realize that adequate energy and nutrient intake is crucial, but it can be difficult to achieve due to fatigue; lack of appetite; lack of time, skill, or interest in food preparation; and/or poor accessibility to nutritious meals. When working with highly trained athletes in these sports, it is important to address these practical issues.

Some athletes may be voluntarily restricting energy intake. Some may fall into a pattern of conscious or unconscious restriction as they try to attain or maintain a low percentage of body fat. Lightweight rowers may restrict energy intake in attempt to make weight for competition.

Overtraining syndrome has no single cause, is difficult to assess and diagnose, and may ultimately end the athlete's career. One of the precipitating factors may be a chronic negative energy balance concomitant with persistent overtraining. Because it is a syndrome, a host of factors may be present, including nutrient deficiencies, immunosuppression, chronic infection, psychological stress, depression, and hormone imbalance (10). Treatment always includes rest, which is very difficult for many athletes to understand or comply with. Restoring energy balance and attaining an appropriate body weight and body composition is a starting point. Maintaining energy balance in the face of eventual increased training is an ongoing issue.

Macronutrients

High-intensity, short-duration athletes need a proper balance of carbohydrate, protein, and fat. Each athlete should be assessed individually, but meeting the minimum macronutrient recommendations must be the foundation of any nutrition plan. Then, the diet plan can be fine-tuned to meet individual needs and preferences.

Sufficient carbohydrate intake is critical for optimal training and performance. It is best to determine and communicate carbohydrate needs based on a gram per kilogram of body weight basis rather than percentage of total energy intake. When energy is adequate, 5 to 7 g of carbohydrate per kilogram per day can be sufficient (11). Sufficient carbohydrate is necessary to replenish muscle glycogen stores, which are depleted by consecutive days of high-volume training.

Part of the training program of a high-intensity, short-duration athlete is to build and then maintain muscle mass. In general, daily protein recommendations for athletes consuming adequate energy range from 1.2 to 1.7 g per kilogram of body weight (12). Because strength is needed to compete in these sports, a general recommendation for high-intensity, short duration athletes is 1.5 g protein per kilogram of body weight per day, which can be adjusted on an individual basis.

Balancing the proper amount of fats in an athlete's diet with the other macronutrients remains a challenge. On the one hand, athletes need to consume enough fat to provide the essential fatty acids and a feeling of satiety after a meal. On the other hand, athletes may need to limit fat consumption so that carbohydrate and protein needs are met but energy intake is not excessive. A good starting point is to recommend that an athlete consume at least 1.0 g fat per kilogram daily. This figure may need to be adjusted on an individual basis but, in general, it provides for an adequate intake of fat and allows the athlete to consume the recommended amounts of carbohydrates and proteins.

However, situations vary and fat intake in elite athletes may range from 15% to as much as 40% of total energy intake (13–16). Some athletes focus on attaining or maintaining a low level of body fat, and restricting dietary fat is a way to restrict energy intake. Other athletes may consume higher fat diets in an effort to meet their high energy needs. When carbohydrate and protein needs are met, fat helps provide the energy that is needed to support such a high level of the training. For these athletes, a higher dietary fat intake is beneficial because, without the fat, they would consume too little energy. It should be noted that the newest guidelines for healthy adults, as outlined by the Institute of Medicine, suggest that fat should comprise 20% to 35% of total energy (17).

For athletes with a justifiably higher fat intake, emphasize moderate amounts of unsaturated fats, especially n-3 fatty acids, and minimize intake of saturated fat. For those who chronically restrict dietary fat, several issues emerge; a restricted fat diet may decrease high-density lipoprotein (HDL) cholesterol (17) and impair immune system function (18). Another concern is that the athlete may be "fat phobic" and develop disordered eating patterns.

Micronutrients

Marginal or frank micronutrient deficiencies are closely related to total energy intake (13–16). For male athletes, when energy intake is adequate, nutrient intake is generally adequate. For female athletes, adequate energy intake may mean adequate nutrient intake. However, if the diet is not nutrient-dense, inadequate intake of the difficult to obtain nutrients—calcium, iron, zinc, and vitamin E—may occur. When energy intake is inadequate, nutrient intake is usually inadequate.

One potential problem is the choice of low nutrient-density foods. Athletes with high energy needs often discover that they must eat a lot of food to maintain energy balance. Some of these athletes choose to eat high-fat, high-sugar snack foods and beverages. Thus, they may consume sufficient energy but not sufficient nutrients.

A multivitamin and mineral supplement is often recommended and may be suggested by the coach as a way for all team members to ensure that they are getting the micronutrients that they need. Although this is well-intended advice, it is important to recognize that inadequate energy intake and/or low nutrient-density foods are the primary problems and nutrient inadequacies are the secondary problem. A multivitamin and mineral supplement addresses only the secondary problem. There is no evidence that athletes who meet all the micronutrient recommendations benefit from a daily multivitamin or mineral supplement.

Hydration

High-intensity, short-duration sports last for less than 30 minutes, so fluid intake during performance is generally not an issue. An exception is 10,000-meter runners, who may drink during races in hot weather. High-intensity, short-duration athletes train for hours, sometimes in warm environments. Therefore, hydration before, during, and after training is important. Lightweight rowers use dehydration as one method for making weight and may restrict fluids, especially during the 24 hours prior to weigh-in.

It is important to balance fluid intake with fluid loss (19). Balance can be monitored by comparing pre- and post-training scale weights and checking urine color, which should be light yellow. Specific fluid guidelines are found in Chapter 6.

Many athletes in high-intensity, short-duration sports find that water is refreshing and sip water during training. Sport drinks provide water as well as carbohydrate. The addition of carbohydrate may help to stabilize blood glucose, provide needed carbohydrate if glycogen stores are low, and add a sweetness that is desirable and palatable. These drinks are popular and can provide additional energy and carbohydrates to athletes who find it difficult to meet their energy needs. Conversely, athletes who are trying to reduce energy intake may not be aware of how many "liquid" calories they are consuming. In some circumstances, it may be appropriate to alternate sport drinks and water. In those who sweat heavily during training, adequate replacement of sodium is needed in addition to fluid.

Total Dietary Intake

Perhaps the most difficult aspect for athletes is combining all of the nutrient recommendations into a flexible eating plan. Requirements can be met by consuming foods and liquids both as snacks and meals. Total energy and macronutrient intake is important but timing is also an issue. In the recovery period, replenishment of glycogen and fluids is critical and should begin immediately after exercise. Because athletes need sufficient carbohydrate, some protein, and fluid quickly, it may be practical to consume sport beverages and/or snacks as soon as training ends. However, in a 24-hour period, athletes must also meet their total energy and carbohydrate needs and they will likely need nutrient-dense meals and snacks to accomplish this. (20,21)

Body Composition

In sports in which the body must be moved quickly over a certain distance, excess body fat may be detrimental because it increases body mass but does not increase power (3). Athletes in high-intensity, short-duration sports talk about a "strength [power] to weight ratio," and the goal is to have a low percentage of body fat and a high percentage of muscle mass. Because many of these athletes are at high levels of training, they cannot realistically increase exercise without increasing the risk for injury. Thus, nutrition often becomes the focus of obtaining a weight and body composition that supports a favorable power-to-weight ratio and, ultimately, a potential performance advantage.

Athletes who focus on attaining and maintaining a low percentage of body fat need nutrition guidance. Without guidance, they may reduce their energy, carbohydrate, and protein intakes too much. Ultimately, their performance will decline. With proper guidance, baseline energy, carbohydrate, protein, and fat needs can be determined and proper reductions can be made. The best time to make major dietary changes and lose weight is during the off-season or the preseason; refinements to the plan can be made during the competition season.

With the exception of downhill mountain biking, most athletes in high-intensity, short-duration sports perform in tight clothing. This places unnecessary focus on the leanness of the athletes, both self-imposed and from coaches, commentators, and spectators. Athletes may feel undue pressure to lose weight, especially if they are not considered to be the "ideal" body composition. Sports dietitians can help athletes understand if and when weight loss is appropriate.

Disordered Eating and Eating Disorders

The pressure to attain and maintain a low percentage of body fat, a focus on body appearance, and the need to make weight are all factors that put some athletes in high-intensity, short-duration sports at risk for developing disordered eating patterns and eating disorders. All athletes should be screened for disordered eating (see Chapter 18).

Lightweight rowing presents a special challenge because of the weight requirement (females less than 130 lb; males less than 155 to 160 lb). Lightweight rowing was developed to accommodate smaller rowers who could not be competitive with larger rowers. Those lightweight rowers who are genetically lean and biologically small can comfortably meet the weight requirement. Unfortunately, some lightweight rowers must go to extraordinary efforts to attain and maintain such weights, and it is those individuals who are most at risk for developing disordered eating patterns and eating disorders.

Determining minimum weights and discussing biological capacity to attain such a weight is crucial. Box 22.1 describes a rower who cannot reach the weight necessary to make the lightweight category without attaining a very low percentage of body fat and who would put her health at risk. The athlete's dilemma is that she may not be competitive with other rowers in the open weight division, so unless she rows as a lightweight, she will not be able to row at all. The dilemma for the sports dietitian is the ethics of working with an athlete who is trying to attain an unhealthy weight. Some choose to do so because the determined athlete will need a professional resource to help reduce the impact of the known risks. Others cannot be comfortable working with such an athlete knowing that health will be endangered. Clark

---

Box 22.1   Minimum Weight Example

Jackie weighs 135 lb and has 13% body fat, but she wants to row on the light-weight team, which has a maximum weight limit of 130 lb. She figures that she should be able to lose 5 lb without a problem, but her coach wants her to talk to the dietitian at the health center before she does.

The dietitian makes some calculations to determine a minimum weight. At Jackie's present weight and body composition, she has approximately 17.5 lb of body fat. (135 lb × 0.13 = 17.5 lb). The dietitian indicates that less than 12% body fat for females (and less than 5% for males) is too low. Using the formula below, the dietitian calculates Jackie's minimum body weight to be 133.5 lb:

$$\text{Minimum body weight} = \text{Lean body mass (lb)}/(1.00 - \text{Minimum body fat \%})$$
$$= 117.5 \text{ lb}/(1.00 - 0.12)$$
$$= 133.5 \text{ lb}$$

To become 130 lb, she would need to go below the minimum body fat recommended for women, lose muscle mass, and/or voluntarily dehydrate. Jackie shares with the dietitian that her menstrual cycle, which used to be regular, is a bit irregular at her current weight and percentage body fat, and that sometimes she gets a little too preoccupied with food. When the dietitian at the health center presented Jackie the "numbers," they both agreed that Jackie should not try to reduce her body weight to 130 lb because she would put her health and well-being at risk.

---

(22) addresses the ethical issues involved in a case study of a 118-lb female coxswain who wanted to attain a weight of 99 lb to qualify for the national crew team.

Dietary Supplements and Ergogenic Aids

Creatine is the most commonly used and studied ergogenic aid for high-intensity, short-duration sports. Beta-hydroxy beta-methylbutyrate (HMB) is also a popular supplement, but there are many fewer studies. In highly trained athletes, creatine and HMB, alone and in combination, do not seem to be detrimental to health (23). Other popular substances include dehydroepiandrosterone (DHEA) and protein, neither of which has been shown to significantly affect gains in lean mass or strength in high-intensity, short-duration activities (24).

Both creatine and HMB increase lean mass and strength gains with resistance exercise (24). Creatine has been shown to improve repeated sprint performance (25), probably by increasing the amount of PCr and accelerating the rate of ATP resynthesis. In one study (5), creatine supplementation increased performance in elite rowers; however, not all studies of rowers have shown this effect (7). The benefit of creatine supplements in swimmers has been unclear. One study suggests that it is ineffective in women (26). This study also found creatine supplements to be effective in men who swam repeated bouts of 10 to 15 seconds, but not in those who swam bouts lasting 30 seconds.

In resistance-trained sprint runners, creatine supplements likely increase lean mass and strength and improve performance. Whether lean mass and strength gains translate into improved performance for athletes in other high-intensity, short-duration sports are not entirely known. It is the promise of improved performance that makes creatine supplements especially attractive. Detailed information about each of the supplements mentioned above can be found in Chapter 7.

Summary

Athletes in high-intensity, short-duration sports train heavily to perform in events that last only minutes. Many of these athletes report daily energy intakes that are less than estimated energy needs, and energy restriction may occur in an effort to attain and maintain a low percentage body fat or, in the case of lightweight rowers, make a weight classification. Assuming that energy intake is adequate, general daily macronutrient recommendations are 5 to 7 g carbohydrate per kilogram body weight, 1.5 g protein per kilogram, and 1.0 g fat per kilogram. Leanness and a low percentage of body fat are emphasized in many of these sports, and some of these athletes are at risk of developing disordered eating patterns and eating disorders.

References

1. Stewart AM, Hopkins WG. Seasonal training and performance of competitive swimmers. *J Sports Sci.* 2000;18:873–884.
2. Hill DW. Energy system contributions in middle-distance running events. *J Sports Sci.* 1999;17:477–483.
3. Williams MH. *Nutrition for Health, Fitness & Sport.* 7th ed. New York, NY: McGraw-Hill; 2005.
4. Spencer MR, Gastin PB. Energy system contribution during 200- to 1500-m running in highly trained athletes. *Med Sci Sport Exerc.* 2001;33:157–162.
5. Chwalbinska-Moneta J. Effect of creatine supplementation on aerobic performance and anaerobic capacity in elite rowers in the course of endurance training. *Int J Sport Nutr Exerc Metab.* 2003;13:173–183.
6. Xia G, Chin MK, Girandola RN, Liu RY. The effects of diet and supplements on a male world champion lightweight rower. *J Sports Med Phys Fitness.* 2001;41:223–228.
7. Syrotuik DG, Game AB, Gillies EM, Bell CJ. Effects of creatine monohydrate supplementation during combined strength and high–intensity rowing training on performance. *Can J Appl Physiol.* 2001;26:527–542.
8. Deutz RC, Benardot D, Martin DE, Cody MM. Relationship between energy deficits and body composition in elite female gymnasts and runners. *Med Sci Sports Exerc.* 2000;32:659–668.
9. Burke LM. Energy needs of athletes. *Can J Appl Physiol.* 2001;26(suppl):S202–S219.
10. Shephard RJ. Chronic fatigue syndrome: an update. *Sports Med.* 2001;31:167–194.
11. Burke LM, Cox GR, Culmmings NK, Desbrow B. Guidelines for daily carbohydrate intake: do athletes achieve them? *Sports Med.* 2001;31:267–299.
12. Position of the American Dietetic Association, Dietitians of Canada, and the American College of Sports Medicine: nutrition and athletic performance. *J Am Diet Assoc.* 2000;100:1543–1556.

13. Leydon MA, Wall C. New Zealand jockeys' dietary habits and their potential impact on health. *Int J Sport Nutr Exerc Metab.* 2002;12:220–237.
14. Papadopoulou SK, Papadopoulou SD, Gallos GK. Macro- and micro-nutrient intake of adolescent Greek female volleyball players. *Int J Sport Nutr Exerc Metab.* 2002;12:73–80.
15. Ziegler PJ, Nelson JA, Jonnalagadda SS. Nutritional and physiological status of U.S. national figure skaters. *Int J Sport Nutr.* 1999;9:345–360.
16. Ziegler P, Sharp R, Hughes V, Evans W, Khoo CS. Nutritional status of teenage female competitive figure skaters. *J Am Diet Assoc.* 2002;102:374–379.
17. Institute of Medicine. *Dietary Reference Intakes for Energy, Carbohydrate, Fiber, Fat, Fatty Acids, Cholesterol, Protein, and Amino Acids (Macronutrients).* Washington, DC: National Academy Press; 2002. Available at: http://www.nap.edu. Accessed November 30, 2004.
18. Venkatraman JT, Leddy J, Pendergast D. Dietary fats and immune status in athletes: clinical implications. *Med Sci Sports Exerc.* 2000;32(7 Suppl):S389–S395.
19. Shirreffs SM. Restoration of fluid and electrolyte balance after exercise. *Can J Appl Physiol.* 2001;26(suppl):S228–S235.
20. Burke LM, Kiens B, Ivy JL. Carbohydrates and fat for training and recovery. *J Sports Sci.* 2004;22:15–30.
21. Ivy JL, Goforth Jr HW, Damon BM, McCauley TR, Parsons EC, Price TB. Early postexercise muscle glycogen recovery is enhanced with a carbohydrate-protein supplement. *J Appl Physiol.* 2002;93:839–846.
22. Clark N. Nutritional concerns of female athletes: a case study. *Int J Sport Nutr.* 1991;1:257–264.
23. Crowe MJ, O'Connor DM, Lukins JE. The effects of beta-hydroxy-beta-methylbutyrate (HMB) and HMB/creatine supplementation on indices of health in highly trained athletes. *Int J Sport Nutr Exerc Metab.* 2003;13:184–197.
24. Nissen SL, Sharp RL. Effect of dietary supplements on lean mass and strength gains with resistance exercise: a meta-analysis. *J Appl Physiol.* 2003;94:651–659.
25. Izquierdo M, Ibanez J, Gonzalez-Badillo JJ, Gorostiaga EM. Effects of creatine supplementation on muscle power, endurance, and sprint performance. *Med Sci Sports Exerc.* 2002;34:332–343.
26. Leenders NM, Lamb DR, Nelson TE. Creatine supplementation and swimming performance. *Int J Sport Nutr.* 1999;9:251–262.

Chapter 23

NUTRITION FOR INTERMITTENT, HIGH-INTENSITY SPORTS

Michele A. Macedonio, MS, RD

Introduction

The term *intermittent, high-intensity exercise* refers to activities that require short periods of all-out effort (eg, sprints of up to 2 to 7 seconds), punctuated with periods of less-intense effort (eg, jogging sustained over 5 to 10 minutes), and low-intensity effort (eg, walking and standing still). Teams sports such as soccer, football, basketball, field hockey, ice hockey, rugby, volleyball, and individual sports such as tennis and squash fall into this category. The stop-and-go nature of these sports often results in impaired performance near the end of the competition and after periods of intense effort. Intermittent, high-intensity sports require a range of exercise intensity from low to very high in varying durations during which all of the major energy systems are tapped.

Soccer has been studied extensively (1–8), providing a base for understanding the physiological demands and nutritional implications of intermittent, high-intensity exercise. Other intermittent, high-intensity sports have been studied (9–18), although each one not as extensively.

Physiological Demands of Intermittent, High-Intensity Exercise

Energy Systems

Athletes engaged in high-intensity intermittent exercise train to improve endurance capacity as well as muscle strength and conditioning. Both anaerobic and aerobic energy production are important. Anaerobic energy production is essential for high-intensity exercise when the demand for adenosine triphosphate (ATP) exceeds the body's ability to produce it aerobically. At the onset of high-intensity exercise, anaerobically produced ATP provides the majority of the ATP used because of the short supply of oxygen. Anaerobic production of ATP continues to play a key role in sustained high-intensity exercise because the demand for ATP is more than can be provided aerobically (see Table 23.1).

Both the intensity and the duration of exercise increase energy demands during vigorous, stop-and-go exercise that lasts for 60 or more minutes (4). For example, soccer encompasses a 90-minute game plus 15 to 30 minutes of warm-up activities prior to match play. Total energy expended during a soccer match is directly related to the distance covered during the 90 minutes of the game, usually 8 to 12 km (5 to 7 miles) (1,3,19).

The relative exercise intensity plays a major factor in determining the fuel mixture during exercise, and is expressed as percentage of maximum oxygen consumption (VO_{2max}), which is influenced by age, sex, genetic makeup, and level of aerobic training (20,21) (see Table 23.2).

The nature of the activity in stop-and-go team sports requires use of both types of muscle fibers (22,23). Fast twitch (FT) fibers exhibit the greatest degree of glycogen depletion after sprint-type activities (24). Costill and colleagues (25) showed that in distance running, glycogen was selectively depleted in slow twitch (ST) fibers but that FT fibers also bore some of the load. From these studies, it seems that ST fibers are activated at lower workloads and that FT fibers are used during two conditions, when ST fibers are depleted of glycogen (26,27) and during high–intensity output (24).

Green et al (14) examined glycogen utilization in the muscle fibers of ice hockey players and found that muscle glycogen depletion averaged 60% and indicated the utilization of both ST and FT fibers, with the greatest decline occurring in ST fibers. There was no apparent difference in glycogen depletion between forwards and defensemen.

TABLE 23.1   Approximate Relative Energy Contribution During 3 Minutes of High-Intensity Exercise

Duration, sec	Anaerobic, %	Aerobic, %
30	80	20
60–90	45	55
120–180	30	70

TABLE 23.2   Muscle Energy Pathways During Activity of Varying Intensity

	Muscle Energy Pathways	Duration of Activity	Type of Activity (% MHR)
Immediate	ATP in muscles	1–6 s	Surges and sprints ($\geq$ 80–90)
	ATP + PCr	7–20 s	
	ATP +PCr + Muscle glycogen	20–45 s	
Short-term	Muscle glycogen	45–120 s	Moderate-intensity running (70–79)
	Muscle glycogen + Lactic acid	120–180 s	
Long-term	Muscle glycogen + Free fatty acids	> 30 minutes, limited by O_2	Low-moderate-intensity running ($\leq$ 69)

Abbreviations: ATP, adenosine triphophate; MHR, maximum heart rate; PCr, phosphocreatine.

Effects of Intermittent, High-Intensity Exercise on Substrate Utilization

The relative contribution of fat and carbohydrate depends on the intensity and duration of exercise (27,28). Endurance exercise training triggers metabolic adaptations that lead to a marked sparing of carbohydrate as a result of a slower utilization of glucose and muscle and liver glycogen during sustained exercise of the same intensity (29,30). Consequently, endurance training leads to a relatively lesser reliance on carbohydrates than on fatty acids during prolonged steady-state exercise. The reduced reliance on blood glucose and muscle glycogen during exercise in a trained state is part of the mechanisms by which exercise enhances endurance. In essence, endurance training helps spare muscle glycogen.

In addition to a relative shift in substrate, the absolute amount of fat used decreases as work rate increases (20,31). Plasma glucose and muscle glycogen utilization both increase in response to an increase in exercise intensity. Plasma glucose contributes approximately 10% to 15% of total energy at all work rates whereas muscle glycogen supplies approximately 60% of the energy requirement in strenuous exercise at approximately 80% of VO_{2max} (20,21).

Bangsbo (5) observed that free fatty acid (FFA) concentration increased during a soccer match, with more increase in the second half than the first. This pattern was attributed to a slower pace during the second half, allowing more blood flow to adipose tissue and possibly promoting a higher FFA release, coupled with hormonal changes. Based on these observations, a high uptake of glycerol in various tissues, primarily the liver, is presumed, indicating that glycerol might be an important gluconeogenic precursor. Blood FFA concentration during soccer is the net result of the uptake of FFA in various tissues and the release from adipose tissue. Ketone bodies may also function as a minor fat source during exercise.

Glycogen is an essential fuel during prolonged vigorous exercise, which is required of athletes engaged in high-intensity intermittent sports. With increasing energy intensity, the percentage of carbohydrate as an energy substrate increases to fuel most of the energy demands of muscle contraction at an intensity near an individual's VO_{2max}. From 40% to 85% VO_{2max}, the relative contribution of fat decreases with a concomitant increase in carbohydrate oxidation. At moderate- and high-intensity exercise (50% to 85% VO_{2max}), plasma fatty acids and muscle triglycerides supply the fats that are oxidized (20,31–33).

In trained athletes, during vigorous exercise there is an initial burst of glycogenolysis and resulting lactic acid production followed by a slowing of the rate of glycogenolysis and a reduction in muscle and blood lactate levels. During match play in stop-and-go sports, intermittent bursts of high-intensity exertion are followed by periods of relative rest and moderate-intensity effort. Aerobic fitness enhances recovery from high-intensity, intermittent exercise through increased aerobic capacity, improved lactate removal, and enhanced phosphocreatine (PCr) regulation (34).

Skeletal muscle contraction and the central nervous system are dependent on carbohydrate as a fuel substrate, but the body's stores of carbohydrate are limited and often the fuel requirements of training and competition for stop-and-go team sports substantially exceed carbohydrate availability. When muscle glycogen stores are depleted, fatigue, both physical and mental, set in and performance is compromised (35–37).

Bangsbo (19) estimated the relative levels of aerobic and anaerobic energy turnover and substrate utilization during soccer based on the cumulative results of various studies. (Refer to Figure 23.1.)

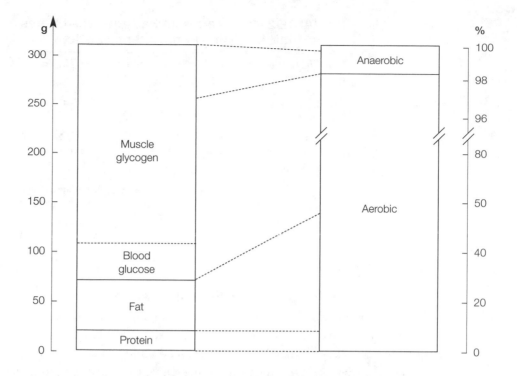

FIGURE 23.1.   Estimated relative aerobic and anaerobic energy turnover and corresponding substrate utilization during a soccer match. Reprinted from Bangsbo J. Energy demands in competitive soccer. *J Sports Sci.* 1994;12(suppl):S10. Used by permission of Taylor & Francis (http://www.tandf.co.uk/journals).

Aerobic Energy System

Attempts have been made to determine the aerobic energy contribution during soccer by measuring oxygen uptake, however, the procedure interferes with normal play and results are most likely imprecise. Heart rate is used to estimate oxygen uptake, but it does not always reflect the actual VO_2. Aside from its use in predicting oxygen uptake, heart rate provides a useful index of the overall physiological demands of soccer (4).

During a match, soccer players spend a significant amount of time working at heart rates estimated to be more than 160 beats/minute or 80% to 90% of maximum (3,38). Intermittent exercise has an effect on oxygen consumption similar to submaximal, continuous running (5). Although anaerobic activity is an important component of soccer, the greater demand is on aerobic metabolism. Considering total distance covered, the ratio of low-intensity to high-intensity activity is 2:1 and the relative time ratio is 7:1 (1). Sprinting occurs less than 1% of total playing time (39). Considering all factors, relative work rates during soccer have been estimated between 70% and 80% of VO_{2max} (3–5). Estimates of VO_{2max} based on many studies of soccer players over the years suggest an average of 60 mL/kg/minute (23). As shown in Table 23.3, a review of research reveals similar heart rate patterns among athletes in other intermittent, high-intensity sports (3,4,10,12,17,40,41).

TABLE 23.3 Heart Rate Patterns of Athletes in High-Intensity, Intermittent Sports

Sport (References)	MHR, %
Soccer (3,4)	80–90
Ice hockey (12)	85–90
Basketball (10)	> 85
Tennis (17,40)	80–85*
Racquet sports including squash, badminton (41)	80–85

*MHR reported in reference 40. In reference 17, heart rate averaged 144 beats/minute.

Anaerobic Energy System

Adenosine Triphosphate and Phosphocreatine

Considerable fluctuations may occur when playing stop-and-go team sports. Although the majority of the exercise in soccer is done at submaximal intensities, high-intensity or all-out exercise plays a crucial role, and players' ability to successfully carry out these high-intensity activities affects the result of the game. PCr concentration fluctuates throughout a soccer match due to the intermittent nature of the game. Despite a small net utilization, PCr plays an important role as an energy buffer providing phosphate for the resynthesis of ATP during the rapid increases in exercise intensity (5,19). Aerobic fitness enhances recovery from high-intensity intermittent exercise through increased aerobic response, improved lactate removal, and enhanced PCr regeneration (34).

Blood Lactate

Blood lactate concentrations have been used as indicators of anaerobic energy production in soccer (3,5). The concentration of blood lactate fluctuates throughout a soccer match. Lactate is metabolized within the active muscle after high-intensity exercise. When intense exercise is punctuated with low-intensity exercise the rate of lactate metabolism increases. Furthermore, lactate released into the blood is taken up by the heart, liver, kidney, and other tissues. Evidence suggests that lactate is an important metabolic intermediate as a substrate for oxidative metabolism in cardiac and skeletal muscle and a precursor for gluconeogenesis (42). Thus, measurements of blood lactate concentration represent the balance of lactate released by muscle and taken up by blood and will not fully reflect lactate production during a soccer match.

It is reasonable to conclude that lactate production may be very high at points throughout a soccer game (3,5). During a tennis match, blood lactate levels were shown to have increased 50% to near, but not beyond, the anabolic threshold (17). The authors attribute this finding to several factors, including a highly trained aerobic system and variations in play that allow blood lactate levels to clear. McInnes et al (10) reported blood lactate levels during basketball averaging 6.8 mmol, indicating that glycolysis is involved in energy production.

Nutrient Needs

Nutrient needs of athletes performing stop-and-go sports, although high, can generally be met with a diet that provides sufficient energy to meet the demands of training and competition. Careful selection based on well-informed choices is the key to meeting the additional nutrient demands. Observations of the dietary practices of athletes engaged in stop-and-go sports suggest that many athletes' diets are inadequate.

Macronutrients

Energy

Energy demands are high due to the intermittent nature of stop-and-go sports, and energy intake must be adequate to support training and competition (43). Several reports suggest that some players may not be meeting optimal nutrient intakes (43–48). Clark reports that professional male soccer players consume between 2,033 and 3,923 kcal/day (44). Data from a Major Indoor Soccer League team revealed that daily energy intakes of male players averaged 2,662 kcal and ranged from 1,618 to 4,394 kcal (45).

It is estimated that a 75-kg male soccer player expends approximately 1,530 kcal per game. Female soccer players experience similar exercise intensity during a match, yet expend less energy than males due to smaller body mass. Brewer (46) reported that at 70% VO_{2max}, energy expenditure during a game is approximately 1,100 kcal. There are reports of insufficient energy intake among female soccer players (48,49).

Data reported in 2003 about collegiate female soccer players indicate that intakes met the Dietary Reference Intakes (DRIs) for total energy (37 kcal/kg of body weight), protein, and fat during the preseason and were significantly more than intakes during the playing season (48). Although protein and fat intakes during the preseason were more than minimum recommendations, carbohydrate intakes were not sufficient to promote glycogen repletion. In this study, protein and fat displaced carbohydrate-rich, nutrient-dense foods, which seemed to meet energy requirements during training but failed to meet carbohydrate and micronutrient recommendations. It is important to note that total energy, carbohydrate, and micronutrient intakes during the season may not have been sufficient to support energy demands and recommended intakes.

An examination of female field hockey players (49) reveals an energy intake less than expenditure, with eight of the nine players attempting to lose weight. Several other observational studies reviewed by Brewer (46) suggest similar trends in the diets of female athletes. Papadopoulou et al (50) assessed the macro- and micronutrient intakes of two national teams of adolescent Greek female volleyball players and found that protein intake was satisfactory (approximately16% of total kcal), but fat intake was generally higher than desired (approximately 37.5% of total kcal) at the expense of carbohydrate consumption (45.9% total kcal), with mean energy intakes less than optimal levels (2,013 kcal and 1,529 kcal, respectively).

Carbohydrate

Maughan et al (51), in a review of studies of cyclists, compared the effects of low-carbohydrate diets vs high-carbohydrate diets on high-intensity exercise. A low-carbohydrate diet (< 10% of total energy from carbohydrate) resulted in reduced endurance time. Conversely, diets that provided 65% to 84% of total energy were associated with increased performance, more consistently so with carbohydrate intakes at the higher end. Maughan et al (51) also noted that a high-protein diet, particularly in conjunction with a low-carbohydrate diet, resulted in metabolic acidosis, which is associated with fatigue. Although many questions about the causal mechanisms remain unanswered, the authors concluded the review with two distinct messages. The first is that it is possible to improve performance of short-duration, high-intensity exercise with a high-carbohydrate, low-protein diet for a few days before competition. Second, performance of this type may be impaired by a high-protein diet with insufficient carbohydrate or an energy-restricted diet in the precompetition period. These are important considerations for athletes who compete in intermittent, high-intensity exercise because of the periods of strenuous demands during competition.

Muscle Glycogen

The demands on muscle glycogen are great and performance is improved when carbohydrate is supplied before and during high-intensity intermittent exercise. Bangsbo et al (52) reports that by increasing the carbohydrate content of the diet from 39% to 65% prior to a soccer match, muscle glycogen levels increased and resulted in a higher work rate and improved intermittent endurance. Akermark et al (53) compared the performance of ice hockey players given a carbohydrate-enriched diet vs a mixed diet. During a 3-day period between two games, players were fed a mixed diet of approximately 40% carbohydrate or a diet of approximately 60% carbohydrate. Distance skated, number of shifts skated, amount of time skated within shifts, and skating speed improved with the higher carbohydrate intake.

Glycogen depletion, a potential factor contributing to fatigue, may seriously limit players' ability to maintain high-intensity work output, particularly during the later stages of the game. Glycogen utilization in leg muscle is markedly increased during bouts of intense exercise. During periods of rest and low-intensity play, glycogen is resynthesized (54). A study of Swedish elite ice hockey players (53) showed that distance and number of shifts skated, the skating speed, and the amount of time skated with shifts, improved with carbohydrate loading prior to activity.

In two separate studies, investigators found low levels of muscle glycogen after completion of a soccer match (22,55) and more use of glycogen in the first half compared with the second half (55). The difference in muscle glycogen measured before and after a match represents the net glycogen utilization and does not fully reflect total glycogen turnover during play (5,19). Toward the end of a match, players experience fatigue and a decrease in performance. Although an exact mechanism for this phenomenon has not been identified, low levels of muscle glycogen are likely a major factor. Saltin (55) observed that players with low levels of glycogen covered 24% less distance, 50% of which was covered by walking. Without sufficient muscle glycogen, exercise is fueled by fat and the intensity of that exercise is typically less than 50% of capacity (20,56).

Blood Glucose

The stored glycogen in exercising muscle provides a major portion of carbohydrate used during a soccer match, but blood glucose also may be utilized by exercising muscles (5) and may, in fact, spare muscle glycogen. As exercise duration increases, carbohydrate from muscle glycogen decreases while that from blood glucose increases (20). Blood glucose concentrations increase during high-intensity intermittent exercise as long as there is sufficient liver glycogen and glucose precursors (3,5).

Hypoglycemia and depletion of glycogen are associated with fatigue and reduced performance. Ferrauti and colleagues (57) assessed the incidence of hypoglycemia in tennis players during repeated tournament and practice matches by examining the change in glucose concentrations over the test period. Results indicate that glucose homeostasis is disrupted several times during tennis tournaments leading to a decrease in glucose concentration and an increased risk of hypoglycemia, especially after a long match and a short break. In the absence of carbohydrate supplementation during extended play, blood glucose can decrease. To reduce the risk of hypoglycemia, a continuous intake of a low–glycemic index carbohydrate is recommended beginning with the third set through the end of the match and during changeovers.

Carbohydrate Recommendations

A 1994 review by Hargreaves (58) presents an overview of the most relevant research results about the role of carbohydrate on soccer players before, during, and after games and intensive training. Hargreaves concluded that a diet of at least 55% of total energy as carbohydrate plus carbohydrate consumed during and after a match would maximize liver and muscle glycogen stores, which will enhance performance of athletes involved in strenuous exercise and training.

Carbohydrate recommendations are expressed on a gram per kilogram basis (59). The current recommendations for athletes engaged in high-intensity, intermittent sports are summarized in Table 23.4 (44,60–67). Specific recommendations should be tailored to the needs of the individual athlete. Before adopting any eating and drinking strategies for immediately before or during a match, players should be cautioned to experiment on training days to establish a comfortable routine to avoid any untoward consequences.

Glycogen Repletion

In spite of measures to minimize glycogen losses, match play drastically reduces glycogen stores. Glycogen depletion is associated with fatigue and a decrease in exercise intensity. Resynthesis of depleted glycogen stores is both an important consideration and a challenge in postexercise recovery. When carbohydrate is supplemented immediately after exercise, the rate of glycogen synthesis and the amount stored is optimal (68), increasing muscle glycogen up to seven-fold (67). The consumption of moderate– to high–glycemic index

TABLE 23.4 Carbohydrate Guidelines for High-Intensity, Intermittent Exercise

	Carbohydrate	Conditions
Training diet	8–10 g/kg body weight (60%–70% total energy)	Adequate energy
Pregame meal	> 200 g	3–4 h prior to competition; low–glycemic index solid carbohydrate may be beneficial
Before exercise	30–60 g	1 h before competition
During exercise	30–60 g/h	6%–8% carbohydrate solution
After exercise	1.2–1.67 g/kg	15- to 30-min intervals for 2–5 h postexercise

Source: Data are from references 44 and 60–67.

foods after exercise may be beneficial (67–69-71). There is a large body of research supporting the need for carbohydrate before, during, and after exercise (see Chapter 2).

Protein

Studies have shown that amino acids can be oxidized for energy during endurance exercise (72) and that amino acid oxidation is inversely related to muscle glycogen availability (73). During team sports of intermittent exercise, muscle glycogen can be depleted depending on the intensity and duration of exercise and pregame glycogen stores. The higher the intensity of exercise, the greater the glycogen utilization and amino acid oxidation. If the amino acids are not replaced via diet, a net loss in amino acids can occur over time, with losses in muscle strength and possibly performance.

Protein recommendations for soccer players have been made on the basis of research that shows the strength component of soccer and the use of protein as an energy source. Lemon (74) concludes that soccer players need more dietary protein than sedentary individuals and suggests a protein intake of 1.4 to 1.7 g/kg/day for competitive soccer players. Lemon cautions against extremely high protein intakes (> 2 g/kg/day) because of possible health hazards and the lack of evidence of performance advantage. A review by Wolfe (75) addresses the use of protein supplements in exercise training and issues the same cautionary note that excessive protein intake may increase the potential for dehydration due to high urea excretion, and may cause gout, liver and kidney damage, calcium loss, bloating, and diarrhea, particularly in at-risk groups such as children, elderly individuals, and those with chronic conditions.

Attention has been given to the possible benefits of combining protein with carbohydrate during exercise to delay fatigue or immediately after exercise to maximize muscle glycogen synthesis (60,76–78). Results have been mixed, with inconclusive evidence to support the addition of protein in the presence of adequate carbohydrate intake.

Fat

Of the three macronutrients, dietary fat plays the smallest role in energy distribution. Fat is certainly an important component of a balanced diet, but the absolute quantity and the percentage of energy distribution contributed by fat should be limited. It is generally recommended that fat should contribute 30% or less of total energy.

To achieve energy intake levels that support weight and weight-training goals, athletes often consume diets high in fat. In a review of the role of dietary macronutrients in optimizing performance, Lambert and Goedecke (60) conclude that consuming a high-fat diet (> 60% of energy from fat) followed by 1-day carbohydrate loading had variable results and is most likely to benefit only ultraendurance athletes.

Among the factors that contribute to less-than-optimal dietary intakes of athletes are travel; all-you-can-eat buffet meals; limited time, facilities, and energy to cook; and insufficient nutrition knowledge. Athletes would benefit from instruction about choosing foods that support both their training and performance goals and their goals for fitness and long-term health.

Dietitians working with athletes who participate in high-intensity intermittent sports should observe the following guidelines about fat intake:

- Determine carbohydrate and protein intakes and then aim for 20% to 35% of energy from fat.

- Limit saturated fats to 10% of energy.
- Emphasize heart-healthy fats.
- Give practical guidelines for food selections that will control the contribution from fat, especially sources of "hidden" fats, such as full-fat dairy products, meats, processed foods, and foods prepared with fat, including restaurant and fast foods.
- Focus on selecting lower-fat protein sources.
- Include tips for choosing foods away from home.

Micronutrients

The energy demands of soccer training and competition are significant and require adequate intakes of all nutrients involved in energy production. There are no known micronutrient needs specific to athletes engaged in high-intensity, intermittent sports. DRIs, which are listed in Appendix A, are therefore appropriate goals for micronutrient intakes (79–82). Fogelholm (83) presents data on micronutrient status and the effects of micronutrient supplementation on exercise performance related to soccer and other team players. In an effort to understand micronutrient needs and intakes of athletes and whether there is any performance benefit to micronutrient supplementation, data were reported from nine studies examining dietary intakes of athletes involved in soccer, football, basketball, hockey, volleyball, and handball, as well as three studies assessing the effect of micronutrient supplementation. The data from these studies suggest that, overall, micronutrient intakes correlate with energy intake. Male intakes were mostly in line with recommendations. Female athletes with energy intakes below 2,400 kcal were more likely to have lower intakes of minerals and trace elements, such as calcium, magnesium, iron, and zinc. The data also suggest that Vitamin B-6 intake was below recommended levels for all groups studied, but this may be due to incomplete data from B-6 nutrient databases.

With regard to supplementation, there was no clear evidence that micronutrient supplementation improved performance of athletes, but the number of subjects studied was small (83). Two exceptions to this conclusion are (a) female athletes with infrequent or irregular menstruation, who may benefit from calcium supplementation to increase bone density; and (b) iron-depleted females (serum ferritin < 12 µg/L), who may benefit from supplementation with 100 mg elemental iron for 1 to 2 months. The iron status of female athletes should therefore be assessed annually.

In general, the micronutrient status of an athlete is directly related to the quality of the dietary intake, especially energy intake. Among the athletes studied by Nutter (49), iron and calcium intakes were 30% less than the recommended levels. Similarly, data collected from male and female team athletes show some areas of concern (84). Low intakes of thiamin were observed in the diets of male athletes. Among female athletes whose daily energy intakes were less than 2,390 kcal, mineral and trace elements, such as calcium, magnesium, iron, and zinc, were suboptimal.

A 2003 investigation by Clark et al (48) of collegiate female soccer players showed that along with insufficient carbohydrate intake, several micronutrient intakes were less than 75% of the DRI pre- and postseason. Among these athletes, a greater consumption of protein- and fat-rich foods displaced more nutrient-dense complex carbohydrates. This becomes particularly troublesome when athletes focus on weight reduction or the maintenance of a low body weight. Fogelholm (83) recommends that nutrition education for soccer players start at an early age and focus on foods and macronutrients. Periodic dietary evaluation and nutrition education by a registered dietitian can detect early trouble signs, help prevent serious nutritional deficiencies, and screen for possible eating disorders.

Fluids

The major causes of fatigue in endurance sports are depletion of muscle glycogen and problems associated with thermoregulation and fluid loss. High-intensity intermittent sports require that players exercise at high intensities for a prolonged period of time, often at elevated ambient temperatures and high humidity. In the case of American football, the added factor of clothing and equipment make heat dissipation, and thus thermoregulation, more difficult (84). The energy demands of stop-and-go sports greatly reduce muscle glycogen stores and fluid reserves, which must be replenished before the next competition. Repletion of muscle glycogen depends not only on carbohydrate intake but also on fluid intake as well because each gram of muscle glycogen is stored with 2.7 g of water.

Studies examining the effects of carbohydrate-electrolyte solutions on performance during high-intensity intermittent exercise found that muscle glycogen utilization was reduced (85), endurance running capacity was improved (86), time to fatigue was delayed, and mental function was improved (35) when a carbohydrate-electrolyte solution was consumed. Under moderate temperatures (10°C or 50°F), the sweat losses of soccer players during a match may be as much as 2 liters (71) and a mean loss of 3 liters or more in the heat (4). When the ambient temperature is more than skin temperature, the body takes on additional heat and thus reduces the capacity to perform prolonged exercise. Players who sweat profusely are likely to become dehydrated and fatigued toward the end of the game. Fluid ingestion in the heat should therefore focus on maintenance of hydration status.

Full rehydration after exercise requires replacement of fluid and electrolytes, primarily sodium, lost in sweat. A study by Shirreffs et al (87) suggests that full rehydration after intense exercise is best achieved when the replacement fluid contains sufficient sodium and is consumed at 150% of the fluid lost through exercise. An investigation examined the effect on gastric emptying of intermittent exercise at varying intensities to simulate a soccer match. Results revealed that a greater volume of carbohydrate-electrolyte solution emptied during the lower-intensity walking trial than during the high-intensity soccer trial, demonstrating that the intensity of activity during this type of stop-and-go team sports is sufficient to slow gastric emptying (88). Details of fluid and electrolyte balance can be found in Chapter 6 and are summarized in Box 23.1 (87,89–94).

Fluid Needs of Young Players

Special consideration and care should be paid to the fluid needs of young athletes, particularly prepubescent youth. During exercise children produce more heat than adults yet have a greater surface area-to-body mass ratio, thus increasing their influx of heat when ambient temperatures are more than skin temperature. In addition, they have less capacity for sweating and take longer to acclimatize to warm weather (95). These factors increase young athletes' risk for dehydration and heat illness. When children become dehydrated, their core temperatures increase faster than dehydrated adults, underscoring the need for strict enforcement of hydration practices. Given the heightened risk of hyperthermia in children, the following precautions and practical measures should be taken:

Box 23.1   Hydration Goals in High-Intensity, Intermittent Exercise

Before Exercise
- Maximize fluid intake during the 24 hours preceding training or competition.
- Drink extra fluid during the last 10–15 min before the game begins.

During Exercise
- Consume fluid early and at regular intervals during exercise.
- Choose cool, flavored beverages that are more palatable and contain 4% to 8% carbohydrate (30–60 g carbohydrate per hour) and electrolytes (0.5–0.7 g sodium per liter of water)

After Exercise
- Achieve rapid and complete repletion of fluid, electrolyte, and carbohydrates lost during training and exercise. Each pound lost is about 480 mL (about 16 oz) of fluid.
- Drink at least a pint (500 mL) of fluid for every pound of body weight lost through exercise.

General Precaution: Alcohol is dehydrating. Avoid alcohol within 72 hours before or after training.

Source: Data are from references 87 and 89–94.

- Five to 8 ounces of fluid should be consumed at least every 15 to 20 minutes during training and exercise in the heat.
- Fluids should be cool and palatable to encourage drinking. In one study, grape was the preferred flavor and the one that lead to the greatest rehydration following mild dehydration (96).
- Clothing should be lightweight and moisture-wicking; Cotton is very absorbent, trapping moisture against the skin, and not recommended as a first layer.
- In warm weather, avoid unnecessary layers of clothing. Soccer goalkeepers should remove the team jersey when wearing the goalkeeper shirt.
- Sweat-drenched clothing should be replaced with dry clothing when possible.
- Reduce intensity of exercise when the relative humidity and ambient temperature are high.
- Allow frequent breaks.
- Provide shelter from direct sunlight during hot weather when on the sidelines.

Summary

The stop-and-go nature of high-intensity intermittent sports places a great physiological and metabolic demand on the body and involves all three energy systems. These sports require bursts of all-out effort interspersed with periods of moderate- and low-intensity effort.

The primary goals of nutrition in such sports is to support peak performance by ensuring adequate amounts of energy and nutrients, the right blend of fuel for a given effort, adequate hydration, and a plan for the rapid replacement of fluids and muscle fuel. Coaches and trainers must take precautions to avoid or minimize some of the pitfalls of high-intensity intermittent exercise, such as fatigue, hypoglycemia, impaired performance, and dehydration and its consequences.

Carbohydrate is the preferred fuel for much of the work in stop-and-go sports and it is crucial to ensure adequate intakes of carbohydrate before, during, and after exercise. The general carbohydrate recommendation is 6 g/kg daily with 8 to 10 g/kg daily recommended during training and competition. The timing of ingestion, as well as the amount of carbohydrate, helps fuel the athlete and enhance endurance and power. Recommended daily protein intake is 1.4 to 1.7 g/kg. Fat should comprise approximately 20% to 35% of total energy intake. When selecting foods, it is important to carefully choose nutrient-dense sources that also provide ample vitamins and minerals, an essential part of fuel production and good health. Fluid intake is critical, especially because many intermittent, high-intensity sports are played in hot and humid conditions.

References

1. Reilly T, Thomas V. A motion analysis of work rate in different positional roles in professional football match play. *J Hum Movement Stud.* 1976;2:87–97.
2. Withers RT, Maricic Z, Wasilewski S, Kelly L. Match analysis of Australian professional soccer players. *J Hum Movement Stud.* 1982;8:159–176.
3. Ekblom B. Applied physiology of soccer. *Sports Med.* 1986;3:50–60.
4. Reilly T. Energetics of high-intensity exercise (soccer) with particular reference to fatigue. *J Sports Sci.* 1997;15:257–263.
5. Bangsbo J. The physiology of soccer—with special reference to intense intermittent exercise. *Acta Physiol Scand Suppl.* 1994;619:1–155.
6. Drust B, Reilly T, Rienzi E. Analysis of work rate in soccer. *Sports Exerc Injury.* 1998;4:151–155.
7. Shephard RJ. Biology and medicine of soccer: an update. *J Sport Sci.* 1999;117:757–786.
8. Bradley G, Toye C. Team play and systems of play. In: *Playing Soccer the Professional Way.* New York, NY: Harper & Row; 1973:105–120.
9. Pincivero DM, Bompa TO. A physiological review of American football. *Sports Med.* 1997;4:247–60.
10. McInnes SE, Carlson JS, Jones CJ, McKenna MJ. The physiological load imposed on basketball players during competition. *J Sports Sci.* 1995;13:387–397.
11. Montgomery DL. Physiology of ice hockey. *Sports Med.* 1988;5:99–126.
12. Akermark C, Jacobs I, Rasmusson M, Karlsson J. Diet and muscle glycogen concentration in relation to physical performance in Swedish elite ice hockey players. *Int J Sport Nutr.* 1996;6:272–284.
13. Houston ME. Nutrition and ice hockey performance. *Can J Appl Sport Sci.* 1979;4:98–99.
14. Green HJ, Daub BD, Painter DC, Thomson JA. Glycogen depletion patterns during ice hockey performance. *Med Sci Sports.* 1978;10:289–293.
15. Green HJ. Metabolic aspects of intermittent work with specific regard to ice hockey. *Can J Appl Sport Sci.* 1979;4:29–34.
16. Konig D, Huonker M, Schmid A, Halle M, Berg A, Keul J. Cardiovascular, metabolic, and hormonal parameters in professional tennis players. *Med Sci Sports Exerc.* 2001;33:654–658.

17. Bergeron MF, Maresh CM, Kraemer WJ, Abraham A, Conroy B, Gabaree C. Tennis: a physiological profile during match play. *Int J Sports Med.* 1991;12:474–479.

18. Smekal G, von Duvillard SP, Rihacek C, Pokan R, Hofmann P, Baron R, Tschan H, Bachl N. A physiological profile of tennis match play. *Med Sci Sports Exerc.* 2001;33:999–1005.

19. Bangsbo J. Energy demands in competitive soccer. *J Sports Sci.* 1994;12(Spec No):S5–S12.

20. Romijn JA, Coyle EF, Sidossis LS, Gastaldelli A, Horowitz JF, Endert E, Wolfe RR. Regulation of endogenous fat and carbohydrate metabolism in relation to exercise intensity and duration. *Am J Physiol.* 1993;265:E380-E391.

21. Roberts TJ, Weber JM, Hoppeler H, Weibel ER, Taylor CR. Design of the oxygen and substrate pathways. II. Defining the upper limits of carbohydrate and fat oxidation. *J Exp Biol.* 1996; 199:1651–1658.

22. Jacobs I, Westin N, Karlsson J, Rasmusson M, Houghton B. Muscle glycogen and diet in elite soccer players. *Eur J Appl Physiol.* 1982;48:297–302.

23. Tumilty D. Physiological characteristics of elite soccer players. *Sports Med.* 1993;16:80–96.

24. Gollnick P, Armstrong R, Saubert IV C, Shepherd R, Saltin B. Glycogen depletion patterns in human skeletal muscle fibers after exhausting exercise. *J Appl Physiol.* 1973;34:615–618.

25. Costill D, Gollnick P, Jansson E, Saltin B, Stein E. Glycogen depletion pattern in human muscle fibers during distance running. *Acta Physiol Scand.* 1973;89:374–384.

26. Gollnick P, Piehl K, Saubert IV C, Armstrong R, Saltin B. Diet, exercise, and glycogen changes in human muscle fibers. *J Appl Physiol.* 1972;33:421–425.

27. Brooks GA, Mercier J. Balance of carbohydrate and lipid utilization during exercise: the "crossover" concept. *J Appl Physiol.* 1994;76:2253–2261.

28. Brooks GA. Importance of the "crossover" concept in exercise metabolism. *Clin Exp Pharmacol Physiol.* 1997;24:889–895.

29. Coggan AR, Kohrt WM, Spina RJ, Bier DM, Holloszy JO. Endurance training decreases plasma glucose turnover and oxidation during moderate-intensity exercise in men. *J Appl Physiol.* 1990;68:990–996.

30. Hurley BF, Nemeth PM, Martin WH III, Hagberg JM, Dalsky GP, Holloszy JO. Muscle triglyceride utilization during exercise: effect of training. *J Appl Physiol.* 1986;60:562–567.

31. Sidossis LS, Gastaldelli A, Klein S, Wolfe RR. Regulation of plasma fatty acid oxidation during low- and high–intensity exercise. *Am J Physiol.* 1997;272:E1065–E1070.

32. Martin WH 3rd, Dalsky GP, Hurley BF, Matthews DE, Bier DM, Hagberg JM, Rogers MA, King DS, Holloszy JO. Effect of endurance-training on plasma free fatty acid turnover and oxidation during exercise. *Am J Physiol.* 1993;265:E708–E714.

33. Weber JM, Brichon G, Zwingelstein G, McClelland G, Saucedo C, Weibel ER, Taylor CR. Design of the oxygen and substrate pathways. IV. Partitioning energy provision from fatty acids. *J Exp Biol.* 1996;199:1667–1674.

34. Tomlin DL, Wenger HA. The relationship between aerobic fitness and recovery from high-intensity intermittent exercise. *Sports Med.* 2001;31:1–11.

35. Welsh RS, Davis JM, Burke JR, Williams HG. Carbohydrates and physical/mental performance during intermittent exercise to fatigue. *Med Sci Sports Exerc.* 2002;34:723–731.

36. Newsholme EA, Blomstrand E, Ekblom B. Physical and mental fatigue: metabolic mechanisms and importance of plasma amino acids. *Br Med Bull.* 1992;48:477–495.

37. Bergström J, Hermansen L, Hultman E, Saltin B. Diet, muscle glycogen and physical performance. *Acta Physiol Scand.* 1967;71:140–150.

38. Smodlaka V. Cardiovascular aspect of soccer. *Phys Sportsmed.* 1978;6:66–70.

39. Bangsbo J, Norregaard L, Thorsoe F. Activity profile of competition soccer. *Can J Sport Sci.* 1991;16:110–116.

40. Therminarias A, Dansou P, Chirpaz-Oddou MF, Gharib C, Quirion A. Hormonal and metabolic changes during a strenuous match. Effect of aging. *Int J Sports Med.* 1991;12:10–16.

41. Docherty D. A comparison of heart rate responses in racquet games. *Br J Sports Med.* 1982;6: 96–100.
42. Brooks G. Current concepts in lactate exchange. *Med Sci Sports Exerc.* 1991;23:895–906.
43. Williams C, Nicholas CW. Nutrition needs for team sport. *Sport Sci Exch.* 1998;11:70.
44. Clark K. Nutritional guidance to soccer players for training and competition. *J Sports Sci.* 1994;12(Spec No):S43-S50.
45. Macedonio M. Nutrition management of the Cleveland Force soccer team. Summary report. Unpublished data. 1987.
46. Brewer J. Aspects of women's soccer. *J Sports Sci.* 1994;12(Spec No):S35-S38.
47. Economos C, Bortz S, Nelson M. Nutrition practices of elite athletes. *Sports Med.* 1993;16: 381–399.
48. Clark M, Reed DB, Crouse SF, Armstrong RB. Pre- and post-season dietary intake, body composition, and performance indices of NCAA division I female soccer players. *Int J Sport Nutr Exerc Metab.* 2003;13:303–319.
49. Nutter J. Seasonal changes in female athletes' diets. *Int J Sport Nutr.* 1991;1:395–407.
50. Papadopoulou SK, Papadopoulou SD, Gallos GK. Macro- and micro-nutrient intake of adolescent Greek female volleyball players. *Int J Sport Nutr Exerc Metab.* 2002;12:73–80.
51. Maughan R, Greenhaff P, Leiper J, Ball D, Lambert C, Gleeson M. Diet composition on the performance of high-intensity exercise. *J Sports Sci.* 1997;15:265–275.
52. Bangsbo J, Norregaard L, Thorsoe F. The effect of carbohydrate diet on intermittent exercise performance. *Int J Sports Med.* 1992;13:152–157.
53. Akermark C, Jacobs I, Rasmusson M, Karlsson J. Diet and muscle glycogen concentration in relation to physical performance in Swedish elite ice hockey players. *Int J Sport Nutr.* 1996;6: 272–284.
54. Nordheim K, Vollestad N. Glycogen and lactate metabolism during low-intensity exercise in man. *Acta Physiol Scand.* 1990;139:475–484.
55. Saltin B. Metabolic fundamental in exercise. *Med Sci Sports Exerc.* 1973;5:137–146.
56. Kirkendall D. Effects of nutrition on performance in soccer. *Med Sci Sports Exerc.* 1993;25: 1370–1374.
57. Ferrauti A, Pluim BM, Busch T, Weber K. Blood glucose responses and incidence of hypoglycaemia in elite tennis under practice and tournament conditions. *J Sci Med Sport.* 2003;6:28–39.
58. Hargreaves M. Carbohydrate and lipid requirements of soccer. *J Sports Sci.* 1994;12(Spec No):S13–S16.
59. Burke LM, Cox GR, Culmmings NK, DEsbrow B. Guidelines for daily carbohydrate intake: do athletes achieve them? *Sports Med.* 2001;31:267–299.
60. Lambert EV, Goedecke JH. The role of dietary macronutrients in optimizing endurance performance. *Curr Sports Med Rep.* 2003;2:194–201.
61. Costill D, Hargreaves M. Carbohydrate nutrition and fatigue. *Sports Med.* 1992;13:86–92.
62. Wright DA, Sherman WM, Dernbach AR. Carbohydrate feedings before, during, or in combination improve cycling performance. *J Appl Physiol.* 1991;71:1082–1088.
63. Maffucci DM, McMurray RG. Towards optimizing the timing of the pre-exercise meal. *Int J Sport Nutr Exerc Metab.* 2000;10:103–113.
64. Coleman E. Update on carbohydrate: solid versus liquid. *Int J Sport Nutr.* 1994;4:80–88.
65. Kirwan JP, Cyr-Campbell D, Campbell WW, Scheiber J, Evans WJ. Effects of moderate and high glycemic index meals on metabolism and exercise performance. *Metabolism.* 2001;50:849–855.
66. Williams MB, Raven PB, Fogt DL, Ivy JL. Effects of recovery beverages on glycogen restoration and endurance exercise performance. *J Strength Cond Res.* 2003;17:12–19.
67. Burke L, Collier G, Davis P, Fricker P, Sanigorski A, Hargreaves M. Muscle glycogen storage after prolonged exercise: effect of the frequency of carbohydrate feedings. *Am J Clin Nutr.* 1996;64:115–119.

68. Ivy J. Optimization of glycogen stores. In: Maughan R, ed. *Nutrition in Sport*. Malden, Mass: Blackwell Science; 2000:97–111. *Encyclopaedia of Sports Medicine,* vol 7.

69. Rankin JW. Glycemic index and exercise metabolism. *Sports Sci Exch.* 1997;10:1.

70. Burke L, Hargreaves M, Collier G. Muscle glycogen storage after prolonged exercise. *J Appl Physiol.* 1993;74:1019–1023.

71. Coyle E. Timing and method of increased carbohydrate intake to cope with heavy training, competition and recovery. *J Sports Sci.* 1991;9:29–51.

72. Evans W, Fisher E, Hoerr R, Young V. Protein metabolism and endurance exercise. *Phys Sportsmed.* 1983;11:63–72.

73. Lemon P, Mullin J. Effect of initial muscle glycogen levels on protein catabolism during exercise. *J Appl Physiol.* 1992;48:624–629.

74. Lemon P. Protein requirements of soccer. *J Sports Sci.* 1994;12(Spec No):S17–S22.

75. Wolfe RR. Protein supplements and exercise. *Am J Clin Nutr.* 2000;72(2 Suppl):551S–557S.

76. Ivy JL, Goforth HW Jr, Damon BM, McCauley TR, Parsons EC, Price TB. Early postexercise muscle glycogen recovery is enhanced with a carbohydrate-protein supplement. *J Appl Physiol.* 2002;93:1337–1344.

77. Davis JM, Welsh RS, De Volve KL, Alderson NA. Effects of branched-chain amino acids and carbohydrate on fatigue during intermittent, high-intensity running. *Int J Sports Med.* 1999;20: 309–314.

78. Lemon PW. Beyond the zone: protein needs of active individuals. *J Am Coll Nutr.* 2000;19(5 Suppl):513S–521S.

79. Institute of Medicine. *Dietary Reference Intakes for Vitamin A, Vitamin K, Arsenic, Boron, Chromium, Copper, Iodine, Iron, Molybdenum, Nickel, Silicon, Vanadium, and Zinc.* Washington, DC: National Academy Press; 2001. Available at: http://www.nap.edu. Accessed November 30, 2004.

80. Institute of Medicine. *Dietary Reference Intakes for Calcium, Phosphorus, Magnesium, Vitamin D, and Fluoride.* Washington, DC: National Academy Press; 1997. Available at: http://www. nap.edu. Accessed November 30, 2004.

81. Institute of Medicine. *Dietary Reference Intakes for Thiamin, Riboflavin, Niacin, Vitamin B6, Folate, Vitamin B12, Pantothenic Acid, Biotin, and Choline.* Washington, DC: National Academy Press; 1998. Available at: http://www.nap.edu. Accessed November 30, 2004.

82. Institute of Medicine. *Dietary Reference Intakes for Vitamin C, Vitamin E, Selenium, and Carotenoids.* Washington, DC: National Academy Press; 2000. Available at: http://www.nap.edu. Accessed November 30, 2004.

83. Fogelholm M. Vitamins, minerals and supplementation in soccer. *J Sports Sci.* 1994;12(Spec No):S23–S27.

84. Kulka TJ, Kenney L. Heat balance limits in football uniforms: how different uniform ensembles alter the equation. *Phys Sportsmed.* 2002;30:29–39.

85. Nicholas CW, Tsintzas K, Boobis L, Williams C. Carbohydrate-electrolyte ingestion during intermittent high-intensity running. *Med Sci Sports Exerc.* 1999;31:1280–1286.

86. Nicholas CW, Williams C, Lakomy HK, Phillips G, Nowitz A. Influence of ingesting a carbohydrate-electrolyte solution on endurance capacity during intermittent, high-intensity shuttle running. *J Sports Sci.* 1995;13:283–290.

87. Shirreffs SM, Taylor AJ, Leiper JB, Maughan RJ. Post-exercise rehydration in man: effects of volume consumed and drink sodium content. *Med Sci Sports Exerc.* 1996;28:1260–1271.

88. Leiper J, Prentice A, Wrightson C, Maughan, R. Gastric emptying of a carbohydrate-electrolyte drink during a soccer match. *Med Sci Sports Exerc.* 2000;33:1932–1938.

89. American College of Sports Medicine. Position stand on exercise and fluid replacement. *Med Sci Sports Exerc.* 1996;28:i–vii.

90. Greenleaf J, Castle B. Exercise temperature regulation in man during hypohydration and hyperthermia. *J Appl Physiol.* 1971;30:847–853.

91. Maughan R, Leiper J. Fluid replacement requirements in soccer. *J Sports Sci.* 1994;12(Spec No):S29-S34.

92. Shi X, Gisolfi C. Fluid and carbohydrate replacement during intermittent exercise. *Sports Med.* 1998;25:157–172.

93. Horswill CA. Effective fluid replacement. *Int J Sport Nutr.* 1998;8:175–195.

94. Burke LM, Hurley JA. Fluid balance in team sports. *Sports Med.* 1997;24:38–54.

95. Climatic heat stress and the exercising child and adolescent. American Academy of Pediatrics. Committee on Sports Medicine and Fitness. *Pediatrics.* 2000;106:158–159.

96. Meyer F, Bar-Or O, Salsberg A, Passe D. Hypohydration during exercise in children: effect of thirst, drink preferences, and rehydration. *Int J Sport Nutr.* 1994;4:22–35.

Chapter 24

NUTRITION FOR ENDURANCE SPORTS

Bob Seebohar, MS, RD, CSCS

Introduction

Endurance events include a broad range of competitions, including marathons, triathlons, long cycling events, ultraruns, and the increasingly popular adventure races (see Box 24.1). This chapter will specifically focus on endurance events lasting 4 or more hours, but many of these same nutrition recommendations can be applied to endurance events lasting less than 4 hours. Some athletes prefer endurance events because of the excitement they generate. In endurance races lasting longer than 4 hours, there is a tremendous sense of accomplishment in just finishing. Winning is not always the goal, as athletes usually encounter unique experiences or failures of some sort before crossing the finish line. How an athlete reacts to the process of the endurance event will dictate his or her success.

To prepare for longer events such as Ironman triathlons or Race Across America, many athletes find it impossible to train the number of miles that they will cover in the race itself. If they did, they risk injury from overtraining. Because most endurance athletes already have a good aerobic base, they prefer to work on specifics in their training, such as improving weaknesses or fine-tuning the biomechanics of their sport(s). Developing a sound nutrition plan during training and racing is of great importance because lack of proper nutrition is one of the most common reasons for an athlete to not finish an event.

Box 24.1   Examples of Endurance Events

- Ultramarathons (such as the Sahara Ultra Run, a 3-day, 117.8-mile run across the Sahara desert)
- Race Across America–RAAM (a coast-to-coast cycling event)
- Ironman triathlons (a 2.4-mile swim, 112-mile bike, and 26.2-mile run)
- Ultraman (a 6.2-mile swim and 90-mile bike on day 1, a 1/1.4-mile bike on day 2, and a 52.4-mile run on day 3)
- Manhattan Marathon Swim (a 28.5-mile swim)

Energy Expenditure and Needs

Endurance athletes predominantly use the aerobic energy system with brief, intermittent involvement of anaerobic energy systems. Actual energy expenditure depends on intensity, duration, and type of activity. Exercise intensities may range between 50% and 90% maximum oxygen consumption (VO_{2max}) for events lasting 4 to 24 hours, with total energy expenditures ranging between 5,000 and 10,000 kcal per day (1).

In a typical endurance event, such as a half-Ironman, ultraswim or ultrarun, the exercise intensity averages 65% VO_{2max} or less, and lipids are the primary fuel source. Although fat oxidation provides the greatest relative contribution to energy expenditure (2), exercise can only be maintained for prolonged periods without the onset of fatigue if sufficient carbohydrate is available (3). In a higher-intensity endurance event, the exercise intensity is often 75% VO_{2max} or more, and carbohydrate is the primary fuel source (4).

Protein does not contribute significantly to energy levels in endurance events. Amino acid oxidation has been shown to contribute up to 15% of the energy used when carbohydrate stores are low (5), but this decreases to 5% when overall energy intake is adequate (6). Following the current guidelines of high carbohydrate consumption before and during endurance events will minimize the contribution from protein as an energy source. Carbohydrates during exercise will supplement muscle and liver glycogen stores and maintain blood glucose concentrations (7).

Nutrient Needs

Endurance athletes spend months to years preparing for their events. Throughout training, these athletes often have specific nutritional goals such as weight loss, altering body composition, eating for recovery, eating to support the immune system, and eating to support the low and high volume and intensity of their training, not to mention eating for overall health. In the past, nutrition guidelines were based only on competition. Endurance events require long training periods. With extended preparation, the focus is broader, not just a few days to a week before the event. Endurance athletes need an overall nutrition plan that begins the first day of training and lasts until well after completion of their last event. This concept is termed *nutrition periodization*.

Nutrition periodization reflects the same principles of traditional physical periodization. It provides a comprehensive plan for athletes because it supports their entire training year and forces them to pay more attention to nutrition. A sound, comprehensive nutrition plan improves performance. The challenge for nutrition professionals is to discuss the overall physical periodization plan first with the athlete and then determine the general and specific nutrient and energy needs that will be required for their sport. Because these needs will fluctuate throughout the training year, it is important to schedule frequent sessions with the athlete, especially when entering a new physical training cycle. The following section will explain the periodization concept and its use by nutrition professionals working with endurance athletes.

Physical Periodization and Nutrition Periodization

Periodization is a program design strategy that promotes long-term training and performance improvements by varying the training specificity, intensity, and volume into different cycles throughout the year. The periodization concept was first applied in the 1940s when Soviet sports scientists discovered that athletic performance was improved by varying the training stresses throughout the year rather than maintaining the same training focus. The East Germans and Romanians further developed this concept by setting goals for the various periods (8). A primary objective of an athlete's training is to reach peak performance at a specific time, usually during the main competition cycle of the year. To achieve this high level of performance, the entire training program must be properly planned so that the development of skills and motor abilities proceeds logically and methodically throughout the year.

The traditional periodization model separates the overall training program into specific time periods (see Figure 24.1). The largest division is a macrocycle, which typically constitutes an entire training year but may be longer for some athletes such as those preparing for the Olympics. Within the macrocycle are mesocycles, each lasting several weeks to several months. The length depends on the goals of the athlete and the number of competitions within the period. Each mesocycle is divided into two or more microcycles that are typically 1 week in length but could last up to 4 weeks. Microcycles focus on daily and weekly training variations.

Periodization normally consists of breaking down the annual plan into shorter, more manageable training phases. This division enhances the organization of training and allows the coach to conduct the program systematically. The annual training cycle is divided into three cycles: (*a*) preparation; (*b*) competition; and (*c*) transition.

Each of the training mesocycles is further broken down into subcycles. For example, the preparation cycle is comprised of general preparation and specific preparation, the competition cycle is comprised of prerace and race, and the transition cycle consists of active recovery. Each subcycle has specific physiologic and performance-related goals.

The planned implementation of the mesocycles and microcycles within a macrocycle is the basis for changing the program design variables. Because it is the intensity and volume of the training program that changes the most, it is important to match these changes with the nutrition support. The nutrition periodization model (see Figure 24.2) should follow the training periodization model, progressing from general to specific to produce the greatest performance gains.

Because each period of the macrocycle has different levels of training intensity and volume, the athlete needs to have slightly different eating plans for each period to meet goals, which might include one or more of the following:

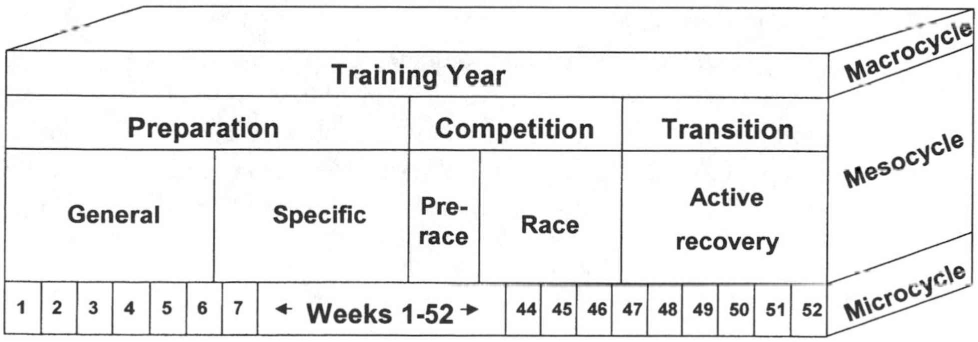

FIGURE 24.1.   Annual physical periodization cycles.

Year-Round Nutrition Principles			Macrocycle
Preparation	**Competition**	**Transition**	Mesocycle
Macronutrient and fluid quantity and timing General and specific eating guidelines-- quality and types		Weight management Variety	Microcycle
Daily macronutrient and fluid needs and recovery nutrition	Carbohydrate loading	Calorie control	

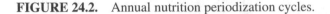

FIGURE 24.2.   Annual nutrition periodization cycles.

- Match energy expenditure
- Create a negative energy balance for weight loss
- Create a positive energy balance that focuses on carbohydrates to increase glycogen storage

It is well-supported that during training or competition an endurance athlete's eating plan may, but not always, include 5 to 19 g of carbohydrate per kilogram of body weight, 1.2 to 3.0 g of protein per kilogram of body weight, and 0.8 to 3.0 g of fat per kilogram of body weight (9–14).

Fluid requirements are presented in specific time intervals and amounts to prevent dehydration throughout the day and during training or racing and will be discussed in each specific periodized training cycle in following sections. In addition, the endurance athlete must compensate for obligatory urine losses incurred during the rehydration process and drink 25% to 50% more than sweat losses to assure optimal hydration 4 to 6 hours after the event (15).

Nutrition is the most commonly overlooked component in an athlete's training program. Most athletes concern themselves with nutrition a week or a few days prior to an event. Doing this may allow the athletes to complete that event, but it will not allow them to achieve peak performance. Proper nutrition throughout the year will not make an athlete stronger or faster by itself, but it will provide the athlete with the correct amount of nutrients that will support training and health, prevent illnesses, change body weight and composition, and improve performance.

Nutrition periodization should be standard practice when working with endurance athletes. The following provides a template of how to structure an athlete's eating plan to support physical training. Keep in mind that the body can absorb about 1 g of carbohydrate per minute of moderately intense exercise (16), so the following are guidelines that should be customized to the athlete's fitness level, sport, body, training, and race conditions.

Preparation Cycle

During the general and specific periods of the preparation mesocycle, training intensity begins low and gradually increases, whereas training volume begins at a moderate level and slowly increases. Most athletes are coming off of their transition cycle, or off-season/active recovery, and are slowly building up their volume but keeping their intensity low to avoid injury. The physiologic goals during this training cycle are to improve cardiovascular endurance and function in preparation for the later, more intense training cycles. During this cycle, the athlete may also be trying to lose weight, which should be done in the beginning of this cycle, not toward the end, because this will compromise speed training, which is introduced in the next cycle.

Daily Macronutrient and Fluid Needs

During the preparation cycle, the following guidelines are recommended:

- Carbohydrate intake should range from 5 to 7 g/kg for moderate-duration and low-intensity training to 7 to 12 g/kg for moderate to heavy training, to 10 to 12 g/kg (or more) for extreme training (4 to 6 hours or more per day) (17).
- Protein intake should range from 1.2 to 1.7 g/kg.
- Fat intake should range from 0.8 to 1.0 g/kg.
- Hydration should be adequate so that urine color is straw colored (pale yellow) throughout the day (18).

Macronutrient and Fluid Timing for Training

Athletes in the preparation period should be advised to do the following:

- Drink 17 to 20 oz of fluid 2 hours before training (18).
- Drink 7 to 10 oz of sport drink 10 to 20 minutes before training (18).
- Consume 30 to 60 g of carbohydrate per hour of training (19) from liquid or solid/semisolid sources. Fluids that contain carbohydrates are highly beneficial during higher intensity training.
- Drink 7 to 10 oz of fluid every 15 to 20 minutes during training (18).
- Drink 20 to 24 oz of fluid for every pound of body weight lost after training (15).
- Within the first 30 minutes after training and at 2-hour intervals thereafter, eat 1.0 to 1.2 g of carbohydrate per kilogram of body weight (17). In addition, eat 6 to 20 g of protein (20) if the training session is longer than 90 minutes.

Endurance athletes typically do not need to consume a pre-exercise carbohydrate feeding if they have an adequate meal before their training session. However, some endurance athletes who are training for longer distances may require more energy prior to a training session. Typically during the first half of the preparation cycle this is not needed but during the latter half it may become more important.

General and Specific Eating Guidelines

The following information should be communicated to the athlete during the sports nutrition consultation to improve health and performance:

- Eat a minimum of 6 to 9 servings of fruit (1 serving = 1 medium fruit; ½ cup chopped, cooked, or canned fruit; ¾ cup of 100% fruit juice) and vegetables (1 serving = 1 cup of raw leafy vegetables; ½ cup of other vegetables, cooked or chopped raw; ¾ cup of vegetable juice) per day to ensure adequate intake of vitamins, minerals, and fiber.

- Choose high-fiber foods such as fruits, vegetables, whole grains, beans, and oats.
- Try new foods and experiment with a variety of different foods and nutritional supplements such as energy bars, gels, and sport drinks to identify those preferred (taste and physical response).
- Find out which nutritional products will be used at the competition events in the upcoming season and try them to see if they are tolerated. Suggest that the athlete use these products during training.
- Consider environmental conditions and adjust fluid intake accordingly.
- Increase variety. Instruct the athlete to rotate through different foods and menus to get more variety and balance in their eating plan and avoid food ruts.

Competition (Prerace) Cycle

During the prerace cycle, the athlete will be increasing training intensity while training volume will be moderate without much increase. The physiologic goals during this cycle are to improve the body's ability to buffer and clear lactate and possibly improve VO_{2max} by performing intense to very intense interval sessions with proper recovery bouts. Energy expenditure is higher during this cycle and a proper energy intake is crucial for the athlete to sustain this higher training intensity. Weight loss should not be a goal during this cycle because it could compromise performance; therefore, weight loss should have taken place during the preparation cycle of training.

Carbohydrate intake should range from 7 to 13 g/kg. As a rule of thumb, because endurance athletes will typically be performing higher intensity training at least 1 or 2 days per week in the form of intervals or repeats, it is wise to instruct them to choose the higher range to maintain adequate glycogen stores on a daily basis. Protein intake should range from 1.4 to 2.0 g/kg. Because athletes are typically performing more strength (hill training) and speed/power (intervals) training during this cycle, the protein intake is increased to prevent muscle protein catabolism as much as possible. Fat and fluid guidelines remain the same as in the preparation cycle.

Daily Macronutrient and Fluid Needs
For athletes in the prerace cycle, the following guidelines are recommended:

- Carbohydrate intake should range from 7 to 13 g/kg.
- Protein intake should range from 1.4 to 2.0 g/kg.
- Fat intake remains the same as in the preparation cycle (0.8 to 1.0 g/kg).
- Fluid guidelines remain the same as in the preparation cycle.

Macronutrient and Fluid Timing for Training
The only significant change in training nutrition during the prerace cycle is the need for pre-exercise carbohydrates and possibly sodium. Athletes will need more energy before exercise, but the addition of protein during exercise is debatable and has not been fully accepted as a standard of practice. Because training intensity is high, energy expenditure will also be high. Nutritional intake must be adequate to support expenditure without experiencing significant weight loss.

Sodium needs depend on many variables, including sweat sodium concentration and losses, sweat rate, environmental conditions, and duration and intensity of exercise. No single sodium recommendation has been established for athletes. Some athletes may need additional sodium during exercise, but they should be cautioned when using a high dose of an exogenous source of sodium because it could shift the electrolyte balance in the body. Adding a modest amount of salt (0.3 to 0.7 g per liter of fluid) may help to offset salt losses through sweat and minimize muscle cramping and hyponatremia (18). It is common practice for endurance athletes to use sodium and electrolyte supplements during training and racing.

General and Specific Eating Guidelines

Topics to be discussed with the athlete during the sports nutrition consultation to improve health and performance include the following:

- Continue to use energy bars, gels, and sport drinks that have worked well in the preparation cycle.
- Eat often. Snacking is beneficial in this cycle to maintain adequate glycogen stores and fluid balance because the athlete will be training 2 to 3 times per day.
- Increase sodium intake.
- Remain in energy balance.

Competition (Race) Cycle

The race season is the peak time of the year and is when endurance athletes put their training program to the test. The physiological goals include improving race performance and ensuring proper and quick recovery. This cycle includes a fairly high level of intensity but a significant reduction in volume. Because of the increased physiological demands of this cycle, an athlete's nutrition leading up to, right before, during, and after a race are extremely important. Many endurance athletes will race 2 to 4 times per month, so the quality and timing of nutrition is of utmost importance.

There is a large range of nutrient needs during this cycle. If an athlete will be racing less than 5 hours, following the lower to mid range of the following recommendations would be ideal. If racing from 5 to 12 hours, use the middle range, and if racing longer than 12 hours, use the higher range. During this cycle, endurance athletes will be competing in many races and some may require the upper end of the following macronutrient and fluid needs to simply maintain adequate energy stores.

Carbohydrate intake should range from 7 to 19 g/kg. Only ultraendurance athletes need to consume more than 13 to 15 g/kg. For most other endurance athletes who are not competing in events for longer than 5 or 6 hours, 12 to 13 g/kg will be adequate, but this is highly dependent on race duration and intensity. Protein intake is the same as the prerace cycle and should range from 1.2 to 2.0 g/kg. Fat and fluid should be increased slightly. Fat intake should range from 0.8 to 2.0 g/kg. The higher range specifically addresses the ultra-endurance athlete who is racing at longer durations and lower intensities. Fluid guidelines should be increased slightly due to increased water loss during competition. In addition, race season normally occurs during the summer months when the heat and humidity index are higher, increasing fluid needs.

Daily Macronutrient and Fluid Needs

The athlete in the race cycle should observe the following guidelines:

- Carbohydrate intake should range from 7 to 19 g/kg.
- Protein intake should range from 1.2 to 2.0 g/kg.
- Fat intake can be increased slightly from 0.8 to 2.0 g/kg.
- Fluid guidelines should be increased slightly to match fluid losses.

Macronutrient and Fluid Timing for Racing

The main difference between the training needs during the prerace and race cycles is the need for more carbohydrate during the race. Longer endurance events and ultraendurance events will require a higher energy intake per hour if the athlete can tolerate it.

- Before the race:
  - Drink 17 to 20 oz of fluid (preferably sport drink) 2 hours before racing (18).
  - Drink 7 to 10 oz of sport drink 10 to 20 minutes before racing (18).
  - Consume 1 to 4 g of carbohydrate per kilogram of body weight 1 to 4 hours prior to the start.
- During the race:
  - Consume 30 to 100 g of carbohydrate (120 to 400 kcal) per hour (19).
  - Drink 7 to 10 oz of fluid every 15 to 20 minutes; include sodium (18).
- After the race:
  - Drink 20 to 24 oz of sport drink for every pound of body weight lost; include sodium (15).
  - Eat 1.0 to 1.2 g of carbohydrate per kilogram of body weight (17) within the first 30 minutes and at 2-hour intervals thereafter. Include 6 to 20 g of protein within the first 30 minutes then a mixed meal 2 hours later. Fat intake should be minimal for 2 to 4 hours.

Carbohydrate Loading

The following guidelines are consistent with the modified carbohydrate loading method, which does not include a severely restricted carbohydrate intake (see Chapter 2 for more on carbohydrate loading). However, although it is standard practice to decrease exercise time and intensity the week before a race, the time presented in the traditional carbohydrate-loading protocol will not correspond with many endurance athletes' training programs the week before a race and therefore is not presented here. If an athlete is competing in a longer-distance race, exercise time will be decreased but possibly not as much as what has been previously described in this protocol by Sherman et al (21). The nutrition professional should be aware of a decrease in exercise duration and intensity during the week prior to an athlete's race but should realize that these variables will differ depending on the length of the event and fitness level of the athlete. Many endurance athletes will take a rest day 2 or 3 days prior to competition, with the day before competition being a light training day at a low intensity.

The following is a carbohydrate-loading regimen to begin 7 days before the race (21):

- Consume 5 g of carbohydrate per kilogram of body weight daily, beginning 4 to 7 days before the race.

- Consume 10 g of carbohydrate per kilogram of body weight daily, beginning 1 to 3 days before the race.

General and Specific Eating Guidelines

For the race cycle, the following guidelines are suggested:

- Increase fluid intake to ensure adequate hydration throughout the day. Use urine color as a marker of hydration status, with straw-colored or clear urine being the goal.
- Use extra sodium if the competition is in a hot and humid environment and/or if the athlete is a heavy, salty sweater.
- Use the energy bars, gels, and sport drinks that have been well-tolerated during previous training cycles.
- Develop a prerace eating routine with specific foods and beverages and specific timing of foods.
- Experiment with a lower-fiber diet to minimize the chances of frequent bowel movements during the race. Use caution so constipation or hemorrhoids do not result.
- Decrease use of hot spices to prevent heartburn or gastrointestinal distress 2 or 3 days before the race (13).
- To promote adequate digestion, absorption, and storage of nutrients, consume the carbohydrate-loading meal 2 nights before the race instead of 1. Given the high anxiety the day before a race, most athletes cannot eat much on race day so smaller, frequent meals consisting of fewer calories is advantageous.
- "Graze" the day before the race on high-carbohydrate, high-sodium, and low-fiber snacks.
- Eat breakfast to minimize endogenous glycogen depletion during sleep.
- Eat only familiar foods, especially on the day of competition.
- Drink fluids that contain sodium. Drinking too much plain water can result in hyponatremia.

Transition/Active Recovery Cycle

When the race season ends, it is time for the athlete to enjoy some much-needed rest from structured training. The volume and intensity of training are both very low because athletes will be recovering from their race seasons and may be working on specific technique weaknesses of their respective sports.

The biggest concern during this cycle is weight gain if the athlete does not decrease the amount of energy eaten to account for the decrease in energy expenditure. Most athletes eat five or more times per day during race season and have a difficult time breaking that habit. This cycle is infamous for weight gain, so the nutrition professional should work closely with the athlete to decrease total energy intake immediately after the race season ends.

Daily Macronutrient and Fluid Needs

For the athlete in the transition/active recovery cycle, intake guidelines are as follows:

- Carbohydrate intake should range from 5 to 6 g/kg.
- Protein should range from 1.2 to 1.4 g/kg.

- Fat should range from 0.8 to 1.0 g/kg.
- Fluid guidelines are the same as outlined in the preparatory cycle.

Macronutrient and Fluid Timing for Training

Because most athletes are not engaged in a highly structured training program during this cycle, it is not necessary to provide specific timing of nutrients. However, the most important nutritional concern during this time is that the athlete still adheres to the fluid guidelines presented in previous cycles, with one exception: there is no need to include the hydration strategies 2 hours before training.

General and Specific Eating Guidelines

The following recommendations should be discussed with the athlete:

- Reintroduce whole foods from all of the food groups to increase variety and balance into the diet.
- Minimize the use of nutrition supplements because extra energy intake is not typically needed during this training cycle.
- Try new foods and new restaurants.
- Decrease energy intake to avoid weight gain.

Table 24.1 summarizes the daily nutrition needs for endurance athletes during all cycles of training.

Nutrition Periodization Concepts That Apply Year-round

Because sports nutrition is a combination of improving health and performance, the following guidelines should be continually emphasized to endurance athletes throughout the year. Many athletes either fall into eating the same foods or eat simply for training year-round, and that is not advantageous from a health perspective.

General and Specific Eating Guidelines

- Focus on variety. Try not to restrict eating to a few food groups.
- Choose foods that have antioxidant properties or activity that contain beta carotene, vitamin C, vitamin E, and zinc.
- Choose more polyunsaturated and monounsaturated fats rather than saturated and *trans* fats.

TABLE 24.1   Daily Nutrition Needs Based on Training Cycles

Cycle	Carbohydrate, g/kg	Protein, g/kg	Fat, g/kg	Urine Color
Preparation	5–12+	1.2–1.7	0.8–1.0	Straw
Prerace	7–13	1.4–2.0	0.8–1.0	Straw
Race	7–19	1.4–2.0	0.8–2.0	Clear/straw
Transition	5–6	1.2–1.4	0.8–1.0	Straw

- If the athlete is taking a multivitamin, encourage them to choose one that has no more than 100% Daily Value (DV) for nutrients. Remember, however, that many sport nutrition products, such as energy bars and recovery beverages, contain high amounts of vitamins and minerals so the athlete may already be consuming higher than usual amounts of these nutrients.
- Encourage the athlete to avoid any dietary supplement that is not completely proven as efficacious and safe. (Research on the efficacy of supplement use in endurance sports is limited.) Taking a dietary supplement without knowing its full effects could have an ergolytic (produces decreases in performance) effect.
- Individualize recommendations. Some athletes will think that a product or specific way of eating is correct because a training partner, friend, or family member follows it.
- Encourage athletes to keep a written 3- to 5-day food diary when eating habits are not going according to plan. (A food diary can also be used to provide constructive feedback when eating habits are good.)

Body Weight and Composition Guidelines

A lower body weight can be beneficial to most endurance athletes because a larger mass can exert a negative impact on performance. However, endurance athletes must be cautious about when they try to reduce body fat during their training year. Energy restriction, resulting in a state of negative energy balance, may impair performance due to: reduction in energy stores, impairment of immune function, alterations in mood, changes in enzyme activity, and structural alterations in the muscle (22).

Because of the negative performance impact weight reduction may have, it is recommended that the athlete only pursue active weight reduction during the transition/active recovery cycle or during the initial part of the preparation cycle. Active weight reduction should not be pursued during the latter half of the preparation cycle or during the competition cycle.

For most endurance athletes who want to reduce weight, a goal of losing 0.5 to 1.0 pound per week is appropriate (23) to minimize losses of muscle glycogen and lean muscle mass, compromised cardiac function, altered ability to maintain body temperature, and muscle cramping due to electrolyte imbalances. Because large changes in scale weight typically reflect changes in fluid balance or glycogen stores, it is recommended that body composition changes be monitored rather than only total body weight.

To attain this weekly goal, a daily negative energy balance of 250 to 500 kcal must be achieved. Because the athlete will be actively trying to lose weight during training cycles that are defined by reduced volume and intensity training, it is recommended that the focus to promote weight loss be primarily from reduced energy intake rather than increased energy expenditure from training. However, nontraining activity, such as walking stairs instead of using an elevator, should be stressed as a way to increase daily energy expenditure.

Altitude

Without previous altitude experience, athletes do not know how their body will react when training and racing at altitudes higher than 8,000 feet (2,400 meters). The following are specific nutrition guidelines to consider when training or racing at altitude:

- Increase fluid intake. With increased breathing due to altitude and physical exertion, the body responds by humidifying the inspired dry air, which produces a greater loss of body fluids. It is recommended that athletes consume 2 to 4 liters of fluid daily when training or competing at altitude.
- Eat small, frequent meals. Anorexia in the initial 72 hours at altitude may decrease energy intake by 40% to 60% compared with that at sea level (24). Small, frequent feedings of beverages and transition foods (mashed potatoes, canned or dried fruit, yogurt, cottage cheese, light soups, instant breakfast drinks) can assist the body in adjusting to unfamiliar altitudes and improve the body's chances of maintaining nutritional balance.

Extreme Environmental Conditions

Physiologically, the most severe stress an athlete can encounter is exercise in the heat (25). Approximately 75% of the energy turnover during exercise is wasted as heat, causing the body's core temperature to increase. In cool environments, most of the body's heat is transferred to the air (26); however, when the environmental temperature exceeds skin temperature, heat is gained and body temperature can increase to dangerous levels.

Hot Environments

Exercising in hot weather puts special emphasis on the importance of adequate hydration and the replacement of glucose during exercise. In hot conditions, water loss through sweat can exceed 2 liters per hour and may peak at approximately 3 liters per hour in an acclimatized athlete (27). Without adequate replacement of lost fluids, circulating blood volume decreases, stroke volume decreases, and heart rate increases, all causing a decrease in circulatory efficiency, which causes fatigue and has been a cause of death in some professional athletes.

When exposed to the heat, athletes often become dehydrated despite the availability of fluids. Regular monitoring of weight should be emphasized, both throughout training cycles and more importantly, during individual training sessions. Pre- and postexercise scale weights are crucial to replenish the increased fluids lost during exercise in the heat. A sport drink supplying 6% to 8% carbohydrate in the form of glucose, sucrose, or maltodextrin has been shown to effectively provide immediate energy and fluid for hydration (28) and should be easily available throughout the training session.

Recommendations made by sports dietitians for endurance athletes training in a hot environment include the following:

- Drink cold fluids and plan for frequent fluid breaks (see Preparation Cycle guidelines).
- Avoid caffeinated, alcoholic, and carbonated beverages.
- Replenish lost electrolytes, specifically sodium, for maximal posttraining session fluid retention.

Cold Environments

The greatest problem with outdoor training in cold environments is hypothermia. During cold training sessions, the body must convert food to heat to maintain the body's core temperature. If heat is being pulled out of the body faster than it can be replaced, the body begins to cool. As the body cools, it automatically begins restricting blood flow to the working muscles, which decreases the quality and quantity of training and racing.

There is no consensus about the most beneficial eating program for athletes training in a cold environment, but there is strong evidence that adequate amounts of carbohydrates are needed (29). The combination of exercise and cold exposure does not act synergistically to enhance the metabolism of fats. Free fatty acid levels may be lower when exercising in a cold compared with a warm environment. It is proposed that cold-induced vasoconstriction of peripheral adipose tissue may account in part for the decrease in lipid mobilization (29).

Recommendations made by sports dietitians for endurance athletes training in a cold environment include the following:

- Drink fluids often. It is still paramount that athletes consume fluid on a regular basis to prevent dehydration because exposure to cold can cause a reduction in the sense of hunger and thirst.
- Weight loss is common during cold-weather training because of the increased energy expenditure. The endurance athlete should follow a normal eating routine as much as possible, including consuming familiar foods, but in extreme conditions freeze-dried or dehydrated foods can be used. Snack on nutrient-dense, high-carbohydrate foods.

Summary

Endurance athletes require well-planned nutrition strategies due to the extreme events in which they are competing. All of the macro- and micronutrient needs, fluid requirements, timing and composition of meals, and overall eating for health can and should be structured so that it fits into the endurance athlete's yearly training program.

Nutrition periodization should be used when working with endurance athletes because these athletes have the most challenges with eating for health and performance throughout the year. Because these athletes follow a highly structured, periodized physical training program, their nutrition must match their training volume and intensity consistently throughout the year. Therefore, the overall goals of nutrition periodization include the following:

- Optimizing athletic performance by matching nutritional intake with the various cycles of the athlete's periodized physical training plan,
- Producing a negative energy balance during appropriate times of the year to produce desirable body weight and body composition changes that will improve health and performance,
- Matching energy intake with energy expenditure to sustain longer and higher quality training sessions,

• Educating the endurance athlete about the importance of cycling their nutrition needs based on their specific training mesocycle or microcycle because of the constant changes in training volume and intensity.

Nutrition periodization is a new concept among endurance athletes, and all athletes will benefit from following some structure with their nutrition. Athletes who have coaches will have a structured and periodized training program in which it will be more realistic for them to adopt many of the nutrition periodization principles. Those without coaches and formal training programs will find some of the guidelines presented more difficult to implement, but they should be encouraged to adopt them at a rate that will be most useful for them in their training.

References

1. Kreider RB. Physiological considerations of ultraendurance performance. *Int J Sport Nutr.* 1991;1:3–27.
2. Acheton J, Gleeson M, Jeukendrup AE. Determination of the exercise intensity that elicits maximal fat oxidation. *Med Sci Sports Exerc.* 2002;34:92–97.
3. Laursen PB, Rhodes EC. Factors effecting performance in an ultraendurance triathlon. *Sports Med.* 2000;31:679–689.
4. Laursen PB, Rhodes EC. Physiological analysis of a high-intensity ultraendurance event. *J Strength Cond Res.* 1999;21:26–38.
5. Dohm GL, Beeker RT, Israel RG, Tapscott EB. Metabolic responses to exercise after fasting. *J Appl Physiol.* 1986;61:1363–1368.
6. Butterfield G. Amino acids and high protein diets. In: Lamb D, Williams M, eds. *Ergogenics: Enhancement of Performance in Exercise and Sport.* Carmel, Ind: Cooper Publishing; 1991: 87–122. Perspectives in Exercise Science and Sports Medicine, vol 4.
7. Burke LM, Cox GR, Culmmings NK, Desbrow B. Guidelines for daily carbohydrate intake: do athletes achieve them? *Sports Med.* 2001;31:267–299.
8. Bompa TO. *Periodization Training for Sports.* Champaign, Ill: Human Kinetics; 1999.
9. Burke LM, Reed RSD. Diet patterns of elite Australian male triathletes. *Phys Sports Med.* 1987;15:140–155.
10. Saris WH, van Erp-Baart MA, Brouns F, Westerterp KR, ten Hoor F. Study on food intake and energy expenditure during extreme sustained exercise: the Tour de France. *Int J Sport Med.* 1989;10(Suppl 1):26–31.
11. Gabel KA, Aldous A, Edgington C. Dietary intake of two elite male cyclists during a 10-day, 2,050-mile ride. *Int J Sport Nutr.* 1995;5:56–61.
12. Garcia-Roves PM, Terrados N, Fernandez SF, Patterson AM. Macronutrient intakes of top-level cyclists during continuous competition—change in feeding pattern. *Int J Sport Med.* 1998; 19:61–67.
13. Eden BD, Abernathy PJ. Nutritional intake during an ultraendurance running race. *Int J Sport Nutr.* 1994;4:166–174.
14. Lindeman AK. Nutrient intake of an ultraendurance cyclist. *Int J Sport Nutr.* 1991;1:79–85.
15. Position of the American Dietetic Association, Dietitians of Canada, and the American College of Sports Medicine: nutrition and athletic performance. *J Am Diet Assoc.* 2000;100:1543–1556.
16. Jeukendrup AE, Jentjens R. Oxidation of carbohydrate feedings during prolonged exercise: current thoughts, guidelines and directions for future research. *Sports Med.* 2000;29:407–424.

17. Burke LM, Kiens B, Ivy JL. Carbohydrates and fat for training and recovery. *J Sports Sci.* 2004;22:15–30.

18. National Athletic Trainers' Association position statement: fluid replacement for athletes. *J Athl Train.* 2000;35:212–214.

19. Tipton KD, Wolfe RR. Protein and amino acids for athletes. *J Sports Sci.* 2004;22:65–79.

20. Murray R, Paul GL, Seifert JG, Eddy DE. Responses to varying rates of carbohydrate ingestion during exercise. *Med Sci Sports Exerc.* 1991;23:713–718.

21. Sherman WM, Costill DL, Fink WJ, Miller JM. The effect of exercise and diet manipulation on muscle glycogen and its subsequent use during performance. *Int J Sport Med.* 1981;2:114–118.

22. Walberg-Rankin J. Changing body weights and composition in athletes. In: Lamb, DR, Murray R, eds. *Exercise, Nutrition and Weight Control.* Carmel, Ind: Cooper Publishing; 1998: 199–236. Perspectives in Exercise Science and Sports Medicine, vol 11.

23. Melby CL, Commerford SR, Hill JO. Exercise, macronutrient balance, and weight control. In: Lamb DR, Murray R, eds. *Exercise, Nutrition and Weight Control.* Carmel, Ind: Cooper Publishing; 1998: 1–60. Perspectives in Exercise Science and Sports Medicine, vol 11.

24. McArdle WD, Katch FI, Katch VL. *Exercise Physiology, Energy, Nutrition, and Human Performance.* Philadelphia, Pa: Lea & Febiger; 1996.

25. Nadel J. Temperature regulation in cold environments. *Sports Sci Exch.* 1988;2:73–76.

26. Williams MH. *Nutrition for Health, Fitness and Sport.* 6th ed. Boston, Mass: WCB McGraw-Hill; 2001.

27. Maughan RJ, Shirreffs SM. Preparing athletes for competition in the heat: developing an effective acclimatization strategy. *Sports Sci Exch.* 1997;10:1–4.

28. American College of Sports Medicine. Position stand on exercise and fluid replacement. *Med Sci Sports Exerc.* 1996;28:i–vii.

29. Doubt TJ. Physiology of exercise in the cold. *Sports Med.* 1991;11:367–381.

Chapter 25

NUTRITION FOR WEIGHT- AND BODY-FOCUSED SPORTS

Satya S. Jonnalagadda, PhD, RD, and Rob Skinner, MS, RD, CSCS

Introduction

Weight- and body-focused sports emphasize strength, conditioning, and body shape to achieve the goals of the sport. Examples include wrestling, martial arts, bodybuilding, gymnastics, and figure skating. Nutrition can have a major impact on the normal growth, development, training, and athletic performance of athletes in these sports (1). To effectively educate athletes and their guardians, parents, coaches, and trainers, nutrition professionals must understand the basis of these sports and the expectations of all the individuals involved. The issues and recommendations discussed in this chapter are based on general recommendations for all athletes but are specific to those participating in weight- and body-focused sports.

Weight- and body-focused sports represent a true integration of mental and physical skills and demand high degrees of strength, flexibility, speed, agility, explosiveness, and concentration (2–10). Athletes participate for various reasons, including self-discipline, physical fitness, artistic and spiritual expression, self-esteem, and self-defense. Plyometric strength, which requires explosive muscular action of the legs, flexible hip and shoulder joints, and agility are required in these sports. In general, weight- and body-focused sports are high-intensity and exhausting sports that demand both physical and mental stamina. Some of these sports have weight categories.

Athletes who participate in weight-restricted and body-focused sports require both aerobic and anaerobic power along with muscular strength, power, and endurance. The specific requirements vary based on the intensity, level, and category of participation. To achieve their desired certification weight, athletes in sports with weight classes may practice dangerous weight-loss techniques. A common belief within the athletic community is that to gain a competitive edge, athletes should compete at a weight category lower than their preseason weight. Consequently, nutritional status and athletic performance may be compromised.

Body Composition

Studies have shown that the body fat content of athletes in weight- and body-focused sports (which is generally less than 20%) is lower than their nonathletic counterparts, perhaps because of the aerobic and anaerobic functions, strength, flexibility, and artistic requirements of the sports, which may predispose these athletes to poor nutritional status (1,5,11–14). The body composition of weight- and body-focused athletes is also influenced by their sports' emphasis on leanness (which many consider a necessary component of performance and appearance), year-round training programs, and the increased demands of growth and development in younger athletes.

Gymnastics, Figure Skating, and Other Aesthetic Sports

Gymnasts and figure skaters are typically shorter-than-average stature. It is unclear whether shorter stature is a result of the sport or inadequate nutrition to support growth, or if shorter individuals are more likely to choose to participate in such sports.

Gymnastics and figure skating are competitive sports that require speed, power, gracefulness, and aesthetic appeal, so particular types of physical shape and strength are necessary. Leanness is particularly valued because the success of these athletes is a function of both technical performance and appearance. For instance, female skaters are smaller, lighter, have less body fat, and are more muscular than inactive females (2,5). Ziegler et al (15,16) assessed male figure skaters with a mean percentage of body fat of 6.5% and females with 17.2% body fat.

Gymnasts have been observed to be significantly shorter and lighter than other athletes and nonathletes (17,18). Beals and Manore (19) reported that female athletes in aesthetic sports, such as gymnastics and cheerleading, weighed significantly less (55 kg) than female athletes in endurance (64 kg) or team/anaerobic (66 kg) sports. Also, the female athletes in aesthetic sports reported a lower desired or ideal body weight (53 kg) than the athletes in endurance (61 kg) or team/anaerobic (62 kg) sports.

Female gymnasts are also characterized by high lean body mass, and a low percentage of body fat compared with nongymnasts. One study reported the mean percentage of body fat of gymnasts age 7 to 9 years was 15% compared with 24% in nongymnasts (18). Lean body composition facilitates performance of artistic maneuvers and is aesthetically appealing. However, it could potentially cause gymnasts to restrict energy intake to improve and enhance appearance and performance.

Low body weight, low percentage of body fat, decreased energy intake, and increased level of physical activity may contribute to the delayed menarche common among female gymnasts and figure skaters. Lower body weights of athletes in aesthetic sports may also contribute to injuries. In one study, significantly more of aesthetic athletes reported sustaining a muscle injury (81%) and/or bone injury (57%) compared with endurance athletes (65% and 29%, respectively) and team/anaerobic athletes (57% and 30%, respectively) (19).

Wrestling

Appropriate body composition is a concern for wrestlers because competitors are matched by body weight and size and athletes must "make weight" prior to each meet. Most wrestlers attempt to maximize amount of lean tissue and minimize body fat and total body weight.

Weight categories range from light (54 kg) to super-heavy (130 kg). Wrestlers typically have very high muscularity, low linearity, and low percentages of body fat: one study reported most wrestlers had less than 10% body fat (range 3% to 13%) (20).

Some wrestlers may try to bulk up to enter a higher weight class and could be stronger in muscle strength per kilogram body weight. During training and competition, however, most wrestlers are very lean. To discourage unhealthful weight-management practices, the National Federation of State High School Associations, the National Collegiate Athletic Association (NCAA), USA Wrestling, and other governing bodies have instituted new rules that include establishment of new weight classes and a new weight-class certification process, and reduced the time between the weigh-in and actual wrestling competition.

Judo and Tae Kwon Do

Similar to wrestlers, judo and tae kwon do athletes can greatly enhance their performance with a lean body composition. Whyte and associates (21) reported that the percentage of body fat for judo athletes was 6.8% for males and 15.7% for females. Likewise, Andreoli et al (22) observed male judo athletes to be lean, with 17.4% body fat (14.1 kg fat mass), 65.3 kg fat-free mass, and 35 kg body cell mass, which represents total mass of metabolically active cells.

Bodybuilding

Bodybuilders have rigorous training schedules, strive for extreme leanness, and have been assessed to have low percentages of body fat, with reports of 7.2% body fat in male bodybuilders and 8.4% body fat in female bodybuilders (23). McInnis and Balady (24) observed bodybuilders to have body mass indexes (BMIs) similar to their sedentary counterparts (31 vs 32); however, the percentage of body fat in the bodybuilders was one third of that in weight-matched sedentary men (8% vs 24%), whereas fat-free mass was 18 kg more for bodybuilders compared with the sedentary subjects (91 kg vs 73 kg).

The bodybuilders engaged, on average, in 1.2 weight-cutting experiences per 6-month bodybuilding season, with a mean weight loss during the competitive season of 6.8 kg and a mean weight gain of 5.9 kg postseason (23,24). Smaller meals (68%) and calorie-counting (56%) were common methods the bodybuilders used to lose weight. Other methods included special diets (18%); fasting (12%); saunas, steam baths, and reduced fluid consumption (9%); and diuretics (6%). To gain body mass, the bodybuilders used amino acids (50%), extra meals (40%), protein powders (32%), liquid supplements (26%), and special diets (11%) (23).

Training

In general, athletes in weight- and body-focused sports need "the balance of a tightrope walker, the endurance of a marathon runner, the aggressiveness of a football player, the agility of a wrestler, the nerves of a golfer, the flexibility of a gymnast, and the grace of a ballet dancer" (25), and they train hard, often beginning when they are very young. These athletes may train year-round for 20 to 36 hours per week, 7 days per week. Their training schedules include aerobic, strength, conditioning, and flexibility exercises along with the sport-specific activities, and many athletes also attend school or work. The time commitment to train and compete presents multiple nutrition-related challenges, especially for younger athletes.

Energy Systems Used in Weight- and Body-Focused Sports

Current understanding of energy balance in weight- and body-focused athletes is limited because few well-designed studies have been published, but it is clear that the energy demands placed on athletes during competition shift and overlap, and that both cardiovascular fitness and upper- and lower-body strength are essential for optimal physical performance. Appropriate training programs should be developed to maximize high power output and increase aerobic power, which delays the onset of metabolic acidosis and fatigue during performance (1,5,26,27).

Muscle cells generate adenosine triphosphate (ATP) through three energy systems: the phosphagen and glycolytic systems, which dominate during strength training, and the oxidative system, which is predominant during aerobic and endurance activity. Power-related elements of weight- and body-focused sports, such as lifting, use the adenosine triphosphate-creatine phosphate (ATP-CP) energy system, whereas speed events mostly use nonoxidative glycogenolysis and glycolysis to power activity.

The physical demands of weight- and body-focused sports are intense, even though the events may not be prolonged or require as much energy expenditure as some other sports. Most weight- and body-focused sports involve short bursts of high-intensity muscular work that rarely last longer than 90 seconds in competition, and these explosive movements place a high demand on the ATP-CP energy system. At the same time, the athlete's aerobic system must allow for quick recovery during brief periods of rest or low- to medium-intensity activity. Energy demands have been hypothesized to be 70% to 90% ATP-CP and 10% to 30% aerobic (28).

Some athletes, such as gymnasts and figure skaters, rely on fast-twitch muscle fibers, which have a limited ability to burn fat in the absence of oxygen. Likewise, judo and tae kwon do are dynamic, physically demanding sports that require complex skills and tactical excellence to succeed. The latter two sports are characterized by short-duration, high-intensity, and intermittent exercises that last less than 10 minutes per match (29). During matches, plasma triglycerides, free fatty acids, glycerol, lactate, ammonia, urea, hypoxanthine, and xanthine concentrations increase, which suggests the roles that carbohydrate, protein, and fat play in meeting the energy needs of athletes during matches (29). Judo and tae kwon do athletes must maintain optimal liver and muscle glycogen and muscle creatine stores to fuel their activity. Energy balance is crucial for athletic performance because prolonged energy deficits have been shown to result in decreases in strength, power, and jump height (5,24,26,30,31).

Macronutrient Recommendations

Energy

Energy and other macronutrient needs vary depending on the sport, the degree of competitiveness, and the athlete's goals. For example, minimal energy intake of high school wrestlers could range from 1,700 to 2,500 kcal/day, and rigorous training may increase the requirement up to an additional 1,000 kcal/day (30). Male bodybuilders may need more than 6,000 kcal/day (32).

In all sports, adequate energy intake is required not only to meet the demands of the activity but also to promote optimal development. An individual athlete's recommended energy intake is influenced by factors such as age, gender, body size and composition, resting energy expenditure, physical activity level, and physiological status. The energy expended during training and competition must be included when calculating recommended total energy intake (5). Body weight, body composition, and dietary intake should be monitored to determine energy balance. Weight-loss practices should be closely monitored, and athletes should be cautioned to lose weight gradually. For individuals seeking to gain weight, energy intakes should start at the low end of the estimated energy intake requirements and gradually increase so that weight gain is slow and maximizes muscle gain while minimizing fat gain (1,5).

Dietary assessment surveys of weight- and body-focused athletes indicate that most consume less than the recommended amount of energy for their age and activity level (5,16,26,30,33,34). Energy deficits as much as 1,500 kcal/day have been found among athletes in weight- and body-focused sports (5). In a study by Fogelholm et al (35), gymnasts and figure skaters had a mean body fat of 17.5% and a mean BMI of 19.6, and their energy intake of 1,682 kcal was deficient relative to their adjusted resting energy expenditure of 1,336 kcal and total energy expenditure of 2,445 kcal. In another study, energy intake of elite male figure skaters and gymnasts was approximately 39 kcal per kilogram body weight (approximately 2,200 kcal/day), whereas energy intake of female figure skaters was approximately 38 kcal per kilogram body weight (approximately 1,600 kcal/day) (36); these levels are also less than the recommended intakes for active males and females. Cupisti et al (37) found that rhythmic gymnasts consumed 28.5 kcal per kilogram body weight per day, with 53% of energy from carbohydrate, 31% from fat, and 15% from protein. In Ziegler and associates' studies of figure skaters (15,16), mean energy intakes were 1,623 kcal for females and 2,433 kcal for males, levels less than the recommended intakes of 2,200 to 2,900 kcal/day for the general population (38).

Energy restriction is one of several techniques used by weight- and body-focused athletes to achieve weight control and maintain a particular body shape. However, at the minimum, these athletes should meet the dietary intake recommendations for the general population: ie, total energy intake of more than 55% carbohydrate, 20% to 35% fat, and 15% to 20% protein. Excessive energy restriction has a negative effect on training and performance, even though athletes may feel lighter when their energy intake is limited. The numerous training and health consequences of excessive energy restriction include nutrient deficiencies, dehydration, fatigue due to muscle and liver glycogen depletion, poor concentration, lack of motivation, delayed puberty, short stature, a decrease in resting energy expenditure, menstrual irregularities, poor bone health, increased incidence of injuries, and increased risk for developing eating disorders (5). (For more information about eating disorders, see the discussion of this topic later in this chapter, as well as Chapter 17.)

Athletes may lose or gain weight because they do not recognize their changing energy needs. Fluctuations in body weight can hinder performance (eg, a weight gain can affect balance, jump, and spin height, whereas a weight loss can result in decreased muscle strength and power). Quality training time, which otherwise could be spent in learning new skills and techniques, may be lost. It is therefore important that athletes maintain energy balance both during the competitive season and during off-season training.

With the time demands of school, practice, optional workouts, and work, many athletes find it difficult to maintain or gain weight without the use of liquid supplements. This can also be true for athletes who are vegetarians and have diets containing less than 20% of energy as fat. Appropriate strategies need to be developed to meet the energy needs of these athletes.

Carbohydrate

Carbohydrate is the primary fuel for athletes in weight- and body-focused sports, which are typically of short duration. Athletes training on successive days must consume adequate carbohydrates as well as energy to minimize the threat of chronic fatigue associated with muscle glycogen depletion (1,39–43). Because body storage of carbohydrate is limited, frequent replacement is recommended. Assuming the athlete consumes adequate energy, a daily intake of 5 to 8 g carbohydrate per kilogram body weight is recommended to ensure adequate glycogen synthesis to replenish muscle and liver glycogen stores (39–43). However, athletes who consume more than the recommended amount of carbohydrate may not consume adequate protein and fat, which are also essential dietary components.

A review of the literature shows that athletes undergoing weight loss (eg, wrestlers) can maintain high-intensity power if carbohydrate intake is 65% or more, possibly because they minimize the loss of muscle glycogen (39–43). One study (26) found that total power and average power produced on the Wingate test (a measure of anaerobic exercise performance) was impaired by 7 days of negative energy balance in male wrestlers consuming a 55% carbohydrate diet; however, no adverse effects occurred in those consuming 70% of energy as carbohydrate. If athletes consume less energy than they expend, it is important to ensure that they incorporate high-carbohydrate foods, which should contribute at least 65% of their total daily energy intake (no less than 5g/kg body weight) (39–43).

Protein

Maintaining the appropriate balance between energy and protein intake is critical for the growth, development, and athletic performance of young athletes (1,44,45). Weight- and body-focused sports require adequate muscle strength and power. Adequate protein and balanced essential amino acid intake are important to stimulate muscle protein synthesis and promote performance. Daily protein intakes of 1.2 to 1.7 g per kilogram body weight have been recommended for athletes in these sports, with intakes more than 2 g/kg/day (ie, 18% of energy intake) showing no additional benefits (44,45).

To determine individual protein requirements, carbohydrate and energy intake must be considered. When adequate calories are consumed to support energy needs, protein can be used for muscle growth and enhancement and the body does not need to rely on it as a substantial source of energy. Sufficient carbohydrate intake promotes muscle protein synthesis. If energy intake is too low, protein will be used for fuel and muscle will be catabolized. In these circumstances, athletes may need to consume 1.5 to 1.7 g protein per kilogram body weight.

Fat

Fat is needed to provide essential fatty acids, to insulate and protect organs, to maintain cell membrane integrity, to facilitate absorption and transport of fat-soluble vitamins, and to synthesize steroid hormones such as estrogen and testosterone (1). Fat also enhances satiety and adds flavor to foods (1). The latter should not be overlooked when educating athletes because it promotes normal food consumption.

Because weight- and body-focused sports require a high strength-to-weight ratio, it is important for athletes in these sports to keep their non-force-producing weight low. Given the anaerobic nature of these sports, fat is not used as a primary fuel source (39,40). Diets containing 20% to 35% of energy as fat are recommended to meet the energy and nutritional needs of individuals and for the prevention of chronic diseases (38). Very low-fat diets (< 10% of energy from fat) and avoidance of animal foods may negatively affect overall health and performance because some fat is needed for the various normal physiological functions (1,39,40).

Micronutrient Recommendations

Energy intake by athletes in weight- and body-focused sports may be insufficient to meet the dietary recommendations for most micronutrients (1,3–5,16,32,34). Although the specific micronutrient needs of these athletes are sparsely reported in the literature, it is reasonable to assume that, at the minimum, they are similar to the needs of the general population.

Compared with the recommended dietary intakes for the general population, athletes in weight- and body-focused sports, especially female athletes, seem to have inadequate intakes of most vitamins and minerals, perhaps because they consume smaller amounts of dairy products, meat (especially red meat), and green leafy vegetables, and eat many low-fat, low-calorie foods (16,18). Weight- and body-focused athletes who restrict energy and fluids may have low intakes of thiamin, vitamin B-6, iron, calcium, zinc, magnesium, sodium, potassium, and chloride. Athletes who avoid animal protein and follow low-calorie or strict vegetarian diets should be monitored for adequate iron, calcium, zinc, and vitamin B-12. Athletes should be encouraged to increase consumption of nutrient-dense foods from grains, vegetables, fruits, dairy products, and meat and meat-alternatives. A multivitamin with minerals is recommended for athletes who consume less than 1,500 kcal per day to ensure overall nutrient adequacy (46,47).

Iron and calcium need special attention. Adequate calcium intake is essential to support proper bone growth and development in adolescent athletes. Although genetics is the greatest factor in the attainment of peak bone mass, nutrition and physical activity also play important roles. Adequate dietary calcium is essential for athletes because inadequate calcium intake increases the risk of stress fractures, reduces bone density, and contributes to the risk for osteoporosis later in life (48,49). Peak bone density is reached during middle to late adolescence, or just at the age when some of these athletes, such as gymnasts and figure skaters, are reaching their peak competitive years. Dietary intakes of these nutrients are typically low in female athletes, and supplements may be recommended (1,15,34).

Many weight- or body-focused athletes do not consume milk or other dairy products because they have lactose intolerance, other self-perceived intolerances, or a belief that all dairy foods are high in fat. It is therefore important to encourage the consumption of foods with high-quality calcium, such as low-fat dairy products or calcium-fortified cereal and grain products, calcium-fortified orange juice, and green leafy vegetables. In a review of dietary intake studies of gymnasts, Nickols-Richardson (18) observed that the diets of gymnasts to be deficient in energy, calcium, and iron, with these athletes having significantly lower intakes than sedentary control subjects or other athletes. Similar deficiencies were observed among figure skaters (15,16).

Adolescent athletes are at increased risk for iron deficiency due to their rapid growth and increased energy requirements (1). The mean intake of iron for female athletes is 6 to 14 mg per day (15,34), which is less than the Recommended Dietary Allowances (RDA) of 15 to 18 mg per day (46). Depletion of iron stores, as indicated by low serum ferritin levels, is a precursor to iron-deficiency anemia. Many athletes in weight- and body-focused sports forego red meat because it is considered high in fat; thus, they need education about incorporating high-quality iron sources in their diet.

Fluid Requirements

Fluid Balance and the Risks of Dehydration

Fluid balance is important for temperature regulation, maintenance of blood volume, muscular endurance, and proper cardiovascular function. Maintaining proper hydration is critical for both optimal athletic performance (50,51) and adequate cognitive performance (52–55; see also Chapter 6). Dehydration reduces body weight, total body water, alters the distribution of body water in the cellular compartments, reduces the hydration of fat-free mass, and alters the density of fat-mass. When dehydrated, athletes experience fatigue, lack of concentration, and a high risk of injury. In trained male power lifters, a small amount of dehydration (1.5%) decreased muscular power by as much as 5% (56). Even with a 2-hour rest and consumption of fluids to regain the 1.5% loss, bench press maximums were still observed to be less than in well-hydrated control subjects.

Athletes in weight- and body-focused sports do not have special fluid needs other than the general fluid guidelines for all athletes, but the age and size of the athlete must be considered when individualizing recommendations. Athletes must be carefully monitored to avoid severe dehydration, which can increase the risk for electrolyte imbalance or kidney failure, or cause death. See Box 25.1 for a list of essential hydration-related responsibilities for the sports dietitian.

Box 25.1   Tips to Ensure Proper Hydration of Athletes

- Educate the athletic team about the consequences of severe dehydration and rapid rehydration.
- Discourage unsafe dehydration techniques.
- Establish fluid consumption schedule for training and competition.
- Communicate with the sports medicine team if hydration problems exist in athletes.

Aesthetic Sports

Athletes in some weight- and body-focused sports, such as gymnasts and figure skaters, may have a difficult time getting access to fluids during training and competition, whereas other athletes may intentionally restrict fluid intake to maintain lower body weights. Coaches are not always in the habit of encouraging athletes to stop for water breaks because this might disrupt practice. In gymnastics and sports with similar competition routines and schedules, the change of rotations and waiting in line for a turn are good times for water breaks. However, athletes in these sports do not like to train with a full bladder or take frequent trips to the bathroom.

Sports with Weight Classes

Many athletes who compete in sports that require specific weight classes believe that competing at a class lower than their off-season weight improves their chances of winning (52–55) by allowing them to gain strength and leverage over opponents. Although dehydration to "make weight" is banned by many sports governing bodies, athletes still report using various dehydration techniques to compete at lower weight classes. For example, in their quest for rapid weight loss to achieve a specific weight class, some wrestlers have used drastic weight-loss methods, including dehydration through excessive sweating, fluid restriction, rubber suits, or sauna use. One study reported that 71% of high school wrestlers used some form of voluntary dehydration such as fasting, spitting, or vomiting, to achieve weight loss, on average, 4 days before competition weigh-in (53).

This type of weight loss is temporary—Clark and Oppliger (57) observed that 25% of dehydrated wrestlers typically regained more than 1.4 kg, usually within days, with a maximum weight gain of more than 8 kg—and can adversely affect performance. Impaired grip strength has been observed in dehydrated high school and college athletes, which could potentially affect their wrestling ability (58).

These dehydration methods can also be extremely dangerous: in 1997, three NCAA collegiate wrestlers died as a result of the dehydration techniques that they used to reduce their body weights (such as restricting fluid and food intake and maximizing sweat losses by wearing vapor-impermeable suits under cotton warm-up suits and exercising vigorously in hot environments) (55,59). Among the three wrestlers, the difference between their preseason weights and their goal competition weights was 30 lb (15% of their total body weight).

With the implementation of minimum-weight programs, some of the rapid weight-loss practices have decreased (60). To encourage this trend, coaches and athletes should be educated to identify appropriate competition weights that are closer to the athletes' body weights and be trained in proper weight-management strategies.

Fluid Sources

Research indicates proper rehydration can occur with many types of fluid (50,51,61). Water, sport drinks, fruit juice, and other fluids should be recommended before, during, and after competition. In addition to water intake, athletes can benefit from the use of sport drinks with added carbohydrate and electrolytes, especially when food intake has been restricted, after prolonged training and exercise, and after increased sweating (50,51,61).

Sport drinks that contain 6% to 8% carbohydrate and some electrolytes along with the fluid seem to work best for hydration and rehydration purposes (50,51,61). Some athletes are concerned with the energy content of sport drinks and must be reassured that the energy content is low while the benefits are high. It should be emphasized to athletes concerned about weight that the calories from sport drinks are typically used for energy during activity rather than stored as body fat.

Because it is important to replace the electrolytes and body fluids lost during weight loss, consumption of sport drinks is especially important for athletes who practice rapid weight-loss techniques to make weight for the competition. In these situations, athletes need to consume the sport beverage before competition and during short breaks in between matches to avoid the adverse consequences of dehydration.

Beverages containing caffeine and alcohol should be avoided because of their diuretic properties (50,51,61). In a recent review of the literature, Armstrong (62) observed that although caffeine consumption (100 to 160 mg) may stimulate a mild diuresis, there is no evidence of a fluid-electrolyte imbalance that is detrimental to health. Athletes are not likely to experience any detrimental fluid-electrolyte imbalances with moderate consumption of caffeinated beverages, but they should be educated about potential problems with high (> 100 mg caffeine/day) intakes.

Foods consumed after training or the weigh-in provide fluid as well as sodium and help contribute to rehydration. Given the nature of these weight- and body-focused sports, the overall low fluid intake associated with them, athletes need to be educated about the importance of proper hydration and water breaks. The sports nutritionist can serve as a resource to reduce health risks associated with restricting food and fluid intake to make weight.

Making Weight

Weight-loss techniques used by athletes in weight-class sports to "make weight" before the weigh-in include fasting, vomiting, binging, diuretics, laxatives, saunas, rubber suits, and steam rooms, and strict avoidance of food and fluids before competition. All of these methods should be discouraged (9,32,55,63,64).

Some athletes think that they can weigh in for a match and then immediately drink water to rehydrate. However, even when adequate amounts of fluids are consumed, a minimum of 6 hours is required to achieve normal hydration levels. During the short time between certification and competition (typically about 4 hours), the consequences of both inadequate hydration and rapid rehydration can have serious effects on an athlete's health. The risks of rapid rehydration include inappropriate fluid shifts, electrolyte imbalance, and decreased performance (50,51,61).

To control the various practices of "making-weight" that lead to dehydration and unhealthful weight loss, minimum weight programs have been implemented to regulate weight practices of athletes in sports with weigh-ins. The NCAA has added a 7-lb weight allowance to each weight class and stipulated that all weigh-ins must be held no more than 2 hours before the start of the competition (8). Additionally, the NCAA requires that body fat of collegiate wrestlers be assessed at the beginning of the season to determine a minimum competitive weight for each athlete (8). The NCAA also prohibits the use of laxatives, emetics, diuretics, excessive fluid and food restriction, self-induced vomiting, hot rooms with temperatures more than 79°F, hot boxes, saunas, steam rooms, vapor-impermeable suits, and artificial rehydration techniques.

Like the NCAA, the National Federation of State High School Associations mandated that all states institute weight-management rules by 2004, with high school wrestlers adopting the NCAA rules. These stringent measures were developed in light of the three deaths of collegiate wrestlers in 1997, but they also respond to weight-cutting patterns observed among high school wrestlers. A study published in 1993 (65) reported that wrestlers typically lost approximately 3.3 kg at the start of the season to make their initial weight class and regained 5 to 6 kg postseason. Additionally, weight lost weekly prior to competition and regained after competition averaged 1.6 kg to 1.9 kg. Among high school wrestlers, 13% to 38% restricted food and fluid three times/week or more, whereas 3% to 5% used saunas and 9% to 20% used rubber or plastic sweat suits to lose weight. Bulimic behaviors were present in 9% of high school wrestlers.

Steen and Brownell (66) observed weight-cutting behaviors to be more extreme among collegiate wrestlers than among high school wrestlers. The largest amount of weight lost by collegiate wrestlers was 7.2 kg compared with 5.2 kg by high school wrestlers, and the use of saunas and rubber and plastic suits was more prevalent among collegiate wrestlers.

Scott et al (60) observed that the NCAA's rule changes were effective in reducing rapid weight gain to 0.66 kg during the 1999 NCAA championships. To achieve weight loss, athletes used running, saunas, exercising in vapor-impermeable suits, swimming, cycling, and laxatives, even though some of these practices were banned by the governing bodies.

In another study of weight-management behaviors of collegiate wrestlers after the implementation of the NCAA weight-control rules, Oppliger et al (67) reported that during the season wrestlers lost 5.3 kg (6.9% of body weight), with a weekly mean weight loss of 2.9 kg (4.3% of body weight). Postseason, wrestlers regained 5.5 kg (8.6% of body weight). Gradual dieting (79%) and increased exercise (75%) were the primary weight-loss methods. However, fasting (55%), saunas (28%), and rubber and plastic suits (27%) were used for weight loss at least once per month. Weight-management behaviors were observed to be more extreme among freshman, lighter weight classes, and Division II wrestlers. Forty percent of the collegiate wrestlers in this study stated that they were influenced by the new NCAA rules and modified their weight-loss practices. However, athletes, trainers, and coaches may need additional education regarding safe weight-loss techniques.

Rapid weight loss can adversely affect various physiological functions, such as fluid and electrolyte balance, thermal regulation, cardiovascular function, and body composition, strength, and power. Dehydration reduces the individual's ability to sustain exercise for longer than 1 to 2 minutes, which means that a dehydrated athlete does not have the endurance to work as hard in repeated bouts during competition. Glycogen stores may also be depleted by exercise-induced dehydration and by food and fluid restriction. Dehydration can produce the loss of sodium, potassium, chloride, and magnesium, which negatively affects muscle function.

Routine urinalysis should be conducted to monitor athletes, especially to identify potentially dangerous rapid weight-loss behaviors. The color of urine indicates how concentrated the urine is. Deep-yellow urine is concentrated urine, a sign of dehydration.

For safe weight loss (no more than 3 lb per week), an individual should minimize water loss via voluntary dehydration and maximize body-fat loss through a sensible, balanced meal plan. Strategies to reduce the risk of pathogenic eating behaviors include de-emphasizing body weight, eliminating group weigh-ins, treating each athlete individually, developing appropriate weight loss goals, and facilitating healthy weight management. To ensure safe weight-control practices, a health care professional should identify an appropriate competition weight and specify rates and limits of allowable weight loss for each wrestler. Coaches and athletes should be trained in proper weight-control strategies (55,59). See Box 25.2 for additional tips for sports dietitians working with athletes in weight-restricted sports.

Dietary Supplements and Ergogenic Aids

Although a nutrient-dense diet plays an important role in optimal performance, many athletes are interested in using ergogenic aids, which are reputed to improve strength, endurance, and energy, as well as result in quick weight loss (68). Some popular supplements are reviewed here. Additional information can be found in Chapter 7.

Creatine

Creatine supplementation has become popular among athletes trying to increase muscle mass (68–70). Limited research suggests that at least part of the increase in body mass associated with creatine supplementation may be due to water retention with a decrease in urinary volume (71). Other research indicates that creatine supplementation increased peak power but did not significantly change percentage body fat or fat-free mass as measured by hydrostatic weighing (71). Once diet and training goals are achieved, creatine supplementation may enhance muscle growth and strength. However, one study showed that during rapid weight loss, creatine might adversely affect muscle endurance during short-duration, high-intensity intermittent exercise (71). These observations are of interest to athletes such as wrestlers, who are often in a dehydrated state, because creatine supplementation requires proper hydration to prevent serious health risks.

Box 25.2   Tips for Making Weight Safely

When working with an athletic team where weight issues are a concern, consider the following suggestions:

- Establish safe weight-loss goals and techniques before the season begins.
- Emphasize healthful and appropriate fat loss vs fluid and muscle loss.
- Discuss the physiology of starvation and dehydration and their effect on athletic performance.
- Discuss the pros and cons of popular ergogenic aids compared with a balanced diet.
- Teach athletes, coaches, trainers, guardians, and parents to recognize disordered eating patterns.
- Communicate with the athlete's team if an individual's weight class seems inappropriate.

Ephedra and Other Herbal Diet Aids

Herbal "diet" teas are commonly used as diuretics, and, in extreme cases, enemas are used in last-minute attempts to make weight. Certain herbal combinations or "stacks," such as ma huang (ephedra), white willow bark (salicylic acid), and kola nut (caffeine), claim to increase metabolic rate and weight loss, but these supplements can be dangerous (72). Ephedra, the herbal form of ephedrine, acts like an amphetamine; the Food and Drug Administration has banned supplements with ephedra. A federal judge struck down the ban for doses of 10 mg or less. Adverse effects of ephedrine include tremors, nervousness, increased heart rate and elevated blood pressure, myocardial infarction, stroke, seizures, psychosis, and death (73). Similar adverse effects are noted with excessive intakes of other herbal diet aids.

Chromium

Chromium functions in carbohydrate, lipid, and protein metabolism; regulates glucose homeostasis; enhances insulin activity, which promotes protein synthesis; and decreases muscle protein breakdown. Athletes who are trying to manipulate their body composition and body weight may avoid many foods that are high in chromium, such as red meat, because these foods are also high in saturated fat. To improve body composition, athletes may use chromium picolinate supplements, but studies have not demonstrated any substantial benefits for losing body fat or gaining muscle (74). Walker et al (74) assessed the effectiveness of 14-week chromium picolinate supplementation (200 µg/day), along with a typical resistance training and conditioning program, on the body composition and neuromuscular performance. No significant changes were observed in body composition or performance variables beyond the changes seen with training alone. Clancy et al (75) and Hallmark et al (76) observed similar results.

Whey Protein and Amino Acid Supplements

Whey protein and amino acid supplements are popular among athletes in the weight- and body-focused sports who want to increase muscle mass. For example, Andersen et al reported that during competition season 58% of bodybuilders took amino acid supplements and 38% used protein powders (23). However, these supplements have not been shown to have any significant effect on lean mass or strength (68).

Individual amino acid supplements, such as branched-chain amino acids, glutamine, and arginine, have not been shown to be effective in stimulating muscle protein synthesis (68). Beta-hydroxy beta-methylbutyrate (HMB), a metabolite of leucine, has been promoted to reduce muscle proteolysis and improve cell integrity (68). However, in trained elite athletes, HMB did not enhance lean body mass, strength, or anaerobic capacity. Limited research suggests HMB has some effect on reducing accumulation of lactic acid and creatine kinase during endurance exercise (68).

Prohormones

Another popular group of supplements, especially in the weight-focused sports, are prohormones, substances that are precursors of testosterone and nandrolone (68,73). These substances include dehydroepiandrosterone (DHEA) and the now-banned androstenedione, androstenediol, and 19-norandrostenedione, which are taken to increase muscle size and strength. However, prohormones have not been observed to raise blood testosterone concentrations, nor have they had any effect on muscle size or strength, and they may pose significant health risks (68).

In recognition of the well-established adverse effects of anabolic steroids, the majority of sports' governing bodies have banned the use of these substances. However, some athletes (up to 29%) in weight- and body-focused sports use anabolic androgenic steroids (77,78). Bodybuilders use anabolic steroids not only to increase lean body mass but also to burn excess body fat (77,79). Evans and Lynch (80) reported that 54% of male and 10% of female bodybuilders used steroids on a regular basis, and such use was perceived as an important factor for winning competitions and providing significant strength. In a study by Cole et al (78), bodybuilders using anabolic steroids were observed to be striving toward an exaggerated mesomorphic physique, while scoring high on the eating disorder inventory. In this study, bodybuilders currently using anabolic steroids wanted to gain about 5.5 kg, despite having the highest current weight, and 85% deliberately increased food intake.

A substantial proportion of bodybuilders (competitive and noncompetitive) have reportedly engaged in pharmacologic manipulation of their physical state. In a study by Evans and Lynch, approximately 10% of bodybuilders reported using insulin to increase body mass and increase muscle size, with some individuals using 10 IU of regular insulin daily during the competitive season (80).

Antioxidants

Because intensive strength-training exercise increases the production of free radicals, supplementation of antioxidants, particularly vitamins E and C, may play a role in reducing muscle fatigue (81). There is limited evidence regarding the benefits of antioxidant nutrients and athletic performance, but there is a growing body of evidence supporting the use of these supplements to prevent exercise-induced oxidative damage to tissues (81).

Supplements for Joint Health

Supplements that promote joint health have recently gained in popularity (68). The main aim of these supplements is to promote joint health by reducing inflammation and the wear and tear caused by overuse. Glucosamine (see Chapter 7), S-Adenosyl methionine, type 2 collagen, and hyaluronic acid are some of the supplement products in this category, which have been shown to have some benefits in individuals with osteoarthritis or joint pain (68).

Meal-Planning Recommendations for Precompetition and Competition

Adequate dietary intake should be promoted as an integral component of athletic training (41), and athletes should be encouraged to experiment with various foods before, during, and after training sessions to determine foods that are satisfying, well-tolerated, and likely to be good choices as competition-day foods. When athletes travel to competitions, access to familiar foods may be limited. To avoid an upset stomach from precompetition jitters, foods and fluids should be familiar to the athlete. Indigestion and impaired performance may be caused by untested foods or beverages. Therefore, planning is the key to success. The sports dietitian can present a sample meal schedule for the day of competition to the coaches and athletes. It should emphasize nutrition conditioning—ie, the same meals and snacks for training and competition. Furthermore, because appetite and hunger are not reliable indicators of nutritional needs, athletes need to be disciplined to eat on a set schedule to maximize their intake and athletic performance. Athletes should be provided with suggestions for high-carbohydrate, low-fat choices when eating out, and they should be taught that carbohydrates are the preferred fuel to supply muscle and liver glycogen, prepare the brain for split-second decisions, and sustain mental concentration.

In weight-class sports, food and fluids are often severely restricted in the days leading up to the event (5,82). On the day of the competition, after the early-morning weigh-in, athletes usually try to consume enough fluids and foods to satisfy their appetite. They are often hungry and thirsty because of the restrictions to make weight, and they may need to be reminded to eat foods high in carbohydrate and low in protein and fat. For some athletes, small amounts of lean protein such as turkey, ham, tuna, or low-fat cheese along with carbohydrate can help settle their stomach and stave off hunger. Popular precompetition carbohydrates are bread, bagels, cold cereal, oatmeal, grits, bananas, crackers, rice cakes, rice, boiled potatoes, pasta, low-fat energy bars, oatmeal cookies, fruits, fruit juices, and sport drinks. If the athlete is nervous and unable to eat solid food before the event, a chilled liquid meal-replacement beverage should be consumed to provide energy and prevent low blood glucose responses.

On the day of competition, the athlete should consume an easily digested, low-residue meal. Liquid carbohydrate meals, whether commercially prepared or homemade, may be suitable. The goal of this meal is to prevent hunger, stabilize blood glucose levels, and provide adequate fluids. Because of the relatively short duration of competitions in weight- and body-focused sports, it is likely that energy requirements the day of competition are not as great as during intense training days, and there are no unique fluid or fuel requirements during the competition in most of these sports. However, between events in a competition, athletes should consume water or sport drink and easily digestible carbohydrate foods such as bagels, English muffins, cereals, crackers, graham crackers, pretzels, fruit (as tolerated), or fat-free yogurt. After the event, sport drinks, fruit juices, and other carbohydrate-containing fluids are important for replenishing muscle and liver glycogen.

To optimize glycogen stores, athletes should be encouraged to eat breakfast, "the most important meal of the day." Athletes may skip breakfast because of time constraints or because they want to limit energy intake, but omitting breakfast hinders glycogen replenishment, especially after an overnight fast. Quick, easy-to-eat breakfasts are available to help rebuild the breakfast routine as well as replenish glycogen stores.

If access to carbohydrate meals during a competition is limited, athletes should ingest 200 to 300 g of carbohydrate 3 to 4 hours before competition. Athletes are typically not hungry after practice and may delay or skip a meal. However, replenishing glycogen stores after practice is critical. Carbohydrate intake (1 to 2 g per kilogram body weight) in the first 2 hours after exercise facilitates rapid glycogen synthesis; therefore, athletes should be encouraged to consume high-carbohydrate foods as soon as possible after training or competing. Frequent small snacks (every 15 to 60 minutes) may be an appropriate strategy (40).

Snack breaks are important for athletes during training and competition. Including a midpractice snack enables the athlete to be more productive and effective throughout training. Snack breaks can be taken between sets or rotations and do not need to take up valuable training and competition time. Snacks should consist of small portions of carbohydrate-rich foods or sport drinks, be convenient and safe to store in a gym bag, and require only moments to eat. Sport drinks, carbohydrate gels, and energy bars are products that can contribute to adequate energy and macronutrient intake before, during, and after training and competition.

Disordered Eating and Eating Disorders

Competitive athletes in some weight- and body-focused sports may be at increased risk of developing disordered eating practices because of the nature and expectations of these sports, in which the perceived ideal body type is thin and lean and aesthetics is a component of success. Athletes compare their body types, start cutting back on the quantity of food they consume, and begin to focus on how much they weigh. Weight becomes a measure of both self-worth and self-esteem, and this measure may last for years after participation in the sport has ended.

Disordered eating patterns not only influence athletes' nutrient intake but also lead to long-term negative physical and psychological health consequences. When coupled with a preoccupation with weight loss, continued restriction of energy, carbohydrate, protein, and fat may place athletes at increased risk for physiological disturbances (83,84). Additionally, weight cycling, which is a common outcome of poor eating patterns, can result in altered aerobic capacity and decreased performance.

Risk Factors

Factors that put athletes at risk of disordered eating and eating disorders include gender (females are more likely than males to develop disordered eating), periadolescent age (ages 9 to 12 years), certain psychological traits, self-esteem issues, pressure from parents, dieting or restrained eating, and lack of knowledge of nutrition and healthful eating practices.

Gender
Disordered eating in female athletes has been reported to range from 15% to 62% (19,31,85,86), and there have been several documented cases of elite female athletes with anorexia nervosa or bulimia nervosa. Beals and Manore (19) reported that 2% to 3% of collegiate female athletes had a clinical diagnosis of anorexia and/or bulimia nervosa, whereas 15% to 30% demonstrated attitudes and behaviors consistent with disordered eating.

Elevated scores on the Eating Attitude Test (EAT) have been associated with energy restriction and a greater probability of an eating disorder (31,85). In one study (19), female athletes in aesthetic sports scored higher on EAT than female endurance athletes and female team/anaerobic athletes, suggesting a higher tendency for eating disorders. In the same study, significantly more athletes in aesthetic sports than in endurance or team/anaerobic sports reported using very-low-calorie diets (< 1,000 kcal/day), fasting, vomiting, and laxatives for weight loss. Additionally, aesthetic athletes were significantly older (13.8

years) than endurance (12.9 years) and team/anaerobic athletes (13 years) when they reached menarche. More athletes in aesthetic sports (4.4%) reported not having a menstrual cycle in the past year compared with athletes in endurance (0.5%) and team/anaerobic (0%) sports (19). These patterns can result in the female athlete triad—disordered eating accompanied by body image distortions (body dysmorphia), amenorrhea, and osteoporosis—which can have a detrimental effect on health and athletic performance (36).

It is well-documented that many female athletes experience amenorrhea and other menstrual dysfunctions (5,87), which may be consequences of low energy intake. The prevalence of menstrual irregularities in athletes is estimated to range from 1% to 44%, compared with 1.8% to 5% in the general population (5,87). Delayed onset of menarche (mean age 13.2 years) has been observed among most female athletes, which is older than that observed among the general population (mean age of menarche 12.43 years) (88). Delayed onset, which can affect the individual's bone mineral density, could be a result of increased physical training or an athlete's low percentage of body fat. Amenorrhea may also be associated with alterations in regional fat distribution and the depletion of fat in the femoral area (around hips, thighs, and buttocks) (87).

Disordered eating and body dysmorphia have also been observed in male athletes in weight- and body-focused sports (5). For example, during the precompetition and competition seasons, male wrestlers in one study consumed half of the recommended energy intake, which led to reductions in prealbumin levels, an indicator of starvation (5). Furthermore, low testosterone levels were noted in these wrestlers, which was associated with a 13% decrease in arm and leg strength and power.

Males typically seem to be concerned about body weight and shape whereas females are often concerned about body weight. Many male athletes in weight- and body-focused sports report body dissatisfaction, known as *Adonis complex* (78). Male body dissatisfaction may be associated with feelings of being underweight rather than overweight, referred to as *reverse anorexia* (an individual's perception that he or she is too small or insufficiently muscular), which has been reported to be most prevalent among bodybuilders (78).

Age

Many young athletes may favor dieting, often beginning before the onset of puberty, as a way to achieve the body type considered most successful in their specific sport (31,36,85,86). Younger athletes may also copy the poor dietary practices of the older and successful athletes in their sport. Dieting, coupled with changes in height, weight, and body shape during puberty, present a challenge to the physical and mental well-being of the athlete.

Davison et al (86) noted that young girls (age 5 to 7 years) participating in aesthetic sports, such as dance, gymnastics, and ice skating, reported significantly more weight concerns compared with girls in nonaesthetic sports, such as soccer, volleyball, track, and girls with no sport participation. Additionally, the young girls in aesthetic sports had significantly higher weight concerns at age 7. These findings suggest that weight concerns are beginning at younger ages and might be linked to participation in certain sports.

Psychological Issues

Some weight- and body-focused sports may attract individuals with predisposition to eating disorders because these sports focus on weight and body shape and emphasize appearance during competition (86). Furthermore, athletes in these sports often have personality traits—such as striving for perfection, obsessive behavior, and attention to detail—that are also characteristic of individuals with disordered eating and eating disorders. These behaviors may lead to more significant health problems, such as the female athlete triad or muscle dysmorphia ("puny muscle syndrome" or "bigorexia," a disorder in which individuals, predominantly males, with muscle dysmorphia are preoccupied with the belief that their bodies are not lean or muscular and perceive themselves to be small or weak) (89).

Restricted Eating/Dieting

Dieting to lose weight is a common practice among weight- and body-focused athletes. Dieting in young athletes, especially females, generally follows puberty by approximately 1 year, and the prevalence of dieting increases with age (5,87). These dieting behaviors may be a result of the increased pressure to remain thin among these athletes, who may seek pathological dieting behaviors, such as starvation and repeated bingeing and purging, as ways of controlling body weight and body fat. It is unclear whether the risk of eating disorders increases as these athletes advance in their athletic career.

Wrestlers and competitive bodybuilders exhibit high levels of restrictive dieting, weight fluctuations, and binge-eating behaviors. Extreme weight-loss practices are often used during preparation to weigh-in for competitions. In a study comparing noncompetitive bodybuilders with sedentary control subjects (90), 81% of the athletes reported frequent concerns with food during training. Compared with the control subjects, the bodybuilders exhibited a higher frequency of dieting (80% vs 28%), weight loss and weight regain of more than 5 kg (82% vs 20%), alcohol abuse (10% vs 0%), and anabolic drug use (15% vs 0%). Among the bodybuilders, episodes of binge eating increased to 10% 1 week before event and 5% the day of event, and further increased to 22% after the event. These athletes expressed a greater drive for thinness, and weight cycling was significantly higher and related to higher levels of body dissatisfaction (90). This pattern of disordered eating attitudes and behaviors, which are practiced to achieve muscle definition and decrease subcutaneous fat for the competition, can potentially result in eating disorders among such athletes (23).

When athletes zealously attempt to achieve a specific weight to compete in a desired weight class, food intake on weekdays can be more restricted than during weekends or after a match or tournament. For example, wrestlers have described "diets" that include no more than 800 kcal per day prior to competition (65–67). Once the competition is over and restricted eating habits cease, the athlete may revert to overconsumption of energy and fat. This scenario may be typical of restricted eating patterns in weight-focused athletes and can increase risk of disordered eating among these athletes, especially during periods of weigh-ins.

Identification and Prevention

It is critical to identify improper eating patterns and behaviors early and prevent them from developing into serious disorders. Common symptoms of overtraining and undereating to make weight are mood swings, fatigue, lethargy, anemia, constipation or diarrhea, decreased libido, and infertility. The dietary habits of athletes should be closely monitored, and athletes should be comprehensively physiologically and psychologically assessed on a regular basis to identify potential problems that can diminish athletic performance and result in short- and long-term psychological, medical, and skeletal repercussions.

Athletes and the teams of people who support them should be educated about sound nutrition practices. An athlete's training program should support a positive and health-enhancing experience, and athletes should acquire the necessary physical and mental tools needed to pursue their goals, secure their well-being, and enjoy their sport. Athletes must learn how to balance meals and stabilize energy and nutrient intake throughout the season. They should be taught that strength training, endurance, motivation, attitude, concentration, and energy levels can be improved by optimizing energy and nutrient intakes. Healthful eating, in turn, allows athletes to train at a more intense level for a longer time, reduces the risk of injury, and promotes happier and healthier athletes. For more on this topic, see Chapter 18.

Other Nutrition Concerns

Achieving the "Ideal" Body Type for Success

Many athletes believe their success in sports is largely dependent on their physical appearance. In their eyes, the best athletes are lean, thin, and powerful. Additionally, athletes are strongly influenced by their coaches, trainers, guardians, parents, and peers. If improper dietary practices occur at home or during training, athletes may adopt similar behaviors. Therefore, athletes and everyone who supports them, including parents and guardians, should be educated about proper dietary practices and helped to recognize that achievement of a certain body type is not always realistic. Certain factors, such as genetics and puberty, cannot be changed. In addition, being lighter or smaller does not always lead to better athletic performances. Nutritional status must be monitored on a regular basis using a combination of dietary, anthropometric, and biochemical assessments.

Consuming a High-Performance Diet

For an athlete, a high-performance diet provides fuel for the working muscles, quick recovery from exercise training, and adequate energy and nutrients for growth, development, and physical training. Because carbohydrate is the preferred fuel for muscles, a diet rich in complex carbohydrates is ideal. Approximately 65% of total energy in an athlete's diet should be from carbohydrate, a minimum of 12% to 15% from protein, and 20% to 25% from fat. Energy intake will vary based on an athlete's size and activity. It is important to emphasize that there are no "good" or "bad" foods.

During practice, athletes should refuel with a snack break after 2½ hours and an additional snack each following hour. Proper hydration is also critical to an athlete's performance.

Training and Competition Meals

During training, nutrition conditioning is recommended to provide consistency for the athletes and to ensure that meals are well-tolerated (23,82). Compared with competition, training is usually a more intense activity over a longer time period, and it is essential for athletes to consume enough food to maintain adequate energy levels while they train.

On competition days, athletes should eat the same types of food they eat on training days. Because of travel schedules and nervousness, athletes may often forego or forget about eating. Planning meals, snacks, and fluids in advance of competition helps ensure that energy needs are met. A good approach is to view every meal during the season as if it were a prematch meal. This perspective is especially valuable because training can be much more intense than the competition itself, and the energy required to improve skills and technique during practice must come from a sound training diet throughout the season.

The meal before competition has two goals: to stabilize blood glucose levels so the athlete does not become hungry, and to ensure optimal hydration. Prematch meals should consist of primarily carbohydrates. Liquid meals can be beneficial.

During competition and between events, sport drinks containing 6% to 8% carbohydrate solution can be effective. These drinks help elevate blood glucose levels and delay the onset of dehydration and fatigue and therefore support the goals of the prematch meal.

Some weight- and body-focused athletes eliminate dairy and red meat from the diet during precompetition because of misconceptions about these foods and their impact on leanness and muscular definition. Dietary calcium, iron, and zinc intakes may be inadequate during the precompetition season or year round, especially for female athletes. Because these dietary inadequacies may negatively affect the health and performance of athletes, increasing intakes of fat-free dairy products and lean red meats should be recommended.

As discussed previously in this chapter, athletes in weight-restricted sports may severely dehydrate themselves to make their weight category for competition. Athletes, parents, guardians, trainers, and coaches should be educated that this practice is not only unhealthy but also unnecessary when individuals choose a realistic weight category and follow an appropriate diet and training strategy. These athletes should be encouraged to maintain proper hydration status and consume at least six to eight glasses of water per day. Fluid intake is especially a concern when athletes train and perform in venues at high altitudes, where dehydration can result from shifts in fluid balance.

Eating when Traveling

Athletes who travel for competition and training, as well as their trainers, coaches, guardians, and parents, should be educated to make wise food choices while on the road (see Box 25.3). These athletes should maintain a high carbohydrate intake, especially prior to competition (91). This can be achieved by increasing their intake of grain products, fruits, and vegetables. When eating out, a high-carbohydrate meal should be chosen over a high-fat meal.

Foodborne illnesses and traveler's diarrhea are commonly encountered when traveling overseas. These conditions may be caused by unfamiliar foods, poor food or water quality, sanitation issues, or the athlete's decreased immunity. To decrease their likelihood of getting sick, athletes should choose foods with which they are familiar, consume only well-cooked foods, and avoid uncooked foods. Athletes should also consider packing nonperishable foods such as breakfast bars, dried foods, pretzels, canned fruit, and sport drinks to be readily available while traveling.

Injuries

Stress and acute fractures, strains, and overuse injuries such as lower-back pain are common injuries among athletes in weight- and body-focused sports. These injuries may be caused by overtraining, reduced physical strength, an unsuitable training environment or

---

Box 25.3   Choosing Healthful Meals and Snacks for Travel and at Competitions

The following are suggestions for teaching athletes to choose healthful meals for travel and for competition:

- Help athletes plan a list of nonperishable foods and fluids when traveling to events.
- Educate athletes about foods that are safe, accessible, and locally available sources of carbohydrate.
- Educate athletes about food safety issues when eating food and beverages from outside of the United States, especially when international travel is involved.
- Educate athletes about available foods, unique cultural habits and practices of different societies when international travel is involved.
- With both domestic and international travel, athletes may need to adapt to different time zones and adjust their eating patterns accordingly. Athletes may need to be educated about consuming small meals at unusual hours of the day until their bodies adapt to the new time zones.
- Discuss fluid needs during travel and identify appropriate choices.

---

training conditions, or misuse of equipment. Inadequate dietary intake can also be a contributing factor. Therefore, it is important to regularly monitor athletes' physical well-being to ensure proper and timely medical attention.

Summary

Adequate dietary intake and fluid status is essential to meet the demands of these weight- and body-focused sports. The athletic team should be educated about proper food choices and fluid consumption before, during, and after training and competition. The use of dietary supplements should be closely monitored and athletes should be educated about the proper use of these products. Sports dietitians should work closely with athletic teams and provide sound nutrition guidelines based on the specific needs of the sport and athlete to promote health and performance (see Boxes 25.4 and 25.5).

Box 25.4   Goals for Working with Athletes in Weight- and Body-Focused Sports

- Emphasize the overall training diet, healthful eating behaviors and maintaining a healthy body composition and weight.
- Rather than the traditional approach of losing weight rapidly to compete in a lower weight class, encourage weight-focused athletes to consider competing in the next higher weight class and reach their body weight based a sound nutrition plan and an appropriate strength-training program.
- Give top priority to establishing a healthy body weight prior to the season. Base the athlete's weight class on body composition and educate on how to maintain that weight during the season through proper diet and training program.
- Educate athletes about signs and symptoms of eating disorders as well as disordered eating patterns and their implications on athletic performance, and overall health and well-being.
- Ask athletes for relevant information regarding the use of anabolic steroids and other illicit drugs and educate them about the consequences.
- Teach athletes to differentiate between fat-free foods and low-calorie, nutrient-dense foods. Help them make food choices that have positive effects on body composition, health, and athletic performance.

Box 25.5   Suggestions for Working with Coaches and Trainers

- Understand that coaches have not traditionally consulted sports dietitians. It is essential to understand the coaching philosophy and the background of the sport.
- Define realistic weight-loss goals with athletes and coaches, and identify the dangers of rapid dehydration and weight-loss techniques and their effects on health and performance.
- Identify the benefits of good nutrition practices, provide nutrition education information at practice sessions, and offer workshops and seminars for the athletic team. Recruit successful athletes to spread the word about the importance of proper nutrition for athletic performance.
- Develop a practical fluid schedule for maintaining proper hydration during training and competition.
- Teach coaches and trainers to recognize the signs and symptoms of eating disorders and whom to refer athletes for help.

References

1. Position of the American Dietetic Association, Dietitians of Canada, and the American College of Sports Medicine: nutrition and athletic performance. *J Am Diet Assoc.* 2000;100:1543–1556.

2. Hawes MR, Sovak D. Morphological prototypes, assessment, and change in elite athletes. *J Sports Sci.* 1994;12:235–242.

3. Kleiner SM, Bazzarre TL, Ainsworth B. Nutritional status of nationally ranked elite body-builders. *Int J Sport Nutr.* 1994;4:54–69.

4. Kleiner SM, Bazzarre TL, Litchford MD. Metabolic profiles, diet, and health practices of championship male and female bodybuilders. *J Am Diet Assoc.* 1990;90:962–967.

5. Loucks AB. Energy balance and body composition in sports and exercise. *J Sports Sci.* 2004;22:1–14.

6. USA Gymnastics Web site. Available at: http://www.usa-gymnastics.org. Accessed May 8, 2004.

7. US Figure Skating Web site. Available at: http://www.usfsa.org. Accessed May 8, 2004.

8. NCAA Wrestling. Rule 3: Weight Certification, Classification and Weighing In. Section 1. Weight Certification. Updated August 17, 2001. Available at: http://www.ncaa.org/champadmin/wrestling/2002_revised_rule3.html. Accessed May 8, 2004.

9. USA National Physique Committee. History of the NPC. Originally printed in Flex Magazine, 1997. Available at: http://www.npcnewsonline.com/new/history.htm. Accessed May 8, 2004.

10. International Judo Federation Web site. Available at: http://www.ijf.org. Accessed May 8, 2004.

11. Frentsos JA, Gaer JR. Increased energy and nutrient intake during training and competition improve elite triathletes' endurance performance. *Int J Sport Nutr.* 1997;7:61–71.

12. Gornall J, Villani RG. Short-term changes in body composition and metabolism with severe dieting and resistance exercise. *Int J Sport Nutr.* 1996;6:285–294.

13. Keim NL, Belko AZ, Barbieri TF. Body fat percentage and gender: associations with exercise energy expenditure, substrate utilization, and mechanical work efficiency. *Int J Sport Nutr.* 1996;6:356–369.

14. Rucinski A. Relationship of body image and dietary intake of competitive ice skaters. *J Am Diet Assoc.* 1989;89:98–100.

15. Ziegler P, Khoo CS, Kris-Etherton PM, Jonnalagadda SS, Sherr B, Nelson JA. Nutritional status of nationally ranked junior US figure skaters. *J Am Diet Assoc.* 1998;98;809–811.

16. Ziegler PJ, Jonnalagadda SS, Nelson JA, Lawrence C, Baciak B. Contribution of meals and snacks to nutrient intake of male and female elite figure skaters during peak competitive season. *J Am College Nutr.* 2002;21:114–119.

17. Nickols-Richardson SM. Body composition issues in women's artistic gymnastics. *J Fam Consumer Sci.* 1997;89:40–45.

18. Nickols-Richardson SM. Dietary intake in young female gymnasts: a summary. *J Fam Consumer Sci.* 1999;91:71–75.

19. Beals KA, Manore MM. Disorders of the female athlete triad among collegiate athletes. *Int J Sports Nutr Exerc Metab.* 2002;12:281–293.

20. Yoon J. Physiological profiles of elite senior wrestlers. *Sports Med.* 2002;32:225–233.

21. Whyte G, George K, Sharma S, Martin L, Draper N, McKenna. Left ventricular structure and function in elite judo players. *J Clin Exerc Physiol.* 2000;2:204–208.

22. Andreoli A, Melchiorri G, Brozzi M, Di Marco A, Volpe SL, Garofano P, Di Daniele N, De Lorenzo A. Effect of different sports on body cell mass in highly trained athletes. *Acta Diabetol.* 2003;40(Suppl 1):S122–S125.

23. Andersen RE, Barlett SJ, Morgan GD, Brownell KD. Weight loss, psychological and nutritional patterns in competitive male bodybuilders. *Int J Eat Disord.* 1995;18:49–57.

24. McInnis KJ, Balady GJ. Effect of body composition on oxygen uptake during treadmill exercise: bodybuilders versus weight-matched men. *Res Q Exerc Sport.* 1999;70:150–156.

25. Aleshinsky SY, Podolsky A, McQueen C, Smith AD, Van Handel P. Strength and conditioning program for figure skating. *Nat Strength Cond Assoc J.* 1988;10:26–30.

26. McMurray RG, Proctor CR, Wilson WL. Effect of caloric deficit and dietary manipulation on aerobic and anaerobic exercise. *Int J Sports Med.* 1991;12:167–172.

27. Thompson JL. Energy balance in young athletes. *Int J Sport Nutr.* 1998;8:160–174.

28. Bellenger S. Wrestling with wrestling. *Train Cond.* 1997;7:50–55.

29. Degoutte F, Jouanel P, Filaire E. Energy demands during a judo match and recovery. *Br J Sports Med.* 2003;37:245–249.

30. Walberg J, Ocel J, Craft LL. Effect of weight loss and refeeding diet composition on anaerobic performance in wrestlers. *Med Sci Sports Exerc.* 1996;28:1292–1299.

31. Nattiv A, Lynch L. The female athlete triad. Managing an acute risk to long-term health. *Phys Sports Med.* 1994;22:60–68.

32. Walberg-Rankin J, Edmonds CE, Gwasdauskas FC. Diet and weight changes of female body-builders before and after competition. *Int J Sport Nutr.* 1993;3:87–102.

33. Benardot D, Schwarz M, Heller DW. Nutrient intake in young highly competitive gymnasts. *J Am Diet Assoc.* 1989;89:401–403.

34. Jonnalagadda SS, Benardot D, Nelson M. Energy and nutrient intakes of the United States National Women's Artistic Gymnastics Team. *Int J Sport Nutr.* 1998;8:331–334.

35. Fogelholm GM, Kukkonen-Harjula TK, Taipale SA, Sievanen HT, Oja P, Vuori IM. Resting metabolic rate and energy intake in female gymnasts, figure-skaters and soccer players. *Int J Sports Med.* 1995;16:551–556.

36. American College of Sports Medicine Position Stand. The female athlete triad. *Med Sci Sports Exerc.* 1997;29:i–ix.

37. Cupisti A, D'Alessandro C, Castrogiovanni S, Barale A, Morelli E. Nutrition survey in elite rhythmic gymnasts. *J Sports Med Phys Fitness.* 2000;40:350–355.

38. Institute of Medicine. *Dietary Reference Intakes for Energy, Carbohydrate, Fiber, Fat, Fatty Acids, Cholesterol, Protein and Amino Acids (Macronutrients).* Washington, DC: National Academy Press; 2002. Available at: http://www.nap.edu. Accessed December 30, 2003.

39. Hargreaves M, Hawley JA, Jeukendrup A. Pre-exercise carbohydrate and fat ingestion: effects on metabolism and performance. *J Sports Sci.* 2004;22:31–38.

40. Burke LM, Kiens B, Ivy JL. Carbohydrates and fat for training and recovery. *J Sports Sci.* 2004;22:15–30.

41. Spriet LL, Gibala MJ. Nutritional strategies to influence adaptations to training. *J Sports Sci.* 2004;22:127–141.

42. Walberg-Rankin J. Dietary carbohydrate as an ergogenic aid for prolonged and brief competitions in sport. *Int J Sport Nutr.* 1995;5(suppl):S13–S28.

43. Burke LM, Cox GR, Cummings NK, Desbrow B. Guidelines for daily carbohydrate intake. Do athletes achieve them? *Sports Med.* 2001;31:267–299.

44. Tipton KD, Wolfe RR. Protein and amino acids for athletes. *J Sports Sci.* 2004;22:65–79.

45. Walberg J, Leidy MK, Sturgill DJ, Hinkle DE, Rithcey SJ. Macronutrient content of a hypoenergy diet affects nitrogen retention and muscle function in weight lifters. *Int J Sport Med.* 1988;9:261–266.

46. Institute of Medicine. *Dietary Reference Intakes for Vitamin A, Vitamin K, Arsenic, Boron, Chromium, Copper, Iodine, Iron, Manganese, Molybdenum, Nickel, Silicon, Vanadium, and Zinc.* Washington, DC: National Academy Press; 2000. Available at: http://www.nap.edu. Accessed May 8, 2004.

47. Institute of Medicine. *Dietary Reference Intakes for Calcium, Phosphorus, Magnesium, Vitamin D, and Fluoride.* Washington, DC: National Academy Press; 1997. Available at: http://www.nap.edu. Accessed May 8, 2004.

48. Cassell C, Benedict M, Specker B. Bone mineral density in elite 7- to 9-year-old female gymnasts and swimmers. *Med Sci Sports Exerc.* 1996;28:1243–1246.

49. O'Connor PJ, Lewis RD, Boyd A. Health concerns of artistic women gymnasts. *Sports Med.* 1996;21:321–325.

50. Shirreffs SM, Armstrong LE, Cheuvront SN. Fluid and electrolyte needs for preparation and recovery from training and competition. *J Sports Sci.* 2004;22:57–63.

51. American College of Sports Medicine Position Stand. Exercise and fluid replacement. *Med Sci Sports Exerc.* 1996;28:i–vii.

52. Marquart L, Sobal J. Beliefs and information sources of high school athletes regarding muscle development. *Pediatrics.* 1993;5:377–382.

53. Marquart L, Sobal J. Weight loss beliefs, practices and support systems for high school wrestlers. *J Adolesc Health.* 1994;15:410–415.

54. American College of Sports Medicine. Position paper on weight loss in wrestlers. *Med Sci Sports Exerc.* 1996;28:ix–xii.

55. Centers for Disease Control and Prevention. Hyperthermia and dehydration-related deaths associated with intentional rapid weight loss in three collegiate wrestlers—North Carolina, Wisconsin, and Michigan, November-December 1997. *MMWR Morb Mortal Wkly Rep.* 1998;47:105–108.

56. Schoffstall JE, Brand JD, Leutholtx BC, Swain DP. Effects of dehydration and rehydration on the one-repetition maximum bench press of weight-trained males. *J Strength Cond Res.* 2001; 15:102–108.

57. Clark RR, Oppliger RA. Minimal weight standards in high school wrestling: the Wisconsin model. *Orthop Phys Ther Clin North Am.* 1998;7:23–45.

58. Alderman BL, Landers DM, Carlson J, Scott JR. Factors related to rapid weight loss practice among international-style wrestlers. *Med Sci Sports Exerc.* 2004;36:249–252.

59. Centers for Disease Control and Prevention. Hyperthermia and dehydration-related deaths associated with international rapid weight loss in three collegiate wrestlers—North Carolina, Wisconsin, and Michigan, November-December 1997. *JAMA.* 1998;279:824–825.

60. Scott JR, Oppliger RA, Utter AC. Body weight changes at the national wrestling tournaments across NCAA divisions I, II, and III. *Med Sci Sports Exerc.* 2002;34(suppl):S26.

61. Shirreffs S, Taylor AJ, Lieper JB, Maughan RJ. Post-exercise rehydration in man: effects of volume consumed and drink sodium content. *Med Sci Sports Exerc.* 1996;28:1260–1271.

62. Armstrong LE. Caffeine, body fluid-electrolyte balance, and exercise performance. *Intl J Sport Nutr Exerc Metab.* 2002;12:189–206.

63. Sossin K, Gizis F, Marquart LF, Sobal J. Beliefs, attitudes and resource of high school wrestling coaches. *Int J Sport Nutr.* 1997;7:219–228.

64. Ziegler P, Khoo CS, Sherr B, Nelson JA, Larson WM, Drewnowski A. Body image and dieting behaviors among elite figure skaters. *Int J Eat Disord.* 1998;24:421–427.

65. Oppliger RA, Landry GL, Foster SW, Lambrecht AC. Bulimic behaviors among interscholastic wrestlers: a statewide survey. *Pediatrics.* 1993;91:826–831.

66. Steen SN, Brownell KD. Patterns of weight loss and regain: has the tradition changed? *Med Sci Sports Exerc.* 1990;22:762–768.

67. Oppliger RA, Nelson Steen SA, Scott JR. Weight loss practices of college wrestlers. *Int J Sport Nutr Exerc Metab.* 2003;13:29–46.

68. Maughan RJ, King DS, Lea T. Dietary supplements. *J Sports Sci.* 2004;22:95–113.

69. Juhn M, Tarnapolsky M. Oral creatine supplementation and athletic performance: a critical review. *Clin J Sport Med.* 1998;8:286–297.

70. Juhn M, Tarnapolsky M. Potential side effects of oral creatine supplementation: a critical review. *Clin J Sport Med.* 1998;8:298–304.

71. Branch JD. Effect of creatine supplementation on body composition and performance: a meta-analysis. *Int J Sport Nutr Exerc Metab.* 2003;13:198–226.

72. Centers for Disease Control and Prevention. Adverse events associated with ephedrine-containing products—Texas, December 1993-September 1995. *JAMA.* 1996;276:1711–1712.

73. Chandler RM, Byrne HK, Patterson JG, Ivy JL. Dietary supplements affect the anabolic hormones after weight training exercise. *J Appl Physiol.* 1994;76:839–845.

74. Walker LS, Bemben MG, Bemben DA, Knehans AW. Chromium picolinate effects on body composition and muscular performance in wrestlers. *Med Sci Sports Exerc.* 1998;30:1730–1737.

75. Clancy SP, Clarkson PM, Decheke ME. Effects of chromium picolinate supplementation on body composition, strength, and urinary chromium loss in football players. *Int J Sport Nutr.* 1994;4:142–153.

76. Hallmark MA, Reynold TH, Desouza CA, Dotson CO, Anderson RA, Rogers MA. Effects of chromium and resistive training on muscle strength and body composition. *Med Sci Sports Exerc.* 1996;28:139–144.

77. Manoharan G, Campbell NP, O'Brien CJ. Syncopal episodes in a young amateur bodybuilder. *Br J Sports Med.* 2002;36:67–68.

78. Cole JC, Smith R, Halford JC, Wagstaff GF. A preliminary investigation into the relationship between anabolic-androgenic steroid use and the symptoms of reverse anorexia in both current and ex-users. *Psychopharmacology.* 2003;166:424–429.

79. Wright S, Grogan S, Hunter G. Body-builders' attitudes towards steroid use. *Drugs: Ed Prev Policy.* 2001;8:91–95.

80. Evans PJ, Lynch RM. Insulin as a drug of abuse in bodybuilding. *Br J Sports Med.* 2003;37:356–357.

81. Powers SK, DeRuisseau KC, Quindry J, Hamilton KL. Dietary antioxidants and exercise. *J Sports Sci.* 2004;22:81–94.

82. Coyle EF. Fluid and fuel intake during exercise. *J Sports Sci.* 2004;22:39–55.

83. Dueck C, Manore M, Matt K. Role of energy balance in athletic menstrual dysfunction. *Int J Sport Nutr.* 1996;6:165–190.

84. Steen S, Oppliger R, Brownell K. Metabolic effects of weight loss and regain in adolescent wrestlers. *JAMA.* 1988;260:47–50.

85. Nattiv A, Agostini R, Drinkwater B, Yeager KK. The female athlete triad. *Clin Sports Med.* 1994;13:405–418.

86. Davison KK, Earnest MB, Birch LL. Participation in aesthetic sports and girls' weight concerns at ages 5 and 7 years. *Int J Eat Disord.* 2002;31:312–317.

87. Moisan J, Meyer F, Gingras S. Leisure physical activity and age at menarche. *Med Sci Sports Exerc.* 1991;23:1170–1175.

88. Chumela WC, Schubert CM, Roche AF, Kulin HE, Lee PA, Himes JH, Sun SS. Age at menarche and racial comparisons in US girls. *Pediatrics.* 2003;111:110–113.

89. Olivardia R. Mirror, mirror on the wall, who's the largest of them all? The features and phenomenology of muscle dysmorphia. *Harv Rev Psychiatry.* 2001;9:254–259.

90. Oliosi M, Grave RD, Burlini S. Eating attitudes in noncompetitive male bodybuilders. *Eating Disorders.* 1999;7:227–233.

91. Nelson-Steen S. Eating on the road: where are the carbohydrates? *Sports Sci Exch.* 1998;11:1–5.

Chapter 26

NUTRITION FOR LOW-ENDURANCE, PRECISION SKILL SPORTS

SALLY HARA, MS, RD, CDE

Introduction

Low-endurance, precision skill sports require fine motor control, coordination, and quick reaction time. Baseball and golf are included in this category. Such sports are typically characterized by low-intensity, noncontinuous activity. This class of athletes usually does not have significantly increased demands for energy or any other macronutrient as other types of athletes may. However, they require anaerobic power (eg, for pitching a fastball, swinging a bat or club, running the bases, throwing a ball a long distance) and general fitness conditioning. Unfortunately, research about the nutritional needs of these athletes is lacking. Therefore, general nutrition guidelines are used and adjusted on an individual basis.

Macronutrient Needs

The macronutrient requirements of low-endurance, precision skill athletes vary with demands of training. In general, they tend to reflect carbohydrate and protein requirements in the low to mid range for athletes. Fat requirements are typically low. However, an individual athlete must be carefully assessed to determine the appropriate macronutrient recommendations and to then tailor these to individual training habits, energy balance, and training goals.

Energy

Honed eye-hand coordination, good concentration, and physical power are important components of low-endurance, precision skill sports. Other components may vary depending on the sport and the athlete's position within the sport. For example, a golfer requires endurance to walk the entire course, whereas a baseball player requires speed to run bases and chase balls.

486

The power component utilizes the phosphate-creatine energy system. For short-term, high-intensity exercise, such as swinging a bat or a club, or sprinting fewer than 100 meters, the phosphate-creatine energy system can produce energy at high rates. Because this is one of the primary energy systems used in low-endurance, precision skill sports, these athletes do not need the large glycogen stores that endurance athletes do. However, the high-intensity, short-duration sprinting often done by baseball players relies on the glycolytic (lactic acid) pathway for the production of adenosine triphosphate (ATP). This requires glucose, which is supplied primarily by glycolysis of muscle glycogen (1–3). Hence, athletes in low-endurance, precision skill sports for which sprinting is a component need to maintain adequate muscle glycogen stores. Golfers do not generally sprint around the golf course, but the duration of their activity requires that they also maintain reasonable glycogen stores. Although low-endurance, precision skill athletes rely less on muscle glycogen than many other types of athletes do, glycogen stores can nonetheless become depleted during training and conditioning sessions (4,5).

Golf and baseball are relatively low energy-expenditure sports when compared with other athletic events. For example, a well-trained tennis player expends more than twice the energy (~12 kcal/minute) as a baseball player in the outfield (~5 kcal/minute). Golf is also a low energy-expenditure sport (~5 kcal/minute), but players expend more energy (~7.6 kcal/minute) if they walk the course or carry their own clubs. Energy needs are more likely to be correlated with body size and composition and, for baseball players, with the position they play (5).

As with any type of sport, energy balance must be considered. The goal is to have adequate fuel available when needed for optimal performance. For this reason, professionals working with low-endurance, precision skill athletes need to be aware of how these athletes distribute their food intake throughout the day. Because such sports typically involve events that last several hours, practice or a game can easily take up the better part of a day. Unless athletes plan carefully, it is easy for them to consume the majority of their food at one meal.

Baseball players are especially notorious for skipping meals. Because they often do not leave the ballpark until 10:00 or 11:00 PM, they have late dinners, may stay up late socializing (often consuming alcohol), and then sleep past noon the next day. They tend to sleep through breakfast, then either grab a quick lunch on the way to practice or eat something at the clubhouse. It is not unusual for players to arrive for late afternoon games having consumed only 500 to 800 kcal of the estimated 3,000 or more kcal required each day; and their athletic performance is compromised by their suboptimal fuel intake. Then they are likely to consume large amounts of food in their postgame meal because they are ravenously hungry.

Redistributing food intake to allow for more fuel to be available before and during the athletes' pregame practice and game could significantly improve performance. Specifically, eating a moderate breakfast and pregame lunch could help increase energy available for play. It could also improve mood and precision of athletic skills, which can be affected if blood sugar levels are low (4).

Another example of poor energy balance is a player who gains excessive weight during the off-season, then attempts to lose weight during training. Such weight gain likely results from decreased activity during the off-season without proportional decreases in food and drink. Professionals working with low-endurance, precision skill athletes should address off-season energy needs and changes in eating habits to prevent unwanted weight gain. If an athlete does need to lose weight at the beginning of a new season, the increased energy expenditure due to training should be considered so as to not to detrimentally underestimate energy needs.

A well-publicized incident is the tragic story of Baltimore Orioles' pitcher Steve Bechler. Bechler was overweight when he reported to spring training in 2003. He voluntarily restricted food and water and took a dietary supplement containing ephedrine (now banned by the Food and Drug Administration [FDA]) in an effort to lose weight rapidly. The combination of hot weather, dehydration, ephedrine, and semistarvation took its toll when Bechler collapsed during practice on February 17, 2003. Bechler's death brought national attention to ephedrine-containing dietary supplements and the practice of crash dieting among athletes. Professionals can help athletes avoid such dangerous practices by providing sound information and guidance regarding energy balance throughout the off-season and during the competitive season (6).

Carbohydrate

Specific carbohydrate guides have not been established for low-endurance, fine motor-skill athletes, so general recommendations are often applied. It is appropriate to recommend approximately 5 to 7 g carbohydrate per kilogram body weight, which is sufficient to maintain muscle glycogen stores (7,8). A diet rich in low-fat, complex carbohydrates is suggested to help maintain muscle and liver glycogen stores, provide adequate fiber, and help with weight maintenance. Athletes who eat a diet including whole grains, fruits, and vegetables have the added benefit of consuming the many micronutrients and phytochemicals contained in these foods. Having adequate carbohydrate available for the duration of the game or practice is essential for preventing hypoglycemia, which could significantly decrease concentration and coordination.

Protein

Current recommendations for protein intake are 1.2 to 1.7 g per kilogram body weight per day (8). Athletes who engage in more strength training have protein needs at the higher end of this range, as do athletes who have insufficient total energy intake. Determining protein needs of individual athletes is dependent on the total energy intake, carbohydrate intake, type of training (degree of strength training and aerobic training), duration of training, and possibly the gender of the athlete (8).

The primary mechanisms influencing protein needs in these athletes are the need to repair exercise-induced microdamage to muscle fibers and the need to support gains in lean tissue mass (8). However, protein can also be used as a fuel source if the total energy intake is insufficient. For this reason, it is important to provide adequate carbohydrate for fuel to spare the protein so it may be used for its other functions. Athletes with decreased energy consumption, often for the purpose of weight loss, may have increased protein needs to prevent muscle wasting.

Athletes should be advised that consuming excess protein will not likely result in greater gains in lean body mass because there is a limit to the rate at which lean tissue can be accrued (8). Additionally, excess protein intake can increase the risks for dehydration, kidney stones, and osteoporosis (1,9–11).

Fat

Many low-endurance, precision skill athletes consume excessive dietary fat. This is especially true for minor league and college athletes who have limited incomes and few cooking skills. High-fat fast food is often considered an affordable option (4). Although fat is an essential part of a normal diet, the long-term negative effects of a high-fat diet are well-established. Athletes are not excluded from the increased risk for cardiovascular disease and cancers associated with high-fat diets. Additionally, when diets are high in fat, carbohydrates—which are the preferred fuel for exercise—are often insufficient.

Conversely, there is no performance benefit associated with a diet containing less than 15% of energy as fat (8). Thus, athletes should consume at least 1.0 g of fat per kilogram of body weight per day. This figure may be adjusted on an individual basis, but it provides for an adequate intake of fat and allows the athlete to consume the recommended amounts of carbohydrate and protein. Professionals should help these athletes identify sources of dietary saturated, polyunsaturated, and monounsaturated fats, and should emphasize consumption of heart-healthy fats.

Micronutrient Needs

Although specific vitamin and mineral needs for low-endurance, precision skill athletes have not been determined, the role of micronutrients in athletes as a whole is well-recognized. Micronutrients are essential for energy production, hemoglobin synthesis, protection from oxidative damage, and bone health (8) and are reviewed in Chapter 5. Even mild deficiencies in some micronutrients (eg, iron, potassium, and magnesium) can result in a decreased ability to concentrate (12–15).

The current Dietary Reference Intakes (DRIs), which are found in Appendix A, are believed to be sufficient to meet the nutritional needs of low-endurance, precision skill athletes. If the athlete's diet is well-balanced and nutrient-dense, then micronutrient needs should be met. However, many athletes have marginal nutrient intakes and may therefore benefit from a multivitamin/multimineral supplement. The adequacy of the athlete's current diet should be assessed and any recommendations for micronutrient supplementation should be made on an individual basis. When recommending multivitamin/multimineral supplements, it is wise to assess nutrients being consumed in fortified foods such as sports bars and sport drinks.

Fluid and Electrolytes

It is well-established that adequate fluid intake is of utmost importance for athletes, and this is especially true for low-endurance, precision skill athletes. These sports often have no time limits and are frequently played in hot and/or humid conditions. As with any sport, performance is optimal when athletes are well-hydrated and is compromised when they are dehydrated. The guiding principle is to match fluid intake to fluid losses. Dehydration can lead to hyperthermia, glycogen depletion, increased heart rate, and even life-threatening heatstroke (1,4,5,8). Athletes need to be educated to recognize the signs and symptoms of dehydration, which include lethargy, headaches, gastrointestinal distress, irritability, low urine output, and dark urine. The need to drink before feeling thirsty should be stressed because adequate fluid intake is ultimately a learned behavior and needs to be practiced (16–18).

Athletes should be well-hydrated before exercising. It is currently recommended that before exercise during which heavy sweating is anticipated, athletes should drink approximately 7 mL per kilogram of body mass (~1 oz per 10 lb of body mass) of water or sport drink 2 hours before exercise. Individuals who sweat profusely may need an additional 3 to 4 mL/kg (0.6 oz/10 lb) within 20 minutes prior to exercise (19,20). Alcoholic beverages are not recommended. More information about fluid intake prior to exercise can be found in Chapter 6.

During exercise, athletes should be encouraged to drink frequently. Unless the weather is exceptionally hot and/or humid, plain water is an excellent choice, although sport drinks containing no more than 8% carbohydrate are also acceptable (4). In very hot and/or humid environments where sweat rates are high, electrolyte and fluid losses become a greater concern (8). Each kilogram of sweat contains approximately 1.5 g of salt, of which 40% is sodium. Therefore, a loss of even 5 kg of water from perspiration corresponds to approximately 8.0 g of sodium depletion (14). Under these conditions, drinking fluids containing replacement electrolytes (especially sodium and potassium) is advised. Sport drinks or an oral electrolyte maintenance solution such as Pedialyte (Ross Products, Abbott Park, IL) are typically good sources.

Postexercise hydration is important to help replace fluid and electrolyte losses. By weighing themselves (in the nude) before and after training and sporting events, athletes can assess postexercise fluid needs. The difference in weight is due to fluid loss. Athletes should consume up to 150% of the weight lost to cover losses in sweat plus obligatory urine production; this means drinking approximately 24 oz of fluid for every pound of weight lost (8,17).

An additional benefit of postexercise hydration in the clubhouse is decreasing thirst, which may otherwise be quenched with alcoholic beverages later. Baseball players are often notorious for late-night drinking (alcohol) after games, especially in the minor leagues. This needs to be addressed when determining fluid and electrolyte needs. It may be prudent for some athletes to begin their day with a sport drink to help replace fluids and electrolytes lost due to alcohol consumption the night before. Tables 26.1 and 26.2 and Box 26.1 offer strategies to help low-endurance, precision skill athletes meet their fluid needs (18–23).

Dietary Supplements and Ergogenic Aids

In the ever-more competitive world of sports, athletes are always looking for an edge to improve their performance. Sports organizations are becoming stricter about the use of

TABLE 26.1   Fluid Guidelines for a Typical Baseball Game

Time	Drink
5 PM	2 cups (16 oz) of sport drink
Game time: 7 PM–10 PM	½ to 1 cup (4 to 8 oz) every 15–20 minutes
After the game	Enough to at least replace lost body weight, (optimally 150% of lost body weight)

Source: Data are from references 18 to 21.

TABLE 26.2   Fluid Guidelines for a Typical Round of Golf

Time	Drink
30–60 minutes before tee time	At least 2 cups (16 oz) of water and a small balanced meal
Just prior to golf round	At least 2 cups (16 oz) water
During play	≥ 6 oz water every 2–3 holes
After the game	Enough to at least replace lost body weight, (optimally 150% of lost body weight)

Source: Data are from references 22 and 23.

Box 26.1   Strategies to Increase Fluid Intake

- Practice scheduled drinking.
- Drink during warm-ups and during breaks in competition.
- Use a sport bottle.
- While exercising, drink a sport drink with a pleasing taste.
- Choose cool fluids, which are usually preferred over warm fluids, and are absorbed better.
- Avoid carbonated beverages because athletes tend to drink less when the beverage is carbonated.

---

drugs such as anabolic steroids. Because of this, many athletes look to dietary supplements as ergogenic aids. Creatine and caffeine are currently popular. The FDA has taken action against two dietary supplements that have been popular in the past, androstenedione and ephedrine. Dietary supplements containing more than 10 mg ephedrine are banned, and warning letters asking companies to cease and desist sales of androstenedione-containing dietary supplements have been issued. Additional information about dietary supplements can be found in Chapter 7.

Creatine

Creatine is one of the most popular dietary supplements, and many baseball players consider it to be an ergogenic aid (24–26). In minor and major league baseball, creatine is often provided to players free of charge in the clubhouse. Although the results are mixed, current research indicates that creatine supplementation does increase performance in some athletes (27–33). No studies, however, have specifically examined the effect of creatine on the performance of baseball players.

Low-endurance, precision skill athletes, particularly baseball players, often use oral creatine monohydrate to enhance the power of their swing. Indeed, many studies of weight lifters and cyclists do support creatine as an effective ergogenic aid for improving performance, enhancing the results of resistance training (27–33), increasing muscle strength and weight-lifting performance (30,31), and increasing the number of maximum repetitions performed to fatigue (28,32). Creatine supplements seem to work by increasing the rate of phosphocreatine resynthesis during the recovery phase of intermittent high-intensity exercise, making repeated bouts of high-intensity exercise possible while delaying muscular fatigue (27,28,33).

Weight gain is a well-documented side effect of creatine supplementation, though its composition remains controversial. There are three leading theories to account for the weight gain: fluid retention, protein synthesis, and improved quality of training, which allows for the development of lean mass. There have been anecdotal reports of muscle cramping, pulls, and strains by athletes who supplement with creatine, but no scientific documentation of this. Some studies indicate that injury rates are no different for athletes supplementing with creatine than for controls (34,35). The majority of research seems to suggest that there are no adverse health effects of long-term creatine supplementation (26,34,36). However, more research in humans is needed to establish long-term safety.

Androstenedione

Androstenedione is a prohormone that has been popularized by some high-profile sports stars, such as professional baseball player Mark McGwire during his homerun record-setting season. His achievements influenced others, including adolescents, to use "andro" (24, 37,38). It has been touted as a "natural" way to boost testosterone levels without the risks associated with anabolic steroid use. Proponents of androstenedione use claim that it can increase lean body mass, strength, and athletic performance. However, a multitude of studies has not supported these claims, showing no performance-enhancing effects (37–44). King et al reported that serum free and total testosterone concentrations were not affected by short- or long-term use of androstenedione (44).

The FDA disagreed with this assessment, stating "The biochemical evidence supporting the effect of androstenedione to raise circulating levels of testosterone and estrogens is strong." It sent letters asking manufacturers, marketers and distributors to cease and desist the distribution of androstenedione-containing dietary supplements. The FDA warns of risks of androgenic and estrogenic effects resulting from the direct conversion of androstenedione to testosterone (45). Several studies report additional concerns about negative health consequences associated with androstenedione supplementation (40,43,44). Androstenedione use has been shown to dangerously alter serum lipid levels—the risk of coronary heart disease increases significantly due to decreased high-density lipoprotein (HDL) cholesterol levels (40). Therefore, because androstenedione has no documented benefit and may result in adverse health consequences, its use should be discouraged. Androstenedione is now banned by the International Olympic Committee and Major League Baseball (45).

Caffeine

Caffeine is widely used by athletes. Some use it as an ergogenic aid to increase power or endurance, while others use it simply as a stimulant to increase alertness and concentration, and to override fatigue (46). As an ergogenic aid, caffeine has been shown effective for increasing endurance and speed for activities lasting longer than 1 minute (46,47). Caffeine is also believed to enhance short-term, high-intensity athletic performance, though there are few well-controlled studies to support this (46–48).

No studies to date have investigated the effect of caffeine on the performance of golfers or baseball players. Of interest, at least two studies concluded that when caffeine and creatine are both consumed, the caffeine counters the benefit of the creatine (49,50).

Caffeine does not seem to cause dehydration or electrolyte imbalance (48,51,52). Evidence suggests that when consumed in moderation, caffeine does not adversely affect sport performance (48). However, it is worth assessing the reason an athlete may be consuming high amounts of caffeine. Sleep deprivation or improper dietary intake or hydration often lead athletes to use stimulants such as caffeine or amphetamines. If this is the case, the athlete should be encouraged to improve sleep and diet habits rather than rely heavily on stimulants. As always, it is wise to assess not only what an athlete ingests, but why. By doing this, the professional can more appropriately coach the athlete toward success.

Special Considerations

Precompetition Meals

Recommendations for precompetition meals depend on the sport and the time of the competition. Golf tournaments typically have relatively early start times to take advantage of daylight hours. Baseball games are often played at night.

Golf

For golfers, a small balanced meal 1 to 2 hours before tee time is suggested (22,23). Refueling during the round is also important in golf because of the duration of the event. Professionals have made various specific recommendations but tend to agree that golfers need to continue to fuel their bodies during play. Variations include bringing along three or four energy bars to consume throughout the round, or eating two snacks—one at the fifth hole and one at the ninth hole. Most agree that fueling around the ninth hole is essential to prevent "bonking" (ie, experiencing extreme fatigue due to hypoglycemia and near depletion of glycogen stores) on the back nine holes. The foods available in the golf clubhouse are not always optimal, so athletes must plan ahead and pack appropriate food options to take with them.

Baseball

Most collegiate and professional baseball games are played at night, and players typically report to the clubhouse 4 to 5 hours prior to game time. The pregame meal should be eaten 3 to 4 hours before the game to allow enough time for food to exit the stomach yet still allow for satiety (5). Food is often provided in the clubhouse, but the selection is not necessarily nutritionally sound (understandably, the major leagues have a greater variety of food available than do minor league or collegiate teams). The pregame meal should be high in complex carbohydrates, moderate in protein, and low in fat, concentrated sweets, and fiber (4). Players need to be coached on how to select appropriate foods. Most minor league and collegiate players would welcome a list of carbohydrate-based meal suggestions that take into account their limited budgets and cooking skills (4).

Given the growing cultural diversity in baseball, ethnic food preferences of the players must be considered. In particular, Hispanic and Japanese preferences may need to be explored.

Athletes prone to gastrointestinal upset resulting from eating before a game should try eating smaller amounts of foods more frequently, avoiding high-glycemic index foods, and/or consuming a sport drink that contains 6% to 8% carbohydrate (14 to 19 g per 8 oz) (4).

Eating on the Road

The frequent travel associated with low-endurance, precision skill sports presents its own set of challenges. Again, amateurs and minor league players are often limited in cash, so fast food and 24-hour diners are common sources of meals away from home. Although it is possible to make low-fat, higher carbohydrate choices at these establishments, it is uncommon for athletes to make the conscious choice to do so. Athletes with higher incomes can afford to eat at fine restaurants, but they do not always choose food that fits into a recommended training diet (4). Some professional baseball players are hiring cooks to help them eat more healthful meals. To meet recommended nutritional intake for optimal performance, many athletes would benefit greatly from professional nutrition coaching, and even then they may have to retrain their taste buds to appreciate lower fat, high-carbohydrate food choices (53).

Postcompetition Eating

Low-endurance, precision skill sporting events can last several hours, and athletes are hungry when competition ends. They should be encouraged to consume high-carbohydrate foods to help replenish muscle glycogen stores. Studies have shown that when adequate carbohydrate is available, glycogen resynthesis is greater during the first few hours after exercise than several hours later (1,4). Thus, eating carbohydrate-rich foods immediately after a sporting event can help athletes recover more quickly and replenish glycogen stores for greater endurance in the near future. Avoiding high-fat foods at this time is also important, because they can slow the absorption of dietary carbohydrates, thus limiting their availability for glycogen synthesis.

Summary

The nutrient and energy needs of low-endurance, precision skill athletes are not extraordinary relative to other types of athletes. A well-balanced diet adequate in energy will likely meet most if not all of these athletes' nutritional needs. General daily recommendations are 5 to 7 g carbohydrate per kilogram body weight, 1.2 to 1.7 g protein per kilogram, and approximately 1.0 g fat per kilogram. Distribute calories throughout the day to ensure that energy is available for training and competition. Matching energy intake with energy expenditure is important, especially during the off-season when training decreases and food intake may remain the same or increase, leading to unwanted weight gain.

Creatine and caffeine are popular supplements. If athletes choose to use dietary supplements to enhance performance, professionals should use sound research to help clarify the risks vs the benefits of supplements. Some of the most valuable types of advice that a nutrition professional working with low-endurance, precision skill athletes can provide are recommendations for specific foods and eating patterns. The nutrition professionals' job is to translate nutrition theory into healthful dietary choices.

References

1. Berning J, Steen S. *Nutrition for Sport and Exercise.* 2nd ed. Gaithersburg, Md: Aspen Publishers; 1998.
2. Hoppeler H, Billeter R. Conditions for oxygen and substrate transport in muscles in exercising mammals. *J Exp Biol.* 1991;160:263–283.
3. De Feo P, DiLoreto C, Lucidi P, Murdolo G, Parlanti N, De Cicco A, Piccioni F, Santeusanio F. Metabolic response to exercise. *J Endocrinol Invest.* 2002;26:851–854.
4. Clark N, Palumbo C. Case problem: nutrition concerns related to the performance of a baseball team. *J Am Diet Assoc.* 2000;100:704–707.
5. Williams MH. *Nutrition for Health, Fitness, and Sport.* 7th ed. Boston, Mass: WBC McGraw Hill; 2004.
6. Raloff J. Homing in on ephedra's risks. *Science News Online.* 2003;163(6). Available at: http://www.sciencenews.org. Accessed December 8, 2004.
7. Burke LM, Cox GR, Culmmings NK, Desbrow B. Guidelines for daily carbohydrate intake: do athletes achieve them? *Sports Med.* 2001;31:267–299.
8. American College of Sports Medicine, American Dietetic Association, Dietitians of Canada. Joint position statement: nutrition and athletic performance. *Med Sci Sports Exerc.* 2000;32: 2130–2145.
9. Amanzadeh J, Gitomer WL, Zerwekh JE, Preisig PA, Moe OW, Pak CY, Levi M. Effect of high protein diet on stone-forming propensity and bone loss in rats. *Kidney Int.* 2003;64:2142–2149.
10. Reddy ST, Wang CY, Sakhee K, Brinkley L, Pak CY. Effect of low-carbohydrate high-protein diets on acid-base balance, stone-forming propensity, and calcium metabolism. *Am J Kidney Dis.* 2002;40:265–274.
11. Barzel US, Massey LK. Excess dietary protein can adversely affect bone. *J Nutr.* 1998;128: 1051–1053.
12. Manore M, Thompson J. *Sports Nutrition for Health and Performance.* Champaign, Ill: Human Kinetics; 2000.
13. Cataldo C, DeBruyne L, Whitney E. *Nutrition and Diet Therapy.* 6th ed. Belmont, Calif: Wadsworth Publishing; 2003.
14. McArdle W, Katch FI, Katch V. *Sports and Exercise Nutrition.* Philadelphia, Pa: Lippincott Williams & Wilkins; 1999.
15. Clarkson PM, Haymes EM. Trace mineral requirements for athletes. *Int J Sports Nutr.* 1994;4:104.
16. Broad EM, Burke LM, Cox R, Heeley P, Riley M. Body weight changes and voluntary fluid intakes during training and competition sessions in team sports. *Int J Sport Nutr.* 119;6:307–320.
17. Hagerman M. *Homeplate Strategy: A Guide to Good Eating for Baseball Players.* 4th ed. Athens, Ohio: Marjorie Hagerman; 1997.
18. Casa DJ. USA Track and Field advisory: proper hydration for distance running. 2003. Available at: http://www.usatf.org/groups/Coaches/library/hydration/ProperHydrationForDistanceRunning.pdf. Accessed December 8, 2004.
19. American College of Sports Medicine. Position stand on exercise and fluid replacement. *Med Sci Sports Exerc.* 1996;28:i–vii.

20. Horswill CA. Effective fluid replacement. *Int J Sport Nutr.* 1998;8:175–195.
21. Casa DJ, Armstrong LE, Hillman SK, Montain SJ, Reiff RV, Rich BSE, Robert WO, Stone JA. National Athletic Trainers' Association position statement: fluid replacement for athletes. *J Athl Train.* 2000;35:212–224.
22. Benzoni J. Golf nutrition: energy tips for consistent golf. Available at: http://www.golfhound. com/golfNutirion.phtml?. Accessed Oct. 9, 2003.
23. Horst LA. Nutritional tips for peak performance. Available at: http://www.lisaannhorst. com/tips/nutritip.html. Accessed Oct. 9, 2003.
24. Brown WJ, Basil MD, Bocarnea MC. The influence of famous athletes on health beliefs and practices: Mark McGwire, child abuse prevention, and androstenedione. *J Health Commun.* 2003;8:41–57.
25. Lawler JM, Barnes WS, Wu G, Song W, Demaree S. Direct antioxidant properties of creatine. *Biochem Biophys Res Commun.* 2002;290:47–52.
26. Poortmans JR, Francaux M. Adverse effects of creatine supplementation: fact of fiction? *Sports Med.* 2000;30:155–170.
27. Branch JD. Effect of creatine supplementation on body composition and performance: a meta-analysis. *Int J Sport Nutr Exerc Metab.* 2003;13:198–226.
28. Iaquierdo M, Ibanez J, Gonzalez-Badillo JJ, Gorostiaga EM. Effects of creatine supplementation on muscle power, endurance, and sprint performance. *Med Sci Sports Exerc.* 2002;34:332–343.
29. Kreider RB. Effects of creatine supplementation on performance and training adaptations. *Mol Cell Biochem.* 2003;244:89–94.
30. Dempsey RL, Mazzone MF, Meurer LN. Does oral creatine supplementation improve strength? A meta-analysis. *J Fam Pract.* 2002;51:945–951.
31. Rawson ES, Voked JS. Effects of creatine supplementation and resistance training on muscle strength and weightlifting performance. *J Strength Cond Res.* 2003;17:822–831.
32. Volek JS, Tatamess NA, Rubin MR, Gomez AL, French DN, McGuigan MM, Scheett TP, Sharman MJ, Hakkinen K, Kraemer WJ. The effects of creatine supplementation on muscular performance and body composition responses to short-term resistance training overreaching. *Eur J Appl Physiol.* 2004;91:628–637.
33. Volek JS, Kraemer WJ. Creatine supplementation: its effect on human muscular performance and body composition. *J Strength Cond Res.* 1996;10:200–210.
34. Schilling BK, Stone MH, Utter A, Kearney JT, Johnson M, Coglianese R, Smith L, O'Bryant HS, Fry AC, Starks M, Keigh R, Stone ME. Creatine supplementation and health variables: a retrospective study. *Med Sci Sports Exerc.* 2001;33:183–188.
35. Greenwood M, Kreider RB, Melton C, Rasmussen C, Lancaster S, Cantler E, Milnor P, Almada A. Creatine supplementation during college football training does not increase the incidence of cramping or injury. *Mol Cell Biochem.* 2003;244:83–88.
36. Farquhar WB, Zambraski EJ. Effects of creatine use on the athlete's kidney. *Curr Sports Med Rep.* 2002;1:103–106.
37. Ziegenfuss TN, Berardi JM, Lowery LM. Effects of prohormone supplementation in humans: a review. *Can J Appl Physiol.* 2002;27:628–646.
38. Gomez JE. Performance-enhancing substances in adolescent athletes. *Tex Med.* 2002;98:41–46.
39. Nissen SL, Sharp RL. Effect of dietary supplements on lean mass and strength gains with resistance exercise: a meta-analysis. *J Appl Physiol.* 2003;94:651–659.
40. Broeder CE, Quindry J, Brittingham K, Panton L, Thomson J, Appakondu S, Breuel K, Byrd R, Douglas J, Earnest C, Mitchell C, Olson M, Roy T, Tarlagadda C. The Andro Project: physiological and hormonal influences of androstenedione supplementation in men 35 to 65 years old participating in a high-intensity resistance training program. *Arch Intern Med.* 2000;160:3093–3104.
41. Ballantyne CS, Phillips SM, MacDonald JR, Tarnopolsky MA, MacDougall JD. The acute effects of androstenedione supplementation in healthy young males. *Can J Appl Physiol.* 2000;25:68–78.

42. Wallace MB, Lim J, Cutler A, Bucci L. Effects of dehydroepiandroserone vs androstenedione supplementation in men. *Med Sci Sports Exerc.* 1999;31:1788–1792.

43. Juhn M. Popular sports supplements and ergogenic aids. *Sports Med.* 2003;33:921–939.

44. King DS, Sharp RL, Vukovich MD, Brown GA, Reifenrath TA, Uhl NL, Parsons KA. Effect of oral androstenedione on serum testosterone and adaptations to resistance training in young men: a randomized controlled trial. *JAMA.* 1999;281:2020–2028.

45. Food and Drug Administration. White Paper: Health Effects of Androstenedione. March 11, 2004. Available at: http://www.fda.gov/oc/whitepapers/andro.html. Accessed July 26, 2004.

46. Paluska SA. Caffeine and exercise. *Curr Sports Med Rep.* 2003;2:213–219.

47. Graham TE. Caffeine, coffee and ephedrine: impact on exercise performance and metabolism. *Can J Appl Physiol.* 2001;26(suppl):S103-S119.

48. Graham TE. Caffeine and exercise: metabolism, endurance and performance. *Sports Med.* 2001;31:785–807.

49. Hespel P, Op't Eijnde B, Van Leemputte M. Opposite actions of caffeine and creatine on muscle relaxation time in humans. *J Appl Physiol.* 2002;92:513–518.

50. Vandenberghe K, Gillis N, Van Leemputte M, Van Hecke P, Vanstapel F, Hespel P. Caffeine counteracts the ergogenic action of muscle creatine loading. *J Appl Physiol.* 1996;80:452–457.

51. Armstrong LE. Caffeine, body fluid-electrolyte balance, and exercise performance. *Int J Sport Nutr Exerc Metab.* 2002;12:189–206.

52. Maughan RJ, Griffin J. Caffeine ingestion and fluid balance: a review. *J Human Nutr Diet.* 2003;16:411–420.

53. Clark N. Eating nutritiously on the road. *Phys Sport Med.* 1985;13:133–139.

At a Glance

The preceding six chapters help professionals understand the physiological and nutritional demands of related sports, but sports dietitians may find that they need a quick and easy reference for a specific sport. The At a Glance section features summaries for 18 sports. The summaries include brief description of the sports and the URLs for Web sites where more information is available. General nutrition guidelines are included and can serve as a basis for an individualized plan. Common nutrition concerns are highlighted and briefly explained. These summaries may be helpful when preparing sports nutrition presentations for teams or as a topical guideline for an individual counseling session with an athlete.

BASEBALL AT A GLANCE

Baseball requires fine motor control, coordination, and reaction time as well as anaerobic power and general fitness conditioning. Professional baseball players begin spring training in February. The regular season is from April to September, followed by postseason play in October and then the off-season. Minor league players "practice, play, eat, sleep, and travel." Collegiate and youth baseball is a spring sport in school, and some players continue throughout the summer in recreational leagues. Learn more about the sport at the Major League Baseball Web site (http://www.mlb.com).

General Nutrition Guidelines

- Energy: Relatively low energy expenditure sport
- Carbohydrate: 5–7 g/kg/day
- Protein: 1.2–1.7 g/kg/day
- Fat: ~ 1.0 g/kg/day

Common Nutrition Concerns

Weight Gain

Professional players may skip meals and then overeat, consume excess alcohol, and eat high-calorie seeds during the game, all habits that can contribute to weight gain. Many overeat and reduce activity during the off-season.

Fluid Intake

Spring training typically takes place in hot and humid conditions, as do many games. Dehydration is a daily concern.

Pregame Meal

Players often arrive for games having not eaten and must eat the food that is accessible, which is often high in calories, fat, sugar, and/or salt. Minor league players have a limited budget and seek out inexpensive food, which is often low in nutritional quality.

Postgame Meal

Late-night eating, large postgame meals, and alcohol intake often result in weight gain. Minor league players typically eat fast food to break up a long bus ride.

Frequent Travel

Frequent travel makes it difficult to maintain a routine and increases exposure to high-calorie foods that are low in nutritional quality.

BASKETBALL AT A GLANCE

Basketball is an intermittent, high-intensity sport requiring strength, power, cardiovascular fitness, agility, and skill. It is usually played in four quarters with a break at half-time, although overtime periods are necessary if the game is tied. All of the body's energy systems are used to fuel the sport—adenosine triphosphate-creatine phosphate (ATP-CP) to jump and pass, the lactic acid system for multiple sprints, and the aerobic system to support several hours of play. The game may be played casually or with great intensity and duration in a variety of venues from the playground to the National Basketball Association (NBA) arena. Learn more about the sport at the NBA's Web site (http://www.nba.com) or the USA Basketball Web Site (http://www.usabasketball.com).

General Nutrition Guidelines

- Energy: Varies depending on the individual, but for players in training, generally a high energy expenditure sport
- Carbohydrate: > 6 g/kg/day; 8–10 g/kg/day during heavy training/competition
- Protein: 1.4–1.7 g/kg/day
- Fat: Remainder of kcal as fat with an emphasis on heart-healthy fats

Common Nutrition Concerns

Energy Intake

NBA players may need 6,000 to 7,000 kcal/day whereas other players, such as high school or recreational players, need considerably less. Low energy and nutrient intakes over the long season may contribute to fatigue, especially during playoffs, and to weight loss.

Carbohydrate Intake

Basketball players need a large amount of carbohydrate daily to replenish glycogen that is used during demanding training sessions and games.

Fluid Intake

Training and games are often held in hot environments. Dehydration can lead to early fatigue and heat illness. Fluid intake should balance fluid losses.

Restoration of Glycogen, Fluids, and Electrolytes

Demanding practices, games, and training sessions deplete glycogen, fluids, and electrolytes. Glycogen stores and fluid and electrolyte losses must be replenished beginning immediately after competition or training. Some postexercise protein consumption is also encouraged. Appetite may be depressed, so liquid meal replacements may become an important option.

BODYBUILDING AT A GLANCE

Bodybuilding is a subjectively judged sport based on muscular development and body presentation. Both males and females participate in contests and there are amateur and professional bodybuilders. Training and nutrition must be well-matched and will vary depending on the demands of the training period—maintaining muscle mass, building muscle mass, tapering (precontest dieting), or cutting weight immediately prior to competition. Learn more about the sport at the International Federation of Bodybuilding and Fitness Web site (http://www.ifbb.com).

General Nutrition Guidelines

Bodybuilders are a variety of weights and sizes, and training and nutrient intakes change as they prepare for contests. Sufficient carbohydrate is needed to meet the demands of training. Protein intakes generally increase during the muscle-building, tapering, and cutting periods. As energy and protein intakes change, the relative contribution of carbohydrates and fats change. These general guidelines must be highly individualized:

- Energy: Energy intake and expenditure must be individually determined. Estimated energy needs are as low as 30 kcal/kg/day for females trying to lose fat weight and maintain muscle mass and as high as 60 kcal/kg/day for males trying to build muscle mass.
- Carbohydrate: 5–10 g/kg/day.
- Protein: 1.4–1.7 g/kg/day (low energy intakes or individual preferences may result in higher intakes—2g/kg/day during lowest energy intake).
- Fat: Remainder of kcal with an emphasis on heart-healthy fats.

Common Nutrition Concerns

Energy Intake

Baseline energy intake varies tremendously and energy needs change as contests approach. Bodybuilders need personalized meal plans that reflect various energy (kcal) levels.

Other Macronutrients

Excessive intake of any one macronutrient may result in a low intake of another. The focus must be macronutrient balance (not just protein intake) with the understanding that the demands of training and competition change the relative balance. Emphasize the importance of carbohydrate and healthful fats for health and performance, as well as an appropriate protein and energy intake.

Fluid Intake

Fluid loss must be balanced with fluid intake. Voluntary dehydration is one method that is used prior to competition and may be dangerous or life threatening.

Lack of Variety

Diets tend to be repetitive and lack variety. Suggestions for foods that contain similar energy and nutrient profiles or meal plans are helpful.

Body Image and Disordered Eating

Due to the nature of the sport, there is a risk for distorted body image and disordered eating.

CYCLING AT A GLANCE

Cycling is a sport of various intensities and durations, from sprinters, whose races last only seconds, to endurance cyclists, such as Tour de France riders, who traverse more than 2,000 miles, much of it over mountainous terrain. Energy and nutrient needs vary according to the type of cycling (eg, track, road racing, mountain biking, and bicycle motocross [BMX]), the demands of training, and the intensity and duration of the race. Learn more about the sport at the USA Cycling Web site (http://www.usacycling.org).

General Nutrition Guidelines

Endurance cycling guidelines can be found under Endurance and Ultraendurance sports in this At-a-Glance section. Sprint cycling is a very high-intensity, short-duration sport, and the general guidelines include the following:

- Energy: Calculate individual needs based on demands of training
- Carbohydrate: 6–8 g/kg/day (often 65% of total calories)
- Protein: 1.2–1.7 g/kg/day
- Fat: Remainder of kcal with an emphasis on heart-healthy fats

Many cyclists fall between the two extremes of sprinting and endurance, and energy and macronutrient requirements must be adjusted accordingly to reflect the demands of training and competition.

Common Nutrition Concerns

Energy and Carbohydrate Intake

Nutrient needs are often high, and a well-balanced diet is important. Distance cyclists need carbohydrate during the ride and must learn to consume food on the bike. Carbohydrate/electrolyte drinks, energy bars, gels, and bananas are some foods that work well, but individual preferences and tolerances must be determined by trial and error.

Fluid Intake

Dehydration is a daily concern. Road and mountain cyclists can carry a limited amount of fluid on the bike but always risk chance of injury when they reach for it. Sweat rates should be calculated and an individualized hydration plan should be developed.

Restoration of Glycogen, Fluids, and Electrolytes

Glycogen stores and fluid and electrolyte losses must be replenished beginning immediately after competition or training. Some postexercise protein consumption is also encouraged. Appetite may be depressed, so liquid meal replacements may become an important option.

ENDURANCE AND ULTRAENDURANCE SPORTS (DISTANCE RUNNING, CYCLING, AND SWIMMING) AT A GLANCE

Endurance and ultraendurance sports include marathons, triathlons, and distance cycling and swimming events. All require year-round training and nutritional support. Training and nutrition must be well-matched and will vary depending on the training period—preparation, pre-race, race, or active recovery. Reducing body fat or weight should be attempted during active recovery or early in the preparation period so that high-volume training or competition is not compromised. Learn more about these sports at the following Web sites: USA Track and Field (http://www.usatf.org/groups/roadrunning), USA Triathlon (http:// www.usatriathlon. org), United States Masters Swimming: Long-Distance Swimming (http://www.usms.org/longdist), and Ultramarathon Cycling Association (http://www.ultracycling.com).

General Nutrition Guidelines

- Energy: High energy expenditure sports
- Carbohydrate: 5–7 g/kg/day when training is reduced and as high as 12–19 g/kg/day during heavy training and racing season. Carbohydrate loading for competition is common.
- Protein: 1.2–2.0 g/kg/day with higher levels consumed during pre-race and racing seasons
- Fat: 0.8–2.0 g/kg/day to match energy expenditure

Common Nutrition Concerns

Energy and Macronutrient Intake

Needs are high and proper food intake must be an integral part of training. A structured eating plan must be developed to support training throughout the year.

Weight Gain

After the racing season is over, energy intake must be adjusted to reflect the decreased volume and intensity of training to prevent unwanted weight gain.

Body Composition

Leanness and low body weight is advantageous in sports in which the body must be moved. Excess body fat can be detrimental because, unlike muscle, it is non-force-producing mass. Rapid weight or fat loss can be detrimental to training and performance, so changes to body composition must be slow. Small reductions in daily energy intake and some increase in activities of daily living will promote slow weight loss. Weight loss is best attempted during the recovery period or early in the preparation period.

Fluid and Sodium Intake

Fluid intake must be balanced to avoid dehydration and prevent hyponatremia. Sodium needs must be individually established. The inclusion of sodium in products taken during training and racing is recommended.

Lack of Variety

Variety and balance can be difficult day after day. Athletes must avoid getting into a rut. Focus on whole foods during active recovery ("off season").

Food Intolerances

Some foods are not tolerated well during competition. Practice using various race foods and beverages during training to prevent problems during competition.

FIELD EVENTS AT A GLANCE

Indoor field events include high jump, pole vault, long jump, triple jump, and shot put. Outdoor field events also include discus, hammer, and javelin throws. Both males and females compete in these events. The necessary athletic skills and body composition differ between jumpers and throwers. Jumpers tend to be leaner because they must move their body through space whereas throwers depend on their strength and body mass to propel an object through space. Jumpers consume less energy than throwers. Learn more about the sports at the USA Track and Field Web site (http://www.usatf.org).

General Nutrition Guidelines

- Energy: Varies depending on the individual and the event
- Carbohydrate: 5–8 g/kg/day
- Protein: 1.2–1.7 g/kg/day
- Fat: Remainder of kcal with an emphasis on heart-healthy fats

Common Nutrition Concerns

Body Composition and Weight Loss

Jumpers are encouraged to have a low percentage of body fat. There is a performance disadvantage to having excess body fat because fat represents non-force-producing mass. A weight-loss plan must allow for sufficient amounts of carbohydrate and protein to support training as well as weight (fat) loss.

High-Fat Diets

Throwers have a tendency to have high-fat diets. Such diets may also be high in saturated fat. All athletes should be aware of the advantages of consuming heart-healthy fats, and substituting such fats for saturated fats should be encouraged. If weight loss is desired, reducing dietary fat would be appropriate.

Fluid Intake

Practices and meets may take place in hot and humid conditions. Fluid loss must be balanced with fluid intake.

FIGURE SKATING AT A GLANCE

Figure skating requires strength, power, and endurance. Individual competitions are held for men and women. Couples compete in pairs and ice dancing and there are team skating competitions. Training starts very early, sometimes at age 3, and many world champions are in their teens. Technique and speed are important, and the degree of skating difficulty increases as skaters become more elite. Artistry plays a critical role and there are many subjective elements considered in scoring. Competitions at the elite level include a short program that is 2 minutes and 40 seconds and a long program that is 4 minutes (females) or 4.5 minutes (males and pairs). Learn more about the sport at the US Figure Skating Web site (http://www.usfsa.org).

General Nutrition Guidelines

- Energy: Individualize based on body composition goals
- Carbohydrate: 5–8 g/kg/day
- Protein: 1.2–1.7 g/kg/day
- Fat: Remainder of kcal with an emphasis on heart-healthy fats

Common Nutrition Concerns

Energy Restriction

Despite the high energy demands of training, many female figure skaters limit energy intake in an effort to attain or maintain a low percentage of body fat. Weight loss must be slow with small restrictions of energy so that muscle mass can be protected and training will not be negatively impacted.

Body Composition

A low percentage of body fat, particularly for females, is considered necessary for success because of the physical demands of the sport and appearance, which is part of the subjective scoring system. The potential for disordered eating and eating disorders is great and early intervention is imperative.

Nutrient Intake

The consumption of nutrient-dense foods is important, especially if energy intake is restricted. Many figure skaters are children and adolescents and need adequate nutrition to support growth and development.

FOOTBALL AT A GLANCE

American football is played by two teams of 11 players each. Each play involves some high-intensity, short-duration activity and there is a short rest period between each play. Professional football games are four 15-minute quarters with a halftime break, but the clock is frequently stopped so the game takes about 4 hours to complete. Body composition varies by position, with receivers being lean and fast whereas linemen depend on their strength and body mass to block. College football players usually have a smaller body mass than professional players and must increase size if they move into the professional ranks. Learn more about the sport at the National Football League Web site (http://www.nfl.com) or Football.com (http://www.football.com).

General Nutrition Guidelines

- Energy: Energy expenditure varies depending on the level of the sport (professional, college, high school, or youth), level of training, amount of muscle mass, growth, etc, and must be individually determined.
- Carbohydrate: > 6 g/kg/day; 8–10 g/kg/day may be needed during rigorous training.
- Protein: 1.4–1.7 g/kg/day.
- Fat: Remainder of kcal as fat with an emphasis on heart-healthy fats.

Common Nutrition Concerns

Energy Intake

Energy intake goals vary among athletes but can be more than 5,000 kcal. Many wish to change body composition by increasing muscle mass (which may require a higher energy intake) or decreasing body fat.

Off-season Weight Gain

Players need to match their off-season energy intake with energy expenditure. Some football players arrive at training camp or spring football practice overweight and out of shape. When this is the case they often look for quick weight-loss methods. Some of these methods may be dangerous, such as voluntary dehydration, use of drugs thought to reduce body fat, and severe restriction of food intake. A nutrition and training plan during the off-season can help athletes prevent unwanted off-season weight gain.

High Fat Intake

Some football players eat out frequently and consume a high-fat, high-saturated fat diet.

Fluid and Electrolyte Intake

Football players may play in hot and humid conditions, often early in the season, before they are acclimated to the heat. Dehydration is a serious and potentially life threatening problem. Pads and clothing compound the situation. Fluid and electrolyte intakes must be balanced with losses. Approximately 10% of players may be "cramp prone" due to large losses of sodium in sweat. They may need additional sodium in addition to fluids to prevent heat cramps.

GOLF AT A GLANCE

Golf is a low-endurance, precision skill sport. It requires fine motor control and coordination. Swinging a club requires power and walking the course (especially if the golfer is carrying clubs) requires general fitness. Golf courses vary in length, but championship courses are approximately 6,000 to 7,000 yards, and an 18-hole course takes several hours to play. Women play shorter distances because of the location of the tees. Professional tournaments include four rounds (72 holes over 4 days) with additional holes played on the last day in case of ties. Learn more about the sport at the Web sites for the Professional Golfers' Association of America (http://www.pga.com) or the Ladies Professional Golf Association (http://www.lpga.com).

General Nutrition Guidelines

Golfers do not have significantly increased demands for energy or nutrients; thus, general nutrient guidelines are used and adjusted on an individual basis.

- Energy: Relatively low energy expenditure sport
- Carbohydrate: 5–7 g/kg/day
- Protein: 1.2–1.7 g/kg/day (often nearer the lower end of the range)
- Fat: ~ 1.0 g/kg/day or remainder of kcal with an emphasis on heart-healthy fats

Common Nutrition Concerns

Energy Intake

The focus is typically on energy balance, although some players may wish to reduce energy intake to lose body fat. Slow weight loss should not affect performance, but severe restriction could lead to inadequate total energy intake and/or low blood glucose, which could negatively affect performance.

Fluid Intake

Golf often takes place in hot and humid conditions. Dehydration is a daily concern and golfers are encouraged to consume fluids between holes.

Precompetition Meal

Players need to eat a meal prior to play because they will be on the course for many hours. Start times vary and may be changed due to weather delays. Breakfast is vital because golfers often start early in the morning. Golfers should have a plan for a pregame meal that considers volume, macronutrient composition, and timing of intake that can be adjusted if the start time changes. Golfers usually carry snacks, such as energy bars or sport drinks, to prevent hunger while playing.

Frequent Travel

Frequent travel makes it difficult to maintain a routine and increases exposure to high-calorie, low–nutrient density foods.

GYMNASTICS AT A GLANCE

Gymnastics involves activities that are typically characterized as high to very high intensity and short duration. In competition, athletes perform and then rest before beginning a new event. Gymnastics requires strength, power, and flexibility. Training is demanding, often involving many repetitions of individual skills or routines, but athletes can rest when it is not their turn to perform. Female gymnasts tend to be shorter and lighter than most other athletes and other females their age. A high percentage of lean body mass and a low percentage of body fat are desirable, not only to perform the skills, but also because such bodies are aesthetically appealing. It is biologically easier for males to attain the currently held "ideal" body type than for females. Learn more about the sport at the USA Gymnastics Web site (http://www.usa-gymnastics.org).

General Nutrition Guidelines

- Energy: Individualize based on body composition goals
- Carbohydrate: 5–8 g/kg/day
- Protein: 1.2–1.7 g/kg/day
- Fat: Remainder of kcal with an emphasis on heart-healthy fats

Common Nutrition Concerns

Energy Restriction

Despite the high energy demands of training, surveys suggest that many female gymnasts limit energy intake. If body fat loss is an appropriate goal, it must be slow with small restrictions of energy so that muscle mass can be protected and training will not be negatively affected.

Body Composition

A low percentage of body fat, which may be difficult for females to attain or maintain, is considered necessary for success because of the physical demands of the sport and appearance. Amenorrhea may be present and is a warning sign associated with excessive energy restriction and/or anorexia. The potential for disordered eating and eating disorders is great and early intervention is imperative.

Nutrient Intake

The consumption of nutrient-dense foods is important, especially if energy intake is restricted. Many gymnasts are children and adolescents and need adequate nutrition to support growth and development.

ICE HOCKEY AT A GLANCE

Ice hockey requires anaerobic power, aerobic conditioning, strength, agility, and speed. Similar to other intermittent, high-intensity sports, there are constant changes in speed and direction, but ice hockey differs from soccer or basketball in that there is full body contact. A game consists of three 16-minute periods, but frequent player substitutions reduce playing time to at least half of the game time. Learn more about the sport at the Web sites for the National Hockey League (http://www.nhl.com) and USA Hockey (http://www.usahockey.com).

General Nutrition Guidelines

- Energy: Varies based on level of training but generally a high-energy expenditure sport
- Carbohydrate: Daily intake > 6 g/kg/day; 8–10 g/kg/day during training and competition to ensure adequate glycogen in quadriceps
- Protein: 1.4–1.7 g/kg/day body weight
- Fat: Remainder of kcal with an emphasis on heart-healthy fats

Common Nutrition Concerns

Carbohydrate Intake

Hockey players need a large amount of carbohydrate daily to replenish glycogen that is used during demanding training sessions and games. Carbohydrate loading seems to be beneficial for performance.

Hydration During Exercise

Hydration during training and competition is important because players can sweat profusely under all of their gear.

Restoration of Glycogen, Fluids, and Electrolytes

Demanding practices, games, and training sessions deplete glycogen, fluids, and electrolytes. Glycogen stores and fluid and electrolyte losses must be replenished beginning immediately after competition or training. Some postexercise protein consumption is also encouraged. Appetite may be depressed. Liquid meal replacements may be beneficial.

MARTIAL ARTS AT A GLANCE

Martial arts is a broad term that describes combat activities. Boxing, fencing, judo, and tae kwon do may be the best known because they are Olympic sports, but there are hundreds of different types of martial arts. Each art is different, but most involve strength, flexibility, and agility, and some also include explosive movements. Many have weight classes and some martial artists use a variety of methods to "make weight." Participants in some competitions, such as judo or tae kwon do, compete several times over the course of a day. Learn more about the sports at the USA Dojo Web site (http://www.usadojo.com).

General Nutrition Guidelines

- Energy: Individualize based on body composition and weight goals
- Carbohydrate: 5–8 g/kg/day
- Protein: 1.2–1.7 g/kg/day
- Fat: Remainder of kcal with an emphasis on heart-healthy fats

Common Nutrition Concerns

Making Weight

As with any sport that has weight categories, rapid reduction of body weight, including extreme methods such as fasting, fluid restriction, or semistarvation, may be an issue. Rapid weight loss is more likely to be detrimental to performance than gradual weight loss. A weight-loss plan must allow for sufficient amounts of carbohydrate and protein to support training.

Nutrient Intake

The consumption of nutrient-dense foods is important, especially if energy intake is restricted. Meal timing and adequacy of intake during meets (multiple bouts during one day) should be addressed.

Fluid Intake

Dehydration is a daily concern. Fluid loss should be balanced with fluid intake. If dehydration is used as a weight-loss method, restoration of fluid and electrolyte balance is critical.

ROWING (CREW) AT A GLANCE

A typical crew race is 2,000 meters lasting 5½ to 8 minutes and requiring strength, power, and endurance. The crew season begins in the fall with preseason training. Winter is a time of intense training and building muscle, while the spring racing season is known for its long daily practices leading up to a rest day and weekend competition. Summer is the off-season. There are lightweight and open (heavy) weight categories. Learn more about the sport at the US Rowing Web site (http://www.usrowing.org).

General Nutrition Guidelines

- Energy: Relatively high energy expenditure sport
- Carbohydrate: 5–7 g/kg/day
- Protein: 1.2–1.7 g/kg/day
- Fat: ~ 1.0 g/kg/day. Fat, in the form of heart-healthy fats, may be increased to meet high energy needs while training but decreased during the off-season.

Common Nutrition Concerns

Energy Intake

Fatigue and lack of appetite may result in involuntary underconsumption of energy. Lightweight rowers may voluntarily restrict energy to make weight.

Making Weight

Lightweight rowers who are genetically lean and biologically small can comfortably meet the requirements for lightweight rowing. Problems with disordered eating and eating disorders occur when extraordinary efforts must be made to attain and maintain a low body weight. Voluntary dehydration may also be an issue.

Consumption of Foods with Low Nutrient Density

Rowers have high energy needs and heavyweight rowers, both males and females, quickly discover that they must eat a lot of food to maintain energy balance. High-fat, high-sugar snack foods and beverages can provide the energy needed but not the nutrients.

Balancing Fluid Intake with Fluid Losses

Dehydration is a daily concern. Rowers have water bottles in the boat during training, but they do not have access to them during long training pieces (approximately 30 to 45 minutes each). It is unlikely that rowers can maintain fluid balance during training.

SOCCER AT A GLANCE

Soccer involves short, intense bursts of activity combined with moderately intense exercise and occasional rest periods. When played outdoors, the field is larger than a football field and the average soccer player will cover between 8 and 12 km (5 to 7 miles) in a game. The game consists of two 45-minute halves with a 15-minute halftime, although the game is shorter for younger players. Learn more about the sport at the Web sites for US Soccer (http://www. ussoccer.com) and US Youth Soccer Association (http://www.usysa.org).

General Nutrition Guidelines

- Energy: Relatively high energy expenditure sport
- Carbohydrate: 6 g/kg/day; 8–10 g/kg/day during training and competition
- Protein: 1.4–1.7 g/kg/day
- Fat: Remainder of kcal with an emphasis on heart-healthy fats

Common Nutrition Concerns

Energy Intake

Energy expenditure is high during training and games. A 75-kg male soccer player may expend more than 1,500 kcal in a game. Many players, both male and female, do not consume an adequate energy intake and this can lead to early onset of fatigue and poor nutrient intake.

Fluid Intake

Players should consume fluid early and at regular intervals during the game. Needs are especially high in hot and humid conditions. Carbohydrate/electrolyte solutions are beneficial during the game. Special attention should be paid to youth soccer players because they do not sweat as much as adults, and the risk for dehydration and heat illness is high. Youth players should consume fluid at least every 15 to 20 minutes during practice and frequently during games.

Restoration of Glycogen, Fluids, and Electrolytes

Glycogen stores and fluid and electrolyte losses must be replenished beginning immediately after competition or training. Some postexercise protein consumption is also encouraged. Appetite may be depressed so liquid meal replacements may become an important option.

Frequent Travel

Frequent travel makes it difficult to maintain a routine and increases exposure to high-energy, low-nutrient density foods.

SWIMMING AT A GLANCE

Swimming is a sport of various intensities and durations. Swimming events can range from 50 and 100 meters (sprints), 200 and 400 meters (middle distances), and 800 and 1,500 meters (distance). Long-distance swimming includes the swim portion of the full triathlon (2.4 miles) and ultraendurance events, such as swimming the English Channel (~ 24 miles). All swimmers have demanding training, so adequate daily energy and nutrient intake is important. Learn more about the sport at the USA Swimming Web site (http://www. usaswimming.org).

General Nutrition Guidelines

Recommendations must be tailored to the individual based on the level of training and the distance. For swimming events ranging from 50 to 1,500 meters, the general guidelines include the following:

- Energy: Calculate individual needs based on demands of training
- Carbohydrate: 5–8 g/kg/day
- Protein: 1.2–1.7 g/kg/day
- Fat: ~1.0 g/kg/day or remainder of kcal with an emphasis on heart-healthy fats

Long-distance swimming guidelines can be found under Endurance and Ultraendurance Sports in this At-a-Glance section.

Common Nutrition Concerns

Energy and Carbohydrate Intake

Energy and nutrient needs are high, and a well-balanced diet is important. Chronic undereating can be a problem. Frequent meals or snacks are important.

Fluid Intake

Dehydration is a daily concern. Thirst is not a good indicator of dehydration and an effort must be made to match fluid loss with fluid intake.

Restoration of Glycogen, Fluids, and Electrolytes

Glycogen stores and fluid and electrolyte losses must be replenished beginning immediately after competition or training. Some postexercise protein consumption is also encouraged. Two-a-day swim practices are often conducted and rapid replenishment of glycogen and fluid balance is critical.

Body Composition

Appropriate percentage body fat varies depending on the distance. Reducing body fat should be a slow process because too great a reduction in energy, carbohydrate, and protein intakes can negatively affect training and performance.

Risk for Disordered Eating and Eating Disorders

Swimmers are at risk for developing disordered eating and eating disorders. Refer to qualified health professionals when necessary.

TENNIS AT A GLANCE

Tennis requires anaerobic power, aerobic conditioning, strength, and agility. The game may be played casually or with great intensity and duration; thus, training and nutrient requirements vary tremendously. One (singles) or two (doubles) players are on each side. Male professional singles players must win three of five sets and singles matches typically last 2 to 4 hours. Females play the best of three sets. Most singles players hit from the baseline and long rallies require excellent fitness. Most tournaments are 1 week in length but major tournaments are 2 weeks long. Recreational players play at a variety of intensities and some do not have significantly increased demands for energy or nutrients. Learn more about the sport at the US Tennis Association Web site (http://www.usta.com).

General Nutrition Guidelines

- Energy: Varies depending on the level of training and the intensity and duration of play. Professional and collegiate players have high energy expenditures.
- Carbohydrate: 5–8 g/kg/day; 8–10 g/kg/day near the end of tournaments
- Protein: 1.2–1.7 g/kg/day
- Fat: ~ 1.0 g/kg/day or the remainder of kcal as fat with an emphasis on heart-healthy fats

Common Nutrition Concerns

Fluid and Electrolyte Intake

Practice and play typically takes place in hot and/or humid conditions. Dehydration is a daily concern. Some players may be "cramp prone" due to large losses of sodium in sweat. They may need additional sodium in addition to fluids to prevent heat cramps.

Restoration of Glycogen, Fluids, and Electrolytes

Demanding practices, training sessions, and match play deplete glycogen, fluids, and electrolytes. Glycogen stores and fluid and electrolyte losses must be replenished beginning immediately after competition or training. Some postexercise protein consumption is also encouraged. Near the end of the tournament, replenishment is especially important for peak performance.

Prematch Meal

Players, especially males, will be on the court for many hours and they need to eat a meal prior to play. Start time may not be known (due to the length of other matches) and play may be stopped and restarted with short notice due to rain. Tennis players should have a plan for a prematch meal that considers volume, macronutrient composition, and timing of intake. The meal can then be adjusted based on start time.

Multiple Matches in One Day

Tennis players may play more than one match in a day. This is especially true for younger athletes who compete in tournaments. "Mini-meals" or snacks may be needed, because sport drinks alone may not be substantial enough.

Frequent Travel

Frequent travel makes it difficult to maintain a routine and increases exposure to high-calorie, low-nutrient density foods.

TRACK EVENTS AT A GLANCE

Track events range from the very fast 100-meter race to the much longer 10,000-meter run or 20,000-meter walking events. Nutrition recommendations must consider the distance involved. Daily workouts are intense. Athletes may compete several times during the course of a day. For most very high–intensity, brief events, diet has less of an impact than other factors such as genetics and training. Compared with distance runners, middle-distance runners have more moderate carbohydrate needs. Learn more about the various track events and the demands of training at the USA Track and Field Web site (http://www.usatf.org).

General Nutrition Guidelines

- Energy: Individualize based on body composition goals
- Carbohydrate (varies depending on training demands):
  - ➤ Very high–intensity, brief events (100–400 meters): 6–8 g/kg/day
  - ➤ High-intensity, short-duration events (800–10,000 meters): 5–7 g/kg/day
- Protein: 1.2–1.7 g/kg/day
- Fat: ~1.0 g/kg/day or remainder of calories after carbohydrate and protein needs are met

Common Nutrition Concerns

Energy Intake

In general, daily energy expenditure is high due to demanding training. Reported daily intakes are often less than estimated needs.

Weight Loss

High muscularity is valued so many track athletes are attempting to lose body fat. Rapid weight loss is more likely to be detrimental to performance than gradual weight loss. A weight-loss plan must allow for sufficient amounts of carbohydrate and protein to support training.

Potential for Disordered Eating or Eating Disorders

Pressure to attain or maintain a low percentage body fat and/or an undue focus on body appearance increase the risk for athletes, particularly female middle-distance runners, to develop disordered eating or eating disorders.

WRESTLING AT A GLANCE

Wrestling involves hand-to-hand combat and requires strength and stamina. A high strength (power)-to-weight ratio is desirable. The sport features weight divisions and some wrestlers "make weight" using drastic measures. Deaths have resulted through the combined use of a variety of techniques including voluntary dehydration and starvation. Rule changes have been instituted to reduce excessive weight loss, including assessing body fat at the beginning of the season, determining a minimum competitive weight, and holding weigh-ins close to the start of competition. No longer just a men's sport, women's wrestling became an Olympic sport in 2004, and the number of high school and collegiate female wrestlers is expected to grow. Learn more about the sport at the Web sites for USA Wrestling (http://themat.com), National Collegiate Athletics Association Wrestling (http://www.ncaa.org/sports/wrestling), and the National Federation of State High School Associations (http://www.nfhs.org).

General Nutrition Guidelines

- Energy: Individualize based on body composition and weight goals
- Carbohydrate: 5–8 g/kg/day
- Protein: 1.2–1.7 g/kg/day (protein requirements may increase to 2g/kg/day during periods of lowest energy intake to achieve weight loss)
- Fat: Remainder of kcal with an emphasis on heart-healthy fats

Common Nutrition Concerns

Energy Intake

Appropriate energy intake must be individually determined. A focus on performance and health, not just weight, can help wrestlers view energy intake from a positive perspective.

Cutting Weight or Making Weight

Weight-cutting practices can be severe and life threatening, although new rules have resulted in less extreme weight-cutting behaviors than in the past. Collegiate wrestlers use more extreme methods than high school wrestlers. Wrestlers in lower weight classes have relatively larger weight changes than those in heavier weight classes. Fasting, fluid restriction, and semistarvation are popular methods to make weight at all levels. Saunas, sweat suits (although banned), and diuretics may also be used. Nutrition counseling across the season is important to develop individualized plans, discuss weight loss methods, and monitor weight changes.

Nutrient Intake

The consumption of nutrient-dense foods is important, especially if energy intake is restricted. Wrestlers have demanding training programs, and sufficient macro- and micronutrient intakes are important to support training, performance, and health. Many wrestlers are adolescents and need adequate nutrition to support growth and development as well.

Fluid Intake

Dehydration is a daily concern. Fluid loss should be balanced with fluid intake. If dehydration is used as a weight loss method, restoration of fluid and electrolyte balance is critical.

Appendix A

DIETARY REFERENCE INTAKES

Dietary Reference Intakes (DRIs): Recommended Intakes for Individuals, Vitamins
Food and Nutrition Board, Institute of Medicine, National Academies

Life Stage Group	Vit A (µg/d)[a]	Vit C (mg/d)	Vit D (µg/d)[b,c]	Vit E (mg/d)[d]	Vit K (µg/d)	Thia-min (mg/d)	Ribo-flavin (mg/d)	Niacin (mg/d)[e]	Vit B6 (mg/d)	Folate (µg/d)[f]	Vit B12 (µg/d)	Panto-thenic Acid (mg/d)	Biotin (µg/d)	Choline[g] (mg/d)
Infants														
0–6 mo	400*	40*	5*	4*	2.0*	0.2*	0.3*	2*	0.1*	65*	0.4*	1.7*	5*	125*
7–12 mo	500*	50*	5*	5*	2.5*	0.3*	0.4*	4*	0.3*	80*	0.5*	1.8*	6*	150*
Children														
1–3 y	300	15	5*	6	30*	0.5	0.5	6	0.5	150	0.9	2*	8*	200*
4–8 y	400	25	5*	7	55*	0.6	0.6	8	0.6	200	1.2	3*	12*	250*
Males														
9–13 y	600	45	5*	11	60*	0.9	0.9	12	1.0	300	1.8	4*	20*	375*
14–18 y	900	75	5*	15	75*	1.2	1.3	16	1.3	400	2.4	5*	25*	550*
19–30 y	900	90	5*	15	120*	1.2	1.3	16	1.3	400	2.4	5*	30*	550*
31–50 y	900	90	5*	15	120*	1.2	1.3	16	1.3	400	2.4	5*	30*	550*
51–70 y	900	90	10*	15	120*	1.2	1.3	16	1.7	400	2.4[i]	5*	30*	550*
> 70 y	900	90	15*	15	120*	1.2	1.3	16	1.7	400	2.4[i]	5*	30*	550*
Females														
9–13 y	600	45	5*	11	60*	0.9	0.9	12	1.0	300	1.8	4*	20*	375*
14–18 y	700	65	5*	15	75*	1.0	1.0	14	1.2	400[i]	2.4	5*	25*	400*
19–30 y	700	75	5*	15	90*	1.1	1.1	14	1.3	400[i]	2.4	5*	30*	425*
31–50 y	700	75		15	90*	1.1	1.1	14	1.3	400[i]	2.4	5*	30*	425*
51–70 y	700	75	10*	15	90*	1.1	1.1	14	1.5	400	2.4[h]	5*	30*	425*
> 70 y	700	75	15*	15	90*	1.1	1.1	14	1.5	400	2.4[h]	5*	30*	425*
Pregnancy														
14–18 y	750	80	5*	15	75*	1.4	1.4	18	1.9	600[j]	2.6	6*	30*	450*
19–30 y	770	85	5*	15	90*	1.4	1.4	18	1.9	600[j]	2.6	6*	30*	450*
31–50 y	770	85	5*	15	90*	1.4	1.4	18	1.9	600[j]	2.6	6*	30*	450*
Lactation														
14–18 y	1,200	115	5*	19	75*	1.4	1.6	17	2.0	500	2.8	7*	35*	550*
19–30 y	1,300	120	5*	19	90*	1.4	1.6	17	2.0	500	2.8	7*	35*	550*
31–50 y	1,300	120	5*	19	90*	1.4	1.6	17	2.0	500	2.8	7*	35*	550*

NOTE: This table (taken from the DRI reports, see www.nap.edu) presents Recommended Dietary Allowances (RDAs) in **bold type** and Adequate Intakes (AIs) in ordinary type followed by an asterisk (*). RDAs and AIs may both be used as goals for individual intake. RDAs are set to meet the needs of almost all (97 to 98 percent) individuals in a group. For healthy breastfed infants, the AI is the mean intake. The AI for other life stage and gender groups is believed to cover needs of all individuals in the group, but lack of data or uncertainty in the data prevent being able to specify with confidence the percentage of individuals covered by this intake.

[a] As retinol activity equivalents (RAEs). 1 RAE = 1 µg retinol, 12 µg β-carotene, 24 µg α-carotene, or 24 µg β-cryptoxanthin. The RAE for dietary provitamin A carotenoids is twofold greater than retinol equivalents (RE), whereas the RAE for preformed vitamin A is the same as RE.

[b] As cholecalciferol. 1 µg cholecalciferol = 40 IU vitamin D.

[c] In the absence of adequate exposure to sunlight.

[d] As α-tocopherol. α-Tocopherol includes *RRR*-α-tocopherol, the only form of α-tocopherol that occurs naturally in foods, and the *2R*-stereoisomeric forms of α-tocopherol (*RRR*-, *RSR*-, *RRS*-, and *RSS*-α-tocopherol) that occur in fortified foods and supplements. It does not include the *2S*-stereoisomeric forms of α-tocopherol (*SRR*-, *SSR*-, *SRS*-, and *SSS*-α-tocopherol), also found in fortified foods and supplements.

[e] As niacin equivalents (NE). 1 mg of niacin = 60 mg of tryptophan; 0–6 months = preformed niacin (not NE).

[f] As dietary folate equivalents (DFE). 1 DFE = 1 µg food folate = 0.6 µg of folic acid from fortified food or as a supplement consumed with food = 0.5 µg of a supplement taken on an empty stomach.

[g] Although AIs have been set for choline, there are few data to assess whether a dietary supply of choline is needed at all stages of the life cycle, and it may be that the choline requirement can be met by endogenous synthesis at some of these stages.

[h] Because 10 to 30 percent of older people may malabsorb food-bound B12, it is advisable for those older than 50 years to meet their RDA mainly by consuming foods fortified with B12 or a supplement containing B12.

[i] In view of evidence linking folate intake with neural tube defects in the fetus, it is recommended that all women capable of becoming pregnant consume 400 µg from supplements or fortified foods in addition to intake of food folate from a varied diet.

[jk] It is assumed that women will continue consuming 400 µg from supplements or fortified food until their pregnancy is confirmed and they enter prenatal care, which ordinarily occurs after the end of the periconceptional period—the critical time for formation of the neural tube.

Source: All tables in this appendix are reprinted with permission from National Academy Press.

Dietary Reference Intakes (DRIs): Recommended Intakes for Individuals, Elements
Food and Nutrition Board, Institute of Medicine, National Academies

Life Stage Group	Calcium (mg/d)	Chromium (µg/d)	Copper (µg/d)	Fluoride (mg/d)	Iodine (µg/d)	Iron (mg/d)	Magnesium (mg/d)	Manganese (mg/d)	Molybdenum (µg/d)	Phosphorus (mg/d)	Selenium (µg/d)	Zinc (mg/d)	Potassium (g/d)	Sodium (g/d)	Chloride (g/d)
Infants															
0–6 mo	210*	0.2*	200*	0.01*	110*	0.27*	30*	0.003*	2*	100*	15*	2*	0.4*	0.12*	0.18*
7–12 mo	270*	5.5*	220*	0.5*	130*	11	75*	0.6*	3*	275*	20*	3	0.7*	0.37*	0.57*
Children															
1–3 y	500*	11*	340	0.7*	90	7	80	1.2*	17	460	20	3	3.0*	1.0*	1.5*
4–8 y	800*	15*	440	1*	90	10	130	1.5*	22	500	30	5	3.8*	1.2*	1.9*
Males															
9–13 y	1,300*	25*	700	2*	120	8	240	1.9*	34	1,250	40	8	4.5*	1.5*	2.3*
14–18 y	1,300*	35*	890	3*	150	11	410	2.2*	43	1,250	55	11	4.7*	1.5*	2.3*
19–30 y	1,000*	35*	900	4*	150	8	400	2.3*	45	700	55	11	4.7*	1.5*	2.3*
31–50 y	1,000*	35*	900	4*	150	8	420	2.3*	45	700	55	11	4.7*	1.5*	2.3*
51–70 y	1,200*	30*	900	4*	150	8	420	2.3*	45	700	55	11	4.7*	1.3*	2.0*
>70 y	1,200*	30*	900	4*	150	8	420	2.3*	45	700	55	11	4.7*	1.2*	1.8*
Females															
9–13 y	1,300*	21*	700	2*	120	8	240	1.6*	34	1,250	40	8	4.5*	1.5*	2.3*
14–18 y	1,300*	24*	890	3*	150	15	360	1.6*	43	1,250	55	9	4.7*	1.5*	2.3*
19–30 y	1,000*	25*	900	3*	150	18	310	1.8*	45	700	55	8	4.7*	1.5*	2.3*
31–50 y	1,000*	25*	900	3*	150	18	320	1.8*	45	700	55	8	4.7*	1.5*	2.3*
51–70 y	1,200*	20*	900	3*	150	8	320	1.8*	45	700	55	8	4.7*	1.3*	2.0*
>70 y	1,200*	20*	900	3*	150	8	320	1.8*	45	700	55	8	4.7*	1.2*	1.8*
Pregnancy															
14–18 y	1,300*	29*	1,000	3*	220	27	400	2.0*	50	1,250	60	13	4.7*	1.5*	2.3*
19–30 y	1,000*	30*	1,000	3*	220	27	350	2.0*	50	700	60	11	4.7*	1.5*	2.3*
31–50 y	1,000*	30*	1,000	3*	220	27	360	2.0*	50	700	60	11	4.7*	1.5*	2.3*
Lactation															
14–18 y	1,300*	44*	1,300	3*	290	10	360	2.6*	50	1,250	70	14	5.1*	1.5*	2.3*
19–30 y	1,000*	45*	1,300	3*	290	9	310	2.6*	50	700	70	12	5.1*	1.5*	2.3*
31–50 y	1,000*	45*	1,300	3*	290	9	320	2.6*	50	700	70	12	5.1*	1.5*	2.3*

NOTE: This table presents Recommended Dietary Allowances (RDAs) in **bold type** and Adequate Intakes (AIs) in ordinary type followed by an asterisk (*). RDAs and AIs may both be used as goals for individual intake. RDAs are set to meet the needs of almost all (97 to 98 percent) individuals in a group. For healthy breastfed infants, the AI is the mean intake. The AI for other life stage and gender groups is believed to cover needs of all individuals in the group, but lack of data or uncertainty in the data prevent being able to specify with confidence the percentage of individuals covered by this intake.

SOURCES: *Dietary Reference Intakes for Calcium, Phosphorous, Magnesium, Vitamin D, and Fluoride* (1997); *Dietary Reference Intakes for Thiamin, Riboflavin, Niacin, Vitamin B6, Folate, Vitamin B12, Pantothenic Acid, Biotin, and Choline* (1998); *Dietary Reference Intakes for Vitamin C, Vitamin E, Selenium, and Carotenoids* (2000); *Dietary Reference Intakes for Vitamin A, Vitamin K, Arsenic, Boron, Chromium, Copper, Iodine, Iron, Manganese, Molybdenum, Nickel, Silicon, Vanadium, and Zinc* (2001); and *Dietary Reference Intakes for Water, Potassium, Sodium, Chloride, and Sulfate* (2004). These reports may be accessed via http://www.nap.edu.

Dietary Reference Intakes (DRIs): Tolerable Upper Intake Levels (UL[a]), Vitamins
Food and Nutrition Board, Institute of Medicine, National Academies

Life Stage Group	Vitamin A (µg/d)[b]	Vitamin C (mg/d)	Vitamin D (µg/d)	Vitamin E (mg/d)[c,d]	Vitamin K	Thiamin	Riboflavin	Niacin (mg/d)[d]	Vitamin B6 (mg/d)	Folate (µg/d)[d]	Vitamin B12	Pantothenic Acid	Biotin	Choline (g/d)	Carotenoids[e]
Infants															
0–6 mo	600	ND[f]	25	ND	ND	ND	ND	ND	ND	ND	ND	ND	ND	ND	ND
7–12 mo	600	ND	25	ND	ND	ND	ND	ND	ND	ND	ND	ND	ND	ND	ND
Children															
1–3 y	600	400	50	200	ND	ND	ND	10	30	300	ND	ND	ND	1.0	ND
4–8 y	900	650	50	300	ND	ND	ND	15	40	400	ND	ND	ND	1.0	ND
Males, Females															
9–13 y	1,700	1,200	50	600	ND	ND	ND	20	60	600	ND	ND	ND	2.0	ND
14–18 y	2,800	1,800	50	800	ND	ND	ND	30	80	800	ND	ND	ND	3.0	ND
19–70 y	3,000	2,000	50	1,000	ND	ND	ND	35	100	1,000	ND	ND	ND	3.5	ND
>70 y	3,000	2,000	50	1,000	ND	ND	ND	35	100	1,000	ND	ND	ND	3.5	ND
Pregnancy															
14–18 y	2,800	1,800	50	800	ND	ND	ND	30	80	800	ND	ND	ND	3.0	ND
19–50 y	3,000	2,000	50	1,000	ND	ND	ND	35	100	1,000	ND	ND	ND	3.5	ND
Lactation															
14–18 y	2,800	1,800	50	800	ND	ND	ND	30	80	800	ND	ND	ND	3.0	ND
19–50 y	3,000	2,000	50	1,000	ND	ND	ND	35	100	1,000	ND	ND	ND	3.5	ND

[a] UL = The maximum level of daily nutrient intake that is likely to pose no risk of adverse effects. Unless otherwise specified, the UL represents total intake from food, water, and supplements. Due to lack of suitable data, ULs could not be established for vitamin K, thiamin, riboflavin, vitamin B12, pantothenic acid, biotin, carotenoids. In the absence of ULs, extra caution may be warranted in consuming levels above recommended intakes.
[b] As preformed vitamin A only.
[c] As α-tocopherol; applies to any form of supplemental α-tocopherol.
[d] The ULs for vitamin E, niacin, and folate apply to synthetic forms obtained from supplements, fortified foods, or a combination of the two.
[e] β-Carotene supplements are advised only to serve as a provitamin A source for individuals at risk of vitamin A deficiency.
[f] ND = Not determinable due to lack of data of adverse effects in this age group and concern with regard to lack of ability to handle excess amounts. Source of intake should be from food only to prevent high levels of intake.

SOURCES: *Dietary Reference Intakes for Calcium, Phosphorous, Magnesium, Vitamin D, and Fluoride* (1997); *Dietary Reference Intakes for Thiamin, Riboflavin, Niacin, Vitamin B6, Folate, Vitamin B12, Pantothenic Acid, Biotin, and Choline* (1998); *Dietary Reference Intakes for Vitamin C, Vitamin E, Selenium, and Carotenoids* (2000); and *Dietary Reference Intakes for Vitamin A, Vitamin K, Arsenic, Boron, Chromium, Copper, Iodine, Iron, Manganese, Molybdenum, Nickel, Silicon, Vanadium, and Zinc* (2001). These reports may be accessed via http://www.nap.edu.

Dietary Reference Intakes (DRIs): Tolerable Upper Intake Levels (UL[a]), Elements
Food and Nutrition Board, Institute of Medicine, National Academies

Life Stage Group	Arsenic[b]	Boron (mg/d)	Calcium (g/d)	Chromium	Copper (µg/d)	Fluoride (mg/d)	Iodine (µg/d)	Iron (mg/d)	Magnesium (mg/d)[c]	Manganese (mg/d)	Molybdenum (µg/d)	Nickel (mg/d)	Phosphorus (g/d)	Potassium	Selenium (µg/d)	Silicon[d]	Sulfate	Vanadium (mg/d)[e]	Zinc (mg/d)	Sodium (g/d)	Chloride (g/d)
Infants																					
0–6 mo	ND[f]	ND	ND	ND	ND	0.7	ND	40	ND	ND	ND	ND	ND	ND	45	ND	ND	ND	4	ND	ND
7–12 mo	ND	ND	ND	ND	ND	0.9	ND	40	ND	ND	ND	ND	ND	ND	60	ND	ND	ND	5	ND	ND
Children																					
1–3 y	ND	3	2.5	ND	1,000	1.3	200	40	65	2	300	0.2	3	ND	90	ND	ND	ND	7	1.5	2.3
4–8 y	ND	6	2.5	ND	3,000	2.2	300	40	110	3	600	0.3	3	ND	150	ND	ND	ND	12	1.9	2.9
Males, Females																					
9–13 y	ND	11	2.5	ND	5,000	10	600	40	350	6	1,100	0.6	4	ND	280	ND	ND	ND	23	2.2	3.4
14–18 y	ND	17	2.5	ND	8,000	10	900	45	350	9	1,700	1.0	4	ND	400	ND	ND	ND	34	2.3	3.6
19–70 y	ND	20	2.5	ND	10,000	10	1,100	45	350	11	2,000	1.0	4	ND	400	ND	ND	1.8	40	2.3	3.6
>70 y	ND	20	2.5	ND	10,000	10	1,100	45	350	11	2,000	1.0	3	ND	400	ND	ND	1.8	40	2.3	3.6
Pregnancy																					
14–18 y	ND	17	2.5	ND	8,000	10	900	45	350	9	1,700	1.0	3.5	ND	400	ND	ND	ND	34	2.3	3.6
19–50 y	ND	20	2.5	ND	10,000	10	1,100	45	350	11	2,000	1.0	3.5	ND	400	ND	ND	ND	40	2.3	3.6
Lactation																					
14–18 y	ND	17	2.5	ND	8,000	10	900	45	350	9	1,700	1.0	4	ND	400	ND	ND	ND	34	2.3	3.6
19–50 y	ND	20	2.5	ND	10,000	10	1,100	45	350	11	2,000	1.0	4	ND	400	ND	ND	ND	40	2.3	3.6

[a] UL = The maximum level of daily nutrient intake that is likely to pose no risk of adverse effects. Unless otherwise specified, the UL represents total intake from food, water, and supplements. Due to lack of suitable data, ULs could not be established for arsenic, chromium, silicon, potassium, and sulfate. In the absence of ULs, extra caution may be warranted in consuming levels above recommended intakes.

[b] Although the UL was not determined for arsenic, there is no justification for adding arsenic to food or supplements.

[c] The ULs for magnesium represent intake from a pharmacological agent only and do not include intake from food and water.

[d] Although silicon has not been shown to cause adverse effects in humans, there is no justification for adding silicon to supplements.

[e] Although vanadium in food has not been shown to cause adverse effects in humans, there is no justification for adding vanadium to food and vanadium supplements should be used with caution. The UL is based on adverse effects in laboratory animals and this data could be used to set a UL for adults but not children and adolescents.

[f] ND = Not determinable due to lack of data of adverse effects in this age group and concern with regard to lack of ability to handle excess amounts. Source of intake should be from food only to prevent high levels of intake.

SOURCES: *Dietary Reference Intakes for Calcium, Phosphorous, Magnesium, Vitamin D, and Fluoride* (1997); *Dietary Reference Intakes for Thiamin, Riboflavin, Niacin, Vitamin B6, Folate, Vitamin B12, Pantothenic Acid, Biotin, and Choline* (1998); *Dietary Reference Intakes for Vitamin C, Vitamin E, Selenium, and Carotenoids* (2000); *Dietary Reference Intakes for Vitamin A, Vitamin K, Arsenic, Boron, Chromium, Copper, Iodine, Iron, Manganese, Molybdenum, Nickel, Silicon, Vanadium, and Zinc* (2001); and *Dietary Reference Intakes for Water, Potassium, Sodium, Chloride, and Sulfate* (2004). These reports may be accessed via http://www.nap.edu.

Dietary Reference Intakes (DRIs): Estimated Energy Requirements (EER) for Men and Women
30 Years of Age[a]

Food and Nutrition Board, Institute of Medicine, National Academies

Height (m [in])	PAL[b]	Weight for BMI[c] of 18.5 kg/m² (kg [lb])	Weight for BMI of 24.99 kg/m² (kg [lb])	EER, Men[d] (kcal/day)		EER, Women[d] (kcal/day)	
				BMI of 18.5 kg/m²	BMI of 24.99 kg/m²	BMI of 18.5 kg/m²	BMI of 24.99 kg/m²
1.50 (59)	Sedentary	41.6 (92)	56.2 (124)	1,848	2,080	1,625	1,762
	Low active			2,009	2,267	1,803	1,956
	Active			2,215	2,506	2,025	2,198
	Very active			2,554	2,898	2,291	2,489
1.65 (65)	Sedentary	50.4 (111)	68.0 (150)	2,068	2,349	1,816	1,982
	Low active			2,254	2,566	2,016	2,202
	Active			2,490	2,842	2,267	2,477
	Very active			2,880	3,296	2,567	2,807
1.80 (71)	Sedentary	59.9 (132)	81.0 (178)	2,301	2,635	2,015	2,211
	Low active			2,513	2,884	2,239	2,459
	Active			2,782	3,200	2,519	2,769
	Very active			3,225	3,720	2,855	3,141

[a] For each year below 30, add 7 kcal/day for women and 10 kcal /day for men. For each year above 30, subtract 7 kcal/day for women and 10 kcal/day for men.

[b] PAL = physical activity level.

[c] BMI = body mass index.

[d] Derived from the following regression equations based on doubly labeled water data:

Adult man: $EER = 662 - 9.53 \times age\ (y) + PA \times (15.91 \times wt\ [kg] + 539.6 \times ht\ [m])$

Adult woman: $EER = 354 - 6.91 \times age\ (y) + PA \times (9.36 \times wt\ [kg] + 726 \times ht\ [m])$

Where PA refers to coefficient for PAL

PAL = total energy expenditure ÷ basal energy expenditure

PA = 1.0 if PAL ≥ 1.0 < 1.4 (sedentary)

PA = 1.12 if PAL ≥ 1.4 < 1.6 (low active)

PA = 1.27 if PAL ≥ 1.6 < 1.9 (active)

PA = 1.45 if PAL ≥ 1.9 < 2.5 (very active)

Dietary Reference Intakes (DRIs): Acceptable Macronutrient Distribution Ranges

Food and Nutrition Board, Institute of Medicine, National Academies

Macronutrient	Range (percent of energy)		
	Children, 1–3 y	Children, 4–18 y	Adults
Fat	30–40	25–35	20–35
n-6 polyunsaturated fatty acids[a] (linoleic acid)	5–10	5–10	5–10
n-3 polyunsaturated fatty acids[a] (α-linolenic acid)	0.6–1.2	0.6–1.2	0.6–1.2
Carbohydrate	45–65	45–65	45–65
Protein	5–20	10–30	10–35

[a] Approximately 10% of the total can come from longer-chain n-3 or n-6 fatty acids.

SOURCE: *Dietary Reference Intakes for Energy, Carbohydrate, Fiber, Fat, Fatty Acids, Cholesterol, Protein, and Amino Acids* (2002).

Dietary Reference Intakes (DRIs): Recommended Intakes for Individuals, Macronutrients
Food and Nutrition Board, Institute of Medicine, National Academies

Life Stage Group	Total Water[a] (L/d)	Carbohydrate (g/d)	Total Fiber (g/d)	Fat (g/d)	Linoleic Acid (g/d)	α-Linolenic Acid (g/d)	Protein[b] (g/d)
Infants							
0–6 mo	0.7*	60*	ND	31*	4.4*	0.5*	9.1*
7–12 mo	0.8*	95*	ND	30*	4.6*	0.5*	**13.5**
Children							
1–3 y	1.3*	**130**	19*	ND	7*	0.7*	**13**
4–8 y	1.7*	**130**	25*	ND	10*	0.9*	**19**
Males							
9–13 y	2.4*	**130**	31*	ND	12*	1.2*	**34**
14–18 y	3.3*	**130**	38*	ND	16*	1.6*	**52**
19–30 y	3.7*	**130**	38*	ND	17*	1.6*	**56**
31–50 y	3.7*	**130**	38*	ND	17*	1.6*	**56**
51–70 y	3.7*	**130**	30*	ND	14*	1.6*	**56**
> 70 y	3.7*	**130**	30*	ND	14*	1.6*	**56**
Females							
9–13 y	2.1*	**130**	26*	ND	10*	1.0*	**34**
14–18 y	2.3*	**130**	26*	ND	11*	1.1*	**46**
19–30 y	2.7*	**130**	25*	ND	12*	1.1*	**46**
31–50 y	2.7*	**130**	25*	ND	12*	1.1*	**46**
51–70 y	2.7*	**130**	21*	ND	11*	1.1*	**46**
> 70 y	2.7*	**130**	21*	ND	11*	1.1*	**46**
Pregnancy							
14–18 y	3.0*	**175**	28*	ND	13*	1.4*	**71**
19–30 y	3.0*	**175**	28*	ND	13*	1.4*	**71**
31–50 y	3.0*	**175**	28*	ND	13*	1.4*	**71**
Lactation							
14–18 y	3.8*	**210**	29*	ND	13*	1.3*	**71**
19–30 y	3.8*	**210**	29*	ND	13*	1.3*	**71**
31–50 y	3.8*	**210**	29*	ND	13*	1.3*	**71**

NOTE: This table presents Recommended Dietary Allowances (RDAs) in **bold** type and Adequate Intakes (AIs) in ordinary type followed by an asterisk (*). RDAs and AIs may both be used as goals for individual intake. RDAs are set to meet the needs of almost all (97 to 98 percent) individuals in a group. For healthy infants fed human milk, the AI is the mean intake. The AI for other life stage and gender groups is believed to cover the needs of all individuals in the group, but lack of data or uncertainty in the data prevent being able to specify with confidence the percentage of individuals covered by this intake.
[a] Total water includes all water contained in food, beverages, and drinking water.
[b] Based on 0.8 g/kg body weight for the reference body weight.

Dietary Reference Intakes (DRIs): Additional Macronutrient Recommendations
Food and Nutrition Board, Institute of Medicine, National Academies

Macronutrient	Recommendation
Dietary cholesterol	As low as possible while consuming a nutritionally adequate diet
Trans fatty acids	As low as possible while consuming a nutritionally adequate diet
Saturated fatty acids	As low as possible while consuming a nutritionally adequate diet
Added sugars	Limit to no more than 25% of total energy

SOURCE: *Dietary Reference Intakes for Energy, Carbohydrate, Fiber, Fat, Fatty Acids, Cholesterol, Protein, and Amino Acids* (2002).

Appendix B

BODY MASS INDEX (BMI) AT SPECIFIC HEIGHTS AND WEIGHTS

Instructions: Find height in left-hand column. Find weight in the row corresponding to height. BMI is the number at the bottom of the column.

Height, in									Body Weight, lb									
58	91	96	100	105	110	115	119	124	129	134	138	143	148	153	158	162	167	172
59	94	99	104	109	114	119	124	128	133	138	143	148	153	158	163	168	173	178
60	97	102	107	112	118	123	128	133	138	143	148	153	158	163	168	174	179	184
61	100	106	111	116	122	127	132	137	143	148	153	158	164	169	174	180	185	190
62	104	109	115	120	126	131	136	142	147	153	158	164	169	175	180	186	191	196
63	107	113	118	124	130	135	141	146	152	158	163	169	175	180	186	191	197	203
64	110	116	122	128	134	140	145	151	157	163	169	174	180	186	192	197	204	209
65	114	120	126	132	138	144	150	156	162	168	174	180	186	192	198	204	210	216
66	118	124	130	136	142	148	155	161	167	173	179	186	192	198	204	210	216	223
67	121	127	134	140	146	153	159	166	172	178	185	191	198	204	211	217	223	230
68	125	131	138	144	151	158	164	171	177	184	190	197	203	210	216	223	230	236
69	128	135	142	146	155	162	169	176	182	189	196	203	209	216	223	230	236	243
70	132	139	146	153	160	167	174	181	188	195	202	209	216	222	229	236	243	250
71	136	143	150	157	165	172	179	186	193	200	208	215	222	229	236	243	250	257
72	140	147	154	162	169	177	184	191	199	206	213	221	228	235	242	250	258	265
73	144	151	159	166	174	182	189	197	204	212	219	227	235	242	250	257	265	272
74	148	155	163	171	179	186	194	202	210	218	225	233	241	249	256	264	272	280
75	152	160	168	176	184	192	200	208	216	224	232	240	248	256	264	272	279	287
76	156	164	172	180	189	197	205	213	221	230	238	246	254	263	271	279	287	295
BMI	**19**	**20**	**21**	**22**	**23**	**24**	**25**	**26**	**27**	**28**	**29**	**30**	**31**	**32**	**33**	**34**	**35**	**36**

continues

Height, in							Body Weight, lb											
58	177	181	186	191	196	201	205	210	215	220	224	229	234	239	244	248	253	258
59	183	188	193	198	203	208	212	217	222	227	232	237	242	247	252	257	262	267
60	189	194	199	204	209	215	220	225	230	235	240	245	250	255	261	266	271	276
61	195	201	206	211	217	222	227	232	238	243	248	254	259	264	269	275	280	285
62	202	207	213	218	224	229	235	240	246	251	256	262	267	273	278	284	289	295
63	208	214	220	225	231	237	242	248	254	259	265	270	278	282	287	293	299	304
64	215	221	227	232	238	244	250	256	262	267	273	279	285	291	296	302	308	314
65	222	228	234	240	246	252	258	264	270	276	282	288	294	300	306	312	318	324
66	229	235	241	247	253	260	266	272	278	284	291	297	303	309	315	322	328	334
67	236	242	249	255	261	268	274	280	287	293	299	306	312	319	325	331	338	344
68	243	249	256	262	269	276	282	289	295	302	308	315	322	328	335	341	348	354
69	250	257	263	270	277	284	291	297	304	311	318	324	331	338	345	351	358	365
70	257	264	271	278	285	292	299	306	313	320	327	334	341	348	355	362	369	376
71	265	272	279	286	293	301	308	315	322	329	338	343	351	358	365	372	379	386
72	272	279	287	294	302	309	316	324	331	338	346	353	361	368	375	383	390	397
73	280	288	295	302	310	318	325	333	340	348	355	363	371	378	386	393	401	408
74	287	295	303	311	319	326	334	342	350	358	365	373	381	389	396	404	412	420
75	295	303	311	319	327	335	343	351	359	367	375	383	391	399	407	415	423	431
76	304	312	320	328	336	344	353	361	369	377	385	394	402	410	418	426	435	443
BMI	**37**	**38**	**39**	**40**	**41**	**42**	**43**	**44**	**45**	**46**	**47**	**48**	**49**	**50**	**51**	**52**	**53**	**54**

Appendix C

THE ENERGY COST OF PHYSICAL ACTIVITY USING METABOLIC EQUIVALENTS

A metabolic equivalent (MET) is a unit of energy relative to the energy cost of sitting quietly (1 MET). One MET is approximately 1 kcal/kg/hr. For the average adult, 1 MET requires approximately 3.5 mL of oxygen per kg of body weight per minute (mL/kg/min). Energy expended by physical activity can be expressed as a multiple of 1 MET. For example, a 5 MET activity requires five times the amount of energy expended as sitting quietly.

METs are most often used in the research setting. The Compendium of Physical Activities was developed to help standardize exercise intensity and estimate energy expenditure in physical activity studies. The first version was published in 1993 and was updated in 2000. The Compendium of Physical Activities Tracking Guide can be downloaded from the Internet (http://prevention.sph.sc.edu/tools/docs/documents_compendium.pdf).

The following table illustrates representative activities at 1.0 to 16.0 METs.

METs	Activity
1.0	Sitting quietly
2.0	Sitting, ice fishing
3.0	Bicycling, stationary, 50 watts, very light effort
4.0	Bicycling, < 10 mph, leisure, to work or for pleasure
5.0	Low impact aerobics
6.0	Bicycling, 10–11.9 mph, leisure, slow, light effort
7.0	Bicycling, stationary, 150 watts, moderate effort
8.0	Bicycling, 12–13 mph, leisure, moderate effort
9.0	Conditioning exercise, stair-treadmill ergometer, general
10.0	Bicycling, 14–15.9 mph, racing or leisure, fast, vigorous effort or running 6 mph (10 min/mile)
11.0	Running 6.7 mph (9 min/mile)
12.0	Bicycling, 16–19 mph, racing/not drafting or >19 mph drafting, very fast
13.0	No activities listed
14.0	Running 8.6 mph (7 min/mile)
15.0	Running 9 mph (6.5 min/mile)
16.0	Bicycling, > 20 mph, racing, not drafting or running 10 mph (6 min/mile)

Reference

Ainsworth BE. The Compendium of Physical Activities Tracking Guide. (January 2002) Prevention Research Center, Norman J. Arnold School of Public Health, University of South Carolina. Available at: http://prevention.sph.sc.edu/tools/docs/documents_compendium.pdf. Accessed August 10, 2004.

Appendix D

CLINICAL EATING DISORDER CRITERIA

Anorexia Nervosa

Individuals with anorexia nervosa are obsessed with the desire to be thinner and intensely fear gaining weight. No matter how thin the individual with anorexia becomes, she or he always "feels fat" and longs to be thinner. The diagnostic criteria for anorexia nervosa, as described in the *Diagnostic and Statistical Manual of Mental Disorders IV* (DSM-IV), are as follows:

- A significant loss of body weight and/or the maintenance of an extremely low body weight (85% of "normal" weight for height)
- An intense fear of gaining weight or "becoming fat"
- Severe body dissatisfaction and body image distortion
- Amenorrhea (absence of three or more consecutive menstrual periods)

Two subtypes of anorexia nervosa have been identified: the "restricting type" and the "binge-eating/purging type." An individual with "restricting type" anorexia nervosa loses weight and/or maintains an abnormally low body weight by means of severe energy restriction and excessive exercise. An individual with "bingeing/purging type" anorexia nervosa also severely restricts energy intake and excessively exercises, but will occasionally binge and subsequently engage in compensatory purging behaviors, such as self-induced vomiting or laxative or diuretic abuse, to control her weight.

Bulimia Nervosa

Individuals with bulimia nervosa engage in regular cycles of bingeing and purging. The diagnostic criteria for bulimia nervosa as described in the DSM-IV are as follows:

- Episodes of binge eating (ie, consuming a large amount of food in a short period of time) followed by purging (via laxatives, diuretics, enemas, self-induced vomiting, and/or excessive exercise) that have occurred at least twice a week for 3 months

- A sense of lack of control during the bingeing and/or purging episodes
- Severe body image dissatisfaction and undue influence of body image on self-evaluation

As with anorexia nervosa, two subtypes of bulimia nervosa have been identified: purging type and nonpurging type. The individual with purging-type bulimia nervosa regularly engages in self-induced vomiting, or the misuse of laxatives, diuretics, and/or enemas, to compensate for his or her bingeing behaviors; whereas the individual with nonpurging bulimia nervosa uses other inappropriate compensatory behaviors, such as fasting or excessive exercise, to compensate for episodes of overeating (but does not regularly engage in self-induced vomiting or the misuse of laxatives, diuretics, and/or enemas).

Binge Eating Disorder

Binge eating disorder has only recently been recognized as a clinical eating disorder (it is sometimes referred to as compulsive overeating). Similar to people with bulimia nervosa, those with binge eating disorder frequently consume large amounts of food while feeling a lack of control over their eating. However, individuals with binge eating disorder generally do not engage in purging behaviors (ie, vomiting, laxatives, excessive exercise, etc). The diagnostic criteria for binge eating disorder as described in the DSM-IV include the following:

- Recurrent episodes of binge eating. An episode is characterized by eating a larger amount of food than normal during a short period of time (within any 2-hour period) and lack of control over eating during the binge episode.
- Binge eating episodes are associated with three or more of the following: (*a*) eating until feeling uncomfortably full; (*b*) eating large amounts of food when not physically hungry; (*c*) eating much more rapidly than normal; (*d*) eating alone because of embarrassment about the amount being eaten; (*e*) feeling disgusted, depressed, or guilty after overeating.
- Marked distress regarding binge eating is present.
- Binge eating occurs, on average, at least 2 days a week for 6 months.
- The binge eating is not associated with the regular use of inappropriate compensatory behavior (ie, purging, excessive exercise, etc.) and does not occur exclusively during the course of bulimia nervosa or anorexia nervosa.

Eating Disorders Not Otherwise Specified

Eating disorders not otherwise specified (EDNOS) is a clinical eating disorder category that was recently added to the DSM-IV to describe individuals who meet some but not all of the criteria for anorexia nervosa and/or bulimia nervosa. The characteristic features of EDNOS are as follows:

- All of the criteria for anorexia nervosa are met except amenorrhea.
- All of the criteria for anorexia nervosa are met except that, despite significant weight loss, the individual's current weight is within the normal range.

- All of the criteria for bulimia nervosa are met except that the binge and purge cycles occur at a frequency of less than twice per week for a duration of less than 3 months.
- The regular use of purging behaviors by an individual of normal body weight after eating small amounts of food (eg, self-induced vomiting after consuming only two cookies).
- Repeatedly chewing and spitting out, but not swallowing, large amounts of food.

Reference

American Psychiatric Association. *Diagnostic and Statistical Manual of Mental Disorders.* 4th ed. Washington, DC: American Psychiatric Association; 1994.

Appendix E

SELECTED SPORTS NUTRITION– RELATED POSITION PAPERS

Joint Position Statements

- Nutrition and athletic performance: position of the American Dietetic Association, Dietitians of Canada, and the American College of Sports Medicine. *J Am Diet Assoc.* 2000;100: 1543–1556. (Reaffirmed in 2005; update in progress.) Available at: http://www. eatright.org. Accessed April 1, 2005.
- Vegetarian diets: position of the American Dietetic Association and Dietitians of Canada. Available at: http://www.eatright.org. Accessed April 1, 2005. See also the accompanying article, "A new food guide for North American vegetarians." Members of the American Dietetic Association can access this article free of charge. To receive a hard copy of this article, send a request along with name and mailing address or fax number to ppapers@eatright.org. Available at: http://www.dietitians.ca/news/ downloads/ Vegetarian_ Food_Guide_ for_NA.pdf. Accessed April 1, 2005.

American Dietetic Association Positions

Available at: http://www.eatright.org. Topics include the following:

- Women's health and nutrition
- Dietary guidance for healthy children aged 2 to 11 years
- Use of nutritive and nonnutritive sweeteners
- Fat replacers
- Food and nutrition misinformation
- Food fortification and dietary supplements
- Nutrition and lifestyle for a healthy pregnancy outcome
- Nutrition intervention in the treatment of anorexia nervosa, bulimia nervosa, and eating disorder not otherwise specified (EDNOS)
- Total diet approach to communicating food and nutrition information
- Weight management

American College of Sports Medicine Positions

Available at: http://www.acsm-msse.org/pt/re/msse/positionstandards.htm. Topics include the following:

- Physical activity and bone health
- Exercise and hypertension
- Appropriate intervention strategies for weight loss and prevention of weight regain for adults
- Exercise and type 2 diabetes

Note: Position papers addressing fluid, electrolytes, and dehydration are referenced in Chapter 6.

Appendix F

SPORTS NUTRITION–RELATED WEB SITES

Aerobics and Fitness Association of America
http://www.afaa.com

Amateur Athletic Union
http://aausports.org

America on the Move
http://www.americaonthemove.org

American Alliance for Health, Physical Education, Recreation and Dance
http://www.aahperd.org

American College of Sports Medicine
http://www.acsm.org

American Council on Exercise
http://acefitness.org

American Diabetes Association
http://diabetes.org

American Dietetic Association
http://www.eatright.org

American Running Association
http://www.americanrunning.org

American Sport Education Program
http://www.asep.com

Australian Institute of Sport
http://www.ausport.gov.au

Body Positive
http://www.bodypositive.com

California Association for Health, Physical Education, Recreation and Dance
http://www.cahperd.org

California Project Lean
http://www.californiaprojectlean.org

Crucible Fitness
http://www.cruciblefitness.com/nutrition/index.htm

Dietitians of Canada
http://www.dietitians.ca

Gatorade Sports Science Institute
http://www.gssiweb.com

Human Kinetics
http://www.humankinetics.com

IDEA Health and Fitness Association
http://ideafit.com

International Institute for Sport and Human Performance
http://darkwing.uoregon.edu/~iishp

International Society of Sports Nutrition
http://www.sportsnutritionsociety.org/site/index.php

Lollylegs—Masters Athletics
http://www.lollylegs.com

Master Track Training
http://www.masterstrack.com/train.html

MomsTeam.com
http://www.MomsTeam.com

National Recreation and Park Association
http://www.nrpa.org

NISMAT Exercise Physiology Corner
http://www.nismat.org/physcor/index.html

The Physician and Sports Medicine
http://www.physsportsmed.com

Runners World
http://www.runnersworld.com

Special Olympics
http://www.specialolympics.org

Sports, Cardiovascular and Wellness Nutritionists
(Dietetic Practice Group of the American Dietetic Association)
http://www.scandpg.org

Sports Dietitians Australia
http://www.sportsdietitians.com.au

SportScience
http://www.sportsci.org

Ultra Marathon Cycling Association
http://www.ultracycling.com

Vegetarian Resource Group
http://www.vrg.org

Note: This list includes Web sites that may be valuable to sports dietitians. The inclusion of a Web site does not constitute an endorsement of that site. At the time of publication, all URLs were correct. This list was compiled by Michael Smith, RD.

INDEX

Page numbers with *b* indicate boxes; with *f,* figures; and with *t, tables.*